A Hitchcock Reader

A Hitchcock Reader

SECOND EDITION

Edited by *Marshall Deutelbaum* and
Leland Poague

WILEY-BLACKWELL

A John Wiley & Sons, Ltd., Publication

This second edition first published 2009
© 2009 Blackwell Publishing Ltd

Edition history: Iowa State University Press (1e, 1986)

Blackwell Publishing was acquired by John Wiley & Sons in February 2007. Blackwell's
publishing program has been merged with Wiley's global Scientific, Technical, and Medical
business to form Wiley-Blackwell.

Registered Office
John Wiley & Sons Ltd, The Atrium, Southern Gate, Chichester, West Sussex,
PO19 8SQ, United Kingdom

Editorial Offices
350 Main Street, Malden, MA 02148-5020, USA
9600 Garsington Road, Oxford, OX4 2DQ, UK
The Atrium, Southern Gate, Chichester, West Sussex, PO19 8SQ, UK

For details of our global editorial offices, for customer services, and for information about
how to apply for permission to reuse the copyright material in this book please see our
website at www.wiley.com/wiley-blackwell.

The right of Marshall Deutelbaum and Leland Poague to be identified as the
authors of the editorial material in this work has been asserted in accordance with the
Copyright, Designs and Patents Act 1988.

Wiley also publishes its books in a variety of electronic formats. Some content that appears in
print may not be available in electronic books.

Designations used by companies to distinguish their products are often claimed as
trademarks. All brand names and product names used in this book are trade names, service
marks, trademarks or registered trademarks of their respective owners. The publisher is not
associated with any product or vendor mentioned in this book. This publication is designed
to provide accurate and authoritative information in regard to the subject matter covered.
It is sold on the understanding that the publisher is not engaged in rendering professional
services. If professional advice or other expert assistance is required, the services of a
competent professional should be sought.

Library of Congress Cataloging-in-Publication Data

A Hitchcock reader / edited by Marshall Deutelbaum and Leland Poague. – 2nd ed.
p.   cm.
Includes bibliographical references and index.
ISBN 978-1-4051-5556-4 (hardcover : alk. paper) – ISBN 978-1-4051-5557-1 (pbk. : alk. paper)
1. Hitchcock, Alfred, 1899–1980–Criticism and interpretation. I. Deutelbaum, Marshall.
II. Poague, Leland A., 1948–
PN1998.3.H58H574 2009
791.4302′33092–dc22

2008041637

A catalogue record for this book is available from the British Library.

Set in 10/13pt Sabon by SPi Publisher Services, Pondicherry, India
Printed in Singapore by Utopia Press Pte Ltd.

001   2009

For those other readers, Joyce and Gregory
M. D.

And for Dennis Poague, master of hawk and handsaw
L. P.

Contents

Preface to the Second Edition

In the twenty years since the initial publication of *A Hitchcock Reader*, Alfred Hitchcock and his films have continued to occupy a central position in cinematic discourse. Viewers and critics *continue* to be fascinated by his films, and filmmakers have increasingly taken him as a model and reference point. This edition of the *Reader* retains the same divisions as the original, with revised or rewritten introductions to each section and updated bibliographies of suggested readings. Most of the original chapters have been retained and several essays added that reflect the key emphases in Hitchcock studies over the past two decades.

John Orr charts the ever-expanding influence of Hitchcock on recent filmmakers and avant-garde artists in "Hitch as Matrix-Figure: Hitchcock and Twentieth-Century Cinema." Where Orr extends Hitchcock studies into the new century, John McCombe looks back to William Wordsworth and Samuel Taylor Coleridge's *Lyrical Ballads* to place *The Birds* within an English poetic tradition wherein the mysterious inexplicably erupts to disturb the taken-for-grantedness of the everyday. The inclusion of chapters by Lucretia Knapp on *Marnie* and Tania Modleski on *Frenzy* illustrates how Hitchcock's later films especially have been the focus of analysis from the perspectives of feminist and queer theory. Raymond Bellour's piece in the revamped "Hitchcock and Film Theory: A *Psycho* Dossier" is now in the company of recent essays by Christopher Morris and Deborah Thomas that reflect how *Psycho* continues to exemplify the complex appeal of Hitchcock's cinematic imagination.

Unfortunately, publishing constraints have required us to eliminate several of the chapters that appeared in the original edition to make room for the newly added ones. Deciding which chapters to omit has been painfully difficult because of the high quality and importance of all the essays that appeared in the first edition.

As in the first edition of *A Hitchcock Reader*, we have regularized spelling and punctuation; we have done our best to regularize documentation formats, though some of the newer items employ "Works Cited" lists, which we have retained. Otherwise, except where authors specifically asked for changes, we have printed the essays as we found them.

Our editorial apparatus has benefited immensely from the advice of Lee Poague's Iowa State colleague Professor Susan Yager. Her editorial suggestions helped us toward the goals of brevity and clarity, and we gladly express our gratitude. Thanks also to Iowa State Professors Lee Honeycutt and Geoff Sauer for last-minute assistance with computer technologies, and to Sheryl Kamps for her help with scanning and formatting.

We are especially grateful to our Blackwell editor, Jayne Fargnoli, for her initial and continued enthusiasm, for her editorial wisdom, and for timely patience; to Ken Provencher, especially for his help in soliciting reviewer feedback; to Margot Morse for her cheerful professionalism; to Nicola Boulton for her help with permissions; to Hilary Walford for her careful copy-editing; to Production Manager Lisa Eaton and Project Manager Linda Auld for keeping things on track; and to all the staff at Blackwell Publishers whose efforts have resulted in a book we are both immensely pleased with.

Marshall Deutelbaum would like to thank his wife, Joyce, for her continuing support and encouragement. In addition, he would like to express his appreciation for Matthew Bernstein's continuous Hitchcockian lures and William B. Covey's endless patience in discussions of all things cinematic. The superb service of the Interlibrary Loan Office of the Purdue University Libraries has been an invaluable resource in this project and many others.

Leland Poague thanks his wife, Susan, for her happy willingness to help him see the *Reader* through a second edition, as she did through the first. Charles Kostelnick, Chair of the Department of English at Iowa State University, deserves thanks for ongoing encouragement and support, as does Michael Whiteford, Dean of the College of Liberal Arts and Sciences, for a research assignment during which much of Lee's work was accomplished. Wayne Pedersen and the staff of the Parks Library Interlibrary Loan/Document Delivery Office at Iowa State University were profoundly helpful and diligent in tracking down articles and books from distant venues. We hope readers of *A Hitchcock Reader* will benefit from their efforts as much as we have.

In the twenty-some years since this book first appeared, we have each taught Hitchcock on numerous occasions, to students at many curricular levels. By way of thanking them all, Lee Poague would like to acknowledge Elizabeth Zimmerman, whose recent independent study of Hitchcock helped him immensely in the task of renewing his engagements with Hitchcock criticism in the midst of his duties as a time-pressed department administrator.

Lee would also like to thank Loring Silet, his team-teaching colleague for most of his thirty-plus years at Iowa State, who often began the semester by invoking the scene in *Rear Window* where Lisa Freemont/Grace Kelly implores L. B. Jefferies/ James Stewart to help her understand what he thinks has transpired across the courtyard: "Tell me everything you saw, and what you think it means."

Most of all, we are grateful to our contributors; thanks are due to all the publishers and authors whose cooperation made both editions of *A Hitchcock Reader* possible. (Special thanks for last-minute assistance are owed to Rebecca Frazier and Stacey Salling at the University of Texas Press.) Likewise, we express gratitude yet again to those helpful colleagues and friends whose contributions to the first edition are acknowledged in the original preface, which we have retained.

Many instructors who used the first edition of *A Hitchcock Reader* responded generously (if anonymously) with advice for revising the book, and their commentary was vital in making our final decisions. To them and to all those who have used the book in the twenty-plus years since it first appeared, we offer a hearty "Thanks!" We hope this second edition will prove as useful as the first.

Marshall Deutelbaum
Leland Poague

Preface to the First Edition

A Hitchcock Reader grew out of our desire as classroom teachers for a comprehensive anthology that could be used as a critical text in introductory or advanced courses devoted to the director's films. We believe, in addition, that many a general "Hitchcock reader" will find most of the essays in this collection exciting and thought provoking for, as they reveal, thinking about Hitchcock's films quickly leads to speculation about larger issues of filmmaking and film culture.

Apart from the occasional special journal issue devoted to Hitchcock, the only real precedent for the present volume is Albert J. LaValley's *Focus on Hitchcock*, now long out of print and compiled before the advent of many of the critical approaches that presently animate Hitchcock criticism. Despite their considerable merits, neither the available biographies of Hitchcock by John Russell Taylor and Donald Spoto, nor the extended, one-volume critical discussion of his films by Claude Chabrol and Eric Rohmer, Raymond Durgnat, and Donald Spoto, nor even the late François Truffaut's lengthy interview book could serve as a central text for the kind of Hitchcock course we have both wanted to teach. The recent rerelease of the five "lost" Hitchcock films – *Rope*, *Rear Window*, *The Trouble with Harry*, *The Man Who Knew Too Much*, *Vertigo* – further reinforces the need we have long felt for an updated Hitchcock anthology representing the rich variety of critical response his films have evoked over the years.

In addition to a book offering critical discussions of Hitchcock's major films and explaining the well-known motifs and themes that have long been associated with them, moreover, we envisioned a collection that, through its choice of essays, would also reflect something of the history of film criticism and theory over the past thirty years, moving from the initial auteurist claims for taking Hitchcock seriously to the more recent psychological, feminist, and Marxist theories that have lately been brought to bear on his films. Thus another goal of this book is to encourage students to become more aware of the traditions and assumptions underlying various perceptions of cinema – that cultural institution in which Alfred Hitchcock plays an historically crucial role. These interests guided us in both the selection and the organization of essays for the collection.

The essays in Part One, "Taking Hitchcock Seriously," for example, introduce readers to the director's visual style and working methods while asking them to ponder their own relationship to the images Hitchcock creates as he develops his abiding themes. The essays in the three sections at the center of the collection offer critical discussion of individual films to be read in conjunction with their screenings. Part Five, "A *Psycho* Dossier," provides an extended consideration of one of Hitchcock's key films from a more thoroughly theoretical position. The Introduction that follows this Preface explains our aims and principles of selection in greater detail.

Because *A Hitchcock Reader* is designed for beginning as well as advanced courses, each of its five sections provides an introduction offering readers an overview of the essays that follow and a context for their consideration. Hitchcock's films are so visually and thematically provocative, however, that no one reading (or sequence of readings) of a given film is ever likely to be exhaustive. For this reason, extensive bibliographies appended to these introductions direct readers to other books and articles relevant to the material in each section. Thus while *A Hitchcock Reader* can be used as the sole text for a course on Hitchcock, these bibliographies suggest additional items that might serve as supplemental readings.

In addition to expressing our appreciation to our many contributors, we would like to thank our editors at the Iowa State University Press, Judith Gildner and Nancy Bohlen, both of whom labored diligently to bring this project to completion. No one labored more diligently or more deserves our thanks than Susan Poague, who typeset nearly the entire manuscript on a personal computer. We are grateful as well to Janet Bergstrom and Thomas Hyde for helping us make important contacts in Paris. Terri Paul, Mary Beth Haralovich, Joseph Kupfer, Dan Miller, Mark Bracher, Rick Altman, William Cadbury, Kathy Sotol, and Dudley Andrew all contributed advice and encouragement. Marian Keane helped provide illustrations. Our indebtedness to many helpful journal editors is evident in our list of permissions; our personal thanks for their cooperation we tender here. Thanks also to Iowa State University Press Director Merritt Bailey for his sustained cooperation and support.

Finally, we would like to thank the anonymous reader who recommended the book's publication and whose editorial judgments proved crucial in helping to determine the final lineup of essays. The difficult task of selecting a small group of essays from the wealth of available material was made significantly easier because we had another opinion to factor in. Thanks again.

Marshall Deutelbaum
Leland Poague

A Brief Chronology

Those films marked with an asterisk (*) were directed by Graham Cutts, with Hitchcock writing scenarios, designing sets, and serving (except in the case of *The White Shadow*) as assistant director. All other films or television programs were directed by Hitchcock himself unless otherwise noted.

1922 *Number 13* (unfinished)
1923 *Always Tell Your Wife* (codirected with Hugh Croise and Seymour Hicks), *Woman to Woman**
1924 *The White Shadow**, *The Prude's Fall**, *The Passionate Adventure**
1925 *The Blackguard**
1926 *The Pleasure Garden* (produced 1925), *The Mountain Eagle* (produced 1925), *The Lodger*
1927 *Downhill, Easy Virtue, The Ring*
1928 *The Farmer's Wife* (produced 1927), *Champagne*
1929 *The Manxman* (produced 1928), *Blackmail, Juno and the Paycock*
1930 *Elstree Calling, Murder!*
1931 *Mary* (German version of *Murder!*), *The Skin Game, Rich and Strange*
1932 *Number Seventeen* (produced 1931), *Lord Chamber's Ladies* (producer)
1934 *Waltzes from Vienna* (produced 1933), *The Man Who Knew Too Much*
1935 *The 39 Steps*
1936 *Secret Agent* (produced 1935), *Sabotage*
1937 *Young and Innocent*
1938 *The Lady Vanishes* (produced 1937)
1939 *Jamaica Inn* (produced 1938)
1940 *Rebecca* (produced 1939), *Foreign Correspondent*
1941 *Mr. and Mrs. Smith* (produced 1940), *Suspicion*
1942 *Saboteur*
1943 *Shadow of a Doubt* (produced 1942)
1944 *Lifeboat* (produced 1943), *Bon Voyage, Aventure Malgache*
1945 *Spellbound* (produced 1944)

1946   *Notorious*
1947   *The Paradine Case*
1948   *Rope*
1949   *Under Capricorn* (produced 1948)
1950   *Stage Fright* (produced 1949)
1951   *Strangers on a Train* (produced 1950)
1953   *I Confess* (produced 1952)
1954   *Dial "M" for Murder* (produced 1953), *Rear Window* (produced 1953)
1955   *To Catch a Thief* (produced 1954), "Revenge," *The Trouble with Harry* (produced 1954), "Breakdown," "The Case of Mr. Pelham"
1956   "Back for Christmas," *The Man Who Knew Too Much* (produced 1955), "Wet Saturday," *The Wrong Man,* "Mr. Blanchard's Secret"
1957   "One More Mile to Go," "Four O'Clock," "The Perfect Crime"
1958   "Lamb to the Slaughter," *Vertigo* (produced 1957), "Dip in the Pool," "Poison"
1959   "Banquo's Chair," *North by Northwest,* "Arthur," The Crystal Trench"
1960   "Incident at a Corner," *Psycho,* "Mrs. Bixby and the Colonel's Coat"
1961   "The Horseplayer," "Bang! You're Dead!"
1962   "I Saw the Whole Thing"
1963   *The Birds* (produced 1962)
1964   *Marnie*
1966   *Torn Curtain*
1969   *Topaz*
1972   *Frenzy* (produced 1971)
1976   *Family Plot* (produced 1975)

Notes on Contributors

RICHARD ABEL is Robert Altman Collegiate Professor of Film Studies in the Department of Screen Arts & Culture at the University of Michigan. Most recently he edited the award-winning *Encyclopedia of Early Cinema* (Routledge, 2005) and published *Americanizing the Movies and "Movie-Mad" Audiences, 1910–1914* (Univ. of California Press, 2006). Currently he is co-editing *Early Cinema and the "National"* (forthcoming from John Libbey) and completing research for *Menus for Movie Land: Newspapers and the Movies, 1911–1915*.

RAYMOND BELLOUR is Director Emeritus of Research at the Centre National de la Recherche Scientifique and the author of numerous books on topics in literature and film, among them *Alexandre Astruc* (Seghers, 1963) and *L'Analyse du film* (Albatros, 1979). The latter recently appeared in English as *The Analysis of Film* (Indiana Univ. Press, 2000). He is the editor of two volumes of *Le Cinéma américain* (Flammarion, 1980) and the author of *L'Entre-images: Photo, cinéma, vidéo* (La Différence, 1990), and *L'Entre-images 2: Mots, images* (POL, 1999). He edited the *Oeuvres complètes* of Henri Michaux (3 volumes) for the "Bibliothèque de la Pléiade" series (Gallimard), and is a co-founder and current editor of the film magazine *Trafic*.

LESLEY W. BRILL is the author of *The Hitchcock Romance: Love and Irony in Hitchcock's Films* (Princeton Univ. Press, 1988) and of numerous essays on film and photography. His latest book is *Crowds, Power, and Transformation in Cinema* (Wayne State Univ. Press, 2006). He teaches at Wayne State University in Detroit.

STANLEY CAVELL is Walter M. Cabot Professor Emeritus of Aesthetics and the General Theory of Value at Harvard University. Among his many books of philosophy, several deal expressly with film, including *The World Viewed: Reflections on the Ontology of Film* (Viking, 1971; enlarged edition, Harvard Univ. Press, 1979), *Pursuits of Happiness: The Hollywood Comedy of Remarriage* (Harvard Univ. Press, 1981), *Contesting Tears: The Melodrama of the Unknown Woman* (Univ. of Chicago Press, 1996), and *Cities of Words: Pedagogical Letters on a Register of the*

Moral Life (Belknap Press, 2004). His most recent book is *Philosophy the Day after Tomorrow* (Harvard Univ. Press, 2005).

VERENA ANDERMATT CONLEY teaches in Comparative Literature and Romance Languages and Literatures at Harvard University. Recent publications include *Ecopolitics: The Environment in Poststructuralist Thought* (Routledge, 1997), *The War against the Beavers: Learning to be Wild in the North Woods* (Univ. of Minnesota Press, 2003), and *Littérature, politique et communisme: Lire "Les Lettres françaises," 1942–1972* (Peter Lang, 2004). She is currently finishing a project entitled *Spatial Fictions*.

MARSHALL DEUTELBAUM is Professor Emeritus of English at Purdue University. His primary research topics are visual design in film and complex narrative structures.

JEAN DOUCHET is a film director, screenwriter, actor, and teacher of film history and filmmaking at "la FEMIS" (École nationale supérieure des méttiers de l'image et du son). He began writing for *Cahiers du cinéma* in 1957. His *Alfred Hitchcock* (Éditions de l'Herne) was first published in 1967; the most recent version appeared in 2006 as *Hitchcock* in the Petite bibliothèque des Cahiers du cinéma series. His monumental *Nouvelle Vague* (Hazan/Cinémathèque française, 1998) appeared in English as *French New Wave* (DAP) in 1999.

NANCY HUSTON was born in Canada and lives in France. The author of numerous books of fiction and non-fiction, she writes in both French and English, translating herself in both directions. She also recently translated André Comte-Sponville's *Little Book of Atheist Spirituality* (Viking, 2007).

THOMAS HYDE has taught film at colleges in Oregon and Ohio. Though he occasionally writes about film, he is currently editing a book of stories about cooking.

MARIAN E. KEANE received her doctorate from New York University and has published on topics in film and philosophy, on film comedy, and on Hitchcock especially. With William Rothman, she co-authored *Reading Cavell's* The World Viewed: *A Philosophical Perspective on Film* (Wayne State Univ. Press, 2000). She provided commentary for the Criterion DVD editions of *The 39 Steps, Spellbound,* and *Notorious.*

LUCRETIA KNAPP is a film, video, and new media artist as well as a specialist in feminist and queer film studies. Her most recent work is *Swim Suit*, an experimental documentary short (distributed in the USA and Canada by Frameline of San Francisco) that is part of a larger work on transgender identity. She teaches video production and digital imaging in the Film Studies Department at Smith College and at the International Center of Photography in New York.

JOHN P. McCOMBE is Associate Professor of English and Associate Director of the University Honors Program at the University of Dayton. His scholarly interests include twentieth-century British literature, post-war Hollywood film, and the intersections of music and literature. His work has appeared in a wide range of literature and film journals including *Twentieth-Century Literature, Cinema Journal, POST SCRIPT,* and the *James Joyce Quarterly.*

JAMES McLAUGHLIN was pursuing a doctoral degree in Film at the University of Iowa until his death in 1995. In addition to his essay on *Shadow of a Doubt*, he published on George Cukor and (posthumously, from his dissertation) on Susan Sontag.

TANIA MODLESKI is Florence R. Scott Professor of English at the University of Southern California. Her *The Women Who Knew Too Much: Hitchcock and Feminist Theory* first appeared in 1988 (Methuen); a second edition (Routledge) came out in 2005. Among her other books are *Loving with a Vengeance* (Archon, 1982; Routledge, 2008) and *Feminism without Women* (Routledge, 1991).

CHRISTOPHER D. MORRIS is Professor of English at Norwich University in Northfield, Vermont. He is the author of *Models of Misrepresentation: On the Fiction of E. L. Doctorow* (Univ. Press of Mississippi, 1991), *The Hanging Figure: On Suspense and the Films of Alfred Hitchcock* (Praeger, 2002), and *The Figure of the Road: Deconstructive Studies in Humanities Disciplines* (Peter Lang, 2006). He is writing books on Mark Twain and on *film noir*.

JOHN ORR is Professor Emeritus in the School of Social and Political Studies at the University of Edinburgh. His *Hitchcock and Twentieth-Century Cinema* appeared in 2005 (Wallflower). His other books include *Cinema and Modernity* (Polity/Blackwell, 1993), *Contemporary Cinema* (Edinburgh Univ. Press, 1998), and *The Art and Politics of Film* (Edinburgh Univ. Press, 2000).

ROBERTA PEARSON is Professor of Film and Television Studies and director of the Institute for Film and Television Studies at the University of Nottingham. Her recent publications include the edited collections *Cult Television* (Univ. of Minnesota Press, 2004) and the forthcoming *Reading* Lost: *Perspectives on a Hit Television Show* (I. B. Tauris, 2008). She is currently editing the Blackwell Companion to Television Genres.

PATRICE PETRO is Professor of English and Film Studies at the University of Wisconsin-Milwaukee, where she is also Director of the Center for International Education. She is the author and editor of several books, including *Aftershocks of the New: Feminism and Film History* (Rutgers Univ. Press, 2002) and *Rethinking Global Security: Media, Popular Culture, and the "War on Terror"* (Rutgers Univ. Press, 2006). She is President of the Society for Cinema and Media Studies.

MICHELE PISO is Assistant Director for Professional Development of the LaGuardia Community College Center for Teaching and Learning. She lives in New York City and is currently doing research in the ethics of food production and consumption.

LELAND POAGUE is Professor of English at Iowa State University. He is the author of books on Frank Capra, Ernst Lubitsch, and Howard Hawks, of the "Hollywood Professionals" volume on Billy Wilder and Leo McCarey, and the co-author (with William Cadbury) of *Film Criticism: A Counter Theory* (Iowa State Univ. Press, 1982). His more recent books include *Another Frank Capra* (Cambridge Univ. Press, 1994) and (with Kathy A. Parsons) *Susan Sontag: An Annotated Bibliography, 1948–1992* (Garland, 2000).

WILLIAM ROTHMAN is Professor of Motion Pictures and Director of the Graduate Program in Film Study at the University of Miami. He is the author of *Hitchcock: The Murderous Gaze* (Harvard Univ. Press, 1982), *The "I" of the Camera: Essays in Film Criticism, History, and Aesthetics* (Cambridge Univ. Press, 1988; second edition, 2004), and *Documentary Film Classics* (Cambridge Univ. Press, 1997). With Marian Keane he co-authored *Reading Cavell's* The World Viewed: *A Philosophical Perspective on Film* (Wayne State Univ. Press, 2000) and has recently edited *Cavell on Film* (SUNY Press, 2005), *Jean Rouch: A Celebration of Life and Film* (Schena Editore and University of Paris-Sorbonne Press, 2007), and *Three Documentary Filmmakers* (SUNY Press, forthcoming).

CHARLES L. P. SILET is Professor Emeritus of English at Iowa State University. He has written widely on film and contemporary literature. His latest book is *The Films of Woody Allen: Critical Essays* (Scarecrow, 2006).

ROBERT STAM is University Professor of Cinema Studies at New York University. Among his numerous books on topics in literature, cinema, and cultural studies are *Reflexivity in Film and Literature: From Don Quixote to Jean-Luc Godard* (UMI, 1985; Columbia Univ. Press, 1992), *Subversive Pleasures: Bakhtin, Cultural Criticism, and Film* (Johns Hopkins Univ. Press, 1989), *Film Theory: An Introduction* (Blackwell, 2000), and *François Truffaut and Friends: Modernism, Sexuality, and Film Adaptation* (Rutgers Univ. Press, 2006). He is the co-editor, among other volumes, of *A Companion to Film Theory* (Blackwell, 1999) and *A Companion to Literature and Film* (Blackwell, 2004).

DEBORAH THOMAS was, until her recent retirement, Professor of Film Studies at the University of Sunderland in the UK. In addition to numerous articles on cinema, especially on Hitchcock and *film noir*, she is the author of *Beyond Genre: Melodrama, Comedy and Romance in Hollywood Films* (Cameron & Hollis, 2000) and *Reading Hollywood: Spaces and Meanings in American Film* (Wallflower, 2001).

ELISABETH WEIS is Professor of Film at Brooklyn College and in the Ph.D. Program in Theater at The CUNY Graduate Center. Weis is the author of *The Silent Scream: Alfred Hitchcock's Sound Track* (Fairleigh Dickinson, 1982) and the co-editor, with John Belton, of *Film Sound: Theory and Practice* (Columbia Univ. Press, 1985). As Executive Director of the National Society of Film Critics since 1974, she edited two of their anthologies: *The National Society of Film Critics on Movie Comedy* (Grossman, 1977) and *The National Society of Film Critics on the Movie Star* (Viking, 1981).

ROBIN WOOD is a Senior Scholar at York University, Toronto, where he continues to teach graduate courses in film. His *Hitchcock's Films* was originally published in 1965; its most recent incarnation, as the Revised Edition of *Hitchcock's Film Revisited*, appeared in 2002. Wayne State University Press has lately issued new editions of his books on Howard Hawks and Ingmar Bergman, as well as the first American edition of *Personal Views*. More recent books include *Sexual Politics and Narrative Film* (Columbia Univ. Press, 1998) and *Hollywood from Vietnam to Reagan ... and Beyond* (Columbia Univ. Press, 2003). He is currently writing a book on Michael Haneke.

MAURICE YACOWAR is Professor Emeritus of English and Film Studies at the University of Calgary. His books include *Hitchcock's British Films* (Archon, 1977), studies of Tennessee Williams, Woody Allen, Mel Brooks, Paul Morrissey, and *The Sopranos*, a comic novel, *The Bold Testament* (Bayeux Arts, 1999), and a biography, *The Great Bratby* (Middlesex, 2008).

Acknowledgments

Jean Douchet's "Hitch and His Public" is reprinted from *Cahiers du cinéma*, no. 113 (November 1960) by permission of the editors.

Maurice Yacowar's "Hitchcock's Imagery and Art" is reprinted from *Hitchcock's British Films* (Hamden, CT: Archon Books, 1977) by permission of the author.

Robin Wood's "Retrospective" is reprinted from the 1977 edition of *Hitchcock's Films* (South Brunswick and New York: A. S. Barnes) by permission of the author.

John Orr's "Hitch as Matrix-Figure: Hitchcock and Twentieth-Century Cinema" is © 2005 by Wallflower Press, London & New York. Reprinted with permission from Wallflower Press.

Lesley W. Brill's "Hitchcock's *The Lodger*" is reprinted from *Literature/Film Quarterly*, vol. 11, no. 4 (1983) by permission of the journal.

William Rothman's "Alfred Hitchcock's *Murder!*: Theater, Authorship, and the Presence of the Camera" is reprinted from *Wide Angle*, vol. 4, no. 1 (1980) by permission of the author and the Johns Hopkins University Press.

Leland Poague's "Criticism and/as History: Rereading *Blackmail*" is reprinted with permission from the author.

Elisabeth Weis's "Consolidation of a Classical Style: *The Man Who Knew Too Much*" is reprinted from *The Silent Scream: Alfred Hitchcock's Sound Track* by permission of Associated University Presses.

Charles L. P. Silet's "Sexuality and Memory in *The 39 Steps*" is reprinted with permission from the author.

Patrice Petro's "Rematerializing the Vanishing 'Lady': Feminism, Hitchcock, and Interpretation" is reprinted with permission from the author.

James McLaughlin's "All in the Family: Alfred Hitchcock's *Shadow of a Doubt*" first appeared in *Wide Angle*, vol. 4, no. 1 (1980-); it is reprinted here (in a slightly longer version) by permission of the author and the Johns Hopkins University Press.

Thomas Hyde's "The Moral Universe of Hitchcock's *Spellbound*" is reprinted from *Cinemonkey*, no. 15 (1978) by permission of the editor.

Richard Abel's "*Notorious*: Perversion par Excellence" is reprinted form *Wide Angle*, vol. 1, no. 1, revised and expanded (1979), by permission of the author and the Johns Hopkins University Press.

Robin Wood's "*Strangers on a Train*" is reprinted from the 1969 edition of *Hitchcock's Films* by permission of the author.

Robert Stam and Roberta Pearson's "Hitchcock's *Rear Window*: Reflexivity and the Critique of Voyeurism" is reprinted from *enclitic*, vol. 7, no. 1 (1983) by permission of the editor.

Marshall Deutelbaum's, "Finding the Right Man in *The Wrong Man*" is reprinted with permission from the author.

Robin Wood's "Male Desire, Male Anxiety: The Essential Hitchcock" first appeared as "Fear of Spying" in *American Film*, vol. 9, no. 2 (1983); reprinted here by permission of *American Film*.

Marion E. Keane's "A Closer Look at Scopophilia: Mulvey, Hitchcock, and *Vertigo*" is reprinted with permission from the author.

Stanley Cavell's "North by Northwest" is reprinted from *Themes out of School: Effects and Causes*, © 1984 by Stanley Cavell. Published by North Point Press and reprinted by permission. All rights reserved. An earlier version of the essay appeared in *Critical Inquiry*, vol. 7, no. 4 (1981). © 1981 by the University of Chicago. Reprinted by permission.

John P. McCombe's " 'Oh, I See....': *The Birds* and the Culmination of Hitchcock's Hyper-Romantic Vision" is reprinted from *Cinema Journal*, vol. 44, no. 3 (2005), pp. 66–80. Copyright © 2005 by the University of Texas Press. All rights reserved.

Michele Piso's "Mark's *Marnie*" is reprinted with permission from the author.

Lucretia Knapp's "The Queer Voice in *Marnie*" is reprinted from *Cinema Journal*, vol. 32, no. 4 (1993), pp. 6–23. Copyright © 1993 by the University of Texas Press. All rights reserved.

Tania Modleski's "Rituals of Defilement: *Frenzy*" is © 1988 by Taylor & Francis Group LLC – Books. Reproduced with permission of Taylor & Francis Group LLC – Books, in the format Textbook via Copyright Clearance Center.

Raymond Bellour's "Psychosis, Neurosis, Perversion" is reprinted from *Camera Obscura*, nos. 3–4 (1979) by permission of the journal and the author.

Christopher D. Morris's "*Psycho*'s Allegory of Seeing" is © 1996 by Salisbury University, Salisbury, MD 21801. Reprinted with permission from *Literature/ Film Quarterly*. Originally published in vol. 24, no. 1 (1996): 47–51.

Deborah Thomas's "On Being Norman: Performance and Inner Life in Hitchcock's *Psycho*" is © July 1997 by *CineAction*. Reprinted from *CineAction*, no. 44 (pp. 66–72), with permission from the author and *CineAction*.

Introduction

To speak of Alfred Hitchcock is to evoke a remarkable series of histories. There is the history of cinema generally, in which Hitchcock plays an exemplary role as a technical and stylistic innovator; there is a history of Hitchcock's films themselves, seen as a matter of decline (for those who prefer his British films) or development (for those who champion his American movies); there is a history of film criticism, especially given Hitchcock's status as a primary test case for the auteur theory, which held that commercial films ("classical films" in more current usage) can and should be discussed in the same terms as were previously reserved for "art" films; and there is a history of contemporary film theory, understood at least in part as involving a return to more sociological and historical concerns after the excesses of auteurism; and so on.

A Hitchcock Reader has a double purpose relative to these histories and at least two audiences. For Hitchcock scholars, *A Hitchcock Reader* retains its value as a summary of some aspects of their academic field. The chapters added to this edition update our presentation of the "Hitchcock conversation" in ways we hope instructors will find helpful. For students, our primary audience, *A Hitchcock Reader* provides a reasonably comprehensive introduction to the field, a map of what may well be for individual readers quite a foreign territory. One goal of *A Hitchcock Reader* is to render the territory less foreign, to encourage students to claim membership in the community of those who have chosen to think long and hard about their relationships to Hitchcock's films and to "Film" more generally. A reader of Hitchcock unfamiliar with the field might well begin with Part One, "Taking Hitchcock Seriously," where the question of whether Hitchcock deserves to be taken seriously is addressed. We presume he does, and want here to specify the principles guiding our selection and presentation of the chapters that follow.

The most basic principle should already be clear: that film study is an *institutional* activity. College-level film courses are offered in numerous departments and programs and from a variety of methodological perspectives. Film is taught as an art form; as an opportunity for cognitive exercise and intellectual development; as a form of mass communication; as a factor in the replication or contestation of cultural wants, needs, and ways of looking. Put another way, film study is not merely "study of films." Rather, like any other academic discipline, film study is defined less by its objects than by the questions that are asked of those objects and of the uses people put them to. It is a mark of the intellectual maturity of film study that contemporary film scholars address these questions so often and so thoughtfully. In that regard the institutional pressures of film study, especially those resulting from the explosion of semiotic and feminist film scholarship in the 1970s, have served us well for insisting that we re-examine our basic assumptions and canonical figures, among whom Hitchcock still retains pride of place.

We take our primary audience to be college undergraduates, many if not most of whom have completed only one or two film courses before taking a junior/senior level class that focuses to a significant measure on Hitchcock. Because many students at this level have not been introduced to the complexities of modern film or cultural theory, we have not included selections especially dependent upon (for example) Lacanian or Derridian semiotics, despite their historical importance to the field. It may be hard to avoid the impression that Hitchcock himself is a deconstructive philosopher of culture; to a post-MTV generation, indeed, Hitchcock's postmodern hybridity may even seem austere, rigorous, almost academic. But the heady mix of mostly continental authorities and concepts often appealed to by critics such as Slavoj Žižek and Tom Cohen seems the wrong place to *begin* an exploration of Hitchcock, because it assumes a sophistication that few undergraduates, in our experience, are likely to possess.

The primary exception to this rule is Raymond Bellour's seminal psychoanalytic study of *Psycho*, for which we have provided options as well as a section introduction designed to assist students who are asked to engage Bellour. One reason we have felt free to address this collection to the general undergraduate audience is our belief that many different courses can be (have been) taught from *A Hitchcock Reader*. For example, only a relatively brief list of supplementary readings stands between this book and a theoretically ambitious investigation of the Hitchcock cinema. We have constantly kept such options in mind in preparing our lists of suggested readings. Although privileging readability may blunt the ideological critique urged either by or against Hitchcock's movies, we believe that critique in both the philosophical and political senses is alive and well in *A Hitchcock Reader*, perhaps even more so in this second edition, where the complexity of Hitchcock's engagements with gender has moved increasingly to the center of attention.

If we have allowed ourselves an overt editorial bias, it has to do with the relationship between formal and historical analysis, modes of approach that are often seen as opposing one another. We take this to be a false opposition, especially when history is understood to be synonymous with ideology. To begin with, every film and every analysis has ideological implications or consequences. Likewise, any analysis of a particular film is logically dependent upon a historical perception of the formal resources of cinema. Noël Carroll has even suggested (in "Film History and Film Theory: An Outline for an Institutional Theory of Film," *Film Reader*, no. 4 (1979)) that such a historical perception of film is an essential factor in answering the question of whether any given film should count as an artwork at all (those do, in Carroll's view, that can be interpreted as repeating, amplifying, or repudiating the traditions of the art form in question). Such perceptions may or may not be difficult to acquire, depending upon how historically precise one wishes to be. At least some descriptions of "the classical narrative cinema," for example, are so paradoxically inclusive – for being so narrowly defined – as to ignore many (if not most) formal or ideological distinctions among periods, genres, or directors. Put otherwise, if the shot/reverse-shot editing figure always "sutures" the viewer into experiencing an illusory plenitude, then there is little to choose between *Blackmail* and *Beach Blanket Bingo*.

Because an underlying assumption of *A Hitchcock Reader* is that finer, more context-specific distinctions need to be made, we have used history – of film generally but also of film criticism and of Hitchcock's own career – as the main organizing principle of *A Hitchcock Reader*. Director-oriented criticism risks reducing every film to a single formal-thematic model, which often amounts to privileging certain films or genres as the theme upon which all other films are read as variations. But, as Robin Wood pointed out long ago, Hitchcock's films possess a remarkable quality of variety and difference: to go from *Vertigo* to *North by Northwest* to *Psycho* is to experience three distinct film-worlds. Indeed, all three films are arguably about the necessity of *distinguishing* among particular views of the world, and about the agonizing difficulty of doing so, and about the temptation to deny difference as a way of avoiding or refusing loss. We hope that an anthology format, a variety of authors, and a largely chronological survey will encourage a genuinely historical yet sustainedly particular view of Hitchcock's films and their possibilities.

Let us not be naive about history in all of this. There are many histories, many *theories* of history, just as there are many Hitchcock films; failure to distinguish among histories can be as problematic as the failure to be historical at all. There is a history of Hitchcock as an empirical individual. There is a history of his filmmaking, which only partly replicates the former. There is a history of the cinema, again only partly coincident with Hitchcock. And there is a history of viewing and criticism as well – for individual viewers and for the film-studies discipline as a whole.

Beyond all that there is a history of culture, to which film studies has shifted much of its focus in the last several decades, especially via the Marxist analysis of culture as both cause and effect, as determined (by modes of material production) and determining (for replicating, for re-presenting those modes in and for individual subjects). Hence the great attraction for film studies, especially for the Marxist and feminist versions of the late 1970s, of the psychological theories of Jacques Lacan, which at the time seemed to offer a concise model for the connection of large-scale social conditions and individual systems of behavior and belief.

In retrospect, the "Lacan" appealed to by early exemplars of this approach was a Lacan of "misrepresentation," to the extent that the allegorical passage (of the developing child, of the infantilized film viewer) from the Imaginary to the Symbolic realms was pictured as a process of serial misrecognitions, the projection and introjection of something like mastery as a means of denying incapacity or lack, all the more to confirm the latter as the (groundless) basis of (patriarchal) social authority. As numerous critics have observed, Hitchcock was nearly always skeptical of social authority. No wonder the feminist imperative to unmask the ruses of patriarchy found its specular match in his movies. (For elaboration of this Lacanian vocabulary, see the Introduction to Part Five, "Hitchcock and Film Theory: A *Psycho* Dossier.")

Yet the paradox by which resistance to patriarchy served (apparently) to validate or venerate yet another cinematic patriarch lent a sense of urgency to feminist questions about political agency and social change. Lacan seemed to *explain* the logic by which patriarchy renewed itself, but apparently lacking in Lacan was a model of reinterpretation that would effectively change our relationships to a particular film or set of films. It is still the case that a primary critical gesture is one of *exposure*, designed as much to show forth the mechanisms of the film/culture relationship as to change them. But even that "showing-forth" is arguably a species of change. One may not be convinced by the Lacanian model invoked throughout Raymond Bellour's reading *of Psycho*, which concludes that "film and cinema" are "the very institution of perversion," as if *Psycho* were subject to, subjects *us* to, "the monolithic power of its ruling signifier," such that our only alternative is to embrace perversion, to be perverse in our turn. But one can hardly deny that, after reading Bellour, our view and experience of *Psycho* will never be, *can* never be, the same.

Bellour's reading of *Psycho* may not explain the film's existence or effects, but his claim to an understanding of *Psycho* is powerful and rests largely on the quality of his formal analysis, his understanding of part/whole relations. This ability of interpretation to induce change, to intervene in the history of the text, of its reception, and of the traditions it inherits, is a historical fact too often overlooked by those who claim history as an antidote to formal analysis. History *is* a species of formalism in that it orders data under explanatory (often narrative) principles and it depends on formal criticism to provide data and to test its explanations.

Predictably, the main task in preparing this second edition of *A Hitchcock Reader* was bibliographic. The "References and Suggested Readings" lists in the first edition of *A Hitchcock Reader* did a surprisingly comprehensive job of presenting the extant English-language scholarship on Hitchcock. In the intervening two decades, Hitchcock scholarship has flourished; its expansion in the first of those decades is helpfully on view in Jane E. Sloan's *Alfred Hitchcock: A Filmography and Bibliography* (Berkeley: Univ. of California Press, 1995). A similar degree of comprehensiveness in the present edition of *A Hitchcock Reader* being impossible for reasons of space, we have been extremely selective.

Because readability was an important criterion in selecting chapters to reprint, it was also a factor in our bibliographic decision making. Even so, we have included some advanced material, especially where the author in question has been important to contemporary Hitchcock studies, such as Slavoj Žižek. Because space was so precious, we decided not to list separately every item in the numerous collections of essays on Hitchcock, though exceptions were made. Similarly, we have generally not listed essays that subsequently became chapters in books about Hitchcock. Where an essay has been reprinted, we tended to favor the most recent or readily available version. When it became necessary, chiefly in Parts One and Four, we also excluded essays listed in Sloan. Indeed, an essay cited in the documentation of any of our chapters will be listed in our bibliographic apparatus only if it is of particular historical importance to Hitchcock criticism. There is a lively Internet version of

"Hitchcock Studies" available online. With apologies to the many authors whose electronically published essays on Hitchcock we reluctantly decided not to list here, we recommend that readers consult the following websites: *Senses of Cinema* (http://www.sensesofcinema.com/), *Bright Lights* (http://www.brightlightsfilm.com/), *The MacGuffin* (http://www.labyrinth.net.au/~muffin/), and the *Alfred Hitchcock Wiki* (http://www.hitchcockwiki.com/hitchcock/wiki/Main_Page).

Immediately following the introduction to Part One, "Taking Hitchcock Seriously," is a list of books and essays that are pertinent to several or all periods of Hitchcock's career. Any journey through Hitchcock should begin here. Sources listed after the introduction to Part Two, "Hitchcock in Britain," are limited to those primarily relevant to that period of Hitchcock's activity. This is also true for those listed after Parts Three through Five, though we will refer from a later list to an earlier one for economy's sake, where an essay appears in an anthology previously cited, for example. We have done our best through brief annotations to identify the topics of entries whose titles are not self-explanatory. In our Part One list of "References and Suggested Readings," we have organized many of the book-length works by generic and topical headings. Though this has resulted in some interesting categorical decisions – listing Michael Walker's wonderfully analytical *Hitchcock's Motifs* under "Reference Works," for example – we believe this arrangement increases significantly the readability and utility of our bibliographic apparatus.

We conclude this Introduction with a final note on "history." For brevity's sake and in deference to Jane Sloan's work, we have not included an exhaustive Hitchcock filmography. Though a dedicated auteur critic could find no better exemplar of directorial authorship in the commercial cinema than Hitchcock, it is increasingly obvious that he did not work alone. Excellent and concise testimony to this effect is found in Susan Schenker's "Plotting the Hitchcock Family" (*Take One*, vol. 5, no. 2 (1976)), which provides a listing by frequency of Hitchcock's collaborative relationships. Not surprisingly for someone whose films are so profoundly concerned with questions of sexuality and marriage, Hitchcock's most sustained collaboration was with his wife, Alma Reville, who received screen credit of several sorts (adaptation, screenwriter, assistant director), always under her maiden name, on eighteen of Hitchcock's fifty-three films, from *The Pleasure Garden* (1926) to *Stage Fright* (1950). Next on the list, again not surprisingly, are two directors of photography, Robert Burks and Jack Cox.

To avoid misrepresentation, we have included screen credits for principal members of cast and crew for all the films discussed at length in this volume. All such entries are found immediately following the first essay treating the film in question in Parts Two through Five. Credits for *Vertigo* follow Wood's "Male Desire/Male Anxiety" chapter; those for *The Birds* appear after the McCombe chapter; those for *Marnie* appear after the Piso essay; those for *Psycho* follow Bellour's chapter. The brief chronology on pages xiii–xiv lists all of Hitchcock's feature films and television shows, keyed as closely as possible to the order of release or initial broadcast. At the very least the chronology stands as a reminder of all that is not covered in this selection of essays; we hope it will also serve as encouragement to further viewing and thinking. Such are both the substance and process of film criticism.

Part One
Taking Hitchcock Seriously

Robin Wood began his landmark 1965 study, *Hitchcock's Films*, with the question: "Why should we take Hitchcock seriously?" In a 1983 article in *American Film* (reprinted here as "Male Desire, Male Anxiety: The Essential Hitchcock" and revised for inclusion in the 1989 edition of *Hitchcock's Films Revisited*), Wood rephrases the question in light of the concept of ideology by asking "Can Hitchcock be saved for feminism?" In 2003 John Belton rephrased the question yet again, explicitly referring to these earlier interrogatives and claiming that such questions have an institutional significance quite apart from "qualities inherent in Hitchcock's films themselves" (p. 21), by wondering "Can Hitchcock be Saved from Hitchcock Studies?"

Though each question is rhetorical – the answer, offered with various degrees of elaboration, conviction, and anxiety, is always affirmative – they are also deeply engaged in crucial moments in the history of Hitchcock criticism. When Wood first posed his question, many (often journalistic) film critics would have answered with a confident "We shouldn't," not by the standards of seriousness of the socially engaged cinema of post-war Neorealism or of "art film" directors like Federico Fellini, Ingmar Bergman, and Michelangelo Antonioni. Similarly, there was a time in the history of film feminism when it was plausible to believe that Hitchcock's films – and maybe the "Classical Hollywood Cinema" in its entirety – were beyond salvation. And in the current "Post-Theory" era, film theory and cultural theory are themselves sometimes accused of "instrumentalizing" or distorting the films under study by imposing frames of reference that are impertinent to the purposes of the films, their makers, or their viewers. But the three questions taken together also attest to the success of Wood's initial argument on Hitchcock's behalf – which claimed on experiential grounds that, seen "without preconceptions," even popular films like Hitchcock's could have "profound implications" (p. 59) as worthy of study as those in the films of Hitchcock's art film contemporaries – because there is, beyond the shadow of a doubt, a discipline of "Hitchcock Studies" of which it is now possible to be wary and in which *A Hitchcock Reader* has played a part.

There are reasons for thinking that Hitchcock generally took *himself* seriously as an artist and also for thinking that he sometimes did not. He was notoriously reluctant,

2 *Taking Hitchcock Seriously*

in any event, to confirm the "metaphysical" pronouncements of cinephile partisans caught up in "the delirium of interpretation" (as Claude Chabrol retroactively describes it; see Vest, 162). That Hitchcock took film seriously *as art* seems evident from his active participation in the (London) Film Society in the late 1920s. Here (per the accounts of Donald Spoto, Tom Ryall, and Patrick McGilligan) Hitchcock would likely have seen German films, like Robert Wiene's *The Cabinet of Dr. Caligari*, Paul Leni's *Waxworks*, G. W. Pabst's *The Joyless Street*, and F. W. Murnau's *Nosferatu*; would probably have seen such Soviet masterpieces as V. I. Pudovkin's *Mother* and *The End of St. Petersburg* and Sergei Eisenstein's *Battleship Potemkin* and *The General Line*; and would have seen films from the French avant-garde and American movies as well, perhaps including Erich von Stroheim's *Greed*. (Hitchcock's interest in the "art film" is also evident in his viewing of Bergman's *The Virgin Spring* and *The Magician* as well as Jean-Luc Godard's *Breathless* and Antonioni's *L'avventura* in the months preceding his decision to make *The Birds*, as Robert Kapsis reports.) Indeed, Hitchcock and several Film Society associates – among them Ivor Montagu, Angus MacPhail, Sidney Bernstein, and Eliot Stannard, all of whom became Hitchcock collaborators – would retire to the flat of filmmaker Adrian Brunel after Film Society screenings to hold "'Hate Parties' to dissect what they had just seen" (McGilligan, 76).

That Hitchcock was eager to be considered an artist of film (of "pure film," as he often put it) is evident in the extent of his cooperation with the young auteur critics at *Cahiers du cinéma* – to the point, as Jean Douchet reports in "Hitch and His Public," of providing a pantomimic "sneak preview" of *Psycho* before it went into production. To be sure, as a filmmaker Hitchcock was always mindful of the press. According to Montagu, Hitchcock saw the press as a primary audience, because of the influence reviewers had on distributors, who controlled what audiences saw (see Kapsis, 21). But his courting of the French film press in the 1950s and 1960s (and theirs of him) was important to the history of cinema far beyond its immediate consequences for Hitchcock.

The "politique des auteurs" advocated by the young *Cahiers* critics was scandalous not because it emphasized the director as the "author" or "artist" responsible for creating a film. Ever since D. W. Griffith declared himself the founder of "the modern technique of the art" of film in his December 3, 1913 advertisement in the *New York Dramatic Mirror*, the idea of the director as "artist" was in the air. As Hitchcock himself made the point in 1927: "Film directors live with their pictures while they are being made. They are their babies just as much as an author's novel is the offspring of his imagination. And that seems to make it all the more certain that when moving pictures are really artistic they will be created entirely by one man" (Spoto, 103). But we note that Hitchcock makes the latter point while comparing American films to British films and "commercially minded" films to "really artistic films for the artistically minded minority" (in the latter case he mentions Debussy and Shelley and Cubist painting; see Gottlieb's *Hitchcock on Hitchcock*, 166–7). So Hitchcock too feared that commerce and art were antithetical. And it was exactly that antithesis that the auteurism of the young *Cahiers* Turks was intent on complicating – by claiming that commercially successful directors like Hitchcock and Howard Hawks were capable of creating morally complex and individually inflected works despite the anti-Hollywood (or anti-American) prejudice that sometimes passed for sophistication at *Sight and Sound* or *Positif*.

Thus, in answering the question "How Could You Possibly Be a Hitchcocko-Hawksian?" André Bazin paraphrases Jean-Paul Sartre to the effect that "Every technique refers back to a metaphysics" as justifying "a vigilant refusal under all circumstances to *reduce* the cinema to the sum of what it expresses" (p. 33). If we understand "expresses" as referring to overt "subject matter," then Bazin's characterization of *Cahiers*-style auteurism entails energetic interpretation; analysis amounts to ascribing "metaphysical" depth to a film by reference to its stylistic parameters. Hence Eric Rohmer and Claude Chabrol can conclude their 1957 *Hitchcock* by saying: "Hitchcock is one of the greatest *inventors of form* in the entire history of cinema.... Our effort will not have been in vain if we have been able to demonstrate how an entire moral universe has been elaborated on the basis of this form and by its very vigor. In Hitchcock's work form does not embellish content, it creates it" (p. 152).

A crucial practice of auteurism, accordingly, involves observing formal similarities within and across a director's entire body of films. For example, in "Hitch and His Public" Douchet sees the "voyeurism" theme migrating from *Rear Window* to *Psycho* via the windows with which both films open. He also sees the criminality of on-screen characters as reflexive; if what they see is what they *want* to see – in both cases, the death of a woman – then their guilt is in some sense our guilt. In passing, moreover, Douchet remarks upon two other Hitchcock motifs: "the call," by which he refers to the many scenes with telephones in Hitchcock; and also what we might call "the vehicular," the fatalistic threat that characters are on the verge of "being carried off, of a skidding that nothing will be able to stop," hence "all the trains, planes, automobiles, skis, boats, bicycles, wheelchairs, etc."

Such formalist observations make more credible the claim that Hitchcock was a decisive factor in producing the films for which he is known. More crucially, they allow for the metaphoric translation by which something more or less literal (a window, a phone, a wheelchair) is read as more significantly figural, as pointing toward some more "serious" or "deeper" meaning. For example, in "Hitchcock's Imagery and Art" (the concluding chapter of *Hitchcock's British Films*, reprinted here as Chapter 2), Maurice Yacowar analyzes the "parallel staircases" of the Newton home in *Shadow of a Doubt* metaphorically: opposed to "the clean public front" stair there is "the dangerous, steep, private back, the latter [of] which Uncle Charlie uses to escape and to threaten Charlie. The two-staired house works as an image of the human psyche and as an image of a societal ideal, both of which project a front that is more attractive and safer than their hidden natures." (Yacowar is obviously indebted to Truffaut's famous "Skeleton Keys" analysis of paired objects and scenes in the film.) Because "Hitchcock exploits the insecurity of his audience" (Yacowar), because his "creation depends on an exact science of the spectator's reaction" (Douchet), such attributions of meaning are interpretively risky, may well seem idiosyncratic or optional in a way that they are not, say, in the Bergman of *Wild Strawberries* or *Persona*. Hence the sense that interpreting Hitchcock's films is more than usually personal, even willful. But recent efforts in the direction of reading Hitchcock's figures – Tom Cohen's two-volume *Hitchcock's Cryptonymies*, but also Peter Conrad's *The Hitchcock Murders* and Michael Walker's *Hitchcock's Motifs* – indicate clearly enough that Hitchcock's complexities are extraordinarily intricate and various.

In "Male Desire, Male Anxiety," reprinted here as Chapter 17, Robin Wood considers Hitchcock's relation to feminism by reference to the concept of "ideological contradiction," especially as it pertains to a picture of the "classical Hollywood film" as more or less homogeneous in its structures and effects. Wood's earlier "Retrospective" – reprinted here as Chapter 3 – appeared at a moment in the institutional shift from auteurism to "Cine-structuralism" or "semiotics," wherein the goal of criticism was no longer the cinephilic elaboration of the admirable unity of style and theme in a given film or group of films but the social-"scientific" demystification of the structures of perception and acculturation ("codes," for short) that underlie the social-political status quo. No doubt the most influential exemplar of this "materialist" critical practice is Laura Mulvey's 1975 *Screen* essay "Visual Pleasure and Narrative Cinema," which employs a version of Jacques Lacan's psychoanalysis to elaborate how gender is encoded in and on film, and not just visually. To the extent that "pleasure in looking" in mainstream cinema "has been split between active/male and passive/female" modes (p. 19), narrative in film is largely a male affair, though its scenarios nearly always "contain" (our term) the female image, either by making a woman the object of sadistic voyeurism, a subject to be investigated or saved *à la film noir*; or by fetishizing her as a perfect erotic spectacle whose very perfection denies the threat of "castration" she purportedly represents. Following Douchet on *Rear Window*, Mulvey sees Hitchcock's *Vertigo* especially as a parable of male complicity in which the viewer (via identification with Scottie) both idealizes and interrogates Madeleine/Judy, with disastrous consequences.

We link Wood and Mulvey for several reasons beyond mere chronology. Though in "Retrospective" Wood defends auteurism against the implication that individual creativity is a trivial concern, he does so by historicizing Hitchcock's cinematic practice. Moreover, his vocabulary at crucial junctures uncannily echoes Mulvey's. His discussion of "Realism," for instance, is obviously part of the same conversation as Mulvey's concluding analysis of the "three looks" of cinema (of the camera, of the audience, of fictional characters at each other); both remark on the illusory "sleight of hand" (Wood) by means of which audiences are induced to identify with characters and hence disavow the materiality of the camera and responsibility of the viewer. Also, Wood's remarks on "the 'look'" and its relation to "the power/impotence obsession" that is typical both of Hitchcock's stories and of Hitchcock's relation to his audience clearly echo Mulvey's discussions of the active/passive duality and of castration. Indeed, Wood depicts Hitchcock as suffering from a "lack" in specifying Hitchcock's "limitations"; Hitchcock is too frequently reluctant "to allow certain disturbing implications to be fully explored" and suffers from a "relative weakness" of the "normative impulse." In essence, Wood claims, Hitchcock's creative energies are negative or critical: "His work typically equates 'normality' with a bourgeois life in whose values the creative side of him totally disbelieves but to which it can provide no alternative."

Wood may be alluding to Mulvey in "Retrospective" or simply drawing (like Mulvey) upon a disciplinary vocabulary already common in Hitchcock criticism ("voyeurism," for instance, or "identification"). What matters most is that both Wood and Mulvey eventually see Hitchcock as what Roland Barthes would call a "limit" case, as a director whose films so completely inhabit and exploit the medium of the "Classical Hollywood Cinema" as to expose its workings and limitations. Mulvey openly follows Douchet's example in seeing *Rear Window* "as a metaphor for the cinema" (p. 23), though her corollary remarks on *Vertigo* and *Marnie* make clear that the "cinema" in question is "Hollywood." In Lacanian terms, writes Mulvey, Hitchcock's "heroes are exemplary of the symbolic order and the law," though the Hitchcock hero is also so voyeuristically fascinated with an eroticized fantasy image that his role is "to portray the contradictions and tensions experienced by the spectator" (p. 23).

As Wood observes, his "Retrospective" description of Hitchcock's skeptical irony is not that far removed from the views of Hitchcock's most rigorous detractors. (Compare David Thomson, whose longstanding distrust of Hitchcock has effectively made him the leader of the loyal opposition: "The master did not film the world; he armored himself against it with bitter homilies and rat-community models" (*Overexposures*, 190).) By the time he comes to write "Male Desire, Male Anxiety," however, Wood too has shifted focus from the question of Hitchcock's individual "psychopathology" to his status as representing, in *Rear Window* and *Vertigo*, "the logic of patriarchy" and of its "original desire," which amounts, given its inevitable disappointment, to an instance of the death drive. Wood credits Hitchcock with revealing the fantastic basis of "romantic love" in divulging Judy's status as Elster's accomplice in the murder of his wife; Scottie's love for "Madeleine" is as fatal to Judy as Elster's cold brutality is to the real Madeleine. And, though Wood disavows the equation of *Rear Window* with cinema *tout court*, however typical it may be of Hitchcock, he still claims that, "at their best, the films dramatize and foreground not merely tensions personal to Hitchcock, but tensions central to our culture and to its construction and organization of sexual difference."

The claim that Hitchcock exemplifies a self-destructive cultural system, however poignantly or tragically, provides a reason for asking "Can Hitchcock Be Saved from Hitchcock Studies?" Though Belton poses that question in an extended review of twenty-first-century Hitchcockiana, clearly his main anxiety about the "instrumentalization" or "commodification" of Hitchcock derives from the "academization of film studies" that was "spurred in part by the rise of Grand Theory in the 1970s" (p. 17). On this latter account Belton explicitly evokes the work of David Bordwell and Noël Carroll, especially their advocacy, in *Post-Theory: Reconstructing Film Studies*, of the prospective benefits of "piecemeal" theorizing, benefits that will follow if film theory and criticism focus more on "middle-level" research problems and less on doctrine (especially as the latter leads to interpretative mimicry: "Lacan in, Lacan out," as Raymond Durgnat put it in *A Long Hard Look at* Psycho (p. 6)). Indeed, what Bordwell and Carroll advocate is akin to what Sidney Gottlieb recommends in calling for a "de-centering" of Hitchcock studies, so that "concern for Hitchcock's distinctive genius" will "be complemented by studies of the various contexts of his work (for example, the artistic and production systems and environments he worked in, his collaborators, his historical milieu, and so on) and a healthy awareness of his artistic limitations, weaknesses, and various missteps as well as his many achievements" (*Gottlieb and Brookhouse*, 17).

We do not claim that John Orr's "Hitch as Matrix-Figure: Hitchcock and Twentieth-Century Cinema" exemplifies Post-Theory as advocated by Bordwell and Carroll, in the sense that Orr rejects as philosophically untenable and methodologically unnecessary most of the "grand" claims of "1975 Film Theory," though he is skeptical on some accounts. To the extent that Orr's first chapter, like the whole of *Hitchcock and Twentieth-Century Cinema*, is explicitly interpretative – most obviously so in his discussion of *The Birds* – it could hardly be otherwise, because it is the business of interpretation to read in the direction of greater meaning, meaning beyond the obvious or literal, though what counts as "serious" or "significant" or "symptomatic" obviously shifts over time. Indeed, in a crucial sense Orr is most timely on these accounts, because one of his primary undertakings is an elaboration of what he calls Hitchcock's "queer aesthetic" (p. 179), especially in regard to *I Confess*, to which he devotes a whole chapter. In Orr's introductory chapter, his emphasis on "subtextual" implications that go "beyond heterosexual romance" is elaborated chiefly by reference to *The Manxman*, a silent film in which "a complicity of looks and signs" suggests "a *dual gaze*," a doubling of desire that "goes beyond narrative's official meaning." (For further elaboration and references, see the Introduction to Part Five: Hitchcock and Film Theory: A *Psycho* Dossier.)

Two other trends in recent Hitchcock criticism are evident in Orr's "Hitch as Matrix-Figure." The more obvious of these is the evocation of the aesthetic and cultural contexts that bear on Hitchcock's accomplishments. Orr's *Hitchcock and Twentieth-Century Cinema* takes strategic advantage of much of the archival work that has been done on Hitchcock since the first edition of *A Hitchcock Reader* appeared, especially those projects involving historical research into Hitchcock's production processes and circumstances. Orr makes frequent reference to Dan Auiler's *Hitchcock's Notebooks* and Bill Krohn's *Hitchcock at Work*, for example, both of which provide fascinating access to Hitchcock's collaborative relationships. In addition, as Orr notes in his first paragraph, Hitchcock is increasingly becoming a "matrix-figure" not only among filmmakers but also among visual artists, as is evident in several museum exhibits and catalogues that detail Hitchcock's relationships to modernist painting in particular. (See *Notorious: Alfred Hitchcock and Contemporary Art*, edited by Kerry Brougher, Michael Tarantino, and Astrid Bowron, *Hitchcock and Art: Fatal Coincidences*, edited by Dominique Païni and Guy Cogeval, and *Casting a Shadow: Creating the Alfred Hitchcock Film*, edited by Will Schmenner and Corinne Granof.) But the main matrix for which Hitchcock is a "matrix-figure" is, per Orr's title, "Twentieth-Century Cinema."

Orr is no less aware than Belton that "Hitchcock's legacy has become a mixed blessing," at least to the extent that "Hollywood, in effect, has commodified [Hitchcock's] memory," yielding "an illusion of progress that masks a compulsion to repeat." But, in saying that "Hitchcock is ubiquitous" at the turn of the century, Orr pictures Hitchcock at the center not only "of his own cinema but of cinema as such."

Though Orr, like Wood, discusses Hitchcock's indebtedness to German Expressionism and to the montage aesthetic of Lev Kuleshov and Sergei Eisenstein – noting how greatly Hitchcock was indebted to early modernism – Orr emphasizes Hitchcock's "translatability." Crucial here is what Orr calls the "precise *translation of vision*" whereby strong auteurs – he specifically mentions Claude Chabrol, Eric Rohmer, Alain Resnais, Roman Polanski, David Lynch, and Peter Weir – "absorb [Hitchcock] into the world of their *own* vision, because they all have a starting point that is independent of his."

Orr also applies the matrix-figure notion to Hitchcock's relationships with collaborators and contemporaries, as if Hitchcock's "centeredness" helps explain his ability to "mediate" or "orchestrate" the contributions of his co-creators. Intriguingly, in chapter two of *Hitchcock and Twentieth-Century Cinema*, "Lost Identities: Hitchcock and David Hume," Orr urges a "transactional" theory of human communication, which "takes place through external relations and through the mediation of objects. These take priority over identity" (p. 32) in Hitchcock and Hume alike. Put otherwise, we should take Hitchcock seriously now – we cannot responsibly do otherwise – because so much of what makes cinema the pre-eminent modern art form came *through* Hitchcock, in that sense *was* Hitchcock.

Orr avowedly pursues his comparison of Hume and Hitchcock at the urging of the French philosopher Gilles Deleuze. So a second trend in contemporary Hitchcock studies for which Orr can stand as token is an accelerating engagement of film study and philosophy. Examples of film scholars who draw upon philosophy in their approaches to Hitchcock, in addition to Orr in his reliance on Hume, are Ken Mogg, who sees Arthur Schopenhauer in particular and "vitalist" philosophy in general as a crucial aspect of what Orr has termed the "buried lineage" (p. 52) of Alfred Hitchcock, and Richard Allen, who derives his concept of "Romantic Irony" from the philosophy of Friedrich Schlegel. (Robert Samuels's *Hitchcock's Bi-Textuality* would also qualify if we take Lacan as a philosopher.) In addition, numerous professional philosophers have turned their attention to Hitchcock. Obviously the most well-known philosopher to take Hitchcock as topic and exemplar is Slavoj Žižek, most notably in his edited collection *Everything You Always Wanted to Know about Lacan (But Were Afraid to Ask Hitchcock)*. Other examples include Robert J. Yanal, in his *Hitchcock as Philosopher*, Irving Singer, in his *Three Philosophical Filmmakers*, as well as the numerous professors who contributed chapters to David Baggett and William Drumin's *Hitchcock and Philosophy: Dial M for Metaphysics*. Pride of place in this tradition goes to William Rothman and his philosophical mentor, Stanley Cavell, whose *The World Viewed* repeatedly references Hitchcock as Cavell pursues his "Reflections on the Ontology of Film."

"After Hitchcock's death in 1980 we might have expected his work to become unfashionable and fade away," writes Orr. Instead, "the impact has intensified." The picture Orr provides of Hitchcock's increasing centrality to world cinema and to world culture more generally means the day has passed when "Hitchcock Studies" is solely responsible for his legacy. Hitchcock's journalistic and academic advocates were profoundly instrumental in shifting Hitchcock's status from "Master of Suspense" to "film philosopher" (Orr, 47), a fact that is beyond regretting or retracting. Put more pragmatically, the only entity who can now displace or decenter Hitchcock will be some "other" Hitchcock. Until then, film criticism seems happily fated to continue its ongoing reassessment of Hitchcock's influence and legacy as successive generations of viewers – at least some of them enrolled in college-level film classes – encounter Hitchcock anew, which means "taking seriously" the critical tradition that *A Hitchcock Reader* has always aspired to represent.

References and Suggested Readings

Reference Works

Leitch, Thomas. *The Encyclopedia of Alfred Hitchcock*. New York: Facts on File, 2002.

Maxford, Howard. *The A–Z of Hitchcock*. London: B. T. Batsford, 2002.

Sloan, Jane E. *Alfred Hitchcock: A Guide to References and Resources*. Berkeley: Univ. of California Press, 1995.

Walker, Michael. *Hitchcock's Motifs*. Amsterdam: Amsterdam Univ. Press, 2005.

Biographies

Chandler, Charlotte. *It's Only a Movie: Alfred Hitchcock, a Personal Biography*. New York: Simon and Schuster, 2005.

Falk, Quentin. *Mr. Hitchcock*. London: Haus, 2007.

McGilligan, Patrick. *Alfred Hitchcock: A Life in Darkness and Light*. New York: Regan/ Harper Collins, 2003.

O'Connell, Pat Hitchcock, and Laurent Bouzereau. *Alma Hitchcock: The Woman behind the Man*. New York: Berkley, 2003.

Spoto, Donald. *The Dark Side of Genius: The Life of Alfred Hitchcock,* centennial edition. New York: De Capo Press, 1999.

Spoto, Donald. *Spellbound by Beauty: Alfred Hitchcock and His Leading Ladies*. New York: Harmony, 2008.

Taylor, John Russell. *Hitch: The Life and Times of Alfred Hitchcock*. New York: De Capo, 1996.

Interviews

Bogdanovich, Peter. *Who the Devil Made It*. New York: Alfred A. Knopf, 1997.

Gottlieb, Sidney, ed. *Alfred Hitchcock: Interviews*. Jackson: Univ. Press of Mississippi, 2003.

Gottlieb, Sidney, ed. *Hitchcock on Hitchcock: Selected Writings and Interviews*. Berkeley: Univ. of California Press, 1995.

Truffaut, François. *Hitchcock*, revised edition. New York: Simon and Schuster, 1984. Originally published as *Le Cinéma selon Hitchcock*. Paris: Laffont, 1966.

Hitchcock at Work

Auiler, Dan. *Hitchcock's Notebooks: An Authorized and Illustrated Look inside the Creative Mind of Alfred Hitchcock*. New York: Spike, 1999.

Auiler, Dan. Vertigo: *The Making of a Hitchcock Classic*. New York: St Martin's Press, 1998.

DeRosa, Steven. *Writing with Hitchcock: The Collaboration of Alfred Hitchcock and John Michael Hayes*. London: Faber and Faber, 2001.

Freeman, David. *The Last Days of Alfred Hitchcock: A Memoir Featuring the Screenplay of "Alfred Hitchcock's The Short Night."* Woodstock, NY: Overlook Press, 1984.

Horton, Andrew. *Henry Bumstead and the World of Hollywood Art Direction*. Austin: Univ. of Texas Press, 2003. A chapter on Bumstead's art direction for several Hitchcock films.

Hunter, Evan. *Me and Hitch*. London: Faber and Faber, 1997.

Kraft, Jeff, and Aaron Leventhal. *Footsteps in the Fog: Alfred Hitchcock's San Francisco*. Santa Monica: Santa Monica Press, 2002.

Krohn, Bill. *Hitchcock at Work*. London: Phaidon Press, 2000.

Leff, Leonard J. *Hitchcock and Selznick: The Rich and Strange Collaboration of Alfred Hitchcock and David O. Selznick in Hollywood*. New York: Weidenfeld & Nicolson, 1987.

Leigh, Janet, and Christopher Nickens. Psycho: *Behind the Scenes of the Classic Thriller*. New York: Harmony Books, 1995.

Moral, Tony Lee. *Hitchcock and the Making of* Marnie. Lanham, MD: Scarecrow Press, 2002.

Rebello, Stephen. *Alfred Hitchcock and the Making of* Psycho. New York: Dembner Books, 1990.

Schatz, Thomas. *The Genius of the System: Hollywood Filmmaking in the Studio Era*. New York: Pantheon Books, 1988. Several chapters treat Hitchcock, mostly in connection with Selznick.

Schmenner, Will, and Corinne Granof, eds. *Casting a Shadow: Creating the Alfred Hitchcock Film*. Evanston, IL: Mary and Leigh Block Museum of Art, Northwestern University, and Northwestern Univ. Press, 2007.

Smith, Steven C. *A Heart at Fire's Center: The Life and Music of Bernard Herrmann*. Los Angeles: Univ. of California Press, 1991.

Vaz, Mark Cotta, and Craig Barron. *The Invisible Art: The Legends of Movie Matte Painting*. San Francisco: Chronicle Books, 2002. Includes discussion of Albert Whitlock's matte paintings for *The Birds, Marnie*, and *Torn Curtain*.

Hitchcock and the Other Arts

Brougher, Kerry, Michael Tarantino, and Astrid Bowron, eds. *Notorious: Alfred Hitchcock and Contemporary Art*. Oxford: Museum of Modern Art Oxford, 1999.

Brown, Royal S. *Overtones and Undertones: Reading Film Music*. Berkeley: Univ. of Calif. Press, 1994. Several chapters discuss Hitchcock's films, and not only those scored by Bernard Herrmann.

Grimonprez, Johan. *Looking for Alfred*. London: Film and Video Umbrella; Ostfildern: Hatje Cantz, 2007. Published in conjunction with an exhibition at the Pinakothek der Moderne.

Leigh, Christian, curator. *Psycho*. New York: KunstHall, 1992. Catalogue of a gallery exhibition.

Leigh, Christian, ed. *Vertigo*. Paris: Edition Thaddaeus Ropac, 1991. Catalogue of a gallery exhibition.

Païni, Dominique, and Guy Cogeval, eds. *Hitchcock and Art: Fatal Coincidences*. Montreal: Montreal Museum of Fine Arts, 2000.

Peucker, Brigitte. *Incorporating Images: Film and the Rival Arts*. Princeton: Princeton Univ. Press, 1995. Discusses dismemberment, *Murder!*, and *Vertigo*.

Peucker, Brigitte. *The Material Image: Art and the Real in Film*. Stanford: Stanford Univ. Press, 2007. Has two chapters on "The Scene of Art in Hitchcock."

Sullivan, Jack. *Hitchcock's Music*. New Haven: Yale Univ. Press, 2006.

Essay Collections

Allen, Richard, and S. Ishii-Gonzalès, eds. *Alfred Hitchcock: Centenary Essays*. London: British Film Institute, 1999.

Allen, Richard, and S. Ishii-Gonzalès, eds. *Hitchcock: Past and Future*. New York: Routledge, 2004.

Baggett, David, and William A. Drumin, eds. *Hitchcock and Philosophy: Dial M for Metaphysics*. Chicago: Open Court, 2007.

Boyd, David, ed. *Perspectives on Alfred Hitchcock*. Boston: G. K. Hall, 1995.

Boyd, David, and R. Barton Palmer. *After Hitchcock: Influence, Imitation, and Intertextuality*. Austin: Univ. of Texas Press, 2006.

Creekmur, Corey K., and Alexander Doty, eds. *Out in Culture: Gay, Lesbian, and Queer Essays on Popular Culture*. Durham, NC: Duke Univ. Press, 1995. Has a "Dossier on Hitchcock."

Deutelbaum, Marshall, and Leland Poague, eds. *A Hitchcock Reader*. Ames: Iowa State Univ. Press, 1986.

Freedman, Jonathan, and Richard Millington, eds. *Hitchcock's America*. New York: Oxford Univ. Press, 1999.

Gottlieb, Sidney, and Christopher Brookhouse, eds. *Framing Hitchcock: Selected Essays from the* Hitchcock Annual. Detroit: Wayne State Univ. Press, 2002.

LaValley, Albert J., ed. *Focus on Hitchcock*. Englewood Cliffs, NJ: Prentice-Hall, 1972.

Raubicheck, Walter, and Walter Srebnick, eds. *Hitchcock's Rereleased Film: From* Rope *to* Vertigo. Detroit: Wayne State Univ. Press, 1991.

Žižek, Slavoj, ed. *Everything You Always Wanted to Know about Lacan (But Were Afraid to Ask Hitchcock)*. London: Verso, 1992.

Book-Length Studies

Allen, Richard. *Hitchcock's Romantic Irony*. New York: Columbia Univ. Press, 2007.

Bellour, Raymond. *The Analysis of Film,* ed. Constance Penley. Bloomington: Indiana Univ. Press, 2000. Originally published as *L'Analyse du film*. Paris: Éditions Albatros, 1979.

Brill, Lesley. *The Hitchcock Romance: Romance and Irony in Hitchcock's Films*. Princeton: Princeton Univ. Press, 1988.

Cohen, Paula Marantz. *Alfred Hitchcock: The Legacy of Victorianism*. Lexington: Univ. of Kentucky Press, 1995.

Cohen, Tom. *Secret Agents*. Minneapolis: Univ. of Minnesota Press, 2005. Vol. 1 of *Hitchcock's Cryptonymies*.

Cohen, Tom. *War Machines*. Minneapolis: Univ. of Minnesota Press, 2005. Vol. 2 of *Hitchcock's Cryptonymies*.

Conrad, Peter. *The Hitchcock Murders*. London: Faber and Faber, 2000.

Corber, Robert. *In the Name of National Security: Hitchcock, Homophobia and the Political Construction of Gender in Postwar America*. Durham, NC: Duke Univ. Press, 1993.

Drumin, William A. *Thematic and Methodological Foundations of Alfred Hitchcock's Artistic Vision*. Lewiston, NY: Edwin Mellon Press, 2004.

Douchet, Jean. *Hitchcock*. Paris: Cahiers du cinéma, 2006. Originally published as *Alfred Hitchcock*. Paris: Herne, 1967.

Dufreigne, Jean-Pierre. *Hitchcock Style*, trans. Simon Pleasance and Fronza Woods. New York: Assouline, 2004.

Duncan, Paul. *Alfred Hitchcock: Architect of Anxiety 1899–1980*. Cologne: Taschen, 2003.

Durgnat, Raymond. *A Long Hard Look at* Psycho. London: British Film Institute, 2002.

Durgnat, Raymond. *The Strange Case of Alfred Hitchcock: Or, the Plain Man's Hitchcock*. Cambridge, MA: MIT Press, 1974.

Finler, Joel W. *Hitchcock in Hollywood*. New York: Continuum, 1992.

Hare, William. *Hitchcock and the Methods of Suspense*. Jefferson, NC: McFarland, 2007.

Haeffner, Nicholas. *Alfred Hitchcock*. Harlow, UK: Longman, 2005.

Hurley, Neil P. *Soul in Suspense: Hitchcock's Fright and Delight*. Metuchen, NJ: Scarecrow Press, 1993.

Kapsis, Robert E. *Hitchcock: The Making of a Reputation*. Chicago: Univ. of Chicago Press, 1992.

Leitch, Thomas. *Find the Director and Other Hitchcock Games*. Athens, GA: Univ. of Georgia Press, 1991.

Modleski, Tania. *The Women Who Knew Too Much: Hitchcock and Feminist Theory*, second edition. New York: Routledge, 2005.

Mogg, Ken. *The Alfred Hitchcock Story*. London: Titan Books, 1999.

Morris, Christopher D. *The Hanging Figure: On Suspense and the Films of Alfred Hitchcock*. Westport, CT: Praeger, 2002.

Orr, John. *Hitchcock and Twentieth-Century Cinema*. London: Wallflower Press, 2005.

Perry, Dennis R. *Hitchcock and Poe: The Legacy of Delight and Terror*. Lanham, MD: Scarecrow Press, 2004.

Phillips, Gene D. *Alfred Hitchcock*. Boston: Twayne, 1984.

Price, Theodore. *Hitchcock and Homosexuality: His 50-Year Obsession with Jack the Ripper and the Superbitch Prostitute: A Psychoanalytic View*. Metuchen, NJ: Scarecrow Press, 1992.

Pomerance, Murray. *An Eye for Hitchcock*. New Brunswick, NJ: Rutgers Univ. Press, 2004.

Rohmer, Eric, and Claude Chabrol. *Hitchcock: The First Forty-Four Films*, trans. Stanley Hochman. New York: Frederick Ungar, 1979. Originally published as *Hitchcock*. Paris: Éditions Universitaires, 1957.

Rothman, William. *Hitchcock: The Murderous Gaze*. Cambridge, MA: Harvard Univ. Press, 1982.

Ryall, Tom. *Alfred Hitchcock and the British Cinema*, with a new introduction. London: Athlone, 1996.

Samuels, Robert. *Hitchcock's Bi-Textuality: Lacan, Feminisms, and Queer Theory*. Albany: SUNY Press, 1998.

Sharff, Stefan. *Alfred Hitchcock's High Vernacular: Theory and Practice*. New York: Columbia Univ. Press, 1990. Close formalist readings of *Notorious, Family Plot*, and *Frenzy*.

Simone, Sam P. *Hitchcock as Activist: Politics and the War Films*. Ann Arbor: UMI Research Press, 1982.

Sinyard, Neil. *The Films of Alfred Hitchcock*. New York: Gallary Books, 1986.

Smith, Susan. *Hitchcock: Suspense, Humour and Tone*. London: British Film Institute, 2000.

Spoto, Donald. *The Art of Alfred Hitchcock: Fifty Years of his Motion Pictures*, second edition. New York: Anchor Books, 1992.

Sterritt, David. *The Films of Alfred Hitchcock*. New York: Cambridge Univ. Press, 1993.

Strauss, Marc Raymond. *Hitchcock Nonetheless: The Master's Touch in His Least Celebrated Films*. Jefferson, NC: McFarland, 2007.

Taylor, Alan. *Jacobean Visions: Webster, Hitchcock, and Google Culture*. Frankfurt: Peter Lang, 2007.

Vest, James M. *Hitchcock and France: The Forging of an Auteur*. Westport, CT: Praeger, 2003.

Weis, Elisabeth. *The Silent Scream: Alfred Hitchcock's Sound Track*. Rutherford, NJ: Fairleigh Dickinson Univ. Press, 1982.

Wood, Robin. *Hitchcock's Films Revisited*, revised edition. New York: Columbia Univ. Press, 2002. Originally published as *Hitchcock's Films*. London: A. Zwemmer; New York: A. S. Barnes, 1965.

Yanal, Robert J. *Hitchcock as Philosopher*. Jefferson, NC: McFarland, 2005

Articles, Book Chapters, and Other References

Allen, Richard. "Daphne du Maurier and Alfred Hitchcock." In Robert Stam and Alessandra Raengo, eds., *A Companion to Literature and Film*. Malden, MA: Blackwell, 2004, 298–325. On *Jamaica Inn, Rebecca*, and *The Birds*.

Allen, Richard. "Hitchcock and Cavell." In Murray Smith and Thomas E. Wartenberg, eds., *Thinking through Cinema: Film as Philosophy*. Malden, MA: Blackwell, 2006, 43–53.

Aumont, Jacques. "Paradoxical and Innocent." In Païni and Cogeval (cited above): 79–99.

Bazin, André, "How Could You Possibly Be a Hitchcocko-Hawksian?" In Jim Hillier and Peter Wollen, eds., *Howard Hawks: American Artist*. London: British Film Institute, 1996, 32–4.

Belton, John. "Can Hitchcock be Saved from Hitchcock Studies?" *Cineaste*, vol. 28, no. 4 (Fall 2003): 16–21.

Belton, John. "Hitchcock and the Classical Paradigm." In Boyd and Palmer (cited above): 235–47.

Blake, Richard A. "Alfred Hitchcock's [Communion of Sinners]." In *Afterimage: The Indelible Catholic Imagination of Six American Filmmatkers*. Chicago: Loyola Press, 2000, 49–86. On *I Confess, Rear Window*, and *The Birds*.

Bordwell, David, and Noël Carroll. *Post-Theory: Reconstructing Film Studies*. Madison: Univ. of Wisconsin Press, 1996.

Cavell, Stanley. *The World Viewed: Reflections on the Ontology of Film*, enlarged edition. Cambridge, MA: Harvard Univ. Press, 1979.

Cohen, Tom. "Political Thrillers: Hitchcock, de Man, and Secret Agency in the 'Aesthetic State.'" In Barbara Cohen, J. Hillis Miller, and Andrzej Warminski, eds., *Material Events: Paul de Man and the Afterlife of Theory*. Minneapolis: Univ. of Minnesota Press, 2001, 114–52.

Deleuze, Gilles. *Cinema 1: The Movement Image*, trans. Hugh Tomlinson and Barbara Habberjam. Minneapolis: Univ. of Minnesota Press, 1986.

Due, Reidar. "Hitchcock's Innocence Plot." *Film Studies*, no. 4 (Summer 2004): 48–57. Challenges audience-centered approaches to Hitchcock.

Ebert, Roger. *The Great Movies*. New York: Broadway Books, 2002. Chapters on *Notorious, Psycho*, and *Vertigo*.

Ebert, Roger. *The Great Movies II*. New York: Broadway Books, 2005. Chapters on *Rear Window* and *Strangers on a Train*.

Edelman, Lee. "Piss Elegant: Freud, Hitchcock, and the Micturating Penis." *GLQ*, vol. 2, nos. 1–2 (1995): 149–77. Discusses *Notorious* and *Psycho*.

Elsaesser, Thomas. "Casting Around: Hitchcock's Absence." In Grimonprez (cited above): 139–61.

Elsaesser, Thomas. "The Dandy in Hitchcock." In Allen and Ishii-Gonzalès, *Alfred Hitchcock* (cited above): 3–13.

Elsaesser, Thomas. "Too Big and Too Close: Alfred Hitchcock and Fritz Lang." *Hitchcock Annual*, no. 12 (2003–4): 1–41.

Gross, Larry. "Parallel Lines: Hitchcock the Screenwriter." *Sight and Sound,* August 1999; Hitchcock supplement, 38–44.

Gunning, Tom. "In and Out of the Frame: Paintings in Hitchcock." In Schmenner and Granof (cited above): 29–47.

Hark, Ina Rae. "Revalidating Patriarchy: Why Hitchcock Remade *The Man Who Knew Too Much*." In Raubicheck and Srebnick (cited above): 209–20.

Hemmeter, Thomas. "Hitchcock's Melodramatic Silence." *Journal of Film and Video*, vol. 48, no. 1–2 (Spring 1996): 32–40. Describes Hitchcock's "modernist" use of melodrama.

Hennelly, Mark M., Jr. "Alfred Hitchcock's Carnival." *Hitchcock Annual*, no. 13 (2004–5): 154–88. Emphasizes *The Ring, Strangers on a Train*, and *Frenzy*.

Lawrence, Amy. *Echo and Narcissus: Women's Voices in Classical Hollywood Cinema*. Berkeley: Univ. of California Press, 1991. Chapters on *Blackmail* and *Notorious*.

Lee, Sander H. "Alfred Hitchcock: Misogynist or Feminist?" *Post Script*, vol. 10, no. 3 (Summer 1991): 38–48.

Leitch, Thomas. "Hitchcock and Company." *Hitchcock Annual*, no. 14 (2005–6): 1–32.

Leitch, Thomas. "The Hitchcock Moment." In Gottlieb and Brookhouse, *Framing Hitchcock* (cited above): 180–205.

Leitch, Thomas. "It's the Cold War, Stupid: An Obvious History of the Political Hitchcock." *Literature/Film Quarterly*, vol. 27, no. 1 (1999): 3–15.

Leitch, Thomas. "McGilligan's Hitchcock and the Limits of Biography." *Hitchcock Annual*, no. 12 (2003–4): 126–46.

McArthur, Colin. "The Critic Who Knew Too Much: Alfred Hitchcock and the Absent Class Paradigm." *Film Studies*, no. 2 (Spring 2000): 15–28.

McDougal, Stuart Y. "The Director Who Knew Too Much: Hitchcock Remakes Himself." In Andrew Horton, ed., *Play It Again, Sam: Retakes and Remakes*. Berkeley: Univ. of California Press, 1998, 52–69. On the two versions of *The Man Who Knew Too Much*.

Mamber, Stephen. "Hitchcock: The Conceptual and the Pre-Digital." *Stanford Humanities Review*, vol. 7, no. 2 (Winter 1999): 128–36.

Metz, Walter. "Modernity and the Crisis in Truth: Alfred Hitchcock and Fritz Lang." In Murray Pomerance, ed., *Cinema and Modernity*. New Brunswick, NJ: Rutgers Univ. Press, 2006, 74–89. Discusses *North by Northwest* and *Shadow of a Doubt*.

Michie, Elsie B. "Unveiling Maternal Desires: Hitchcock and American Domesticity." In Freedman and Millington (cited above): 29–53. Discusses *Shadow of a Doubt* and *The Man Who Knew Too Much* (1956).

Mulvey, Laura. "Visual Pleasure and Narrative Cinema." In *Visual and Other Pleasures*. Bloomington: Indiana Univ. Press, 1989, 14–26.

Naremore, James. "Hitchcock and Humor." In Allen and Ishii-Gonzalès, *Hitchcock* (cited above): 22–36.

Naremore, James. "Hitchcock at the Margins of Noir." In Allen and Ishii-Gonzalès, *Alfred Hitchcock* (cited above): 263–78.

Poague, Leland. "Hitchcock and the Ethics of Vision." In William Cadbury and Leland Poague, *Film Criticism: A Counter Theory*. Ames: Iowa State Univ. Press, 1982, 91–155.

Robinson, M. J. "The Poetics of Camp in the Films of Alfred Hitchcock." *Rocky Mountain Review*, vol. 54, no. 1 (2000): 53–65. Emphasizes *Stage Fright, The Birds*, and *Marnie*.

Rothman, William. *The "I" of the Camera: Essays in Film Criticism, History, and Aesthetics*, second edition. New York: Cambridge Univ. Press, 2004. Chapters on *North by Northwest, Vertigo*, "The Villain in Hitchcock," and "Thoughts on Hitchcock's Authorship."

Sandler, Kevin S. "The Concept of Shame in the Films of Alfred Hitchcock." *Hitchcock Annual*, 1997–8, 137–52.

Sarris, Andrew. "The American Cinema: Directorial Chronology 1915–1962." *Film Culture*, no. 28 (1963): 1–68. Expanded as *The American Cinema: Directors and Directions 1929–1968*. New York: E. P. Dutton, 1968.

Sarris, Andrew. *"You Ain't Heard Nothin' Yet": The American Talking Film: History & Memory 1927–1949*. New York: Oxford Univ. Press, 1998. "The Directors" chapter discusses Hitchcock.

Singer, Irving. *Three Philosophical Filmmakers: Hitchcock, Welles, Renoir*. Cambridge, MA: MIT Press, 2004.

Sipière, Dominique. "What Hitchcock Taught Us about Whodunits." In François Gallix and Vanessa Guignery, eds., *Crime Fictions: Subverted Codes and New Structures*. Paris: Presses de L'Université Paris-Sarbonne, 2004, 149–55.

Sklar, Robert. "Death at Work: Hitchcock's Violence and Spectator Identification." In Boyd and Palmer (cited above): 217–34.

Smith, Murray. *Engaging Characters: Fiction, Emotion, and the Cinema*. Oxford: Oxford Univ. Press, 1995. *Saboteur* and *The Man Who Knew Too Much* (1956) are repeatedly discussed.

Smith, Susan. "The Spatial World of Hitchcock's Films: The Point-of-View Shot, the Camera, and 'Intrarealism.'" *Cineaction*, no. 50 (September 1999): 2–15.

Stam, Robert. "Hitchcock and Buñuel: Authority, Desire, and the Absurd." In Raubicheck and Srebnick (cited above): 116–46.

Sterritt, David. "The Diabolic Imagination: Hitchcock, Bakhtin, and the Carnivalization of Cinema." In Gottlieb and Brookhouse (cited above): 36–67.

Strauss, Marc. "The Painted Jester: Notes on the Visual Arts in Hitchcock's Films." *Journal of Popular Film and Television*, vol. 35, no. 2 (Summer 2007): 52–6.

Stromgren, Dick. "'Now to the Banquet We Press': Hitchcock's Gourmet and Gourmand Offerings." In Paul Loukides and Linda K. Fuller, eds., *Beyond the Stars III: The Material World in American Popular Film*. Bowling Green: Bowling Green State Univ. Popular Press, 1993, 97–105.

Swaab, Peter. "Hitchcock's Homophobia: The Case of *Murder!*" *Perversions*, no. 4 (Spring 1995): 6–40. Discusses homosexuality in Hitchcock generally.

Thomson, David. "Hitchcock." *Sight and Sound*, January 1997, 26–30.

Thomson, David. *Overexposures: The Crisis in American Filmmaking*. New York: William Morrow, 1981. Chapters on Hitchcock and *Psycho*.

Toles, George. *A House Made of Light: Essays on the Art of Film*. Detroit: Wayne State Univ. Press, 2001. Chapters on *Psycho, Rear Window*, and "Mother Calls the Shots: Hitchcock's Female Gaze."

Truffaut, François. "Skeleton Keys." *Film Culture*, no. 32 (Spring 1964): 63–7.

Walker, Michael. "The Stolen Raincoat and the Bloodstained Dress: *Young and Innocent* and *Stage Fright*." In Allen and Ishii-Gonzalès, *Alfred Hitchcock* (cited above): 187–203.

White, Patricia. "Hitchcock and Hom(m)osexuality." In Allen and Ishii-Gonzalès, *Hitchcock* (cited above): 211–27.

Wollen, Peter. "Hitch: A Tale of Two Cities." In Allen and Ishiii-Gonzalès, *Hitchcock* (cited above): 15–21.

Wood, Robin. "Hitchcock and Fascism." *Hitchcock Annual*, no. 13 (2004–5): 25–63.

Zirnite, Dennis. "Hitchcock, on the Level: The Heights of Spatial Tension." *Film Criticism*, vol. 10, no. 3 (Spring 1986): 2–21.

Žižek, Slavoj. *Enjoy Your Symptom! Jacques Lacan in Hollywood and Out*, revised edition. New York: Routledge, 2001. An added chapter, "Why is Reality Always Multiple?," asks "Is There a Proper Way to Remake a Hitchcock Film?"

Žižek, Slavoj. "Everything You Always Wanted to Know about Schelling (But Were Afraid to Ask Hitchcock)." In Jason M. Wirth, ed. *Schelling Now: Contemporary Readings*. Bloomington: Indiana Univ. Press, 2005, 31–44.

Žižek, Slavoj. *Looking Awry: An Introduction to Jacques Lacan through Popular Culture*. Cambridge, MA: MIT Press, 1991. "One Can Never Know Too Much about Hitchcock" emphasizes *Vertigo* (the theme of "The Woman [who] does not exist") and *The Birds* (the Lacanian connection of the anamorphic "blot" to the "maternal superego").

Chapter One
Hitch and His Public

Jean Douchet
TRANSLATED BY VERENA ANDERMATT CONLEY

A reading of this article is forbidden to those who have not yet seen *Psycho*.[1]

Which does not mean that others are obliged to read it. It is, however, impossible to study the film without unveiling its secret. And to know that would deprive the reader, as a future spectator, of a major part of his pleasure. I know this from experience. During his last interview, Hitchcock told Domarchi and myself about his film, and he mimed it to us from one end to the other, in an extraordinary fashion.[2] For more than one hour we watched *Psycho* being born, sequence by sequence, and at times shot by shot. I truly say *being born,* since this took place in October of 1959 and Hitchcock did not begin to shoot until November. And now, in his screening room at Paramount, we had the impression of seeing the film for a second time. We were cut off from part of the terror that seized the other spectators.

A Magical Art

But this terror is the primary, if not the ultimate goal pursued by Hitchcock. Even in his most inconsequential interviews he likes to reveal to what extent, for him, creation depends on an exact science of the spectator's reaction. Not for financial reasons (he was even quite sure that *Psycho* would be a failure), nor even for promotional reasons (though he admirably uses publicity, and we know, since *North by Northwest*, what he thinks of it), but because he attributes a mission to "suspense." And this mission is cathartic. The spectator has to "undo his repressions" in a psychoanalytical sense, confess himself on a logical plane, purify himself on a spiritual level. Hitchcock depends therefore on the active participation of the public.

The proof? *Rear Window*. It is there that Hitchcock elaborates his very concept of cinema (that is to say of cinema in cinema), reveals his secrets, unveils his intentions. James Stewart, a news photographer, is before everything else a spectator. This is one of the reasons why he is seen bound to his wheelchair. Through him, Hitchcock intends to define the nature of the spectator and, especially, the nature of a Hitchcockian spectator. The latter is a "voyeur." He wants to experience (sexual) pleasure (*jouir*) through the spectacle. What he looks at on the screen (in other words, what Stewart watches in the building on the other side of the courtyard) is the very projection of himself. Only the latter is capable of interesting him. In one way or the other, it is himself that he comes to see. A spectacle which, after all, would quickly become dull if some special matter, some mystery, would not happen to capture his attention entirely. From then on, his understanding is fixed on this idea which becomes an obsession. Reasoning and deduction are subordinated to subjectivity, to feelings of desire and fear. The more he desires or fears, the more his expectation will be rewarded and beyond all his hopes. Stewart so ardently desires that a crime take place that the crime does materialize and approach him. In a Hitchcock movie, the spectator creates the suspense. It does nothing but answer his own summons. (Remember, too, Doris Day, the spectator, in *The Man Who Knew Too Much*.) In other words, Hitchcock first excites vile and low feelings in his public and authorizes it through his spectacle to satisfy these urges. The impression of horror the spectator then feels brings forth other feelings in him, noble and pure, which alone are capable of destroying the initial urges. More than a therapy, cinema, here, is a truly magic art.

The Three Realities

All of which sends us back to the intention of the author. Hitchcock intends to unveil reality and have us discover it in three ways. Three, like the three blinds which go up, one after the other, in the very first shot of *Rear Window*. The first reality, evidently, is that of the everyday world which is immediately recognizable by the spectator. Hence the care which Hitchcock accords it. Because it functions as a stable basis for his construction, the filmmaker has not ceased to depict reality with a great deal of truth. For him, the fake is intolerable. Even less the arbitrary. (We are far from Clouzot's *Diaboliques*.) Never, ever, does Hitchcock deceive the spectator. At times he lulls, sometimes willingly, the spectator's attention (the way he lulls Stewart at the moment the crime takes place in *Rear Window*), but he always leaves him information enough. The spectator can, if he desires it, reconstitute in his thoughts the events which have taken place. This observation is of the utmost importance for *Psycho*, where everything, to the least detail, is explained clearly. Nothing is therefore less justified than the accusations of implausibility that some direct toward Hitchcock.

The second reality, the second set of blinds, opens onto the world of desire. It is thus that the building on the other side of the courtyard appears. Everything that takes place in the everyday world of Stewart's apartment inscribes itself there, projects itself as if on a screen. The apartment itself is shown in multiple examples, each populated by forms and animated by the forces which have brought them into being. These form-forces personify secret thoughts, mental attitudes, and especially the desires of our hero. And in this world they possess a real existence and an active power. Like an immense mirror, put up in front of the quotidian reality, the world of desire inverts situations as well as thoughts. Thus, the Kelly–Stewart couple (paralyzed) and the other, Raymond Burr and his bedridden wife. Thus also the existence of Stewart's latent desire to rid himself of Kelly, a desire which Raymond Burr acts out. These form-forces of desire constitute the primary element of any Hitchcock movie. A psychoanalyst will see in it the figure of culpability. However, never before *Psycho* had our filmmaker made it so evident. Here, the form is endowed with a terrifying force.

Finally, the third reality, the intellectual world. The latter is the main support beam of the Hitchcockian *oeuvre*, the perpendicular which links the two parallel universes and thus allows them to communicate. It is on this beam that the film-maker relies for all his films. It is therefore via this intermediary world that Stewart, confined in his quotidian universe (and that is the reason why we do not leave his living room throughout the movie), is able to see through to the world of desire. As spectator, what does our hero see? What he believes to be the quotidian world, though it is only his own reflection. But the world of desire soon unveils his true nature. A horrible action takes place in it, one which the hero has not seen but suspects. From then on his attention is awake, his intellect at the service of his self-interest. If Stewart, on the basis of the slightest clues, leads his investigation according to the logical process of induction and deduction, it is not that he pursues a noble goal. To the contrary, he seeks less to reveal the light than to penetrate the darkness, the darkness in which the murderer envelops himself, though his presence is nevertheless betrayed by a cigarette. In brief, he examines the objective givens (*les données objectives*) only to please his own subjectivity, or even better, to satisfy an even sicker curiosity. (Understood from this perspective, the publicity about *Psycho* imagined by Hitch becomes a chief element in the movie: the public must want to feel fear.) Once this happens, the audience deprives itself of its most important weapon, lucid understanding. The audience is as unprotected as a savage, subject to great ancestral fears. Its reason voluntarily loses itself in the irrational, surrenders itself without defense (like Janet Leigh under the shower) to the almighty power of the occult.

In front of the menacing Shadow of the murderer, who, having come from the world of desire, suddenly invades his quotidian universe, the flashes of the camera seem to Stewart laughably ineffectual. This purely material light cannot suffice to protect him. "Each is caught in his own trap," we hear it said in *Psycho*. The Hitchcockian spectator more than anyone else. Because of this intellectual distance (represented by the courtyard), Stewart, at the height of curiosity, wants Kelly to cross it. He then releases what occultists and magicians fear the most: the blow in return. Now, if the reader is willing to be convinced that *Rear Window* illustrates the very concept of Hitchcockian cinema, then he can summarize what precedes in these terms: Stewart is like the projector; the building opposite like the screen; then the distance which separates them, the intellectual world, would be occupied by the beam of light. If the reader also remembers that Stewart is first the spectator, he can conclude that the hero "invents his own cinema." But is that not the very definition of a "voyeur," the very core of morose gratification?

From Contempt to Complicity

So? We have to push our investigation of this intellectual world even further. First of all, the more this investigation concentrates on an object of desire or fear, the more intense it becomes, the more the force of this intensity animates the form which it brought into being. At the same time, the force becomes more precise and grows stronger. Thus in *Psycho*. Assume that Stewart has descended from the screen of *Rear Window* to take his place in the theater, that he has become each one of us, a spectator. His voyeur's appetite finds nourishment in the opening of *Psycho*. Indeed, the camera penetrates indiscreetly into a room with lowered shades, in the middle of the afternoon. And in this room there is a couple on a bed, embracing, kissing, demonstrating a great physical attraction. From then on, he feels frustrated. He would like "to see more." Even if John Gavin's bare chest could possibly satisfy half the audience, the fact that Janet Leigh is not naked is hardly tolerated by the other half. This awakened desire must logically find its conclusion at the end of Janet's journey. She will be naked, completely, offering herself entirely. The sexual act which will be perpetrated on her will also be extreme – therefore, a wish fulfillment beyond all hopes.

But let us get back to the beginning of the movie. The spectator's feeling toward Janet is one of envy and contempt at the same time. A woman who accepts a sleazy hotel room in the middle of the afternoon in her own provincial town is not worthy of esteem. He may therefore ascribe to her his worst instincts – among others, his unconscious desire, which he does not dare to act out in real life, that of theft. Indeed, back at her desk, Janet witnesses an important transaction of cash. The spectator, who is beginning to get bored by these banal business scenes, wishes for something to happen. And precisely – why not? – that Janet Leigh take the money for herself. Since the transaction is irregular, there would be no proof, and the owner of the money is truly loathsome. Luckily, her boss has her carry the money to the bank. The amount is $40,000. In addition, the events take place on a Friday: the theft will not be noticed until the following Monday. So Janet takes the money. And here she is, on the road.

A cop stops her: a simple verification of identity. A disquieting feeling overcomes us. This feeling increases. The cop follows her. What does he want from her? Has the theft already been discovered? But from now on we ardently desire that she succeed. We are with her with all our heart. But this altruistic thought covers our very own crime, which Janet Leigh has to assume. Under the guise of sympathy, it hides a vile desire – a desire which will be realized: the cop abandons his pursuit.

(Why did he abandon her? There are, of necessity, three explanations. One, psychological: this woman seems distraught; moreover, she is pretty. It is normal that a cop – who is nevertheless a man – hopes that she will ask him to help her. But she does not ask. Another logic: as a highway patrolman, the state of fatigue of Janet Leigh intrigues him. Professional reasons oblige him to observe her behavior for fear that she may provoke an accident. But, she provokes none. Finally another, an occult, reason. The very appearance of the cop, similar to that of the cops in Cocteau's

Orpheus, belongs to the domain of the fantastic. He is both conscience and Angel of Order, sent for a last attempt at salvation. But he cannot save that which does not want to be saved. If the reader-spectator imbues himself with magical ideas, he understands that the hostile flow from the audience prevents the Angel from accomplishing his mission. Hence, in Hitchcock, the extreme importance of the call, the appeal, often symbolized by the telephone. That is how, in *Rear Window*, Stewart, seeing Kelly at the murderer's place, at the same time provokes and calls the latter. Inversely, the murderer calls Stewart before coming. In *Psycho*, the fact that the sheriff calls Bates in the second part of the film strangely illuminates what such calls represent in the occult order. One can converse only between equals, from man to man, from angel to angel, or from God to Satan (*North by Northwest*). By contrast, man may appeal to superior powers, whether good or evil. Teresa Wright in *Shadow of a Doubt*. Farley Granger in *Strangers on a Train*.)

Salvation being rejected by us, and therefore by Janet Leigh, she is given up to nocturnal powers, is incapable of enduring the radiance of light; from now on she falls prey to any delirium. Her state of fatigue makes us wish that she would stop. Hence our relief when she comes to a motel. But the unusual and mysterious aspect of the place and of its host provoke in us a mute anguish. We have the premonition of a danger, the more so as Janet Leigh is alone in this sinister place, alone in her room, with the window wide open, while she tries to hide her money (our money). And can't she find a better place to hide it than in plain sight, on the nightstand? From then on, we fear the worst. We fear that while she has dinner someone will steal the bank notes. And because we fear everything, her conversation with Perkins seems too long to us. We wish to see this fear verified. Our desire *to see* will increase even more: Perkins, like ourselves, is a voyeur and watches his client undress. Is there going to be a rape or a theft (*viol ou vol*)?

Neither one nor the other, but worse. Because our desire and our fear do not know yet in which object to invest, because they are still vague in our mind, the form they take is also vague – a kind of shadow, an ectoplasm. But, exacerbated by our long wait, they are at the height of their intensity. Also, the force we have transmitted to this form will be of a terrifying power. The form-force then accomplishes its crime.

(Let no one tell me that I extrapolate. On the one hand, I describe only what one sees and what each spectator may have felt. On the other hand, I point out that *Psycho* was shot in forty-one days. But this scene itself, which lasts only forty-five seconds on the screen, took six days to film. Hitchcock has carefully explained the difficulties he and Russell, his director of photography, had in rendering this indefinite form. He wanted no special effects but insisted that the effects be the result of lighting itself. In short, he had a very precise idea about arriving at this indefinite form. Let us give him the benefit – which he claims vigorously elsewhere – of knowing what is needed and of not shooting anything that is not rigorously necessary.)

A crime at one and the same time hallucinating and fascinating. A crime which Perkins tries to efface out of filial devotion. And while he does so, we enter completely into his thoughts. We witness his sordid household chores; we accept that Janet Leigh, wrapped in a transparent shower curtain, really becomes what she represented for us, a form. We are simply anxious for this operation to be over. Moreover, we fear that another driver, lost on this little-frequented road, will discover the crime. A fear heightened even more when Perkins, having made a rapid inspection of the room to see if he has not forgotten an object belonging to Janet, does not see *our* money.

(Which shows that Janet had found the best hiding place for it. "To appreciate *Psycho*, one needs a great sense of humor," states Hitchcock. Especially some Hitchcockian humor, which consists, as we know, in reversing wishes, that is to say in realizing them in a way contrary to our expectations. Besides, is not inversion our filmmaker's favorite system?)

But Perkins retraces his steps, sees the package, and takes it. We hope that he will see the money and keep it, in short, that the murder will have its material justification. But, since he also throws it into the trunk, together with the corpse and the other belongings of the victim, we feel at the same time relieved. Perkins pushes it all into the viscous, sleepy waters of a marsh. The car sinks halfway in. "Let us hope that it disappears," we think. At last it sinks completely, definitely. We utter a sigh of relief. Darkness – or our subconscious – has swallowed forever, we think, our complicity in the theft.

Return to the Everyday World

But to arrive at that, we have become accomplices in a crime. We have gone up one step on the ladder of culpability. I do not think that it would be useful to summarize the rest of the film in detail. What is important to perceive above all is the process of Hitchcock's creative faculty: how Hitch uses the spectator for the internal progression of the film, how he plays on his desires and fears. To understand this, one need only analyze his own reactions at the moment when the private detective arrives. The viewer understands why the form-force, when it surges for the second time, will have become very precise, though it still remains mysterious. After this test, he has one desire only: to flee. To flee the motel and its inhabitants. But the machinery he himself has set in motion cannot be stopped. From now on, paralyzed, riveted to his chair, he reaches the limits of fear. The more so as he learns that the presumed murderer has been dead for ten years. This is the utter rout of his logical mind, the disturbance of his intellectual world. Henceforth, for the spectator, everything becomes a terrifying business. It is enough for him to see some simple thing, be it the most banal, to become afraid. Each new shot is an instrument of fear. He is left with one attitude only: that of prayer and blind faith. He hopes with all his might that Vera Miles, Janet Leigh's sister, come in search of her, will be saved. These noble and disinterested feelings, together with his fear, which has reached the height of its paroxysm, make it necessary that the form-force be revealed at last, its true face in the light. It is vanquished.

Hence the necessity, after this trying incident at the end of the night, at the end of the world of desire, of returning to our quotidian world. This task may be incumbent only upon the intellectual world, but devoid of any passion, detached from subjectivity, freed of all unhealthy curiosity. In short, a task for scientific reasoning.

This is the reasoning of the psychiatrist's discourse. From then on, freed, the spectator can contemplate the object of his fear, this form-force, which seems like a nocturnal bird, to be stuffed and fixed upon a wall. And then, it excites in him an immense compassion. Compassion which the form-force attempts to refute by making believe that he wants to provoke it. ("I am not going to move. They all look at me. This fly is going to continue to walk on my hand. And they will say, he is not even capable of harming a fly.") And our pity is perhaps the only chance for salvation for this form-force which appears to be forever damned, its possibility of returning from the dark, like the car that a huge chain pulls out of the black waters of the marsh.

The Ideal Vehicle

Thus, after the example of *Psycho* and by adopting solely the point of view of the audience, it becomes easier to understand the multiple relations which exist, in Hitchcock's *oeuvre*, between the three realities. If the spectator belongs to the everyday world, it is evident that the screen unveils the world of desire. Is it not the screen's very property to be populated by forms animated by forces? These forms, though untouchable, possess a reality. So, if the spectator finds on the screen the exact reflection of his quotidian universe, he immediately communicates with the latter. If he feels that appearances have not been falsified in order "to get" him, he cannot "pull away." He is carried off in a fatal movement. The more so as, on this screen, Hitch wants to provoke what the spectator does not dare to do in his everyday reality. The spectator participates more and more intensely in these forms charged with assuming his impulses and secret dreams. He no longer looks objectively at the appearances of everyday reality but receives them subjectively. However, these appearances do not change intrinsically. It is the spectator who transforms them, who changes their lighting. To the point where, at last, the screen becomes for him the sole reality. His ultimate goal is to penetrate it.

The ultimate vehicle which links those two worlds and allows them to communicate (the spectator with the screen, the quotidian world with the world of desire) is evidently the intellectual world. In fact, for Hitchcock it is a question of giving it a function of transmission. And the term "vehicle" seems to be the only one to account for all the trains, planes, automobiles, skis, boats, bicycles, wheelchairs, etc., which haunt his universe. We receive them not only as a sign of passage from one world to the other but especially as a sensation. A sensation of being carried off, of a skidding that nothing will be able to stop anymore. They give the very impression of fatality. The reader will have been quick to remember the multiple variants which Hitch loves to introduce into this theme which is so dear to him. But never, perhaps, has he so completely and so well "dreamed" of it as in *Psycho*. The slow and wonderful drive of Janet Leigh allows for the material and intellectual passage from one world to the next. From objectivity to pure subjectivity. In general, in Hitchcock the human body is the first vehicle. (Hence the condemnation of dancing, which allows the body to slide and to be carried off – the Stork Club in *The Wrong Man,* the dance at the afternoon tea in *Vertigo,* as well as the waltzes of the merry widows in *Shadow of a Doubt*.) By extension, any vehicle which contains a body becomes for the latter a new body. This is why Janet Leigh, when changing cars, expresses her profound desire to change bodies, personalities. She wants to save a love, pure in itself, from the sordid material circumstances which accompany it. But, far from wanting to struggle to achieve noble conditions for this love, she looks only for purely external expedients. Far from trying to change herself, she believes that by changing the material wrapping her wish will be granted.

A World of Harshness

If I believe truly that the occult is at the basis of Hitchcock's universe, it is not that I am impassioned with the esoteric nor even that I think that it is fundamental for the director. But, simply, it is a way of understanding which permits the artist's imagination the greatest possibilities of revery. In addition, as this doctrine does not contradict other systems of knowledge, it allows for an extremely varied vision of the world adapted to the real temperament of the creator. It is certain that one can content oneself with psychoanalysis in order to comment on Hitchcock. I do not, however, believe that psychoanalysis suffices to explain the invention of forms and their internal dynamics.

Hitchcock's work has always depicted in a certain manner the duel of Light and Shadow, therefore of Unity and Duality. The very first shot of *Psycho*, which follows the abstract credits by Saul Bass, uncovers a large plain surrounding a banal city in a very raw light. It seems that everything here is immutable and must give a feeling of eternity. Subtitles specify the place, the time, and the date. Opposed to this light, from the second shot on, is the absolute darkness of a room into which we penetrate with the camera to discover a bed and lovers in embrace. In two shots, Hitchcock expresses his purpose: *Psycho* will talk to us about the eternal and the finite, of existence and of nothingness, of life and of death, but seen in their naked truth. Nothing can please in *Psycho*, which is the inverse of *Vertigo*. The latter was built upon seduction, hence upon makeup, appearances, the joining of images, in short, upon attraction. Here, everything is based on crudity (and we are spared no detail in that regard), on faces without makeup, on the clash of montage (a montage, cutting like a knife). This trip toward death must produce only fear, and it must produce that fear through its harshness.

Notes

1. This article is the last in a series begun under the title: "The Third Key of Hitchcock," *Cahiers du cinéma*, nos. 99 and 102.
2. *Cahiers du cinéma*, no. 102.

Chapter Two

Hitchcock's Imagery and Art

Maurice Yacowar

Of the twenty-three feature films that Hitchcock directed in his first fifteen years, none is without some interest and some lively personal character. Hitchcock was Hitchcock from the outset – perceptive, progressive, playful, in his mischievous machinations against the simple securities of his audience, yet profound in the implications of his ironic stance. The early films show the same thematic concerns for which his later work is known, and the same expertise.

As in his later work, Hitchcock often paralleled characters of ostensible innocence and guilt to dramatize the thin line that separates man from his pretensions to purity. Thus we have Patsy Brand contrasted to Jill Cheyne in *The Pleasure Garden*, the romantic policeman contrasted to the Lodger, and the two men of *The Manxman*. In *Easy Virtue*, *Rich and Strange*, *The Skin Game*, and *Jamaica Inn*, figures of simple innocence are inadvertently seduced into criminal complicity. These foreshadow the drama of Bruno and Guy in *Strangers on a Train*.

Often the Hitchcock innocent is drawn into evil by boredom, which functions as the image of moral lassitude. Thus we have the passionless marriages of *The Pleasure Garden*, *The Manxman*, and *Sabotage*; the premature marriages in *The Ring*, *Easy Virtue*, and *The Skin Game*; and the boredom which prompts the girl to flirt with the artist in *Blackmail*. Hitchcock realizes how dull morality is and how exciting sin is. His delight is to make his moral points through exciting fictions, reminding his audiences of the difficulties and pain of the moral life – albeit in his delightful way. These marriages foreshadow the cold, antiromantic situations that are developed in *Notorious*, *North by Northwest*, and *Topaz*.

Because innocence and guilt are so radically intertwined, a Hitchcock hero never enjoys a simple success. The innocent will die along with the guilty: the native girl in *The Pleasure Garden*, the pirate in *Rich and Strange*, Stevie Verloc in *Sabotage*, as later the children and Annie in *The Birds*, and Marion Crane will *after* she has resolved to surrender to police in *Psycho*. For man's laws fail in the allocation of justice.

In *Rope*, Jan asks playfully of a friend's description of her: "Did he do me justice?" Rupert replies sharply: "Do you deserve justice?" From the lovers of *The Pleasure*

Garden through the murderers of *Family Plot*, Hitchcock's heroes are of at best a dappled virtue, and his villains of civilized elegance. Indeed, his villains are often extremely sympathetic people, as Verloc is, or Fane of *Murder!* Even the nasty Levet in *The Pleasure Garden* is allowed a death of charming civility.

Hitchcock's justice is tricky, poetic rather than legal. For his world is full of uncertainty. *Shadow of a Doubt* may seem to have a happy ending, but the killer is eulogized by the small town, and an innocent man was fed to an airplane propeller by mistake. Similarly in *Blackmail*, the murderers go free while a small-time blackmailer is killed in their stead. Even the happy endings, then, refuse the confidence of a secure order. No simple justice, no simple psychology, can be sustained in Hitchcock's world of quicksand insecurity. So almost all Hitchcock's films end on an uncertain image, from the new lovers in *The Pleasure Garden* to the mass of abiding doom at the end of *The Birds*. And in *Frenzy*, Blaney establishes his innocence by performing the crime for which he was wrongly sentenced; no matter that the woman he attacks in Rusk's bed is already dead.

Hitchcock often uses the X image to express his sense of man as a complex of innocence and evil. Thus in *The Pleasure Garden* we found the two women forming an X to suggest their equivalence in their lover's mind; the husband moves to kill his wife in order to complete the X, in response to his murdered mistress's imagined demands. In *Blackmail* a similar editing completes an X between the corpse's hand and the policeman's, where the plot develops the illegality of police activities and the criminal parodies justice. The X imagery is developed most fully, of course, in *Strangers on a Train*.

Perhaps Hitchcock presents two different concepts of man's makeup. First, opposite tendencies may unite to form a single, composite whole, as the ladies do in *The Pleasure Garden* and as the strangers on a train do. Here the X would represent the unity of opposite motions and values in human nature. Similarly, in *I Confess* an X variant, the cross, unites Father Logan and killer Keller in a criminal sacrament that costs them Alma (the soul in its earthly existence). But, in the second image of human nature, opposite wholes are parallelled. Charlie and Uncle Charlie in *Shadow of a Doubt* are parallel opposites, albeit with such similarities as name, selfishness, vanity, and telepathic connection. They are not a unity. The good Charlie may have some flaws and the evil Uncle Charlie some elegant pretense to justice in his effect, but the characters are clearly separable and they diverge by the impulse of their respective wills. So too in *Psycho*, Norman Bates pretends to be an X with his mother, but she is innocent, misrepresented even after she was murdered by her spoiled, jealous son. Norman and his mother are antitheses who only intersect in Norman's malevolent rationalizing. The bantering and bickering lovers in Hitchcock's romances (*Champagne*, *Mr. and Mrs. Smith*) and in his thrillers (*The 39 Steps*, *Saboteur*, and on through *Marnie*) are spirited strokes who discover themselves fulfilled as Xs.

The other quintessential Hitchcock image is the staircase. Again, the early films show ample use of this device for which his later work is known. Whether upward or down, Hitchcock's stairs take his characters and his audience to the fears, dangers, and rewards of self-discovery. The most common staircase shot is downward through a seeming spiral, which leaves the impression of stairs within stairs. One finds this shot from *The Lodger* through *Vertigo*. As an emblem it recalls Peer Gynt's onion, concentric layerings around a void, with the addition of the danger that height always means in Hitchcock.

The occasional round staircase, as in *The Pleasure Garden* and *Secret Agent*, also suggests a plunge through layers of one's self. There are even three staircases in *Waltzes from Vienna*: the rickety ladder down which Schani's rival carries the heroine in the opening fire scene; its parallel, the ladder the girl climbs at the end to save Schani from the duel and to reclaim him romantically; and the palatial staircase down which the Count rolls his valet to a piano riff, an image of their difference in privilege and station. In *Juno and the Paycock* the stairs provide a single straight and dark descent from the family warmth to the cold public funeral and to their dispossession.

In *Shadow of a Doubt* Charlie's home has two parallel staircases, the clean public front and the dangerous, steep, private back, the latter which Uncle Charlie uses to escape and to threaten Charlie. The two-staired house works as an image of the human psyche and as an image of a societal ideal, both of which project a front that is more attractive and safer than their hidden natures.

Stairs compel movement and, with it, fear, as in Constance's ascent to Murchison's office in *Spellbound*, and Arbogast's in *Psycho*. The camera (the maker) has a liberty over space and stairs that the character has not. Hence the open, expressionistic staircase in *The Lodger* and the brittle one in *Number Seventeen*. Hitchcock's stairs image both man's composition and the rigors and fears of his rise or plunge to awareness. The danger that always lurks around the stairs is the anxiety that undercuts all confidence (in the Hitchcock vision), all sense of secure footing, and that provides both the central metaphor and title for *Downhill* and for *Vertigo*. The source of the latter was a novel titled *Between Two Deaths*, but "Vertigo" conveys Hitchcock's primary interest: man's uncertainty in stepping between two moments of living.

Hitchcock's art is based on the dramatic appeal of the insecure. In the first place, his characters are typically secure people whose footing is swept out from under them. Thus Patsy loses her independence in *The Pleasure Garden* and the hero loses his whole world in *Downhill*. Sanders loses his station in *The Ring* and the fisherman his bliss, friend, and wife in *The Manxman*. Love provides only a false sense of security in *The Pleasure Garden*, *The Farmer's Wife*, *The Manxman*, and *Champagne*, where the reconciled lovers begin to quarrel anew over their marriage arrangements. And in *Mr. and Mrs. Smith* a marriage suddenly ceases to exist.

Nor is there security in the social contract. The processes of justice go awry in *Easy Virtue*, *Blackmail*, *Juno and the Paycock*, *Murder!* And in the thriller series from *The Man Who Knew Too Much* through *The Lady Vanishes* the individual's private life is shattered by the social processes that are supposedly functioning to protect him. Hence Hitchcock's frequent twist where the hero is threatened by the police as much as by the enemy: *The Lodger*, *Blackmail*, *The 39 Steps*, *North by Northwest*, *Psycho*, *Frenzy*. Virtue and Hitchcock's justice are endangered by the merely human law. Joe in *The Lodger* eventually subordinates his romantic interest to his public duty. But not until *Frenzy* will we have a Hitchcock policeman whose arrival at the truth is based upon his sense of the criminal potential within himself.[1]

For the others, the police are sheep (*The 39 Steps*) or careless shots (*Strangers on a Train*). In *The Trouble with Harry* the springy villagers have but a single fear – discovery by the sheriff's deputy, a cold Puritan named Calvin whose resurrections are confined to antique autos.

Hitchcock usually presents his theme of man's limited freedom in society as a conflict between love and duty. The tension is between love and friendship (a personal duty) in *Downhill*, *The Manxman*, and *The Farmer's Wife*. In the policeman drama the hero must choose between what his job requires and what his heart (and the lady) deserve: *The Lodger*, *Blackmail*, *Young and Innocent*, *Sabotage*, *Stage Fright*, *The Paradine Case*. The spy thrillers adjust the love versus duty debate to the tensions of the cold war, where the hero must choose between his personal love and his international duty: *Foreign Correspondent*, *Notorious*, *North by Northwest*, *Torn Curtain*, *Topaz*. Another form of this debate is the conflict between privacy and public involvement. Although the fullest presentation of this theme is in *Rear Window*, it is fully developed in both versions of *The Man Who Knew Too Much*, *Secret Agent*, *Sabotage*, and *The Lady Vanishes*. Possibly its earliest statement, however, is in the scene of the switchboard operator in *Easy Virtue*.

But if love and citizenship are two areas in which Hitchcock afflicts his characters with insecurity, the most dramatic is the family relationship. Richard Roud relates the motif of parental tyranny to the espionage plots:

> Even his domestic dramas involve a kind of espionage in the sense that his characters, having discovered frightening realities buried beneath the surface, are obliged to turn spy themselves in order to discover the whole truth. Often it has something to do with the past, the past that comes back to confound the present, to compromise the future.[2]

Thus we find so many tyrannical parents in Hitchcock's work, as we have noted in our discussion of *Downhill*. Cruel fathers spring readily to mind: *Downhill*, *Champagne*, *The Manxman*, *Waltzes from Vienna*. Then there are the treacherous father surrogates in *Sabotage*, *The Lady Vanishes*, and *Jamaica Inn* (particularly after Hitchcock's revision of the villain in the latter). Even where the parent figures are not oppressive or negative, the parent must be abandoned at least temporarily, as in *Young and Innocent*. The family is presented as a fragile, sometimes false and always vulnerable, unit in all Hitchcock's thrillers of the late 1930s. In *Psycho* we have a pervasive feeling of parental oppression, by Marion Crane's mother, Sam's father, and the happiness-buying Texas daddy; but in the main thrust of the film, it is the sick son who projects his guilt and inhibitions upon his parental image. The parent is blamed for the child's violent weakness.

In this respect one of the key Hitchcock films is his comedy *The Trouble with Harry*. A little boy discovers a man dead in the forest; it's his stepfather, unknown to the boy. The dead Harry Warp harmonizes the entire community as each member assumes guilt for this death and they all combine to conceal him. In one shot the corpse is so arranged that his feet and legs seem to complete the body of the little boy (Jerry Mather), whom we see from the waist up. Later we see the Captain (Edmund Gwenn) dozing in his rocker; we see all but the Captain's feet, but on the wall behind him we see the shadows of the corpse's feet. These two shots prove Roud's point. The dead complete and shape the living, but the living can make their own use of the dead.

Thus we have the fatal "haunting" of Levet in *The Pleasure Garden*, the heroine's haunting by her past in *Easy Virtue* and in *Blackmail*, and the community's haunting by the past in *Juno and the Paycock* and *The Skin Game*. The individual can succumb to the pressure of his past – or blame it for his own weakness. But the haunting can work as a regeneration, as it does in *The Trouble with Harry*. In *The Farmer's Wife*, too, the dead wife's message provides a new lease of life for her husband, as the lovers' exile will in *The Manxman*. As Roger Thornhill emerges chastened and solidified by his false death in *North by Northwest*, Richard Hannay assumes a responsibility from the death of the strange woman at the start of *The 39 Steps*; so do Ashenden and his lady from Caypor's death in *Secret Agent*. Even in *Waltzes from Vienna*, Schani descends through the hell of the pastry cook, abandoned suitor, duelling rake, and disowned son to emerge an Orphic hero. Hitchcock's hero can prove himself by surviving the tribulations that befall him (or that he claims to inherit).

Even more than the insecurity of his characters, though, Hitchcock exploits the insecurity of his audience, hence his penchant for subjective shooting angles. His early films abound with attempts to depict the character's mind through what he sees. Hence, too, Hitchcock's penchant for expressionistic devices. The camera and printing tricks of *The Lodger*, the hallucinations of *The Pleasure Garden*, *Downhill*, and *The Ring*, the swoop in *Young and Innocent*, all serve as nonrealistic rhetoric to dramatize the character's state of mind. Hitchcock used images of the concrete to express the reality of the imagination. As Tom Ryall points out, "the openings from *The Lodger* (1926), *The Manxman* (1928), and *Blackmail* (1929) could be documentaries of the newspaper industry, the fishing industry and the police force respectively."[3] So, too, Hitchcock's delirium sequences document the hot currents of the character's mind. Durgnat's distinction between Hitchcock's "piercing realism" and his "vibrant irrealism" is a merely formal distinction, for Hitchcock's basic interest has always been in how our perceptions reshape our world. His realism constantly shades off into the expressionistic imagery and extravagant technical devices by which he conveys the realism of the emotional state. So his aquarium explosion of Picadilly Circus in *Sabotage* ranks with the best documentary poetics of Vertov.

Hitchcock continually violates his viewer's expectations. Thus we have the romantic deflations in *The Pleasure Garden* and *Champagne* and the surprise of Drew's innocence in *The Lodger*. Where the genre requires a fight, Hitchcock will provide a comic fight, as in *Downhill*, *Number Seventeen*, *Waltzes from Vienna*, and *The Lady Vanishes*, for there is no room in Hitchcock's world of vertiginous insecurities for the conventional fight, which makes its protagonists appear efficient.

And from time to time Hitchcock allows his comic spirit, the vision of an anarchic principle at the heart of the universe, to run free. So we get the chaotic consequences of the courtships in *The Farmer's Wife*, the fumbling villains of *The Man Who Knew Too Much*, and old Ben in *No. 17*. Of course, these comedies of chaos are only lighter versions of Hitchcock's essential vision that man's civilization is underpinned by chaos, as we have it in *The Pleasure Garden*, *Downhill*, *The Manxman*, *Champagne*, *Rich and Strange*, *Murder!*, *The 39 Steps*, and *Sabotage*. In his later work, Marion Crane must die *because* she is played by the star, Janet Leigh. For Hitchcock's films are a relentless assault upon the viewer's security, as well as his moral assumptions.

The English films also prove that from the outset Hitchcock's technical innovations were close to the thematic center of the work. The experimental devices of *The Lodger* and *Blackmail* served those films' basic themes, the preoccupation of the former with the misleading power of perception, and of the latter with the obscurities and difficulties of communication. Then, too, the scenes with off-camera orchestras in *Juno and the Paycock* and *Murder!* were the pivotal points in the psychological development of the narratives. This observation serves as well when we approach Hitchcock's later work.

For example, his massive orchestration of birds for *The Birds*, a staggering technical challenge, is an assertion of the power of the human enterprise in the face of the film's assault upon man's pre-Copernican arrogance. The technical challenge in *Lifeboat* is analogous to its political theme, the fatal isolation of the Allies and their need for a selfless unity. The continuous shooting of *Rope*, which Hitchcock calls his "abandonment of pure cinema" because it eschewed his normal dependence upon dramatic editing, grows out of both the title image – something continuous that will tie one up – and the main theme of the film – the continuity of word into deed; a murderous human reality is spun out of a musing that was considered safely theoretical.[4] The restricted isolation of the camera in *Rear Window* relates to that film's central concern: the distinction between respecting one's brother's privacy and meeting his needs for a keeper. What Durgnat calls Hitchcock's "calmly hermetic aesthetic satisfaction" might be better considered as his passionate synthesis of idea, irony, and technique.[5] In his achievement of the emotional idea and the intellectual image he meets the aim of that other great film editor, Eisenstein. By so brilliantly uniting idea, image, and emotion, Hitchcock has come to make our nightmares for us with a clarity and thrust no other filmmaker has commanded.

Hitchcock's ironic detachment also explains those moments in his work where we see the seams of his craft, where his technical work may seem to be rough. One lesson which the British films should teach us is that Hitchcock always knows what he is doing. His plots are carefully crafted. For example, he has Drexler rehearse the orchestra of Strauss Sr. so that their surprise performance of Schani's new waltz will not seem implausible. And, where Hitchcock's technical work seems shoddy, what we really have is not a craftsman nodding but an artist extending his resources. Where Hitchcock's craft seems loose, we usually find his technique subserving his content, his literal realism shading off into vibrant metaphor.

To put it another way, it is safe to assume that what seems to be a Hitchcock error is likely our failure to work out what he is doing. In *The Lady Vanishes*, for instance, the palpably false opening shot and the unreal proportions of the departing train are typical of how Hitchcock extends his realism into expressionism – only to be charged with poor technique. This liberty came from the German cinema. Thus Fritz Lang inserts a jarring interlude of false scenery into a key moment of *Rancho Notorious*.

William Johnson describes Hitchcock's "failure" in *Marnie*:

> It so happens that there are certain departments in which Hitchcock has a patently blind eye. These include the phony backdrops that grate like TV commercials (especially in color), the bits of rapid montage that do not quite fit together, and the two-shots that are held so long that they almost ossify.[6]

The false backdrops in *Marnie* are a concise image of the heroine's predicament: she lives in dislocation from her surroundings and from her own past. The false backgrounds provide a physical expression of the disjunction in her mind. Thus the first false back-projection scene is her first scene aboard Forio, when she is enjoying an artificial respite from her alienation. A loud, rhetorical swell in the music coheres with the rhetoric of the false background. The second is the scene at her mother's home, where the ships' dock is flat and false behind the tenement. The painted ships loom larger than life and paler, imaging the phantom sailor unacknowledged from her past. The false register of both backgrounds moves the shots from setting to active symbol. A false front stands behind the Rutland building, a building stripped of its back, or a foreground unsupported by an integrated backing, as Marnie is. Mark varies this motif by giving Marnie a $42,000 ring instead of a family heirloom; he wants her to "have something that never belonged to anyone before." The line jocularly refers to her thefts, poignantly recalls her childhood, without a bed of her own, and provides another instance of an object without a past, a foreground without an integrated background.[7] Similarly in *Torn Curtain* the palpable falseness of the garden path up which Newman leads Andrews (Hud leads Mary Poppins) undercuts the noble pretense of the hero's ambitious venture. And what Samuels finds to be the "contentless virtuosity" of *North by Northwest* is the heart of the film: the film's central theme/effect is that total dislocation which the complacent hero and the typically injudicious cinema audience share.[8] As the title tells us, the film deliberately pursues a fantastical course.

It is similarly wrong to consider Hitchcock a craftsman first and only secondarily, accidentally as it were, an artist. From his first feature on, even through that period of self-conscious "respectable" adaptation, Hitchcock's films had something to say, sometimes an obvious message (*Easy Virtue*, *Lifeboat*) but more often an integrated theme (*Pleasure Garden*, *Downhill*). Only because form is content can Hitchcock say "I am interested not so much in the stories I tell as in the means of telling them."[9] Structure is theme in *Psycho*, *Vertigo*, *The Trouble with Harry*, but also as early as *The Pleasure Garden*, *Downhill*, and *The Ring*.

The early films are also notable for their ambitious conception. Though working in an unacknowledged medium, Hitchcock showed himself a serious artist even then. For Hitchcock, popular film is art. His art is the manipulation of the audience's emotions and fantasy through a variety of felt dangers and thrills, to send his viewers out at the end, calm of mind, all smugness spent, ready to brave the hairline moralities of real life. In his early films Hitchcock also dealt with the responsibilities of the artist. The dance-floor meat markets of *The Pleasure Garden*, *Downhill*, and *Champagne* and the squared circle of *The Ring* are fairly tawdry arenas of human enterprise. But even in those settings it is possible for an individual to achieve art, to fulfill his own creative and expressive impulses, and to establish a community with an audience.

The laughing clown in *Blackmail* provides the neatest statement Hitchcock makes about art. Coherent with the fertility of silent montage, the portrait gains new meaning from each juxtaposition, each context, yet it maintains the same detached, ironic stance regardless of its changing set. When all about are noisy, loud, ambiguous, Hitchcock's mute jester remains silent. Yet the portrait is eloquent in its accusatory stare, its lively eye, its shameless traditional garb. Beyond the inflections of that painting in the story itself, Hitchcock devotes himself to a career of critical irony that will be independent of changes in mode and in medium. The jester retains his acrid independence even when stored in the vaults of the most conventional (the police station; the commercial bastions of light, diversionary cinema).

From *Murder!* we can infer why Hitchcock was never to stray into the esoterica of Bergman, late Godard, or even the Penn of *Mickey One*. For *Murder!* is the drama of an artist who takes his artistic skills and interests into the prosaic business of real life. In *Murder!* some fulfill themselves through art (the theater folk), some conceal themselves in their art (the transvestite trapeze artist), but the noblest and most gifted turn their art to the service of humanity (Sir John), to the discovery of truth and self-knowledge and the saving of lives – from prison and from boredom. The West End artist-aristocrat brings his style and sensitivity to the service of the hurly-burly world.

For Hitchcock, life is a matter of drawing art and reality together. In *Stage Fright*, Eve Gill comes from a separated family, a realistic but theatrical father and a whimsical but prosaic mother. Eve's salvation lies in ordinary Smith, a policeman who plays the piano, and in her own abilities at acting and setting scenes. The clues point to the guilt of the Marlene Dietrich figure, but, as her song warns us, she is too lazy to be either criminal or moral. The real villain is the Richard Todd character. He is unable to distinguish pretense (art) from reality, so he kills for Dietrich and is ultimately prepared to kill Eve to prove his own insanity. As befits his unharmonized dichotomy, he is chopped in half by the safety curtain on the theater stage.

For Hitchcock, art is to come from life (*Waltzes from Vienna*). But often life emulates art, as in the film parodies in *Sabotage*, *Saboteur*, and *North by Northwest*. Art at its best will cultivate, free, and invigorate the human spirit, both the emotion and the will, as the cartoon does for Sylvia in *Sabotage*. Sometimes art will deliver a narrow truth, as Mr. Memory does, or deliver one from bondage, as the child is freed by song and by shot in the two versions of *The Man Who Knew Too Much*. But its deeper function is to free the emotions. So Hitchcock often sets up a theatrical situation to expedite a character's physical escape: *The Pleasure Garden*, *Downhill*, *The Ring*, the fashion show in *The Lodger*, the auction in *The Skin Game*, Roger Thornhill's auction in *North by Northwest*, the ballet in *Torn Curtain*. In *Vertigo* even more fully than in *Murder!* and *Stage Fright*, Hitchcock explores the corollary danger: losing one's self in the act of performance. Hence the penultimate image in *Psycho*: Norman Bates dissolves into the skull; the hidden reality overwhelms the muted, visible reality; the role overtakes the self. But, like the Todd figure in *Stage Fright*,

Norman Bates lost the sense of where lie and art were to be distinguished. Upon this distinction and interplay Hitchcock thrives for fifty years of splendid filmmaking.

Hitchcock's genius lies in his synthesis of mind, eye, and heart in the dynamic film experience. Some critics prefer the craft of the American period over the English or the profundity of the later American films over the earlier diversions. William Pechter prefers Hitchcock's detailed realism of the English thrillers and bemoans his loss of contact with his audience in the American period. But even in 1931 C. A. Lejeune was to complain of Hitchcock's lack of "the warm humanity of a director like Griffith" and "Pabst's psychological insight":

> His figures are photographic records of synthetic men, not men of flesh-and-blood trans-
> lated into the medium of the motion picture.... The fault with Hitchcock's unreality lies
> in the fact that he has been essentially a director of realistic films; his subjects have been
> intimate, detailed and individual. He has dealt with one man, not with men.[10]

Pechter harkens back to the golden age of the thrillers and Lejeune cavils before them, but both find Hitchcock naturalistically unsatisfying. Nor could anyone accuse the golden thrillers of realism!

Surely the realism of Hitchcock ranges from the physical settings of *The Lodger* to the imaginative inner worlds of *Downhill* and *The Ring* and between those poles throughout his later career. Always he is a poet and always he is engaged with the moral and perceptual nature of man. The early films are full of emotionally charged scenes, it is true: the praying scene, the fevered kiss, the final killing in *The Pleasure Garden*, or the private reconciliation of old Strauss in *Waltzes from Vienna*. But there is a well of feeling in Lydia's scenes with the coffee cups in *The Birds* too. The films of Alfred Hitchcock are rich enough, varied enough, yet of a spiritual piece, to make their total enjoyment preferable to any arbitrary choice of preferences. One can watch Hitchcock's British films in order to come to a better understanding of the American ones. But also because they are so good in themselves, so moving, so thoughtful, and so much fun.

Notes

1. See Leland A. Poague, "The Detective in Hitchcock's *Frenzy*," *Journal of Popular Film*, vol. 2, no. 1 (1973): 47–59.
2. Richard Roud; "In Broad Daylight," *Film Comment*, vol. 10, no. 4 (1974): 36.
3. Tom Ryall, "Durgnat on Hitchcock," *Screen*, vol. 16, no. 2 (Summer 1975): 123. Hitchcock told Leslie Perkoff: "I would like to make documentary films, because here you have
   states of action or movement which can easily [be] treated by photography and cutting.
   But a cataclysm in any film, for example, is akin to documentary material. It begins with
   the camera and goes directly to the cutting-room." This is in "The Censor and Sydney
   Street," *World Film News* (March 1938): 4. Hitchcock here yearns for the fantastical
   opportunities provided by documentary! He exploited them most obviously in the plot
   line and settings of *Rich and Strange* and in the opening scenes of *Champagne*, *Blackmail*,
   The Manxman, *The Wrong Man*, etc.

4. Peter Bogdanovich, *The Cinema of Alfred Hitchcock* (New York: Museum of Modern Art, 1963), 28.

5. Raymond Durgnat, *The Strange Case of Alfred Hitchcock* (London: Faber, 1974), 367.

6. William Johnson, "*Marnie,*" *Film Quarterly*, vol. 18, no. 1 (1964): 38–42.

7. David Thomson provides a more general interpretation of the device in *Movie Man* (London: Secker and Warburg, 1971), 72.

8. Charles T. Samuels, "Hitchcock," *Encountering Directors* (New York: Putnam, 1972), 301. Of course, Hitchcock is famous for the painstaking attention he gives his work before going on the set. See the following articles from *American Cinematographer* as evidence: Hilda Black, "The Photography is Important to Hitchcock: *I Confess*" (December 1952): 524–5, 546–7, 549; Frederick Foster, "'Hitch' Didn't Want It Arty" (February 1957): 84–5, 112–14; Charles Loring, "Filming *Torn Curtain* by Reflected Light" (October 1966): 680–3, 706–7; Herb Lightman, "Hitchcock Talks about Lights, Camera, Action" (May 1967): 332–5, 350–1.

   Hitchcock's famous preplanning and subsequent appearance of casualness about the actual shooting may have contributed to the ready disdain for his technical "sloppiness." It certainly alienated André Bazin (see his "Hitchcock vs. Hitchcock" in *Cahiers du Cinéma in English*, no. 2: 51–60).

9. Bazin, 55.

10. William Pechter, *Twenty-Four Times a Second* (New York: Harper & Row, 1971), 175–94. C. A. Lejeune, *Cinema* (London: Maclehose, 1931): 11–12.

Chapter Three
Retrospective

Robin Wood

One can usefully begin by considering the two major aesthetic influences on Hitchcock's work. In the early years of his career, when his creative personality was in the process of formation, he made two films (in fact, his first two completed films as director, *The Pleasure Garden* and *The Mountain Eagle*) in German studios; the contact seems to have confirmed an interest in the potentialities of Expressionism that was already present (he speaks, in the Truffaut interview book, of Lang's *Der mude Tod* as one of his first important cinematic experiences). A little later, he discovered the Soviet cinema, which confirmed for him the crucial importance of montage, its centrality to what he wanted to do. The Expressionist influence is already very plain in *The Lodger* (1926); the importance to Hitchcock of montage is also implicit there, waiting to be developed. The film was also Hitchcock's first suspense thriller and first great commercial success: the coincidence of all these factors was obviously crucial in determining the development of his career.

"Expressionism" evades simple definition, but a central impulse was clearly the attempt to "express" emotional states through a distortion or deformation of objective reality, "expression" taking precedence over representation. The continuing dominance of such an aesthetic aim in Hitchcock could be suggested by innumerable examples, of varying degrees of subtlety, from any of the films; it is enough here to mention the most obvious, the red suffusions in *Marnie*, which have nothing to do with representing "reality" and everything to do with communicating the heroine's subjective experience.

The importance to Hitchcock of Soviet montage theory is, if anything, even more obvious. The affinities become plain if one begins to analyze the Odessa Steps massacre in *Potemkin* as if it were a Hitchcockian suspense piece. Almost everything in the sequence works effectively in that way (and this partly accounts, of course, for its extraordinary emotional power): perhaps the most striking single example is the famous incident involving the baby's pram, where Eisenstein's fragmented editing is devoted to the buildup and release of tension on a basis of will-it-or-won't-it? All the techniques deployed in the Odessa Steps sequence could be paralleled somewhere in Hitchcock, even the one potentially most disturbing to the audience's involvement on a "Realist" level, overlapping montage: in the sequence of the riding accident in *Marnie*, the camera covers (by a variety of technical means – both tracking and zooming) the same stretches of ground over and over again to convey the effect of time agonizingly "stretched" at a moment of supreme fear and anguish.

A central characteristic of Expressionism (as a cinematic movement) is the distortion of the "reality" the camera records or the creation of a world phenomenologically remote from the reality recognized by our senses; a central characteristic of montage theory is the creation of concepts that have no necessary phenomenological equivalents in what was actually presented before the camera. These two movements represent, in their very different ways, the two main lines of opposition to the notion of film as an inherently "realistic" medium: their emphasis is on artifice rather than representation. In Hitchcock's cinema, their "artificiality" is intensified by the fact that both techniques are divorced from their original ends. Expressionism was a "high art" movement rooted in a specific time and place, a specific *angst*; Soviet montage was associated with revolution and propaganda, with the task of making the principles underlying the revolution intelligible, cogent, and concrete. Hitchcock in a sense perverted both, employing their techniques (or his own modification of them) in the creation of popular bourgeois entertainment. Obviously, any innovation, its expressive possibilities established, becomes public property, a part of the complex apparatus of the cultural tradition, capable of being put to uses far beyond those that stimulated its evolution. Yet I find it significant – having in mind the whole Hitchcock *oeuvre* – that he should build the foundations of his style out of elements inherently "artificial," borrowed from cultures other than his own and detached from the conditions that originally gave them their meaning.

Doubtless, scholars more intimate than I am with Hitchcock's British period will be able to trace the process of absorption into his style and method of these major influences. For my purposes, to illustrate their fusion in his work and the purposes to which he put them, his first sound film, *Blackmail* (1930), offers a convenient and striking example. Consider the famous scene – it is repeatedly cited in textbooks on film history with reference to the development of sound – where the heroine, who has stabbed a would-be rapist to death, is forced to listen to a gossipy woman talking garrulously about the murder. The scene unites a number of thematic and stylistic elements central to Hitchcock's work: the bourgeois family involved in daily routine (in this case breakfast) contrasted with the extraordinary and disturbing, which exists nonetheless in their midst and for which one of them is responsible; the action presented through the consciousness (and to some extent the eyes) of the distraught heroine (who, like her successors through *Shadow of a Doubt* to *Psycho*, combines bourgeois "normality" with a romantic/dramatic situation, hence is an ideal identification figure); the knife on the breakfast table, to which the camera (that is, the heroine's consciousness) obsessively returns; close-ups of the woman's lips moving as she chatters on; the gradual distortion of her voice to an unintelligible gabble out of which only the word "knife" emerges clearly, "cutting through" the scrambled sound track. Here montage combines with the Expressionist distortion of physical reality to communicate a character's subjective experience directly to the spectator; to involve us in that experience;

to confirm what is already encouraged by the construction of the scenario, the empathic identification of spectator and character.

My use of the term "artificial" (intended as descriptive rather than evaluative – though I shall argue that the particular artificiality of Hitchcock's cinema carries with it certain weaknesses and limitations) inevitably raises many of those questions about "Realism" that haunt contemporary film criticism; here I can only touch on them in a way that I am aware leaves major theoretical issues unresolved. I will mention in passing, however, that the Realism debate seems frequently clouded by a failure to distinguish sufficiently two main ways in which the cinema can be spoken of as a "Realist" art form – the two being neither incompatible nor necessarily, beyond a certain primitive point, interdependent. The cinema derives from two major sources, the invention of photography and the nineteenth-century novel. From the former comes the simple, basic notion of film "Realism": the camera records the reality in front of it. From the latter comes a much more sophisticated and complex notion of "Realism," bound up not so much with literal visual representation as with the audience's involvement in the movement of a narrative, the illusion that we are experiencing "real life." The potentiality for confusion can be suggested by pointing out that the Odessa Steps massacre or the horse accident in *Marnie* is "Realist" in the former sense only in the most barely literal way but intensely "Realist" in the latter sense: the reality the camera records has very little to do with the illusion the audience experiences. Hitchcock's cinema is either the least or most "Realist," depending on which definition you are using.

In order to define its artificiality more precisely, I want to draw on certain key notions and motifs that recur almost obsessively in Hitchcock's interviews. His own statements about his work are – if one is ready to make connections and read between the lines – more illuminating than I used to give them credit for: both for what they reveal and for what they conceal, the two aspects being significantly related.

First, one cannot leave the question of Hitchcock's debt to the Soviet cinema without considering the importance he attaches (from his point of view, quite rightly) to the famous Kuleshov experiment. A close-up of the actor Mosjoukin was intercut with various objects which the editing implied he was looking at (a baby, a corpse, a bowl of soup); the audience is supposed to have admired his expressive acting, although in fact the same close-up was used each time and when the shot was taken the actor didn't know what he was meant to be looking at. Both the alleged results and the theoretical validity of the experiment have been called into question (notably by V. F. Perkins in *Film as Film*); what concerns us here is not what the experiment actually proved but what lessons Hitchcock drew from it. He drew two which are absolutely central to the development of his art. First, the Kuleshov experiment suggests the possibilities of editing for deceiving the spectator, for playing tricks with time and space. It is a lesson he could have learned equally from Eisenstein: witness, again, the Odessa Steps sequence, where the spatial relationships of the various characters are never clear (in fact, clearly didn't exist in terms of staged action), where the audience's sense of the length of the steps and the progress of the soldiers is consistently undermined, where the woman whose child falls *behind* her as they flee from the soldiers is subsequently shown going *down* the steps to retrieve his body.

Spatial deception through editing is common practice in Hitchcock. For illustration, one needn't go to any of the famous set pieces. Consider the apparently simple moment in *Notorious* where Ingrid Bergman, having stolen Claude Rains's key from his key ring, is surprised by him as she holds it in one of her hands (we aren't allowed to be sure which). He, affectionate but gallant, wants to kiss her fingers; he uncurls one hand, and, after kissing it, makes for the other. She flings her arms round his neck, drops the key behind his back, and pushes it under a chair with her foot. Filmed by, say, Preminger, in a single-take long-shot from across the room, this simple action would be ludicrously implausible: Bergman would have, first, to crane her neck over Rains's shoulder to see where the key had fallen (and, short as the actor was, this would involve some craning); she would then have to wrap one leg around his body to maneuver her foot into position, then move the foot several inches to conceal the key (which would not be very effectively concealed anyway) – and all this, of course, without Rains noticing. Hitchcock breaks down the incident into a characteristically detailed and fragmented montage, culminating in a close-up of the foot pushing the key, both bodies out of the frame: it is doubtful, such are the tension and involvement generated by this admirable scene, whether any spectator at the time questioned the plausibility of the action.

The other lesson is even more significant. The emotions Mosjoukin was felt to be expressing (tenderness, sorrow, hunger, or whatever) must obviously have been supplied by the spectator from his own fund of stock responses to babies, corpses, and bowls of soup: the principle of audience identification is already implicit in the Kuleshov experiment. Again, it is also implicit in Eisenstein, and a sequence such as the Odessa Steps (which supplies the audience with a careful selection of identification figures) suggests the relationship between the two "lessons": it is the spectator's emotional involvement that carries him over the deceptions and the artifice, making him ready to accept as "real" an action that patently isn't, even in the limited sense of being performed in spatial and temporal continuity. The relationship is in fact even closer: the fragmentation of the Eisenstein sequence and the spatial/temporal disorientation (as in certain of Hitchcock's *tours de force* – the shower murder in *Psycho*, where the blows are never seen actually to connect, the horse accident in *Marnie*) actually *increase* the spectator's sense of confusion and panic.

The relationship between identification and the ready acceptance of sleight of hand might be investigated through innumerable examples of Hitchcock's work. One general point emerges clearly: Hitchcock has grasped that the identification principle can work in this elemental/elementary way only when very simple and basic feelings are involved – often primitive feelings (especially terror) rooted in direct physical sensation. Otherwise, identification (empathy, as opposed to the kind of sympathy we may feel for the characters in, for example, a Renoir film) is a doubtful and complicated phenomenon that has to be built very subtly. There may be a reason beyond that of mere technical obviousness why many people are so alienated by the artificial devices of *Marnie*: that, in the very nature of the central character and her predicament, total identification is impossible. One can study the care with which Hitchcock builds identification, when he can't rely on "primitive" emotions, in the first scene of *Psycho*, where every stylistic decision and every step in the construction of the scenario can be seen as part of a process whereby Hitchcock prepares for that identification with Marion Crane on which the effect and essential meaning of the entire film depend (on whatever level of seriousness we feel it as working). The opening is not a single take (as my own treatment of it might seem to imply – an error perpetuated in Raymond Durgnat's interesting recent book, *The Strange Case of Alfred Hitchcock*) but a series of shots linked by almost imperceptible dissolves and one awkward cut (presumably from a location to the studio set) just before the camera moves in through the open window. The captions identifying place, date (but not the year), and time of day confirm the impression of "documentary" realism given by the location work; the dissolves subliminally convey the sense of covering a lot of territory, the progress towards the window seeming ambiguously arbitrary and purposive. The spectator (even if he missed the advance publicity) has been alerted to expect some kind of horror movie by the title and by Bernard Herrmann's opening music, but Hitchcock's insistence on the ordinary and "real" temporarily lulls him – under cover of which Hitchcock can begin at once to play on his voyeuristic tendencies. As the camera takes us in through the open window into the dark hotel bedroom, the lighting is subtly modified: the effect is of our eyes becoming adjusted to the dark after the sunshine outside. When Sam says, "You never did eat your lunch," Hitchcock cuts in a close-up of the sandwich lunch on the bedside table: the shot is obviously superfluous in terms of the conveying of information, but it corresponds closely to the movement of our consciousness: if we were in the room and heard Sam say that, we would instinctively glance at the lunch. When the lovers lie down again on the bed, the camera moves in as though to lie down with them: from being invisible spectators actually in the room, we are led to become participants. Then, when Marion springs up in recoil, the camera abruptly recoils too, closely mirroring her movement: our participation begins to be given a clear bias which is developed through the remainder of the scene. There are no shots that are strictly subjective, but the camera repeatedly favors Marion and her viewpoint. She is privileged with close-ups (notably on "I'll lick the stamps," where the music also endorses our romantic sympathy for her position and attitude) or shown in profile; we look at Sam, on the other hand, in medium long-shot and *almost* as through her eyes (notably on his, "Well, all *right*," as he surrenders to her demand for "respectability" with a submissive gesture of the hands). In fact, the first clearly subjective shot in the film is withheld until the moment when Marion's car is stopped at the traffic lights and she sees her boss crossing in front of her – by which time the movement of the scenario, the editing, the placement of the camera, the music, have thoroughly but unobtrusively determined our relationship to her and to the action.

Hitchcock's attitude toward actors – another, though seldom so explicit, recurrent theme of his interviews – follows logically from the centrality to his art of the Kuleshov experiment. One can make a broad distinction (and it is intimately bound up with certain aspects of the "Realism" debate) between directors who work collaboratively with actors and directors who use actors to execute a preconceived plan or idea: Renoir, Hawks, McCarey against von Sternberg, Antonioni, Hitchcock. To von Sternberg, actors were "puppets": he claimed that every detail of Dietrich's performances in their films was created by him, down to the smallest gesture or flicker of expression. Arthur Penn aptly described the actors in Antonioni's films as "beautiful statuary." Hitchcock has denied saying that "actors are cattle": what he said was that they should be *treated* like cattle. The former trio seek to discover what an actor can give and then encourage him to give it, within the limits of an overall conception which is relatively loose: one knows, for example, that some of McCarey's best scenes were improvised on the set, that *La Règle du jeu* changed and grew during the course of shooting, that Hawks and his cast more or less made up *Hatari!* as they went along, within the loose framework of a hunting season. The spectator won't find in a Hitchcock film (or only very rarely) the continuous invention of detail, the spontaneous bits of business, that make *La Règle du jeu, Rio Bravo, Once upon a Honeymoon* so inexhaustibly alive; I find that Hitchcock's films go "dead" on me more easily. The broad distinction is between actor-centered cinema and image-centered cinema. The former implies a "humanist" philosophy and a certain form of "Realism." It also carries a logical thematic extension: the characters of Hawks, Renoir, and McCarey experience and express at least a relative freedom (literally, of movement within the frame; spiritually, of moral choice); the films of these directors are centered on values of generosity and affection between people, on the possibility of contact and reciprocal relations. In contrast, the characters of von Sternberg, Antonioni, Hitchcock are, typically, trapped, isolated, unable to communicate; there is a strong emphasis on impotence (the word to be understood in its general sense, though its specifically sexual overtones are not inappropriate).

To define and exemplify Hitchcock's image-centered concept of cinema, one need not adduce specimens of Kuleshovian editing: one need not look beyond the first shot of *Marnie*. Its primary function is to arouse the spectator's curiosity/voyeurism, though it also introduces certain important thematic motifs; its method involves the virtual elimination of the actor or of acting. Each precisely calculated detail in the action, the *décor*, and the camera movement conveys a precise idea or represents a strategy in the Hitchcockian game of audience manipulation (at this stage of the film taking the form of teasing). The close-up on the yellow bag tells us the bag is significant without giving us any clue as to why; as the camera slows and the figure walks on, our chief desire is to see her face – a desire Hitchcock systematically frustrates until, like Michelange in *Les Carabiniers*, we want to climb in through the frame and run ahead to take a look. She has black hair, so it can't be Tippi Hedren; except that it is so very black, and so glossy, that it may be dyed, so perhaps it *is* Tippi Hedren after all. We want the camera to catch up with her again so that we can get a better look: perhaps she will stop and turn. Hitchcock accordingly slows the camera down even more, eventually stopping it altogether; then, just as she turns and we might see her face (even at a distance) in profile, he cuts. Our curiosity is increased by other factors in the scene which are revealed as she moves further from the camera: the time of day (apparently very early morning), the station platform (completely deserted, without even a porter in sight, so she will have to wait a long time for a train), the way she is walking very straight and precariously along a yellow line, like a girl balancing on a tightrope. The "corridor" pattern of converging, receding lines (tracks, empty trains, the edges of the platform), familiar from *Vertigo* and taken up recurrently later in the film (the hotel corridor, the honeymoon ship, Mrs. Edgar's street), has an immediately expressive impact with its suggestion of a trajectory, introducing the "journey" motif on which the film is built. There is no purer example of the Hitchcock shot: the execution of a complex of ideas, with audience response a crucial determining concern.

The characteristics of Hitchcock's cinema so far described make logical another recurrent theme of his interviews: the repeated assertions that he is not really very interested in the actual shooting because he knows, with the completion of the shooting script, shot by shot what the film will be like: the filming is merely the mechanical execution of a precise blueprint. One takes this with at least one pinch of salt. On the one hand, it helps to explain the unevenness of so many Hitchcock films, the process of shooting providing no compensation for a failure of interest at the planning stage. Were all those slack sequences in *Topaz* – that look as if they'd been shot and thrown together by a television crew during the director's absence – really planned shot by shot? Perhaps so; the slackness could be accounted for by assuming that Hitchcock wasn't interested in them at the planning stage and, because he isn't a McCarey, could instill no life into them during shooting. On the other hand, one needs to account for the numerous superb performances in certain films where the acting quite transcends any Kuleshovian trickery. Hitchcock might, of course, have anticipated Grant's performance in *North by Northwest*, and even Bergman's in *Notorious*, from prior knowledge of the players. But Joseph Cotten in *Shadow of a Doubt*? Robert Walker in *Strangers on a Train*? Anthony Perkins in *Psycho*? One might account for them by the hypothesis that, because Hitchcock isn't interested in acting, certain actors, left to their own devices, are able to seize their chances and create their own performances independently; there is more reason to deduce that there are certain performances – or, more exactly, certain *roles* – which arouse in Hitchcock a particular creative interest.

Minor reservations apart, however, the films convincingly bear out the notion of detailed preplanning – especially the set pieces of what Hitchcock calls "pure cinema," a concept that invariably turns out to be based on the possibilities of montage. This accounts for Bazin's famous disillusionment when he visited Hitchcock on location for *To Catch a Thief* and found the *metteur en scène* apparently very little concerned with what was currently being shot. It is also the ultimate confirmation of our sense of Hitchcock's conception of cinema as an artificial construct – the most artificial, perhaps, short of animation (which something like the horse accident in *Marnie* strikingly resembles). This goes some way towards explaining the paradox that Hitchcock's cinema, dedicated so singlemindedly to the total entrapment of the spectator in an emotional experience, is also the easiest mentally to deconstruct. It is a truism that works of art can give pleasure on different levels, depending on a variety of factors: familiarity with the work, familiarity with its background and context, familiarity with its conventions; personal temperament; degree of intellectual awareness; the mood of the moment. The sorts of pleasure afforded by Hitchcock's films are unusually disparate, even contradictory: one might assume they would be mutually exclusive. There is the pleasure derived from experiencing the films in a state of total submission, carried through step by step in the scenario, shot by shot in the montage, in intense emotional participation; there is the pleasure of total awareness of how everything is done, the pleasure usually termed "aesthetic," wherein one delights in the skills of Hitchcock's technical mastery (when it works). Happily, the complexity of the human organism and its responses is such that even such seemingly opposed experiences can operate simultaneously (though each will modify the other). This is in fact implicit in my parenthesis above on Hitchcock's mastery ("when it works"): our intellectual awareness that something "works" (on which that apparently purely "aesthetic" delight rests) inevitably refers to an emotional level of response, the only level on which (at least in a Hitchcock movie) the concept of "working" can be validated.

* * *

So far, this attempt at a more precise and concrete definition of the nature of Hitchcock's art than *Hitchcock's Films* originally offered might seem to lead logically either to the traditional rejection or denigration of it as the work of a skillful technician and manipulator or to the type of analysis favored by the semiological school of "materialist" critics which would bypass questions of individual creativity and personal response, seeing the films as part of a "social process." The latter, certainly, would produce its revelations: one looks forward (not without trepidation) to accounts of, say, *Vertigo* and *Psycho* along the lines of Stephen Heath's remarkable reading of *Touch of Evil* in the Spring 1975 issue of *Screen*. But it is my contention that, however completely "coded" a work of art can be demonstrated to be, at its heart (if it is alive) is individual creativity, and it is with the nature of the creative impulses embodied in it that we must ultimately be concerned. This is not to talk naively about "genius" in a way that suggests that works of art spring spontaneously out of the artist's head via some process of immaculate conception. That Hitchcock's American period is in general richer than the British (a proposition I see no reason to retract or modify) can doubtless be attributed as much to a complex set of interacting determinants as to personal development; similarly, a complete account of any one of the great Hitchcock films would have to see it as the product of an intricate network of influences, circumstances of production, collaborations, happy confluences. But at the center of that network is – must be – a particular creative personality. The *auteur* theory, concerned to trace relationships between films and between different aspects (style, structure, theme) of the same film, exaggerated the degree of individual determination in the process of making it possible to define it; the current swing of the critical pendulum overcompensates for this by seeking to deny the individual altogether.

As soon as one begins to contemplate Hitchcock's work thematically, it becomes evident that its technical elaborations, the manifest desire to control audiences, have a thematic extension: they are determined, in other words, not simply by conscious commercial strategy but by powerful internal drives and pressures of the kind that never operate exclusively on a conscious level. The desire to control, the terror of losing control: such phrases describe not only Hitchcock's conscious relationship to technique and to his audiences but also the thematic center of his films. The personal relationships that fascinate Hitchcock invariably involve the exercise of power, or its obverse, impotence; in many cases, a power drive that seeks to conceal or deny or compensate for a dreaded impotence, the perfect metaphor for which is provided by the "double" Norman Bates of *Psycho*: the young man terrified of women and the exaggeratedly "potent" monster wielding the phallic knife. This relationship-pattern, with its possible permutations and variations, links films as apparently diverse as *Notorious*, *Rope*, *Rear Window*, *Vertigo*, *Psycho*, and *Marnie*: on the whole, the more the plot structure allows it to dominate, the richer, more forceful, more fully achieved is the film. *Notorious* – one of Hitchcock's finest works, of which we still await an adequate account – derives its fascination from its complex shifting of power-and-impotence relationships, involving all four of the principle characters, and from certain suggestive Freudian overtones related to this: the key Ingrid Bergman steals from Claude Rains to give to Cary Grant, the bottle in the cellar which Grant discovers and which contains Rains's secret "potency" (in the form of uranium ore).

The scene of the party in Rains's house suggests the central importance in Hitchcock of a motif peculiarly appropriate to the cinema, the "look," and its relation to the power/impotence obsession. It also suggests that the common simplistic association of subjective camera with audience identification (which parts of *Hitchcock's Films* may have done something to encourage) needs careful qualification. During the early part of the scene, we are placed, in turn, in the positions of Bergman, Grant, and Rains as they watch each other across the room, through the throng of guests, each for his or her own reasons apprehensive; the spectator is led to participate in the tensions expressed through the pattern of interchanged looks rather than to identify with a particular character. The look expresses both dominance (the power of watching) and helplessness (the impotence of separation); by the use of subjective shots, Hitchcock at once makes the tension personal to himself (camera as the director's eyes) and transfers it to the audience (camera as eyes of the spectator).

The close connection between this and the voyeuristic tendencies so often noted in Hitchcock's cinema is obvious. Again, perhaps, the most vivid single instance is in *Psycho* (significantly, among the most intensely personal of all his films, and the one in which he was most singlemindedly dedicated to manipulating his audience): the close-up of Norman's eye as he watches through his peephole and the cut to a subjective view of Marion undressing, so that the eye becomes both ours and Hitchcock's. The whole of *Rear Window* can be seen as an elaboration of this principle, the James Stewart character combining certain aspects of the roles of spectator and *metteur en scène*. The notion of impotence is concretely embodied in the broken leg; the people Stewart watches are at once dominated imaginatively by his consciousness (like Marion, they don't know they are being watched) and forever beyond his control.

To trace the creative drives behind Hitchcock's films to sources in psychopathology (possible, after all, to some degree with *any* artist) does not necessarily invalidate the emphasis placed in my book on their therapeutic impulses: indeed, it could logically be felt to strengthen this emphasis by giving the therapeutic impulses a particular focus or motivation. I still feel that the Hitchcock films I most admire are centered on a movement toward health via therapy and catharsis. I have, however, become much more keenly aware of a need to insist on sharp discriminations – a need to stress the limitations of Hitchcock's art and to distinguish the work (a small proportion of the total *oeuvre*) that succeeds in transcending them.

The limitations are of two kinds, though perhaps not entirely unconnected. There is, first, the somewhat equivocal relationship between Hitchcock the artist and Hitchcock the showman-entertainer. Obviously, the two can never be cleanly separated, nor would it be desirable that they could be, as their interrelationship is in many ways crucial to the robustness of Hitchcock's work. One can, nevertheless, set up fairly obvious polar opposites: the intensely involved personal art of *Vertigo*, say, as against the businessman who lends his name to anthologies of largely trivial horror stories or the comic fat man who introduces the Hitchcock half-hour on television. Between the two, however, lie areas where the relationship becomes problematic. What concerns me here is the way in which some of Hitchcock's finest work is flawed by compromises that, in an artist free of "commercial" constraints, would appear neurotic, the result of a reluctance to allow certain disturbing implications to be fully explored, but which Hitchcock encourages us (sometimes, in interviews, explicitly) to regard as the result of external pressures, fears of alienating his audiences (the two motivations are not, of course, incompatible). There is a whole series of Hitchcock films which work magnificently up to a point, arousing complex and disturbing emotions, achieving a rich – and often very subversive – suggestiveness, and then evade their own implications by a sudden simplification. I have already touched in *Hitchcock's Films* on the two most striking instances, *Strangers on a Train* and *Torn Curtain*. The former offers the neatest example of all, because one can point to the exact moment where the film goes wrong (which is also where it departs most decisively from its source, Patricia Highsmith's novel) – the scene where Guy *doesn't* murder Bruno's father. Here and in *Torn Curtain* Hitchcock's reluctance to explore or acknowledge the disturbing implications of his hero's behavior results in a curious paralysis at the center of the film: neither one thing nor the other, the hero ends up nothing, and interest is displaced onto Bruno (in *Strangers*) and onto peripheral characters (in *Torn Curtain*). If in *Strangers* the simplification takes the form of trying to pass off Guy as a conventional hero, in *Shadow of a Doubt* it takes the opposite form of turning the film's most complex and ambivalently viewed figure (Uncle Charlie) into a mere monster for the last third. *Psycho* is much nearer to being a masterpiece (the first half, up to the point where Marion's car sinks into the swamp, is certainly among the most extraordinary achievements of the American cinema). Yet even here one cannot but feel a lapse to a lower level of interest, with conventional detective-story investigation, "flat" characters (Sam and Lila), and scenes (especially those involving Sheriff Chambers) that could easily come from one of the less distinguished of Hitchcock's TV shows. (The film picks up again, superbly, with Lila's exploration of Norman's home.)

The second limitation is more damaging: I would define it as the relative weakness in Hitchcock's art of the normative impulse. That great art strives – however implicitly – toward the realization of norms seems to me axiomatic, though the principle I am stating is frequently misunderstood or misrepresented. It is not a matter of whether a work is "optimistic" or "pessimistic" and certainly not a denial of the validity of a tragic vision of life. It is a matter of the nature of the creative impulse, which, to flourish, must be rooted in a sense of at least a *potential* normality for which to strive, values by which to live. "Normality" here must not be understood in terms of the reaffirmation of established values, least of all the norms of bourgeois society: Godard's *Tout va bien*, for example, answers perfectly to my concept of "normative" art, though its tone is not optimistic and it proposes no clearly definable solutions to the problems it raises; if I place beside it, as another essentially "normative" work, Bergman's *The Silence*, I shall perhaps sufficiently have safeguarded myself against simplification and parody.

It is not really paradoxical that Hitchcock's art is usually at its most creative when his material permits or encourages the most complete immersion in the abnormal. If creativity is, almost by definition, a striving towards norms, this implies a process, a *moving through*. The problem with Hitchcock is that the movement seems almost always blocked. His work typically equates "normality" with a bourgeois life in whose values the creative side of him totally disbelieves but to which it can provide no alternative. The couple in *Rich and Strange* pass through a series of disruptive experiences only to return, at the end of the film, to precisely the sterile existence of the beginning: all they have learned is to be afraid of the unfamiliar. The pattern established here is fundamental to Hitchcock's work: bourgeois "normality" is empty and unsatisfying, everything beyond it (or, more importantly, *within* it, secreted beneath its surface), terrifying. This explains why Hitchcock's most satisfying endings are those that express catharsis without reimposing a defined "normality" – at once, necessarily, the bleakest and most "open": the opening of the window and firing of the gun at the end of *Rope*; the car being withdrawn from the swamp at the end of *Psycho*; above all, the end of *Vertigo*. And, if this last remains, unchallengeably, Hitchcock's masterpiece, this is surely because there the attitude to the unknown and mysterious is not simply one of terror but retains, implicitly, a profound and disturbing ambivalence.

It is symptomatic that the most obvious legacy of Hitchcock's Jesuit education should be the lingering fascination with Hell and damnation, often concretized in the detail of the films. When Uncle Charlie arrives in Santa Rosa (*Shadow of a Doubt*), the whole image is darkened by the black smoke from the train, and the character is thereafter repeatedly shown with smoke hanging around him from his cigarette; when Bruno pursues Miriam through the Tunnel of Love (*Strangers on a Train*) his boat is named Pluto; when Marion Crane tells Norman Bates that she "thought she must have gotten off the right road," he replies that "Nobody ever comes here unless they've done that." It is to these "damned" characters (ambiguously lost souls or devils) that Hitchcock's strongest interest gravitates, giving us some of the most vividly realized performances in his films; one looks in vain for any compensating intimation of Heaven. Hitchcock seems interested in the "normality" presented by the films only when he can treat it satirically, as with the "society" party of *Strangers on a Train*. *Shadow of a Doubt* is especially interesting here, as it is one film in which Hitchcock is supposed to create small-town life affectionately. In fact, the family the film depicts consists of a collection of more-or-less caricatured individuals, each of whom inhabits a private, separate dreamworld, the mother nostalgic for her youth and her adored younger brother, the father living in a fantasy world of detective fiction and real-life crime, the younger daughter perpetually immersed in books. The film is rich in amusing detail, and the early scenes of Uncle Charlie's intrusion into the small-town world are genuinely disturbing and subversive; but it would be difficult to claim either that the family life presented offers much in the way of affirmation or that the film suggests any possible alternative that isn't corrupt or "evil." Uncle Charlie, characteristically, brings life and excitement into an inert world, but proves to be a devil who must be destroyed: the sense of emptiness with which one is left at the end is closely bound up with the film's association of excitement with corruption, with Hitchcock's habitual distrust of the forces of the Id.

If I were to undertake a revision of *Hitchcock's Films*, the chapter that would call for the most modification would be that on *The Birds*, a film about which my feelings continue to be both mixed and fluctuating. It seems in some ways Hitchcock's most important, most "serious" film: the film in which he is most overtly concerned to elaborate a view of the universe. What is ultimately wrong with it is not that the eye too easily penetrates the technical trickery but that, for all the audacity of the conception and the consistent interest of the execution, the characters and their relationships are too slight to sustain the weight of significance implicitly imposed on them, too slight ever adequately to represent humanity and human potential; and there is no sign that Hitchcock can conceive of human potential positively in more adequate terms. The development the film appears to offer – the stripping-away of the veneer of complacent superficiality – never really materializes, at least not very impressively. One is left with a sense of discrepancy between the film's grand postulate – the threatened end of civilization and perhaps of humanity itself – and the actual created civilization and humanity presented in it. The weakness can be localized specifically in the perfunctory treatment of the children, in Hitchcock's notable failure to respond to the notion of renewed potential they and the school might have represented, his reduction of the concepts of education and childhood – the human future – to the automatic reiteration of an inane jingle. It is because the film fails to achieve the dimensions of tragedy (which depends on concepts of positive value) that it seems so perilously to border on the sadistic – the sadism directed ultimately, perhaps, at the audience. The film suggests, strongly, that the artificiality of Hitchcock's cinema, which I have attempted to define stylistically, has ramifications far beyond the "unnatural" surface of the films: he seems unable to create a "normal" life, whether actual or potential, of any richness or density, a point that holds whether one understands "normal" in the conventional, bourgeois sense or in my sense of "moving towards new norms."

Chapter Four

Hitch as Matrix-Figure: Hitchcock and Twentieth-Century Cinema

John Orr

This book is being written adjacent to a framed Hitchcock image that hangs at a right angle to the desktop, on the far wall of the room. His thriller set in a Manhattan apartment, *Rope* (1948), inspires the image. It displays a coiled rope, double-knotted, looping down level with a diagonal fold in a scarlet curtain. Suspended between the two knots is another loop in the center of the frame that looks like a hangman's noose. It is not a specific image from the film but an image keyed in by the strangulation that begins it so shockingly; an image conveying the feel and menace of the Hitchcock narrative, not only in this film but also throughout his long career. It signifies, at the very least, killing and retribution, crime and punishment, guilt and judgment. Yet the image is no abstract signifier: it is concrete and immediate as Hitchcock's images are. It sends a direct signal to the senses. Hitchcock once said that his films were intended to create goose bumps on the neck of the spectator. Glancing across at this image is a clear and present reminder of his intent.

The motif is a screen print by Sam Ainslie, who displayed it in an exhibition at the Glasgow Print Studio in Autumn 2003 called simply *HITCH*. Other Scottish artists, among them Steven Campbell, Peter Howson, Ray Richardson, and Adrian Wiszniewski, also created images triggered by other famous films: *Spellbound* (1945), *Strangers on a Train* (1951), *Vertigo* (1958), *North by Northwest* (1959), *Psycho* (1960), *The Birds* (1963), *Torn Curtain* (1966). The media varied, from screen and digital print to photopolymer and oil or acrylic on canvas. All were images that departed from the photographic still, as signs of Hitchcock's cinema taken over into other visual forms. Yet this translation is testament to the enduring power of his moving images. There are few film directors in the world, past or present, who could prompt such a testament. And this exhibition, modest in scale but marvelous in execution, is only one indication of what can be done. It was not the first nor will it be the last "translation" of Hitchcock out of cinema. Hitch has been inspiration to a number of multimedia and installation events, the best known perhaps being Douglas Gordon's *24-Hour Psycho* at the London Hayward Exhibition *Spellbound* in 1996, which slowed Hitchcock's film down to a speed of two frames per second (see Mulvey). Three years later the MOMA Oxford Exhibition with contributions from filmmakers and other visual artists marked the Hitchcock centenary in the UK. Not to be outdone, a Francophone exhibition premiered in Montreal in 2000 was then displayed at the Pompidou Centre in Paris, with Hitchcock film excerpts, storyboards, and publicity stills set alongside work from many great visual artists of the twentieth century.

Legacies

If he is transferable in this way across visual forms, Hitchcock is more transferable *within* the form where homage and pastiche abound. This periodic transfer started in a big way while he was still alive, no more so than in the French New Wave, where François Truffaut, who wrote on Hitchcock and did a series of famous interviews with him, also made a quartet of homage films – *Fahrenheit 451* (1966), *The Bride Wore Black* (1967), *Mississippi Mermaid* (1969), and *Finally Sunday!* (1983). The authors of the best Hitchcock study ever, Eric Rohmer and Claude Chabrol, went on to use his themes and motifs just as closely in their own films. As if to announce future intent, Chabrol had early on paid mock homage to Hitchcock (who of course tried to appear in each of his pictures), by advertising his book on Hitchcock in his 1959 film, *Les Cousins*; the sad provincial hero (Gérard Blain) can be seen at one point in a bookshop browsing a copy of the Rohmer – Chabrol tribute! Elsewhere in Paris, documentary filmmaker Chris Marker, who worked mostly on social and political themes, paid a succinct double-homage to *Vertigo*, first with the memory-haunting sequences of his short film *La Jetée* (1962) and then twenty years later with the San Francisco sequence of the *Vertigo* tour in his compelling documentary *Sans Soleil* (1985).

But Hitchcock made an even stronger impact on the future of box-office cinema. The creation of the James Bond series in the 1960s, for example, was made possible only by the dynamism and drive of his earlier spy thrillers from *The 39 Steps* (1935) right through to *North by Northwest*, the immediate inspiration. American directors also paid their respects. In 1958 Stanley Donen reunited Cary Grant and Ingrid Bergman for *Indiscreet*, a film that echoed their dazzling roles in Hitchcock's *Notorious* (1946), and followed it in 1963 with *Charade* with Grant playing opposite Audrey Hepburn in clear echoes of *To Catch a Thief* (1955). At the start of the 1960s *Psycho* reinvigorated the Hollywood horror genre and cleared the way for the 1970s sensation narratives of Brian De Palma, George A. Romero, and John Carpenter. In terms of its attention to place and detail and its powers of horror, it found a much worthier successor in William Friedkin's Washington-based fable *The Exorcist* (1973). Meanwhile, *The Birds* was a key source for many spectacle-disaster movies premised on special effects that lit up Hollywood in the late 1970s and have been big box-office ever since. Filmed on location in San Francisco, *Vertigo*, Hitchcock's great study of erotic obsession, became the unwitting Ur-text for wilder things in the work of Brian De Palma: in his lurid incest drama *Obsession* (1976) and his pseudo-erotic shocker *Body Double* (1984), which also cannibalized *Rear Window* (1954). It also surfaces through the dubious homage of Paul Verhoeven's bombastic, soft-core *Basic Instinct* (1992), sadly box-office gold and also filmed on San Francisco locations. More San Francisco homage duly came from other glossy pictures, the smart suspenseful *Jagged Edge* (1987) with Glenn Close and Jeff Bridges reprising the roles (with genders reversed) of defense lawyer and defendant in *The Paradine Case* (1947), and soon after the nonsensical *Final Analysis* (1992) with Richard Gere and Kim Basinger.

After Hitchcock's death in 1980 we might have expected his work to become unfashionable and fade away. But since then, as we have seen, the impact has intensified. Hollywood, in effect, has commodified his memory and homage has become obsessive. There were two sequels to *Psycho*, the first with Anthony Perkins in a 1983 reprise of his role as Norman Bates, the second in 1986 where Perkins was not only Bates again but also directed and shot at the start a strange homage to the bell-tower scene that ends *Vertigo*. As if not to be outdone, there has been a 1999 remake of the original *Psycho* by Gus Van Sant that copies it with some key variations but also films it, inexplicably, in color. (It could be argued that Van Sant's real attempt to recapture the sheer horror of the Hitchcock film comes in his 2003 meditation on the Columbine High School massacre, *Elephant*.) Earlier *Psycho's* horror lineage had spread into the 1960s renaissance of European cinema with powerful repercussions. Its narrative momentum seems essential to Roman Polanski's South Kensington chamber-drama *Repulsion* (1965) filmed just five years later. Elsewhere, its Gothic reanimation of the dead Mother, whose skull is superimposed on the face of the hapless Norman sitting in his prison cell, has been seen as a source of the identity-superimpositions in Ingmar Bergman's more abstract and enigmatic *Persona* (1966) (see Ness, 181–2). We could also make the case that Bergman's late German psycho-drama *From the Life of the Marionettes* (1980), with its deranged businessman who murders a prostitute whom he mistakes for his hated spouse, is a key link between the Hitchcock classic and David Lynch's disturbing, psychogenic *Lost Highway* (1996).

Elsewhere Canadian directors who generally cast a quizzical Northern eye over the genre habits of their American neighbors have produced ingenious variations. Set in Toronto, David Cronenberg's car fetish film *Crash* (1996), with its destructive pairing of Eros and technology, is one of the most powerful renderings of North American apocalypse since *The Birds*. In Francophone Canada, *Le Confessionnal* (1995) by Robert Lepage exposes as false the division between homage and originality. His film was not only a conscious sequel to the Quebec thriller *I Confess* (1952) but alternates dramatically between then and now (1989) in its time sequence to intimate much darker secrets than the ones Hitchcock had uncovered. Daringly, it also integrates shots from the Hitchcock original with an invented story around the making of the film in which Hitchcock is treated as a fictional character. Not to be outdone, his fellow Canadian Atom Egoyan, strongly influenced by Hitchcock in his memory films *Exotica* (1994) and *The Sweet Hereafter* (1997), then adapted a Jack Trevor story of an Irish girl in Birmingham, *Felicia's Journey* (1999), where he has a stout reclusive killer from a past age called Hilditch (Bob Hoskins), smother-loved as a child by his mother and reared on her strange cooking lessons, a figure who seems a slyly affectionate portrait of a gastronomic Hitchcock transformed into one of his own villains. In Egoyan's perverse equation Hilditch, we might speculate, equals Hitch.

Meanwhile back in Hollywood the third screen remake of John Buchan's *The Thirty-Nine Steps* was slated for production with Robert Towne directing (the first, of course, being Hitchcock's 1935 adaptation). Of course there had been an unofficial one in 1990 by the talented Australian Peter Weir. Weir had used the handcuff motif of Hitchcock's film – where the fugitive couple are literally stuck with one another – as metaphoric inspiration for *Green Card* (1990), a smart romantic comedy about a furtive French migrant and his American "wife" in New York trapped by their planned marriage of convenience. Subsequently Weir culled the major themes of fear and trauma from *Spellbound* and *Vertigo* to make his haunting story of a plane crash survivor (Jeff Bridges) in *Fearless* (1993), again with homage sequences in San Francisco using special effects. Another haunting reprise came in 1988 with Roman Polanski's *Frantic*, where an American doctor (Harrison Ford), speaking no French, arrives with his wife (Betty Buckley) at dawn in an eerie unsettling Paris for a conference-cum-holiday. He enjoys neither, as his wife disappears as soon as they have unpacked in their hotel. The sudden kidnapping with its political agenda echoes Hitchcock's color remake of his *The Man Who Knew Too Much* (1956) with like family kidnapping and like American doctor, James Stewart this time, in Marrakech. Ford's tenacious paranoia and key perception lapses mirror those of his famous predecessor, though Polanski of course has his own ingenious variations. At the cruder end of the market, Andrew Davis, who made his blockbuster *The Fugitive* (1993) by hyping up all the elements of the Hitchcock chase into manic proportions for (again) Harrison Ford, then went on to remake *Dial "M" for Murder* (1950) by changing the title to *A Perfect Murder* (1998), changing locations from London to New York and casting Gwyneth Paltrow as a dead ringer for Grace Kelly. If anything the film shows us just how much Paltrow and Michael Douglas pale by comparison with Kelly and Ray Milland in the original.

Not to be outdone, the French have come up with more subtle variations. Veteran Eric Rohmer's *L'Anglaise et le Duc* (*The Lady & the Duke*, 2001), based on a Scottish noblewoman's diary of danger in the French Revolution, strongly echoes Hitchcock's only major costume film, the star vehicle for Ingrid Bergman, *Under Capricorn* (1949), set in nineteenth-century Australia and shot in a London studio. As if to pay homage to that artifice, Rohmer, the great realist, changes tack and gives us a studio movie for the digital age with painted scenery and computer-generated images. In 1998, Nicole Garcia's ambitious *Place Vendôme* updates the Hitchcock thriller to the shadowy world of European diamond merchants, and also remakes *Vertigo* in Paris by focusing on the female figures of Hitchcock's plot, reworking in French terms an imaginary rivalry between a real Madeleine Elster (whom we see in *Vertigo* only as a corpse) and her young rival-imitator, Judy Barton (Kim Novak). On one reading, Garcia's film, recycling Bernard Herrmann's *Vertigo* music for its vertiginous sequences, is a conscious reversal of Hitchcock's tragic ending, a fable of female redemption in which Marianne (Catherine Deneuve) rescues both herself and her young impostor, Nathalie (Emmanuelle Seigner) from a double betrayal (see Kline, 36–9). We add another reference point. The substance of Deneuve's central performance as an abject, betrayed alcoholic who finds renewed hope seems to owe much to the commanding figure of Bergman in *Under Capricorn* and *Notorious*, who of course had found similar redemption in impossible circumstance. Finally Gilles Mimouni's elegant thriller *L'Appartement* (1997) pays simultaneous homage to Hitchcock *and* Truffaut by subjecting Hitchcock's doubling and voyeur motifs, and his *mise-en-scène*, to hyperactive Truffaut-like camerawork. The dazzling result is an eclectic style mix that crosses *Rear Window* and *Vertigo* with Truffaut's *La Peau douce* (1964).

Other names and titles could be added to the list at the turn of the century. In East Asia, we could cite Chinese filmmakers like Wong Kar-Wai, who used *Notorious* as a model for his poetic memory film *In the Mood for Love* (2000), or Lou Ye, who made *Suzhou River* in the same year and set it in contemporary Shanghai as a conscious homage to *Vertigo*. An even stronger link can be found in the disturbing Japanese shocker, Takashi Miike's *Audition* (2000), which integrates elements of *Psycho* and *Vertigo* with aspects of the Japanese ghost narrative perfected by Kenji Mizoguchi's classic *Ugetsu Monogatari* (1953). A composed fable of pure terror, Miike's film shows us a film producer obsessed with auditioning an unknown for a new film at the same time as for the role of his new wife. The chosen one – slim, beautiful, modest, deferential, and dressed in virginal all-white – is not, however, what she seems. As the object of the producer's constant obsession, she echoes the role of Madeleine Elster in *Vertigo*, a contemporary Japanese version of a beautiful ghost. Yet the climactic violence comes from a different Hitchcock tradition. True, it has its portents early in the film, but when it erupts it is still as shocking, as unexpected, as psychically disturbing as the killings in *Psycho*. In both his late films Hitchcock plays in different ways on the elusive relationship of appearance and reality, and Miike's film blends their legacy with a chilling composure.

The salient point here is not the formation of any one Hitchcock school of filmmaking, but the enduring power of his themes and images everywhere. At the turn of the century Hitchcock is ubiquitous. As we shall see, the 1990s revival of film noir, or neo-noir, could well be called post-Hitchcock noir, a crossover genre that blends noir and Hitchcock motifs that in the 1940s had stood in opposition to one another. In Joel and Ethan Coen's black-and-white pastiche movie *The Man Who Wasn't There* (2001), set in post-war California, noir themes of adultery and murder echoing Billy Wilder's classic *Double Indemnity* (1944) are shot on location in Santa Rosa, the small town north of San Francisco that had been the famous site of Hitchcock's *Shadow of a Doubt* (1943). And Hitchcock's film had in turn been an inspiration to the location shooting in Californian Noir used from 1944 onwards by Wilder, Robert Siodmak, and Otto Preminger. Preminger's cynical smalltown melodrama, *Fallen Angel* (1945), is a prime and triumphant case in point.

We can see here, witnessing this immense overload, that Hitchcock's legacy has become a mixed blessing. There have been many inspirational movies, and many new directions fired up by his supreme example. On the other hand, homage often shades into imitation or pastiche into repetition, both a temptation for directors to bump up their credentials when they are seeking an easy way out. There is always the thrill of mystery at the center of Hitchcock's work and the lure in a less censored age governed by speed and information of opening out the Hitchcock narrative, making it faster and more explicit, stepping up the suspense, cranking up the violence, but equally junking the well-made story, the articulate dialogue, the nuances of editing, the formalisms of *mise-en-scène*. Generally the effect is the opposite of what is intended. What shows through instead with this contagion of imitation is a time illusion of "progressive cinema," of moving things one stage on for a new age and a new generation, an illusion of progress that masks a compulsion to repeat, a compulsion indeed that is often threadbare, an easy addiction in which "inspiration" is too easily an excuse for lacking vision. As opposed to the illusion of the step forward, however, there lies perspicacity in the shift sideward, the incorporation of Hitchcock into a strong existing auteurist vision. Notable here is a sharing of key qualities, the use of the camera to replicate fundamentals of human vision in the exploration of cinematic space and of narrative to replicate fundamental rhythms of everyday life; the attention to detail in *mise-en-scène*, and respect for the power of the spoken word as well as the image. It is out of these qualities that the essential Hitchcock elements of the extraordinary flow – mystery, memory, suspense, ambivalence, terror.

In this respect we can note a precise *translation of vision* among some directors who take Hitchcock in their own direction. Several figures stand out: Chabrol, Rohmer, Resnais, Polanski, Lynch, and Weir. They are all successors to him precisely because they are all *unlike* him. That is to say, they absorb him into the world of their *own* vision, because they all have a starting point that is independent of his. At a glance, therefore, we can easily compare Hitchcock's films to theirs. Yet, once we have made surface comparisons, we will soon find depth and complexity to keep us guessing. For, critically speaking, we are always in parallel worlds. The same sensation occurs when taking Hitchcock *backward*. Rolling back in time, he had a big legacy to inherit and would have been nothing without it, a legacy unusual for an Anglo-American director of his time that sprang from his early cinephile enthusiasms in 1920s London. It was indeed varied: the surrealist impulse of Luis Buñuel and Salvador Dalí countered by the montage aesthetics of Lev Kuleshov and Sergei Eisenstein, and then the key inheritance of Weimar cinema, especially the work of Friedrich Wilhelm Murnau and Fritz Lang, that lasted throughout his professional life. Surrealism, Soviet montage, expressionism: great moments of early modernism and all blended seamlessly into the Hitchcock *oeuvre*.

At the same time his contemporaries have always loomed large. It is easy to imagine Hitchcock and Buñuel looking closely at each other's films throughout their dazzling careers and then duly taking note. Truffaut has pointed to *Shadow of a Doubt* as inspiration for Buñuel's Mexican murder drama *The Criminal Life of Archibaldo de la Cruz* (1955) (Truffaut, 266). Toward the end of his career Hitchcock professed great admiration for *Tristana* (1968) and *That Obscure Object of Desire* (1977). Elsewhere, the steely eroticisms of American film noir ran in counterpoint to the erotic romance of American Hitchcock while Hitchcock duly donated his flight motifs to successors in post-war British film before his departure for American shores. In the capable hands of directors like Carol Reed and Alberto Cavalcanti they flourished without him. Likewise you could say that on the British front Hitchcock continually traded motifs and images with Michael Powell, and on the American front with Orson Welles. Like him both had absorbed the vision of German expressionism and then went on to develop distinctive films of their own out of its broad legacy. Yet it was Hitchcock who hogged the limelight as Welles was pilloried for *The Lady from Shanghai* (1948) and Powell attacked at the end of the next decade for *Peeping Tom* (1960). Most critics today would value both films highly but that would have been no consolation to Powell or to Welles back then. By contrast, Hitchcock always knew how to play safe when in doubt without compromising his vision. He was shrewd enough and lucky enough to escape opprobrium for his controlled provocations. Yet provocations they were. To challenge the conventions and the censorship of the time, cinematic and social, yet always communicate directly with a mass audience: such a working mandate linked Hitchcock to another Hollywood contemporary of European origin he greatly admired, Billy Wilder. Both were determined to test the edges of Hollywood censorship while challenging their audiences, but always doing so through well-constructed, emotionally absorbing films. If Hitchcock has a rival in this sense, it is not Welles or Lang, who experienced mixed fortunes in Hollywood. It was the writer/director of *Double Indemnity, The Lost Weekend* (1945), and *Sunset Boulevard* (1950). Working within the studio system, Hitchcock, like Wilder, used its strength and money astutely to keep a grip on his mass audience. If he flopped at the box office when he went back to post-war London to make the ambitious *Under Capricorn*, Hitchcock knew how to bounce back on returning to Hollywood with *Strangers on a Train*. If *Vertigo* proved too obscure for audiences in 1958, *North by Northwest* and *Psycho* would soon have them on the edge of their seats.

This intermingled history sets up our main metaphor. In discussing *Rear Window*, Rohmer and Chabrol called James Stewart as L. B. Jefferies, the photographer with prying eyes, a "matrix-figure," whose gaze dominates the enclosed space of the Greenwich Village courtyard, where the spectacle of murder unfolds (Rohmer and Chabrol, 124). It is a brilliant metaphor, but perhaps does not go far enough. For in the history of Western cinema Hitchcock himself became something of a matrix-figure. Indeed, the lean figure of Stewart as the tall, wheelchair-bound photographer is a mirror image of his short, portly director seated in the director's chair, orchestrating the space and spectacle of his vision. The image is enduring: Hitchcock at the center not only of his own cinema but of cinema as such. Through his work so much of the entire life of Western cinema has been nurtured and dispersed. So much shock, so much suspense, so much montage, so much mystery, so much watching, so much doubling, so much disaster, so much redemption: it all goes back to him. Or rather, because it also precedes him, it all goes through him. That enables us to look at this special link between Hitch and his fellow-filmmakers as a form of fate that ties in through echo and repetition down the years. In the last century the fate of Hitchcock and cinema were inextricable. In this century the odds are that they will continue to be so.

The other Hitchcock connection lies in the way he refashioned the relationship between auteur and genre. The Hitchcock "thriller" or "romance" had an authorial mark that was unmistakable. As a towering figure in mid-century Hitchcock thus mediates the future, between a system of cinephile authorship and a Hollywood genre system reworking plots and narratives from written sources in fiction or drama that brighten the faces of studio producers. From 1940 he worked within popular genre to turn it around, but from *Rear Window* onward to *Marnie* (1964) he effectively transcended it. Though he had begun to produce his own films successfully after his break with David O. Selznick in 1947, he was never a financially independent director and during the crisis afflicting the twilight of his career after *Marnie* he made no attempt to move in that direction. Indeed he had little conceptual relationship to New American Cinema of the 1970s, though the inspired acting of Karen Black, Barbara Harris, and Bruce Dern in *Family Plot* (1976) shows clear dramatic crossover. Indeed, the aging Hitchcock had taken a tumble as New American Cinema began to prosper. Production delays in 1963 had meant the ambitious *Marnie* was largely confined to studio sound stages, much to its detriment, and its US box-office failure meant difficulties in funding later projects. He then turned back to previous British concerns, including a wish to film John's Buchan's 1924 thriller *The Three Hostages*. One of his great, unrealized ambitions late in life was to film J. M. Barrie's ghost play *Mary Rose* (1920). It seems in retrospect to have been a nostalgic gesture and it was blocked by MCA-Universal when he intended it as a follow-up to *Marnie* (Krohn, 278). In an era that seemed to be slipping away from him he filmed mundane Cold War thrillers like *Torn Curtain* and *Topaz* (1969) before returning to London to film one of his powerful British pictures – *Frenzy* (1972).

Yet the prehistory of *Frenzy* as a different (and aborted) project to be shot in New Jersey and New York City – *Kaleidoscope* – suggests that, after the drearily orthodox *Torn Curtain*, Hitchcock *did* want to update his filmic style, late in life, to absorb the European modernisms of the 1960s. The bold experiments in form by Michelangelo Antonioni and Jean-Luc Godard that he watched avidly in the mid-1960s were a special inspiration. A serial-killer story like the later *Frenzy* (and inspired by the life of British murderer Neville Heath), this was to be a location shoot with sequences featuring male and female nudity, natural light, experimental color, and handheld camera (see Auiler, 443–5, 547–8). Horrified by the explicit nature of the material and the unorthodox means of shooting, MCA executives, including Lew Wassermann, redirected Hitchcock away from this cutting-edge innovation to the banal disasters of *Topaz* and away from his quest to prove to himself and his audience that he was the equal of the new European innovators. Fragments of a draft screenplay written by Hitchcock himself suggest a fascinating scenario (Auiler, 279–89). Yet the irony was that, with *Vertigo*, *Psycho*, and *The Birds*, Hitchcock had already proved his modernist credentials without fully realizing it. As we shall see, *The Birds* equals any film anywhere of its decade in its artistic confrontation with the risks of nature and the perils of modernity. In truth, Hitchcock had already made his point. At the same time the studio knock-back on the *Kaleidoscope* project, for which in 1967 Hitchcock had already done initial filming, was a heavy blow to both personal morale and artistic freedom. By shooting *Frenzy* in London he was able to escape the studio's prying eyes, but also reverted to shooting narrative for a less experimental kind of film. Ironically, he also reclaimed his full auteurism by strengthening his position as a stockholder in MCA, too late to prevent the jettisoning of *Kaleidoscope* or *Mary Rose*, but salvaging without a doubt his twilight contribution to 1970s cinema.

Though he seldom took a screenwriting credit, Hitchcock was also a matrix-figure in another sense – at the center of everything he filmed, at the center of a product he nurtured into existence on all levels – adaptation, treatment, storyboarding, costuming, screenplay, shooting script, design, *mise-en-scène* and editing. His preparation was meticulous and, for some, too mechanical. True, his time with hands-on producers Michael Balcon at British-Gaumont and then with Selznick in Hollywood had sometimes constrained his options. Yet he would still try, creatively speaking, to flesh out his role as director to the full: to orchestrate everything in minute and precise detail using his main actors, writers, and his many brilliant collaborators. In America Hitchcock found such lasting and creative collaborators in art director Robert Boyle, music composer Bernard Herrmann, costume designer Edith Head, cinematographer Robert Burks, and editor George Tomasini. All were treated as creative colleagues and as instruments of his cinematic design, all as invaluable specialists bringing texture and detail to his vision. Between these two roles, instrument and collaborator, his collective work ethic ensured there was never a lasting contradiction. In the intense American period between 1940 and 1963, filmmaking became a continuous process achieved without any significant break. To this end, he would almost always overlap his films, starting work on *North by Northwest*, for example, when *Vertigo* was still in post-production or discussing *Marnie* with screenwriter Evan Hunter on set while filming *The Birds* (even though Hunter was fated not to last the course with his adaptation of Winston Graham's novel). Naturally Hitchcock was not "original," if we demand a writer-director who uses original material with few literary sources and still carves a dynamic career out of modest budgets. He was, for sure, no John Cassavetes or Ingmar Bergman. He was the product of a studio system, which he then manipulated triumphantly to his own ends. That in itself was no mean achievement. The question of originality can never produce open and shut answers. We must remember that Shakespeare had pillaged history chronicles, the Renaissance, the classics, and the plays of fellow dramatists to forge the greatest theater ever written in the English language. Everything, as Hitchcock knew, came from somewhere else, but you could always imprint it with your own signature.

Hitchcock and Modernity

In the course of his career we can take the easy divide, 1939, between British and American Hitchcock as a watershed, as the start of something more profound. In the British phase of the 1930s there had been a penchant for suspense, smart spy stories, and a passing, often quirky commentary on the English class system. In the American phase he gets serious. Suspense modulates into psychodrama as the complexities of crisis situation deepen. Here his narratives rotate around a recurring theme – the internal violation of bourgeois order. It is a violation that has a variety of sources, a multitude of causes. Three overlapping forms stand out in the American period. The first is the threat from without (political) that becomes a threat within (social); the second is the threat from within (individual) that highlights the failure of social order; the third lies in the failures of the law itself. The first form works through the anti-Nazi phase of the 1940s from *Foreign Correspondent* (1940) to *Notorious*, where Hitchcock's traitors are bourgeois renegades, closet Nazis who have retained their charm and social manners but have lost all sense of humanity. The second profiles the psychotic killers of *Shadow of a Doubt, Spellbound, Rope*, and *Strangers on a Train*, whose motives are purely individual but whose action also springs from a proto-Nazi contempt for humanity, killers who feel the masses are inferior beings and that they, in contrast, are exceptional ones who rise above such mediocrity. The third phase shows the law as either inept or corrupt or indifferent, or a combination of all three: such variations run through *Saboteur* (1942), *Shadow of a Doubt, The Paradine Case, I Confess, Dial "M" for Murder, Rear Window, The Man Who Knew Too Much*, and *The Wrong Man* (1956). More oblique signs of ineptness are also present in *Vertigo, North by Northwest, Psycho*, and *The Birds*. The trend has a long history. In *Dial "M" for Murder* Chief Inspector Hubbard (John Williams) not only rescues Margot (Grace Kelly) from the gallows at the last minute; he is also rescuing the law, which includes himself, from near-fatal stupidity. In *Frenzy*, twenty years later, Inspector Oxford (Alec McCowen) more or less pulls the same last-minute rabbit out of the hat, trapping cheery cockney Bob Rusk (Barry Foster), the serial killer and rapist for whom his grumpy double, Richard Blaney (Jon Finch), had been stupidly mistaken, but only after Blaney has escaped from prison hospital to take his revenge.

While Orson Welles was a more dynamic and forceful critic of the cupidity of the law, in films like *Touch of Evil* (1958) and *The Trial* (1962), Hitchcock was not far behind, working through understatement or humor rather than confrontation. In the era of the studio code he had little choice. But, as the code started to fray at the edges in the late 1950s, the limitations of the law loom larger in his films: in *The Man Who Knew Too Much* the official indifference to the kidnapping, in *The Wrong Man* the cheap corner-cutting and false accusation that leads to quick prosecution, in *Vertigo* the postmortem on Madeleine's "death" that never considers foul play, in *North by Northwest* the cynicism of Cold War espionage in which individuals are dispensable, in *Psycho* the official complacency that has never investigated the darker side of Norman Bates, in *The Birds* the police failure to recognize impending catastrophe. Hitchcock was not only fascinated by the failures of the law. The law was a flawed mediator, in his vision, between the public and the intimate spheres of the modern world. Even if it proves itself absolutely right, which is not all that often, Hitchcock calls into question its procedures, its judgment, its powers. Yet this vision is slow-burning, something in fact that precedes American Hitchcock. It starts back on the streets in London with his silent film *The Lodger* (1926) and a basic pattern emerges that informs many of the early pictures.

In *The Lodger* Ivor Novello is very nearly the victim of mob justice before he reveals he is an aristocrat seeking the serial killer for whom he is mistaken, the monster who has numbered the lodger's sister amongst his many victims. Hitchcock then comes in closer to confront the shortfall of the law. In the stunning volte-face that ends *The Manxman* (1928), the lawyer-become-judge takes charge of the case of his ex-lover, who has tried to commit suicide (a crime at the time) after being left with his illegitimate child. He then acknowledges his part in the build-up to the attempted "crime" and proceeds to peel off his wig and stand down in front of an astonished court to seek conciliation with the accused wife and her bemused husband. If this is the law court as pure theater, then Hitchcock repeats it in *Murder!* (1930), where the ambivalent and effeminate Sir John, an upper-class enforcer who finally reverses a wrong-woman murder sentence, does so only because he had earlier capitulated in the jury room to the guilty verdict of his fellow-jurors. Pursuit of the real murderer, Handel Fane (a cross-dressing actor and trapeze artist), then becomes a form of dubious atonement. Hitchcock also produces more secretive scenarios. In *Blackmail* (1929) and *Sabotage* (1936) his detectives may not be smart enough to prevent wrongdoing but they are shrewd enough to cover up the killings by the wronged women whom they covet, getting them off the hook in order to hook them. In *Young and Innocent* (1937), by contrast, the police are quintessential clueless coppers: not only do they allow the man they wrongly suspect of murder to escape; they also allow him to be aided by the daughter of the Chief Constable, who never believes his offspring capable of such complicity. Hitchcock's police detectives have never been too bright, but, equally, some have a hidden agenda and others are devious. Standard cop thrillers with solid enforcer-heroes are a world away from his vision. Investigation, official or otherwise, is ever undermined by the investigator's blemished vision. And lawyers come off no better: in *The Paradine Case* defense lawyer Anthony Keane (Gregory Peck) makes a public fool of himself by falling in love with his client Maddelena Paradine (Alida Valli), believing her innocent of murder when she is in fact guilty. He then disintegrates in court as Valli dramatically confesses, under his foolhardy interrogation, to the crime of which she stands accused.

Hitchcock's world of the law is generally one of shortfall investigators sometimes finding the guilty innocent or more often finding the innocent guilty. In any event, the relationship between law and justice is wickedly dysfunctional, and as his career progresses the vision gets darker. Yet Hitchcock never makes the mistake of treating the error of misidentification as all too obvious. He makes sure misperception is a mistake his audience could easily make themselves, one that *anybody* could make, even when they have the advantage his narration gives them at critical moments over toiling investigators. And when he has a successful investigator, like Jefferies in *Rear Window*, Hitchcock ensures that his hero is blemished in other ways. The intersection of an intimate life and a public life, the point where for better or worse the law intervenes, is the means by which Hitchcock's vision forges a wide linkage – that of modernity to its destiny or fate. The intimate life of the modern is a flawed and fragile thing open to the ebb and flow of a dangerous life, never set in stone. Here Hitchcock works in two key areas where his vision overrules convention and produces some startling results – sexuality and the family.

At the center of Hitchcock's vision of sexuality are variations on heterosexual romance, which take pride of place in his work. Romance can be hectic (*The 39 Steps*), therapeutic (*Spellbound*), redemptive (*Notorious*), erotic (*North by Northwest*), or tragic (*Vertigo*). All work within the boundaries of the Studio code and official censorship, though often at their very edge. There is a dynamism and depth here in Hitchcock intimacies that go way beyond standard forms of melodrama or romantic comedy. All are richly subtle, unexpected variations on the expected. But Hitchcock also goes further in his use of subtext, which augments the more obvious forms of romance through sexual variation. Although, for example, the steamy hotel-room scene that opens *Psycho* involves a single woman and divorced man, the sweaty secrecy of the assignation implies a liaison between a single woman and a *married* man, that is to say, the scene as evidence of adultery. In understated ways Hitchcock always tries to extend the range of what is possible. (At the end of *North by Northwest*, when he was not allowed to show Cary Grant and Eva Marie Saint climbing into their Pullman berth and kissing horizontally unless they were finally married, he retaliated with the closing shot of their train rushing into a tunnel at the moment of embrace.) By the time of *Frenzy*, made for Universal in 1972 when the Hollywood studio code had collapsed into a more liberal ratings system, the rape-murder sequence at the core of the picture is much more graphic and disturbing than anything Hitchcock had previously shown onscreen. But that is also because the romance motif in his work had by this time also gone out the window. Nearing the end of his career, he became truly (and briefly) explicit. *Psycho*, made only twelve years earlier, seemed the height of discretion by comparison.

Yet for Hitchcock Eros is usually inseparable from love. The opening of *Psycho* may be steamy but there is also deadness in the knowing solitude of its lovers, an excess of familiarity where love and Eros are dying simultaneously. Hitchcock was more in his element in showing the *first* encounter of romance, an encounter that is also a feature of motion, circulation, and the speed of modernity. In his sound features the romance of the first romance narrative, *The 39 Steps*, takes place under the duress of hectic flight, a motif repeated Stateside in the wartime *Saboteur* and then more powerfully in the Chicago-bound train of *North by Northwest*, where his erotic couple consummate their discreet one-night stand. Elsewhere the first encounter of Grant and Ingrid Bergman in *Notorious* at a late night party gains its full resonance only from the drunken car ride afterwards, while the infatuation of James Stewart with Kim Novak in *Vertigo* is inseparable from his car stalking and furtive following through the streets of San Francisco. And the fugitive romance of Bergman and Gregory Peck in *Spellbound* is enhanced by their train escape from New York. In all five films, love and Eros fuse *only* through the auto-motion of the modern machine, the intimate stillness of the lovers at times set against the recurrent movement surrounding them. By contrast, in the narratives of enclosed mansions or rooms, in the Manderley of *Rebecca* (1940) or the prison encounters of *The Paradine Case*, in the apartments of *Rope, Dial "M" for Murder*, and *Rear Window*, love is rendered sterile, entropic, dissipated. Eros is either stillborn or else it is seen as a lingering menace, not a salvation. With the truly romantic couple, only some defining instance of modernity's motion tips the balance into Eros. It traverses a no-man's-land of uncertainty, of bodily and psychic tension that has its own adrenaline rush; which Cary Grant and Eva Marie Saint convey to its full in their train encounter to end all train encounters, a *mise-en-scène* so sensual and yet so effortless it is often copied but never repeated.

Elsewhere there is a grey area in Hitchcock's vision that goes beyond heterosexual romance. It is not strictly homosexual but rather a template for a *triangulation of desire* or love triangle that works uneasily, or not at all, within heterosexual format. The term "bisexual" barely does justice to it. Its first explicit appearance is in his last silent film, *The Manxman*. On the face of it this is a romantic drama in which two close friends on the Isle of Man, Philip (Malcolm Keen), a lawyer, and Pete (Carl Brisson), a fisherman, are both attracted to the same girl, Kate (Anny Ondra), with damaging consequences. Yet embedded in the film is a subterranean sense that its close male friendship is more than meets the eye. The lawyer's wordless, furtive gaze signifies clear attraction to his handsome fisherman pal, who seems too naive to notice the difference between friendship and desire, and in turn is attracted to Kate, whom he later marries. Yet during their courtship the girl *has* noticed her suitor's "closeness" with the lawyer and the lawyer's covert jealousy. When Pete goes off to sea, Phil takes his place as rival for the girl, whom he seduces, transferring affection from male to female. When false news arrives of Pete's death at sea, Kate exclaims, "At last we're free!" (It is an ambiguous cry of relief echoed in two later films, *The Paradine Case* when Alida Valli confesses to her husband's killing as a ploy intended to "free" the love of Louis Jourdan, and in the like words of Anne Baxter to Montgomery Clift after Villette's death at the start of *I Confess*.) In all three films, the same motif is broached: sexually ambiguous elimination of "the rival." In *The Manxman* the gestural language of silent film makes this more visually explicit. The naive handsome fisherman is a dual object of desire, the object of a *dual gaze*, who does not understand desire: the fullness of *their* knowledge, however, makes of his best friend and girlfriend (both desiring him) partners in a complicity of looks and signs that goes beyond narrative's official meaning. For the girl, inciting the lawyer's transfer of affection from Pete (where it is something unspoken) to her (where it is openly displayed) means the elimination of a rival sexuality *even if* it is at the expense of a naive first lover. It is a pure, ambiguous exchange (also an exchange of class from proletarian to bourgeois, signifying her social ambition). For Hitchcock it is a prototype for much to come. The knowing couple trade their love rivalry for the hapless Pete into a love for each other in his absence, where he becomes the excluded other. And there is no road back. Yet, when he does come back (since the report of his death was false), he continues to "love" Kate as his wife and "love" Philip as a friend. The result: impasse.

The Manxman's love triangle sets up many of American Hitchcock's dramas of torn loyalty, in *Rebecca* (must the new Mrs. de Winter, in taking on the role of Rebecca, take on her sexuality too?), *Rope, Strangers on a Train*, or, more obliquely, *The Paradine Case* and *I Confess*. In *The Paradine Case*, with its post-war English setting, official disclosure at the murder trial reveals a husband jealous of his young wife's affair with his valet. Subtext hints suggest that Maddalena Paradine may have poisoned her rich husband to free his handsome valet, Latour, from sexual domination by his master. In subtext, and subtext only, the condemned woman has killed the man she married so as to "liberate" her reluctant lover from a very different sexual identity. There are minor traces too in the Tippi Hedren films, *The Birds* and *Marnie*, subtle shadings where, as Melanie and Marnie, Hedren inspires not only jealousy in other women close to the men with whom she is involved but also, one suspects, a sneaking affection for her bold intimacy with men they once desired.

In *The Birds* the framing-together of the rival women in Annie's house where Melanie stays while visiting Mitch has a tense intimacy that is resolved only by Annie's horrific death in the bird-attack. Suzanne Pleshette as Annie and Diane Baker as cousin Lil in *Marnie* are both dark-haired women full of face and body with strong jawlines, in contrast to Hedren – blonde, thin-faced, slim-bodied. If they physically resemble one another in that contrast, Hitchcock lets the ambiguity linger. Have they passed in their affection from the man each has given up on, to the beautiful woman – Hedren – who has taken their place? Or are they hopelessly undecided? As Lil's face is pressed in long shot to an upstairs window of the family home, gazing in quiet desperation at the departing Mark and Marnie, we might ask which of the two she will miss the most. It is, of course, subtext, a back-story that stays incomplete, something unspoken. But in Hitchcock you feel it is palpably there, adding yet another tangled layer to unresolved questions of jealousy. In his unrealized 1967 *Kaleidoscope* Hitchcock appears to continue with the drama of torn loyalty but set it out explicitly. His vision of the charming psychopath killer Willie, so attractive to women, was also intended to deepen the subtle homosexual profiling he had developed for Bruno in *Strangers on a Train*.

If Hitchcock cues the multiple sexualities of our age from within the studio code, his later work also comments on the frailties of that most revered of institutions, the family. The 1950s and 1960s were – in official discourse at least – the golden age of the nuclear family, the married couple with (usually) two children, advertised as the ideal model for a modernizing capitalist society. It has long since become an ideal clouded by extreme skepticism, and is now a minority preference in many Western societies at the start of the new century. In mid-century the nuclear family had been seen by social commentators as the key to a stable life in a rapidly modernizing world. By the turn of the century it has become a domestic arrangement in free-fall. If Hitchcock displays it under extreme duress, showing external pressures that threaten to bring it down – the kidnapping in *The Man Who Knew Too Much* or the unjust arrest in *The Wrong Man* – you feel it also because he has a sense of its inherent fragility. *The Birds* brings such brittleness to fruition in the attack on the Brenner home, where, under total strain, the "family" without a male head (the dead father's portrait hangs on the wall) has reconstituted itself with Melanie as its ambiguous fourth element. At times she seems like a long-lost daughter to Lydia Brenner but also like a long-lost mother to Lydia's young daughter, Cathy: she seems at times like a sister to Mitch but also, at times, like his lover. In crisis, there is no fixity of definition. There is an echo of this alarming lack almost immediately in *Marnie* when Mark takes his new wife back to her old home in Baltimore, where she becomes once more her mother's daughter to replace the young surrogate (neighbor's) daughter who has replaced her in her absence. There is the same quartet effect in the framing – females of three generations and the male as outsider, an effect reinforced by Marnie's flashback scenes of the sailor who had attacked her mother when she was a child.

In all these films Hitchcock stresses the horrific vulnerability of children, avoiding standard Hollywood cuteness or sentimentality in the power of his images. The attempted murder of the girl-child, niece Charlie in *Shadow of a Doubt*, the ruthless kidnap of the McKennas' son in *The Man Who Knew Too Much*, the blank incomprehension of the Balestrero children in *The Wrong Man* as their family life falls apart, the childhood toys in the attic of *Psycho's* childlike killer Norman Bates, the horrific attacks on the schoolchildren in *The Birds*, and the terrified witnessing of the Brenner daughter Cathy, the trauma of the childhood flashback scene that ends *Marnie*; Hitchcock does not spare the weak and the innocent. Conversely, he reserves his most acid observations for matrimony and the childless household. Here the final icing on the cake (or arsenic in the coffee cup) is the loveless marriage in *Frenzy*. It is a fate the wrong man accused of murder and the police inspector who hounds him both share, while the actual killer, who searches out "relationships" through a marriage bureau, is incapable of any intimacy bar torture and killing. The wrong man's marriage has failed miserably and he is childless. The inspector's domestic life, equally childless, is a bizarre round of culinary experiences orchestrated by his dotty wife. But the horror of the rape/killing by Rusk in the marriage bureau of Brenda Blaney is intensified by dark dramatic irony. Brenda is working professionally to prop up an institution – marriage – that has failed her personally: for her pains she is faced by the nightmare client who will rape and strangle her. And her ex-husband will be accused of the killing. The symbolic site of restoration (marriage matching) becomes a crime scene of utter spoliation. Brenda's devotion to a faltering cause is the cause of her own death, a bleak vision in a dark film to round out a deepening pessimism about modern life. It was a relief that Hitchcock could end his career with a sharp comedy, *Family Plot*, in which intimacy did work, but only because its couples were loving partners in crime.

Modernity and Catastrophe: *The Birds*

The Birds is a late summation of many great things in Hitchcock – above all his cinematic style, his deep knowledge of film and his dark vision of modernity. It is a film in which all of these come to fruition, and come together. He displays his use of style at its strongest where it prompts multiple readings of narration through a designed interplay of artifice and reality. At the same time he blends together the historical high points of modernist filmmaking – the silent cinema of the 1920s that produced surrealism, expressionism and montage with the abstract, ambiguous intimacies of European film circa 1960, particularly the work of Bergman, Resnais, and Antonioni that he had seen prior to the making of *The Birds*. He thus shoots a film on location in California's Bodega Bay that is contemporary in every sense of the word and convinces us of its setting as a small fishing town, which naturalizes its characters, its topography, and its sense of place. Yet it is also a *constructed* film that switches in the same sequence from exterior shots to studio shots with rear projection, from the actual town center to its replication in a studio back lot, from naturalistic landscapes to multiple matte compositions that atmospherically resemble them. Its terrifying vision of the birds as a force of nature unleashed on the human world is made possible only through the use of special effects. In short it makes us aware, just as much as *Rear Window* or *Vertigo*, that it is pure cinema.

The story, of course, is not his and came from the pen of Daphne du Maurier in 1951. Hitchcock claimed to Truffaut that he could hardly remember the original, but her short narrative, set in a remote Cornwall village, has many of his incidents that fired his visual imagination – the besieged family in their farmhouse with birds stabbing with their beaks at the front door and swarming down the chimney, and a neighboring farmer brutally pecked to death. Yet in Evan Hunter's screenplay his American family is a different kind of family: more prosperous, more sophisticated, and the central characters are the film's own. If the Brenner family – Lydia (Jessica Tandy), Mitch (Rod Taylor), and Cathy (Veronica Cartwright) – are the film's very own, then so is its sophisticated intruder, Melanie Daniels. Moreover, the coastal setting and its abstract *mise-en-scène* seem to come less from anything du Maurier wrote than from recent films Hitchcock had seen by Antonioni – *L'avventura* (1960), *La notte* (1961) – and Bergman – *The Seventh Seal* (1958) and *Through a Glass Darkly* (1960). In both his films Bergman had used Swedish coastal settings. *The Seventh Seal* with its allegorical story of medieval plague and divine judgment was remembered by many for the game of chess Bergman's crusading knight plays and loses with the figure of Death on the seashore. Like *The Birds* it was apocalyptic yet psychologically complex. In Hitchcock's film we get a different kind of duel with Death played out by the seashore, in the world of the present where the enemy is not the plague but the attack of the birds. To make it contemporary we can think of Bergman's other film, *Through a Glass Darkly*, which, despite its biblical title, is a contemporary story of madness within a close-knit family at their summerhouse on a remote island. Karin (Harriet Andersson) is a young married woman who undergoes complete breakdown and then seduces her teenage brother, to the consternation of her ineffectual husband and hypocritical father. In the cracks of the wall in an attic room to which Karin retreats, she claims to hear God's voice speaking to her, a voice that triggers her madness. In the attic room of Brenner's home that Melanie Daniels enigmatically visits the morning after the bird attack, she is confronted by the avian creatures, which have infiltrated the cracks and fissures of the roof. They all but destroy her. Karin's traumatic collapse at the end of Bergman's film is mirrored in Melanie's traumatic collapse at the end of *The Birds*. And, after several days of enduring live birds being thrown at her for the montage of the attack sequence, Tippi Hedren had collapsed as much as her character, Melanie. For the scenes in long shot where she is carried downstairs from the attic by Mitch her rescuer and revived on the living-room couch, Hedren was no longer there, away recuperating and replaced on set by a double.

Antonioni's *L'avventura* provides a different angle of inspiration not only through its coastal landscapes of Sicily and the Lipari islands but also through its use of Monica Vitta as Claudia, a young Roman sophisticate out of her depth and out of sorts in a remote world that was not her own. Her uncertain affair with Sandro (Gabriele Ferzetti), fiancé of her disappearing best friend, seems a model for the drained, edgy relationship of Melanie with Mitch, though not the one Evan Hunter had envisaged when he referred to the couple in his screenplay as "screwball lovers." Though the film starts out in San Francisco mining the familiar vein of romantic comedy, Hitchcock gradually turns it after her arrival in Bodega Bay into something different, cooler and more fragmented, with uncertain emotions. The picnic sequence on the cliff that Hitchcock wrote into the final script, much to Hunter's dismay, with its couple framed together through high-angle shots of the coastline, echoes in its framing the tense ambiguous relationship of Vitti and Ferzetti in *L'avventura* as they scour remote cliffs in search of Anna. In his next film, *La notte*, Antonioni experimented with the novelty of electronic music on his soundtrack. Hitchcock decided to do the same with great success on his picture, creating artificial bird screeches and dispensing with a musical score. Yet this malaise of the emotions that Hitchcock takes from Antonioni and Bergman is only a prelude to a wider catastrophe, that of the massed avian attack. Both the European filmmakers then went on to make oblique studies of failed intimacy within the shadow of the nuclear age – Antonioni in *L'eclisse* (1962), Bergman in *The Silence* (1963) – but their coolly apocalyptic fables here are in complete contrast to Hitchcock's visceral and sensuous vision of a universal terror. In preparing and executing this, he goes back to earlier inspirations at the start of his life in cinema.

Before we turn to this, let us remark on the figural similarities of Vitti and Hedren, beautiful and sophisticated, incongruously overdressed and framed by rock, coastline, and water. In the location shooting there is a strong naturalistic element to Antonioni's abstract and painterly design, showing his origins in Italian neo-realism. For the outboard motor sequence in *The Birds*, however, where Melanie rents a boat and speeds across the bay to take Mitch by surprise and deliver the caged lovebirds to his house as his sister's birthday present, there is a distinctly artificial feel amid the natural setting, something uncanny. Hedren looks like an A-list model straight off the catwalk. (The incongruity recalls Tallulah Bankhead in Hitch's wartime drama *Lifeboat*, as survivor of a U-boat attack adrift in the Atlantic in a mink coat and looking as if she had just come from a Broadway first night; by the end of both films, of course, the clothes of Hedren and Bankhead are in tatters.) In the boat sequences across the bay and back, the alternation within sequence between long-shot location-takes and medium or close shots of Melanie with studio back projection sets up a strange counterpoint. The latter were visually enhanced at the time by a transition from a blue- to a new yellow-screen technology using sodium lamps for superior back projection, an innovation that cut out color seepage and gave greater clarity and definition to composite images. Its effect here is to give to Hedren's screen image, her image of arrival in Bodega Bay – swept-up honey-blonde hair, unlikely fur coat, and pale-green suit – a luminous quality that is not shared by any of the locals. In fact she fits the description given earlier to Madeleine Elster in *Vertigo*, that of a "beautiful ghost." Who is she, exactly? Where has she really come from? Is she really earthed, truly grounded? Or is she another San Francisco ghost like the one Hitchcock had manufactured for his earlier picture? Another way to put it is this. Is it the bird attacks that finally make her human, and the creatures of the sky that bring her down to earth? Or more precisely, does the first gull that swoops down on the boat and draws blood from her forehead prove to us literally that she is flesh and blood?

Hitchcock's interest in the existential modernisms of Antonioni results in the blending of two key techniques in the making of *The Birds*. It becomes one of his most improvised films, with many last-minute changes, and Hitchcock eliminates all the rational or allegorical explanations, or hints of them, for the bird Blitzkriegs that are present in the different drafts of Evan Hunter's screenplay (Krohn, 238–43). The film was shot in the autumn (1962) of one of the century's gravest political crises, the Cuban Missile affair, which many commentators at the time feared could result in nuclear war between the United States and the Soviet Union. Though this would certainly have charged the atmosphere of Hitchcock's filmmaking in Northern California, the final cut shows no direct sign of it. Hitchcock eliminated politics just as he eliminated science fiction. The attacks for him were ineffable terror, the sum of all catastrophes in the modern age emanating here from a natural source, unpredictable and possibly without end. It is why in the age of global terror networks and the misplaced responses they elicit – both adding dangers at the start of this century to the existing threat of nuclear war – his film will continue to have such a steely resonance. For it intimates the detail of terror on a local scale but makes its import universal. It is something that happens here (Bodega Bay) but it could also happen anywhere, and may well go on to do so. As fellow-creatures the attacking birds remind us of the powers of human destruction, but, as the winged creatures of nature, the even greater power of natural catastrophe. Of course the two are often conjoined. In the age of man-made climate change where our energy excesses intimate disaster for us in different forms – pollution, heat, drought, fire, floods, tempests, hurricanes – there is no clear divide between nature and culture in the realm of catastrophe. In Hitchcock's masterpiece the situation is likewise. His film may be based on barely plausible assumptions about birds, despite the growing incidence of isolated attacks on humans, but it continues to resonate as a masterwork that contains the sum of all our fears.

This is a horror film about plausible horrors, and there is an upending of the natural order that is truly Shakespearean in its effect. It is understandable, therefore, that new modernist aesthetics bringing in the 1960s were necessary but not sufficient for the film's ambition. Hitchcock also went back to his cinematic roots. His artifice-location counterpoint that drives one off against the other links him back more firmly to the film aesthetics of an earlier age: to expressionist art and, conversely, the technical power of editing. Edvard Munch's famous painting, *The Scream*, textured much of the art design of Robert Boyle, and was then transferred to storyboards plotting in detail the human reaction to bird attack. The diving swoop of a single gull, whose beak slashes Melanie's forehead as she brings her boat back round the bay to harbor, is a quick, precise image. It recalls in its surreal power of shock the famous shot of a razor slitting the eyeball at the start of *Un chien andalou* (1929), the sharp incisive motion that produces the shock incision. The use of quick-fire montage in the attack sequences recalls Eisenstein's editing in his silent classic, *Battleship Potemkin* (1925). In the schoolhouse attack we could say that Hitchcock restages and transforms the Odessa Steps massacre into a mass attack where, miraculously, all the victims survive their wounds. Later, for the attic attack on Melanie, the scissors in the cutting room are out again, and this time working overtime.

In *Battleship Potemkin* Eisenstein uses quick orchestrated montage to indicate the different phases of revolt, where there are two staged and starred contrasts, the first the mutiny that starts below decks on the battleship with the saga of maggot-filled meat, the second the counter-attack on shore by armed Cossacks, a phalanx moving mechanically in step who drive the panicking crowd before them down the steep city steps. It is a source of the Hitchcock "open and shut" contrast, the mutiny at first interior within the crews' quarters, but the shore massacre exterior, in the open public places of the city by the shore of the Black Sea. (In his open schoolhouse sequence, Hitchcock pays homage to *Battleship Potemkin* by transforming the shattered lens of the woman's fallen pince-nez on the Steps, a famous image, into the shattered, fallen glasses of a besieged girl as she runs into town.) The sense of live terror in both films is quite remarkable. Just as Hedren suffered trauma for her live acting, so Eisenstein's shooting on the real location is rumored to have created casualties among his stampeding extras. (In Hitchcock's flight sequence, of course, the birds are shot separately and matted on during editing.) The double montage in *The Birds* goes in the opposite direction, spatially, from *Battleship Potemkin*: from the open space of the road descending into town to the enclosed attic of the Brenner home to which Melanie ascends in anticipation of her fate. If Eisenstein's progression is closed to open, Hitchcock's is open to closed. As opposed to rapid alternation between long and close shots in the schoolhouse flight, the enclosed sequence of the attic attack is done through the quick-fire matching of close shots as Melanie is pinned against the door; fragments of her body under attack, swift cutting between head and feet, or between the arm arcing the torch in desperate defense and reverse POV shots as the birds strike. (Here the shower-scene in *Psycho* is echoed by Melanie's gradual fall under stabbing beaks whose sharp movement resembles the striking knife of Marion Crane's killer.) In *Marnie* Hitchcock would soon repeat this double montage with Hedren through an open-to-closed chronology that gives us the open, exterior montage of the hunt – fragmenting the tragic fall of her beloved Forio as it hits a fence and falls beneath her – to the closed interior montage of the childhood flashback, memories of being trapped in a room with her mother and her mother's sailor client. This is cutting in rhythmic repetition, in which the first foreshadows the second and the second echoes the first, the flashing fragmentation of distorted bodies in conflicting motion: in the first sequence horse and rider, in the second child, mother, and sailor. Both end in tragic death.

The *mise-en-scène* of the schoolhouse attack also shows us exactly what defines Hitchcock's method of filming, the switch back and forth between objective and subjective shots. The jungle gym scene is a key prelude to the sequence: Melanie sits outside the school smoking on a bench, waiting for Annie's class to finish, her back to the fence enclosing the gym behind her. Hitchcock sets up ambiguous montage: he cuts back and forth from medium close-ups of the waiting Melanie to the scattered arrival of birds on the climbing frame behind her. Here the audience is privileged at first by shots of what happens behind her back without her knowledge. Melanie's face is clouded by a growing anxiety, but, since she never turns round, it is never clear at what point she first senses what we are seeing. Is the anxious look a sign of what she currently sees or what she remembers from the picnic attacks on the previous day? We only know for sure when she finally sees the creatures above through a special eye-line match. She glances up and left of screen. The match cut shows a panning shot of a single bird flying left to right behind her. Her eyes follow its flight. The bird alights on the frame where hundreds are now perched. Turned around in the reverse angle cut, she is now standing in horror. Her shock is mirrored in ours, and this is the point at which Hitchcock clearly sutures her point of view and that of his audience. She may have missed the first feathered arrivals we have clearly seen, but we have also missed, during the camera's focus on her, the mass arrival that makes the left-to-right pan end in shock revelation for her and for us.

Even in these sequences, where Hedren is the focus of our attention, there is always a steely objective element in Hitchcock's camera. She may dominate the early part of the film but even then she is a figure of mystery. We never see her at work or at home, with family or with friends, and we are encouraged to see her as object, to try and figure her out, never to feel fully familiar with her. Later of course her stark individuality is drowned in collective events and collective trauma. At key junctures the major moments of catastrophe are seen from afar. The bird attack that starts outside the schoolhouse ends with the explosion at the gas station whose deadly consequence Hitchcock's camera shows from a high-angle Godlike point of view, in the sky above the town. Elsewhere Melanie is also limited in her role as a filter of the collective gaze. It is Lydia Brenner, not she, who drives out to the Glaiser farmhouse and discovers the farmer's mutilated corpse with its pecked-out eyes. Later the brunt of the practical fight against the birds comes from Mitch, who then occupies center frame, and at the end, even when Melanie has recovered consciousness after the attic attack, she looks comatose in her bandaged head and shredded clothes, barely alive. As the family act and talk around her, she hardly seems to have a consciousness at all. This constant shifting of focus, even when there is a dominant field of vision, suggests a framing of Hitchcock's method in terms of what some critics have called an aesthetic of "intrarealist" effect (see Sallitt, and also Smith). To see this composite blending, technically complex, is to guard against the dangers of seeing in his camera either a purely omniscient gaze or a purely subjective cinema of obsession.

This leads us onto a final point. *The Birds* is a very salient feature about the limits of perception or, more precisely, the unfinished translation of fragmented perceptions into a conceptual ordering of things. In the film no one can give a final answer to explain the unexpected attacks. No one can predict when they will start or when they will end. All this is finally beyond human understanding. The attacks are in no way supernatural – there is no get-out clause here – and yet no convincing reason for them can be given. This is truly tough for Hitchcock's audience; tougher than in any other film, because the result of the actions we cannot explain is catastrophe. And here it is collective; it affects us all. This, momentously, is the high point of Hitchcock's art and also the most troubling. Here it is not the ordinary things of daily life that elude both the film's victims and the audience watching them: it is something more powerful. Indeed, it is so powerful it shatters the usual irony of limits that Hitchcock's philosophy places on perception. For in general his cinema leads us by varying degrees to the same endpoint. There will always be something new and different in experience to elude us, and yet we (audience and heroes alike) will always try to master it. In most of his films his subjects do eventually succeed, but only at great cost to themselves. Yet in his later films they usually fail, and the limitation becomes a source of anguish, to us as well as to them. That anguish is a key to the philosophy of life expressed so powerfully in his art: to its wider implications we must now turn.

Works Cited

Auiler, Dan. *Hitchcock's Notebooks: An Authorized and Illustrated Look inside the Creative Mind of Alfred Hitchcock*. New York: HarperEntertainment, 2001.

Kline, T. Jefferson. "Recuperating Hitchcock's Doubles: Experiencing *Vertigo* in Garcia's *Place Vendôme*." *Studies in French Cinema*, vol. 3, no. 1 (2003): 35–46.

Krohn, Bill. *Hitchcock at Work*. London: Phaidon Press, 2000.

Mulvey, Laura. "Death Drives: Hitchcock's *Psycho*." *Film Studies*, no. 2 (Spring 2000): 5–14.

Ness, Richard. "Hitchcock, Bergman, and the Divided Self." *Hitchcock Annual*, 2002–3, 181–203.

Rohmer, Eric, and Claude Chabrol. *Hitchcock: The First Forty-Four Films*, trans. Stanley Hochman. New York: Frederick Ungar, 1979.

Sallitt, Daniel. "Point of View and 'Intrarealism.'" *Wide Angle*, vol. 4, no. 1 (1980): 39–43.

Smith, Susan. "The Spatial World of Hitchcock's Films: The Point-of-View Shot, the Camera, and 'Intrarealism.'" *Cineaction*, no. 50 (September 1999): 2–15.

Truffaut, François. *The Films of my Life*, trans. Leonard Mayhew. New York: De Capo Press, 1994.

Part Two
Hitchcock in Britain

If critics refused for so long to consider Hitchcock as a serious artist, they merely reflected the pose of popular entertainer that the director carefully created for himself during the years he worked in the British film industry. Early in his career, Hitchcock appears to have realized that his own best interests lay in aligning himself – at least in words – with those who believed that the making of movies depended upon the production of entertainment, not art. As John Russell Taylor recalls in his biography of the director, Hitchcock "often said that one of the great misfortunes was when someone had the bright idea of calling the place that films were made a 'studio,' with all its artistic overtones, rather than a factory" (p. 41). This is not to suggest, however, that Hitchcock was indifferent to the aesthetics of the medium. Working in Germany on *The Blackguard* (1925) gave him ample opportunity to observe film production at the UFA studios at Neubabelsberg, where he watched F. W. Murnau shooting the innovative *The Last Laugh*. Furthermore, Hitchcock attended screenings of other aesthetically innovative European films throughout the remainder of the decade as a member of the (London) Film Society (see Sexton). Thus, even as a neophyte director, Hitchcock was in all likelihood well aware of the artistic issues and achievements that animated continental filmmakers as the silent film flowered into a supplely expressive medium.

As biographical evidence suggests, however, Hitchcock quickly learned that similar artistic aspirations on his part were a liability in the no-nonsense business of British film production. No one made this clearer than C. M. Woolf, the head of the company that handled distribution for Hitchcock's employer, Gainsborough Pictures. Woolf declared the first three films Hitchcock directed to be uncommercial and shelved them. Though the films had received favorable reactions at press screenings, Woolf judged them too arty for general audiences. Thus, while the major trade journal, *The Bioscope*, called *The Lodger* "a directorial triumph" in its September 16, 1926 issue, declaring that "it is possible that this film is the finest production ever made," Woolf withheld *The Lodger* from release to theaters until February 14, 1927. Only the intervention of Michael Balcon, the head of Gainsborough, made the film's release possible. He hired Adrian Brunel and Ivor Montagu, ironically two of the founders of the Film Society, to work with Hitchcock in improving the film. Together, they eliminated many intertitles, added atmospheric title cards designed by E. McKnight Kauffer, and rephotographed a few sequences. Finally, six months after its press preview, *The Lodger* was released, to popular acclaim.

For the next six years, Hitchcock worked for British International Pictures, joining them in 1927 for a salary that made him the highest-paid director in England. Despite his salary, Hitchcock lacked the authority to control his projects, and the quality of his films varied greatly. In 1933 Hitchcock teamed again with Balcon and Montagu at Gaumont–British Pictures for the first four of the thrillers that would securely establish his international reputation: *The Man Who Knew Too Much* (1934), *The 39 Steps* (1935), *Secret Agent* (1936), and *Sabotage* (1936).

Even at this late date, however, Hitchcock was not entirely free of the arbitrary control of distributors. His successful reunion with Balcon and Montagu for *The Man Who Knew Too Much* also reunited him with C. M. Woolf, who again acted as their distributor. Despite the success of *The Man Who Knew Too Much*, Woolf canceled the production of *The 39 Steps* after reading the script prepared by Hitchcock and Montagu and tried to set the director to work, instead, on a musical called *The Floradora Girl*. Only Balcon's return from the United States managed to set *The 39 Steps* into production as he overruled Woolf.

Hitchcock appears to have realized fairly early in his career that his survival in the film industry depended upon both the commercial success of his films and the public's awareness of him as a director. The international success of his thrillers of the middle and late 1930s consolidated Hitchcock's reputation within the industry as a commercial director and attracted the interest of Hollywood producers. Since the later 1920s Hitchcock had also worked just as hard at making himself a household name for reviewers and the general public. Even the caricature profile by which Hitchcock is still known was invented by him for this purpose and mailed out to recipients in the form of a jigsaw puzzle as a Christmas greeting in 1927. In recalling Hitchcock's problems with C. M. Woolf during this time, Ivor Montagu told interviewers for *Screen* that it was only through such shrewd self-promotion that Hitchcock was finally able to gain some measure of control over his work by the late 1930s. As Montagu explained, Hitchcock designed his films to win good press notices so the public would quickly learn his name:

> The public did not generally know who directed the films they saw, but they had seen Hitchcock's name in the Press. The result was that every group that was floating a new company during the Quota Act wanted Hitch under contract in order to attract money. Hitch was able to go from company to company improving his position and contract each time. This is the way his career was made. (Wollen et al., 80)

While the public learned his name and face, Hitchcock made sure that neither they nor those for whom he worked would learn of his underlying artistic interests. These were increasingly hidden during the 1930s within the codes of the classical narrative film. Yet, as the following six chapters devoted to his English films attest, critics have come to recognize the abiding marks of Hitchcock's artistic concerns, even if practical need eventually forced him to deny their existence. As Lesley Brill argues, Hitchcock's self-conscious manipulations of the thriller's conventions in *The Lodger*, along with his formalist experiments, encourage viewers to reflect upon the film's double status "as a work of art as well as a representation of life." Thus, while Hitchcock may have learned to hide behind the public reputation of a popular entertainer in order to survive within a crudely commercial industry that viewed art with mistrust, critics have come to insist that he nevertheless inscribes himself as an artist, frame by frame, within the continuity of his films.

It should not be surprising, then, that these six chapters repeatedly rely upon the close analysis of images and patterns of cutting to identify and discuss Hitchcock's artistry. At a thematic level, this artistry often defines itself through references to the stage and to acting, references that, as William Rothman suggests in his discussion of *Murder!*, permit Hitchcock to differentiate his interests from those of the established theatrical tradition. Thus, in treating the stage as a subject, *Murder!* articulates "its reflections on its nature as a film."

As Hitchcock's repeated troubles with C. M. Woolf suggest, he was prudent to subdue his overtly self-conscious manipulation of the medium during these years. Elisabeth Weis's discussion of this process in relation to Hitchcock's use of sound in *The Man Who Knew Too Much* carefully explains how these formal experiments drew increasingly less attention to themselves as Hitchcock learned to motivate their innovative qualities within the framework of the classical cinematic codes. By so doing, Hitchcock could appeal to the mass audiences satisfied by a story told at breakneck speed, while at the same time rewarding the minority audiences who took pleasure from his testing of the medium's expressive possibilities.

Thinking about Hitchcock's films therefore invites a double awareness of his skills both as a commercial director able to entertain an international audience and, within these limits, as an original artist, actively engaged in exploring the narrative and stylistic possibilities of the medium. As Leland Poague argues in his discussion of *Blackmail*, a similar doubleness necessarily informs every interpretative endeavor as well, as each critic's particular take on a film is shaped by and responds to the history of that film's critical reception. Thus, in their respective chapters on *The 39 Steps* and *The Lady Vanishes*, Charles L. P. Silet and Patrice Petro urge readers to look beyond received interpretations of these films to consider how both assert a place for feminist values in what many have taken to be Hitchcock's resolutely paternalistic films.

As indicated by the titles of many of the entries in this section's "References and Suggested Readings," there is continuing critical interest in locating the origins of Hitchcock's visual style and thematic concerns, both in his experiences in Germany before making *The Lodger* and in the changes that were made in adapting well-known literary works into screenplays. Read in chronological order, the essays on *Sabotage* listed as supplemental reading comprise a continuing discourse about the ins and outs of Hitchcockian adaptation. Bill Krohn addresses the adaptation question in a considerably more sophisticated manner (in "*I Confess* and *Nos deux consciences*") by suggesting that Hitchcock's themes developed to fullness over a number of films as the director tinkered with their enactments, in particular stories and stars, and their implications. Thus the theme of the man accused of a crime he did not commit begins, Krohn argues, in Hitchcock's second film, *The Mountain Eagle* (1926), and slowly evolves as it is reworked in the films that follow, reaching its full design only in *The Man Who Knew Too Much* (1934).

Also elaborated in *Sabotage* and of increasing interest to critics of Hitchcock's British (or, per Charles Barr, his "English") films is Hitchcock's obvious interest in the connections between the political and the technological, between social control and mass communications. Thus *Blackmail* begins with a police "flying squad van" receiving a radio message directing officers to arrest a miscreant, and a major turn of events, as Poague observes, involves Alice White's claim that she has seen every film worth seeing. When her detective date expresses his eagerness to see "Fingerprints" all the same, because the producers are bound to get the police-procedural details wrong, Alice replies that, to be on the safe side, they had hired a real criminal to direct the picture.

The conflation of the cinematic and the criminal implicit in the reference to an outlaw auteur comes to explosive fruition, we might say, in *Sabotage*, where the saboteur character owns and runs a cinema, which serves literally to screen his destructive political activities. Ironically, the cinema exacts revenge when his wife, whose younger brother had died in the explosion of a bomb he had been sent to deliver, seems inspired by the onscreen murder of "Cock Robin" in a Disney cartoon to stab her husband with a carving knife (see Susan Smith for a thorough analysis of the scene's numerous complexities). Though Hitchcock may have understood himself as a singing bird whose wooing of the public was constantly at risk of sabotage at the hands of pinch-penny producers or distributors, so that he cloaked his cinematic subversiveness in the guise of commercial entertainment, in *Sabotage* he puts the screen on screen in ways that twenty-first-century critics find increasingly fascinating. Indeed, the intersection of Conrad and Hitchcock has proven especially productive among critics for whom conceptualizing the complex relationships between mass-culture modernity and the art of film is a top-priority critical task.

References and Suggested Readings

Allen, Richard. "*The Lodger* and the Origins of Hitchcock's Aesthetic." *Hitchcock Annual,* 2001–2, 36–78.

Allen, Richard. "Sir John and the Half-Caste: Identity and Representation in Hitchcock's *Murder!*" *Hitchcock Annual*, no. 13 (2004–5): 92–126.

Barr, Charles. *English Hitchcock*. Moffat, Scotland: Cameron & Hollis, 1999.

Barr, Charles. "Hitchcock and Powell: Two Directions for British Cinema." *Screen*, vol. 46, no. 1 (Spring 2005): 5–14.

Barr, Charles. "Hitchcock's British Films Revisited." In Andrew Higson, ed., *Dissolving Views: Key Writings on British Cinema*. London: Cassell, 1996, 2–19.

Barr, Charles. "Writing Screen Plays: Stannard and Hitchcock." In Andrew Higson, ed., *Young and Innocent?: The Cinema in Britain, 1896–1930*. Exeter: Univ. of Exeter Press, 2002, 227–41.

Beckman, Karen. "Violent Vanishings: Hitchcock, Harlan, and the Disappearing Woman." *Camera Obscura*, no. 39 (September 1996): 79–103. On *The Lady Vanishes*.

Brent, Jessica. "Beyond the Gaze: Visual Fascination and the Feminine Image in Silent Hitchcock." *Camera Obscura*, no. 55 (January 2004): 77–111.

Brophy, Stephen. "The Use of Glass in Alfred Hitchcock's *Blackmail*." *Cineaction*, no. 50 (September 1999): 20–3.

Cohen, Tom. "Hitchcock and the Death of (Mr.) Memory (Technology of the Visible)." In *Anti-Mimesis from Plato to Hitchcock*. New York: Cambridge Univ. Press, 1994, 227–59.

Cohen, Tom. "Graphics, Letters, and Hitchcock's 'Steps.'" *Hitchcock Annual*, 1992, 68–105.

Cohen, Tom. "Sabotaging the Ocularist State." In *Ideology and Inscription: "Cultural Studies" after Benjamin, De Man, and Bakhtin*. New York: Cambridge Univ. Press, 1998, 169–200. On *Sabotage*.

Combs, Richard. "Hitchcock's German Double." *Sight and Sound*, vol. 59, no. 4 (Autumn 1990): 220–1. Compares *Murder!* and *Mary*, the German-language version of the former.

Devas, Angela. "How to Be a Hero: Space, Place and Masculinity in *The 39 Steps* (Hitchcock, UK, 1935)." *Journal of Gender Studies*, vol. 14, no. 1 (March 2005): 45–54.

Drumin, William A. "*Sabotage*: Chaos Unleashed and the Impossibility of Utopia." In Baggett and Drumin (cited in Part One): 3–16.

Durgnat, Raymond. "The Business of Fear." *Sight and Sound*, August 1999; Hitchcock supplement, 2–11.

Eyüboglu, Selim. "The Authorial Text and Postmodernisms: Hitchcock's *Blackmail*." *Screen*, vol. 32, no. 1 (Spring 1991): 58–78.

Fleishman, Avrom. "*The Secret Agent* Sabotaged?" In Gene M. Moore, ed., *Conrad on Film*. Cambridge: Cambridge Univ. Press, 1997, 48–60.

Fuller, Graham. "Mystery Train." *Sight and Sound*, January 2008, 36–40. On *The Lady Vanishes*.

Garncarz, Joseph. "German Hitchcock." *Hitchcock Annual*, 2000–1, 73–99.

Glancy, Mark. *The 39 Steps*. London: I. B. Tauris, 2003.

GoGwilt, Christopher Lloyd. "The Geopolitics of Screenplay: Sabotage from Joseph Conrad to Alfred Hitchcock." In *The Fiction of Geopolitics: Afterimages of Culture, from Wilkie Collins to Alfred Hitchcock*. Stanford, CA: Stanford Univ. Press, 2000, 160–98. Mostly on *Sabotage* and *Young and Innocent*.

Gottlieb, Sidney. "Early Hitchcock: The German Influence." In Gottlieb and Brookhouse (cited in Part One): 35–81.

Hark, Ina Rae. "Keeping Your Amateur Standing: Audience Participation in Hitchcock's Political Films." *Cinema Journal*, vol. 29, no. 2 (Winter 1990): 8–22. Emphasizes *The Man Who Knew Too Much* (1934) and *The 39 Steps*.

Hemmeter, Thomas. "Adaptation, History, and Textual Suppression: Literary Sources of Hitchcock's *Sabotage*." In John D. Simmons, ed., *Literature and Film in the Historical Dimension*. Gainesville, FL: Univ. Press of Florida, 1994, 149–61.

Jenson, Paul M. *Hitchcock Becomes "Hitchcock": The British Years*. Baltimore: Midnight Marquee Press, 2000.

Krohn, Bill. "*I Confess* and *Nos deux consciences*." In Schmenner and Granof (cited in Part One): 49–61.

Mogg, Ken. "Hitchcock's *The Lodger*: A Theory." *Hitchcock Annual*, 1992, 115–27.

Mogg, Ken. "Hitchcock the Cockney: *No. 17* (1932)." *The MacGuffin*, no. 5 (November 1991): 15–20.

Mogg, Ken. "Mood Swings: Hitchcock's *Young and Innocent* (1937)." *The MacGuffin*, no. 13 (August 1994): 12–25.

Mogg, Ken. "South by Southeast: Hitchcock's *Rich and Strange*." *The MacGuffin*, no. 22 (May–August 1007): 17–24.

Morgan, Jack. "Alfred Hitchcock's *Juno and the Paycock*." *Irish University Review*, vol. 24, no. 2 (September 1994): 212–16.

Morris, Christopher D. "The Allegory of Seeing in Hitchcock's Silent Films." *Film Criticism*, vol. 22, no. 2 (Winter 1997–8): 27–50.

Osteen, Mark. " 'It Doesn't Pay to Antagonize the Public': *Sabotage* and Hitchcock's Audience." *Literature/Film Quarterly*, vol. 28, no. 4 (2000): 259–68.

Phillips, Louis. "The Hitchcock Universe: Thirty-Nine Steps and Then Some." *Films in Review*, vol. 46, nos. 3–4 (March–April 1995): 22–7.

Roth, Marty. "Hitchcock's Secret Agency." *Camera Obscura*, no. 30 (May 1992): 34–49.

Ryall, Tom. *Alfred Hitchcock and the British Cinema*. (Cited in Part One.)

Ryall, Tom. *Blackmail*. London: British Film Institute, 1993.

Schneider, Lisa. "*The Woman Alone* in Conrad and Hitchcock." In Gene E. Moore, ed., *Conrad on Film*. Cambridge: Cambridge Univ. Press, 1997, 61–77.

Sexton, Jamie. "The Film Society and the Creation of an Alternative Film Culture in Britain in the 1920s." In Andrew Higson, ed., *Young and Innocent?: The Cinema in Britain, 1896–1930*. Exeter: Univ. of Exeter Press, 2002, 291–305.

Smith, Susan. *Hitchcock: Suspense, Humour and Tone*. (Cited in Part One.) See chapter one: "A Cinema Based on *Sabotage*."

Strauss, Marc Raymond. *Alfred Hitchcock's Silent Films*. Jefferson, NC: McFarland, 2004.

Street, Sarah. "The Lodger." In Jill Forbes and Sarah Street, eds., *European Cinema: An Introduction*. Hampshire, UK: Palgrave, 2000, 67–78.

Taylor, John Russell. *Hitch: The Life and Times of Alfred Hitchcock*. (Cited in Part One.)

Telotte, J. P. "The Sounds of *Blackmail*: Hitchcock and Sound Aesthetic." *Journal of Popular Film and Television*, vol. 28, no. 4 (Winter 2001): 184–91.

Welsh, Alexander. "A Talking Film." In *George Eliot and Blackmail*. Cambridge, MA: Harvard Univ. Press, 1985, 3–18.

Williams, Evan. "*The Lady Vanishes* (1938): An Appraisal." *The MacGuffin*, no. 9 (May 1993): 17–20.

Wollaeger, Mark. *Modernism, Media, and Propaganda: British Narrative from 1900 to 1945*. Princeton: Princeton Univ. Press, 2006. Chapters on *Sabotage* and on *Bon Voyage* and *Aventure Malgache*.

Wollen Peter, Alan Lovell, and Sam Rohdie. "Interview: Ivor Montagu." *Screen*, vol. 13, no. 3 (Autumn 1972): 51–70.

Yacowar, Maurice. *Hitchcock's British Films*. Hamden, CT: Archon Books, 1977.

Chapter Five
Hitchcock's *The Lodger*

Lesley W. Brill

Following its director's lead, most critics identify *The Lodger* as the "first Hitchcockian" film.[1] In his third feature-length movie, Hitchcock made his first venture into what Maurice Yacowar calls the "genre of suspense," dealt with the theme of the unjustly accused innocent for the first of many times, and exhibited the conspicuous technical flash that has done so much for him at the box office. Despite its acknowledged importance as an early marker in Hitchcock's career, however, *The Lodger* has received little attention – a few short essays and the inconclusive remarks critics make as they bustle past it *en route* to the films they really want to talk about.[2] It deserves more careful scrutiny. Its significance in Hitchcock's career is underrated if it is regarded as little more than his first work of suspense. It displays, additionally, the mythic echoes, the complication of characterization, the self-conscious attitude towards its own formulae, and the social themes that run through Hitchcock's work for a half-century following.

The shaping mythic structure in *The Lodger* and in Hitchcock's films generally has gone virtually unnoticed. This aspect of *The Lodger* appears as a modern version of the Persephone (or Proserpine) myth; but, as a broad tendency in Hitchcock's art, it is perhaps best called "romance," in the sense of a narrative genre strongly informed by folklore and fairy tale, classical myth, certain stories in the Bible, and the literary derivatives of all of them. The structures of comic romance in particular – with its sprawling quests, miraculous coincidences, fearsomely evil antagonists, and emblematic marriages – organize the narratives and imagery of most of Hitchcock's films.

Since Hitchcock has reworked the Persephone myth according to the conventions of a commercial film of 1926, it may be useful to review the original briefly before examining its metamorphosis in *The Lodger*. The daughter of Zeus and Demeter, Persephone is seized and carried down to Hades by Pluto while she is gathering flowers with her handmaidens. Demeter seeks her vainly until Zeus convinces Pluto to release her. But, because she ate part of a pomegranate while in the underworld, Persephone is doomed to spend a portion of each year in Hades. She is thus associated mythologically with the appearance and growth of vegetation, especially flowers, in the spring and summer and with its dying and disappearance in fall and winter. It may be relevant to *The Lodger* that Persephone's abductor is invisible and not able to be propitiated by sacrifice.

In *The Lodger* Hitchcock changes the actors from gods into men and locates the action entirely upon earth. The essential features of the underlying myth are further obscured by the circumstance that the film starts in the midst of the story that it returns to complete only in a late flashback. By the end of the movie we understand the sequence of events in the Lodger's quest to be as follows. The Lodger is dancing with his sister at her coming-out ball when a mysterious hand turns off the ballroom lights. When they are turned back on, his sister is discovered to have been murdered in his arms. His mother has thereby suffered a shock that will send her to her death also, but before she dies she asks her son to promise to pursue "the Avenger," whose triangular mark and signature were found by the body of her murdered daughter. (All this information is imparted by the flashback.) The Lodger's sister proves to be the first of a series of golden-haired girls murdered by the Avenger, and the geographical pattern of these killings brings her brother to the neighborhood of the Buntings in anticipation of the next crime. He takes rooms in the Buntings' house, where his suspicious behavior and his growing closeness to Daisy Bunting bring him under the scrutiny of a police detective suitor. He is arrested, escapes in handcuffs, and is nearly killed by a mob that believes him to be the Avenger; but the police detective learns just in time that the real Avenger has been caught and rescues him from the mob. He marries Daisy or becomes engaged to her – it is not quite clear – and takes her home to his magnificent mansion. There, in the last sequence, he entertains his awed working-class in-laws and embraces his bride while "TONIGHT GOLDEN CURLS" flashes in the London background as it did in the opening sequence.

The echoes of the Persephone myth are a bit confused, but suggestive. Like Demeter's daughter, the Lodger's golden-haired sister is assaulted, while in the company of an attendant crowd, by an assailant who seems to rise up from the underworld and disappear as abruptly as he came. The Lodger descends into the strange dark world of London (the film is subtitled "A Tale of the London Fog") and rescues another golden-haired girl, with whom he returns to the bright and (socially) higher world of his home. The Demeter-figure, the Lodger's mother, has transferred her authority as searcher to her son, and the Persephone-figure is abducted in the person of his sister and recovered in the person of his new wife; but, despite these and other alterations of the original myth, the outlines remain.

The imagery that dresses the plot is evocative of the mythic antecedent of the film. The ball at which the Lodger's sister is murdered is brilliantly lit and shot from predominantly low camera angles, which make it appear to be a brighter, higher world than the dark, foggy London into which the Lodger descends on his quest. Darkness, as a mysterious hand that turns off the lights just before the murder of the Lodger's sister, erupts to seize the first Persephone-figure and the second is carried up from the persistently shadowy world of her parents' flat to the brilliant mansion in which she clearly belongs. The insatiability of the Avenger associates him with the unpropitiable king of the underworld. He commits his crimes in the darkness of Tuesday nights against golden-haired girls, emblems of the light (the flashing sign advertising

"Golden Curls" is literally embodied in light). Daisy, in keeping with this imagery, is generally shot in bright light and shown full of gaity. Her name emphasizes her relationship to Persephone. In this very sparely titled silent, Hitchcock insists upon its significance with a pair of titles, at least one of which is entirely superfluous from a narrative standpoint, which say only "Daisy." The presence of her parents in the final sequence suggests that she, like Persephone, will have to return occasionally to a lower world; not a symbolic Hades, perhaps, but a place closer to the underworld than the Lodger's mansion. "All stories have an end" reads the title that introduces the last sequence. It thus emphasizes the formulaic quality of Hitchcock's film, the fact that it is a story somehow like "all stories." As it concludes, the golden-haired Daisy is in her lofty brilliant palace, the Avenger is out of business, and "TONIGHT GOLDEN CURLS" is again flashing in the background, but this time promising an imminent marital embrace rather than murder on a dark bridge over a symbolic Styx. "The End" is superimposed, significantly, on a shot of luxuriant foliage tossing in the wind. Summer has returned.

It is worth observing that the influence of the Persephone story may also account in part for one of the more puzzling details of *The Lodger*, its evocation of Christ on the cross when its hero is trapped on the spikes of an iron fence. The story of Christ, like that of Persephone, has to do with descent and return, death and resurrection. Its evocation in a narrative infused with those themes, then, seems consistent and appropriate. As I shall argue later, it is fitting for other reasons as well.

How the Persephone myth came to be embodied in *The Lodger* is a question that is beyond the scope of this chapter. Several general points about its presence can be made, however. First, the mythic elements of plot and imagery are artifacts of the film only; they are not to be found in the novel by Marie Belloc-Lowndes on which the movie is loosely based. Second, the outcropping of such mythic bedrock recurs in Hitchcock's films throughout his career. Wicked stepmother figures in *Rebecca* and *Under Capricorn*, echoes of *Job* in *The Wrong Man* and of the fall from Eden in *Frenzy*, the romantic quests of *The 39 Steps* and *Sabotage* are a few among many examples. Third, the mythic component of the film clarifies the import of certain details – Daisy's name and the foliage behind the final title, for example – and solidifies the coherence of its plot.

When we turn to other aspects of *The Lodger* we again see that it often anticipates its director's later films. The almost schematic but nevertheless complicated treatment of characters is thoroughly Hitchcockian. The contrast between the Lodger and Joe, his rival, organizes the characterization of all the important figures. Ordinary looking, somewhat burly, and unmistakably middle class, Joe carries himself with a rough cordiality against which the Lodger's dark, slim beauty and gentle reserve appear exotic. Though the camera is manipulated to give the Lodger an air of menace, his actions are characteristically protective. The scene in which he is discovered with Daisy in his arms after she has been frightened by a mouse typifies his solicitousness, as does his expression of distaste when he rushes into the hall after hearing a scream and finds Joe jocularly handcuffing Daisy to the newel post. Earlier Joe cheerfully declares, "After I put a rope around the Avenger's neck, I'll put a ring on Daisy's finger." As this remark and the handcuffing suggest, Joe extends his hunt-and-catch profession into his courtship. When he later puts handcuffs on the Lodger, he symbolically links Daisy and his rival as victims of his assaults. In contrast to Joe's rough clutching, Hitchcock sets a delicate symbol of the subtle intimacy growing between the Lodger and Daisy. During the scene in which they play chess, the Lodger and Daisy sit facing each other over a small table. Behind the table the arch of a fireplace rainbows between the two players and expresses, in contrast to the opposition of the chess game, a joining, a coming-together. (Hitchcock was to use this symbol of lovers' concord again, for example, in *Secret Agent* (1936), when the arch of a bridge in the backgound pairs Mr. and Mrs. Ashenden as they confess their love for each other and in *Saboteur* (1942), when the lovers are framed at a crucial moment in their relationship by an arched door.)

Evidently somewhat older than Daisy, Joe seems to be associated as much with her parents as with her. The Lodger, on the other hand, is Daisy's age and has virtually no social contact with her parents, who are suspicious of him. Like Daisy's parents, Joe is solidly middle class. The Lodger, for most of the film, has the air at once of a criminal and of a gentleman. He will prove to be the latter, of course, but for most of the story it is his equivocal status as much as his gentility that contrasts with the social clarity of the representative of law and order who is his rival. An indication of both their social status and the eventual outcome of their rivalry may be found in Hitchcock's characteristically symbolic use of stairs and interior levels. He generally shows Joe coming down the outside steps that lead from street level to the basement kitchen of Daisy's parents. There Joe visits Daisy and socializes with her parents. The Lodger's rooms are upstairs, and, as a consequence, we usually see him ascending. Daisy's parents seem uneasy in that part of the house, and Joe is there only twice, both episodes of sharp hostility. Only Daisy appears to be a comfortable and welcome visitor to the second floor.

The association of Joe with downstairs and the parents and the Lodger with upstairs and Daisy has both social and archetypal consistency. If Daisy recalls Persephone, she also reminds us of Cinderella with the Lodger as her prince. The dress that the Lodger buys her serves as a glass slipper, a token of her suitability for a more refined world. The Lodger realizes while watching Daisy in the fashion show that she belongs in a mansion on a hill rather than a shabby flat along the Embankment. It is worth noticing that stories like "Cinderella" usually contain a female blocking figure – a stepmother, wicked witch, or jealous hag. Hitchcock mildly evokes such a figure in Daisy's mother, who distrusts and fears the Lodger and resists the budding affection between him and Daisy. Until the very end of the movie she favors Joe's suit almost to the point of collaboration. Daisy's father, though he is partly under his wife's sway, seems more inclined to trust the Lodger, and in the last scene he nudges his wife clownishly in the ribs to draw her attention to the tenderness between the two lovers. His action pointedly parallels an early scene in which Daisy's mother had nudged him during some amorous play between Daisy and Joe.

In general outlines the Lodger anticipates many of Hitchcock's protagonists at the outset of their careers. Somewhat isolated and under unjust suspicion, he is also attractive, unmated, of marriageable age, and inappropriately tied in some sense to family members whom he ought to be leaving for a spouse. (In the Lodger's case the ties consist of the memory of his dead sister and the promise to his mother; but the late flashback to his dancing with his sister suggests the mild retardation of development that Hitchcock often gives his main characters at the beginnings of his films.) Daisy, too, needs to escape her somewhat protracted dependence on her parents, while Joe serves as an early example of a typical Hitchcockian Mr. Wrong – wrong age (a little too old), wrong class, wrong style, wrong intuitions. Such is the stuff of Hitchcock's triangular configurations of characters: Sir John, Diana, and Fane in *Murder!* (1930); Robert Tisdall, Erica, and her father in *Young and Innocent* (1937); Jack, Charlie, and Uncle Charlie in *Shadow of a Doubt* (1943); Roger Thornhill, Eve Kendall, and Vandamm in *North by Northwest* (1959) – one could go on and on. Looking back across more than fifty films, one sees only a handful of exceptions to the disposition of characters that Hitchcock worked out in *The Lodger*. Joe must lose, the Lodger must triumph, and Daisy must find the arms of her proper gentleman prince.

Joe and the Lodger are rivals not only for Daisy but also in their pursuit of the Avenger. Their portrayal as hunters of the murderer involves them with the more general question of how society as a whole responds to the crimes. The reaction of London at large to the Avenger's crimes is the theme of the opening movement of the film. In the first shot the head of a light-haired young woman fills the frame; we see her scream. Immediately a crowd gathers to gape at the victim, newspaper reporters phone their central offices, presses roll, and distribution trucks rush into the streets. "Tuesday's my lucky day," crows a paper seller. Radio accounts are broadcast and eagerly consumed. For his amusement and to the alarm of a witness giving a statement to the police, a bystander at the scene pulls his coat across his face and pretends to be the murderer. Later we will see a young man play the same joke on a chorus girl in the show "Golden Curls" – ironically, for she proves to be the Avenger's next victim. The sequence that conveys society's response to the murders runs surprisingly long and gains emphasis from the repetition of several series of similar images.

Why this concern with social response? Part of the answer is, I believe, the obvious one: Hitchcock devotes the opening of the film – second in rhetorical importance only to its end – to social reactions because the murders have great significance for the whole society; they are not represented as an isolated aberration. Furthermore, the opening sequence establishes the extremes of an isolated individual and an unparticularized crowd between which the central concerns of *The Lodger* lie. First we see the face of a single woman, screaming for help that does not come; then we witness the social appropriation of her tragedy by crowds of people whose identities flow together as smoothly as the dissolves of the radio listeners' faces. Between the solitary victim and the crowds, and illuminated by both perspectives, are the central figures of the film.

London's response to the murders is to make of them entertainment, a source of titillation for the idly curious. Details both in the opening and in later sequences indicate that the amusement the people of London find in the Avenger's murders is related to the voyeurist pleasures they take in fair-haired young women more generally. The murders occupy an extreme place on a scale of entertainments, but the important point is that they are on a scale at all. The film does not portray them as socially incongruous acts. "Golden Curls," with its blond chorines, represents one aspect of the general fascination with fair young women; Daisy's job as a model is another. The pictures in the Lodger's rooms suggest that golden curls are consumed even in middle-class houses, and their sexy (in one case sadistic) renditions relate them to the Avenger's monstrous obsession. Even the Lodger is implicated. "Beautiful golden hair," he says, stretching his hand toward Daisy's head. The most suggestive indication that the Avenger's criminal passion has ordinary analogues occurs when the Lodger first kisses Daisy: the camera is very tight on Daisy's face, which is framed obliquely and lighted like the faces of the Avenger's victims.

Joe's attitude toward the Avenger is determined by both his public and his private interests. From the public viewpoint, as a police detective, Joe regards the Avenger with the amused interest of London at large. He bets Daisy's father that the criminal will be caught before the next Tuesday and is delighted to be assigned to such an entertaining and well-publicized case. But he has private interests as well, interests foreshadowed more clearly than he understands when he makes his remark about putting a rope around the Avenger's neck and a ring on Daisy's finger. This personal interest climaxes with Joe's arrest of the Lodger. The Lodger and Daisy, out together despite the opposition of Daisy's mother, are confronted by Joe as they sit together on a park bench. Joe irritably claims that Daisy is *his* girl, the Lodger rises indignantly, and Daisy tells Joe that she never wants to see him again. She and the Lodger walk off, leaving a disconsolate Joe sitting on the bench alone. Head hanging, he gazes absentmindedly at the footprints of the just-departed Lodger, which (thanks to some deft lab work) begin to fill with inculpating images of his rival. Suddenly "on the track" of the Avenger, Joe rushes off to get a warrant for the search of the Lodger's rooms that leads to his arrest. The sequence makes the self-interest of Joe's suspicion unequivocal. Like the rest of London's citizens, Joe finds the Avenger murders a source of entertainment; and, like the newspaper people and the radio broadcasters, he also finds in the crimes furtherance of his private interests.

Almost alone in London, the Lodger has an entirely serious interest in the Avenger's crimes. This fact, along with their contest for Daisy, brings him into conflict with Joe. For, unlike Joe – and London at large – the Lodger expects no personal profit or pleasure from his pursuit of the Avenger. Already a victim of the Avenger through the deaths of his sister and mother, he will suffer again in his "crucifixion" by the tavern mob. From the social as well as the mythological perspective, then, the association of Christ and the Lodger is appropriate. The Lodger's sister is the first, and the Lodger himself is the last, to suffer from the Avenger's crimes. In his dedication to pursuing the criminal and in his near dismemberment by the mob, he may be seen as a redemptive figure, one who suffers not on his own behalf but in place of the truly guilty, the society that gave rise to the Avenger and is implicated by association in his crimes. The fact that the Avenger is apprehended at the same time the Lodger is arrested and attacked by the mob underscores the redemptive aspect of the Lodger's sacrifice. The explicatives in the detective's two titles during this sequence are perhaps more resonant than usual: "My God, he is innocent" and "Thank God I got here in time."

Joe, who incites the mob against the Lodger, also rescues him from them. As clearly as Hitchcock renders the contrasts between his central male characters, he does not make either one uniformly vicious or valiant. Not only does Joe, in an act of personal and professional integrity, save his rival, but he is allowed to attract some empathy throughout. When Daisy returns Joe's cookie-dough heart and, more clearly, when she rejects him after he has discovered her with the Lodger on the bench, we are likely to sympathize with his disappointment even while finding it mildly comic. For all his rough edges, Joe behaves in a straightforward manner and has an unfeigned affection for the heroine of the film. The Lodger, on the other hand, carries a slight stain of the vigilante and outlaw, however just and gentle the main lines of Hitchcock's drawing show him.

The mild suggestions of tarnish on the hero of *The Lodger* must not be exaggerated, however, or the central themes of the film are rendered incoherent. It grossly deforms the tone of the Lodger's characterization to argue that "the Avenger is only doing on a larger scale what the hero, the avenger, would do."[3] One critic actually makes the Lodger more culpable than the Avenger: "He intends to kill the killer, and his crime – not of passion or a deranged mind ... is a carefully premeditated act of hatred."[4] Such interpretations turn the diffident figure portrayed by Ivor Novello into something like Hawthorne's Roger Chillingworth, a revenge-obsessed monomaniac. We do not know, in fact, that the Lodger "intends to kill the killer"; he never says so, and his possession of a gun is hardly conclusive proof of such an intention. To equate the Avenger with the hero asks us to forget that the former is a madman who has killed innocent young women and the latter is the grieving brother of one of his victims.

Although she appears on first consideration to be the most clearly stereotyped figure in the film, Daisy's character nonetheless includes rich complications. A golden girl living below her natural station, she is surprisingly receptive to Joe's rather coarse attentions, especially early in the film. At the same time, she often retreats from him for no apparent reason. Her readiness for love precedes the arrival of its proper object, and her on-and-off responsiveness comes on the one hand from her desire and on the other from her intuition of the detective's unsuitability. When the Lodger arrives, Daisy immediately feels the pull of his attraction. Her prior involvement with Joe and her confusion about her own feelings lead to some intricate choreography. After Joe has angered her by playfully handcuffing her, for example, Daisy kisses him (in front of an approving mother) by way of forgiveness. Having done so, she immediately detaches herself and skips upstairs to the Lodger, leaving behind a puzzled detective and perhaps a puzzled film audience as well. Daisy's ambivalent interest in the two men lasts until nearly the end of the film. It is echoed by triangular composition within the film frame and by prominent details of the sets – repeated shots of the chandelier, for instance, with its three glass shades. Medium shots very frequently include three figures. The triangles that decorate the titles and the Avenger's triangular logo underscore the broad implications of the love triangle as a motive for the action of the film.[5]

Daisy is both the likely prey of the Avenger and the protector of the Lodger. Thus she is potentially victim and savior, a young woman murdered or a wife – only at the end of the film can we be sure which possibility will be realized. (The prolonging of suspense implies substantial similarity between two roles that coexist so persistently.)

When Daisy finally goes home with the Lodger, she has found someone like her in the most crucial ways. She protects her protector and, a revitalizing-Persephone figure herself, marries another redemptive figure. At the risk of belaboring a point, Hitchcock's treatment of the relation between Daisy and the Lodger again anticipates his later films. Love in Hitchcock's work is nearly always mutually healing and transforming. The gallant heroes who carry away their loves need to be lifted up and carried themselves; without each other, both lovers in most Hitchcock films are misplaced and alienated.

Without each other they are also endangered. The on-screen murders of the two fair-haired young women and the arrest of the Lodger dramatize the vulnerability of the unprotected to misdirected erotic energies. The second murder occurs, significantly, after the victim and her boyfriend have quarreled and separated in anger, leaving her exposed to the sexual madman who stalks the London fog. It is hard to judge how far to push the implications of the fact that the Avenger's first victim, the Lodger's sister, is murdered while dancing in her brother's arms; but the suggestions that arise from her "coming-out ball" seem clearer. *The Lodger* is concerned both with right courtship and marriage and with the dangers of growing up and going out. In *Easy Virtue* (1927), *Notorious* (1946), *Psycho* (1960), and *Frenzy* (1973) the theme recurs: men and women – especially women – face terrible dangers from the distorted amorous impulses of other people when they are away from or fail to find their proper mates. Daisy and the Lodger might well look gratefully heavenward as they stand in each other's arms at the end of their adventures.

Among other themes and motifs typical of Hitchcock's art is a clear sense of physical geography and an equally clear sense of social geography, class consciousness; both do a great deal to define the ambiance of *The Lodger*. Hitchcock's famously unenthusiastic view of the police appears clearly in this early film, as does his less well-known but more consistent demophobia. (In a Hitchcock film any group of people larger than roughly half a dozen registers as a mob – conformist, unimaginative, inhumane. A curious variant on this pattern occurs in *The Birds*, in which the peaceful intimacy of a pair of lovebirds is set against the mob frenzy of the flocks that attack Bodega Bay.) These themes do not appear as emphatically in *The Lodger* as they do in other Hitchcock movies, but their presence demonstrates again how early in his career he found his central concerns.

Equally typical and of considerably more importance in *The Lodger* is Hitchcock's self-conscious treatment of the mystery genre, the playfulness with which he treats its more conspicuous conventions and his systematic manipulation of the audience's expectations. As the subtitle promises, most of the photography is dismally atmospheric. The murders are portrayed by the stylized heads of screaming women and there is a memorable low-angle shot of a line of police marching through the night. Hitchcock relentlessly uses the conventions of the murder mystery to cast suspicion upon the Lodger. He appears first, shrouded in fog and masked by his muffler, on the Buntings' doorstep just after the gaslights have abruptly gone off in the house. The Buntings, of course, live at No. 13. His rooms are full of spooky shadows. He behaves eccentrically: sneaking outside in the middle of the night, carelessly leaving money lying about his room (an idea Hitchcock repeats in the opening of *Shadow of a Doubt*), and making oracular pronouncements about the concerns of Providence. Radical camera angles and suggestive cutting give innocent gestures an aura of menace. Obvious examples include the occasions when the Lodger reaches for a poker to stir the fire and when he tries the bathroom doorknob while Daisy is in the tub (another idea, the vulnerability of a bathing woman, that Hitchcock was to use effectively later in his career). The famous shot through the ceiling of the room below the Lodger's chambers casts further suspicion on him.

The obvious conclusion that these sequences show the unreliability of appearances has been drawn often enough. Equally, however, they show the unreliability of the conventions of the genre. In doing so they emphasize the self-consciousness of the film, its tendency to draw the viewer's attention to its status as a work of art as well as a representation of life. *The Lodger* gives its audience the sort of images they can easily recognize as conventional; Hitchcock did not invent the game, but he played it enthusiastically throughout his career. In *The Lodger* Hitchcock's manipulations of the conventions of the mystery thriller enrich the other modes of the film. A modern mystery story encompasses the shape of an ancient myth; an entertainment based on Jack the Ripper portrays a society titillating itself with accounts of murders. There is a mild suggestion that such imitation and social appropriation help people to deal with the fear engendered by violent, random crimes. The two men who mimic the Avenger in the film both intend to produce the relief of laughter, though neither meets with overwhelming success. What is true of the social transformations of the Avenger's crimes within the film is true of the film itself. It too makes of murder an entertainment; it too transforms anxieties into stylized, distanced, cathartic representations. "The technique of art and the technique of life," as Sir John calls this mingling of real and fictional events in *Murder!*, blur and twine in *The Lodger*.

While the film, like the media it portrays, exploits the sensational appeal of homicide, it also brings to its subject a complex personal and social understanding quite unlike media accounts. The voyeuristic eyes suggested by the rear windows of the newspaper van represent only too well the public perspective on violent crimes, then and now.[6] But Hitchcock's early silent turns its eyes to the more human perspective of Joe, the Lodger, Daisy, and her parents. *The Lodger*, like most of Hitchcock's films for the next half-century, is a love story in which suspense and loss occasion resolution and marriage. It is, additionally, a self-conscious narrative turning its gaze inward at itself as well as outward at its characters and action. In doing so it asks, in contrast to the blankly staring eyes of the newspaper van, what it is and who is watching.

Hitchcock has complained that the presence of Ivor Novello as leading man compelled an exonerating ending for the film.[7] The changes he made in adapting the novel to the screen bring the narrative into a shape so characteristic of his later work, however, that I think we can discount as superficial the influence of the matinée idol on *The Lodger* as a whole. What Hitchcock changed, and kept, in Marie Belloc-Lowndes's novel shows clearly his characteristic romanticism, social concerns, and self-consciousness as a storyteller. The center of attention in the novel, and the source of most of its point of view, is the landlady, Mrs. Bunting; in the film the center of attention shifts to the three younger people; and the point of view, with a few interruptions, is objective. The film adds Daisy's job as a model, a change that emphasizes her natural nobility. It changes the Lodger from a sham to a real gentleman and from a murderer to the innocent pursuer of the Avenger. As it makes him into a type of Christ, it also removes a theme of religious dementia that is prominent in the novel. From a few mild hints in the Lowndes story the film develops the involvement of Daisy and the Lodger, and it adds entirely the rivalry between the Lodger and Joe. Hitchcock kept most of the details that in the novel eventually reveal the Lodger's true identity as the murderer, but in the film they are used deceptively to suggest a spurious guilt. The film preserves almost unchanged from the novel the gossipy interest of media and populace in the Avenger's crimes, but it pushes the implications of that interest harder. The flashback to the sister's coming-out exists only in the film, of course, as does the associated imagery invoking the Persephone myth. The changes that Hitchcock made in adapting the novel all incorporate the themes and motives that were to characterize his entire career. In Marie Belloc-Lowndes's story he found, not those concerns, but materials to be reshaped and converted. At age twenty-seven Hitchcock showed a remarkably secure grasp of what were to be his central artistic preoccupations for the next fifty years. His conceptions were clear, and he was confident enough to treat a popular novel by a well-known writer with extreme freedom. One might add in closing that such license with his sources is also characteristically Hitchcockian.

Notes

1. In François Truffaut, *Hitchcock* (London: Panther Books, 1969), 48, Hitchcock calls *The Lodger* "the first true 'Hitchcock movie.'"
2. Since I wrote this chapter, William Rothman has published *Hitchcock: The Murderous Gaze* (Cambridge, MA: Harvard Univ. Press, 1982), which includes an extended treatment of *The Lodger*. He is concerned largely to discuss "the relationship of author and viewers" in that film. His analysis thus overlaps only slightly with the subjects of my discussion.
3. Maurice Yacowar, *Hitchcock's British Films* (Hamden, CT: Archon Books, 1977), 40.
4. Donald Spoto, *The Art of Alfred Hitchcock* (Garden City, NY: Doubleday, 1976), 7.
5. Yacowar discusses "the contrast of circle and triangle shapes," 38.
6. Hitchcock discusses this shot in Truffaut, 50.
7. Truffaut, 48–9.

THE LODGER (Gainsborough, 1926). *Producer*: Michael Balcon, *Script*: Alfred Hitchcock, Eliot Stannard, from the novel by Marie Belloc-Lowndes, *Assistant Director*: Alma Reville, *Photography*: Baron Ventigmilia, *Editor*: Ivor Montagu, *Sets*: C. Wilfred Arnold, Bertram Evans, *Players*: Ivor Novello (the Lodger), June (Daisy Bunting), Marie Ault (Daisy's mother), Arthur Chesney (Daisy's father), Malcolm Keen (Joe). 100 minutes.

Chapter Six

Criticism and/as History: Rereading *Blackmail*

Leland Poague

In a chapter on *Psycho* that appeared in the first edition of *A Hitchcock Reader*, I discuss a view of the relationship of an artwork to its historical (genetic) context that assumes, of a given text, that it has (in the words of Tony Bennett) a "once-and-for-all existence, a once-and-for-all relationship to other texts which is marked and determined by the circumstances of its origin."[1] Once a regressive text, always a regressive text.[2] Such a view of art history or of history generally is remarkably and obviously problematic; disallowing significant change effectively disallows "history" at all. A hopeful response to this problem as it bears on film criticism is seen in the fact that film scholars have lately doubled the history question by acknowledging that at least two histories are involved in any interpretative act: the history of the text itself and the history of the reader or viewer. As Stephen Crofts has recently made the point in *Wide Angle*: "Not only the author and the text, but just as importantly, the reading must be seen as historically and culturally shaped. Time and place will, almost always, divide the moment of production from the moment of reading. The 'meaning' of any text will thus vary...."[3]

A similar, though far more fully worked-out model of this "dualistic" or "relational" view of art history (one I propose to explore briefly and very provisionally in the following remarks on Alfred Hitchcock's *Blackmail*) is that suggested in the "reception theory" of Hans-Georg Gadamer and Hans Robert Jauss. Crucial to the work of both is a view of interpretation as a process, an explicitly historical process, that mediates or holds in tension the two historical moments or perspectives ("horizons") that might otherwise be taken as mutually exclusive, the "present" of the work and the "present" of the reader. The underlying theoretical point is simple, however complex its implications may be: our sense of the past is always already influenced by our present understanding of the world (we see the past through the present); and yet our present understanding of the world is itself always already influenced and determined by the past (we see the present through the past). Among Gadamer's contributions to the debate over the relation of history to understanding is the suggestion that we need to see past and present as involved in dialogue with one another; hence his interest in the concept of "tradition" as the arena where such "conversation" takes place.[4] Each interpreter "speaks" from his or her own historically situated present, as does the past itself, but the cumulative presence of many "speakers" serves as a check on interpretation, as a means of insuring that no one interpretation is crippled by its own preconceptions or subjectivity, however unavoidable preconceptions must be. Jauss, then, extends Gadamer's notion of dialogue, which Gadamer applies to all interpretative contexts, to more explicit questions of literary history.

Without elaborating further on the precise nature of that extension (Jauss wishes to allow for criticism of the tradition, even to the point of forgetting it), I wish to extract from Jauss two key interpretative principles to guide the following discussion of Hitchcock's *Blackmail*. One involves the question/answer nature of the past/present dialogue "according to which the past work can answer and 'say something' to us only when the present observer has posed the question that draws it back out of its seclusion" in the past.[5] Each work is thought of as answering to some prior (historical) question; thus interpretation involves reconstruction of the question, though such reconstruction need not rely particularly on evidence external to the text beyond that implicit in its generic and linguistic circumstances (see Jauss, 24; also Gadamer, 335–6). The second principle I would extract from Jauss is the crucial importance of the tradition of criticism itself as being nearly synonymous with the history of the work's "reception." Precisely because of its crucial status as an early instance of sound on film, there exists a sustained tradition of commentary on *Blackmail*. By and large I see the present remarks as an extension and contribution to that tradition of reception – though my primary focus will be on elucidating two questions (and their implications) that *Blackmail* may be understood as answering. In the process I hope to make the degree of my critical (historical) indebtedness clear.

Discussion of *Blackmail* generally begins with the curious fact that Hitchcock shot the film twice – or at least in such a way as to produce two distinct versions (one silent, one sound) where only one had been initially authorized.[6] We might say that in filming *Blackmail* twice Hitchcock attempted to avoid the question that sound posed. But the sound-on-film version of *Blackmail* is so extraordinary – to the point of seeming retroactively "modernistic" after the advent of filmmakers like Jean-Luc Godard – that "avoidance" is hardly an appropriate characterization of Hitchcock's accomplishment. Indeed, *Blackmail* is often taken to be a sustained reflection on the possible relations of sight to sound, of visual to aural aspects of film style, and we can usefully discuss the film by exploring the view that takes *Blackmail* as Hitchcock's answer to the question of the meaning and uses of sound in the cinema.

At least to judge by the promises splashed across its original advertisements – "The First Full Length All Talkie Film Made in Great Britain," "Our Mother Tongue As It Should Be Spoken," "Hold Everything Till You've Heard This One" – *Blackmail*'s original audience may well have approached the film with an expectation of fullness, of plenitude, of transparence: no longer would cinema be hampered by the partiality of its representation of the real, by the divorce of voice from speaker. But Hitchcock promptly counters this expectation in the first reel, which depicts the apparently routine location and apprehension of a criminal by a Scotland Yard "flying squad." The sequence moves (literally, many of the shots having been taken through the windshield of the moving police van) with a freedom and speed characteristic of the late silent period: there are sound effects, to be sure, and musical accompaniment, but no effort is made to eliminate moments when conversation is filmed though not recorded. Hitchcock even plays with the sound/silence distinction at the end of the sequence when the film's heroine, Alice White, shares a whispered joke with a police sergeant: we hear the resulting laughter, but cannot share in it for having missed the joke, just like Frank, Alice's detective sweetheart, who can do no more than join weakly in the laughter to cover his discomfort at being excluded from the gag. This play with sound is not limited, however, to the film's opening few moments. We can describe the film as having five primary "movements" each of which is characteriz-able (at least in part) by particular variations on the sound/silence relationship.

Part One: detection (directions are received by wireless as the flying squad van is *en route*), apprehension and arrest, interrogation, incarceration, relaxation (as the detectives clean up at the end of their shift). Synchronized conversations are kept to a minimum in this section, and the conversations we do hear (often spoken by char-acters with their backs to the camera) are partial or indistinct. Here visuals carry the primary burden of information.

Part Two: Alice's date. She meets Frank in the lobby of Scotland Yard headquar-ters (Frank and a colleague pass through glass doors to get to her, the doors serving almost as a dividing line between silence and sound). Frank and Alice quibble about Frank's being half an hour late. Leave the Yard. Ride the underground to another section of London (Hitchcock makes his cameo appearance as a fellow passenger) and make their way to an upper floor of a crowded restaurant. They argue about what to do for the evening: shall they see a detective film (a "picture") or not? Frank in frustration (and self-confidence) walks out on Alice, assuming (perhaps) that she will follow him and apologize, only to see her leave the establishment on the arm of another man. Alice's date then continues (what she and the second man do is unspecified) and concludes at the man's flat, just around the corner from Alice's King's Road home where her parents run a news agency and tobacco shop. The man, an artist, invites her to see his studio. Alice hesitates. Crewe (the artist) speaks briefly to a passerby. Alice and Crewe ascend to his flat. Drinks. Music. Attempted rape. Death.

Throughout this part of *Blackmail* synchronized sound and conversation are cru-cial to the development and understanding of the course of events. The dialogue, as often noted, verges on the banal, but that very banality is crucial to an understand-ing of character and action. The catch here, as in most of the film, is that dialogue works at several levels at once, banality at one level thus becoming significance at another. Example: Alice thrice changes her mind about going to the cinema. The third time Frank assumes she is being either flighty or playful, hence his theatrical exit. The viewer, by contrast, knows that Alice's playfulness is of a different, poten-tially more serious order. We have seen the note in Alice's purse, and the exchange of glances between Alice and Crewe. Visuals thus set dialogue in context; but the interaction is mutual – dialogue sets visuals in context as well, and as crucially.

Part Three: Alice's nightmare, the most frequently discussed section of the film. Here we find some of the most often cited instances of visual and aural distortion in all of Hitchcock: the neon cocktail shaker that Alice "White" ("Gordon's White Purity") sees transformed into a neon carving knife mechanically, repeatedly stabbing at the "cock" in "cocktail"; the chirping birds in Alice's bedroom upon her return home, their chirps increasingly amplified as Alice "wakes up" (Alice pretends to be asleep when her mother enters and uncovers the bird cage; Alice's bedclothes are printed in a tree branch motif, as if she were herself a bird); the word "knife," repeated over and over again by a local gossip discussing the prior evening's crime, amplified and abstracted from the surrounding conversation until it seems (to Alice, framed in close-up) a shout of accusation; and so on. It all has a subjective, dreamlike quality to it, a quality confirmed by the fact that the sequence may be said to begin when Alice emerges in her slip from behind the curtains of Crewe's bed; progresses for what seems a somnambulist's eternity as she walks from Crewe's flat to her own home (which she had earlier described as being just around the corner) and as she gets back into bed, re-emerges, and goes down for breakfast; and concludes with the famous clanging doorbell, which announces the entrance of Frank and the beginning of the film's next-to-final section.

Intercut with Alice's sleepwalking is another sequence of events – the landlady's report of the crime (she seems completely unfamiliar with the telephone and can barely make herself understood) and the initial stages of the investigation, including Frank's discovery of Alice's glove on the floor beneath the cartoon nude she and Crewe had painted only hours before. Without doubting the "reality" of these events, it is also reasonable to see them as internal projections of Alice's fevered conscious-ness (akin to Marion Crane's "fine soft flesh" soliloquy in *Psycho*), which reading is confirmed by the cut from Alice screaming at the sight of a drunkard's arm to the landlady (similarly framed) as she screams at the sight of Crewe's dead body, as if the landlady were herself a figure of Alice's guilty conscience. Synchronous dialogue plays very little part in this section of *Blackmail*.

Part Four: Frank enters the shop to ask Alice about the glove, immediately followed by Tracy, the blackmailer, as if Tracy were shadowing him, as if Tracy were his shadow (as he had been earlier, of Alice: we see the shadow of his hat on the door of Crewe's flat as Alice leaves – which hat closely resembles Frank's). Tracy wants money for his silence (Tracy has the other glove, the twin of the one Frank found), though he couches his demand in terms of doing "business" (telling Frank and Alice they are fortunate he found the glove instead of someone else: "there are some men who would make money" but he "couldn't do a thing like that"). Tracy invites himself to breakfast. The police interrogate the landlady at Scotland Yard headquarters and decide to bring Tracy in for questioning ("Let's hear what he's got to say"). Frank receives a phone call in the booth inside Mr. White's shop – evidently, to judge by Frank's subsequent actions, instructions to arrest Tracy on the testimony of Crewe's landlady. Tracy threatens to implicate Alice ("She was there too"); Frank replies that his word, and Alice's, "are a bit better" than that of a jailbird. Tracy, desperate, bolts through a back window. The chase leads to the British Museum; Alice writes her confession. Tracy falls through the glass of the cupola over the museum's reading room.

Language, both written and aural, is perhaps more crucial to this section of *Blackmail* than to any of the other four segments, though its significance seems often to be overlooked. Partly this involves the necessary "indirection" of much of the dialogue, especially that connected with Tracy's blackmail scheme. But not all the dialogue in this section is indirect in the same manner. Consider, for example, the dialogue that follows Frank's phone conversation with Scotland Yard.

It is a commonplace of *Blackmail* scholarship that Frank and Alice turn the tables on Tracy, becoming blackmailers themselves in the process. But this is not what happens. The case against Tracy has nothing to do with Frank and Alice. Frank simply undertakes to carry out the order for Tracy's arrest. Tracy wants to escape before additional police arrive and threatens to talk. Frank offers no payment in return for Tracy's silence, nor does he request payment in return for his (he refuses Tracy's offer to return Frank's initial payment); Frank simply offers threat for threat, sound for sound, his word as opposed to Tracy's. Moreover, at this point, Frank does not rule out testimony from Alice (she will "speak at the right moment"), though he perhaps assumes, falsely, what her testimony will be. Indeed, Frank's guilt and Tracy's are far more a matter of things not said, of things elided or presumed, than the contrary. Perhaps Frank's greatest failing is not his "holding back" of evidence (if Frank were not Alice's sweetheart, we would simply have, at least to this point, an instance of a cop collecting evidence, part of his job, and confronting a suspect, i.e., Alice, with it). Rather, Frank's most overtly culpable gesture is his willingness, with only a moment's hesitation, to pay the blackmail price Tracy asks, as if he believed all along that Alice was indeed guilty. Yet all he really has to go on is the fact of Alice's glove and the memory of Alice and Crewe departing the restaurant in high good spirits.

Tracy's case (our reading of his case) depends even more upon ellipsis and inference than Frank's. His anxious response to the threat of arrest far exceeds the obvious gravity of the situation confronting him. He still has Alice's other glove, has witnesses to his "friendship" with Alice and Frank, has considerable evidence that Alice herself will awaken from her trance and tell the truth (as she tries to do). So what is he trying to hide? We never know for sure, but it is clear that his relationship with Crewe significantly predates the evening of Alice's visit to Crewe's flat (the landlady tells Crewe that Tracy had called several times; Crewe seems to know Tracy when hailed on the steps of his apartment building). Perhaps Tracy is already in the blackmail business, even before Crewe takes Alice up to his flat. So we cannot simply say that it is the silence of Frank and Alice that drives Tracy to his death. Indeed, his death is directly coincident with his own attempt to turn tables: he pauses in his flight to accuse Frank, cringes as his pursuers rush toward him, and breaks through the glass of the dome. (Again the figure of ellipsis: Hitchcock's framing here, as later in *Vertigo*, makes it impossible to determine whether Tracy really trips or whether the glass merely gives way as Tracy shifts his weight.)

Part Five: After writing her confession, Alice stands up into the nooselike shadow cast by the window next to her. Dissolve, then, to the Scotland Yard plaque, after which Alice enters and asks to see the chief inspector. She is required to fill out a form, waits until an escort arrives to lead her to the inspector's office, and is finally shown into the presence of Frank and his superior. Frank attempts to stall her confession, asking if it is "worthwhile" (given the Yard's presumption that Tracy was the murderer); Alice herself delays a moment by saying how hard it will be to speak the truth – at which point the phone rings and the inspector turns Alice over to Frank, who then escorts her to the outer lobby. *En route* Frank pockets her note (the form she filled out), and she confesses that she "didn't know" what she was doing the night of Crewe's death. In the lobby the police sergeant jokes once again with Alice, aloud this time rather than in a whisper: if she told Frank who did it (in the sense of solving the mystery rather than of confessing to the crime), then Scotland Yard will soon have women detectives. And the joke is clinched when Alice sees Crewe's "Laughing Harlequin," along with the cartoon nude of her that she and Crewe had painted the night of his death, carted together, back to back, into the silent depths of Scotland Yard.

How can we construe the foregoing sequence of cinematic events as offering an answer to the question of the value of sound on film for the development of film language or of Hitchcock's particular ideolect or form of film speech? Two kinds of answer to this question are commonly available in the tradition of reception of *Blackmail*. One is to assert that Hitchcock's play with the silence/sound relationship in *Blackmail* amounts to an indictment of "the limitations of verbal communication" (hence of the expectation that sound would be "all talking" and hence "all answering").[7] In this respect Hitchcock can be compared (as Marsha Kinder and Beverle Houston have done) to Crewe's "Laughing Harlequin" – both remain essentially silent, but in their silence they mock the expectation "of poetic justice and the effectiveness of verbal communication" (p. 58). Such an answer, we might say, depends upon seeing Hitchcock as the cause and *Blackmail* the effect, so that the unconventional or unexpected use of sound is taken primarily as a token of authorial autonomy and control. Another kind of answer takes the opposite tack and assigns causality to character subjectivity, as if film sound were only partially, at one remove, under directorial control. In *Hitchcock's British Films*, for example, Maurice Yacowar draws an insightful analogy between the workings of language in the world of *Blackmail* and the workings of the law: each depends upon the characters who use it, rather than upon the director *per se*. Thus Alice's personal association of the word "knife" with her stabbing of Crewe "corrupts the function of 'knife' in social language, as Frank's personal twist will corrupt the social function of justice later."[8] A third kind of answer to the question of Hitchcock's valuation of sound combines the first two, again by means of analogy.

Rather than see sound as more or less exclusively at the mercy of Hitchcock's authorial will or as subordinate to or determined by the lives and actions of characters in the depicted world of the film, we can have it both ways (as Deborah Linderman does) by pressing the analogy between Hitchcock and Crewe's "Harlequin" or, at least, between Hitchcock and Crewe. Both are artists who use the language of cinema, of visual and aural representation (Crewe both paints and sings), which language is itself a kind of law (at least in the scenario provided by Lacanian psychology), to pervert or deny the full (if unspeakable) humanity of Alice White – just as Frank, at film's end, denies her the opportunity to redeem herself through confession. In part what *Blackmail* represents *is* silence, if not of the audience, at least of Alice White. In this view the distance between Crewe's (apparently failed) attempt at rape and Frank's (successful) attempt to silence Alice is minimal. And the difference between Hitchcock and Crewe is only a little less so. The key difference here is that Hitchcock is himself confessing (knowingly or not) to the coercive power of his art, including its power, via an illusory expectation of visual and aural plenitude, over him. At best the film is a species of joke or witticism, *re*pressing by *ex*pressing: "The film perpetuates with great wit an intertextual ethos of repression of the feminine by raising the sophistication of its own level of desire whereby the ultimate blackmail is that proffered by the text to its proper character."[9]

One need not concur with (or, for that matter, fully comprehend) the Lacanian logic invoked by Linderman's essay on *Blackmail* to find it intriguing and suggestive, though her emphasis on the question of Alice's confession seems somewhat skewed if Alice has nothing to confess – that is, if Alice is to be seen as so thoroughly a prod-uct of the "male gaze" as to be nothing more than a (scandalous) token of "differ-ence." But Linderman's "doubling" of the notion of authorship (as if the scene in Crewe's apartment has two authors, Crewe and Hitchcock, each of whom ultimately succumbs to the seductive power of his art) raises a second question to which *Blackmail* may be read as answering, though neither the film nor this particular reading of it can stand as a final or complete answer, that is, the question of the relationship of public to private as mediated by the notion of art.

The question comes to mind under the influence of Fredric Jameson's lengthy and thoughtful review of William Rothman's *Hitchcock: The Murderous Gaze*, itself a thorough and thoughtful reflection upon the nature of Hitchcock's artistic and cine-matic accomplishments. Neither Rothman nor Jameson is easily summarized, but what I would take from both relates to the notion of "doubleness" urged above in connection with Gadamer and Jauss. Briefly put, Jameson understands Rothman as offering an "allegorical" reading of Hitchcock that depends on the very nature of the medium itself, almost on its "historical" nature, as figured for both Rothman and Jameson by the fact of the camera itself, which always exists in two worlds at once – the real world, wherein "the camera is the instrument of a real relationship between author and viewer," and the film world, in which "the camera has the power to penetrate its subjects' privacy, without their knowledge or authorization."[10]

Each film always takes place in both worlds, thus always tells two stories, one involving the relationships of characters to each other, the other involving our rela-tionship as viewers to Hitchcock as the author-in-the-text; hence "the content of the film is an allegory of the latter's form, or to be more precise, the events within the film are an allegory of the latter's consumption."[11] Jameson doubles all this one step further by offering a "genealogical" reading of Hitchcock, which he means to stand as corrective to Rothman. That is, Jameson wants to ask the question of the historical "conditions of possibility" in which such films could be made or, once made, could be read as Rothman reads them. And that condition of possibility, for Jameson, is late-stage capitalism, especially urban capitalism, wherein human relationships and functions (even within particular individuals) are divided, differentiated, alien-ated. Thus Jameson cites the later Metz ("The Imaginery Signifier") to confirm the almost schizophrenic character of the film-viewing experience (equally active and passive) and correlates this with the equally schizophrenic character of modern urban living, wherein so many of our actions and perceptions seem just as automatic, just as "material and anonymous," as the experience of film viewing itself, as if each (capitalism, cinema) called forth the other. Only under such circumstances, or so I take Jameson to imply, can the question of the relation of public to private be asked. I believe that Hitchcock asks it in *Blackmail*.

The relationship of public to private in *Blackmail* is especially complicated. For example, the film's opening sequence, the arrest and interrogation of some sort of criminal, seems on first viewing a remarkably "public" event – indeed, the intrusion of public authority into a private life. But through the course of the film the whole sequence takes on a very "private" quality via its relationship to Frank, who seems at first simply an actor in the public drama but for whom the drama takes on an increasingly private and personal significance. Partly this has to do with the reso-nances established retroactively with later scenes: Frank's pocketing of the criminal's gun recalls (and vice versa) the moment when he pulls Alice's glove from his coat pocket in the phone booth of her father's shop; his helping the crook to get dressed recalls his deference to Tracy while Tracy has the upper hand; the rock thrown through the window anticipates Tracy's exit through the window of the Whites' dining room – not to mention the criminal's addictions to newspapers and cigarettes (Alice's father runs a news agency and tobacco shop). But mostly it has to do with the degree of Frank's displeasure when Alice refuses to take an interest in the detective film he looks forward to seeing. He may be confident the filmmakers will get the details wrong, but Frank takes an obviously personal interest in the film nevertheless, as if it were a genuine token of himself. Perhaps it will be a silent film about the arrest and interrogation of a dangerous criminal. Perhaps we have just seen it.

A similarly private addiction to cinema can be seen to motivate Alice as well. One reason she gives for wishing to skip "Fingerprints" is the contention that she has "seen everything worth seeing." Her father's tobacco shop, moreover, is literally awash in what might well be fan magazines; and the walls of Alice's bedroom are covered with male pinups or publicity photos, presumably of film stars (among which the photograph of Frank in his Bobby uniform seems decidedly dour and out of place; indeed, it hangs on a different wall, by itself). Alice does not seem especially interested in Crewe as a sexual partner or life mate. Indeed, as Frank is on the verge of leaving their table at the restaurant, she offers a sincere apology, as if not wanting really to offend him. But once he is gone, the prospect of acting out the flapper role seems irresistible and relatively harmless – hence her departure with Crewe, hence her willingness to go up to his flat. Once there, furthermore, it is the prospect of being pictured, of being sketched, that catches her fancy; she becomes the "Miss Up to Date" of whom Crewe sings.

Artist or no, Crewe is also caught up in the scenario. After he first kisses Alice, Crewe seems alternately encouraged and slightly disgusted with himself (recall the way he jams his hands into his pockets), the remorse recalling Alice's apology to Frank in the restaurant. But, again like Alice, Crewe cannot resist "playing" along. He returns to the piano and grabs Alice's dress from the dressing screen, eventually tossing it away (it lands, apparently, on the painting of the "Laughing

Harlequin," as if to confirm Alice's secret desire to be framed or Crewe's desire to frame her). The catch, for both of them, is that such a "private" use or abuse of art is self-destructive. They play a scene on the screen provided by the draw curtains of Crewe's wall bed; but the scene is too private, too intense, yet also too much under the sway of public models that do not seem private enough, for misrepresenting each person's better self, or for disallowing its representation at all. Perhaps what they need is an audience beyond each other. The real nightmare, as both Frank and Alice learn at film's end, is not having an audience that will listen or can be trusted.

A major thread of Rothman's general case on Hitchcock is exactly concerned with the question of audience, of Hitchcock's need to elicit its recognition, of him and of its own complicity in the institution of cinema, as if his "privacy" behind the camera were both a privilege and a burden, a burden made somehow easier to bear "in public," on the screen. No absolute resolution of the public/private dilemma seems possible. However "public" a film like *Blackmail* may be, nothing disallows a view that construes it as symptomatic of Hitchcock's "private" obsessions. Nor is it a matter of an absolute split between artist (privacy) and audience (publicity). Alice and Frank are clearly identified as "viewers"; even Frank's gestures of control toward Tracy and Alice are directed by superiors (in each case a phone call from or to headquarters does the job). But Crewe is an instance of an artist enthralled by his own art (as if the cartoon nude of Alice were a factor in his arousal); and Hitchcock's cameo appearance, on the one hand a token of his artistry, depicts him as a reader, not as a writer. Perhaps the ideal circumstance (for Jameson, Rothman, and Hitchcock) is a world wherein everyone is both reader and writer, both viewer and director, where public and private are not two sides of an absolute antithesis. The world of *Blackmail* is not that world. But within that world (and within our own) it counts for something that Hitchcock willingly inscribes a version of himself on screen, facing us directly, and as one of us, as a reader: indeed, as someone who reads in public. By contrast, Crewe's tokens of artistry, his paintings, are singular, in that sense destined for private (capitalist) consumption – and his posture toward his audience is neither direct (he faces away from Alice as she changes behind the screen, though the screen itself betokens the fact that he could confront her more directly, more honestly) nor is it self-conscious in a sense analogous to that evinced by Hitchcock. Crewe does not stand to his paintings as Hitchcock stands to Crewe, which is to say that Crewe takes little note of the negative implications or consequences of his actions, for himself or for Alice, his audience, apart from the private workings of his own desire. Let us say he has no sense of history, of inference, of narrative: his world is static, like the mask on the wall of his flat that silently, blindly, gazes over the scene of seduction – or like the equally static (if gigantic) Egyptian head that gazes past the fleeing Tracy in the British Museum. It is not running that kills Tracy, after all, but stopping. Movies move, with or without sound, and minds with them: that's the heart of the matter. In *Blackmail* Hitchcock refuses to be stopped by sound, though he welcomes it as an additional source of cinematic complexity, to be thought with, and thought about.

Perhaps the anxiety of criticism – the disquiet in many quarters at the thought of endless interpretation – follows from exactly this insight: movies move, time passes, views change. The literary/historical work of Gadamer and Jauss, appropriated here to the context of film criticism, offers us a perspective on the process of change that acknowledges the obligation we have to account for both difference (the sense in which a film answers as much to its own questions as to ours) and identity (the sense in which our reading is always *our* reading).[12] We discharge that obligation, or so I take them to imply, by means of a properly historical reading. In a curious way such a reading, if this "rereading" of *Blackmail* is any test, involves a chronological reversal. The "present" of my own reading is my confrontation with the immanent facts of *Blackmail*, with "the film itself," though the film has a past inscribed within its very structure of issues, in the questions it addresses. The background or "past" of my reading, by contrast, is provided by the efforts of other critics, many of them my contemporaries, whose efforts serve as both encouragement and corrective to my own, which in turn may serve as encouragement and corrective to theirs. In other words, one cannot *avoid* living historically: every reading is always situated, always takes place in particular circumstances. To "read historically" encourages one to become more aware of those circumstances, though history teaches us that such awareness can never be final or complete. Perhaps we should think of the desire for completion, the desire to give a particular text a once-and-for-all meaning, as a form of historical blackmail, blackmailing history, soliciting its silence – of which *Blackmail* teaches us to be wary.

Notes

1. Tony Bennett, *Formalism and Marxism* (New York: Methuen, 1979), 69.
2. On the denial of history, see Kristin Thompson and David Bordwell's critique of Noël Burch in "Linearity, Materialism and the Study of Early American Cinema," *Wide Angle*, vol. 5, no. 3 (1983): 4–15.
3. Stephen Crofts, "Authorship and Hollywood," *Wide Angle*, vol. 5, no. 3 (1983): 21.
4. Hans-Georg Gadamer, *Truth and Method* (New York: Crossroad, 1975), 331, 345. An excellent summary of Gadamer is that by David Couzens Hoy in *The Critical Circle: Literature, History, and Philosophical Hermeneutics* (Berkeley: Univ. of California Press, 1978).
5. Hans Robert Jauss, *Toward an Aesthetic of Reception*, trans. Timothy Bahti (Minneapolis: Univ. of Minnesota Press, 1982), 21.
6. On the production history of *Blackmail*, see Charles Barr, "*Blackmail*: Silent and Sound," *Sight and Sound*, vol. 52, no. 2 (1983): 189–93.
7. Marsha Kinder and Beverle Houston, *Close-Up: A Critical Perspective on Film* (New York: Harcourt Brace Jovanovich, 1972), 53.
8. Maurice Yacowar, *Hitchcock's British Films* (Hamden, CT: Archon Books, 1977), 106.
9. Deborah Linderman, "The Screen in Hitchcock's *Blackmail*," *Wide Angle*, vol. 4, no. 1 (1980): 28.
10. William Rothman, *Hitchcock: The Murderous Gaze* (Cambridge, MA: Harvard Univ. Press, 1982), 102.

11.   Fredric Jameson, "Reading Hitchcock," *October*, no. 23 (1982): 38.
12.   On the notions of "identity" and "difference," see Fredric Jameson, "Marxism and Historicism," *New Literary History*, vol. 11, no. 1 (1979): 41–82.

BLACKMAIL (British International Pictures, 1929). *Producer*: John Maxwell, *Script*: Alfred Hitchcock, Benn W. Levy, Charles Bennett, from the latter's play, *Photography*: Jack Cox, *Editor*: Emile de Ruelle, *Sets*: C. Wilfred Arnold, Norman Arnold, *Music*: Campbell and Connely, arranged by Hubert Bath and Henry Stafford, *Players*: Anny Ondra (Alice White), Joan Berry (Alice's voice), Sara Allgood (Mrs. White), John Longden (Frank Webber), Charles Paton (Mr. White), Cyril Ritchard (Crewe), Donald Calthrop (Tracy). 82 minutes.

Chapter Seven

Alfred Hitchcock's *Murder!*: Theater, Authorship, and the Presence of the Camera

William Rothman

Murder! is, arguably, the masterpiece of Hitchcock's early work. The philosophical dimension implicit in such films as *The Lodger* and *Blackmail* becomes explicit in the arguments between Sir John, the playwright protagonist, and the cunning and articulate Handell Fane, against whom he is pitted. *Murder!*'s philosophical concerns are those of all of Hitchcock's films and include the conditions of human identity; the relationships among love, desire, murder, dreams, madness, and theater; and the nature of views, visions, and fantasies. Underlying the film's arguments, and manifest in them, are its reflections on its nature as a film. The arguments between Sir John and Handell Fane about the conditions of art, and the film's testing of those arguments, are placed within a series of invocations of theater, which in turn are performed in the context of *Murder!*'s insistence on its own decisive separation from theater.

This chapter will focus on *Murder!*'s extraordinary climax and conclusion. Through a close and reflective "reading" of this passage, we may begin to appreciate how the film declares itself as a film, how it poses and addresses its central question, *What is it one views or makes when one views or makes a film?* And perhaps this reading may also help us to learn a lesson about the seriousness of the thinking that some works of "classical cinema" have inscribed within their forms and the seriousness with which films like Hitchcock's call for being viewed if their thinking is to be acknowledged and not falsely reduced to a set of "codes."

Before we begin this detailed reading, it will be helpful to offer a brief synopsis of the film up to its climax. Edna Druce, an actress, is found murdered, an empty brandy glass beside her. All evidence suggests that the murderer is Diana Baring, a rival actress. At her trial Diana offers no defense other than that she remembers nothing. The scene shifts to the jury room, where those jurors inclined to believe in her innocence are persuaded, one by one, to change their votes. Reluctantly, Sir John too agrees to go along with the guilty verdict. At home in his bathroom, however, musing in a celebrated stream-of-consciousness voice-over, he berates himself for failing to convince the other jurors of Diana's innocence. The thought strikes him that the real murderer is the man who drank the brandy. He vows to embark on his own investigation, intending to expose this villain.

Sir John's project embeds a characteristically Hitchcockian nest of ambiguities and ironies.[1] Sir John's passionate struggle with his own dark double is also his investigation of Diana's mysterious nature and his courtship and seduction of her. But, if Sir John desires Diana as his lover and bride, he also eyes her as a man of the theater would: he wishes to make her the star of his next production, to cast her *on stage* as the woman he loves. Sir John is swept up within a chain of events that would make a perfect piece of theater, a play that could be called "The Inner History of the Baring Case." Sir John is an actor in these events, but he also undertakes to assume, in effect, their authorship. But, within the world of *Murder!*, "The Inner History of the Baring Case" is not merely an imaginary play: as the film unfolds, it gradually becomes clear that Sir John actually *is* immersed in writing a play that follows the events surrounding the murder point by point. When the film ends with a view of the curtain falling on a performance of Sir John's new play, we take this to *be* "The Inner History of the Baring Case" itself.

Sir John's investigation leads to the discovery of a crucial clue, the murderer's cigarette case. Sir John visits Diana in prison, hoping that, confronted with this object, she will break her silence and speak the name of the murderer. This "Prison Visit" scene is followed by a brilliant passage that might be called the "Play Scene," in which Sir John invites Handell Fane, the man named by Diana, to audition for the part of the murderer in his new play. Sir John and Handell Fane are locked in a struggle that is, at one level, a struggle for authorship of "The Inner History of the Baring Case."[2] At another level, it is a struggle for superiority as artists. When Fane does not break down as he reads the incriminating lines Sir John has written for him, Sir John is momentarily bested: he is reminded that he is powerless to make events come out as he wishes, powerless to write the ending of his new play without Fane's collaboration. The "Play Scene" sets the stage for the film's climax, in which the struggle between Sir John and Handell Fane is decided.

The scene shifts to the circus where Fane has returned to his former job as a most singular trapeze artist. Accompanied by Markham (the stage manager of Diana's theater company who acts as Dr. Watson to Sir John's Sherlock Holmes throughout the investigation), Sir John enters Fane's dressing room. Fane puts the finishing touches on a letter, seals it, and rises in welcome. Spotting a bottle of brandy on the table, Sir John says, with an undercurrent of accusation, "I suppose you find brandy steadying for the nerves." But he cannot comprehend the secret meaning in Fane's reply ("Mine's very nervy work, you see, Sir John. You never know what may happen"), for Sir John indeed does not know what "nervy work" Fane's performance is destined to be.

In the first part of Fane's performance, he exhibits himself as a spectacle of sexual ambiguity, making a series of theatrical entrances. He enters, in succession, the camera's field of vision, Sir John's view, and the "stage" of the circus ring.

A large black region momentarily eclipses all else in the frame. Almost immediately, this "shadow" reveals itself to be a figure in a huge feather headdress. As this figure – it appears to be a woman – walks into the depths of the frame, blackness consumes less and less of the screen. The effect is that of the raising of a curtain.[3] Finally, "she" turns and we recognize this figure to be Handell Fane.

The second entrance follows immediately. An elephant parades from background to foreground, screen left to screen right, blocking Fane from our view. As Sir John steps into the frame, the elephant moves by, repeating the "curtain-raising" effect. Fane now turns, making his theatrical entrance into Sir John's view.

As the band starts up its haunting refrain, Sir John takes a step toward Fane, who turns away disdainfully then steps forward into the circus ring, presenting himself to the audience at large. This third entrance sets up the climax of the first part of Fane's performance: he opens his cloak and displays himself, a man/woman (and, in his feathered costume, also a man/bird).

Fane's form of theater is solitary. It does not consist in the enactment of roles but in theatrically displaying *himself*. He is a creature whose unfathomable sexuality condemns him to live and die outside the human community, a Hitchcockian "Wrong One."[4] Fane's performance is a ritual in which he exhibits his condition theatrically and seals his cursed fate. In *Murder!*, Fane's kind of theater stands opposed to the performance of which Diana Baring dreams.[5] It is rather kin to the death-in-life, the madness, represented by Diana's imprisonment. Fane is condemned to the cruel, inhuman gaze of his audience.

In the second part of Fane's performance – his high-wire act – Hitchcock intercuts shots of Sir John and Markham, Sir John and Markham placed within the audience at large, and the audience's views of Fane (these last represent both the general audience's views and Sir John's private views from his special place within the larger audience). The key to this sequence, which establishes a Hitchcockian paradigm, is that it images Fane's act in sexual terms.[6] This passage reveals Fane's passion and ecstasy as, absorbed in his performance, he appears as if on the threshold, then in the grips, of orgasm. The quasi-sexual performance on the trapeze culminates the self-exhibition of the first part of Fane's act. His "nervy work" calls for him to get "all worked up" before a heartless audience.

The climax of Fane's performance takes place only after he has completed a series of feats that compose the main body of his act. First, he climbs the high pole. This accomplished, he looks down. We cut to the circus ring from Fane's point of view, then to Sir John and Markham attentively watching. Fane drops his feather head-dress, dries his hands, grasps the bar, and begins swinging. Twin spotlights cast pools of light, with Fane appearing as a shadow in each pool, creating the image of a pair of watching eyes.[7] This part of the sequence ends with Fane soaring through the air, to ringing applause.

On this sound, Hitchcock cuts to Fane. He is swinging, but remains stationary in the frame, while the world, as an out-of-focus backdrop, passes first downward then upward before our eyes. This vertiginous effect signals the loosening of the world's grip on him. In his ecstasy, he turns inward and at the same time looks triumphantly into the camera.

From Sir John and Markham looking on uncomprehendingly, Hitchcock cuts to a closer view of Fane, the world again passing vertiginously through the frame. His face now registers great tension and anguish: his ecstasy is also a passion. We cut again to Sir John and Markham, still oblivious to Fane's condition, then back to Fane. His face is in dark shadow, but, as the world rises up through the frame, it becomes lit by harsh glare. At this decisive moment, the camera penetrates Fane's subjectivity and frames a series of three visions.

In the first, we see Sir John in close-up, looking slightly off to the left, superimposed on the world passing through the frame. (At one point, a string of lights momentarily crosses his face, creating an image of a death's head grin. This effect anticipates the ending of *Psycho*, when the dead mother's and Norman's grins are momentarily superimposed.)

Do we take it that, in his anguish and ecstasy, Fane literally *sees* Sir John's face before him? We may be tempted to say that this is a superimposition of what Fane hallucinates (Sir John's face) and what he literally sees (the world passing before his eyes). The hallucinatory aspect of this image is what leads me to call this a *vision* rather than a *view*. But perhaps Fane suffers no hallucination at this moment, the image of Sir John's face corresponding to nothing that Fane either sees or imagines. Perhaps this superimposition simply serves Hitchcock as a conventional shorthand for indicating that, at this moment of inwardness, Fane is haunted by Sir John, transfixed by his image. Then again, perhaps this shot represents a real view of Sir John at this moment – this view the camera's, and corresponding to the view of no one within the world of the film – superimposed over Fane's real view. Then this shot would correspond to no "private" experience of Fane's at all but only serve as Hitchcock's reminder to us that, while Fane has turned inward, Sir John is still watching.

The status of this frame and its relation to Fane's subjectivity are precisely ambiguous. This may be an "inner vision" projected *from within* Fane's imagination, or this frame may itself be projected *onto* Fane's imagination, Fane being subjected to this image as we are. We cannot say whether, in effect, Fane's imagination subjects us to this image or is subjected to it. But then again, we do not really know who or what the figure of Handell Fane represents, what his subjectivity comes to. What *is* Fane's relationship to the camera (to the film's author and viewers)? Who is subject to whom? And in a frame that contains a vision, whom or what does the camera represent?

One fact at least is clear. Whatever Sir John is envisioned as looking at, he is not envisioned as looking at the camera. In this oblique framing, his gaze does not confront the camera and poses no threat to it. Fane envisions Sir John as having no power to confront his gaze, having no power to penetrate or possess him with his gaze. In Fane's vision, Sir John's powers are inferior to his own.

From the first vision, we cut back to Fane, wide-eyed, his face half in light and half in shadow. Then we are presented with Fane's second vision: a close-up of Diana looking into the camera, her face likewise superimposed over the world passing through the frame.

In his second vision, Diana comes to Fane as a goddess who compels men's gaze. In Fane's first vision, Sir John was looking off, his eyes averted from the camera. In retrospect, we take it that Sir John, as envisioned by Fane, is held spellbound, like Fane himself, by a vision of Diana. But also, Diana looks right into the camera: within Fane's vision she penetrates his gaze as if she possessed the inner world of his imagination. Fane's vision of Diana appears as if it were a projection of the gaze of this goddess, as if it were she who conjured this vision of herself into being. But through what agency does this apparition really come to Fane? If it is projected from within his imagination, he is also subjected to it. And is it possible that Diana's powers really are magical, as Fane imagines them to be? After all, when the camera earlier penetrated the privacy of her prison cell, Diana looked up at it, violence in her eyes, as if confronting what disturbed her absorption: when we viewed her through the cell window, she appeared to possess the power to imagine, to penetrate, even to conjure, our views. What powers are natural for a being framed by the camera who is attuned to, and may be in league with, the agency that presides over that framing?

When we cut back to Fane, his eyes are almost completely shut, as if entranced by the voice of a siren. If he now abandoned himself completely to his vision, of course, he would fall to a violent death. But he does not black out. He opens his eyes and again looks up at the camera. But does this gesture break the spell cast by Diana's gaze as Fane envisions it, or does he bid his visions to continue? Does he look into the camera in defiance of Diana or at her bidding?

In the following frame, nothing is superimposed on Fane's vertiginous view of the world. Does this mean that this shot represents no vision at all? I prefer to think of this frame as representing a vision of nothingness. It is not simply devoid of a super-imposed human countenance; the blurred images that pass before Fane's eyes are charged symbolically, and admit of a reading, like a dream. The shadowy pole; the curious bell-like hanging lights (suggestive of both death bells and wedding bells, and also invoking sightless eyes); the death's head grin; finally, the blurred image of a couple: this vision is charged with signifiers of the realm of human sexuality from which Fane is irrevocably estranged and charged as well with images of death.[8]

This vision of nothingness sums up Fane's nature in his own eyes and – as he imagines – in Diana's eyes. This vision of nothingness is also Fane's vision of his own fate. Death is Fane's mark: in the world, Fane spells death, and only his own death can release him from his curse.

The series of Fane's visions now complete, Hitchcock cuts to an "objective" view. Fane lands on the high platform, relinquishes his grip on the bar, passes a rope through his hands, and turns to acknowledge his audience. The second part of his performance is successfully completed, but his strength is spent. His hands hang limp, and he seems to be suffering overpowering vertigo. Can he go on?

If Diana died in Fane's place, he would be responsible for her death. His vision of Diana is a guilty one. Since it is, in effect, as a ghost that she appears to him, her death would not free him from her gaze but condemn him to being forever haunted. His vision of Diana brings home to him that his desires can never be satisfied and mocks his nothingness. It is as if Diana's envisioned gaze represented Diana's own revenge against him. It corresponds precisely to Diana's nightmare visions of her guards, which were central to the design of the "Prison Visit" sequence. Diana's imprison-ment is the death-in-life of madness, but Fane, condemned to and by his visions, is also imprisoned, also mad, also already dead. Release from prison promises Diana a cure, while Fane's curse can be lifted only if his visions relinquish their hold on him.

Fane cannot bear his guilty vision of Diana, but this vision also arises out of his desire. He does not wish to be freed from it. I imagine him unwilling, for example, to confess and put himself at the mercy of a court, for I take it that he cannot abide bearing witness to the union of Sir John and Diana. Only through suicide can he keep faith with Diana without denying his desire. Death is the fulfillment of his calling.

First and foremost, Fane's suicide is a private act, admitting no audience. We might think of Diana as Fane's real audience, but the "Diana" Fane envisions as bearing witness to his death and the "Fane" who is possessed by this vision of Diana are not separate beings who could stand in the relationship of audience and theatrical performer. For this Diana is also within Fane, and this Fane within Diana. Diana's possession of Fane's act, which her gaze indeed also calls forth, does not make it a piece of theater, does not mitigate against its essential privacy. Diana can no more really sit in Fane's audience than we can.

On the other hand, Fane does perform his suicide in the most theatrical way possible and in a public arena before an audience that is hushed and waiting for the death-defying climax of his act. Fane's private act of tying the noose with spellbinding deliberateness, slipping it over his neck, and jumping off the platform is also a consummate piece of theater that brings down the house. True, we can imagine that Fane must "work himself up to it," overcoming his fear of death as though it were stage fright. Nonetheless, when Fane grabs the rope and passes it slowly through his hands, hardly appearing to attend to it, giving no sign of awareness that he is in the presence of an audience, the theatrical effect is stunning. But, insofar as Fane's private act is also theater, who is its intended audience? We comprehend what is about to happen only an instant before Sir John does. At precisely the moment when it appears that Sir John has finally understood, Hitchcock cuts to Fane, who only now openly discloses that he is tying a noose. It is as though he defers this revelation until his obliviousness first impresses itself on Sir John, then addresses this revelation directly to him. When we now cut to Sir John, it is apparent that Fane's masterful theatrical stroke has its intended effect. Fane's suicide, at one level a completely private act, is also a demonstration, directed to Sir John, of the power his art holds over him. Sir John has taken his place as a spellbound member of Fane's audience. Fane has demonstrated that his theater is superior. Fane's art is triumphant.[9]

From Sir John, taut with anticipation, we cut back to Fane. He tightens the noose around his neck and jumps. Hitchcock (tactfully? theatrically?) holds this framing so that the rope swings back and forth across an empty frame as Fane dies off-screen. If Fane's suicide is addressed specifically to Sir John, it is also addressed to the circus audience at large, the audience within which Sir John has assumed a place. To this audience and to Sir John within it, Fane's gesture says: "All along, what you have really wished to view is my death. Your monstrous desire for the sight of blood is what drew you to the spectacle of my degradation. Here is the authentic climax of my act. Are you ready to confront your real desire?" In a rapid montage, Hitchcock details the audience's reactions of shock and ecstasy. Fane's audience breaks down, running amok. No one present can claim to be his superior. Fane's case is proved.

Fane's gesture is the dramatic climax of *Murder!*. Handell Fane is a figure of heroic stature who dwarfs Sir John, and his suicide casts a pall over the film. Even if *Murder!* ended with an unambiguous image of Diana freed and united romantically with Sir John, it would not have the feeling of a conventional happy ending. The film does not end in this way, however. Rather it presents an image of Sir John and Diana embarked on living happily ever after, then decisively draws back from that image, framing it and disavowing its reality.

After a brief transitional passage in which Sir John reads out loud Fane's suicide note, which fills in the gaps in his understanding of the mystery, we dissolve to the prison gate. This dissolve creates an air of unreality, in part because of the framing's invocation of a stage set viewed from across the barrier of the proscenium. The sense of unreality is also due to this image's clear repetition of the shot that opens the "Prison Visit" sequence. The effect is uncanny when Sir John enters this frame from below and walks into its depths. It is as if he crosses the barrier separating the stage from the world. He passes from the region of the camera, the region where *his* view and *ours* are one, to enter a space still haunted by his gaze. It is as if he were a dreamer who awakens and passes into the world of his own dream. In the depths of this charged frame, Sir John and Diana join in an embrace.

There is a slow dissolve to a much closer view of the couple locked in an embrace, the new view placing them in the back seat of a limousine. We can sum up one effect of this dissolve by saying that we do not know whether there are two embraces or only one.

The dissolve underscores the discontinuity between these scenes even as it smoothly bridges them, denying their real separation. The dissolve also calls attention to itself, on the one hand by its extreme slowness and on the other by its invocation of the passage in which the camera penetrated the privacy of Diana's prison cell.

Diana is in tears. They are tears of thankfulness: she is sitting beside her hero, in freedom. But to whom does she give thanks? And does she also weep for Handell Fane, whose love was responsible for her ordeal but who finally sacrificed himself, allowing her to assume this place? In any case, we recognize this as the conventional moment for Sir John to declare his love and propose marriage.[10] But what Sir John says is, "Now my dear, you must save those tears. They'll be very useful – in my new play."

By referring to it simply as his, Sir John claims sole authorship of this play. But if this play is indeed "The Inner History of the Baring Case," Sir John claims responsibility, not only for a work of theater, but for the conclusion to the real events surrounding the murder. Claiming sole authorship of this double conclusion, Sir John fails to acknowledge Handell Fane – fails to recognize the significance of Fane's final gesture and his own need for Fane's collaboration. This failure, I take it, confirms that he is not, finally, Fane's equal. Nor is he Diana's equal, in his continuing failure to acknowledge her. And, if Sir John also means by his "new play" their *marriage*, then Diana will surely need all the tears she can muster for it. Like Alice at the end of *Blackmail*, Diana is condemned to a relationship that denies her freedom and from which there is no escape. Alice bears the brunt of mocking laughter and knows that the joke is on her, but Diana is cut off at this moment from our privileged vantage and does not yet know her condition of bondage. She weeps tears of joy, although she is imprisoned in a relationship with a man who claims to be her master; who subjects her to the dictates of his imagination, confining her within its frame; and who directs her to serve his art and his desire.

Sir John takes Diana's hand. As she gazes happily at him, he rests his face against her, pressing his lips to her hair. Looking right into the camera, he gives a half-smile, in a shot precisely echoing the ending of *The Lodger*. His open eyes and smile reveal that Diana's complete absorption in this present moment is not his own. His smile expresses his self-satisfaction in completing his project, and it shows him looking ahead to enjoying the fruits of his success. But we cannot say whether his look is addressed to the camera, or whether he is blind to the presence and agency it represents. Does his look acknowledge that he knows we are watching, or is he so absorbed at this moment, not with Diana's real presence, but with the scene he is imagining (whether or not it is Diana's erotic proximity that intoxicates him, freeing his fantasy), that he can look right into the camera without recognizing it? Is Hitchcock, and are we, his coauthors in the scene that is about to be enacted, or do we bear witness, with Hitchcock, to his continuing *hubris*?

From this intimate view, Hitchcock dissolves to an extreme long shot of Sir John. As harmonious music plays, Markham – dressed as a butler – opens the door to the room. Diana makes her entrance, attended by Dulcie Markham in a maid's uniform. Sir John holds out his hand and Diana steps toward him. He takes her hand, the Markhams looking on.

The dissolve suggests that this is precisely the scene Sir John imagines when he looks up at the camera, smiling. We take it that this is a tranquil coda set in the future, when Sir John and Diana are husband and wife and the Markhams are impressed into a nonthespian service more in line with their talents. As Sir John kisses Diana's hand, the camera begins to track out. At first, this movement strikes us as a gracious and tactful acknowledgment of this couple's wish for privacy. The suggestion is that we are viewing the prelude to an act of lovemaking and that we have arrived at a conventional happy ending. Sir John and Diana appear poised for the kiss that signifies that they are destined to live happily ever after, their blissful future to commence forthwith in privacy. An implication of this suggestion is that Sir John's half-smile is retroactively revealed to have been in anticipation of this ending and in particular the scene about to take place out of the camera's purview.

However, as the camera continues moving out, it crosses the barrier of a proscenium and stops only when the proscenium emblematically frames the view that a moment before had filled the screen. Within this frame-within-the-frame, Sir John and Diana, tiny figures in the distance, kiss. The curtain rings down to applause from an unviewed audience, the image fades out, and a title announces the end of the film.

This scene that we took to be real is retroactively revealed to be staged. Nor is this just *any* scene: it is, we take it, the final curtain of "The Inner History of the Baring Case." The implication is that Sir John's half-smile was in anticipation of the completion, production, and performance of his new play. This play ends with the perfect fulfillment of Sir John's wishes, but what does the ending of his play signify in reality? How do events really end within the world of the film? Does this staged kiss correspond to a real kiss, one that anticipates a real act of lovemaking? Yet no real kiss could coincide with this kiss performed in the public space of Sir John's theater, under his direction. The kiss in reality is the stuff from which Sir John creates his play's ending. The real kiss, on the other hand, is at the service of the staged kiss, which presents itself to its audience as at the service of nothing outside itself. Within the play, the final kiss signifies the lovers' mutual acknowledgment of their love and their equality in marriage. But the real kiss serves an art that Sir John claims as his alone, not acknowledging Diana as his partner. In completing "The Inner History of the Baring Case," Sir John completes his creation of himself as a character fated for the heaven-on-earth of marriage to Diana. But, in finishing his play, Sir John also completes his break with that character. Sir John's play ends with the lovers joined in an embrace that is forever, but Hitchcock does not claim that the "real" events of his narrative end that way. *Murder!* disavows Sir John's ending as the film's own. Then what is Hitchcock's ending, and why does he close his film with this disquieting camera movement, rather than, for example, a direct dissolve from Sir John and Diana in the limousine to the stage with the camera from the outset beyond the proscenium?[11]

An answer that suggests itself is that this camera movement declares that all our views of the world of the film have really been views of scenes staged by Sir John. That is, perhaps at every moment the camera could have pulled out to reveal the proscenium of Sir John's theater. Perhaps Sir John's highbrow shocker/blood-and-thunder melodrama/aerial act/Shakespearean tragedy/romantic comedy *is* the film we have just viewed. Perhaps Sir John's and Hitchcock's authorships are really one and we are seated in the phantom audience whose applause resounds as the curtain rings down.

But we have already pointed out that Sir John's and Hitchcock's endings do not coincide. If there is any gesture within the world of the film that calls for comparison with the camera's final gesture or the series of gestures it culminates, it is performed by Handell Fane, not Sir John. *Murder!* acknowledges Fane's suicide in its ending, as "The Inner History of the Baring Case" cannot, because nothing in Sir John's play corresponds to Hitchcock's camera. Sir John's authorship is not Hitchcock's authorship. The audience for "The Inner History of the Baring Case" is not in our position, as *Murder!*'s viewers, to acknowledge an author in the camera's framings. *Murder!*'s invocations of the stage are framed by, and frame, a succession of views that can be identified with no piece of theater, real or imagined. In the camera's gestures, Hitchcock's authorship is declared and our acts of viewing acknowledged. *Murder!* ends with a gesture that is its most decisive declaration that what Hitchcock has made, and we have viewed, is not a piece of theater but a *film*. *Murder!* leaves its viewers with the question, What is it that one views or makes when one views or makes a film?[12]

Notes

1. In certain ways, Sir John's project is modeled on the protagonist's project in *The Lodger*. Hitchcock, I take it, is always attentive to the ironies in the relationship between the projects of his "characters" and his own authorship.
2. In his doctoral dissertation, "Fearful Symmetries," submitted to the NYU Cinema Studies Department in 1979, David Corey studies the roles played by struggles for authorship within Hitchcock's narratives.

3. This "curtain-raising" effect, already employed in *The Lodger*, becomes a staple Hitchcockian technique.

4. The concept of the "Wrong One" is developed in *The Murderous Gaze*. I adopt this chilling term from a number of Hitchcock films, most notably *The Wrong Man* and *Psycho* ("Did she look like a Wrong One to you?") and the teleplay "Breakdown."

5. *Stage Fright* follows *Murder!* in the central importance it gives to this dialectical opposition between contrasting forms of theater.

6. Compare, for example, the climactic struggle between the two Charlies in *Shadow of a Doubt*, the fight on the merry-go-round at the end of *Strangers on a Train*, and the shower murder sequence in *Psycho*.

7. This is a modified form of a "joke" first used in *The Lodger*. A truck carrying bales of newspapers drives into the depths of the frame. Two heads, visible through the oval windows in the back of the vehicle, swing back and forth, providing the van with a pair of watching eyes.

8. This shot exemplifies an important Hitchcockian mode of symbolic representation. The presentation of Sebastian's discovery of Alicia's betrayal in *Notorious* is one of the most prominent examples of this mode. When the camera pans across the floor of the wine cellar until it frames the telltale stained drain, our view represents Alex's literal one, but it is also a symbolically charged vision. Through its veiled sexual references, it invokes a scene of lovemaking between Alicia and Devlin that Alex imagines or fantasizes or dreams. The climax of *Vertigo*, with Judy/Madeleine's vision of the black-robed nun, is another example. Cf. my "Alfred Hitchcock's *Notorious*," *Georgia Review*, vol. 29, no. 4 (1975). Readers might find it edifying to compare this essay with Richard Abel's essay on *Notorious* (Chapter 13, below).

9. The theatrical gesture as instrument of instruction plays a crucial but rarely recognized role in the characteristic Hitchcock film. This is a point developed at length in *The Murderous Gaze*.

10. Precisely this occurs in *North by Northwest*, although with a singular twist.

11. This camera movement echoes the one that closes *The Lodger* and anticipates the ending of *The 39 Steps*. *The 39 Steps* ends with Mr. Memory's death, the Professor's damnation, the union of Hannay and Pamela, and society's indifference as it turns its attention to the chorus line. But we might also say that it ends with a movement of the camera, by which it pulls out to hold its final framing. When the camera pulls out at the end of *Murder!*, it discloses that the lovers locked in an embrace are really on-stage, acting. Their "union" takes place in the sight of society, although society is present, not as witness and celebrant, but only as audience. *The 39 Steps* reverses this. Hannay and Pamela are not revealed to be acting on stage in front of an audience. We alone view their embrace. Our view is conjoined with theirs as they step back to take in the moving spectacle of Mr. Memory's death. Our condition as viewers is joined with theirs. Their final embrace is no piece of theater. The camera's final gesture calls upon us to reaffirm our bond with Hannay. If we affirm our community with Hannay and Pamela, we exempt ourselves from Hitchcock's indictment of the unviewed audience within the hall and fulfill our calling.

We cannot be satisfied when Handell Fane dies unacknowledged and Sir John persists and prevails in his hubris. But, while the ending of *The 39 Steps* is not that of traditional comedy, its melancholy aspect in no way prevents it from giving us pleasure. There is justice in this world's fate. Hitchcock too must be satisfied with the fate of his subjects in this world: the Professor's challenge to his authorship has been defeated and punished, and those who acknowledge his higher power have been saved. The camera's final movement in *Murder!* confronts us with our continuing failure to acknowledge the film's author. But the final gesture of the camera in *The 39 Steps* grants us satisfaction. Why should Hitchcock not give his blessing to those who "identify" with Hannay, who join in affirming this film's author?

12. This question identifies one of the main burdens of *The Murderous Gaze* as a whole: the task of articulating the answer to this question that is inscribed within Hitchcock's *oeuvre*.

MURDER! (British International Pictures, 1930). *Producer:* John Maxwell, *Script:* Alma Reville, Alfred Hitchcock, Walter Mycroft, from the novel *Enter Sir John* by Clemence Dane [Winifred Ashton] and Helen Simpson, *Photography:* Jack Cox, *Editors:* René Marrison, Emile de Ruelle, *Sets:* John Mead, *Players:* Herbert Marshall (Sir John Menier), Nora Baring (Diana Baring), Phyllis Konstam (Doucie Markham), Edward Chapman (Ted Markham), Esmé Percy (Handell Fane). 92 minutes.

Chapter Eight

Consolidation of a Classical Style: *The Man Who Knew Too Much*

Elisabeth Weis

In a generally favorable contemporary review of *The Man Who Knew Too Much* (1934), Forsyth Hardy observed that "with *Murder!* in mind, the surprise of the film is the absence of any expressive use of sound."[1] If by "expressive" sound Hardy is referring to virtuoso effects, then he is right; there is nothing equivalent to the choric chanting in *Murder!* or the knife sequence in *Blackmail*. However, Hitchcock is still very much experimenting with sound in *The Man Who Knew Too Much* – in less obvious ways. With this film Hitchcock finds a successful formula that will enable him to develop his concerns with the deeper impulses of human behavior without resorting to noticeable expressionistic devices. It is the first film in the classical style that will characterize such films as *Young and Innocent* (1937), *The Lady Vanishes* (1938), *Foreign Correspondent* (1940), and *Mr. and Mrs. Smith* (1941).[2]

The classical method requires Hitchcock to manipulate his sounds within a realistic context. On the stylistic level this means that he has to provide a literal pretext for any exaggerated use of sound. On the thematic level, the method requires the incorporation of the aural effects into the plot itself, so that they are so obvious and so essential that they do not jar with the style of the rest of the film.

One means of amplifying a sound with a literal source is to find a plausible second sound that provides an aural correlative for the original sound. This substitution technique is akin to the use of "objects as visual correlatives" that Andrew Sarris has observed in Hitchcock's films.[3] In *The Man Who Knew Too Much*, vases serve this function during a shoot-out at the spies' hideout at Wapping. The director wants to show that the spies are gradually being overcome by the police who are firing at them through the windows, but he does not want to eliminate his few spies too soon lest he also eliminate the suspense. He therefore uses vases, which line the room's shelves, as a visual substitute for and aural extension of the destruction being sustained. Hitchcock presumably does not want actually to depict the violence of the spies' deaths; not only does Hitchcock prefer implication but also Hollywood's gangster films had recently created a revulsion in England against excessive violence. He was able to suggest the impact of the bullets by showing the shattering and toppling of vases (just as Howard Hawks had shown Gaffney's murder through indirection in *Scarface* two years earlier by having the camera follow a bowling ball released by the murdered man to its target, where a last pin wavers and finally topples). Similarly, the sounds of gunshots from down the street, even if realistic (at this time sound-effects recordists had to find substitutes for the sounds of shots, because recording the real sound would have blown out their sensitive equipment), were multiplied and amplified by the sounds of numerous vases shattering and crashing to the floor. In much the same way, Hitchcock uses crockery during a donnybrook in *Young and Innocent* and balloons during a birthday party in *The Birds* to intensify the effects of destruction.

The other way to manipulate sounds within realistic limitations is carefully to control the use of ambient noise, that is, the sounds that might occur naturally in the background of a given location. Background noises can be juggled quite extensively before the audience will notice them. Hitchcock was fond of saying that a "decisive factor" in *The Man Who Knew Too Much* was "the contrast between the snowy Alps and the congested streets of London," which he told Truffaut was a "visual concept [that] had to be embodied in the film."[4] For the transition between the Swiss and the British scenes Hitchcock dissolves from snowy mountains to a night shot of Piccadilly Circus and from the jingle of sleigh bells to the noise of traffic. Otherwise, he barely indicates any visual congestion of London. He depends much more on sound for ambience.

For instance, when the film's two heroes, Lawrence and Clive, first arrive at Wapping, the soundtrack is busy with boat whistles, hand-organ music, car horns, and traffic, but we see little activity. (Of course, this is the more economic way of creating ambience in a tightly budgeted studio.) As the men walk upstairs and wait outside a dentist's office that is a front for espionage activities, Hitchcock keeps up the level of ambient noise. However, while we wait outside with Lawrence once Clive has gone into the office with an unsavory-looking dentist, Hitchcock eliminates all but a few token exterior noises to focus our concentration on the closed door. Our expectations are rewarded with a scream (Clive's), which confirms our fears about both assassins and dentists. (An earlier association between the assassin and dentistry is suggested when Lawrence's daughter observes that she does not like the assassin because he uses too much brilliantine and has too many teeth.) It is important to the film that Wapping is the kind of seamy location in which a scream goes unheeded. The plausibility of its going unnoticed by the outside world has been increased by the introduction of that world as a noisy location.

In Hitchcock's American remake of *The Man Who Knew Too Much* (1956), it is the first setting (in this version, Marrakesh) that is noisy and London that is quiet.[5] Hitchcock emphasizes the congestion of Marrakesh by staging the murder of the spy in the marketplace. Contrasted with the noisy setting is the placidity of the Jimmy Stewart character – Hitchcock has specifically described his character to Truffaut as "an earnest and quiet man" (Truffaut, 170). The manipulation of the ambient noise to underline this contrast is done with great care. For instance, there is a scene in a police station in which Stewart and his wife talk with a police officer. The shots alternate between the couple's view of the policeman, which includes a view through the window of the busy city, and the policeman's view of the couple, who are sitting across from him before a blank wall. Although the ambient noise should theoretically not vary, in fact, Hitchcock raises the traffic noise when we see the city and lowers it significantly when we are looking at Stewart. I have described this detail to distinguish between the early and later appearances of the classical style. The manipulation of ambient noise is already present in the 1934 film but in relatively crude form. Later versions of Hitchcock's techniques are almost always more refined.

If the technical aspects of the classical style are superior in the second version, however, those thematic aspects that the films share are already fully developed in the first. That is to say, Hitchcock has so neatly incorporated his thematic elements into the plot and characterization that they are all but invisible to the viewer who does not want to look for them. The point where the themes all coalesce is the famous Albert Hall sequence, in which a diplomat is to be assassinated. The spies plan to have the sound of the assassin's gunshot at the concert hall masked by the sound of cymbals crashing, so that the structural climax of the film corresponds with the musical climax of a dramatic cantata being performed. At the concert is a woman, Mrs. Lawrence, who knows about the plot but has been warned that her intervention would mean the death of her kidnapped daughter. Thus her last-second scream, which saves the diplomat, is also the thematic climax of a film whose moral dilemma has been a couple's choice between the life of their daughter and that of a famous diplomat, between the family and the state, between love and duty. The choice between screaming and remaining silent is related to one of the film's major concerns: the contrast between silence and oral expression that differentiates the spies from the heroes of the film. Furthermore, the concert sequence creates a conjunction of music and murder, the one a sign of order, the other a sign of chaos. The silence-versus-expression antinomy operates on an individual level. The music-versus-murder antinomy operates on a social level. These two antinomies merge at the concert sequence, which poses in concrete terms the central tension of this and other Hitchcock films: the problem of how to reconcile the need for social order with the need for personal expression. As my analysis will show, on the social level Hitchcock is more or less on the side of control; on the personal level he is more or less on the side of expression.

The silence-versus-expression motif is developed through contrasts of characters. *The Man Who Knew Too Much* is the first of Hitchcock's films to suggest that for criminals to be effective they must work quietly, a concept that is most fully and literally developed in *Family Plot*, where the kidnappers always remain mute in their dealings with lawmen. In both films, silence is associated with single-minded dedication to one's task. Noise and talking reveal espionage activities and must be avoided at all costs. The spies would not have known that the Lawrences "knew too much" in the first place if Lawrence had not talked too loudly about it in a hotel hall in Saint Moritz. Even shooting is to be avoided if possible. The spies battle Lawrence and Clive in their church with chairs rather than guns because they do not want the police to hear. During the brawl the woman spy tells the organist to play a hymn to cover up the sound of the scuffle. The spies engage in the final shoot-out with the police only because their hideout has been discovered. Thus it is altogether appropriate that their assassination attempt involves their concealing a gunshot under the sound of crashing cymbals. Similarly, it is appropriate that their kidnapping involves keeping the Lawrences quiet. Despite the film's title, it is not the Lawrences knowing too much, so much as their telling anyone, that concerns the spies. The idea of "keeping your mouth shut" is literalized by Hitchcock, who has Lawrence tell Clive to do precisely that after Clive has had his tooth extracted in the cause of their search for the daughter.

The most efficient, and the quietest, character in *The Man Who Knew Too Much* is the woman spy, who, even after being shot, dies without a sound, and who spends a good deal of time trying to prevent her brother, Abbott, the spy ringleader, from getting sidetracked from his work. Talking too much is Abbott's fatal flaw. It is also what gives him (as played by Peter Lorre) his personality because it humanizes him. He likes to chat, to make puns, and to laugh. He is so identified by his musical Swiss watch that, when Lawrence is searching for him in the hideout-church, his presence can be revealed by the sound of the watch chiming while he is still off-screen.

Keeping quiet involves controlling one's emotions. Abbott tells Lawrence, "You should learn to control your fatherly feelings and not drop things on the floor," and challenges the father not to give away his feelings when he is reunited with his daughter in the spies" hideout. That reunion sequence is matched later against the scene of the woman spy's death, in which Abbott cannot entirely suppress his despair.

In *The Silent Scream* I have suggested that silence is a symptom of moral paralysis; in *The Man Who Knew Too Much* it is also a sign of emotional paralysis. For Hitchcock implies that always keeping quiet requires the unhealthy suppression of emotions. Unlike the spies, the Lawrences are talkers. Volubility is a sign of emotional life, of spontaneity, of irrepressibility. In the second scene of the film, the skeet-shooting finals between Mrs. Lawrence and Ramon (who, it will turn out, is the spies' assassin), the Lawrence daughter spoils her mother's shot by talking too much. The mother remarks, "Let that be a lesson to you not to have children." Like most jokers, she is partly serious, although her actions for the rest of the film show that she prefers life, and having a daughter, to winning. (She does win in the "contest" that involves a life, rather than just winning an artificial game.) A moment later it is the mother who is shushed by the crowd for talking too much (as she is saying that she will "disown the child" if she loses), and the assassin wins the championship. There is a structural connection linking the first two confrontations between these two sharpshooter-antagonists. At the skeet-shooting match the daughter's speaking makes the mother miss a shot. At Albert Hall the mother's screaming makes the assassin miss.

Thus the concert sequence, which is usually considered merely a clever device for producing suspense, is related to the tension in the rest of the film between keeping quiet and revealing one's feelings. (More obviously, the concert sequence is also a confrontation between the good and evil forces.) At the concert the mother is torn between two forms of behavior – one trained, one instinctual. The audience sympathizes with both. One choice is not to disturb a concert, not to make a fool of oneself in public – a behavior pattern that has been instilled in us from an early age. The other choice is the impulse to cry out at a moment of danger. When the mother screams in the nick of time to prevent the assassination, she is not so much going against maternal instinct (by risking the life of her child) as responding to the more immediate instinct of wanting to save the ambassador's life. Thus her behavior here is one and the same healthy expression of emotion as her daughter's talking at the shooting match, and both are opposed to the unnatural repression of emotion typical of the spies.

The two screams elicited by the spies at different points in the film provide a measure of the extent to which anarchic forces have intruded into civilization. The spies' threat moves from an isolated room in a seamy suburb to an Albert Hall concert at the political and cultural center of British society. If a scream goes unheeded when emitted from a slum dentist's office, it is altogether conspicuous and inappropriate at a concert, and that is why it is an effective means for Mrs. Lawrence to save a diplomat's life.

The whole notion of staging the film's climax at a concert is particularly useful because Hitchcock can work with the concept of musical order in two ways, stylistic and thematic. A comparison of the role of music in both versions of the film reveals once again that, while both thoroughly develop the thematic associations of music, the second is a decided improvement on the first in its stylistic use of music. Hitchcock has said that "the first version is the work of a talented amateur and the second was made by a professional" (Truffaut, 65). He was, as usual, assessing his films only according to their craftsmanship, and in that area he is certainly right. In both films the stylistic function of the music is to create suspense. Music is such a useful tool for Hitchcock because a piece of music has its own structure, a pre-established order against which he can time the struggles of his characters.

Truffaut and Hitchcock together have quite thoroughly analyzed the improvements in the second version of the concert sequence itself (Truffaut, 63–5). They have not so thoroughly discussed the preparation for the sequence, however. In the British version of the film Hitchcock gives us little chance to hear the musical phrase during which the shot will be fired. A considerable portion of the piece ("The Storm Cloud Cantata" by Arthur Benjamin) is played under the opening titles, but it stops short, just before the last four notes that make up the crucial phrase. The four notes in isolation are first heard just before the concert, as Abbott plays them for the assassin (really for the audience, of course) on a record player. The American version is much more sophisticated aurally and visually in acquainting the audience with the music so that the suspense can be milked. Just a look at the scene in which the spies play the record reveals the added clarity of Hitchcock's later version – a clarity evidently based on a greater self-awareness of the elements of his own style. In the later film the spies provide the context of the musical phrase, and they play the record twice. In the first version the playing of the record is photographed in deep focus, so that we may watch the expressions of the father and daughter in the center and depth of the image, with Abbott and the assassin less conspicuously located on either side of the frame and nearer the camera. In the second version Hitchcock simplifies the shot (the three spies in it are all looking at the phonograph; the hostages are not seen), thereby forcing us to pay closer attention to the music. There is no emotional distraction.

Formal considerations aside, Hitchcock established with the first *Man Who Knew Too Much* the thematic role that classical music would usually play from then on in his films; the concert is a staid ritual of refined society. During the film's violent confrontations the spies use music to cover their activities. Their first assassination is that of a British spy in Saint Moritz who is shot while he is dancing with Mrs. Lawrence. Hitchcock does not emphasize the point, but this assassination, too, is concealed by music. The gunshot occurs on a musical beat, and the sound heard is not of a bullet but of window glass breaking. Even the victim himself looks down with surprise, after not noticing for a moment that he is wounded. As noted above, the spies try to cover the noise of the brawl in their church with music. At the end of the hymn, the organist plays a solemn amen. Church music is, of course, even more staid than choral music, and so we experience a frisson of pleasure when Lawrence earlier gets the chance "naughtily" to sing false words to a hymn while he is trying to warn Clive of their danger. (It is the same antiauthoritarian pleasure we get out of seeing grown men and women fighting in church.) Their disregard for the normal lyrics of the hymn may be seen as a foreshadowing, like the daughter's talking during the match, of the mother's "naughty," antisocial scream during the concert. The disrespect for music by the so-called moral forces in the film is continued, in a minor way, even during the final shoot-out, when two policemen, commandeering one citizen's parlor, use his piano as a barricade after the first policeman has scolded his younger partner for playing a few notes by saying, "This is a scrap, not a … concert."

The evil forces cover their activities with a front of respectability (religious and cultural). By contrast, the good side has to be disrespectful to cultural institutions to preserve them. The conjunction of music and murder is one of Hitchcock's many ways of showing that evil lurks very near the surface of respectability. Just as the attachment of Mrs. Lawrence's knitting to the coat of someone about to be killed juxtaposes "the domestic and the sinister," so the interruption of music by assassinations suggests that domestic and national security are very fragile illusions – as tenuous as a thread of yarn that breaks when a man dies; that security and control are gained at the cost of repressing natural instincts; and that a scream may be more civilized than a cantata.[6]

Notes

1. Forsyth Hardy, "Films of the Quarter," *Cinema Quarterly*, no. 3 (Winter 1935): 119.
2. Films that combine classical and subjective techniques in varying proportions include *The 39 Steps* (1935), *Sabotage* (1936), *Saboteur* (1942), *Lifeboat* (1943), *Dial "M" for Murder* (1954), *To Catch a Thief* (1955), and *The Man Who Knew Too Much* (1956).
3. Andrew Sarris, *The American Cinema* (New York: E. P. Dutton, 1968), 58.
4. François Truffaut, *Hitchcock* (New York: Simon and Schuster, 1967), 61; originally published as *Le Cinéma selon Hitchcock* (Paris: Robert Laffont, 1966).
5. In the American version the characterizations of the heroes are more complex, and there is an added subjective component. See Elisabeth Weis, *The Silent Scream: Alfred Hitchcock's Sound Track* (East Brunswick, NJ: Fairleigh Dickinson Univ. Press, 1982), 163.

6. Raymond Durgnat, *The Strange Case of Alfred Hitchcock* (Cambridge, MA: MIT Press, 1974), 123.

THE MAN WHO KNEW TOO MUCH (Gaumont-British, 1934). *Producers*: Michael Balcon, Ivor Montagu, *Script*: A. R. Rawlinson, Charles Bennett, D. B. Whyndham-Lewis, Edwin Greenwood, Emlyn Williams, *Photography*: Curt Courant, *Editor*: H. St C. Stewart, *Sets*: Alfred Junge, Peter Proud, *Music*: Arthur Benjamin, Louis Levy, *Players*: Leslie Banks (Bob Lawrence), Edna Best (Jill Lawrence), Peter Lorre (Abbott), Nova Pilbeam (Betty Lawrence), Hugh Wakefield (Clive), Pierre Fresnay (Louis Bernard), Frank Vosper (Ramon). 75 minutes.

Chapter Nine

Through a Woman's Eyes: Sexuality and Memory in *The 39 Steps*

Charles L. P. Silet

The 39 Steps is often credited with being the first really successful "Hitchcock" film, the one that brought together for the first time all of those dramatic elements for which Hitchcock became justly famous: the innocent man pursued by both police and criminals, the Hitchcockian blonde who educates the hero in the ethics of sexuality, the foregrounding of art via themes of theatricality. Indeed, William Rothman's discussion of the film in his recent *Hitchcock: The Murderous Gaze* gains much of its considerable force by simultaneously confirming and denying the typicality of *The 39 Steps* – seeing it as Hitchcock's first real seriocomic "thriller" but explicitly contradicting the commonplace that reads Richard Hannay, the film's hero, as an early version of the Cary Grant figure whom Hitchcock both condemns and redeems in the series of films stretching from *Suspicion* through *Notorious* and *To Catch a Thief* to *North by Northwest*. In *The 39 Steps*, as Rothman reads it, the series of awakenings that Hannay undergoes does "not add up to a conversion. There is no article of faith he comes into or loses. He receives no edification, but then again he stands in need of none: Hannay is perfectly all right as he is."[1]

Rothman is not literally accurate here: Hannay has much to learn if he wishes to clear himself of the charge of murder lodged against him after "Annabella Smith" is found knifed to death in his London flat. He needs to learn who lives at Alt-na-Shellach, for example; he needs to learn that Professor Jordan is the ringleader of "the 39 steps" spy organization; he needs to learn that the police who arrest him at the political rally are not police but Jordan's henchmen; he needs to learn where and how Jordan will pick up the Air Ministry secrets that he plans to spirit out of the country. But Hitchcock presents us with a kind of "MacGuffin" or displacement in *The 39 Steps*, which makes it difficult to see the relationship between the film's overtly political intrigue and its primarily sexual thematic matrix. We might say that education in *The 39 Steps* is construed less in terms of self-criticism, as in *North by Northwest*, than as a matter of memory, such that it is less what Hannay says than what he remembers (or can remember) that counts; and what he has to remember is primarily a series of male/female encounters that mark the progress of his redemption from a charge of woman-killing to his implied union with Pamela, as if Hitchcock were thereby acknowledging the value of women on behalf of a (male) society that treats women, and especially marriages between men and women, as traps to be avoided.[2]

The opposition between sexual equality and the values of the dominant culture is first sketched out in the music-hall scene that opens *The 39 Steps*, though the opposition between what are essentially masculine values and sexual honesty is repeated throughout the film in a series of scenes that invariably turn on or have recourse to overtly sexist jokes or assumptions – the scene between Hannay and the milkman, for instance, or that with Hannay and the corset salesmen on the Highland Express. The music-hall scene is especially important, however, for happening twice, at the film's beginning as well as, in a modified or displaced form, at its conclusion. And its first instance, together with the following scenes between Hannay and Annabella Smith, provides clear evidence of the displacement of sex by politics (and vice versa) that structures the film.

Thus the first question put to Mr. Memory in the initial music-hall scene is asked by a woman – "where's my old man been since last Saturday?" – though the overt honesty, even anger, of her question is met with deaf ears. "A serious question, please," replies Mr. Memory. More "serious" questions follow – most of them having to do with British sporting events – though one of those, asked *by* a woman, effectively reasserts the link between private facts of sexuality and more public forms of knowledge: "Who was the last British heavyweight champion of the world?" She receives three answers: Henry VIII, "my old woman," and Bob Fitzsimmons, the latter of whom defeated Jim Corbett in October of 1897. The first two answers are offered as boisterous jokes; taken together they envision sex as a kind of national/ dynastic battleground. Indeed, it is a repeatedly unanswered sex question – "How old is Mae West?" – that initiates the drunken brawl that Annabella's pistol shots then accelerate into a panic. And the sense in which Mr. Memory's species of sexual propriety (the questions he will not answer) is representative of the culture of his audience is indicated by the master of ceremonies, who boasts that Mr. Memory has willed his brain to the British Museum, as if it were a national treasure, part and parcel of the nation's larger recall of itself.

A similar pattern of sexual jokes and unanswered questions – leading again to sexual violence – is evident in the scenes leading from the Music Hall to Hannay's flat and finally to Annabella's death. Once outside the Music Hall Annabella asks Hannay if she can go home with him (so as to evade pursuit by Jordan's henchmen). In a bemused tone Hannay replies "it's your funeral" – not knowing that the violence jokingly hinted at in the sex/death commonplace will soon come back to haunt him. As they board the bus to go back to Hannay's flat, and we catch a glimpse of Hitchcock walking by, we can also see, if we are careful, a sign on the bus that reads "Cooperative Permanent." Hannay clearly at this point sees Annabella's companionship as a very temporary affair. But the subsequent course of events – her hiding in the shadows of Hannay's sitting room, her request that Hannay turn the mirror to the wall, her insistence that Hannay not answer the incessantly ringing telephone, her tale of espionage and a nation at risk that Hannay brushes off as a "spy story," the symptom of "persecution mania," cautioning her to be more careful in choosing her gentlemen friends – makes of Annabella a very "permanent" companion, an indelible fixture of Hannay's memory. Indeed it is for remembering his own response to Annabella – a memory that takes the form of Annabella's ghostly presence in Hannay's field of vision: "The police would not believe me any more than you did" – that Hannay decides to flee London, to take Annabella's task upon himself, to become her "co-operative."

Hannay thus begins his journey with a sense of urgency and danger. It will be a matter of life or death before he is through – and a matter of sexuality, marriage, and women as well. Significantly, Hannay's next encounter with a woman follows almost immediately upon his departure from the company of the joking underwear salesmen whose compartment he has shared on the Highland Express – as if in rejecting their sexual ethics he were fated henceforth to depend upon women and their world for his survival. Out in the train corridor Hannay is stopped by a uniformed porter who inquires if he will take tea in the dining car. Hannay replies that he will, but in replying notices police moving through the train. Desperate, Hannay enters a compartment not his own, sits down next to its only occupant, a blonde young woman reading a book, whom we later recognize as Pamela, takes her into his arms, and rather forcefully kisses her. During the kiss the woman's glasses slip between the embracing couple and disappear. The police in the corridor pass by the couple as one of the uniformed Bobbies cracks that "someone in there is getting a free meal." The remark carries a double meaning, and the other police*men* smile at the off-color joke. The remark also brings back to mind the cluster of associations of meals, domesticity, sex, marriage, and couples that have already passed in the film. Particularly important here is the disappearance of the glasses, perhaps suggesting that Pamela will be barred from reading about the murder as the salesman had done and will need to draw her own conclusions when she encounters Hannay again. Another possibility has to do with the whole idea of Hannay's education and awakening. By the end of the film Hannay will be forced to see the film world clearly, especially its underlying sexual dynamics, which he accomplishes in (metaphorical) part by borrowing a pair of women's opera glasses in the Palladium sequence (our kinship with Hannay throughout the film will be confirmed by our sharing his point of view here). The single image we take away from the kissing scene is a vivid one of Pamela's right eye expressing a sense of fear while Hannay's head obscures the rest of her face. It is an image that will haunt both *Vertigo* and *Psycho*.

Hannay immediately apologizes for his actions, once the police have passed by, confesses that he is in danger, and pleads with Pamela not to betray him. The police return at this moment to ask if either of them has seen a man pass by. The man in front of her is the one they are seeking, Pamela tells them. Providentially, the railway porter enters at this moment to announce that tea is served. It is all the diversion Hannay needs to open the exterior door of the compartment and swing himself to the outside of the train. In the chase that follows, the police stop the train, allowing Hannay to get off and hide among the girders of the bridge spanning the Firth of Forth.

Hannay's next encounter with a female, the crofter's wife, begins by seeming chance, as did the first two. Hannay hikes down a hill and meets John, the dour crofter, who agrees to put him up for the night. For a second time Hannay pays for assistance; the milkman, while verbally refusing the pound note Hannay offers to borrow his white hat and coat, neatly takes, folds, and pockets the bill while announcing that he may need the same sort of assistance some day. The association of money with escape also brings it into a relationship with sex and marriage. John goes beyond the amiable banter of the milkman as his avarice is linked with his strangely obsessive jealousy. One might ponder the rather odd attraction afforded to him by bringing a handsome outsider into contact with his young and impressionable wife. After all, he could easily refuse to harbor Hannay: the money seems slight enough reason when one considers the extremity of his jealousy. There is obviously something more to his motives.

According to Hitchcock, this whole scene was derived from an off-color story that was a favorite of his. In his interview with the late François Truffaut he tells the joke about the old, black-bearded, extremely austere South African Boer and his sex-starved wife. The latter slaughters a chicken and bakes her husband a chicken pie for his birthday, only to be scolded for killing the bird without his permission. The night is stormy and suddenly a stranger arrives at the door and requests shelter. The man is let in and offered some of the pie, but the Boer won't let him have very much. The woman, in Hitchcock's words, is "hungrily eyeing the stranger, wondering how she can get to bed with him." The husband suggests that the stranger sleep in the barn; the wife insists that all three get into bed together. Finally the woman sends the husband out to check the rest of the chickens and tells the stranger "Come on, now's your chance." And the stranger hops out of bed and gulps down the rest of the chicken pie.[3]

The point of the dirty story is to show how both the sex-starved wife and her grasping husband get their comeuppance at the hands of a stranger. By contrast with the crofter, however, Margaret is not the cartoon caricature of the joke merely brought to life on film. She seems genuinely compassionate and even is willing to risk her husband's wrath, which she has surely experienced before, in order to help the stranger escape. There are parallels in this scene to the one between Hannay and Annabella. Margaret prepares a meal of fish for Hannay, as he had for Annabella; both strangers confess their involvement in something mysterious; both seem exotic to their host/hostess and bring the latter a break in the monotony of their lives. In both scenes there is an implied sexual element, seen in Annabella's initial proposition and in Hannay's rather uncharacteristic attempts to manipulate Margaret's obvious loneliness and longing to his benefit. Also like Annabella, Hannay withdraws the sexual suggestion as he genuinely learns to appreciate Margaret's unselfish cooperation, even to the point of helping him escape. Hannay thus plays both roles – host/guest, male/female – and learns from the women in both instances. Annabella teaches Hannay to attend to what people say: her warnings prove accurate, the spies are indeed dangerous, and Hannay does have to watch out. Margaret teaches Hannay a certain humility, as she willingly sacrifices herself for his well-being.

Rather than being an illustrated dirty joke, then, the scene at the crofter's becomes an object lesson in a bad marriage and provides a counterpoint for the

Hannay/Pamela scenes later on. The crofter and his wife are truly chained together in a terrible sort of bondage. The cavalier quips of the milkman and the badinage of the traveling salesmen on the train become the horror of the Margaret/John relationship; it is the worst example of a marriage we will see in the film.

After the three retire for the night, Margaret and John to their marriage bed, Hannay to the box bed, the police arrive. For the second time in the film Hannay is awakened by a woman and sent on his way. The pattern that emerges here is not only that women (especially Annabella) alert Hannay to the dangers of the world but also that they are capable of saving him from danger altogether, as we later see in Pamela's case. In a final gesture Margaret gives Hannay her husband's overcoat because Hannay's jacket is "so terrible light." The coat provides an image of her protectiveness, her desperate need to care for someone. As Hannay leaves he kisses her and tells her that he will never forget her. After the door has closed on his exit, Margaret turns slowly toward the camera as Hitchcock lovingly captures her gentleness and goodness in a silent-screen image worthily reminiscent of Murnau or Griffith.

Hannay's subsequent flight from the crofter's cottage takes him over more ragged countryside to the door of the Professor's house, the goal of his journey so far, where Hitchcock provides him with yet another object lesson in sexual politics.

It is instructive that the most English of couples in the film are the spies, the Professor and his wife.[4] Even as he conveys his annoyance at Hannay's sudden appearance, which might jeopardize his upper-class cover, Professor Jordan notes in his civilized way that he does not know what his wife and daughter would think. Just as the Professor is handing Hannay a gun and suggesting that he might want to blow his brains out for the sake of convenience, Mrs. Jordan sallies in, irritated that she and the other guests are being kept waiting at the dinner table. Glancing quite calmly at the gun in Jordan's hand, she asks if Hannay will be staying for lunch. The Professor does not think so. The husband/wife relationship here raises the question of marriage as a kind of screen or cover and opens the possibility of seeing below the surface of another relationship. If Margaret and John hid their feelings, they were nevertheless right below the surface. The Professor and his wife demonstrate how layers of refinement can disguise depths of evil.

The conclusion of the sequence at Jordan's mansion – the "death" of Hannay – jerks us both backward and forward. The Professor shoots Hannay to eliminate the risk of disclosure; the film cuts to John and Margaret as she confesses she gave the stranger his coat with the Bible in the pocket, a confession that earns her his abusive blows in return; the soundtrack delivers laughter as we cut to the police station and a close-up of the Bible with the Professor's bullet lodged in it. The sheriff's joke about some of those hymns being powerful hard to get through also provokes the ironic realization that John's religion has done some good after all, though only through Margaret's intercession. Indeed, the contrast of Margaret and Annabella, to this point, indicates that women may function as sources of liberation as well as of confinement or entrapment. This zigzagging between these seemingly contradictory states, freedom and bondage, will continue throughout the film, with Pamela finally uniting the two themes by providing freedom *through* confinement.

The next significant male/female encounter in the film follows Hannay's escape from the sheriff and his participation, handcuffs and all, in a Salvation Army parade. Once he has left the marchers he ducks into a doorway labeled "Assembly Hall" to elude the police. As he does so, Hannay is promptly seized by a woman who announces that they have been waiting for him and pushes him out onto a stage where another woman beckons him to be seated. After a mumbled introduction by another man and with some prompting from the woman seated next to him, Hannay finally rises to make a speech. However, as he is beginning to say how pleased, and perhaps relieved, he is to be on that stage before this audience, the blonde from the train enters the hall in the company of a man, presumably the politician whom Hannay has been mistaken for.

Both Hannay and the woman seem surprised to see each other. Hannay continues to speak – to the effect that as long as he is on this stage he is delivered from the cares, and also the dangers, of the day; about his ride on the Highland Express; about the bridge at the Firth of Forth, in the process recalling (to his mind and ours) the location of his first meeting with the blonde woman. Meanwhile Pamela starts up the side aisle to get help – at which point she encounters two of the Professor's men. Mistaking them for policemen (though they most resemble Gestapo agents with their long leather coats), she confides to them that Hannay is an escaped criminal. They follow her back up the side aisle while Hannay, seeing this, becomes all the more impassioned about banishing cruelty and fear and oppression and of knowing how it feels to have the whole world against you. It is a compilation/distillation of Hannay's experience so far and suggests a change in his perspective. His world has widened and he has been made aware, as have we, of something missing in his life – passion and commitment. He now accidentally dangles the loose handcuff (the sheriff only managed to close one of the manacles before Hannay bolted) as an image of his incompleteness, of his need of another. As he finishes the speech he tries to exit through the front of the hall, but the pressing crowd pushes him back into the waiting arms of the Professor's thugs. Desperate, Hannay turns to Pamela, imploring her to call the High Commissioner of Canada, thus unwittingly implicating her (as Annabella had more knowingly implicated Hannay) in the effort against Jordan. The "police," accordingly, ask Pamela to come along as well.

And again it is a woman who helps Hannay to escape. Angry or not, haughty or not, Pamela is far more observant than Hannay (the result of prior experience – of memory?) in noticing first that the car has passed the local constabulary. Her saying so forces their captors to fabricate a story about having to take them to Inverary, and it is Pamela who precipitates Hannay's decision to run for it when she subsequently notices the signpost indicating that the car is not heading in the direction of Inverary at all. Hannay is quick to pick up on the implications of her observations and asks to see the warrant for his arrest – at which moment he begins to whistle the Mr. Memory tune from the Music Hall sequence. In spite of the fact that he has been among the spies before, it is not until he is with Pamela that he begins the process of unraveling the mystery of their "39 steps" organization. The reappearance of this little music-hall tune symbolizes the beginning of what proves to be Hannay's final awakening. It is vitally important that the first appearance of it should be with Pamela – as if she were responsible for his memory.

Hannay follows up his original request to see the warrant by betting Pamela that the police are not police at all, that they work for a man whose little finger, right hand, is missing something. Hannay gets slugged for his trouble (like Margaret for hers?). As Hannay says "I win," Pamela looks at him in shock (as if she too had been slugged?). She is now consciously aware that things are not always what they seem. Hannay reintroduces the joke motif as the car skids to a stop amid a flock of sheep. Lots of detectives he quips. Getting out of the car to clear the road, one of the spies fastens the other handcuff to Pamela's wrist, remarking that she is now a special constable and that Hannay will stay with her. Or go with him, Hannay says, exiting the other side of the auto.

This brilliant stroke of handcuffing Hannay and Pamela brings together a number of themes associated with sex and coupling and marriage that have become established features of the film.[5] The comic spectacle of two adults of the opposite sex handcuffed together, especially the subsequent episode of Pamela removing her hosiery, suggests both the dirty-joke motif as well as the issue of eroticism as previously represented by the Mae West reference, by Annabella's come-on to Hannay, by the brassiere/girdle images associated with the salesmen on the train, by the crofter's sexual possessiveness and voyeurism, and so on. It also brings forward once again the many direct references to marriage – the milkman's, the salesman's "my wife – burr," John and Margaret, the Jordans – all people tied or chained together. The loose cuff, shiny and circular, suggests a wedding ring, as well as whatever level of commitment and bond goes with it – or should.

The escape scene also recalls Hannay's earlier flight as he drags Pamela over waterways and across terrain resembling that which he encountered after fleeing the crofter's. The most important section of this sequence takes place as Hannay and Pamela walk along the fog-enshrouded road. Hannay whistles the Mr. Memory tune; Pamela tells him to stop. Throughout this scene she snaps back at Hannay, suggesting her mettle and independence of spirit. She asks him why he is doing all of this if he cannot possibly escape; Hannay tells her to keep such questions for her husband. The implication is strong by film's end – given the film's underlying concern with sexuality generally and marriage especially – that he will indeed become her husband, so the remark here is both appropriate and prophetic, like the remark to Annabella about her funeral. Hannay now mentions that the two men who captured them were not police, and Pamela asks when he noticed – to which Hannay replies that she too should have seen that they were impostors: it was right under her nose, he tells her, suggesting that she needs to observe things more carefully. While criticizing her, he also compliments her on her observation that they were not going in the right direction, which he admits he had not seen. When he now tells her the spy story for the third time, she responds as before by comparing his confession to an espionage thriller. As if on cue, Hannay tries a new tack and becomes menacing, taking on a melodramatic stance reminiscent of Annabella's death scene in which her choking and overacting followed soon upon Hannay's remark that *her* explanation sounded like a spy story. Hannay's allusions to archfiends and defenseless women elicits Pamela's mildly unconvincing assertion that she is not at all frightened – at which point she sneezes, breaking Hannay's theatrical moment and pose. Genuinely exasperated at Pamela's refusal to believe him, Hannay seizes her by the coat and tells her seriocomically to do everything he tells her to, and quickly. In the last line of the scene Hannay confesses that, after all, he likes her pluck. He then begins to whistle the Memory tune as the scene fades.

Two important points about this encounter stand out. One is that Pamela is not much put off by any of Hannay's ruses, being neither scared, nor convinced, nor even very angry at him – all of which points to their growing relationship of commitment. Secondly, Hannay openly admits to Pamela that he admires her spirit, an admiration grounded in Hannay's experience and memory. He has been surrounded by assertive women all along; Annabella is a spy whose financial cynicism seems more assumed than real; Margaret in her quiet way shows enormous daring by defying John; even Mrs. Jordan snaps at the Professor for keeping lunch. Pamela's grit becomes attractive to Hannay here because he has encountered other women with similar toughness and because Pamela is both desirable and unattached. Hannay's remark, then, is more than incidental. It sets up the sequence at the inn where Pamela will finally believe Hannay and acknowledge her love for him.

The next woman on Hannay's itinerary is the innkeeper's wife and we are asked to judge whether or not she is as perceptive as the rest of the women in the film in her assessment of the lovers, despite their quite evident antagonism. There are several occasions when the landlady sees through the obvious. For example, when Hannay and Pamela feign coziness in front of the fire as the landlady brings in the tray of food, Hannay remarks that they are "warming" themselves – to which the landlady replies "I can *see* that." What she "sees" is the young couple warming themselves in a sexual way. Perhaps this explains why the promised nightgown never appears: the landlady assumes Pamela will not really need it. In the landlady we also have another instance of someone who finds humor in sex – though not of the smirking variety seen elsewhere in the film. Her humor is more knowing and romantic in tenor. Hers is a woman's view of sexuality and its awkwardnesses that recalls especially Margaret's impassioned naivety about beautiful women and painted toenails. Where men seem incapable of dealing with their sexuality except through crude, even brutal joking, women in *The 39 Steps* learn to accept sexuality with understanding. When finally told by Hannay that he and Pamela are a runaway couple on their wedding night, a story he fabricates to cover Pamela's gaff in recalling the landlady as she is about to leave the room, the landlady responds by saying that she knew it all along.

What the landlady understands as a question of intimacy in marriage, Pamela understands as a more immediate question of sex. It is instructive that she never appears to fear for her life from Hannay but is terrified of spending the night sleeping with him. Sex is a more powerful fright than death (cf. the crofter's relief at learning that Hannay is wanted for murder and is not seducing his wife). The sex question finds visual expression when Hannay drags Pamela upstairs at the inn. As they enter the room, framed in the doorway, their arms outstretched but manacled together, they frame the double bed between them. Once inside the room there is also the question of how they will sleep. As with Annabella and later at the crofter's, Hannay will sleep fully clothed, but there is a good deal of banter in this later scene about Pamela's taking off her wet clothes. Pamela refuses all suggestions that she remove her wet skirt, though Hannay assures her of his indifference: "I don't mind." It is a throwaway line that rather succinctly sums up the ambivalence of this scene. Hannay *really* does not mind. He is man of the world enough not to be shocked by female nudity but is also tired enough and gentleman enough not to have any sexual designs on Pamela. At least not on this particular night. Given his previous behavior and the calming effect his gestures of concern have on Pamela, we have to trust his good manners here.

Witness, for example, the rapid change in attitude Pamela undergoes in the scene where she does remove her stockings. In part, the scene's impact reinforces the erotic references in the film and reminds us of the jokelike ridiculousness of the spectacle of two adults handcuffed together. Pamela's awkwardness in removing her stockings with Hannay's cuffed hand trailing across her bare legs is both comic and erotic. Hannay's limp hand, only once showing any interest in Pamela's knee, is ample visual proof of Hannay's sincerity about not being a sexual threat. And when Hannay helps her hang up the stockings, her thank you is much quieter and more heartfelt than her no thank you was when he offered to help remove her hose. The change in mood here is remarkable; Pamela has seen something that will prepare her for the bantering scene on the bed and the final revelation disclosed by the conversation she later overhears as the spies phone Mrs. Jordan from the bar below.

When Hannay suggests going to bed, Pamela once again reacts according to type, though he quickly soothes her by declaring a truce, to the battle of the sexes presumably, and announcing that all he wants is a good night's sleep. The truce allows both of them to enjoy the long and rather amusing story Hannay tells about his life of crime. Pamela even has to suppress a laugh at one point to keep Hannay from realizing that she is enjoying the story and thereby relaxing in his company. The jokes about the Cornish Bluebeard remind us again of the sex/death/joke connection and highlight the series of "stories" Hannay has been telling since he began his flight. The sad tale of his life apparently puts Pamela to sleep, and as they both settle down the film fades to the scene of Professor Jordan's oddly emotional and moving farewell to his family as he departs for London.

The departure of the Professor takes us back to the inn and Pamela's escape from Hannay. Once Pamela awakens, she turns her attention to removing her hand from the cuff, which she does with some pain. As she is about to put on her hose, preparatory to leaving the room and the sleeping Hannay, she hears a noise downstairs in the bar. Stealing out onto the landing she overhears the phone call from the spies to Mrs. Jordan, a portion of which confirms Hannay's story. As the garrulous barkeep is about to reveal the whereabouts of Hannay and Pamela, his wife appears and like an avenging angel whisks the inquiring spies out into the night, declaring that there will be no after-hours drinking. And warming to her husband as she closes the door, she smiles and coos to her "old fool" about not wanting to give away the young lovers, to which he also smiles and looks heavenward. Overhead, Pamela hears all this and returns to her room a changed woman, now protective in her turn rather than combative – as if having suddenly seen all of Hannay's previous actions anew, in a new light, an act of memory, the precedent for which we have already seen in Hannay's memorial envisioning of Annabella after her murder. Smiling down at the sleeping Hannay, Pamela now pulls the blanket over him. She then settles herself on the bench at the foot of the bed, thus reversing the sleeping arrangement of Hannay and Annabella earlier.

When Hannay awakens the next morning, he glances at the empty handcuff, then to the open door. He smiles to himself, unconcerned if not philosophical about Pamela's escape; the smile almost betokens admiration. As he glances to the foot of the bed, however, Pamela sits up and returns his smile in full measure. He is puzzled. "What's the idea? How did we get out of these?" "*We* didn't, I did" she replies, maintaining the tone of verbal give and take that has characterized their relationship all along. Pamela tells Hannay how she discovered the truth and of her decision to stick around. Her volunteering to stay with him and help him constitutes a commitment on her part that Hannay will acknowledge and accept in the final frames of the film. She also, for the second time, supplies him with information that will aid him to expose the spies and clear himself. She also confesses that she has been a fool and apologizes for doubting him, a gesture he humbly accepts by telling her that it really is all right. The mood of companionship and mutual acknowledgment continues as Hannay gently suggests they get moving if they are to get ahead of the spies whom he thinks are still asleep at the inn. When Pamela says that they left last night, however, Hannay explodes and becomes his old self again, calling her a "button-headed little idiot" for failing to understand the gravity of the situation. Hannay's outburst here reminds us that love will not entirely alter these characters we have come to know. It is also an assurance that one of the strengths of their relationship is their ability to remain individuals within it, even though Hannay still has a murder charge hanging over his head – as he points out to Pamela. Her response, like Hannay's to Annabella, is to suggest they contact the police rather than take personal responsibility for foiling Jordan's espionage scheme.

The scene shifts to London, where it is Pamela's turn to discover the futility of dealing with the police, and specifically with their inability to believe her story. It is as if they cannot take her seriously – as Mr. Memory would not take seriously the woman who first rose to question his authority, his knowledge, in the film's opening scene.

The final sequence of *The 39 Steps*, at the Palladium, brings the film full circle. The laughing, smoking "Crazy Months" audience, although more genteel than their Music Hall predecessors, still recalls, if only by virtue of what its members choose to view and laugh at, the earlier crowd. Again we follow a central character into the theater, only this time it is Pamela, not Hannay, and she is also followed by police (as Annabella followed Jordan's thugs). At first Pamela cannot find Hannay, but by going to the balcony she spots him from above, as we first saw Annabella in a shot from above. Furthermore, Hannay is sitting pretty much in the same location as earlier. Except this time he is not just observing but looking for something specific.

He borrows a woman's opera glasses, as if to signify his adoption of a woman's vantage point, through which (and only through which) he espies the stunted maleness figured in Professor Jordan's little finger. Pamela arrives and asks Hannay what he will do, just as Mr. Memory's tune strikes up. The puzzle is complete. That is what he has not been able to get out of his head: the tune, Annabella, the Music Hall ... the memories come in rapid succession. Again Hannay raises the woman's opera glasses. What he sees is the Professor signaling to Mr. Memory with a pocket watch, suggesting it is time to go and implying, perhaps, that Mr. Memory's memory has fallen under an hypnotic spell. "I've got it," Hannay announces, just as police storm down the side aisle (recalling Pamela at the political rally). Confronting the police, Hannay tries one last time to tell his story. Again, disbelief follows upon propriety. In desperation Hannay charges back into the audience and challenges Mr. Memory to explain "the 39 steps," which, after brief hesitation, he starts to do. Again shots ring out; Mr. Memory is hit; Jordan leaps from the balcony; again an audience panics. The police – brought there unwittingly, though providentially, by Pamela, as if to witness Hannay's redemption from guilt – close in on Jordan as the curtain falls.

The delicacy of the film's concluding sequence is hard to capture in words. On the one hand, Mr. Memory's backstage, confession-like recitation of the Air Ministry secrets redeems Hannay and confirms the liberating power that the exercise of memory can have, and almost offhandedly resolves the "spy" plot. As if to confess and confirm their own memories – Hannay's of all the women he has encountered, Pamela's of Hannay – each quietly seeks the other out, their hands entwining as the image fades. Hannay and Pamela thus come together voluntarily, without the restrictions that manacle the other couples in the film, a fact symbolized by the now dangling and useless handcuff that hangs between them as they stand together, backs to the camera.[6]

On the other hand, as William Rothman points out, the recollections invoked in the final shots, specifically those connotations clustered around the initial music-hall sequence, carry decidedly negative implications, evidenced chiefly by the line of high-stepping, barely clad chorines visible in the background while Mr. Memory confesses to Hannay. Their presence is intended to calm panic and to reassert the music-hall norm, sexuality as gag or display, as something not serious, which replaces or displaces the life-or-death drama just enacted (it literally takes the place previously occupied by Mr. Memory and Professor Jordan). Thus it matters tremendously that in the film's last frame Hannay and Pamela displace the dancing chorines in our field of vision. What we remember of them, what they might be remembering of themselves, stands literally opposed to the vision of women on view to the world of the film. Hannay and Pamela embody the secret of sexual equality and acknowledgment represented by the memories they bear and bear witness to. And, whether they are members of another world or worldview, ours perhaps, depends on us, on the views we take and find memorable. In the words of William Rothman: "The camera's final gesture calls upon us to reaffirm our community with them. If we do so, we exempt ourselves from Hitchcock's indictment of the unviewed audience within the hall. We fulfill our calling as viewers" (p. 172).

Notes

1. William Rothman, *Hitchcock: The Murderous Gaze* (Cambridge, MA: Harvard Univ. Press, 1982), 125. The contents of this chapter as well as its form owe much to Rothman's excellent chapter on *The 39 Steps*.
2. Maurice Yacowar touches on this theme lightly in his discussion of the film in *Hitchcock's British Films* (Hamden, CT: Archon Books, 1977), 185 and *passim*.
3. François Truffaut, *Hitchcock* (New York: Simon and Schuster, 1967), 66.
4. Donald Spoto briefly deals with this point in his analysis of *The 39 Steps* in *The Art of Alfred Hitchcock* (New York: Hopkinson and Blake, 1976), 42–3.
5. See also Raymond Durgnat's ideas on handcuffing in *The Strange Case of Alfred Hitchcock* (Cambridge, MA: MIT Press, 1978), 129–30.
6. Stuart Y. McDougall writes about some of these same ideas, although his main point is to compare the adaptation of Hitchcock's film from the John Buchan novel; cf. "Mirth, Sexuality and Suspense: Alfred Hitchcock's Adaptation of *The Thirty-Nine Steps*," *Literature/Film Quarterly*, vol. 3, no. 3 (1975): 232–9. For an additional essay on the theme of adaptation, see also Jocelyn Camp, "John Buchan and Alfred Hitchcock," *Literature/Film Quarterly*, vol. 6, no. 3 (1978): 230–40.

THE 39 STEPS (Gaumont-British, 1935). *Producers*: Michael Balcon, Ivor Montagu, *Script*: Charles Bennett, Alma Reville, Ian Hay, from the novel by John Buchan, *Photography*: Bernard Knowles, *Editor*: Derek N. Twist, *Sets*: Otto Werndorff, Albert Jullion, *Music*: Louis Levy, *Costumes*: J. Strassner, *Players*: Madeleine Carroll (Pamela), Robert Donat (Richard Hannay), Lucie Mannheim (Annabella Smith), Godfrey Tearle (Professor Jordan), Peggy Ashcroft (the crofter's wife), John Laurie (the crofter), Wylie Watson (Mr. Memory). 86 minutes.

Chapter Ten

Rematerializing the Vanishing "Lady": Feminism, Hitchcock, and Interpretation

Patrice Petro

I

Whose desire does narrative speak? Does classical film narrative produce pleasure solely for the male spectator? Is all representation of female desire hopelessly caught within relations that situate man as bearer of the look, as the active and desiring viewer, and woman as merely the passive object of his gaze?

Ever since Laura Mulvey advanced this reading of classical cinema in "Visual Pleasure and Narrative Cinema," feminist theorists have returned to Hitchcock's films in an effort to address the question – and discern the possibility – of female desire in narrative.[1] This is not to suggest, however, that feminist theorists have reached any agreement about Hitchcock, narrative, or visual pleasure; indeed, the polemics that continue to rage on these issues, in and of themselves, raise further questions about the very function of feminist interpretation. Raymond Bellour, for example, agrees with Mulvey that Hitchcock's films inevitably reduce woman to the passive object of the male gaze. In his interpretation of *Marnie*, Bellour maintains further that Hitchcock's fascination with woman's image characterizes Hollywood cinema in general, where the "man-subject-behind-the-camera" guards against the disturbing fact of sexual difference by producing images of woman that define her desire in terms of his own. Reformulating the question Freud posed long ago ("What do women want?"), Bellour asks:

> What is orgastic pleasure for woman? What is the nature of her desire? ... This question is raised in two movements.... The first of these movements consists in the activation of an irreducible difference: "the dark continent of female sexuality" for Freud, the privilege granted to woman with respect to pleasure for Lacan (with its reverse side of ignorance ...); in Hollywood cinema [this movement involves the] extreme condensation of sexuality in the woman's body image. The second movement effects a calculated reduction of this magnified difference based on a single element: of which the woman's sexuality ... constitutes, for the man, a visible reversal, the mirror image.[2]

Where the representation of female desire effectively "vanishes" from Bellour's thinly veiled auteurist analysis of visual pleasure, it rematerializes in Tania Modleski's appropriation of a different practice and a different question for feminist interpretation. Countering Bellour, she argues that, in order for woman to mold her image according to man's desire, "she must first ascertain what that desire is. And given the complex and contradictory nature of male desire, it is no wonder that women become baffled, confused.... Although women have not had the chance to articulate the problem as directly as men have, they could easily ask Freud's question of the opposite sex: what is it they want?"[3] Rather than construct classical film narrative as monolithic or invariant, Modleski seizes upon its contradictions, which allow female desire to "speak," however tentatively or provisionally. To be sure, Modleski does not deny the force of Bellour's analysis of male power and pleasure in the cinema and in culture. Yet, rather than reproduce male Oedipal narratives in her own critical analyses, she interprets classical films differently so as to forge and identify a place for female subjectivity. As Modleski suggests: "Current film theory tends to agree with Roland Barthes that all traditional narratives re-enact the male Oedipal crisis.... While I do not mean to underestimate the strength of this position – we do, after all, live in a patriarchal society – I believe that we occasionally encounter a film which adopts a feminine viewpoint and allows the woman's voice to speak (if only in a whisper), articulating her discontent with the patriarchal order" (p. 34).

Such a film, for Modleski, is Hitchcock's *Rebecca* (1940). But, in my view, a much more forceful and less equivocal example of a female Oedipal (even anti-Oedipal) narrative is the film directed by Hitchcock two years earlier, *The Lady Vanishes* (1938). Despite the interest *The Lady Vanishes* might hold for feminists, and despite its canonical status as Hitchcock's penultimate British film, it has, of yet, received little critical attention. To date the most sustained and interesting close reading of the film is Raymond Durgnat's. While suggestive in his remarks about the film's maternal register – implicit in aspects of the Miss Froy/Iris relationship – Durgnat chooses to emphasize the film's historical and political import for its contemporary British audience.[4] He clearly acknowledges the questions and enigmas raised by *The Lady Vanishes* and attempts to interpret them without reducing their significance to a single or coherent meaning. Nevertheless, his contention that the film's secret tune is merely an element of the film's overall "musical atmosphere" and his suggestion that none of the characters (and particularly Iris) undergoes any profound change in the narrative are two readings my own analysis will contest.

If the title of *The Lady Vanishes* raises the question of woman, it also seems to suggest an inevitable narrative resolution: the "lady," the woman, the secret support of narrative and symbolic order must vanish from representation in order for the narrative to contain the threat she poses by virtue of her sexual difference. While a feminist analysis cannot entirely dismiss such a resolution, it is also important to stress that the film does not present the heroine's progression toward Oedipus and heterosexual union in a straightforward or inevitable way. Instead, *The Lady Vanishes* explores female desire both within and on the margins of Oedipal/paternal relations, occasioning a textual movement through which affectual desire is activated for the spectator by focusing upon the heroine's search for the mother and for what rapidly becomes the lost object of her original desire.

This affectual or original desire, it must be emphasized, is not exclusively a function of the spectator's identification with the heroine or of the heroine's desire for reunion with the mother. As Julia Kristeva explains, desire is never simply desire for an object (whether that object be the mother or the father) but also for an experience that precedes object choice and sexual differentiation (a desire rooted not in identification but in its dissolution).[5] The heroine's desire for that which exists on the boundaries of the Oedipus complex might be said to carry with it both the pleasurable experience of rhythm and movement as well as the threat of horror, fear, and psychosis that follows upon the dissolution of identification and representation. This double desire – desire for an object and desire for desire itself – is set into play for both the heroine and spectator of *The Lady Vanishes* through a musical theme. And quite appropriately, for music carries with it perhaps the least obvious reference to objects and the strongest reference to emotion and affect, serving to mark the heroine's erotic development and to foreground the role of the nonrepresentational (affect, rhythm, movement, drive) in addition to the representational (*mise-en-scène*, characters, plot) in the desiring process that is cinema. That this music is ultimately portrayed as lending fundamental support to the film's depicted (symbolic, economic, and political) order cannot be denied. It is nonetheless significant that the heroine never violently repudiates the maternal figure (as the Joan Fontaine character repudiates Mrs. Danvers in *Rebecca*) but activates the emotive power of maternal psychic energy in order to resist patriarchal definitions that seek to deny both her vision and her memory.

II

Over the credits that open *The Lady Vanishes* is the musical strain associated with Miss Froy, a phrase later identified as the secret tune carrying important information for European security. The camera reveals a serene mountain landscape, then passes over the results of a recent avalanche before the image dissolves to the chateau and then to the chateau lobby. The first human to interfere in the tranquility of this landscape is Miss Froy, the film's maternal figure, although she is soon forgotten in the pace of events that follow. After checking in at the desk, Miss Froy exits: two men enter and announce that an avalanche has blocked the railway lines, with the result that all passengers will be stranded at the chateau overnight. The composed *mise-en-scène* and melodious soundtrack give way to a cacophony of languages, sounds, and movements – to spatial and aural confusion. Miss Froy could thus be said to disturb the narrative's previously established order. And, indeed, what follows upon her departure is a rather fragmented introduction to the sexual "deviations" of the various characters: Caldicott and Charters, the two British gentlemen who bicker like a stereotypical married couple, are terrorized by the sexuality of the maid whose room they must share; "Mr. and Mrs." Todhunter, a couple who are involved in an extramarital affair, have lost the passion and intimacy they once had; Iris and her two girlfriends, whose bodies are displayed in a fragmented, specular series of shots, discuss the limitations of Iris's upcoming marriage to a British blue blood (Iris announces,

"I shall take the veil ... and change my name to Mrs. Charles Fotheringale.... I've no regrets. I've been everywhere, done everything.... What is there left for me but marriage?" – to which one of her friends responds, "Couldn't you get him to change *his* name instead?"); and Gilbert, a professional musicologist recording the ancient folk music of Central Europe, who interrupts the guitar serenade that enraptures Miss Froy and soothes Iris, both of whom occupy rooms directly beneath his.

Gilbert's music is, importantly, quite different from the music associated with Miss Froy. Serene, dangerous, and mysterious, Miss Froy's music carries with it what Kristeva has termed "abjection," the threat of horror, silence, and death as visualized in the strangulation of the lone guitarist who first performs it. In contrast, Gilbert's rendition of the ancient folk music of Central Europe is in no way natural, expressive, or evocative: he forces the rather reluctant servants to engage in a dance routine that he alone orchestrates and manipulates. His intent in performing this music is articulated, moreover, as a desire to preserve and promote the "ancient" sexual/ social relations of patriarchal culture (the dance Gilbert orders up, he explains to the chateau manager, is "the dance they danced when your father married your mother"), and thus Gilbert is implicated in what Kristeva in *Powers of Horror* calls the desire "to know everything, to know, in particular, what seems to be lacking in his mother or could be lacking in himself" (p. 34). Explicitly represented as competing with the guitar serenade, Gilbert's music so annoys Iris that she reports Gilbert to the management. In retaliation, Gilbert forces himself into her room, tosses his cane onto her bed (only after he kisses it), and challenges her to get rid of him. As representative of the patriarchal order, Gilbert's music (not to mention his rather obnoxious behavior, noisily singing, brushing his teeth, and running the bathwater) sets up a strong polarity between himself and Miss Froy, respectively distinguishing and identifying the paternal and maternal registers of the film.

These different registers in *The Lady Vanishes* are explored both in image and in music, which is to say, in both representational and nonrepresentational ways. Iris's initial resignation in the face of Oedipal imperatives, her apparent need to aspire to heterosexual union as expressed in her conversation with her girlfriends, is in fact reinforced by the accompanying images that abstract and fragment her body in erotic display (a display, it may be added, that even embarrasses the manservant when he delivers a rather large bottle of champagne that punctuates her image). This visual fixing of the female figure is nevertheless disrupted by the musical strains associated with both Gilbert and Miss Froy. And yet, rather than identify initially with the musical values associated with Gilbert (values that attempt to fix female positions in a hierarchical and paternalistic fashion in a way not unlike the images that fragment Iris's body), Iris will choose instead the maternal strain associated with Miss Froy. To be sure, Iris's choice for the maternal register is already anticipated by her relationship with her two girlfriends (she kisses them on the forehead and says, "Goodnight, my children"); she will nonetheless opt for maternal identification only after meeting Miss Froy again and sharing with her the experience of a different time and, indeed, a different desire.

Once the avalanche has been cleared and the passengers are able to proceed to London, yet another dislocation, again initiated by Miss Froy, disrupts narrative and spatial order. As Iris bids farewell to her friends, Miss Froy interrupts to ask if anyone has seen a piece of her luggage. Receiving only a quizzical response, Miss Froy walks away. Iris suddenly discovers that Miss Froy has inadvertently dropped her glasses and in returning them to her is struck on the head by a falling window box apparently intended for Miss Froy. (As a sign of female subjectivity, the glasses might be said to emphasize the risks involved when woman appropriates the gaze, especially when that woman is named "Iris.") Unable to delay the train's departure so that Iris might regain composure, Miss Froy assures Iris's friends that she will look after their companion and the two women board the train together. Now guided by Miss Froy, Iris embarks on a journey that leads her away from Oedipal desire and toward a desire characterized by delirium, displacement, and the threat of madness.

Iris's unsteady vision, evoked through a superimposed image of train wheels, smoke, and faces, suggests an aberration in her mental processes and calls into question for the spectator the "reality" of the sequence that follows. Significantly, this is the sequence where Iris and Miss Froy introduce themselves and share a conversation over a cup of tea. Iris introduces herself by situating her identity within the terms of patriarchal relations ("My name is Iris Henderson. I'm going home to get married"). Miss Froy, by contrast, introduces herself as a governess, but a train whistle drowns out her voice as she speaks her name. Struggling to make herself heard, Miss Froy pronounces her name precisely, but when Iris mistakes the assonance of "Froy" for "Freud," Miss Froy rhymes her name explicitly with "joy." Unmarried yet still maternal, joyful yet facing the constant threat of death as a secret agent, Miss Froy exists, not within patriarchal relations, but on their margins. Her recommendation to Iris that she have children may therefore be understood as a plea for a nonpatriarchal definition of motherhood, since Miss Froy herself performs a maternal function outside of marriage. Indeed, her very inability to speak her name situates her identity within a maternal realm that borders the unnameable, where subject identities exist, but only barely so.

This sequence of their meeting, the memory of which will later haunt Iris, is also rendered in ambiguous terms, bounded as it is by shots of train wheels that introduce, close, and reintroduce narrative action. As I have suggested, the first shot of train wheels is relayed from Iris's point of view: a superimposed image of smoke, faces, and train wheels, coded to be read as dreamlike, is followed by a shot of Iris waking from sleep. The shot of train wheels that closes the sequence is, by contrast, not superimposed and not coded as "unreal," and yet, like the first, it is followed by a shot of Iris waking from sleep. The organization of this sequence suggests the possibility that Iris has only imagined her encounter with Miss Froy, and that only upon waking from (her second) sleep does she regain "proper" consciousness. The dreamlike quality of their meeting is thereby reinforced cinematically, visualized as an intersection between the glimpse of a real object and a hallucination. Only the trace of Miss Froy's name on the dining-car window will reactivate the truth of their encounter for Iris (and by extension for the spectator), serving to verify not only Miss Froy's existence but Iris's perception as well.

That Iris's desire for and identification with Miss Froy takes place on a train suggests a further variation in the film's maternal register. The temporality of the train ride, in addition to representing a "male" register of time as linear, progressive, and teleological, also initiates a kind of rhythm that provides for Iris's entry into an earlier psychic realm, a realm of undifferentiated sexuality and temporality.[6] (Indeed, even when Iris is brought back into line with the paternal symbolic system, that is, even when she transfers her focus of desire from Miss Froy to Gilbert, the train is again dislocated and driven off the main rails. Male authority, it seems, must assert itself far more forcefully if narrative closure or resolution is to be enacted.) Where the chateau is somewhat static, confining, and baroque, the train allows for movement and rhythm. And where the artificial architecture of the chateau contributes to the representational potential of the characters, individuating them from their environment, the rhythm of the train serves as the site for Iris's projection of her desire, where what is repressed at the level of the narrative (the representation of Iris's desire for the mother) re-emerges through the *mise-en-scène* as hallucination, revealing Iris's desire to be analogous to that which psychoanalytic theory attributes to an inaugural loss (the loss of sexually undifferentiated affectual feelings that exist prior to maternal or paternal object choices), a loss upon which desire, language, and meaning are subsequently founded.

In direct opposition to Mulvey's and Bellour's analysis of visual pleasure in the cinema – where desire is understood to be rooted in a hierarchical system in which the man is the bearer of the look, the woman the object of his gaze – Iris initiates the investigation into Miss Froy's disappearance and controls through her gaze the narrative search for the lost object that is also a woman. Although Iris's attempt to account for Miss Froy is clearly mistrusted by the other characters within the fiction, read symptomatically her look offers resistance to the assertion that woman's status in the cinema is to be objectified as spectacle according to the masculine structure and motive of the cinematic gaze. In fact, Dr. Hartz's attempt to produce such a reading of Iris's investigating gaze, that is, his attempt to name female subjectivity as a sign of illness ("There was no Miss Froy," he tells her, "only a vivid, subjective image"), is likewise rendered suspect in the narrative. Not only is Dr. Hartz sinister, associated with the menace to international security; his theory is also understood by other characters (and, indeed, by the spectator) to be overly indulgent and dismissive of Iris's real experience. (When Iris tells him that one of the passengers has remembered Miss Froy, he replies: "My theory was a perfectly good one – the facts were misleading." The "facts" of woman's experience, it seems, are all too frequently passed over by psychoanalysis.) And when the doctor, in collaboration with the magician, substitutes Mme. Kummer for Miss Froy, Iris not only refuses to accept the substitution as a valid representation of the real object of her desire, but she also rejects the attempt to dematerialize her vision, to explain it away: she remembers and describes Miss Froy's dress exactly, down to the small blue handkerchief in her breast pocket.

Iris's refusal nevertheless carries with it the possibility of terror, where the lack of a signifiable object (Does Miss Froy exist? Is she an illusion?) calls attention to the basis of desire in that which exists prior to the selection of an object for desire. Iris's vision of Miss Froy is projected onto the faces of the other passengers, transforming her desire into an apparition materialized in the environment. The environment itself thus becomes threatening, causing Iris temporarily to suffer despair, isolation, and mental enclosure. Iris's state of delirium lasts only a short time, for she immediately pulls back from the threat of madness, from a desire that has foundered on drive and affect. Joining Gilbert, who advises her to make her mind "blank," she desperately tries to repress her memory and her vision. Gilbert's incessant talk about his father ("it's surprising how many great men began with their fathers") – that is, his attempt to bring her into line with the paternal order – leaves Iris unmoved. She returns to the topic of Miss Froy and lapses into hysteria when Miss Froy's name reappears on the dining-car window. Importantly, this hysteria is attributed, not to her confusion about the boundary between subject and object, self and other, but to her conviction that a real object actually exists. Aggressively seizing control of the situation, Iris demands that the group take immediate action and pulls the emergency brake to halt the train when no action is forthcoming. With that gesture, she faints.

The potential danger of the female look is contained from this point on, as Iris's return to "mental health" becomes dependent on her alliance with Gilbert, to whom is delegated the gaze. Significantly, Iris's alliance with Gilbert does not follow the pattern of *Marnie*, where the female character ultimately aligns herself with the person functioning in the role of psychoanalyst.[7] Gilbert adopts the posture, not of the psychoanalytic interpreter, but of the quintessential British investigator: he plays Holmes to Iris's Watson and appropriates the investigating gaze while she remains the less privileged, if still inquisitive, sidekick.

Now constituted as a team, Gilbert and Iris search the train together for Miss Froy and stumble across Signor Doppo's "Vanishing Lady" apparatus. A mysterious figure whose presence seems weakly motivated in terms of the central narrative enigma, Signor Doppo, or perhaps more precisely his apparatus for dematerializing the female figure, nonetheless serves a crucial function in realigning Iris's desire. After "disappearing" into the magician's apparatus, Iris emerges only to be subdued (explicitly cast by Gilbert in the Watson role) and brutalized (she tumbles to the ground and is attacked by birds!). As a metaphor for the cinema itself, Signor Doppo's "Vanishing Lady" apparatus effects an inversion of Iris's previous image: her investigating gaze is made passive, her desire is transformed according to patriarchal definitions of female sexuality. The title *The Lady Vanishes*, and the narrative's substitution of various female figures (Mme. Kummer for Miss Froy, the "nun" for a counterspy), could in fact be read as a self-conscious reference to the Méliès 1896 substitution-trick film, *The Vanishing Lady*, where the theatrical magician's attempt to master the threat posed by woman by making her vanish via the techniques of cinematic reproduction points to a fundamental relationship between the absence of woman and visual pleasure.[8] This magical aura of cinematic reproduction, when joined with the interpretative power of psychoanalysis in *The Lady Vanishes* (Signor Doppo works with Dr. Hartz in abducting Miss Froy), seems to suggest an even more insidious relationship between technologies that attempt to erase female desire or subjectivity by excluding it from representation.

It would be a mistake, however, to take this reading at face value and to assume the narrative logic of *The Lady Vanishes* (or classical narrative cinema in general) to work simply to recuperate female desire and make it submit to male authority, for a number of disturbances continue to riddle the film's portrayal of gender relations long after Iris has transferred her desire from Miss Froy to Gilbert. To be sure, Iris's brush with madness, the result of Dr. Hartz's reading of her symptoms, renders her susceptible to psychoanalytic suggestion. (When Dr. Hartz says he has poisoned their drinks, Iris passes out and Gilbert merely feigns sleep. When Gilbert discovers that the drinks were perfectly harmless, it is Iris alone who becomes the object of ridicule, engaging as she does in strenuous exercises to keep from falling asleep, a state she associates with madness.) Gilbert, moreover, clearly initiates all further narrative action: it is he who risks death by climbing through the train window to silence Mme. Kummer and he who steers the train back to the main line. Points of female resistance to male authority nonetheless remain, notably in the figure of the "nun," whose high-heeled shoes counter her saintly and servile image and whose muteness serves, not as a sign of (female) hysteria or aphasia, but instead as a disguise that allows her to assume a degree of control and narrative mastery.

Most important, however, is the presence of Miss Froy, who, despite the machinations of doctors, magicians, and self-centered British travelers, refuses to disappear. Entrusting Gilbert with protecting and transmitting crucial narrative information musically encoded in a tune, she attempts to transform the paternal register of the film by bringing it into contact with a distinctly maternal realm. Miss Froy, a governess and a music teacher, and Gilbert, a professional musicologist, are thereby linked through the song that opens and initially disrupts symbolic order. Fittingly enough, Gilbert forgets the tune once he has consummated his union with Iris; that is, once Iris has "vanished" from her fiancé's sight and affirmed her desire for Gilbert, Gilbert loses the memory of the maternal realm passed on to him. Quite appropriately, he can only reproduce the "Wedding March" at the foreign office. Nonetheless, the maternal strain is reactivated in the final sequence of the film, and again by Miss Froy, only this time she does not simply hum or listen to it but plays it on the grand piano in Whitehall. Maternal psychic energy, in the service jointly of patriarchy and the "mother country," thereby emerges as the ultimate – and no longer secret – support of both narrative and symbolic order.

III

The guiding question that opened this chapter – Whose desire does narrative speak? – was meant to raise the issue of psychoanalytic and cinematic discourses in relation to the theorization of female subjectivity. The received psychoanalytic interpretations of cinematic identification and visual pleasure leave no doubt that desire in narrative is fundamentally masculine. And yet, as my analysis of *The Lady Vanishes* suggests, narrative can – and often does – produce a place, however provisionally, for woman to tell her story and speak of her desire. Iris's initial refusal to accede to Oedipal imperatives by focusing her desire on Miss Froy instead of Gilbert, for example, sets into play the terms of her identification with maternal psychic energy – an identification that has the effect of interrupting her Oedipal "normalization" and revealing a desire rooted, not in repression, but in resistance. That is to say, Iris's desire for the mother is not a desire for the utilitarian, social, and symbolic aspect of motherhood as defined by patriarchy but for the negating side of her symbolic position. It is significant, therefore, that Iris's brush with madness, her movement away from the maternal and toward a state of undifferentiated (that is, as yet unsexed) desire, does not situate her desire outside of Oedipus and representation. On the contrary, it leads her to confront the patriarchal symbolic order and to refuse its definitions, which exclude a place for her identity, her experience, and her memory. While not entirely "progressive" in its representation of female desire (Iris does, after all, shift her erotic attachment from the maternal to the paternal figure and relinquish her aggressive and investigating gaze), *The Lady Vanishes* nevertheless opens up a space where female desire can be articulated, where the female figure can exercise some of the narrative control traditionally denied to her.

References to magic, cinema, and psychoanalysis in *The Lady Vanishes* also expose the discursive mechanisms whereby the female subject is conventionally reproduced. *The Lady Vanishes* can, therefore, be read as rendering visible those discourses and modes of analysis that assume female subjectivity to be illusory and static rather than culturally and materially produced by a number of specific textual, discursive, and institutional practices. While the narrative development of *The Lady Vanishes* clearly works to fix and center traditionally patriarchal female and male positions, it also explores the negative side of this Oedipal paradigm – the maternal power to refuse, withdraw from, and disturb the symbolic space. Miss Froy, for example, while never exceeding the boundaries of symbolic relations as defined by patriarchy, nonetheless offers resistance to them, impeding Iris's erotic development by putting into play through her own ambivalent maternal function the possibility of a different desire.

My own interpretation of *The Lady Vanishes*, I must emphasize, should not be taken as a neutral or even exhaustive reading of the film (even if such a thing were possible). Indeed – and this must be kept in mind when consuming or producing textual criticism – there are political implications in every interpretative act, whatever meaning that interpretation seeks to bestow. This is not meant to suggest, however, that all readings should be regarded as of equal value, for readings can be assessed politically only in terms of their consequences in and for the present. Durgnat's interpretation of *The Lady Vanishes*, for example, is decidedly not a feminist reading of the film. While he certainly raises a number of interesting and clearly useful ideas for feminist criticism, his own position remains markedly idiosyncratic and less concerned with those issues that a feminist criticism would – indeed, must – seize upon.

Furthermore, in contrast to Mulvey's and Bellour's negative appraisal of the possibility for female desire to speak in narrative, as a feminist critic I prefer to follow the interpretative procedure outlined by Modleski and recently expanded upon by Teresa de Lauretis.[9] Their view that psychoanalysis and the cinema can and do address the experience of the female subject (even if they often will not or do not) and their contention that feminist practice must construct that experience in criticism and in narrative are, for me, absolutely uncontestable tenets for feminist interpretation. Rather than assume systems of signification (whether classical narrative, psychoanalytic theory, or cinematic reproduction) to be fixed in relation to female subjectivity and rather than attempt to place woman somewhere outside of narrative or representation, feminist criticism would do better to disrupt the prevailing array of discourses so as to produce new subject identities and, above all, new forms of political alliance through which moments of historical rupture might be constituted. It goes without saying that, in following through with such an interpretative project, feminist criticism would also have to bypass debates over the inherent meaning of Hitchcock's films for women; the point is that meanings do not inhere in texts alone nor can they be prescribed or assured for once and all time.[10] The notion I have entertained throughout my analysis of *The Lady Vanishes* – namely, that its narrative and visual organization reflects upon and transforms representational and theoretical discourses (the cinema and psychoanalysis respectively) so as to reveal and reconstitute them – must therefore be qualified and restated. That is to say, it is not cinematic narrative alone but feminist criticism that reveals and reconstitutes the cultural and ideological discourses that texts refer to and engage. Because a text's political effects are produced only in acts of viewing, analysis, and interpretation, feminist critics must therefore attend to the experiences of women as spectators and adopt an active position toward textual phenomena. It seems to me that the task of rematerializing the "vanishing lady" has to begin by wrenching so-called classical films from the ways in which they are customarily received so as to mobilize them in different, and more politically relevant, directions.

Notes

1. Laura Mulvey, "Visual Pleasure and Narrative Cinema," *Screen*, vol. 16, no. 3 (Autumn 1975): 6–18.
2. Raymond Bellour, "Hitchcock, The Enunciator," *Camera Obscura*, no. 2 (1977): 85–6.
3. Tania Modleski, " 'Never to Be Thirty-Six Years Old': *Rebecca* as Female Oedipal Drama," *Wide Angle*, vol. 5, no. 2 (1983): 38.
4. Raymond Durgnat, *The Strange Case of Alfred Hitchcock* (Cambridge, MA: MIT Press, 1974), 142–63. Maurice Yacowar, in *Hitchcock's British Films* (Hamden, CT: Archon Books, 1977), also discusses the "maternal" implications of Miss Froy in *The Lady Vanishes*, but he conflates maternity and "family" and finds the latter notion altogether unproblematic; hence my own reading of the film cuts directly against the grain of his.
5. Julia Kristeva, "Something to Be Scared Of," in *Powers of Horror: An Essay on Abjection* (New York: Columbia Univ. Press, 1982), 32–55. See also her "Ellipsis on Dread and the Specular Seduction," *Wide Angle*, vol. 3, no. 3 (1979): 45–6.
6. Julia Kristeva, "Women's Time," *Signs*, vol. 7, no. 1 (1981): 16. See also Tania Modleski's discussion of time and memory in her "Time and Desire in the Woman's Film," *Cinema Journal*, vol. 23, no. 3 (1984): 19–30.
7. For an interesting analysis of *Marnie* see Mary Ann Doane, "The Dialogical Text: Filmic Irony and the Spectator," Ph.D. dissertation, University of Iowa, 1979.
8. See, e.g., Lucy Fischer, "The Lady Vanishes: Women, Magic, and the Movies," *Film Quarterly*, vol. 33, no. 1 (1979): 30–40; and Linda Williams, "The Film Body: An Implantation of Perversions," *Cine-Tracts*, vol. 3, no. 4 (1981): 19–35.
9. See Teresa de Lauretis's discussion of "Semiotics and Experience" in *Alice Doesn't: Feminism, Semiotics, Cinema* (Bloomington: Indiana Univ. Press, 1984), 158–86.
10. I am indebted to Tony Bennett for this formulation. See his "Marxism and Popular Fiction," *Literature and History*, vol. 7, no. 2 (1981): 138–65.

THE LADY VANISHES (Gainsborough, 1938). *Producer*: Edward Black, *Script*: Sydney Gilliatt, Frank Launder, Alma Reville, from the novel *The Wheel Spins* by Ethel Lina White, *Photography*: Jack Cox, *Editors*: Alfred Roome, R. E. Dearing, *Sets*: Alex Vetchinsky, Maurice Cater, Albert Jullion, *Music*: Louis Levy, *Players*: Margaret Lockwood (Iris Henderson), Michael Redgrave (Gilbert), Dame May Whitty (Miss Froy), Paul Lukas (Dr. Hartz), Cecil Parker (Mr. Todhunter), Naugton Wayne (Caldicott), Basil Radford (Charters). 97 minutes.

Part Three
Hitchcock in Hollywood

It is arguable that Hitchcock never left Britain entirely behind him. As Philip French observes, Hitchcock continued to rely on British (and French) novels or stories late into his Hollywood career: *Stage Fright, The Trouble with Harry, The Birds, Frenzy,* and *Family Plot* all derive from English literary sources. And Hitchcock never hesitated to cast his films – even those set primarily in America – with British actors: Claude Rains and Cary Grant in *Notorious*; Leo G. Carroll in *Spellbound, Strangers on a Train,* and *North by Northwest*; Cary Grant and James Mason in *North by Northwest*; Sean Connery in *Marnie*, and so on. Yet Hitchcock's move to Hollywood seems in retrospect an inevitable step in his development. He had done as much in Britain as he could. Indeed, the successful series of films from *The Man Who Knew Too Much* through *The Lady Vanishes* threatened to lock him forever into the comedy-thriller format. Moreover, Hitchcock got his start in cinema working for the London office of Famous Players–Lasky ("You might say I had an American training," as Hitchcock put it in the Truffaut interview (p. 125)), and he obviously reveled in the technical opportunities that working in Hollywood made available to him. But more than technology was involved in Hitchcock's decision to leave Britain. As Philip French remarks: "America was a place of reality and dream for Hitchcock.... He saw in the freer, larger, more dangerous, more socially mobile American society the possibility of discovering the objective correlatives for his powerful feelings about violence and sexuality" (p. 117). Only in Hollywood, or so French implies, could Hitchcock's agonized Britishness find its full expression.

At least initially, however, Hitchcock found himself no less restricted in Hollywood than he had been in England. While his contract with David O. Selznick was handsome enough, he soon realized that his new employer took as much interest in his day-to-day work as had his English producers. It made little difference that Selznick genuinely meant well in his concern about every detail for the production of *Rebecca* (1940), Hitchcock's first Hollywood effort. Selznick rankled Hitchcock by forcing him to adhere to a script as close to Daphne du Maurier's novel as the Production Code Administration would permit and by his protracted search for the actress to play the title role. Hitchcock responded to Selznick's intrusive supervision by slowing down the speed at which he worked and shooting only enough footage to ensure that the film could be cut together only as he wished. Selznick, who had been used to having alternate takes to cut together, found himself stymied. Yet, for all of this, Selznick's interference was far less than it might have been had he not been so busy attending to the final details of *Gone with the Wind*, which occupied most of his attention during this time.

Worse than his intrusions was Selznick's ultimate failure to provide the stability that Hitchcock had hoped for. In 1940 Selznick began to dismantle Selznick International Pictures as part of a plan to minimize the taxes he would have to pay on the extraordinary profits from both *Gone with the Wind* and *Rebecca*. Then, worn out from the demands of the business, he finally closed his studio at the end of 1941 and gave up active production for three years. He retained, however, some personal contracts with performers and directors, including Hitchcock, for his new company, David O. Selznick Productions. So began a series of lucrative loan-outs as Selznick made deals for Hitchcock to work elsewhere. Thus, while he made *Rebecca* directly for Selznick, Hitchcock was loaned out to Walter Wanger for *Foreign Correspondent* (1940), to RKO for *Mr. and Mrs. Smith* (1941) and *Suspicion* (1941), to Universal for *Saboteur* (1942) and *Shadow of a Doubt* (1943), and to Twentieth Century-Fox for *Lifeboat* (1944) before actually working for Selznick again on *Spellbound* (1945).

While these loan-outs gave Hitchcock the welcome opportunity to familiarize himself with the superb technical facilities of the industry, he was not always able to develop the scripts for these films in advance or do as much preproduction planning on each project as he would have liked. In addition, he came to resent the profits Selznick made by hiring him out to others, often for twice his own salary. All these inconveniences continued even during his final two films for Selznick. *Notorious* (1946) was sold as a package to RKO with its script virtually complete, while *The Paradine Case* (1947) was shot entirely under Selznick's aegis. As had been the case with *Rebecca*, Hitchcock chafed under Selznick's constant supervision, though it too might have been more oppressive had the producer not been preoccupied with making *Duel in the Sun*.

(In the midst of these loan-outs, Hitchcock made two films for the British war effort. Leaving postproduction work on *Lifeboat* to his wife, he flew to England to direct the pair of brief, French-language three-reelers intended by the British Ministry of Information to support the Free French cause. The films, *Aventure Malgache* and *Bon Voyage*, both of which employ intricate flashbacks, were shot quickly during January and February 1944, with casts made up largely of French actors who had escaped to England after the fall of France. Though announced in the press, their existence was quickly forgotten – even by Hitchcock scholars! – until their release in 1990 by their original sponsor, the Ministry of Information.)

In December 1947 Hitchcock ended his association with Selznick to become his own independent producer. Together with his trusted English friend Sidney Bernstein, he established Transatlantic Pictures and directed *Rope* (1948) and *Under Capricorn* (1949), both of which were distributed by Warner Bros. Though he would not work with Selznick again, Hitchcock later alluded to his unhappiniess with him by making

Lars Thorwald, the killer in *Rear Window* (1954), resemble Selznick and by having Roger Thornhill in *North by Northwest* (1959) reflect upon how his middle initial, "O," meant nothing – an allusion to Selznick's decision early in his career to adopt "O" as his middle initial in the belief that it would make his name sound more distinguished. Yet, however unhappy Hitchcock may have been during these years because of Selznick's policies, the fact remains that this was a period of great personal growth for him as he tested the technical facilities of the industry, extended his exploration of the formal properties of the medium, and immeasurably deepened the implications of his recurrent themes.

Often Hitchcock spoke freely about the technical means available to him in Hollywood for heightening effects. He repeatedly explained, for example, how he managed to put a light bulb in a glass of milk in *Suspicion*; or devised the elaborate crane shot in *Notorious* that ends in a close-up of the wine-cellar key clutched in Alicia Huberman's hand; or constructed for *Rope* an intricate series of rheostats that smoothly modulated the New York City backdrop – from late-afternoon sunshine, to dusk, to a darkness set off by the miniature lights of studio skyscrapers. He discussed his continuing formal experiments in the medium less frequently, however, merely acknowledging *Lifeboat* as a problem in filming in a restricted set, describing the Dali-designed dream sequence in *Spellbound* as an attempt to render a dream in a hard-edged style, or categorizing the long takes of *Rope* and *Under Capricorn* as problems in coordination and execution. The more subtle details of these experiments he left unmentioned.

One can clearly see the need to go beyond Hitchcock's own guarded words about his work in the case of a film like *Rope*. Though Hitchcock dismissed his attempts at filming it in reel-long, ten-minute takes as a "stunt" in his discussion of the film with François Truffaut, the extraordinary care he takes to explain how he attempted to make the film's continuity appear seamless (by using a close-up of an actor's jacket to hide the reloading of the camera between reels) opens a series of questions for any student of cinema about the basic principles of the classical Hollywood style. If only because such long takes preclude the shot/reverse-shot cutting that is classicism's mainstay, Hitchcock's practice in *Rope* deserves closer scrutiny for what it may reveal about alternative systems of *mise-en-scène*.

In fact, disguising the end of one reel and the beginning of the next in the manner Hitchcock describes happens only part of the time in *Rope*. Not only does an undisguised straight cut early in the film move viewers directly into the apartment at the moment of the strangulation murder, but reel openings later are used to supply important reverse-shots that the long-take format otherwise denies. In one instance, the opening of a new reel suddenly isolates Mrs. Wilson as she begins to clear the chest in which the body has been hidden. The audience is left to wonder whether Brandon or Philip will notice her before she can lift the chest's lid. More importantly, the opening of a new reel coincides with the key dramatic moment when Rupert Cadell (James Stewart) realizes that Philip is lying about never having wrung the neck of a chicken. One reel ends on Philip as he denies the action; the next begins as essentially a reverse-shot of Rupert's reaction as he realizes that Philip is dissembling and begins to be suspicious of him. In this, as in its method of valorizing different areas of the apartment at different times through its *mise-en-scène*, *Rope* merits closer attention for what its formal properties can reveal to us about the making and reading of cinematic narratives.

As the chapters in this section reveal, the growing formal sophistication of Hitchcock's Hollywood films is accompanied by a deepening of their thematic resonances as well. Thus in writing about Bruno and Guy in *Strangers on a Train* (1951), Robin Wood identifies one essential Hitchcockian theme – "that ordered life depends on the rigorous and *unnatural* suppression of a powerfully seductive underworld of desire" – which is easily as applicable to the lesson young Charlie learns from her same-name uncle in the earlier *Shadow of a Doubt*. Similarly, James McLaughlin reads out from young Charlie's experience the recurring motif of later films in which powerful women are punished for desiring autonomy. As Richard Abel demonstrates through a sensitive structural reading of *Notorious*, such large-scale parallels between Bruno and Guy and the two Charlies are also illustrative of the more particular dynamics of cinematic coding and *mise-en-scène* that Hitchcock employs to establish and play upon the echoing psychological relationships among an individual film's cast of characters.

Indeed, this close relationship of psychological theme and symbolic visual form in Hitchcock's 1940s films reaches a culmination of sorts in *Spellbound*, where questions of visualization and displacement, of guilt conjured up and denied – questions that will eventually inform such films as *Rear Window* and *Vertigo* – become overt subject matter. Even here Hitchcock both disguises and declares his artistry: disguises it by engaging Salvador Dali to design the film's most overtly "artistic" sequence, John Ballantine's "dream" recollection of the murder of Dr. Edwardes, as if thereby to efface or downgrade his own authorship; but Hitchcock also quietly declares his authorial autonomy by rewriting the popular Freudian scenario of the "talking cure" to suit his own thematic ends. As Thomas Hyde observes in his discussion of the film, "the cure for John's amnesia is not found on the analyst's couch but rather emerges from a series of experiential trials culminating in John's physically re-enacting the episode which originally triggered his disturbance." Freudian psychoanalysis, at least in *Spellbound*, provides Hitchcock less with a master system than with yet another metaphoric framework through which to explore the visual and moral dynamics of the world he puts in view.

Though the relative commercial failures of *Rope* and *Under Capricorn* as the 1940s ended cost Hitchcock his own production company, the popular success of *Strangers on a Train* in 1951 assured him of another successful decade as an independent producer. Indeed, the decade in question was the decade in which Hitchcock began the series of masterpieces – from *Rear Window* through *Marnie* – for which he is chiefly known today. But between Hitchcock's 1939 arrival in Hollywood and the 1954 production of *Rear Window*, Hitchcock directed sixteen feature films, many of which are generally considered equally as masterful as his better-known movies. *Rebecca* has become a central text among feminist and lesbian Hitchcock scholars, as the film in which Hitchcock's ambivalent relationship with the "female Gothic" or the "woman's film" was established as central to his subsequent accomplishments. *Shadow of a Doubt* is generally accounted his most endearingly and disturbingly "American" film. *Spellbound* and *Notorious* gave Hitchcock the chance to work with Ingrid Bergman and to pose questions about what we might call the "sanity" of patriarchal gender relationships as those were complicated (perhaps "poisoned") by the tensions and stresses of the Second World War. And *Rope* has become a crucial site for considering the figural relationships between cinematic and sexual "connotation," given the way Hitchcock's technical *tour de force* apparently served to divert attention from the erotic implications of the homosocial relationships among Brandon, Philip, and Rupert Cadell.

The films of this period are also, by and large, the films that inspired Hitchcock's French partisans to insist that Hitchcock was a major force in world cinema, as James Vest has shown. Eric Rohmer and Claude Chabrol's *Hitchcock*, for example, discusses only one film (*Rear Window*) from among those typically seen as Hitchcock's major works of the late 1950s, and their book concludes with a lengthy analysis of *The Wrong Man*, which they see as a culminating achievement: "we are pleased to be able to conclude our study of [Hitchcock] with a film that not only brings together the themes scattered throughout his work but also eloquently proves that the attempt to illuminate the depths of his work was worth the effort" (p. 145).

To be sure, as John Orr points out, Rohmer and Chabrol were astonishingly prescient in describing *Rear Window* as "The Matrix-Figure," as a film about "the very essence of cinema, which is *seeing, spectacle*" (p. 124); their subsequent references to Kant and Leibnitz and Plato and their elaboration of the film's theological dimension as a treatise on the conflict of neighborliness and solitude set precedents for decades of commentary to come. But their points of Hitchcockian reference are *Strangers on a Train, I Confess*, and *The Wrong Man*. Put otherwise, the Hitchcock of his first Hollywood period was already an artist of true significance, even if the list of suggested readings below seems relatively brief by comparison to those for Parts Four and Five. However, many of the more recent critical studies devoted to Hitchcock – beginning with Tania Modleski's *The Women Who Knew Too Much* in 1988 – pay considerably more attention to this period than is evident below (Modleski discusses *Rebecca, Notorious*, and *Stage Fright*, and Orr devotes extended attention to *Notorious, The Paradine Case*, and *I Confess*.) It seems highly probable that the films of this era of Hitchcock's career will become ever more important to Hitchcock Studies in the decades ahead.

References and Suggested Readings

Anderegg, Michael. "Hitchcock's *The Paradine Case* and Filmic Unpleasure." *Cinema Journal*, vol. 26, no. 4 (Summer 1987): 49–59.

Auxier, Randall E. "Democracy Adrift in *Lifeboat*." In Baggett and Drumin (cited in Part One): 159–73.

Barton, Sabrina. "Crisscross: Paranoia and Projection in *Strangers on a Train*." In Creekmur and Doty (cited in Part One): 216–38.

Barton, Sabrina. "Hitchcock's Hands." In Gottlieb and Brookhouse (cited in Part One): 159–79. Emphasizes *Shadow of a Doubt*.

Berenstein, Rhona J. "Adaptation, Censorship, and Audiences of Questionable Type: Lesbian Sightings in *Rebecca* (1940) and *The Uninvited* (1944)." *Cinema Journal*, vol. 37, no. 3 (Spring 1998): 16–37.

Berenstein, Rhona J. " 'I'm not the Sort of Person Men Marry': Monsters, Queers, and Hitchcock's *Rebecca*." In Creekmur and Doty (cited in Part One): 239–61.

Biderman, Shai, and Eliana Jacobowitz. "*Rope*: Nietzsche and the Art of Murder." In Baggett and Drumin (cited in Part One): 33–45.

Britton, Andrew. "Hitchcock's *Spellbound*: Text and Counter-Text." *Cineaction*, nos. 3–4 (Winter 1986): 72–83.

Carringer, Robert L. "Collaboration and Concepts of Authorship." *PMLA*, vol. 116, no. 2 (March 2001): 370–79. On *Strangers on a Train*.

Cragle, Chris. "Rough Trade: Sexual Taxonomy in Postwar America." In Donald E. Hall and Maria Pramaggoire, eds., *RePresenting Bisexualities: Subjects and Cultures of Fluid Desire*. New York: New York Univ. Press, 1996, 234–53. On *Strangers on a Train*.

Dellolio, Peter J. "Expressionist Themes in *Strangers on a Train*." *Literature/Film Quarterly*, vol. 31, no. 4 (2003): 260–9.

Deutelbaum, Marshall. "Seeing in *Saboteur*." *Literature/Film Quarterly*, vol. 12, no. 2 (1984): 56–64.

Doane, Mary Ann. "Female Spectatorship and Machines of Projection: *Caught* and *Rebecca*." In *The Desire to Desire: The Woman's Film of the 1940s*. Bloomington: Indiana Univ. Press, 1987, 155–75.

Edwards, Kyle Dawson. "Brand-Name Literature: Film Adaptation and Selznick International Pictures' *Rebecca* (1940)." *Cinema Journal*, vol. 45, no. 3 (Spring 2006): 32–58.

Fabe, Marilyn. "Hollywood Auteur: Alfred Hitchcock's *Notorious*." In *Closely Watched Films: An Introduction to the Art of Narrative Film Technique*. Berkeley: Univ. of California Press, 2004, 135–51.

Fawell, John. "*Stage Fright*: Alfred Hitchcock's Fear of Acting." *Film Criticism*, vol. 26, no. 1 (Fall 2001): 25–41.

Fletcher, John. "Primal Scenes and the Female Gothic: *Rebecca* and *Gaslight*." *Screen*, vol. 36, no. 4 (Winter 1995): 341–70.

Flitterman-Lewis, Sandy. "To See and not to Be: Female Subjectivity and the Law in Hitchcock's *Notorious*." *Literature and Psychology*, vol. 33, nos. 3–4 (1987): 1–15.

French, Tony. " 'Your Father's Methods of Relaxation': Hitchcock's *Shadow of a Doubt*." *Cineaction*, no. 50 (September 1999): 43–5.

French, Philip. "Alfred Hitchcock: The Film-Maker as Englishman and Exile." *Sight and Sound*, vol. 54, no. 2 (Spring 1985): 116–22.

Gallafent, Ed. "Black Satin: Fantasy, Murder, and the Couple in *Gaslight* and *Rebecca*." *Screen*, vol. 29, no. 3 (Summer 1988): 84–103.

Gallafent, Ed. "The Dandy and the Magdalen: Interpreting the Long Take in Hitchcock's *Under Capricorn* (1949)." In John Gibbs and Douglas Pye, eds., *Style and Meaning: Studies in the Detailed Analysis of Film*. Manchester: Manchester Univ. Press, 2005, 68–84.

Gordon, Paul. "Sometimes a Cigar is not Just a Cigar: A Freudian Analysis of Uncle Charles in Hitchcock's *Shadow of a Doubt*." *Literature/Film Quarterly*, vol. 19, no. 4 (1991): 267–76.

Hall, Sheldon. "*Dial 'M' for Murder*." *Film History*, vol. 16, no. 3 (2004): 93–108.

Hark, Ina Rae. " 'We Might Even Get the Newsreels': The Press and Democracy in Hitchcock's World War II Anti-Fascist Films." In Allen and Ishii-Gonzalès, *Alfred Hitchcock* (cited in Part One): 333–47.

Hatt, Harold. "*Notorious*: Penance as a Paradigm of Redemption." In John R. May, ed., *Image & Likeness: Religious Visions in American Film Classics*. New York: Paulist Press, 1992, 126–34.

Hemmeter, Thomas. "Hitchcock the Feminist: Rereading *Shadow of a Doubt*." In Gottlieb and Brookhouse (cited in Part One): 221–33.

Hemmeter, Thomas. "Twisted Writing: *Rope* as an Experimental Film." In Raubicheck and Srebnick (cited in Part One): 253–65.

Hollinger, Karen. "The Female Oedipal Drama of *Rebecca* from Novel to Film." *Quarterly Review of Film and Video*, vol. 14, no. 4 (1993): 17–30.

Hughes, Rowland. "Shadows and Doubts: Hitchcock, Genre, and Villainy." In Stacy Gillis and Philippa Gates, eds., *The Devil Himself: Villainy in Detective Fiction and Film*. Westport, CT: Greenwood, 2002, 107–19.

Jacobowitz, Florence. "Seeing and Believing: Sid Bernstein's German Atrocities Film and the Question of Hitchcock's Participation." *Cineaction*, no. 50 (September 1999): 86–88.

Jacobowitz, Florence. "*Under Capricorn*: Hitchcock in Transition." *Cineaction*, no. 52 (June 2000): 18–27.

Kaplan, E. Ann. "Melodrama and Trauma: Displacement in Hitchcock's *Spellbound*." In *Trauma Culture: The Politics of Terror and Loss in Media and Literature*. New Brunswick, NJ: Rutgers Univ. Press, 2005, 66–86.

Krohn, Bill. "Ambivalence (*Suspicion*)." *Hitchcock Annual*, 2002–3, 67–116.

Krohn, Bill. "*I Confess* and *Nos deux consciences*." In Schmenner and Granof (cited in Part One): 49–61.

Lawrence, Amy. "American Shame: *Rope*, James Stewart, and the Postwar Crisis in American Masculinity." In Freedman and Millington (cited in Part One): 55–76.

Light, Allison. "*Rebecca*." *Sight and Sound*, May 1996, 28–31.

Lowry, Stephen. "Image, Performance, Text: Star Acting and the Cinematic Construction of Meaning." In Paul Goetsch and Dietrich Scheunemann, eds., *Text und Ton im Film*. Tübingen: Gunter Narr Verlag, 1997, 285–95. On *Suspicion*.

McElhaney, Joe. "The Object and the Face: *Notorious*, Bergman and the Close-up." In Allen and Ishii-Gonzalès, *Hitchcock* (cited in Part One): 211–27.

Martin, Adrian. "Luminous Alicia, Sore Devlin, Poor Alex: Around *Notorious* (1946)." *The MacGuffin*, no. 10 (August 1993): 14–25.

Mayne Judith. "Narratives of Ambivalence." In *Private Novels, Public Films*. Athens, GA: Univ. of Georgia Press, 1988, 127–54. On *Rebecca* and *Mildred Pierce*.

Mahoney, MaryKay. "A Train Running on Two Sets of Tracks: Highsmith's and Hitchcock's *Strangers on a Train*." In William Reynolds and Elizabeth A. Tembley, eds., *It's a Print!: Detective Fiction from Page to Screen*. Bowling Green, OH: Bowling Green State Univ. Popular Press, 1994, 103–14.

Miller, D. A. "Anal *Rope*." In Diana Fuss, ed., *Inside/Out: Lesbian Theories, Gay Theories*. New York: Routledge, 1991, 119–41.

Mogg, Ken. "Hitchcock's *Stage Fright*: An Appreciation." *The MacGuffin*, no. 2 (February 1991): 11–16.

Mogg, Ken. "The Lost Paradise: Hitchcock's *The Paradine Case* (1947)." *The MacGuffin*, no. 12 (February–May 1994): 12–21.

Mogg, Ken. "The Million Pound Mystery: Hitchcock's *Suspicion* (1941)." *The MacGuffin*, no. 7 (May–August 1992): 11–22.

Morrison, James. "Hitchcock's Ireland: The Performance of Irish Identity in *Juno and the Paycock* and *Under Capricorn*." In Allen and Ishii-Gonzalès, *Hitchcock* (cited in Part One): 193–210.

Perkins, V. F. "*I Confess:* Photographs of People Speaking." *Cineaction*, no. 52 (June 2000): 28–39.

Philips, Gene D. "Dance with the Devil: *Strangers on a Train* and *Playback*." In *Creatures of Darkness: Raymond Chandler, Detective Fiction, and Film Noir*. Lexington: Univ. Press of Kentucky, 2000, 202–22.

Polan, Dana. "The Light Side of Genius: Hitchcock's *Mr. and Mrs. Smith* in the Screwball Tradition." In Andrew Horton, ed., *Comedy/Cinema/Theory*. Berkeley: Univ. of California Press, 1991, 131–52.

Pomerance, Murray. " 'Don't understand, my own darling': The Girl Grows Up in *Shadow of a Doubt*." In Frances Gateward and Murray Pomerance, eds., *Sugar, Spice, and Everything Nice: Cinemas of Girlhood*. Detroit: Wayne State Univ. Press, 2002, 39–53.

Pressler, Michael. "Hitchcock's *Suspicion*: Reading between the Lines." *Studies in the Humanities*, vol. 31, no. 1 (June 2004): 99–104.

Rappaport, Mark. "*Under Capricorn* Revisited." *Hitchcock Annual*, no. 12 (2003–4): 42–66.

Renov, Michael. "From Identification to Ideology: The Male System of Hitchcock's *Notorious*." *Wide Angle*, vol. 4, no. 1 (1980): 30–7.

Roche, Mark W. "Hitchcock and the Transcendence of Tragedy: *I Confess* as Speculative Art." *Post Script*, vol. 10, no. 3 (Summer 1991): 30–7.

Rohmer, Eric, and Claude Chabrol. *Hitchcock: The First Forty-Four Films*. (Cited in Part One.)

Rubin, Martin. *Thrillers*. New York: Cambridge Univ. Press, 1999. A chapter on "The Classical Period" adduces Hitchcock repeatedly; Part III includes "The Psychological Crime Thriller: *Strangers on a Train* (1951)."

Smith, E. W. "Thereby Hangs a Tale: Rope in the Hands of Plautus, Porter, and Hitchcock." *Arachne*, vol. 5, no. 1 (1998): 53–78.

Thomas, Deborah. "Confession as Betrayal: Hitchcock's *I Confess* as Enigmatic Text." *Cineaction*, no. 40 (May 1996): 32–7.

Thomas, Deborah. "Psychoanalysis and Film Noir." In Ian Cameron, ed., *The Book of Film Noir*. New York: Continuum, 1993, 71–87. Discusses *Shadow of a Doubt*.

Thompson, Kristin. "Duplicitous Narration and *Stage Fright*." In *Breaking the Glass Armor: Neoformalist Film Analysis*. Princeton: Princeton Univ. Press, 1988, 135–61.

Truffaut, François. *Hitchcock*, revised edition. (Cited in Part One.)

Wallace, Lee. "Continuous Sex: The Editing of Homosexuality in *Bound* and *Rope*." *Screen*, vol. 41, no. 4 (Winter 2000): 369–87.

White, Patricia. "Female Spectator, Lesbian Spectator." In *Uninvited: Classical Hollywood Cinema and Lesbian Representability*. Bloomington: Indiana Univ. Press, 1999, 61–93. On *Rebecca*.

Wings, Mary. "Rebecca Redux: Tears on a Lesbian Pillow." In Liz Gibbs, ed., *Daring to Dissent: Lesbian Culture from Margin to Mainstream*. London: Cassell, 1994, 11–33.

Wolitzer, Meg. "*Shadow of a Doubt:* Fat Man and Little Girl." In David Rosenberg, ed., *The Movie that Changed my Life*. New York: Penguin, 1993.

Wollen, Peter. "*Rope:* Three Hypotheses." In Allen and Ishii-Gonzalès, *Alfred Hitchcock* (cited in Part One): 73–86.

Wood, Bret. "Foreign Correspondence: The Rediscovered War Films of Alfred Hitchcock." *Film Comment*, vol. 29, no. 4 (July–August 1993): 54–58.

Wood, Robin. "Hitchcock and Fascism." *Hitchcock Annual*, no. 13 (2004–5): 25–63.

Wood, Robin. "*Rebecca* Reclaimed for Daphne du Maurier." *Cineaction*, no. 29 (August 1992): 97–100.

Worland, Rick. "Before and after the Fact: Writing and Reading Hitchcock's *Suspicion*." *Cinema Journal*, vol. 41, no. 4 (Summer 2002): 3–26.

Chapter Eleven

All in the Family: Alfred Hitchcock's *Shadow of a Doubt*

James McLaughlin

So fruitful of conjecture is the text of the family. (Elizabeth Hardwick, Sleepless Nights*)*[1]

"This family has just gone to pieces." With those words, Charlie, the eldest daughter of Mr. and Mrs. Joseph Newton of Santa Rosa, California – she's eighteen years old and named after her uncle – recumbent in her bedroom in that very position described by Freud as being so conducive to the relaxation of the ego's vigilance over the unconscious, begins her grievance against a family that provides her with everything, not the least of which is disgust.[2] The idea of the family is a very important one in the films of Alfred Hitchcock; so is the idea of disgust. What we find is that the two ideas are very much related. Like everything else in Hitchcock, the family is not innocent: besieged by malevolent forces from without, it also engenders murderous feelings from within, and these two phenomena are intimately linked. The image that accompanies this obsession with the family and its filthy dynamics is, of course, that of the house. The façade of the Newton family home in *Shadow of a Doubt* is composed of sweetness and sunshine; behind it, however, lies, in the words of Uncle Charlie, "a foul sty."

Both Charlie and her uncle are introduced in the film in exactly the same manner: after a few introductory shots of their respective towns, Santa Rosa and Philadelphia, the camera cranes in on their bedroom windows and, after a cut, continues tracking in to approach their reclining figures on their beds. In this cinema of the bedroom that Hitchcock's films often turn out to be, this camera movement, in its Peeping Tom way, allows a nearness of observation that watches, that spies, that comes closer in order to see better. The camera's indiscreet curiosity creates suspicions of illegitimacy – the suspicion that the two houses are hiding something vaguely sinister, which must be exposed. The Philadelphia boardinghouse shelters Uncle Charlie, who, we learn, more than vaguely sinister, is actually suspected of murder by two cops who subject him to relentless surveillance. The Santa Rosa home shelters Charlie (along with the rest of her family), who becomes, in the obscure equation proposed by the insinuating camera movement, a criminal too. The exact nature of her "crime," however, is not immediately apparent and is never explicitly stated. Yet the film provides numerous hints from which we can construe the reason for Charlie's association with criminality. In these early scenes, this coupling of the two characters lying in beds separated by a continent is the most striking indication of the relationship that exists between them; there is a sly hint that what Charlie and her uncle are thinking about while lying in bed is the other in bed – that is, of being with the other in bed. Incest is a barely suppressed presence in the film whose unconscious enactment certainly incriminates Charlie; and incest is a metaphor that conveys precisely the transgressive power of Charlie's fierce attachment to desires of which her uncle, as we will see, is the emblem.

The union of Charlie and her uncle is impugned as unhealthy from the start. The two characters are thought to be "sick." In the Philadelphia sequence, the landlady of the boardinghouse asks Uncle Charlie: "You look kinda tired to me. Are you sick?" On the train that carries Uncle Charlie to Santa Rosa, the porter and the passengers speak of how ill he is. When he alights from the train with the assistance of his fellow passengers onto that irremediably unpopulated Santa Rosa train station, Charlie is the sole person who sees him – she asks him if he is sick. When the Santa Rosa sequence begins, Charlie's father, Joe, in his first communication with his daughter, asks her if she is feeling well. (This occurs before Charlie complains about the ills of her family, which she thinks is sick.)

The intense togetherness of uncle and niece is registered then in fantasies of incest and illness and identity of name. Yet the insistence on their closeness goes still further. "We're more than an uncle and niece," Charlie says at one point, "we're sort of like twins." Hitchcock is fond of characters who resemble one another – twins, doubles, cases of mistaken identity pervade his work. It is as if he were mocking all bourgeois conceptions of the individual as a single, solitary self. For Hitchcock, the individual is often a charismatic organization of two.

Yet the charismatic becomes problematic – by becoming vividly vampiristic. "We have the same blood," is Charlie's arresting phrase, and her uncle's resemblances to the most famous of all vampires, Count Dracula, abound in the film. Like Dracula, Uncle Charlie comes from "the East." Like Dracula, he possesses a fearsome grip – Charlie twice complains that he hurts her when he grabs her.[3] Like Dracula, he is associated with the dead and the dark. (There are those great stretches of night in *Shadow of a Doubt*, those realms of darkness that haunt the day without yielding an hour and disappear eventually only in the new night of death.[4]) When Uncle Charlie speaks to the landlady of the boardinghouse, he sounds barely alive, indeed looks barely alive, until she pulls down the window shade. We see the darkness cover his face. Thereupon, Uncle Charlie springs up from the bed with a startling automatism and throws his glass against the wall: the darkness, with its magnetic obscurity, attracts and provides him with an explosive revivification. Like Dracula, he can mysteriously disappear. When the detectives pursue him in the beginning of the film, he eludes them, and we see him watching them from the top of a building. Later, when the detectives visit the Newton home posing as "pollsters" sent by the National Public Survey to interview "the representative American family," one of the detectives bets Charlie that her uncle is not in her bedroom where she thinks he is.

The detective is correct: Uncle Charlie unexpectedly enters the second floor through the doorway from the outside staircase. This phantom-like quality of Uncle Charlie is emphasized again in the shot where we see only his reflection on his niece's graduation picture – as if he were a disembodied spirit. There is even a direct reference to Dracula in the film. One of the detectives requests that Ann, Charlie's bibliophilic younger sister, tell Saunders "the story of Dracula."

His most important similarity to Dracula, however, is that Uncle Charlie is summoned by his niece. Charlie stresses the fact that her uncle "heard" her, that there is a kind of mental telepathy between them. She wanted him to come and, miraculously, he came. "To be in tune with another person who is on the other side of the country – it's all mental," she states. Similarly, Dracula does not invite one into his castle; one must make the first move and cross the threshold. The presence of Dracula is unconsciously wished for by the other characters in the novel. Dracula also communicates telepathically with women and has strong affinities with children and madmen.

Dead, but still with us, still with us, but dead. (Donald Barthelme, The Dead Father)[5]

Charlie's monologue in her bedroom in the presence of her father about the stagnation of family life continues thus:

CHARLIE: It's been on my mind for months. You sort of go along and nothing happens. It's in a terrible rut. What's going to be our future?
FATHER: Well, I just got a raise at the bank.
CHARLIE: How can you talk about money when I'm talking about souls? We eat, we sleep, and that's about all. We don't really have any conversations. We just talk.
FATHER: And work.
CHARLIE: Poor mother. She's not an ordinary mother. We ought to do something for her.
FATHER: And what do you propose to do?
CHARLIE: Nothing I suppose. We'll have to wait for a miracle.
Mother appears.
MOTHER: My, those back stairs sure are steep.

There is then a short exchange between the mother and father about Charlie's health. Then,

CHARLIE: I'm going to send a telegram. There's only one person who can save us. A wonderful person who will come and shake us all up....

Charlie's summoning of her uncle is a way, she hopes, of curing the Newtons of the debilitation induced by the inertia of family living in smalltown America: the endless repetition of mundane events, the joyless performance of ever so quotidian tasks. It is also a way of "doing something" for her mother. There is a very interesting equation established between Charlie's desire to cure her family and her desire to "do something" for her mother – it is as if the two desires were one and the same thing. Charlie's notion of the family is conflated with the mother, not the father; she seems to think her family would be better off without him. "What destructiveness is implied in our desire to make life extraordinary," writes Philip Rieff, and Charlie's destructiveness is aimed, like a gun, at her father.[6] Her wish for the presence of her uncle is another shot, more subtle but also more damaging than the first, at her father, who is vulgarly concerned with money, not with "souls." The implication is that her father just does not "do" enough for her mother, while her uncle will. There is an undeniable tug underlying Charlie's remarks, with a hint of the father's inadequacy, sexual and otherwise.

So the serene surface of the Newtons' family life is disturbed by an undertow of Charlie's unmistakable, barely conscious, hostility directed at her father, which is why, I think, Joe is such an insignificant figure in the film, a real cipher. The daughter's repressed rage radically diminishes the stature of the father. In addition, a slighter, more overt hostility, in the form of insult, is directed at Joe by the other female members of the household and by Uncle Charlie. Ann tells her father when he returns home from the bank carrying a digest of detective stories titled *Unsolved Crimes*: "Here I am only a child and I wouldn't be caught reading the things you do." After dinner, Mrs. Newton (Emma) gives her brother her husband's newspaper and pillow and the best chair. Uncle Charlie does not heed Joe's advice not to throw his hat on Charlie's bed. He also usurps Joe's position at the dinner table and treats him like one of the children. Joe receives his gift from Uncle Charlie at the same time the children receive theirs, while the mother and Charlie are regaled with a much more elaborate presentation. Uncle Charlie also embarrasses Joe in the bank in which he works by talking very loudly to him about embezzlement, and he further mortifies Joe by intimating in the presence of the bank's president that Joe is "looking out" for the latter's job.

The father becomes the presence that is really an absence. When Uncle Charlie arrives in Santa Rosa – preceded by ominous clouds of black smoke emitted by the train that carries him – and first meets his sister Emma, he declares: "Stop. You're Emma Spenser Oakley, not Emma Newton, of 46 Burnham Street.... The prettiest girl on the block." (Those vapors of Uncle Charlie, the billowing clouds of smoke and gas – obscure, opaque, shadowy – permeate this film so insidiously and resemble, with their elusiveness and their delicacy, the singular strength of their progenitor.) Joe does not exist for his brother-in-law, nor does the reality of his marriage to Emma. Charles strips his sister of her marital status and attempts to return to the world of their childhood. He even presents Emma with photographs of their parents taken in 1888. "It was a wonderful world. Everybody was sweet and pretty then," he says, and it is this world he is trying to re-create. This sense of returning, at least in fantasy, to a golden age by visiting Santa Rosa is also conveyed by Uncle Charlie's voice when he speaks to the telephone operator. It is his voiceover of "Santa Rosa," pronounced in a tone of exquisite elegiac yearning, that begins the Santa Rosa section of the film: he is, in a sense, giving us Santa Rosa, a Santa Rosa without Joe Newton.

However, the superior transgression against the father occurs when Uncle Charlie takes Joe's newspaper to construct a house in order to hide from the Newtons a report that might reveal his culpability in the murder of three rich widows. Each of the children mentions that their uncle is destroying "father's paper." This paper house is an exemplary image of the institution of the family whose fragility is guaranteed by dad's flimsy materials. The image also suggests a criminality concealed in the family's very construction.

Two other remarks further suggest that Joe is an absence, a lack, a big hole in the Newton family edifice. His neighbor Herb tells him, after some prank involving soda in Joe's coffee: "For all you knew, you might just as well be dead now." Charlie, at another point, irate at her father's conversation with Herb, screams: "Can't you two stop talking about killing people?" – to which Joe responds: "We're not talking about killing people. I'm talking about killing him and he me."

The rich widow weeps with one eye and laughs with the other. (Proverb)[7]

The father then is "dead," a soft murder for which Charlie's wish for her uncle's appearance is primarily responsible. And we have Uncle Charlie aching to take his place. Charlie's wish for the presence of her uncle is enough to create the reality – mental states produce physical events – but the reality so summoned appears in not quite the way that is expected, since the wish for it is strongly mixed with a good dose of guilt over the anger she feels toward her family, especially her father. Uncle Charlie is far from being the "wonderful person" she thinks. He does kill, and this time not in fantasy, what are called "merry widows." Now why are they labeled that and why do they disgust Charles so much that he feels compelled to murder them? One resonant scene occurs in the bank president's office. The wife of the bank president, accompanied by her widowed friend, Mrs. Potter, visits her husband's office to ask him for money. "One good thing about being a widow, Mr. Oakley," Mrs. Potter says to Uncle Charlie, "is that you don't have to ask your husband for money." What makes this widow "merry," and threatening, is her independence, financial and otherwise, from her husband. Uncle Charlie, in his diatribe against these "fat, faded, wheezing animals," distinguishes between "town women" and "city women" (shades of *Sunrise*), the latter being "useless women." (Charlie protests: "They're alive. They're human beings!" "Are they, Charlie?," her uncle responds.) "Their husbands dead, made so much money." Their widows are now "eating the money, drinking the money, they stink of money." These women, in other words, are enjoying an "unheard-of totality of pleasures – a [real] banquet."[8] Charles delivers his jeremiad in extreme close-up by which he acquires an exceptional ferocity. It is this pronounced fear of women with money, of women with any kind of power, which is essentially a fear of women's sexuality, that reverberates throughout and indeed structures so many of Hitchcock's films. (It similarly structures Bram Stoker's novel, *Dracula*.) It is a fear of, at once, wide scope and terrible specificity: a fear marking every gesture, undermining every speech, permeating every shot, and haunting every scene.

Charlie Newton exhibits qualities shared by those famous hysterical patients of Freud. Freud described those women as follows:

> I have described the patient's [Elisabeth von R.] character, the features which one meets with so frequently in hysterical people and which there is no excuse for regarding as a consequence of degeneracy: her giftedness [*"She's got brains,"* *Joe says of Charlie*], her ambition, her moral sensibility, her excessive demand for love which, to begin with, found satisfaction in her family, and the independence of her nature which went beyond the feminine ideal and found expression in a considerable amount of obstinacy, pugnacity and reserve.[9]

Freud's psychomoral prescription for women and his polite misogyny are apparent in this passage; Hitchcock's are no less apparent in his films, with the difference that Hitchcock's misogyny is hardly polite. Charlie also seeks to go "beyond the feminine ideal," the ideal embodied by that "town woman," her mother. She wants to escape the stultifying routines of family life in smalltown America. In fact, what she is really after is the independence and power of the "merry widow." Her uncle consecrates those wishes by placing on her finger the ring of the widowed woman he has murdered.[10] This unhealthy, unholy union – it is as if they are getting married – of her and her uncle, of her feminine and masculine halves, must be broken in order to allow the holier one of her and Graham. The masculine half of Charlie's personality seeks those "masculine" traits of independence and power; and it is this phallic, striving half that is really the cause of the aggression unleashed against her family and, ultimately, herself. The unconscious guilt she feels over the "destruction" of her family eventually deflects the course of her anger and redirects it toward herself. Charlie's wish to escape the family and its mediocrity is, as the progress of the film makes quite clear, a death wish. The masculine desires that gnaw at her, feed off her, vampiristically suck her blood ("How's your throat?," a friend of Charlie's asks her in one scene), and almost kill her are those desires she eventually overcomes by pushing her uncle off his train to land in front of an oncoming one. The moment of their abolition occurs on that powerful, moving, black vehicle that brought Uncle Charlie to Santa Rosa and now brings him to his death.

Single women with money (or some kind of power) are deadly in Hitchcock; they provoke uncontrollable anxiety in men, which turns to murderous rage. They are regarded as inhuman and unnatural, unhinging both the social and natural orders. Those famous Hitchcock heroines who appear in the films made after *Shadow of a Doubt*, like Alicia Huberman (*Notorious*), Miriam Haines (*Strangers on a Train*), Judy Barton (*Vertigo*), Marion Crane (*Psycho*), Melanie Daniels (*The Birds*), Marnie Edgar (*Marnie*), and Brenda Blaney (*Frenzy*), are "mature" women – that is, they possess the independence and power of the "merry widow," for which Charlie merely yearns and certainly does not possess. (That lack in Charlie constitutes her youth and "innocence." Innocence in quotes because even to yearn for independence is enough to contaminate any woman in Hitchcock's world.) This maturity makes them all, so to speak, notorious – that is, criminal: in essence, to be a woman is a crime. And the punishment for that crime calls forth an impressive array of disciplinary techniques: Alicia is punched in the face and poisoned; Miriam is strangled; Judy is dragged to the top of a church bell tower off which she falls and dies; Marion is stabbed to death; Melanie is attacked by birds and pecked until she is unconscious (Annie Hayworth is pecked until she is dead); Marnie is tormented psychologically; and Brenda is strangled. Charlie is herself gassed, tripped down a flight of stairs, and almost thrown in front of a speeding train. And the "merry widows," of course, are murdered.

Uncle Charlie, the embodiment of his niece's phallic desires, lands in front of an oncoming train; Charlie herself, in the final scene of the film, lands on that pedestal upon which "Averageness" – her mother – has been firmly enthroned throughout the course of the film. (In the last shot of the film, Graham is looking up at Charlie.) "Average families are the best," Graham tells Charlie at one point. The film is a chart of her progress from rejection of her family and her premonitions of her future status within it to wholehearted acceptance of her mother's position. The repressed violence implicit in her desire for freedom and independence not only "kills" her father but thereby converts her mother into a "widow." As I suggested earlier, Charlie's remarks imply a world without the father, which would be the world of the merry widow, a world of unheard-of pleasures. This is the world she wants for herself and her mother. In fact, this world of incredible pleasures is obtained when she exists alone with her mother; it is equivalent to the bliss obtained in that golden age of the pre-Oedipal. Such is the nature of the extraordinary life Charlie seeks.

At the same time, however, that Charlie converts her mother into a "widow," she also prepares her mother for death at the hands of the "merry widow murderer," her uncle (that is, her phallic desires). She learns to her horror that by "killing" her father she would also be "killing" her beloved mother. It is her uncle's closeness to her mother that terrifies Charlie – "Keep your hands off my mother," she warns him – and motivates her attempts to drive him out of town. Her love for her mother proves stronger than her love of independence and reconciles her to her mother's position. The ambivalent nature of Charlie's phallic wishes – that they kill both the father (desired) and the mother (undesired) – is reflected in the contradictory makeup of Uncle Charlie himself, who not only embodies Charlie's phallic yearnings but also voices the fears that those yearnings provoke.

Needless to say, Emma does not share her daughter's perception of family life as stagnant and hardly aims to suppress the presence of her husband. Yet an obscure vision of the world of the "merry widow" nevertheless also motivates Emma to a limited extent: she participates in the demeaning of her husband and is brought to tears at the departure of her brother. At one point she addresses Joe and Charles, standing side by side, as "the two men in my life," a remark that attests to the strength that Charles has in her life, as strong as that of her own husband. (Charles eventually leaves her, however.) Though Emma has become too much of a "town woman" for her to treat her daughter's unrest too seriously, she still betrays traces of that unrest, as, by implication, does every woman.

Yet the last scene of the film is so maliciously ambiguous. In medium-shot we see Charlie on the right, Graham on her left, standing a bit behind her so that he is looking up to her. There is a church in the background. We hear organ music and the voice of an off-screen priest extolling the character of Uncle Charlie during his obsequies.

PRIEST: Santa Rosa has gained and lost a son. A generous, kind....
CHARLIE: *(whose voice overwhelms that of the priest)* He hated the whole world. He said people like us had no idea of what the world is like.
GRAHAM: It's not as bad as all that.
PRIEST: ... their sterling characters....
GRAHAM: Sometimes, the world needs a lot of watching. It goes a bit crazy now and then, like your Uncle Charlie.
PRIEST: ... the beauty of their souls, the sweetness of their characters live on with us forever.

Hitchcock is not only convicting civilization of its illusoriness – the priest, stalwart representative of society's moral values, eulogizes a murderer – but is also, in effect, marrying Graham and Charlie. There they stand, the redoubtable couple, churched and together, the detective and his recently "cured" wife, with all contaminating traces of her uncle's influence – that is, of her own disturbing desires – expunged; she is (they hope) clean. Yet their "marriage" occurs during a funeral. Is the implication that wedlock really is deadlock? Are Charlie's fears about the killing mediocrity of family life being ever so underhandedly confirmed? Those desires of independence and freedom almost do kill her; yet she rids herself of them only to land in the tomb of marriage and family life – so she really has not escaped death after all. Hitchcock, like God, loves a joke; and divine jokes, as the Greeks knew so well, are often the cruellest.[11]

Hitchcock's indictment of the family as a trap, if not a tomb, is suggested in another way. When Graham proposes marriage to Charlie in an earlier scene, the door of the garage in which they are standing slams shut. Hitchcock also indicts the family as a fount of criminal mischief. In this last scene, Graham and Charlie are a couple formed by a kind of secret complicity in the death of her uncle; they achieve a composure at once silent and sinister, secure in their private knowledge that their "marriage" is founded on a murder. Criminality's presence, at first suggested behind the façade of the Newton family home then concealed in the construction of the paper house, remains undisclosed in this apotheosis of the couple that concludes the film. Criminality, Hitchcock insists, hides within domesticity; or, to put it another way, domesticity is merely the most hidden criminality.

And it is no accident, given the fears shaping the film, that Charlie finds herself married to a detective, a cop, a representative of Law and Order. Graham affirms that "the world needs a lot of watching." What needs watching, in other words, are those women who yearn to exceed their juridical limits – consignment to husband and family – as Charlie once did and perhaps will do again. (It is remarkable how obsessed Hitchcock is with this theme of watching and investigating women and how he develops it further in the films that follow *Shadow of a Doubt*.) Part of the "nasty taste" (Robin Wood's phrase) that lingers after seeing this film consists of the fear that these illicit desires of women are not easily eradicated, that the family Charlie and Graham are going to form will produce offspring who will inevitably have the same unruly desires that their mother once did.[12] In the novel *Dracula*, Jonathan Harker, a man whose wife has been bitten by the Count, writes about vampires in his journal: "Just as their hideous bodies could only rest in sacred earth, so the holiest love [marriage] was the recruiting sergeant for their ghastly ranks."[13] Similarly, the "recruiting sergeant" for the vampires torturing this very martial film is the holy locus of the family. The family itself, by its mere existence, produces those phallic/feminine desires it hopes to keep under wraps. But those desires have a way of breaking through and throwing everything into question – like the startling image of the waltzing merry widows erupting like a hysterical symptom at four distinct points during the course of the film – a disturbance of the narrative flow that is very unusual in a film of the 1940s. It is this cycle – the perpetual repetition of banal existence of the family, that generates the wish to escape and destroy it, that instills guilt for having the wish, that distorts the effect of the wish, that brings near death and a return to the family – that elicits Hitchcock's most profound disgust and transforms the family into the great Unsolved Crime. The fact that woman triggers this process makes her into a criminal, but she is a crime that can be "solved" – by means of marriage and a husband, or a brutal death.

One significant feature of the Law and Order that Charlie's phallicness threatens is the order of Time. What time is it? This insistent, if mute, question haunts the world of *Shadow of a Doubt* and indeed of many other Hitchcock films. When Uncle Charlie presents the Newton family with gifts, he gives Joe a watch. When Herb first appears in the film, he asks Joe the time. When Charlie rushes off to the library, there is a shot of the town clock. And the name of the sordid nightclub to which Uncle Charlie takes his niece is the 'Til Two Club. One implicit answer provided by the film to that nagging question is, it is bedtime, that is, the time of sleep, the time of the dream, the time of wish fulfillment. (Remember that the two characters, Charlie and her uncle, begin the film lying in bed.) Sleep puts to sleep the time machine; sleep also brings an end to uprightness. Indeed one could view the film as Charlie's progress from lying down, dreaming, and leaving the bed to standing upright (with her husband), as erect as the columns of the church in front of which she stands at the end of the film. The world of the bed attempts to subvert the world of the upright – horizontal versus vertical. And the world of the bed is also the world of sick sexuality, the world of female sexuality, whose fiendish energy (so perceived by Hitchcock) breaks the bounds, breaks apart and levels the order of the Father, the order of Law and Time. Small wonder that his film is populated by cops, priests, and soldiers.

For Alfred Hitchcock, family relationships are a source of endless provocation. The family, in the course of its normal and natural existence, produces the most oppressive of tensions and the calm matter-of-factness with which it does so is what makes it so frightening. "It's not the horrible which shocks," writes Adorno, "but its self-evidence."[14] In *Shadow of a Doubt*, the family with its glow (its halo) may seem like a warm bath, but it all too readily becomes a swamp of frustrated yearnings, breeding demons of female emancipation whose ferocity it is barely able to contain. The representative American family, in short, is the true horror of the film.

I had a family. They can be a nuisance in identity but there is no doubt no shadow of a doubt that that identity the family identity we can do without. (Gertrude Stein)[15]

Notes

1. Elizabeth Hardwick, *Sleepless Nights* (New York: Random House, 1979), 107.
2. Sigmund Freud and Josef Breuer, *Studies on Hysteria*, trans. James Strachey (New York: Avon Books, 1966).
3. Hands have a special authority in Hitchcock's films, and the vampirism pervading those films is given its paradigmatic expression in the form of the grip. Cf. the shot of Bruno's hand retrieving the cigarette lighter from the sewer in *Strangers on a Train*; Bruno stomping on Guy's hands in the same film as Guy desperately holds on to the merry-go-round as it swings out of control; Uncle Charlie squeezing the napkin in *Shadow of a Doubt*; Babs, dead, clutching Rusk's stickpin so tightly in *Frenzy* that he has to break her fingers in order to retrieve it; and the striking opening shot of *Vertigo* of the criminal's hand grasping the ladder.

    Characters embracing, as many people have noticed, often lovingly resemble a strangling: Henrietta's initial appearance in *Under Capricorn*, in which she places her hands on the neck of her lover/husband, Sam Flusky; Kendall and Thornhill on the train in *North by Northwest*; also Vandamm's hand on Eve's neck at the auction in the same film.

    Think also of the results of so many of the murders or near murders – a stunning shot of the victim's hand with the fingers resolutely outstretched and far apart, a hand that, in its shock, no longer grasps: Marion's hand during the stabbing in the shower in *Psycho*; Melanie's and Mitch's hands, pecked in *The Birds*; Brenda's hands during the strangling in *Frenzy*; and Bruno's fist opening at the end of *Strangers on a Train* to reveal the cigarette lighter. Hitchcock's characters often seem spellbound – like Uncle Charlie and his automatism mentioned above – in the grip of something or other; and it seems as if the aim of murder is to break the grip of whatever or whomever the murderer thinks, consciously or not, is feeding on him.
4. A phrase from Michel Foucault, *Madness and Civilization*, trans. Richard Howard (New York: Vintage Books, 1973), 110.
5. Donald Barthelme, *The Dead Father* (New York: Farrar, Straus, and Giroux, 1975), 3.
6. Philip Rieff, "Fellow Teachers," *Salmagundi*, no. 20 (1972): 34.
7. Quoted in Hardwick, 62.
8. A phrase I borrow from Roland Barthes, *A Lover's Discourse*, trans. Richard Howard (New York: Hill and Wang, 1978), 119. In this connection we might ask why Hitchcock's characters are always eating. The appetitive mode predominates, and after the bedroom, the dining room is probably Hitchock's most favorite setting. References to food and eating are innumerable. Some outstanding examples: "You never did eat your lunch today, did you?" are the first words spoken in *Psycho*; there are the disgusting meals prepared by the inspector's wife in *Frenzy*; Rusk, again from *Frenzy*, is the owner of a produce-distributing company who is often seen biting into a piece of fruit (Is there a sly homosexual reference here? Rusk as the big Fruit?); Bruno and Guy meet in the dining car of the train in *Strangers on a Train*; the townspeople of Bodega Bay stand in a diner and watch the birds attack in *The Birds*; very erotic exchanges take place around the dinner table in *Notorious* and *North by Northwest* (Eve Kendall: "I never discuss love on an empty stomach"); and in *Shadow of a Doubt* when Uncle Charlie overhears Joe and Herb mention that the other suspected "merry widow" murderer walked into the propeller of a plane, he declares: "I could sure eat a good dinner today."

    That eating is connected to vampirism (feeding on someone) seems obvious, but exactly how it is connected, I am uncertain. There are, I am sure, other meanings attached to this hunger that rages throughout Hitchcock's work. This endnote, along with the others, states in a very speculative way, as something to think about, various themes entwined in Hitchcock's films that should be explored more thoroughly than they have been.

9. Freud and Breuer, 202.

10. Hitchcock's world is populated by glowing objects, of which the ring is one, objects possessed by light as if radioactive (like the wine bottles in *Notorious*), acquiring a life as eerily vivid as that of the protagonists. In *The American Cinema* (New York: E. P. Dutton, 1968) Andrew Sarris has written: "Hitchcock's objects are never mere props of a basically theatrical mise en scène, but rather the very substance of his cinema. These objects embody the feelings and fears of characters as object and character interact with each other in dramas within dramas" (p. 59).

   But why? Why do objects figure so luminously and become the "very substance of his cinema"? One possible answer lies in Hitchcock's connection to Expressionism. Everyone seems to agree on Hitchcock's debts to that artistic movement, a movement that, to speak very simplemindedly, emphasized the subjective over the objective, that attempted "to 'express' emotional states through a distortion of objective reality" (see Robin Wood, Chapter 3 above).

   Yet Expressionist inwardness, it seems to me, necessarily makes objects seem like characters and characters seem like objects. Theodor Adorno has written: "The more the I of expressionism is thrown back upon itself, the more like the excluded world of things it becomes.... Pure subjectivity, being of necessity estranged from itself as well as having become a thing, assumes the dimensions of objectivity which expresses itself through its own estrangement. The boundary between what is human and the world of things becomes blurred" (Theodor Adorno, *Prisms*, trans. Samuel and Shierry Weber (London: Neville and Spearman, 1967), 262).

11. To modify a phrase of Hannah Arendt's in *Men in Dark Times* (New York: Harcourt Brace Jovanovich, 1968), 98.

12. Robin Wood, *Hitchcock's Films*, 2nd edn. (London: A. Zwemmer, 1969), 69.

13. Bram Stoker, *Dracula* (1897; reprint New York: Dell Books, 1977), 330.

14. Adorno, 248.

15. See Judith Therman, "A Rose is a Rose is a Rose is a Rose Gertrude Stein," *Ms.*, vol. 2, no. 8 (1974): 54.

SHADOW OF A DOUBT (Universal, 1943). *Producer*: Jack H. Skirball, *Script*: Thornton Wilder, Alma Reville, Sally Benson, from a story by Gordon McDonnell, *Photography*: Joseph Valentine, *Editor*: Milton Carruth, *Sets*: John B. Goodman, Robert Boyle, R. A. Gausman, E. R. Robinson, *Music*: Dimitri Tiomkin, *Costumes*: Adrian, Vera West, *Players*: Joseph Cotton (Charles Oakley), Teresa Wright (Charlie Newton), Patricia Collinge (Emma Newton), MacDonald Carey (Jack Graham), Henry Travers (Joe Newton), Hume Cronyn (Herb Hawkins). 108 minutes.

Chapter Twelve

The Moral Universe of Hitchcock's *Spellbound*

Thomas Hyde

One would hardly want to rank *Spellbound* (1945) as one of Hitchcock's richest or most perfectly conceived films. Even the Master himself (he can be puckishly agreeable when offered negative opinions of his work) told Truffaut in his interview book that it was "just another manhunt story wrapped up in pseudo-psychoanalysis."[1] Truffaut, concurring, dismisses the film as "somewhat of a disappointment" after a few brief exchanges. Robin Wood in his *Hitchcock's Films* devotes but a short paragraph to *Spellbound*, citing the incongruous Dali dream sequences and a troublesome "split in the thematic material" between the growth of the relationship of Ingrid Bergman and Gregory Peck and the progress of the murder plot.[2] The film has its share of other weaknesses; Truffaut (assisted by Hitchcock) catalogues most of them: the Hollywood treatment of psychoanalysis in parts of Ben Hecht's script; Miklos Rozsa's grotesquely overdramatic score; Gregory Peck's insufficiently convincing portrayal of a potential madman-murderer. Yet the presence of flaws hardly justifies a lack of critical press, especially when a virtue can be produced for every flaw (not the least of which is Ingrid Bergman's exquisite, dimensional performance), and particularly when the so-called flaws are often as interesting as the virtues. It is worth looking at *Spellbound* to discover what it is that makes it so pleasurably and uniquely a Hitchcock film.

As the precursor of *Vertigo*, *Psycho*, and *Marnie*, *Spellbound* is Hitchcock's first film to deal with pathological mental cases and, even more prominently than in these or in any others, with psychoanalysis. Here John Ballantine, who suffers from amnesia, assumes for a time the identity of a Dr. Edwardes, who is scheduled to replace the head of an insane asylum, a Dr. Murchison. The possibility is raised later that Ballantine murdered Dr. Edwardes and took over his identity out of guilt. Ballantine undergoes a journey through a series of mental as well as physical landscapes in order to trace down the clues to his real identity and to uncover the roots of his debilitating guilt complex. In all this he is aided by a psychiatrist, Dr. Constance Peterson, and by her mentor, Dr. Alex Brulov. In the end Dr. Murchison is exposed as the real murderer.

Now it is significant that in a film about psychoanalysis the cure for John's amnesia is not found on the analyst's couch but rather emerges from a series of experiential trials culminating in John's physically re-enacting the episode that originally triggered his disturbance – the murder of Dr. Edwardes on the ski slope at Cumberland. Here, as elsewhere, Hitchcock seems to be responding to the common belief that the psychiatric patient can be cured of his deep problems by just talking them out. But this does not necessarily mean that Hitchcock is attacking psychoanalysis itself. Rather, as treated in the film, psychoanalysis becomes a figure that Hitchcock employs to express his disapproval of certain kinds of attitudes and assumptions associated with its application, so as to bring out the real issues with which he is concerned. Psychoanalytic practice is a vehicle for making an artistic statement; it is both MacGuffin and metaphor. It is not really even John Ballantine's film, for, while the sensational psychoanalytic murder-mystery plot holds our immediate surface attention, Hitchcock's sustained, essential focus here is on the emotional and moral development of Constance Peterson in her relation with Ballantine. The film depicts a learning process, not only that of Ballantine's recovery of his lost identity by following his guilt feelings to their unconsciously repressed source but that of Constance forging a new identity by tapping a suppressed capacity within herself for feeling and committed action. What is being emphasized and approved here by Hitchcock is Constance's trusting involvement with John.

Ultimately more absorbing than the determination of John's innocence is their personal transformation – becoming integrated within themselves and so redeemed for each other. Our interest in this is mediated less by the suspense elements through which Murchison's ostensible guilt is revealed than by the undercurrent of implication whereby a more basic, universal culpability is exposed in each of the characters. *Spellbound* shows the unwarranted guilt complex to be a much rarer phenomenon than we might be inclined to suppose. In exploring the question of the appropriateness of one's feelings of guilt and self-doubt, *Spellbound* suggests a relation between moral and mental health that receives its most comprehensive exposition later in the character of *Psycho*'s Norman Bates. Hitchcock seems to be saying that guilt may be damaging when it remains beyond one's ability to act on it, but also when it is absent or unheeded. Guilt can be a healthy signal to direct one's awareness to what is, in Hitchcock's moral universe, a potential for moral error native to the human condition.

One of the major themes pointed up consistently in the film is the inadequacy of intellectual analysis when it is divorced from compassionate, understanding involvement. This is introduced in the initial sequences as the classic opposition of book knowledge versus experiential knowledge, connected with the education of Constance Peterson. The film begins with Mary Carmichael, an inmate of the hospital, whom we see display a rather thinly concealed hostility toward men (she nuzzles up to Harry the aide, then scratches his arm). In the subsequent session with Constance she then tells of another would-be seducer who got his moustache bitten off for his trouble. Taking the bait Hitchcock dangles for the amateur psychiatrist here, we can infer that Mary encourages men to accept this role in order to punish them and that it indicates some deeply rooted sexual conflicts in Mary, possibly Oedipal in nature, possibly having to do with forbidden childhood feelings toward a father figure that she has not yet been able to overcome. Although she may desire a mature relationship with a man, she cannot accomplish it under the contradictory terms she has established. Constance seems the cool, rational opposite of Mary. Starched and stiff in her white hospital coat, Constance's backed-off, cerebral, patronizing stance contrasts sharply with Mary's cultivated attractiveness and her passionate, lascivious behavior ("Psychoanalysis bores the pants off me!"). Mary reacts to Constance's unfeeling attempts at analysis by throwing a book at her and calling her "Miss Frozen-Puss."

If we have not already guessed it, when Constance next spurns Dr. Fleurot's advances we become aware that her detached, clinical attitude is not reserved solely for her professional relationships, but extends to the private ones as well. Fleurot lectures her on her "lack of human and emotional experience." "It's rather like embracing a textbook," he says. "You're exactly like Miss Carmichael. I'd like to throw a book at you – but I won't." Despite Fleurot's vicious, juvenile sniping at her later and his subsequent jealousy, we can appreciate his frustration and see that he is basically correct in his estimation of her. She has evidently been dependent on books as the source of her knowledge of human behavior at the expense of direct, intimate experience. (In this respect, Constance is related to the know-it-all, bookish little sister figures such as Ann in *Shadow of a Doubt* and Barbara in *Strangers on a Train*.) And she *is* like Mary Carmichael in exhibiting a milder form of Mary's hysteria. We are, after all, given no indication that Fleurot does not genuinely care for her, even though in his approach he resembles more than slightly the masher from Philadelphia and the house detective in the Empire Hotel. Constance may understandably be repulsed by his aggressive moves, but the fact is, her aggressive rejection of him is symptomatic of her ignorance of certain legitimate human needs and obligations, not only those of others, but her own as well.

Moreover, Constance is to be seen as accountable for this in a way in which Mary is not; Constance has no excuse for not regarding the responsibility to be aware of her own and others' emotional requirements. She is not prevented from investigating and evaluating her own responses, as Mary is by her mental condition. Constance's detachment and frigid demeanor, the complacent, presumptuous distancing of herself from human contact, is tantamount to the sin of pride. It is a willed and willing choice on her part, and this neglect of worldly knowledge is especially debilitating in a person of her profession, dedicated to helping people with serious problems of their own. The starting point for the evolution of Constance's trust in instinct and passion is her "love at first sight" introduction to Dr. Edwardes in the dining room at the asylum. The turning point, however, comes with her choosing to disregard reason and accompany Edwardes rather than revealing him to the police when he leaves the asylum. It is appropriate that the awakening in Constance of a person of open feeling should proceed from a spontaneous decision that logical calculation would have counselled her to avoid. For Constance, Dr. Edwardes's book on the guilt complex, which she thinks she ought to read, is superseded by an immersion in first-hand experience.

Having witnessed her obliviousness to the needs and motives of others, we now observe Constance's blindness to her own emerging feelings, her self-deception with regard to her reasons for staying with John in his hotel room in New York. She tells him she has come to help him, but only as a doctor, and as they embrace she murmurs,

"It has nothing to do with love, nothing at all, nothing at all." Our interpretation of this transparency has been prepared for in previous scenes depicting her romantic distraction with John. What is at stake here is her ingrained definition of herself, her confidence in her intellectual and professional competency, her maintenance of a customary, secure decorum. Her precarious illusion of aloofness from and control over her world is being threatened by the passionate feelings involuntarily called forth from her. Her basic assumptions having been called into doubt, her circumvention here follows the same pattern as John's amnesia: the blocking-off (more consciously impelled in Constance than in John) of the recognition of fallibility for fear of disturbing one's stable orientation to an imposed, faulty conception of reality. Constance's turning-away from the haven of established authority is the right move to make, but with it comes the shocking awareness of the illusion of her own autonomy, to be replaced slowly by a more true, more sober vision of the limitations of personal freedom and independence.

As Constance progresses in discovering her capacity for the expression of feeling, we are made very conscious of her vulnerability in extending herself to John. Our responses to this are mixed. On the one hand, there is the matter of John's innocence or guilt in respect to killing Edwardes. We are warned by Dr. Murchison that John is a "paranoid imposter" and that he is certainly guilty of dispatching Edwardes. Dr. Alex's condemnation of Dr. Edwardes for harboring John ("What kind of doctor is it that wants to bring a dangerous patient into a bowling alley?") also accents Constance's impulsiveness and seems to cast doubt on her ability to judge wisely. She does underestimate Alex in his ability to "put two and two together." He has seen through their husband-and-wife story, and in the apparently menacing scene with John and the razor, where we are made the victims of our own expectations, Dr. Alex accordingly turns the tables on John. Constance subsequently tells Alex, "I couldn't feel this way about a man who was bad, who had committed a murder," an indication of her gain in self-perception in acknowledging the demands of her emotions. Yet it also seems at this point that she has swung too far in the direction of relying exclusively on instinct and emotional prejudice in evaluating John's character. Alex *is* wrong, however, in censuring her emotional fidelity to John, and Constance must abandon the paternal possessiveness and protection of Alex, and the kind of reserved authority he stands for, in favor of a more mature and responsible relationship with John. Constance's problem here still is her lack of self-doubt, her lack of an accurate perspective on the scope of her actions and abilities with respect to the scope of circumstance, the way things operate in the world. She is correct in remaining with John and helping him to handle what her psychological probing has released. She must come to feel the full impact of what it means to be responsible for penetrating to the deepest center of one's selfhood and to realize the problem of coping with what one finds there. Just as the turning point of John's rejuvenation occurs on the ski slope in the revelatory return to the childhood source of his guilt complex, so Constance begins her real transformation immediately after this, with the numbing shock that the happy ending to their romance and the vindication of her plans and efforts have been overturned by the emergence of the fact that Edwardes was murdered. Her reaction, looking up at John but not meeting his eyes, reflects her realization that, despite having uncovered the origin of John's complex, despite the voice of her intuition, she could still be wrong about his capacity for evil. The vision of doors swinging open at her first kiss with John is replaced by the vision of cell doors swinging closed, the end to which her presumption has led her. Her distress in her subsequent scene with Alex marks the critical point of her diminishment at the perception of her own certain guilt: in being responsible because of pride, self-interest, and complacency for bringing about the reversal of her own intentions and for assigning the man she loves to a fate her efforts were designed to avoid. Having now been humbled by the vision of her own culpability and the complexities of character and situation of which she had not been aware, the way has been prepared for her to form a more realistic, adjusted idea of herself and the life she has been leading. Her traumatic downfall has also been her salvation. She is now able to return to life and to act in accordance with a greater awareness of the moral weight of involvement, the implications and consequences of her action, and the limitations of her abilities.

Particularly enigmatic here is the problem of John's behavior, his response to certain stimuli, the matter of his guilt. John's amnesia, we are told, is the result of the repression of memory by the subconscious mind in order to evade damaging self-incrimination arising out of a past childhood event. We find that John did indeed kill his brother in a boyhood accident, and the similarity of Edwardes's death at Cumberland provoked the amnesia as a defense. But, along with the repression or guilt, a simultaneous desire for and fear of punishment manifests itself obliquely in John's actions, a tension of anxiety that is linked to aggressive and sexual energy. John's taking-on of Dr. Edwardes's identity can be interpreted as an unconscious desire to be exposed and to confess. There is an implied parallel here with Garmes, whose example lends weight to the suspense at Constance's involvement with John. Like John, Garmes suffers from a guilt complex; he believes himself to have killed his father. Constance's counsel to Garmes is a rather unhelpful assurance: "People often feel guilty about things that happened in their childhood." Prevented from confronting and confessing the source of his very real guilt, Garmes eventually finds a punishing, destructive outlet for his anxiety, a possibility we later feel is imminent in John. Constance's dismissal here is a further symptom of her overall naivety. She is ignorant of the meaning and importance of guilt related to crimes, real or imagined, since she has not faced the possibility of sin in herself. She is mistaken about the nature of one's experience of guilt. What she has to learn is that guilt is not explained away or suppressed, for it will surely break out again, and, while it may be mistaken and damaging to blame oneself for unconscious intentions or acts for which a person cannot be held responsible, to be without a sense of guilt or doubt may be equally invidious.

Unlike Garmes's, John's guilt seems to have sexual dimensions that are manifested more clearly on the surface. John's repressed feelings on occasion erupt past his normal exterior in displaced, hostile outbursts of aggression when triggered by the reminders of the guilty incident of his brother's death – dark lines and the color white. These signs almost always appear when he is in the company of Constance. The first time this occurs, John's "spell" is brought on as a result of what is supposed to be a swimming pool that Constance has drawn on the white tablecloth. However, the drawing is also clearly vaginal in shape. In other instances, she discourages his forceful advances in order to interrogate him about his guilty past. John subsequently falls into his trance, and, apparently influenced by the earlier denial of his gratification, his subconscious aggressions emerge in resentment: "If there's anything I hate it's a smug woman!" John's outbursts here resemble those of Fleurot. John, a medical student, is connected with Fleurot by Dr. Murchison's comment too, that Fleurot exhibits "the manners of a medical student" in regard to his bitter remarks directed at Constance. John's treatment of Constance suggests that he too harbors an immature attitude toward women and sex, one that links him to Fleurot, the house dick, and the masher. John's relationship with Constance, to be healthy and lasting, must be free of the taints of exploitation and self-indulgence. John must come to dissociate aggression from sex and to expend those aggressive energies in useful labor – as Alex points out to Constance: "There's lots of happiness in working hard – maybe the most." Perhaps we are to see that John is not to be considered responsible for this behavior, in the same way as Constance's other admirers in the film, because of its origin in his unconscious guilt problems. If this is so, then the solving of John's guilt complex by the divulging of its origin in childhood fears (punishment grossly out of proportion to offense = undue guilt) implies that John's aggression-sex problems are also on the way to being healed. The last scene of the film, showing John taking a more suitable, responsible stance toward marriage, can be interpreted as indicating the growth of John's edification that has coincided with Constance's development in the film.

The thematic and moral issues raised by the interaction of characters and situations in *Spellbound* are summarized in two major pairs of scenes incorporating subjective camera shots occurring near the beginning and end of the film and serving as reference marks against which may be measured the progress of the characters and the advancement of the film's statement. The first pair of incidents, in retrospect, calls our attention to the progress of Constance as, from her point of view, the camera tracks up the stairs of the asylum to bring into central notice the door of Dr. Murchison's room. In both cases, it is Constance's willing choice to climb the stairs and confront what is beyond the door that is the major issue. Throughout the film John has been associated with guilt, aggression, emotion, and with downward movements, descending inside himself, into his dreams, uncovering his subconscious and repressed memories, and discovering his relation to this inner life. Constance has been associated with self-certainty, reserve, and reason, and with ascending movements, moving outward to experience in the world, to encounters with others, expanding her consciousness of the potential for both love and destruction in human character and human relationships. Here in the initial instance it is the false Dr. Edwardes who waits on the other side of the door. She is unaware of the dangers and complications her involvement with him may entail: she is only vaguely conscious of the nature and force of her newfound feelings to which she will accede. She crosses to the library first to get Dr. Edwardes's book, a symbol of her diluted life of intellectual retreat. She chooses to cross the threshold, and, as she faces John across another doorway, her real motives begin to become clear: "I thought I wanted to discuss your book with you – I'm amazed at the subterfuge." This is the beginning of self-revelation. The second tracking shot, reminding us of the first and its associated implications, calls our attention to the progress that has been made, the difference in Constance. In this case, it is the duplicitous Dr. Murchison who inhabits the room, and Constance, having suffered through the experiencing of guilt in herself and in John, is now fully armed with the knowledge of what she is doing and its possible consequences. Where in the first scene the essential rightness of following her instinctual desires was emphasized, her choice to enter the room this time is a measure of her realization of the depth of complexity and responsibility that such a commitment necessitates.

The final set of scenes recapitulates cinematically the major themes developed within the film: the deception of appearances, the untrustworthiness of authority, the nature of guilt and sin, and the moral responsibility of human involvement. They occur from the point of view, first, of John Ballantine and, second, of Dr. Murchison. In the context of the first shot, Ballantine has descended the stairs at Dr. Alex's home to confront Alex at his desk, again across a doorframe. John is in one of his trances, his hand clutching a razor, which we are made to think he will use on Alex, since he has just spared the sleeping Constance. The situation is symbolic of the primal scene, with John competing with a father-figure for the possession of Constance. As John raises to his lips the glass of white milk, which we know will serve to fuel the fire of his aggressions, the camera is John's eyes. Alex is seen through the bottom of the glass as the milk gradually rises up and the screen fades to white. What we learn, of course, is that the threat, while real enough by itself, was not to be carried out so inevitably as we thought. With the drugged glass of milk, the distinctions between victim and victimizer begin to break down, but with the advantage here on the side of the one most consciously aware of the deep motives and vulnerability of others.

Likewise, in the final confrontation between Constance and Dr. Murchison, it is Constance who must put what she has learned about herself on the line by trusting in her intuition of its applicability to Murchison. The situation here is advanced a rational and moral notch from the previous one. Like John, Constance must face down the figure of fatherly authority in order to win her lover, but here the similarity ends. She knows that Murchison is the murderer of Edwardes and is aware of what may be the ultimate consequences to herself of this act of emotional fidelity to John. Murchison proves his skill at analysis by correctly interpreting the dream that damns him as guilty, parallel to Alex's deciphering of John's illness and unconscious intent in the former scene. The gun, seen from the subjective point of view of Murchison, corresponds to the glass of milk as the externalization of apparent danger. As the gun and camera follow Constance across the room, she appeals to Murchison on the basis of logic not to commit a second murder, for, she says, considering his mental condition at the time, he would not be accounted guilty or responsible for the first. As with Garmes and later with John, the resort to reason proves inadequate. Murchison, having failed to admit his own moral condition to himself, is done in by his own complacency. The light of truth bursts in through the hole in Constance's reasoning, inflaming his sense of guilt rather than absolving it. The destructive pointer of blame, associated now with self-righteous authority, comes round to confront itself, and ourselves.[3]

The simplistic question, then, of the efficacy of reason over emotion has been transcended in the course of the film through its demonstration of the imperatives of self-awareness, love, and responsible involvement with others. More humbly conscious of their own capacity for error and the nature of the world's demands, Constance and John deserve to be reunited, saved for a better life. Rather than kiss and part, like the other couples in the train station, their approved example is to kiss and remain, in faith and trust, together.

Notes

1. François Truffaut, *Hitchcock* (New York: Simon and Schuster, 1967), 118.
2. Robin Wood, *Hitchcock's Films* (New York: A. S. Barnes, 1977), 44.
3. Robin Wood says of this shot that "it is one of the rare instances I can think of in Hitchcock of a *pointless* use of identification technique, since none of us want to shoot Ingrid Bergman and we feel no connection of any kind with the murderer" (p. 44). I disagree that there is a lack of connection. It is just that the connection is of an odd sort. The shot involves a *disparity* between our feelings and Murchison's action that is very much to the point. True, we don't want to kill Ingrid Bergman: neither, really, does Murchison. The gun suddenly turned on *us*, though, brings home, if just for an instant, the enormity and reality of suicide. This puzzling personal threat, brief and implausible as it may be, gives us a shock, disturbs our security, and mobilizes a self-preservation response so different from the one of the head we are supposed to be in that it forces us to query Murchison's reasons with a sense of urgency that no other treatment of the scene could provoke.

SPELLBOUND (Selznick, United Artists, 1945). *Producer*: David O. Selznick, *Script*: Ben Hecht, Angus McPhail, from the novel *The House of Dr. Edwardes* by Frances Beeding (pseud. of Hilary St. George Saunders and John Palmer), *Photography*: George Barnes, *Editors*: William H. Ziegler, Hal C. Kern, *Sets*: James Basevi, John Ewing, Emile Kuri, *Music*: Miklos Rozsa, *Costumes*: Howard Greer, *Dream Sequence*: Salvador Dali, *Players*: Ingrid Bergman (Dr. Constance Peterson), Gregory Peck (John Ballantine), Leo G. Carroll (Dr. Murchison), Norman Lloyd (Garmes), Michael Chekhov (Dr. Alex Brulov), Rhonda Fleming (Mary Carmichael), John Emery (Dr. Fleurot). 111 minutes.

Chapter Thirteen

Notorious: Perversion par Excellence

Richard Abel

Notorious is the proper name for such a grim fairy tale, not only because of its "tainted" heroine and its outrageous plotting but principally because of a perversion of the conventional fairy-tale narrative, perversions in the ritual of sexual coupling, and a consequent rupture in audience identification or spectator placement. Perversions make *Notorious* (1946) one of Hitchcock's most deceptive and disturbing films.

To begin with, let us accept Peter Wollen and John Fell's simplified schema of the Proppian fairy-tale structure.[1] A task is set for the hero by a dispatcher (father or family). If he performs it successfully, the hero will be rewarded – the gift of the heroine. The task is to liquidate a lack, to find and return an object of desire or possession (sometimes the heroine herself), which has usually been separated from the dispatcher by a deceitful villain. In his quest, the hero sometimes receives the aid of a helper or magical agent. After setbacks and delays, the hero vanquishes the villain, retrieves the object, and claims his reward.

In *Notorious* this basic structure undergoes striking transformations. The task or quest can be divided into three parts. Initially, Prescott (the dispatcher) sends Devlin (the hero) to retrieve Alicia Huberman (the object/heroine) from her traitorous father and drunken playmates – led by a gentle old sugar daddy yachtsman. The task is quickly performed – with a midnight punch, a morning glass of orange juice, and the "right words" from a surreptitious recording. There is no reward here. Or, more precisely, Devlin and Alicia are on the point of rewarding one another, with one another, when Prescott separates them (the interrupting phone call). The separation apparently results from the appearance of Alexander Sebastian (the villain), but actually he is introduced by Prescott and his men (becoming known through their words). A specific task now is set for the heroine, and the hero is reduced to functioning as her helper (at the riding club their dress codes even imply a sex role reversal – Alicia in hat and tie, Devlin hatless and tieless). She is to discover a secret/object the villain possesses. Through trickery, Prescott, with Devlin's tacit consent, turns Alicia (disguised in her former state) over to Sebastian. A "perversion" of the conventional structure is already apparent: the reduction/submission of the hero, the transformation of the heroine from object to subject/agent (but through deliberate "tainting"), the deception played on the villain. The dispatcher Prescott manipulates all for his own ends and seems about to reward no one.

Alicia performs her task and passes on the key to the secret (hand to hand, bottle for bottle) through Devlin to Prescott. Undeceived at last, Sebastian, aided by a devilish mother, traps the heroine in his "castle" and turns her into a "sleeping beauty." The final task is assumed by Devlin alone. No longer directed by the now ignorant Prescott, he drops his guise and enters the "castle" as the "knight in shining armor" to awaken and rescue the "damsel in distress."[2] Alicia helps him now with even more secrets and, at the last moment, Sebastian abets their escape only to be sacrificed for their "happiness." The conventional structure reasserts itself, with an important difference. The dispatcher is replaced by the villain – as manipulator and, more importantly, as the one who rewards: it is Sebastian who now authorizes (reluctantly) the reunion of hero and heroine. Despite this change in function, Devlin and Alicia abandon him to death ("That's your headache").

Read in this fairy-tale form, *Notorious* can be said to distribute its main characters along the axis of parents versus children.[3] Special prominence is given the "father" figures who function through sets of oppositions and substitutions.[4] There are three crucial "father" figures. The first serves immediately to define Alicia – the daughter of a traitorous father, she is "guilty" politically, a "marked woman" by association. The syntagmatic repetition in sequence 1 (shots 1–3, 4–6) clearly substitutes her for the expected father as court adjourns. Several sequences later, however, the association is presented as false (the recorded voices), and Alicia is allied ("a job") with Devlin and, through him, with a second "father," his boss, Prescott. The job can "make up for her father's peculiarities," and the death of her father (also made known through Prescott) transforms/"frees" her ("it's as if something had happened to me, not him"). Her new identity emerges in love for Devlin. The absent, denied father is replaced momentarily by the hero (marked as early as sequence 5 when, over the recorded voices of daughter denying father, Devlin approaches Alicia and positions himself beside her).[5] In the midst of external dangers, a couple is formed – a standard Hitchcock theme.

In accepting Alicia, however warily, Devlin acts for himself against a second "father" figure, the dispatcher, Prescott. In effect, he violates "the law of the father."[6] The retribution is swift and humiliating. The dispatcher-father ignores the changed identity of the heroine, sets up the villain as the (semic) antithesis of the hero (short/tall, fair/dark, elderly/young, warm/cold, charming/sarcastic), and gives the heroine to him instead of to the hero (Alicia matching Alex).[7] Submissive, impotent, castrated (the celebratory bottle of wine left behind with Prescott), Devlin joins Prescott in perversely using Alicia, turning her back into what she is not.[8] To restore Alicia and re-establish their sexual union, Devlin must again violate the "law of the father" and act on his own.[9] When he does, in the end, the "castle" opens miraculously for him, and even Sebastian accedes to his demands. Through the act of defying both "father" figures, the couple reforms – in guilt.

The villain introduces a further acting-out of parental defiance. In accepting the disguised Alicia, Sebastian, too, acts for himself and against the wishes of a dominant mother. Because mother and son already form a "complete" couple in the "castle,"

Alicia intrudes as a powerful rival ("You are jealous of her just as you've been jealous of every other woman who's shown an interest in me").[10] Her presence betrays the double function of the villain – he is both son and "husband" to the mother. He, too, acts the "father." The function is marked by his age ("tired ... this business makes me feel old and look old"), his friendship with Alicia's father, his oppositeness to Prescott. As the antithetical "father" who is actually son, Sebastian makes the "castle" the site of a perversion that is as much sexual as political.[11] By unlocking the door to the cellar, Devlin and Alicia expose the secret, the "other" bottle of wine, which marks the false love between her and Sebastian and the explosive love (incest) that unites mother and son. Once Sebastian realizes the secret is out (in a reverse transfer of knowledge), authority shifts from the motherless, mateless Prescott to this "unwholesome" couple of mother and son. Consequently, it becomes "right" that these false "parents" are defied and abandoned, that this "tainted" couple (politically, morally, and sexually) is replaced by a "purified" one.

This ritual of couple formation at the expense of the family (father/mother) also operates within a more specific system of the film: the stance and gesture of characters within the space of the frame and the syntagmatic placement of that positioning.[12] Devlin's submission to Prescott and, consequently, to his rival, Sebastian, is articulated paradigmatically across a series of related sequences. In sequence 5, Alicia had come out of her room to join Devlin and take the job he offered; in sequence 15, she again comes out of her room to face Devlin and now Prescott behind him. It is Prescott she asks to help clasp her necklace (cf. Devlin's earlier "gift" of the scarf round her waist); and, when Devlin moves to the left behind his boss, Prescott is positioned between them and warns them to "keep shy of one another." When Alicia comes to the office with Sebastian's marriage proposal in sequence 19, again Prescott is positioned between the two, syntagmatically (looking screen left towards Alicia and screen right towards Devlin). Once more he separates them, doubly, crucially, when his off-screen agreement to her marriage speaks through Devlin's silence. Suppressed, deprived of power and desire, Devlin yields his position beside Alicia to Sebastian, beginning with the staged incident at the riding club. In sequence 14, a shot of Devlin sitting alone screen left at a bar table is separated by a fade from the next shot of Alicia sitting alone screen right at a restaurant table. Sebastian enters and assumes the screen-left position opposite Alicia that Devlin had previously filled (cf. sequence 7 at the outdoor café). Again at the racetrack Devlin yields the position screen left opposite Alicia to Sebastian. Finally, in the cellar confrontation, Devlin and Alicia are positioned spatially and syntagmatically opposite Sebastian until a three-shot centers Devlin between wife and husband. His departure leaves Alicia and Sebastian together but separated through intercutting.

Hero and villain now take exactly opposite actions in the face of "parental" authority. Betrayed by Alicia, Sebastian returns to Mother. From Sebastian's point of view, a shot of Alicia in bed is replaced by one of his mother in bed (sequence 29 to sequence 31). As she listens to the tale of her son's "foolishness," a mid-shot of Mother dissolves into and out of a full shot of Alicia sleeping unaware, confirming the displacement and marking her threat to Alicia through enclosure. After circling Sebastian (in a movement peculiarly similar to Devlin's circling Alicia after she consents to the job – sequence 5), Mother positions herself screen right opposite her son and resumes control over him, speaking her murderous plan through his silence. Later, in a *mise-en-scène* (sequence 38) that explicitly contrasts the actions of hero and villain, Devlin faces his "father" for the last time. Devlin's screen-left position repeats Sebastian's, while Prescott's screen-right position in bed matches the mother's. Only here Devlin is standing and Prescott, in contrast to the mother's "gangster-style" smoking, is contentedly munching on cheese and crackers (an image at odds with the continual comments on his handsomeness). "Father" and "mother" functions seem iconically reversed. The decision to check on Alicia (to rescue her) is Devlin's, not Prescott's ("Go ahead *if you want*" – emphasis added). Although Prescott consents, Devlin's action is independent and threatens the operation to the point where only Alicia's information saves it from irreparable bungling. Thus, these paradigmatic sequences of "child" confronting "parent" have pointedly opposite conclusions. Submitting to mother (playing "father") leads the villain to his death, while defying the "father" (playing "mother") leads the hero to the heroine and their union/happiness.

The "figure" of the hero and heroine's sexual union is established in the famous long-take "nuzzling" shot on the balcony in sequence 10. There the codes and signifiers made pertinent are character position (Devlin screen left facing Alicia screen right), gesture (kissing, gazing into one another's face and eyes), voice (low, soft whispering), camera position (medium close-up to close-up), camera movement (dolly-in from medium close-up to close-up and follow-dolly to sustain the close-up), and cutting (uninterrupted long take).[13] The disappearance of that moment, the disintegration of their union, is articulated in their very next sequence together through reversals in the signifiers of each of the pertinent codes. After learning what her job entails, Devlin returns to Alicia on the apartment balcony. Now their positions are reversed; there is no dolly-in from the mid-shot; the look and kiss are denied; the voices are raised; and, when Devlin refers coldly to her promiscuous past, the shot is broken by a cut to Alicia alone in close-up. The signifiers conspire their separation. The purpose of the film will be to reconstitute that first moment by reinventing the specific instances of the pertinent codes.

The ritual of the hero and heroine's progress from separation to reunion can thus be traced through the pertinent codes of their remaining sequences together. At the racetrack, for instance, a mid-shot places them side by side, Devlin screen left and Alicia screen right (matching Sebastian and his mother in the off-screen private box behind them). This time, however, they do not face one another; again there is no dolly-in from mid-shot; and, when Alicia reports the addition of Sebastian "to her list of playmates," the shot now is broken by a cut to Devlin alone in close-up. A new variation in the codes of character position and cutting emerges. The next shot shows Alicia in close-up as she suddenly turns (in profile facing screen left) to snap at Devlin's sarcastic response. The return cut to Devlin shows him from Alicia's point of view, also in profile facing screen left. The intercut profiles and disorienting change in camera position mark the force of her desire and his refusal. After another mid-shot of the two, the same profiles are repeated in an alternating series until Alicia in close-up turns forward and hides her look behind a pair of binoculars.[14] The alternation continues through another shift in camera position (to an extreme close-up of

Alicia) that accompanies her gesture of lowering the binoculars and her gaze. When she suddenly turns to the left in profile again ("Is that all you have to say?"), the point-of-view shot of Devlin's profile returns, but he now turns forward as if finally to look at her. The expectant reciprocity of looks is denied, however, by his words ("Dry your eyes, Baby, it's out of character") and a cut to Sebastian coming forward through the crowd. When the mid-shot returns, Devlin has turned his back to the camera while Alicia remains facing forward, and Sebastian enters to stand between and separate them.

Later in the "castle" wine cellar, suddenly the moment nearly erupts in the form of a ruse after the two are discovered by Sebastian. The series of alternating shots between Devlin and Alicia kissing and Sebastian looking on gives way momentarily to several privileged close-ups of their embrace. All but two of the pertinent codes return (camera movement and lack of cutting). Devlin's look (still quizzical but affected) and Alicia's breathy cry ("Oh, Dev!") briefly mark the rediscovery of desire. But the cutting allows Sebastian once more to intervene and the alternating series to resume its dominance. The final meeting on the park bench reconfirms their separation, but the last shot of the sequence announces a shift. An unexpected change in camera position suddenly puts Devlin in close-up profile looking right – the paradigmatic opposite of his position in the racetrack sequence and the perfect complement to Alicia's profile looking left. As much as his anxious glance after her, it marks his change of mind and the possibility of reunion.

Finally, in the rescue sequence, as Devlin enters the "castle" bedroom where Alicia has been held captive, all the signifiers of the pertinent codes are reinvented. The sequence begins as a variation on sequence 5, when Devlin entered Alicia's bedroom in Miami. Once again he approaches her bed to save her from the "intoxications" of drinking (the liquor of her "playmates"/the drugged coffee of the "castle"). Almost immediately the intercutting between them gives way to a re-creation of the moment on the balcony – in mid-shot Devlin (screen left) leans over Alicia (screen right); the camera dollies into close-up; Devlin looks intently at her and places his head on the pillow to touch her lips; he whispers to her gently; the shot is unbroken as the camera dollies out slightly and tilts up for Devlin to sit her up in bed. What had taken a half-dozen sequences to accomplish earlier (rescue, job acceptance, love) is telescoped into six shots, Devlin's continuous movement right towards Alicia and the single long-take shot of their reunion. The only variation in the pertinent codes is a cut to an extreme close-up of the two embracing (as in the cellar sequence) and a cut back to the close-up as they cross the room (the follow-dolly returns, sustaining their close-up embrace) to the door. The extreme close-up is marked by an 180-degree track-pan that reverses their position within the frame, effectively transposing the earlier signifiers of separation into signifiers of union (Alicia screen left now ends the shot murmuring, "you love me"). The "figure" of union re-emerges from a synthesis of previous variations and inversions of the pertinent codes. Instead of moving right toward the dispatcher-father and separation, as in sequence 12, the reunited couple moves left to face the villain in the final confrontation.

The villain's position with regard to the hero and heroine creates a perversion of the conventional audience identification that operates in the "classical" American cinema.[15] The balcony sequence of "nuzzling" already pushes audience identification to the point of excess, arresting us in fascination of "the perfect image." Hitchcock himself has described it as a "ménage à trois" – of hero, heroine, and spectator.[16] The erotic pleasure of the moment is ours as much as theirs for our being absorbed so closely and at such length in the embrace (that it is Cary Grant and Ingrid Bergman we are joining is no small matter). The desire to see the couple reunited is no less than our desire to repeat that "ménage à trois" moment of pleasure. And is it not intensified by the "tainting" of the heroine – masked by our desire to "save" her, "purify" her, have her for ourselves? Thus do we (males, at least) become rapt voyeurs, and the narrative, the quest, is propelled by our desire. "Performance as a remembering, the production of a memory."[17]

In the racetrack sequence we suddenly discover that the villain is not only the antithesis/complement to the hero and dispatcher-father but our opposite/second as well. As we watch Devlin and Alicia for signs of reawakening love, Sebastian watches too – behind them and for exactly the opposite reason. A voyeur like ourselves, he watches, not out of desire, but out of fear. Interrupting the hero and heroine, he becomes our enemy as well – the source of hindrances, delays, and threats to the couple's reunion and our pleasure. At the party our expectant watching is paralleled, even taken over (in point-of-view shots) by Sebastian's scrutiny; and in the cellar again he intervenes – from the other side – to separate Devlin and Alicia and repress our renewed pleasure.

The villain's position is troubling for us in another way as well. Though politically and morally contemptible, his gentlemanly attitude toward Alicia at first contrasts with that of Devlin's caddishness. His love perhaps is even stronger than Devlin's – that is, his defiance of Mother versus the hero's submission to "father." Furthermore, the film suddenly allows him the status of subject during the sequence when he discovers Alicia's betrayal of his love. As spectators we are made to share that feeling of betrayal. He is victimized nearly as much as Alicia, and doubly victimized when he submits to the power of Mother again.

The final sequence brings our conflicting responses to a head. Although he has nearly murdered the heroine and still is motivated by his own desire to survive, the villain now fulfills our desire by helping Devlin and Alicia escape the "castle." He speaks the words we want to hear (even Mother wants to hear), words that will open the door for them. When Devlin locks the car door on him (shot from his point of view) and speeds off with Alicia smiling, Sebastian is abandoned and deceived once more. And the film keeps us behind with him. As Sebastian turns to walk back to the "castle," moving from close-up (looking off left after the departed car) to long shot, the camera begins to dolly slowly after him. The movement inexorably closes off the space around him, seems to "push" him towards the fatal door, as if operating out of *our* desire to get rid of him. The contradiction rubs; we have become the agents of death for the character whose action has fulfilled what we so desired – the reunion of hero and heroine, the re-creation of "the perfect image." The rub worsens when we realize that the close-up (privileging his feeling of doom) and the dollying camera that follows him (echoing the dollies associated with Devlin and Alicia) equally make us share his approaching death. The closure we had sought, indeed are responsible for, rips us asunder.[18] Where earlier defiance of the "father" split hero and heroine, this act of defiance splits us, the spectators. The guilt the hero and heroine have incurred by their defiance is displaced through the villain onto us.

Notorious – the pleasure that turns perverse.

Notes

1. Peter Wollen, "*North by Northwest*: A Morphological Analysis," *Film Form*, vol. 1, no. 1 (1976): 32, 34. John Fell, "Vladimir Propp in Hollywood," *Film Quarterly*, vol. 30, no. 3 (1977): 20. For analyses based on A. J. Greimas and Tzvetan Todorov (which also support this reading of *Notorious*), see Alan Williams, "Structures of Narrativity in Fritz Lang's *Metropolis*," *Film Quarterly*, vol. 27, no. 4 (1974): 17–24, and Charles F. Altman, "Classical Narrative Revisited: *Grand Illusion*," *Film Studies Annual* (West Lafayette: Purdue University, 1976): 87–98.
2. Bruno Bettelheim, *The Uses of Enchantment* (New York: Knopf, 1976), 111–16, 225–36. Bettelheim analyzes this kind of fairy tale in terms of Oedipal conflicts and resolutions.
3. Roland Barthes, *S/Z* (New York: Hill and Wang, 1974), 35–6.
4. Cf. Raymond Bellour, "Le Blocage symbolique," *Communications*, no. 23 (1975): 242–50.
5. In one shot the camera dollies back in front of Devlin as he moves away from the phonograph; in the next the camera dollies in (from Devlin's point of view) toward Alicia's bedroom door as she comes forward brushing her hair. Just before it stops in a mid-shot of her in the doorway, however, Devlin enters from the left foreground to stand beside her and turn back towards the camera – the shot shifts internally from subjective to omniscient point of view, from the level of the diegesis to the level of the discourse.
6. Charles Altman explains the Lacanian basis of this concept in "Psychoanalysis and Cinema," *Quarterly Review of Film Studies*, vol. 2, no. 3 (1977): 250–60.
7. Barthes, 67–8.
8. More than any other Hitchcock film (except perhaps *Vertigo*), the text repeatedly makes the heroine the victim of men's actions.
9. From another perspective, the text works according to our expectations of how a certain "star" behaves: it presents Cary Grant initially as "not-Cary Grant" and narrates his becoming "Cary Grant."
10. This form of the Hitchcock couple reaches its apotheosis in *Psycho*.
11. Cf. *North by Northwest*, where the villain Vandamm is brother, "husband," and "father" to his sister; "father" and "lover" to Leonard; "father" and brother-in-law to Valerian.
12. In a slightly different form, William Rothman postulates a similar ritual pattern in "Alfred Hitchcock's *Notorious*," *Georgia Review*, vol. 39, no. 4 (1975): 885. It should be remarked that the initial version of my own chapter was presented as a paper on "Hitchcock's *Notorious*: Myth and Ritual" at the 1977 convention of the Midwest Modern Language Association. As I was reworking the paper to submit to *Wide Angle*, Dudley Andrew suggested that I take a look at Rothman's essay. Doing so helped me to differentiate more clearly my own "structuralist" analysis of the film from his "phenomenological" analysis. Accordingly, the version that I submitted to *Wide Angle* included some half-dozen endnote references to Rothman's essay, most of which highlighted the distinctions between my analysis and his. Following an editor's request for fewer citations, I deleted all but one of the Rothman notes. Given an opportunity to reconsider the

matter further before publication, I would have reinserted at least one of those deleted notes and called attention to the very different analytical methods of our two essays.

13. At least four of the six (character position, camera position, voice, camera movement) are established even earlier in the second sequence at Alicia's party in Miami.

14. A fine irony here. The object of Alicia's gaze, the horse race, is reflected on her lenses and literally denies her look (to Devlin and to us). Similarly, Sebastian uses his binoculars to hide from his mother his attempt to watch Alicia and Devlin.

15. "Narrativisation is the complex operation of the film as narrative and the setting of the spectator as subject *in the operation*...." Stephen Heath, "Film Performance," *Cine-tracts*, no. 2 (1977): 12.

16. François Truffaut, *Hitchcock* (New York: Simon and Schuster, 1967), 327–8.

17. Heath, 13.

18. The locus of the difference between the subject of the enounced and the subject of the enunciation shifts onto us. Cf. the outrageous "ménage à trois" that ends *Psycho*.

NOTORIOUS (RKO, 1946). *Producer*: Alfred Hitchcock, *Assistant Director*: William Dorfman, *Script*: Ben Hecht, *Photography*: Ted Tetzlaff, *Editor*: Theron Warth, *Sets*: Albert S. D'Agostino, Carroll Clark, Darrell Silvera, Claude Carpenter, *Music*: Roy Webb, *Costumes*: Edith Head, *Players*: Ingrid Bergman (Alicia Huberman), Cary Grant (Devlin), Claude Rains (Alexander Sebastian), Leopoldine Konstantin (Mrs. Sebastian), Louis Calhern (Paul Prescott). 101 minutes.

Chapter Fourteen

Strangers on a Train

Robin Wood

The first shots introduce us to two pairs of men's feet as their owners arrive at a station. The two are characterized by means of their shoes: first, showy, vulgar, brown-and-white brogues; second, plain unadorned walking shoes. A parallel is at once established in visual terms: or, more precisely, a parallel is imposed by the editing on what would otherwise be pure contrast. Each shot of the first pair of feet is promptly balanced by a similar shot of the second. On the train, we are shown the feet again, moving to the same table. It is always Bruno's feet that we see first – he arrives at the station first, he sits down first; it is Guy's foot that knocks his accidentally, under the table, leading directly to their getting into conversation. Thus Hitchcock makes it clear that Bruno has not engineered the meeting, despite the fact that he knows all about Guy ("Ask me anything, I know the answers") and has the plan for exchanging murders ready to hand: it is rather as if he is waiting for a chance meeting he knew would come. This gives us, from the outset, the sense of some not quite natural, not quite explicable link between the two men.

The contrast between them is developed explicitly in the dialogue. Guy is planning a career in politics: in Hitchcock's films, politics, government, democratic symbolism (the Statue of Liberty in *Saboteur*, the US Capitol in this film, Mount Rushmore in *North by Northwest*), are always associated with the idea of an ordered life, set against potential chaos. Bruno, on the other hand, has been expelled from three colleges for drinking and gambling and lives mostly for kicks. Guy wants to marry Ann Morton, a senator's daughter; Bruno is associated with his mother (by means of the ornate tiepin, a gift from her, which bears his name). Bruno, despite the fact that he has flown in a jet and driven a car blindfolded at 150 mph and has a theory that "you should do everything before you die," envies Guy: "I certainly admire people who do things"; and, "It must be pretty exciting being so important – me, I never do anything important." We register this sense of impotence as probably, at bottom, sexual: it links up with Bruno's voyeuristic prying into Guy's love life.

Yet, behind the contrast, the parallel established by the editing of the opening shots becomes manifest. Both men, like so many of Hitchcock's protagonists, are insecure and uncertain of their identity. Guy is suspended between tennis and politics, between his tramp wife and his senator's daughter, and Bruno is seeking desperately to establish an identity through violent, *outré* actions and flamboyance (shoes, lobster-patterned tie, name proclaimed to the world on his tiepin). His professed admiration for Guy is balanced by Guy's increasing, if reluctant and in part ironically amused, admiration for him. Certainly, Guy responds to Bruno – we see it in his face, at once amused and tense. To the man committed to a career in politics, Bruno represents a tempting overthrow of all responsibility. Guy fails to repudiate Bruno's suggestive statement about Miriam ("What is a life or two, Guy? Some people are better off dead") with any force or conviction. When Bruno openly suggests that he would like to kill his wife, he merely grins and says, "That's a morbid thought"; but we sense the tension that underlies it. When he leaves the train he is still laughing at Bruno, but he leaves his lighter behind. This lighter, on which our attention has already been focused by a close-up and some commentary in the dialogue, is to be of crucial importance in the plot. It was given to Guy by Ann Morton, and bears the inscription "A to G" with two crossed tennis rackets: it is through his tennis that Guy's entry into politics has become possible. Guy's forgetfulness at this moment belies his dismissive joking air when Bruno asks if he agrees to the exchange of murders ("Of course I agree – I agree with *all* your theories"). He is leaving in Bruno's keeping his link with Ann, his possibility of climbing into the ordered existence to which he aspires. The leaving of the lighter is one of the visual equivalents Hitchcock finds for the interior, psychological analysis of the Patricia Highsmith novel that was his source.

Guy, then, in a sense connives at the murder of his wife, and the enigmatic link between him and Bruno becomes clear. Bruno is certainly a character in his own right, realized in detail with marvellous precision; but he also represents the destructive, subversive urges that exist, though suppressed, in everybody: he is an extension, an embodiment, of desires already existing in Guy. In their first conversation, as they face each other, the cross-cutting between them gives us Guy's face unshadowed, Bruno's crossed with lines of shade like the shadow of bars. He is continually, in these early stages of the film, associated with shadows and with darkness; the development of the film can partly be seen in terms of his forcing himself into the light for recognition. He understands Guy's darker motives better than Guy does himself: "Marrying the boss's daughter – the shortcut to a career." Nothing later in the film, and especially not the uneasy, formal relationship between the lovers, contradicts this assessment.

The next sequence introduces us to Miriam and defines Guy's position more clearly. Miriam – hard, mean, slovenly, at once contemptible and pathetic in her limitations – is one of those Hitchcock characters created in the round with the utmost economy in a few seconds: a gesture of the hands, a drooping of the mouth, a slovenly way of turning the body, dull yet calculating eyes peering shortsightedly through her glasses. She is more than a character. We are introduced to her in the record shop where she works, and the association of her with revolving objects (taken up later in the fairground sequence) suggests the futile vicious circle of her existence, the circle from which Guy wishes to break free. We have already seen Guy's lack of insight into other people in his inability to deal firmly with Bruno, and seen too that this lack is basically one of self-awareness; so we have no difficulty in accepting the premise of his involvement with Miriam.

After the row in the record shop, during which Guy "warns" Miriam and shakes her violently, the phone call to Ann: "You sound so savage, Guy" – "I'd like to break her foul, useless little neck ... I said I could strangle her" – shouted over the roar of an approaching train. Cut to Bruno's hands – his mother has just manicured them, and he is admiring them, flexing the fingers. The cut finally clinches the relationship between the two men, making Bruno an agent for the execution of Guy's desires.

The fairground and amusement park is a symbolic projection of Miriam's world: a world of disorder, of the pursuit of fun and cheap glamour as the aim of life, of futility represented by the circular motion of merry-go-round and ferris wheel that receive such strong visual emphasis in almost every shot. The whole sequence is realized with a marvellous particularity and complexity. Through Miriam, Hitchcock evokes a whole social milieu, smalltown life in all its unimaginativeness and restriction. The sequence is introduced by the longshot of Miriam's home, from Bruno's viewpoint as he waits for her to emerge: respectable-looking, white-fronted house, mother sitting outside on porch, calling, "Now don't be out late" to Miriam as she runs down the steps with her two boyfriends, holding hands, giggling childishly. We think back to the sullen girl in the record shop. At the fairground, she makes the boys buy her an ice-cream cone, talking at the same time about hot dogs, and they tease her about eating so much. We remember that she is pregnant. She talks about her craving – the boys laugh: "Craving for what?" She turns, gazing around the fairground through her glasses, licking at her ice cream like a spoiled schoolgirl, looking at once childish and sensual, and her eyes fix on Bruno, watching her from a distance. Not only is the character rendered with precision: an attitude to her is precisely defined, an attitude totally devoid of sentimentality, astringent yet not without pity. She is not pathetic in herself (she is never aware of needing anyone's compassion), but her situation – the narrow, circumscribed outlook, the total lack of awareness – is both pathetic and horrible. And what is being defined, ultimately, is the world from which Guy is struggling to escape: contaminated by that world (remember the impurity, exposed by Bruno, of his motives for wanting to marry Ann), he cannot free himself cleanly as he wants.

The sequence of events leading up to the murder throws further light on both Miriam and Bruno: the strangling is invested with a clear sexual significance. Miriam, at her first glimpse of Bruno, sees something more intriguing – more *dangerous* – than she can find in her two very unmysterious boys. She gives him the come-on, unmistakably, demanding to go to the Tunnel of Love loudly, so that he will hear. As her boys fail to ring the bell at the "Test Your Strength" machine, she looks around for him, and when he materializes mysteriously on her other side, she smiles at him. He shows off his strength to her ("He's broken it!"), first proudly flexing his hands, which are emphasized by the low camera angle, afterwards waggling his eyebrows at her. Then the merry-go-round: circling motion, raucous music, painted, prancing horses, more flirtation from Miriam. She calls – loudly again, like an announcement – for a boat ride. More revolving in the backgrounds as they get the boats: the ferris wheel behind Bruno, huge waterwheel beside the Tunnel of Love ahead of Miriam.

From here, the sexual symbolism accumulates strikingly. They pass through an archway to the boats, above which is written "Magic Isle" – where Miriam will shortly be murdered; the boats cross the lake, enter the tunnel (where Bruno's shadow ominously overtakes Miriam's), out again onto the lake. Miriam runs away on the isle, purposely losing the boys. Then a lighter is thrust before her face and struck, "A to G": "Is your name Miriam?" "Why, yes," she smiles seductively, and Bruno drops the lighter and strangles her.

Her glasses fall off, one lens shatters, and the murder is shown to us reflected in the other lens, inverted and distorted. The lens itself recalls lake and tunnel and is a further sexual symbol. The shot is one of the cinema's most powerful images of perverted sexuality, the murder a sexual culmination for both killer and victim. It ends with Bruno's hands enormous in the lens as he moves back from the body. We see the lighter, "A to G," on the grass, and remember Guy's words on the phone: "I could strangle her." Having retrieved it, Bruno returns to his boat through a chaos of promiscuity – pairs of lovers on the grass all around: the chaos world has been finally defined, the "Magic Isle" becomes an island of lost souls. The association of sexual perversion with the sense of damnation will be taken up again more forcefully in *Psycho*. Bruno, with his close relationship with a crazy mother, is an obvious forerunner of Norman Bates.

As he leaves the fairground, Bruno helps a blind man across the road. At the time, it seems merely a cleverly ironic touch, a trifle glib; but in retrospect it takes on a deeper meaning. Henceforth Bruno will be haunted by the memory of Miriam's eyes looking at him through her glasses in which the lighter flame is reflected; his helping of a blind man with dark glasses is an act of unconscious atonement. The sequence ends with Bruno looking at his watch: cut to Guy, on a train, looking at *his*: the visual link again used to enforce the connection between them.

Later, we see Guy reaching his rooms in Washington. On one side of the street, stately, respectable houses; towering in the background, on the right of the screen, the floodlit dome of the US Capitol, the life to which Guy aspires, the world of light and order. On the other side of the street, deep shadow and tall iron-barred gates from behind which Bruno calls. The light-and-darkness symbolism – Guy turning from the lighted doorway of the house towards the shadow, away from the Capitol dome – is simple, but not naive or ridiculous, and handled naturally and unobtrusively. Bruno beckons, a shadow among shadows. Again we see him with bars across his face: at the start of the ensuing dialogue he is behind the bars, Guy in the open. He gives Guy the glasses, reminds him about the lighter – "I went back for it, Guy." Guy is horrified. Then: "But, Guy, you *wanted* it.... We planned it together.... You're just as much in it as I am.... You're a free man now." The phone rings in Guy's rooms, a police car approaches, stops outside, and Guy promptly joins Bruno behind the bars, in shadow: a free man. He says, "You've got me acting like I'm a criminal," and we have a subjective shot of the police from Guy's position behind the bars. The scene gives a beautifully exact symbolic expression to Guy's relationship to Bruno and what he stands for.

More light and darkness in the next sequence: Guy answers his phone, Ann tells him to come around. Right of screen: a large, lighted lamp, Guy holding the receiver to his ear, Ann's voice coming through. Left of screen: heavy shadow, Miriam's glasses dangling downwards in Guy's other hand. The hands remind us of a pair of scales. We then see Guy and Ann together for the first time, and Hitchcock shows us their rather remote, uneasy relationship. Ann strikes us as the older, certainly the maturer, the more completed: the dominant partner. Their kiss lacks real intimacy or tenderness. She tells him she loves him and he replies, "Brazen woman, I'm the one to say that": an odd, endistancing, defensive kind of joke. As Ann, her father, and her sister Barbara break the news, and Guy makes a feeble attempt at surprise, our view of the lovers' relationship is confirmed by Ann's obvious suspicions that Guy has killed Miriam: she tells him, with heavy significance, "She was strangled"; and she is visibly relieved when he explains his alibi. If the world from which Guy wishes to escape is defined for us by Miriam, then Ann – formal, rather hard, rather cold, in Ruth Roman's unsympathetic performance – defines the life to which he aspires: a life of imposed, slightly artificial orderliness. As for his guilt, Hitchcock makes it very clear that what he cannot bear is, not the idea that he has been indirectly involved, at any rate by desire, in the death of a human being, but the fear of being found out: it is the only feeling he reveals in his conversation with Bruno and all that he and Ann reveal in this scene. The moral point is made clearly when Senator Morton rebukes Barbara for saying of Miriam, "She was a tramp," with the remark, "She was a human being." The rebuke, for the audience, has relevance to the lovers as well.

Yet, despite the critical attitude adopted toward the lovers' relationship, we are made aware of its importance for Guy. Ann is more than a way to a career; she represents in herself something of the ordered world he aspires to. Thus the kiss that closes the sequence, which Guy, eyes looking straight into the camera, scarcely returns, is in contrast to the kiss that opened it: the *potentialities* of the relationship are threatened by the concealment of his involvement in Miriam's murder.

In the ensuing sequences Bruno increases the pressure on Guy to murder his father. First, the phone call to Ann's house: Guy hangs up. Second, the scene where Guy and Hennessy (the detective detailed to watch him) walk together past the Capitol building. In the setting of spacious, ordered architecture, Guy says, "When I'm through with tennis I'm going into politics," and looks across to see Bruno watching from the steps, tiny in long-shot. Third, the letter from Bruno pushed under Guy's door. Fourth, the scene where Ann sees Bruno for the first time. She and Guy are in the Capitol building when Bruno calls Guy from among the pillars: "You're spoiling everything.... You're making me come out into the open." Fifth, Guy receives the plan of and key to Mr. Anthony's house. Then, at last, the famous shot of Bruno watching Guy at the tennis court, all other heads turning to follow the ball, Bruno's conspicuous because motionless, his eyes fixed on Guy: a moment at once funny and unnerving. He now manages to meet Ann while Guy practices.

These scenes work beautifully in terms of suspense, but here as elsewhere it is necessary to ask, Of what exactly does this suspense consist? We feel uneasy, not just because pressure is being brought to bear on Guy to make him commit a murder, but rather because what he wants to hide is indeed "coming out into the open." Think back to a character I have hitherto neglected: Ann's sister, Barbara. In the first scene at

Senator Morton's house, Barbara's function is clearly to express, directly and unhypocritically, what everybody – including the spectator – is slightly ashamed to find themselves thinking: that it is really an admirable thing from all points of view that Miriam is dead. Her frank and shocking remarks recall Bruno's justification of killing – "Some people are better off dead" – and therefore involve the spectator with Bruno; they also prompt the senator's rebuke – "She was a human being." In other words, conflicting, apparently mutually exclusive, responses are set up in the spectator, with disturbing results. We respond strongly to Barbara's no-nonsense honesty, but we are made ashamed of that response. This conflict within the spectator is the essence of the ensuing suspense: we, as well as Guy, are implicated in Miriam's murder. Bruno's symbolic progress, each step bringing him closer and clearer – telephone, distant figure, close figure lurking among shadowy pillars, figure sitting in full sunlight, young man in conversation with Ann, intruder from the chaos-world into the world of order – represents the emergence of all we want concealed: our own suppressed, evil desires.

Bruno's appearance at the party marks his final eruption into the world of order: the demand for recognition of the universality of guilt by a world that rejects such an assumption. The centerpiece of the scene – in some respects of the whole film – is Bruno's near strangling of Mrs. Cunningham. It derives its disturbing power again from a subtly aroused conflict, the attractiveness and the danger of that connivance at common guilt that Bruno represents. First, we are disarmed by Bruno's casually irreverent deflation of a dignified, self-righteous judge: how is he able to sit down to dinner after sentencing someone to death? The way the judge responds to the insolent question plainly makes the point that his way of life depends on such questions never being asked. The lightly humorous treatment releases us from some of the uneasiness we feel at responding to Bruno and prepares us for the next step – Bruno's conversation about murder with Mrs. Cunningham.

Here the underlying assumption of the film (subversive, destructive desires exist in all of us, waiting for a momentary relaxing of our vigilance) becomes explicit. Mrs. Cunningham's denial that *everyone* is interested in murder breaks down abruptly when Bruno asks if there have not been times when she has wanted to kill someone – *Mr.* Cunningham, perhaps? There follows the richly comic exchange of murder methods, culminating in Bruno's demonstration of silent strangling – the method he used on Miriam – with Mrs. Cunningham as guinea pig. As his hands close on the old woman's throat, Barbara comes up behind her, Bruno sees her and, for the second time, is reminded by her (dark hair, round face, glasses) of Miriam. He goes into a "sort of trance," Mrs. Cunningham is nearly killed, and the sequence ends with Barbara, who has realized that Bruno was really strangling *her*, in tears. The scene is a superb example of the Hitchcock spectator trap. First, belief in established order has been undermined in the deflation of the judge; then the dialogue with Mrs. Cunningham and her friend, because of its light tone, gives us license to accept the notion of common guilt as something of a joke, to connive at it, allowing ourselves to be implicated in the "game" of murdering Mrs. Cunningham, who is anyway a rich, trivial, stupid old woman. Then abruptly the joke rebounds on us – we have nearly been implicated in another murder: swift modulation of tone has seldom been used to such disturbing effect. We are horrified to find that we have momentarily identified ourselves with Bruno (the sequence contains a number of subjective shots where we are placed in his position). We have the feeling, even, that we, through a lack of vigilance, have released these destructive forces by conniving at them. But the final emphasis is on Barbara, and we recall that earlier it was she who was used to make explicit our conventionally suppressed feeling that Miriam's murder was all for the best. She seemed before to give validity to the release of the anarchic forces of desire; now she is punished by the very forces she helped release, and we with her. The scene leads us straight to the essence of Hitchcock, the view that ordered life depends on the rigorous and *unnatural* suppression of a powerfully seductive underworld of desire, and we see the reason for the stiff formality of the world of order in the film.

The scene is rich in other ways too. The three minor characters, the judge, Mrs. Cunningham, and her friend, are realized with marvellous economy and precision, the realization being, as always, as much a crystallization of an attitude toward them as the objective description of character; there is nothing indulgent about the humor with which these representatives of the world of order are presented. The incident also further illuminates Bruno, whose symbolic function in the film is by no means undermined by the fact that he is also a character created in the round. Mrs. Cunningham, like Bruno's mother, is rich, spoiled, foolish, and indulgent; he is able to handle her so adroitly because he is used to managing his mother, manipulating her reactions. This is the kind of relationship he can manage, a relationship based entirely on power, wielded through a combination of cunning and insidious, self-insinuating charm – his ability to involve others in his sickness. Finally, the sequence shows the toll his life and actions are taking of him, his thoroughgoing cynicism and complete lack of remorse belied by his obsession with Barbara's (that is, Miriam's) glasses and neck, the ineradicable memory of that other relationship expressed in the shot of his anguished face as he tries to strangle Mrs. Cunningham. As his hands are pulled away from her throat, he falls back in a swoon.

It is the near strangling of Mrs. Cunningham that forces the spectator to come to terms with his attitude toward subversive desire and prompts Guy, under pressure from Ann, to divulge the truth to her – without, however, acknowledging any personal guilt, of which he obviously remains quite unaware. He tells Ann, "I'd do his murder, he'd do mine"; to which she responds, suggestively, "What do you mean – *your* murder, Guy?" Her first reaction was, "How did you get him to do it?" The removal of doubts between the lovers marks a necessary stage in the action. Their relationship is now on a surer footing, giving Guy the strength to take steps to extricate himself. The next sequence, in which he visits Mr. Anthony's house at night, is a turning point and a critical crux.

The emphasis is, again, on suspense: in successive shots we see Guy take the gun Bruno has sent him, elude his "tail" by using the fire escape, and cross the moonlit lawn of the Anthony grounds in long-shot, like a shadow. We do not know at all clearly what he intends to do or what will happen to him. Suspense is built up as he enters the house (using the key Bruno has sent), consults Bruno's map to find the father's room, encounters a snarling mastiff on the stairs, subdues it, finds the room, transfers the gun (hesitating for a moment with it in his hand) from his breast pocket to his side pocket, creeps into the bedroom, approaches the bed, calls in a whisper,

"Mr. Anthony ... I want to speak to you about your son ... about Bruno." Then the dark figure on the bed switches on a lamp and reveals himself as Bruno.

At first glance this seems, indeed, to be that "mere" suspense that is all Hitchcock's detractors see in his films: externally applied, rather cheap. And if we assume that Guy knows precisely what he is going to do in Mr. Anthony's house, the criticism is unanswerable. Hitchcock is cheating, basing the suspense on a deliberate misleading of the spectator. There are, however, points that suggest that this is too superficial a reading: that Guy has indeed made up his mind to visit Mr. Anthony, but there remains a possibility, right up to the moment of hesitation outside the bedroom door, that he will change his mind and shoot him. With this in mind, the sequence assumes quite a different aspect.

The first hint comes in fact several scenes earlier when Guy is talking to Hennessy in his rooms before the party. The camera looks down as Guy opens the top drawer in which Bruno's gun is lying, and we see the two men, with the gun strongly emphasized in the foreground of the screen. Guy has just been telling Hennessy he will have an early night: he is in fact planning to visit the Anthony house. But they are now discussing Hennessy's suspicious colleague, Hammond, and, as we see the gun in the drawer, Hennessy says, "He doesn't trust anybody – not even himself." The whole shot is framed and directed in such a way as to give a particular significance to the remark, linking it with the gun. Then, in the house, we have the moment of hesitation itself. This is either the decisive moment of the scene or a very cheap trick indeed: cheap, because it falsifies a character's behavior for the sake of producing a shiver – if the gesture does not imply uncertainty as to what to do with the gun, then it has no meaning at all. Finally, shortly after the discovery that it is Bruno on the bed, Guy tells him, "You're sick," adding, "I don't know much about those things...." It is the nearest to an explicit statement in the film of that lack of self-awareness so plentifully illustrated elsewhere. The "suspense" of the sequence, then, has a point: the spectator's uncertainty as to what Guy is going to do corresponds to the character's own inner uncertainty. And the moment of final decision is the turning point of the film: henceforward, Bruno is openly *against* Guy, no longer wanting anything but revenge. The conflict has changed levels, and the struggle for self-preservation is the price Guy must pay for his involvement; an involvement partly expiated by the decision taken outside Mr. Anthony's bedroom.

But, this said, it must then be admitted that to raise such doubts is to acknowledge a dissatisfaction with the sequence. Guy's uncertainty is not sufficiently realized, a fault due perhaps to the limitations of Farley Granger as an actor, which led Hitchcock to put more weight on that one gesture with the gun than it can stand. But the criticism is of a misjudgment, a local failure of realization, not a major lapse in artistic integrity. [– Now I'm not so sure. The compromise over the hero figure that fatally flaws *Torn Curtain* offers a close parallel, and one cannot but feel that Hitchcock's uncertainty of handling in the scene of Guy's visit to Bruno's house has its roots in his fears of the effect of so morally dubious a "hero" on box-office response. "Major lapse in artistic integrity" is perhaps not too strong a description. – R.W. 1968.]

* * *

Ann's interview with Bruno's mother is the next step in the working-out of the situation on its new level, the protagonists now ranged openly against one another. In Mrs. Anthony's insanity we see (as we are to see it later, more extremely, in the amalgam of Norman Bates and his mother at the end of *Psycho*) the ultimate extension of the chaos-world. The woman's very existence depends on the complete rejection of all value judgments, the final denial of responsibility. In fact, "irresponsibility" is the word she uses to excuse Bruno: with a smile of maternal indulgence, a little knowing shake of the head, she says, "Sometimes he's terribly irresponsible." To which Ann returns a moment later, "He's *responsible* for a woman's death."

The famous cross-cutting between the tennis match and Bruno's journey with the lighter gives us a very different sort of suspense – simpler, less disturbing than before, as befits this phase of the action. The tension we feel now is not uncomplicated by conflicting responses (who has not *wanted* Bruno to reach the lighter?), but the struggle has become clear and simple, the forces of good and evil are now separate and clearly aligned. Despite this, some very interesting points arise.

First, the development of that elementary yet elemental light-darkness symbolism: Guy fights for victory on the brilliantly sunny tennis court as Bruno struggles to reach the lighter that has slipped through a grating down a drain. One does not want to reduce the film to simple, pat allegory (Hitchcock resolutely defies any such treatment), but the cutting between sunny open court and shadowy enclosed drain carries powerfully evocative overtones: underlying the whole action of the film, we can see as its basis the struggle for dominance between superego and id. Secondly, we remember that tennis has been established from the start as Guy's means of access to the ordered world, his ladder from the previous life with Miriam to his projected political career; it is therefore appropriate that his fate should depend now on his ability at tennis. Furthermore, this test is made explicitly one of character, even of character development. Guy, in his desperation to finish the match in time, has to change his whole manner of playing (as the commentator points out) – he abandons his usual cautious long-term strategy in favor of a "grim and determined" open battling style. His whole career – even the desire to marry Ann – has been a matter of careful strategy: now he is forced to fight openly for what he wants. Thirdly, it is significant that the outcome of the entire film should be made to depend upon the retrieving of the lighter, symbol of Guy's involvement with Bruno, of his placing himself in Bruno's hands. Great emphasis is laid on it – and on the "A to G" inscription – every time it appears. It is Guy's strongest *concrete* link with the ordered world; now he must reenter the chaos-world in order to retrieve it, thereby risking final submersion.

The fairground climax gives us the ultimate development of that world in its magnificent symbol of the merry-go-round that gets out of control. Guy struggles for his life – for more than his life – on the insanely whirling machine beneath the metallic hoofs of hideously grinning and prancing dummy horses: the horses on which Bruno, with Guy's implicit consent (the lighter), set about "seducing" Miriam. Guy is denied the satisfaction – we are denied the release – of a straightforward victory: the merry-go-round terrifyingly breaks down, Guy is thrown clear, Bruno is crushed under the wreckage. He dies obstinately refusing repentance, and Guy seems involved forever. Then, as he dies, Bruno's hand opens: the lighter is in his palm.

The very last scene of the film (where Guy and Ann move away pointedly from a friendly clergyman on a train) shows us, with light humor, Guy, united with his senator's daughter, resolutely – even somewhat extremely and rigidly! – resisting the possibility of further temptation. The stiff unnaturalness of the couple's behavior is perfectly logical: Guy's involvement with Bruno has been worked out in action – he has never faced its implications, and his personality remains to the end unintegrated, his identity still potentially unstable, the threat of disorder to be held back only by rigid control.

Strangers on a Train draws together many themes already adumbrated in earlier films, which will be taken further in later ones: the theme of what Conrad calls the "sickening assumption of common guilt" (developed especially in *Psycho*); the theme of the search for identity (*Vertigo*); the theme of the struggle of a personality torn between order and chaos (perhaps the most constant Hitchcock theme); and, in close conjunction with this, the notion of experience therapy – the hero purged of his weaknesses by indulging them and having to live out the consequences (*Rear Window*). We find here, too, the characteristic Hitchcock moral tone: the utterly unsentimental and ruthless condemnation of the forces that make for disorder, coupled with a full awareness of their dangerously tempting fascination, a sense of the impurity of motives. Does Guy love Ann, or is she merely the way to success? Clearly both: good and evil are inseparably mixed. And, running through the film, there is that Hitchcockian humor that itself represents a moral position: it is the manifestation of his artistic impersonality, of his detached and impersonal attitude to themes that clearly obsess him. Yet the film leaves one unsatisfied (not merely disturbed). The fault may lie partly with the players: Farley Granger, a perfect foil to John Dall in *Rope*, is too slight a personality to carry much moral weight, so we feel that Guy's propensity for good or evil is too trivial: Ann (Ruth Roman) is a cold, formal woman, so there is little sense, at the end, that Guy has won through to a worthwhile relationship. There is not enough at stake: his triumph over too slight an evil (in himself) has won him too equivocal a good. Consequently, the effect seems at times two-dimensional, or like watching the working-out of a theorem rather than a human drama; and the film, if not exactly a failure, strikes me as something less than a masterpiece.

One has no qualifications about Robert Walker's Bruno or about any of the scenes built around him. The film's two classic sequences, in fact, seem to me the first fairground sequence and the scene of the Morton's party. Here the characteristic Hitchcockian moral tone is felt in all its disturbing complexity.

STRANGERS ON A TRAIN (Warner Bros., 1951). *Producer*: Alfred Hitchcock, *Script*: Raymond Chandler, Czenzi Ormonde, Whitfield Cook, from the novel by Patricia Highsmith, *Photography*: Robert Burks, *Editor*: William H. Ziegler, *Sets*: Edward S. Haworth, George James Hopkins, *Music*: Dimitri Tiomkin, *Costumes*: Leah Rhodes, *Players*: Robert Walker (Bruno Anthony), Farley Granger (Guy Haines), Ruth Roman (Ann Morton), Leo G. Carroll (Senator Morton), Patricia Hitchcock (Barbara Morton), Laura Elliot (Miriam Haines), Marion Lorne (Mrs. Anthony). 101 minutes.

Part Four
The Later Films

In *The Strange Case of Alfred Hitchcock*, Raymond Durgnat divides Hitchcock's career into thirteen periods or "lives," the divisions corresponding roughly to successive changes in Hitchcock's studio affiliations – from Gainsborough to British International to Gaumont-British to Gainsborough to Selznick to Warner Bros., and so on. Clearly Durgnat's polemical purpose in so doing – as his subsequent realignment of Hitchcock's career by theme and genre indicates – was to counter the then-prevailing wisdom, which preferred British Hitchcock to Hollywood Hitchcock and identified the former almost exclusively by reference to the comedy thrillers made for Gaumont-British and Gainsborough – that is, the films from *The Man Who Knew Too Much* (1934) to *The Lady Vanishes* (1938).

In *Hitchcock: The Murderous Gaze* William Rothman also undertakes a revision of the Hitchcock canon. He discusses five films in depth – *The Lodger, Murder!, The 39 Steps, Shadow of a Doubt, Psycho* – in support of his claim that "*Psycho*'s position is already declared, indeed already worked out, in *The Lodger*," (p. 2), as if period distinctions among Hitchcock's films finally ought not to matter much. Rothman's running commentary on Hitchcock's development does not divide up the British filmography as neatly as Durgnat does; Rothman discusses the English period in generic and thematic rather than chronological terms. But, in his culminating discussion of *Psycho*, Rothman still sketches an account of Hitchcock's American period that suggests four phases akin to Durgnat's chronological scheme. These are the films of the 1940s, from *Rebecca* (1940) through *Stage Fright* (1950), which Rothman describes by and large as "a time of searching" (p. 246) during which Hitchcock worked out the terms of his relationship to Hollywood and to America; the films of the early 1950s, from *Strangers on a Train* (1951) through *Dial "M" for Murder* (1954), wherein we see "the full flowering of [Hitchcock's] mature art" (p. 246); the "mature period" proper, beginning with *Rear Window* (1954) and identifiable largely with Hitchcock's Paramount films through *Psycho* (1960), though both *The Wrong Man* (Warner Bros.) and *North by Northwest* (MGM) are usually included in the category; and the final films, beginning with *The Birds* (1963), in which the rapport of audience and auteur that had characterized Hitchcock's previous period broke down, in part at least because Hitchcock slowly lost the services of his closest collaborators – Cary Grant, Grace Kelly, Robert Burks, Bernard Herrmann.

Readers of *A Hitchcock Reader* will have noticed that our own division of Hitchcock's career into three periods – the British, the Hollywood, the "later films" – is at best a rough approximation of such organizational schemes as those of Durgnat and Rothman, far plainer than Durgnat's "Plain Man's Hitchcock." But we really had a second history in mind beyond or behind that of the films themselves – the history of Hitchcock criticism, especially that which developed in the English-speaking world in response to the radical rethinking of Hitchcock initiated in the middle and late 1950s by the young Parisian Turks at *Cahiers du cinéma*.

Five names are crucial here, though each in odd ways (for references see the introduction and bibliography of Part One). The *Cahiers* ringleaders were clearly Eric Rohmer and Claude Chabrol, as evidenced by the publication in 1957 of their *Hitchcock*. The oddities here are two. The book concluded with a relatively lengthy discussion of *The Wrong Man*, at the time Hitchcock's latest film, though not one highly regarded by the English-language press; and the book itself was not available in English until 1979. François Truffaut, under the sometimes discomfited tutelage of André Bazin, was also a Hitchcock partisan, though his book on Hitchcock did not appear until 1966 (1967 in English). But Truffaut's general influence on English-language film scholarship, in particular his championing of auteur criticism, gained crucial currency through his filmmaking (*The 400 Blows* was released in 1959) and through the work of Andrew Sarris (whose auteurist pantheon of the American cinema first appeared in *Film Culture* in 1963). Jean Douchet played the crucial role of extending the "Catholic/mystical" reading of Rohmer and Chabrol to the post-*Wrong Man* films in a series of three essays published in *Cahiers* in 1959 and 1960. While ranging widely in his references to Hitchcock's *oeuvre* (partly in homage to Rohmer and Chabrol), Douchet devotes his most concerted attention to three films – *Rear Window, North by Northwest*, and *Psycho* – all from Hitchcock's mature period. Lastly, there is Robin Wood, whose "Psychanalyse de *Psycho*" (which eventually became the crucial chapter in his 1965 *Hitchcock's Films*) appeared as the lead article in the same number of *Cahiers* (no. 113) as the last of Douchet's three pieces.

Facts of language and timing are crucial here. English-language Hitchcock criticism through the middle 1970s is largely a debate between those, like Wood, who found the *Cahiers* approach to Hitchcock to be a great advance, and those like Penelope Houston, the editor of *Sight and Sound*, who found the *Cahiers* line irredeemably silly and inflated for proclaiming Hitchcock as profound and profoundly a film artist as Bergman or Antonioni. It is highly ironic – highly Hitchcockian – that many parties to the debate over Hitchcock's authorship and stature, especially its more journalistic American participants, had never read its central documents; hence the importance of Robin Wood, who stood, for a time, as the only "original" bridge between Hitchcock's French-speaking partisans and his typically more skeptical English-speaking reviewers.

Moreover, the crucial period during which the debate took place was 1960 through 1963 – that is, between *Psycho* and *The Birds*. Under the influence of Douchet and Wood, a central canon of Hitchcock texts was forming: *Vertigo, North by Northwest*, and *Psycho* were all vivid in memory, though *Vertigo*, like *Rope, Rear Window*, the remake of *The Man Who Knew Too Much*, and *The Trouble with Harry*, would soon be withdrawn (hence "lost") from circulation – partly for legal reasons but also in the hope that they would prove a valuable legacy (as they did) for Hitchcock's heirs. The question of Hitchcock's artistic stature was thus ripe for the asking, the lines were clearly drawn, and, with the release of *The Birds* in 1963 and *Marnie* the following year, the battle was joined in earnest.

In retrospect the lines were far too narrowly drawn. In its original edition Wood's book covered only seven films in detail: *Strangers on a Train, Rear Window, Vertigo, North by Northwest, Psycho, The Birds*, and *Marnie*. But to say that the lines were drawn too narrowly is not to imply that the films included within the canonical circle were unworthy of the attention they received, however historically contingent that attention may initially have been. They are *still* the films most frequently attended to. Witness the work of Raymond Bellour, whose close readings of *North by Northwest, Psycho, The Birds*, and *Marnie* far exceed in rigor and complexity the original ambitions of the *Cahiers* crew. Or consider Tania Modleski's "Resurrection of a Hitchcock Daughter (2005)," a retrospective chapter included in the second edition of *The Women Who Knew Too Much*. Though she cites and discusses a significant number of latter-day Hitchcock scholars (Slavoj Žižek, Robert Kapsis, Susan Smith, Lee Edelman, Lucretia Knapp, Rhona J. Berenstein, Susan White), her consideration of "how feminist scholarship on Hitchcock has fared" (p. 125) since her book first appeared focuses chiefly on *The Birds* and *Marnie*, though *Rear Window* and *Rebecca* are also crucial.

A consequence of allowing this historical focus on the canonical "later films" to determine our choice of essays is the necessity of slighting some films from the same period – most regrettably *To Catch a Thief* and *The Trouble with Harry* – that have not figured so prominently in the tradition of Hitchcock criticism. But the alternative was to misrepresent, or under-represent, that tradition. We found the prospect of providing multiple perspectives on the canonical later films especially compelling for providing readers with an opportunity to see the tradition in action. Though the terms of argument established by reference to such films as *Vertigo* and *Psycho* have proven appropriate across the whole range of Hitchcock's works, as a glance at nearly any essay in this anthology will confirm, for brevity's sake we have chosen to introduce the chapters in this part by following a single thread. We might call it, in a backhanded reference to Henry James via Penelope Houston, "the figure in the carpet."

In his discussion of *Strangers on a Train*, Robin Wood dwells on the "ironic" quality of the film, what Wood calls its "characteristic Hitchcock moral tone: the utterly unsentimental and ruthless condemnation of the forces that make for disorder, coupled with a full awareness of their dangerously tempting fascination." Some difficult questions are involved here. In what sense can a film be "aware"? By what property of act or action can a film utter a "condemnation"? Or is Wood treating the film itself as a "speech act," as communicating its author's state of mind? Or, to take a second example, consider the following passage from David Kehr on the topic of Hitchcock's "lost films":

In these films, Hitchcock can be seen doing what he refused to do in life: acknowledging his status as a creator and struggling to come to terms with that status. Though art isn't always the primary theme, it is always closely related to the perennial thematic center of Hitchcock's work: the problem of guilt. If Hitchcock always refused to confess his artistry – and went to maniacal lengths to protect himself from the accusation – it's because art was Alfred Hitchcock's dirty secret, his original sin. (p. 10)

But how does a film "acknowledge" or "confess"? And how does a director get a film to do such things or get film critics to attribute them? That is, by what logic do critics like Wood and Kehr propose to discern the "figure" of the director within the complex thematic/formal weave of the cinematic "carpet" bearing his signature?

At heart such discernment or attribution depends on or interprets a commonsense analogy implicit in the terminology of screen credits: "Directed by Alfred Hitchcock." Pictures do not take themselves – cameras must be pointed, "directed" – so it is easy to think of the camera as an embodiment of its director's gaze or intention. A photograph necessarily implies or "connotes" a photographer. But it is a curious property of photographs, or at least of the responses they typically evoke, to connote "photographer" by exclusion. What we typically see within the frame is the "subject" of the photograph – a room, a scene, a street, a face – the photographer is out of frame, "off-screen." Hence the somewhat paradoxical fact that film authorship is perceived simultaneously as both an active and a passive undertaking – active for taking photographs, passive for taking no visible part in them.

This basic paradox of authorship is often repeated in reference to the spectator and to what critics have understood as conventional habits of viewing. Hollywood films have long been subject to charges of escapism; of promoting vicarious experience, chiefly through the mechanism of viewer/character "identification"; of manufacturing an ersatz world, which viewers respond to passively, as if the film world were as real and as intractable as the world of their daily lives, though the film world is also experienced as having been cut to the measure of desire – so that film viewers are encouraged in this sense to desire their own passivity, as if the world "as it is" were always already "desirable."

In the 1980s and 1990s such charges were renewed and rewritten in light of advances in the realms of semiotics, psychoanalysis, and feminism, as the Robin Wood and Marian Keane chapters on *Vertigo* and the Michele Piso and Lucretia Knapp analyses of *Marnie* well attest (see the introduction to Part Five for further elaboration of the psychological background to some of these views). But the basic equation here has been relatively constant: authorial self-effacement, the director's retreat behind the image, is taken to encourage viewer "passivity" before the image. By the same token, authorial self-assertion, the director's calling attention to the fact of his or her direction, to the fact that what we are watching is not a real world but a film world, is taken to encourage in viewers an "active" and "self-aware" form of spectatorship. This formulation of the relation of author, film, and viewer explains the central importance attached by most latter-day critics to textual "reflexivity": only by showing an active form of directorial or spectator self-consciousness at work (or so goes the argument) can critics justify their desire to analyze and to make positive claims about the likely cultural effects of the films on which they have chosen to focus. Several of the following chapters are exemplary instances of this approach to film criticism.

The *locus classicus* here – as the Robert Stam/Roberta Pearson chapter and the first part of Robin Wood's contribution to this part confirm – is *Rear Window*, the very title of which, as Stam and Pearson elaborate it, "evokes the diverse 'windows' of the cinema: the cinema/lens of camera and projector, the window in the projection booth, the eye as window, and film as 'window on the world.'" But two such analogies are crucial, each of which bears on the activity/passivity dilemma.

One of these (first elaborated by Jean Douchet in "Hitch and His Public") is the viewer/character analogy: Jefferies (James Stewart) in his wheelchair is similar to the viewer in his or her theater seat, isolated, motionless, passive, yet intensely, "voyeuristically" interested in the events that transpire on the apartment window "movie screens" opposite his own rear window. But, as Stam and Pearson read the film, this habit of voyeuristic looking is then called into question by means of a second analogy, that of Jefferies and Hitchcock. Each is a photographer; each depends for a living on his ability to capture the bizarre and exciting on film. By thus splitting the directorial function, Hitchcock evinces a degree of self-consciousness that eludes Jefferies until late in the film, when he watches his own surrogate, Lisa (Grace Kelly), searching the apartment where Jefferies believes a murder has taken place. When Thorwald returns and catches Lisa in the act, however, Jefferies is forced to confront the very fear his voyeurism had sought to mask or ignore – his fear of sexual intimacy with Lisa. For once he wishes he were close to her, and he cannot be. Moreover, this implicit critique of the Jefferies character effects a realignment of the operative analogy. No longer is it viewer/character or character/director; now it is a viewer/director analogy. By thus allying himself with his audience, Hitchcock encourages a species of viewer self-consciousness akin to the actively reflexive self-consciousness embodied in *Rear Window* itself.

A similar logic runs through the chapters by Keane and Stanley Cavell, though modified in at least two ways. *North by Northwest*, as Cavell reads it, presents us with three director surrogates, as opposed to *Rear Window*'s one – the Professor (Leo G. Carroll), who invents a fictitious government agent to divert attention from the real agent played by Eva Marie Saint; Philip Vandamm (James Mason), the master spy who falls for the Professor's ruse and whose henchmen effectively "cast" Roger Thornhill (Cary Grant) in the "George Kaplan" role; and Roger Thornhill/Cary Grant, himself a director and victimizer, especially of women, but the only one of the three director surrogates who earns the right to direct himself, for having been so thoroughly the victim of the others. (Is this why, of the three, Grant is most closely allied with Hitchcock, as if Hitchcock too were a victim?) A similar doubling of director surrogates is also evident in *Vertigo*, as both Wood and Keane observe; Scottie's efforts to remake Judy as Madeleine are disturbingly akin to Elster's original casting of Judy in the very same role; in each case a species of murderousness is at work.

The primary difference between Cavell and Keane, on the one hand, and the kind of reasoning represented by Pearson and Stam, on the other, involves essentially different understandings of the "ontology" of the cinematic image. Pearson and Stam clearly assume, as do many of the writers they cite, that "activity" of a certain type ought to be valorized or encouraged – an activity of aesthetic, political, and sexual self-criticism by contrast with the viewer "passivity" or "complicity" allegedly encouraged by most instances of the "classical narrative cinema." Paradoxically, one component of this passive acceptance of mainstream cinematic conventions is the oft-repeated contention that "looking" in the Hollywood film is split along conventional sexual lines: males (Hitchcock, the typical viewer) are the active and controlling lookers, females merely the passive objects of the male gaze, as Laura Mulvey famously put it. It is hardly the case that Keane and Cavell are unmindful of the authority and activity of Hitchcock's authorship. Each proposes to speak of Hitchcock's authorship on his behalf, as if Hitchcock were using them to lodge his claims to artistic authority. But each also goes on to declare that on one crucial account Hitchcock's authorship is passive, and positively so.

That is, Cavell and Keane introduce another level to discussions of activity and passivity by dwelling on the identities of the beings who inhabit the worlds of the films under scrutiny. In his chapter on *North by Northwest*, for example, Cavell declares "Cary Grant" to be a primary subject of the film, one of its primary sources (as much a source as *Hamlet*). Similarly, in her reading of *Vertigo*, Keane declares the "flesh and bloodness" of Kim Novak and James Stewart (qualities brought out in them by the photographic power of the camera's gaze) to be as much the subject of Hitchcock's meditations as the more overtly dramatic events their characters enact. Partly what Cavell and Keane have in mind here involves an artistic persona, a set of connotations built up around an actor or actress through the course of a career. Cavell is explicit on this account in tracing the history of Grant's earlier work with Hitchcock and also with Howard Hawks.

But equally important is what Keane (citing Cavell) calls "photogenesis," by which she refers to the fact that *Vertigo*, like most Hitchcock films, is especially dependent for its meaning upon particular faces, particular physiognomies (even if the parti-cular face in question, as Cavell has it in discussing *North by Northwest*, is the face of the world itself). One of the chief differences between theater and cinema for both Keane and Cavell is the fact that, in Cavell's words, "film actors and their characters get stuck to one another" and are thus inseparable. *Hamlet* will always be *Hamlet*, whoever plays the title role. But there is no *Vertigo* apart from Novak and Stewart. This argument underlies Keane's view that Hitchcock's remarkable and sustained attention to faces and expressions in *Vertigo* (especially in those moments when Judy or Scottie stares directly into the camera) amounts to a declaration of authorial pas-sivity before the world, a realization and recognition of the contingency of the cin-ematic medium. As Keane phrases it, "Hitchcock can place his subjects in worlds tailor-made for the emergence of their inner selves, but he does not have the power to invent these beings." It is precisely for denying the flesh and bloodness of Judy Barton that Scottie stands condemned at the end of *Vertigo*; it is precisely in acknowl-edging the flesh and bloodness of Kim Novak, James Stewart, and Cary Grant that Hitchcock evinces his most profound and moving understandings of the medium of cinema, of its paradoxical capacity to be actively passive, or passively active, as if to challenge those very categories of being or perception. Hitchcock shows us a way of looking at the world in these later films that is far more reflective and confessional than many are willing to grant. We might say, echoing Keane's characterization of Scottie in *Vertigo*, that in his later films Hitchcock is exploring the feminine regions of himself, his own sensitivity and passivity and bitterness before the world, as if he too were a vengeful "bird," poised and hovering above an uncomprehending community.

Much of the credit for locating this feminist strain in Hitchcock goes to Tania Modleski, though she often refers to François Truffaut's remarks on *Rebecca* in his interview with Hitchcock to confirm her claim that it was Hitchcock's explicit encounter with "the feminine discourse of du Maurier's Gothic novel" (Modleski, 42) that established Hitchcock's "true subject and his true method" (p. 134). Indeed, that Hitchcock disavowed his authorship of *Rebecca* – "It's not a Hitchcock picture," he told Truffaut (p. 127) – establishes its centrality to his subsequent career, where "psychological ingredients ... initially discovered in the Daphne du Maurier novel" (p. 129) increasingly take the place of thriller-style "suspense." Hence, for Modleski, Hitchcock's authorship – as *Frenzy* makes appallingly if poignantly clear – is almost literally a matter of (textual) incorporation and (gender) role reversal. Indeed, the thesis of *The Women Who Knew Too Much*, she declares in the book's first paragraph, is that "Hitchcock's great need ... to insist on and exert authorial control can be related to the fact that his films are always in danger of being subverted by females whose power is both fascinating and seemingly limitless" (p. 1). Even when dead, like Babs Milligan in *Frenzy*, they often have an uncanny power to avenge themselves on their patriarchal oppressors.

Hence the striking fact that "*feminists* have found themselves compelled, intrigued, infuriated and inspired by Hitchcock's works" (p. 1). In calling herself "a Hitchcock Daughter," Modleski invokes the concept of identification (of "family romance" too). And, if she is generally clear that Hitchcock as "cine-master" is a paternal figure, it is one who identifies himself on numerous occasions with a feminine perspective. Even in *Frenzy*, it is Inspector Oxford's acceptance of his wife's viewpoint on the murder of Brenda Blaney – however cautious he is about ingesting Mrs. Oxford's continental cooking – that leads him to return to Rusk's scene-of-the-crime apart- ment, thereby putting an end to Rusk's serial sex crimes and clearing Richard Blaney of multiple murders. That hardly makes *Frenzy* a celebration of feminism, though Modleski construes the depth of its disgust with sexuality as symptomatic of the "boundary confusion" attendant upon the "sexual and social liberation" of the early 1970s, hence of patriarchy's vulnerability in the face of undying feminist resistance.

A key term in Modleski's discussion of *Frenzy*, as in Lucretia Knapp's of "The Queer Voice in *Marnie*," is "ambivalence," an ambivalence (in Modleski) bearing exactly on the intersection of identification and incorporation. Mythically speaking, Modleski reads the "savage" equation of women with food in *Frenzy* as expressing, in reverse, a male fear of being consumed; in psychoanalytic or developmental terms, "incorporation may be seen as a preliminary stage of identification" or intersubjectiv- ity that seeks as much to "appropriate" or "assimilate," even to "preserve," femininity as to "destroy" it – "hence that curious mixture of 'sympathy and misogyny' found in [Hitchcock's] films." As well as, we might also add, the necessity repeatedly seen in Hitchcock of finding (or hearing) a female('s) voice. That such voices and characters nearly always suffer repression in Hitchcock's films is less surprising than the fact that viewers are often called upon to acknowledge female victimization and to admire the courage of these women in the face of oppression, an admiration, as Modleski and Knapp both attest, that may extend to Hitchcock via the character/director analogy; if we admire Marnie as (in Knapp's term) an "outlaw" – as in some sense both Mark and Hitchcock do as well – then we may identify, however ambivalently, with Hitchcock's peculiar brand of "outlaw" authorship. As Knapp puts it: "Hitchcock's films are of great interest because, for him, there is nothing sacred about the heterosexual narrative." So perhaps "the queer voice in *Marnie*" is as much Hitchcock's as Marnie's.

A main difference between Modleski and Knapp is that Knapp applies "ambivalence" almost exclusively to descriptions of the traumatic mother–daughter relation in *Marnie*, while Modleski applies it to male–female relationships more generally. Though Modleski started her own labyrinthine journey through Hitchcock by investigating how mother–daughter relationships between the second Mrs. DeWinter and "assorted mother – substitutes" (p. 44) in *Rebecca* enact a gothic version of the "female oedipal journey," Knapp takes exception to her arguably oversimple equation of pre-Oedipal mother–daughter "fusion" and female bisexuality. As Modleski concedes in "Resurrection of a Hitchcock Daughter (2005)," such an equation risks seeing female homosexuality as instancing "arrested development" (p. 143). Like many feminists, Modleski employs the "bisexuality" notion as a way of explaining the variability of female spectatorship and identifications and as a utopian marker of a world less polarized by gender anxieties and inequities. Knapp writes from an explicitly lesbian perspective, however, for the purpose of showing how Hitchcock's "gender play" – as in the enigmatic nursery rhyme that opens and closes the film's action, for example, or in the rivalry verging on same-sex attraction between Marnie and Lil – creates "a space for Marnie outside the dualistic economies of patriarchy," because Marnie herself "plays" with gender stereotypes; though feminine in appearance and demeanor, she is an active agent of desire whose deepest longings are female-oriented.

The Birds, writes John Orr in "Hitch as Matrix-Figure" (see Part One), "is a late summation of many great things in Hitchcock," among which he includes Hitchcock's "cinematic style, his deep knowledge of film and his dark vision of modernity" and also "of all catastrophes in the modern age," especially those resulting from humankind's erasure of the "divide between nature and culture in the realm of catastrophe." The modernity in question in Orr's analysis of *The Birds* is chiefly that of the 1920s avant-gardism of Eisenstein's *Battleship Potemkin* and the apocalyptic 1950s and 1960s art-film modernism of Ingmar Bergman and Michelangelo Antonioni. While agreeing with Orr that *The Birds* is an exemplary instance of artistic self- consciousness, John McCombe locates Hitchcock's modernity within the context of British Romantic Poetry, especially the visionary and apocalyptic and aesthetically self-conscious practice of William Wordsworth and Samuel Taylor Coleridge. An obvious connection here is the way Coleridge's Ancient Mariner (in his "Rime of the Ancient Mariner") suffers the revenge of Nature after his killing of an allegorical albatross, which can be seen as anticipating the revenge that Nature visits upon the inhabitants of Bodega Bay after Melanie Daniels delivers her allegorical "lovebirds" to Cathy Brenner. More to the point, as both Orr and McCombe explicitly avow, is the way *The Birds* evokes the problematic link between vision and understanding. No less than *Rear Window* or *Psycho*, *The Birds* is a film about seeing, about "eyes," about the vulnerability and contingency of perception; but in posing an interpretative question (why do the birds attack?) that so obviously resists solution, Hitchcock raises further questions about the determination of human and narrative causality and about the human institutions – the art world and educational establishments among them – charged with balancing the claims of nature and culture in a time and place when the balance is obviously distorted, perhaps beyond redemption.

Three closing cautions are in order here. Two of these are urged by Robin Wood in his chapter on *Vertigo*. (1) In discussing Hitchcock's authorship we are not primarily concerned with the artist's private life; the films he made are "public" in the sense that we are all free to ponder their meaning. We may finally want to attribute that meaning to Hitchcock, to believe in our heart of hearts that Hitchcock would confirm our interpretations; but no better confirmation exists (or is likely to) than actively attentive reviewings of the films themselves. (2) We need also to be cautious in presuming that Hitchcock's films are typical – each of the others or any of the "classical Hollywood cinema." As Wood points out, to follow Bellour in describing all Hollywood films as "machines for producing the couple" is to deny many essential differences and to restrict severely the opportunities available to viewers and critics.

The third critical caution emerges from Marshall Deutelbaum's historical study of the circumstances surrounding the production of *The Wrong Man*. In one crucial detail, Hitchcock's artistic practice refused the self-effacement typical of Hollywood; in the vast majority of his films Hitchcock puts in a cameo appearance at one point or another. Quite often such appearances explicitly identify Hitchcock as an artist – helping the musician with his timing in *Rear Window*, for example, or climbing aboard a train with a string bass in *Strangers on a Train*. But Hitchcock ostensibly eschews the role of artist in his introductory comments to *The Wrong Man*, where he promises that *this* story, unlike his "thrillers," is "a true story, every word of it." In so doing, however, Hitchcock only further reinforces his status as a fabulist, as a practitioner of the craft of fiction, because most of what makes *The Wrong Man* a Hitchcock film, as Deutelbaum demonstrates, had nothing to do with the facts of the case on which it is based. Latter-day audiences might well be excused for missing that, for treating *The Wrong Man* as they would any other Hitchcock film. It remains a striking footnote to the history of Hitchcock's relation to his public that no one among the film's original audience (to judge by contemporary reviews) seems to have noticed what is arguably Hitchcock's most overt challenge to his audience, his most explicit claim to the acknowledgment of his authorship: he tells a familiar story *his way*, playing havoc with the well-publicized facts of Emmanuel Balestrero's case for the sake of his artistic vision. But, as another of Hitchcock's fabulist/surrogates once put it in bringing to life another case history: "Here I was born, here I died; you took no notice." The caution here? Trust not the teller but the tale.

References and Suggested Readings

Allen, Jeanne Thomas. "Looking through *Rear Window*: Hitchcock's Traps and Lures of Heterosexual Romance." In Diedre Pribram, ed., *Female Spectators: Looking at Film and Television*. London: Verso, 1988, 31–43.

Allen, Richard. "Avian Metaphor in *The Birds*." In Gottlieb and Brookhouse (cited in Part One): 281–309.

Allen, Richard. "Hitchcock after Bellour." *Hitchcock Annual*, 2002–3, 117–47. On *The Birds* and *Psycho*.

Barr, Charles. *Vertigo*. London: British Film Institute, 2002.

Bellour, Raymond. "Hitchcock – Endgame." In Allen and Ishii-Gonzalès, *Alfred Hitchcock* (cited in Part One): 179–84. On *Family Plot*.

Belton, John, ed. *Alfred Hitchcock's* Rear Window. New York: Cambridge Univ. Press, 2000.

Belton, John. "The Space of *Rear Window*." In Raubicheck and Srebnick (cited in Part One): 76–94.

Bergstrom, Janet. "Enunciation and Sexual Difference." In Constance Penley, ed., *Feminism and Film Theory*. New York: Routledge; London: British Film Institute, 1988, 159–85. On Bellour, *The Birds*, and *Marnie*.

Berman, Emanuel. "Hitchcock's *Vertigo*: The Collapse of a Rescue Fantasy." In Glen O. Gabbard, ed., *Psychoanalysis and Film*. London: Karnac, 2001, 29–62.

Berry, Sarah. "'She's Too Everything': Marriage and Masquerade in *Rear Window* and *To Catch a Thief*." *Hitchcock Annual*, 2001–2, 79–107.

Bingham, Dennis. "Hitchcock and Biopics." *Acting Male: Masculinities in the Films of James Stewart, Jack Nicholson, and Clint Eastwood*. New Brunswick, NJ: Rutgers Univ. Press, 1994, 69–83.

Bordwell, David. "The Viewer's Activity." *Narration in the Fiction Film*. Madison: Univ. of Wisconsin Press, 1985, 29–47. On *Rear Window*.

Bordwell, David, and Kristin Thompson. *Film Art: An Introduction*, eighth edition. Boston: McGraw Hill, 2008. The "Film Criticism" chapter discusses *North by Northwest* as exemplifying "The Classical Narrative Cinema."

Boyd, David. *Film and the Interpretive Process: A Study of* Blow-Up, Rashomon, Citizen Kane, 8½, Vertigo *and* Persona. New York: Peter Lang, 1989.

Brill, Lesley. "Packs, Predators, and Love in Hitchcock's *North by Northwest*." *Crowds, Powers, and Transformation in Cinema*. Wayne State Univ. Press, 2006, 121–42.

Bronfen, Elisabeth. "Risky Resemblances: On Repetition, Mourning, and Representation." In Sarah Webster Goodwin and Elisabeth Bronfen, eds., *Death and Representation*. Baltimore: Johns Hopkins Univ. Press, 1993, 103–29. On *Vertigo*.

Brown, Royal S. "Music and/as Cine-Narrative or: *Ceci n'est pas un leitmotif*." In James Phelan and Peter J. Rabinowitz, eds., *A Companion to Narrative Theory*. Malden, MA: Blackwell, 2005, 451–65. On *North by Northwest*.

Brown, Royal S. "The Music of Vertigo." In *Feature Film, a Book by Gordon Douglas*. London: Artangel Afterlives, Book Works, and Galerie du jour-Agnès B., 1999, 5–8.

Busch, Justine E. A. "The Centre Cannot Hold: Betrayals in Alfred Hitchcock's *Topaz*." *Cine-action*, no. 66 (April 2005): 29–41.

Butte, George. *I Know That You Know That I Know: Narrating Subjects from* Moll Flanders *to* Marnie. Columbus: Ohio Univ. Press, 2004. A chapter on "Comedy, Film, and Film Comedy" discusses "Hitchcock's Cary Grant Films," while the chapter on "Deep

Intersubjectivity and Masquerade" discusses "Hitchcock's *Marnie*, The Maternal Gaze, and Masquerade."

Cameron, Ian, and Richard Jeffery. "Universal Hitchcock." In Deutelbaum and Poague (cited in Part One): 265–78.

Carroll, Noël. "*Vertigo* and the Pathologies of Romantic Love." In Baggett and Drumin (cited in Part One): 101–13.

Columpar, Corinn. "*Marnie*: A Site/Sight for the Convergence of Gazes." *Hitchcock Annual*, 1999–2000, 51–73.

Cooper, David. *Bernard Herrmann's* Vertigo: *A Film Score Handbook*. Westport, CT: Greenwood Press, 2001.

Cowie, Elizabeth. "Rear Window Ethics." In Jeffrey Geiger, and R. L. Rutsky, eds. *Film Analysis: A Norton Reader*. New York: W. W. Norton, 2005, 475–93.

Deleyto, Celestino. "Focalization in Alfred Hitchcock's *The Birds*." *Miscelanea*, vol. 15 (1994): 155–91.

Deutelbaum, Marshall. "Logical Dream/Illogical Space: Set Design as Narration in a Key Sequence in *Vertigo*." *Hitchcock Annual*, 2002–3, 204–12.

Dick, Bernard F. "Hitchcock's Terrible Mothers." *Literature/Film Quarterly*, vol. 28, no. 4 (2000): 238–49.

Durgnat, Raymond. *The Strange Case of Alfred Hitchcock: Or, the Plain Man's Hitchcock*. (Cited in Part One.)

Edelman, Lee. "Hitchcock's Future." In Allen and Ishii-Gonzalès, *Alfred Hitchcock* (cited in Part One): 239–58.

Edelman, Lee. "*Rear Window's* Glasshole." In Ellis Hanson, ed., *Out Takes: Essays on Queer Theory and Film*. Durham, NC: Duke Univ. Press, 1999, 72–96.

Fawell, John. *Hitchcock's* Rear Window: *The Well-Made Film*. Carbondale: Southern Illinois Univ. Press, 2001.

Flory, Dan. "Hitchcock and Deductive Reasoning: Moving Step by Step in *Vertigo*." *Film and Philosophy*, no. 3 (1996): 38–52.

Flory, Dan. "*Vertigo*: Method, Obsession, and Human Minds." In Baggett and Drumin (cited in Part One): 115–27.

Gabbard, Glen O. "*Vertigo*: Female Objectification, Male Desire, and Object Loss." *Psychoanalytic Inquiry*, vol. 18 (1998): 161–7.

Gilmore, Richard A. "A *The Usual Suspects* Moment in *Vertigo*: The Epistemology of Identity." *Doing Philosophy at the Movies*. Albany: State Univ. of New York Press, 2005, 33–56.

Greig, Donald. "The Sexual Differentiation of the Hitchcock Text." *Screen*, vol. 28, no. 1 (Winter 1987): 28–46. On Bellour's Hitchcock.

Gunning, Tom. "The Desire and Pursuit of the Hole: Cinema's Obscure Object of Desire." In Shadi Bartsch and Thomas Bartsherer, eds., *Erotikon: Essays on Eros, Ancient and Modern*. Chicago: Univ. of Chicago Press, 2005, 261–77. On *Vertigo*.

Harvey, James. *Movie Love in the Fifties*. New York: Alfred A. Knopf, 2001. Chapters on *Vertigo*, "Hitchcock's Blondes," and "Janet Leigh and *Psycho*."

Hinton, Laura. "A Woman's View: The *Vertigo* Frame-Up." *Film Criticism*, vol. 19, no. 2 (Winter 1994–5): 2–22.

Holland, Norman N. "*Vertigo*: One Viewer's Viewing." In *Meeting Movies*. Madison, NJ: Fairleigh Dickinson Univ. Press, 2006, 36–53.

Horwitz, Margaret. "*The Birds*: A Mother's Love." In Deutelbaum and Poague (cited in Part One): 279–87.

Houston, Penelope. "The Figure in the Carpet." *Sight and Sound*, vol. 34, no. 4 (Autumn 1963): 159–64.

Hutchings, Peter. "*Frenzy*: A Return to Britain." In Charles Barr, ed., *All Our Yesterdays: 90 Years of British Cinema*. London: British Film Institute, 1986, 368–74.

Jameson, Fredric. "Spatial Systems in *North by Northwest*." In Žižek, *Everything You Always Wanted to Know about Lacan (But Were Afraid to Ask Hitchcock)* (cited in Part One): 47–72.

Kalinak, Kathryn. "The Language of Music: A Brief Analysis of *Vertigo*." In *Settling the Score: Music and the Classical Hollywood Film*. Madison: Univ. of Wisconsin Press, 1992, 3–19.

Kaplan, E. Ann. "The Maternal Melodrama: The 'Phallic' Mother Paradigm: *Now Voyager* (1942) and *Marnie* (1964)." In *Motherhood and Representation: The Mother in Popular Culture and Melodrama*. London: Routledge, 1992, 107–23.

Kehr, David. "Hitch's Riddle." *Film Comment*, vol. 20, no. 3 (May–June 1984): 9–18. On the "lost" Hitchcock films.

Lee, Sander H. "Existential Themes in the Films of Alfred Hitchcock." *Philosophy Research Archives*, vol. 11 (March 1986): 225–44.

Leff, Leonard J. "Hitchcock at Metro." In Deutelbaum and Poague (cited in Part One): 41–61.

Lefebvre, Martin. "Conspicuous Consumption: The Figure of the Serial Killer as Cannibal in the Age of Capitaism." *Theory, Culture & Society*, vol. 22, no. 3 (2005): 43–62. On *Frenzy*.

Lehmann, Ulrich. "Language of the PurSuit: Cary Grant's Clothes in Alfred Hitchcock's *North by Northwest*." *Fashion Theory*, vol. 4, no. 4 (2000): 467–85.

Leigh, Christian. "Double or Nothing: Alfred Hitchcock's (Subversive) Cinema: Notes on a Damaged 'Machine.'" In Leigh (cited in Part One): 8–25.

Leitch, Thomas. "It's the Cold War, Stupid: An Obvious History of the Political Hitchcock." *Literature/Film Quarterly*, vol. 27, no. 1 (1999): 3–15.

Lesser, Wendy. "Hitchcock's Couples." In *His Other Half: Men Looking at Women through Art*. Cambridge: Harvard Univ. Press, 1991, 121–44. Mostly on *North by Northwest*, *Vertigo*, and *The Man Who Knew Too Much* (1956).

Lightning, Robert K. "A Domestic Trilogy." *Cineaction*, no. 50 (September 1999): 32–42. On *The Man Who Knew Too Much* (1956), *The Trouble with Harry*, and *The Wrong Man*.

Linderman, Deborah. "The Mise-en-Abîme in Hitchcock's *Vertigo*." *Cinema Journal*, vol. 30, no. 4 (Summer 1991): 51–74.

Lippe, Richard. "Kim Novak: *Vertigo*, Performance and Image." *Cineaction*, no. 50 (September 1999), 32–42.

Manlove, Clifford T. "Visual 'Drive' and Cinematic Narrative: Reading Gaze Theory in Lacan, Hitchcock, and Mulvey." *Cinema Journal*, vol. 46, no. 3 (Spring 2007): 83–108. On *Vertigo*, *Rear Window*, and *Marnie*.

Maxfield, James F. "A Dreamer and his Dream: Another Way of Looking at Hitchcock's *Vertigo*." In *The Fatal Woman: Sources of Male Anxiety in American Film Noir*. Madison, NJ: Fairleigh Dickinson Univ. Press; London: Associated Univ. Presses, 1996, 84–94.

McElhaney, Joe. "Fascination and Rape: *Marnie*." In *The Death of Classical Cinema: Hitchcock, Lang, Minnelli*. Albany: State Univ. of New York Press, 2006, 85–139.

Meola, Frank M. "Hitchcock's Emersonian Edges." In Gottlieb and Brookhouse (cited in Part One): 113–31. On Hitchcock's "Americanness."

Modelski, Tania, *The Women Who Knew Too Much*, second edition. (Cited in Part I.)

Mogg, Ken. "Defending *Marnie* – and Hitchcock." *Hitchcock Annual*, 1999–2000, 74–83.

Mogg, Ken. "The Fragments of the Mirror: *Vertigo* (1958) and its Sources." *The MacGuffin*, no. 11 (November 1993): 7–22.

Mogg, Ken. "The Gioconda Smile: Archetypes in/of Hitchcock's *Rear Window* (1954)." *The MacGuffin*, no. 23 (November 1997): 7–26.

Mogg, Ken. "The Man Who Knew Too Little: Hitchcock's *The Wrong Man* (1957)." *The MacGuffin*, no. 6 (February 1992): 17–25.

Mogg, Ken. "Submission, Containment, Liberation: Hitchcock's *Torn Curtain* (1966)." *The MacGuffin*, no. 8 (November 1992–February 1993): 12–23.

Mogg, Ken. "The Universal Hitchcock: *The Trouble with Harry*." *The MacGuffin*, no. 21 (February 1997): 9–25.

Naremore, James. *Acting in the Cinema*. Berkeley: Univ. of California Press, 1989. Chapters on *Rear Window* and *North by Northwest*.

Naremore, James, ed. North by Northwest: *Alfred Hitchcock, Director*. New Brunswick, NJ: Rutgers Univ. Press, 1993.

Ngai, Sianne. "Moody Subjects/Projectile Objects: Anxiety and Intellectual Displacement in Hitchcock, Heidegger, and Melville." *Qui Parle*, vol. 12, no. 2 (Spring–Summer 2001): 15–55. Treats *Vertigo* at length.

Nichols, Bill. "For *The Birds*." In *Ideology and the Image: Social Representation in the Cinema and Other Media*. Bloomington: Indiana Univ. Press, 1981, 133–69.

O'Brien, Geoffrey. "Hitchcock: The Hidden Power." *New York Review of Books*, 15 November 2001, 22–3. On *Vertigo*.

Odabashian, Barbara. "The Unspeakable Crime in Hitchcock's *Rear Window*: Hero as Lay Detective, Spectator as Lay Analyst." *Hitchcock Annual*, 1993, 3–11.

Oliver, Kelly, and Benigno Trino. "Mad about Noir: Hitchcock's *Vertigo*." In *Noir Anxiety*. Minneapolis: Univ. of Minnesota Press, 2003, 97–114.

Paglia, Camille. *The Birds*. London: British Film Institute, 1998.

Palmer, R. Barton. "Lost in the Dark: The Noir Thriller." In *Hollywood's Dark Cinema: The American Film Noir*. New York: Twayne, 1994. 105–38. Discusses *Vertigo*.

Palombo, Stanley R. "Hitchcock's *Vertigo*: The Dream Function in Film." In Joseph H. Smith and William Kerrigan, eds., *Images in Our Souls: Cavell, Psychoanalysis, and Cinema*. Baltimore: Johns Hopkins Univ. Press, 1987, 44–63.

Peek, Wendy. "*Cherchez la Femme: The Searchers, Vertigo*, and Masculinity in Post-Kinsey America." *Journal of American Culture*, vol. 21, no. 2 (Summer 1998): 73–87.

Perlmutter, Ruth. "*Rear Window*: A 'Construction Story.'" *Journal of Film and Video*, vol. 37, no. 2 (Spring 1985): 53–65.

Pisters, Patricia. "New Subjectivity in Cinema: The Vertigo of Strange Days." In Willem van Reijen and Willem G. Weststeijn, eds., *Subjectivity*. Amsterdam: Rodopi, 2000, 283–314.

Poague, Leland. "Engendering *Vertigo*." In Gottlieb and Brookhouse (cited in Part One): 251–80.

Pomerance, Murray. "A Clean, Well-Lighted Place: Hitchcock's New York." In Murray Pomerance, ed., *City that Never Sleeps: New York and the Filmic Imagination*. New Brunswick, NJ: Rutgers Univ. Press, 103–17. Mostly on *The Wrong Man* and *North by Northwest*.

Pomerance, Murray. "Finding Release: 'Storm Clouds' and *The Man Who Knew Too Much*." In James Buhler, Caryl Flinn, and David Neumeyer, eds., *Music and Cinema*. Middletown, CT: Wesleyan Univ. Press, 2000, 207–46.

Pomerance, Murray. " 'The Future's Not Ours to See': Song, Singer, Labyrinth in Hitchcock's *The Man Who Knew Too Much*." In Pamela Robertson Wojcik and Arthur Knight, eds.,

Soundtrack Available: Essays on Film and Popular Music. Durham: Duke Univ. Press, 2001, 53–73.

Pomerance, Murray. "Hitchcock Quotes." *Quarterly Review of Film and Video*, vol. 23, no. 2 (2006): 139–54. On *The Man Who Knew Too Much* (1956).

Pomerance, Murray. "Two Bits for Hitch: Small Performance and Gross Structure in *The Man Who Knew Too Much*." *Hitchcock Annual*, 2000–1, 127–45.

Potts, Neill. "Character Interiority: Space, Point of View and Performance in Hitchcock's *Vertigo* (1958)." In John Gibbs and Douglas Pye, eds., *Style and Meaning: Studies in the Detailed Analysis of Film*. Manchester: Manchester Univ. Press, 2005, 85–97.

Preminger, Aner. "François Truffaut Rewrites Hitchcock: A Pygmalion Trilogy." *Literature/Film Quarterly*, vol. 35, no. 3 (2007): 170–80.

Rhu, Lawrence F. "From Cyprus to Rushmore." In *Stanley Cavell's American Dream: Shakespeare, Philosophy, and Hollywood Movies*. New York: Fordham Univ. Press, 2006, 105–35.

Rothman, William. *Hitchcock: The Murderous Gaze*. (Cited in Part One.)

Saito, Ayako. "Hitchcock's Trilogy: A Logic of Mise en Scène." In Janet Bergstrom, ed., *Endless Night: Cinema and Psychoanalysis, Parallel Histories*. Berkeley: Univ. of California Press, 1999, 200–48. On *Vertigo*, *North by Northwest*, and *Psycho*.

Salotto, Eleonor. "She's Not There: *Vertigo* and the Ghostly Feminine." In *Gothic Returns in Collins, Dickens, Zola, and Hitchcock*. New York: Palgrave Macmillan, 2006, 101–17.

Shaffer, Lawrence. "Obsessed with *Vertigo*." *Massachusetts Review*, vol. 25, no. 3 (Autumn 1984): 383–97.

Sharff, Stefan. *The Art of Looking in Hitchcock's* Rear Window. New York: Limelight Editions, 2004.

Sharrett, Christopher. "The Myth of Apocalypse and the Horror Film: The Primacy of *Psycho* and *The Birds*." In Gottlieb and Brookhouse (cited in Part One): 355–72.

Shetley, Vernon. "The Presence of the Past: *Mulholland Drive* against *Vertigo*." *Raritan*, vol. 25, no. 3 (Winter 2006): 112–28.

Sikov, Ed. "Unrest in Peace: Hitchcock's Fifties Humor." In *Laughing Hysterically: American Screen Comedy of the 1950s*. New York: Columbia Univ. Press, 1994, 150–78.

Silver, Alain. "Fragments of the Mirror: Hitchcock's *Noir* Landscapes." In Alain Silver and James Ursini, eds., *Film Noir Reader 2*. New York: Limelight Editions, 1999, 107–27.

Smith, Allan Lloyd. "*Marnie*, the Dead Mother, and the Phantom." *Hitchcock Annual*, 2002–3, 164–80.

Smith, Julian. "The Strange Case of Lars Thorwald: Rounding up the Usual Suspects in *Rear Window*." *New Orleans Review*, vol. 19, no. 2 (Summer 1992): 21–9.

Staiger, Janet. "Toward a Historical Materialist Approach to Reception Studies." In *Interpreting Films: Studies in the Historical Reception of American Cinema*. Princeton: Princeton Univ. Press, 1992, 81–95. On *Rear Window*.

Stern, Emil. "Hitchcock's *Marnie*: Dreams, Surrealism, and the Sublime." *Hitchcock Annual*, 1999–2000, 30–50.

Sterritt, David. "Alfred Hitchcock: Registrar of Births and Deaths." In Gottlieb and Brookhouse (cited in Part One): 310–22. On *Family Plot*.

Street, Sarah. "The Dresses had Told Me: Fashion and Femininity in *Rear Window*." In Belton, *Alfred Hitchcock's* Rear Window (cited above): 91–109.

Suárez Sánchez, Juan A. "The Rear View: Paranoia and Homosocial Desire in Alfred Hitchcock's *Rear Window*." In Chantal Cornut-Gentille D'Arcy and José Angel García Landa, eds., *Gender, I-deology: Essays on Theory, Fiction and Film*. Amsterdam: Rodopi, 1996, 359–69.

Thomas, Deborah. "How Hollywood Deals with the Deviant Male." In Ian Cameron, ed., *The Book of Film Noir*. New York: Continuum, 1993, 59–70. Discusses *The Man Who Knew Too Much* (1956).

Truffaut, François. *Hitchcock*, revised edition. (Cited in Part One.)

Veith, Lynne S. "Restored to Color: Ghosts of Art Past in Hitchcock's *Vertigo*." *Stanford Humanities Review*, vol. 7, no. 2 (Winter 1999): 137–49.

Vest, James M. "The Controller Controlled: Hitchcock's Cameo in *Torn Curtain*." *Hitchcock Annual*, 1998–99, 3–19.

Vest, James M. "Reflections of Ophelia (and of Hamlet) in Alfred Hitchcock's *Vertigo*." *Journal of the Midwest Modern Language Association*, vol. 22, no. 1 (Spring 1989): 1–9.

Walker, Michael. "*Topaz* and Cold War Politics." *Hitchcock Annual*, no. 13 (2004–5): 127–53.

Walker, Michael. " 'A Hitchcock Compendium': Narrative Strategies in *Torn Curtain*." *Hitchcock Annual*, no. 14 (2005–6): 95–120. Compares *Torn Curtain* to *Psycho*.

Weis, Elisabeth, and Randy Thom. "The City That Never Shuts Up: Aural Intrusion in New York Apartment Films." In Murray Pomerance, ed., *City that Never Sleeps* (cited above): 215–27. Discusses *Rear Window*.

White, Susan. "*Vertigo* and the Problem of Knowledge in Feminist Film Theory." In Allen and Ishii-Gonzalès, *Alfred Hitchcock* (cited in Part One): 279–98.

Williams, Dan. *North by Northwest: Director, Alfred Hitchcock*. London: York Press; Harlow: Pearson Education, 2000.

Williams, Tony. "*Vertigo*: Authorship as Transformation." *Cineaction*, no. 50 (September 1999): 56–9.

Wollen, Peter. "Compulsion." *Sight and Sound*, April 1997, 14–19. On *Vertigo*.

Wood, Michael. "Fearful Cemetery." In Freedman and Millington (cited in Part One): 173–80. On *Family Plot*.

Wood, Michael. "No Second Chances: Fiction and Adultery in *Vertigo*." In Nicholas White and Naomi Segal, eds., *Scarlet Letters: Fictions of Adultery from Antiquity to the 1990s*. Basingstone: Macmillan; New York: St Martin's Press, 1997, 189–98.

Wood, Robin. "Looking at *The Birds* and *Marnie* through the *Rear Window*." *Cineaction*, no. 50 (September 1999): 80–5.

Žižek, Slavoj. "*Vertigo*: The Drama of a Deceived Platonist." *Hitchcock Annual*, no. 12 (2003–4): 67–82.

Chapter Fifteen

Hitchcock's *Rear Window*: Reflexivity and the Critique of Voyeurism

Robert Stam and Roberta Pearson

I chose this picture of all the films I have made, this to me is the most cine-matic. (Alfred Hitchcock)[1]

"We've become a race of Peeping Toms." (Stella in Rear Window*)*

Hitchcock's characterization of *Rear Window* as the "most cinematic" of his films points to its most striking feature: its status as a brilliant essay on the cinema and on the nature of the cinematic experience. A paradigmatic instance of reflexivity, the film performs the metalinguistic dismantling of the structures of scopophilia and identification operative in dominant cinema generally and in Hitchcock's own films particularly, even while exploiting those very structures. The film focuses attention on what Geoffrey Nowell-Smith calls the "intersubjective textual relation," the relationship between the film and the spectator.[2]

Jean Douchet, writing in *Cahiers du cinéma* in 1960, was among the first to point out the reflexive dimension of *Rear Window*. Douchet compared the protagonist, played by Jimmy Stewart, to a projector, the building across from his window to the screen, and added that the Stewart character is a spectator who "makes himself his own cinema."[3] Most critics have accepted Douchet's equation of the protagonist with director/spectator but have not gone on to detail the technical means and theoretical implications of that equation. Our purpose here will be to examine *Rear Window* not only as a reflexive film-about-film but also as a multitrack inquiry concerning the cinematic apparatus, the positioning of the spectator within that apparatus, and the sexual, moral, and even political implications of that positioning.

The film's action is circumscribed within a single set, an elaborately constructed block of Greenwich Village apartments surrounding a courtyard. All the events take place either in the apartment of the protagonist, a freelance photographer named L. B. Jefferies (James Stewart), or in the courtyard and neighboring apartments. The rear window of Jefferies's apartment overlooks an architectural triptych of three buildings. The right-hand building houses a struggling composer and a couple, while the left-hand building houses a pair of newlyweds and a woman with a pet bird. But the film concentrates especially on the characters living opposite Jefferies: the sculptress on the first floor, her neighbor "Miss Lonelyhearts," the dancer "Miss Torso," and the salesman Lars Thorwald and his invalid wife. An unhappy couple with a dog and two "party girls" fill the other apartments.

The film's diegesis spans four days in the life of Jefferies, emphasizing his interactions with the visiting nurse Stella (Thelma Ritter), his girlfriend (Grace Kelly), and his detective friend Doyle (Wendell Corey), along with various neighbors, particularly Lars Thorwald (Raymond Burr). Temporarily immobilized by an accident, Jefferies spends his time spying on his neighbors. Stella arrives to feed and massage him and lectures him for preferring to watch the titillating acrobatics of Miss Torso rather than marry the mature and beautiful Lisa. That same night, Lisa arrives, argues with Jeff about marriage, and leaves in anger. After her exit, we hear a crash and a scream which we later learn to have signalled the demise of Mrs. Thorwald. Jeff alternately dozes and watches Thorwald, who repeatedly ventures out into the rain with a large suitcase. The last of his departures, this time accompanied by a woman, finds Jeff asleep.

On Thursday, Jeff begins spying on Thorwald in earnest, first with binoculars and then with a telephoto lens. Thorwald's actions – washing a knife and a saw, tying up a trunk – strike him as suspect. On sketchy evidence, he decides that Thorwald has murdered his wife. Lisa initially mocks his suspicions, but Jeff finally convinces her and recruits her as partner in the investigation. The next day, he attempts to convince Detective Doyle, but Doyle, after a minor investigation, concludes that Thorwald is innocent. Jeff and Lisa momentarily abandon their investigation, but the murder of a dog rekindles their suspicions. Thorwald must have killed the dog, they reason, because it had been digging around Mrs. Thorwald's corpse.

On Saturday, Jeff and Lisa begin to pressure Thorwald. Jeff lures him away from the apartment complex to allow Lisa and Stella to forage for clues. Lisa surreptitiously enters Thorwald's apartment where she finds the most vital clue – Mrs. Thorwald's wedding ring. Since no "normal" woman would travel without her wedding ring, she can only have been murdered. Thorwald returns before Lisa can effect her escape, however, and she is saved only when the police arrest her for breaking and entering. Stella departs to post bail, leaving Jeff exposed to Thorwald, who has now spotted Jeff as his antagonist. A confrontation ends with Jeff's falling out of the rear window and Thorwald's arrest. An epilogue intimates that Jeff and Lisa have reached tentative accommodation concerning their relationship.

The title *Rear Window*, apart from the literalness of its denotation, evokes the diverse "windows" of the cinema: the cinema/lens of camera and projector, the window in the projection booth, the eye as window, and film as "window on the world." The apartment complex, for its part, forms an artistic as well as a social microcosm. Its Greenwich Village setting metonymically evokes "artistic milieu," and its residents take pictures, sculpt statues, compose music, and perform roles. Like the cinema, the complex "englobes" the signifiers of other arts. The architectonic stylization and painterly artifice of the set betray what is transparently a studio product. Its inhabitants, furthermore, together reproduce the division of labor typical of Hollywood studio production. Virtually all the members of this *cinemato-graphicum mundi* are artists, or actors, or are engaged in an entertainment-related profession.

The composer and Miss Torso are involved in the performing arts, the sculptress in a plastic art. Thorwald sells costume jewelry, with its connotations of glamor and artifice. While we never learn the occupations of Miss Lonelyhearts or the newlyweds, they participate in the theatricality of everyday life, acting out charades for Jeff's benefit and ours, the groom carrying his bride over the threshold and Miss Lonelyhearts staging a dinner for an imaginary male companion. Within this interplay of art and experience, every human gesture becomes potentially transmutable into a kind of entertainment.

The very language of *Rear Window* resonates with the terminology of entertainment. Lisa speaks of the "opening night" of Jeff's final week "in a cast." Pulling the drapes, she tells Jeff that the "show is over" and promises "coming attractions." The film highlights the intertext of this entertainment through self-referential allusion. The sequence of slides that Jeff projects calls attention to the static photograph as the primordial point of departure for cinematic illusion. Lisa's speculation that the dog might have been killed because he "knew too much" alludes to a title Hitchcock liked so much he used it on two occasions. More importantly, the film foregrounds the generic intertext in which fiction films operate. The world across the courtyard is presented as a series of framed genre pantomimes in which accompanying music largely substitutes for a dialogue track. Jefferies begins, prior to picking up the telephoto lens, by watching what amounts to an early silent "tableau" film, stylistically characterized by long-shot and static camera. The performing inhabitants of the various apartment/frames, meanwhile, seem to have strayed directly from the various genres of the classic Hollywood film.[4] Miss Lonelyhearts is borrowed from an earnest 1950s social realist film like *Marty*; Thorwald comes from a murder mystery; the dog couple comes from a domestic comedy. The songwriter belongs in a musical bio-picture such as *Till the Clouds Roll By*. Laboring away at his compositions, he provides commentative music for Jeff's "film" as well as our own. (Surrogate artist, he clearly stands in for Franz Waxman, whose work he literally performs, much as Jefferies stands in for Hitchcock, and his final version of "Lisa" exactly coincides with the conclusion of the film.) Miss Torso, finally, belongs in an MGM musical, when not in 1950s soft-core porn. A vulgar utopian, she transforms the quotidian – brushing her teeth, checking the refrigerator – into musical-comedy-style song and dance.

As *magister ludi* of these cinematic games, Jefferies clearly functions as substitute director/auteur. Hitchcock presents us with a protagonist whose activities partially analogize and at times literally mimic those of the director. Jefferies the photojournalist, like Hitchcock, is both artist and technician, professional and visionary. Lisa's succinct résumé of his activities – "going from one place to another taking pictures" – applies equally to Hitchcock. Within the fiction, moreover, Jefferies enjoys partial directorial control over his "film," since binoculars and telephoto lens facilitate a multiplicity of setups and perspectives. His narrative and actantial function, finally, consists in persuading a number of characters, let us call them "spectators," to look where he has looked before. He channels and guides their glance, framing their vision and imposing his interpretation.

Surrogate for the director, Jefferies functions on a deeper level as a relay for the spectator. Indeed, Jefferies and the apartment complex taken together may be taken to prefigure what has come to be called, after Jean-Louis Baudry, the "cinematic apparatus," that is, the instrumental base of camera, projector, and screen as well as the spectator as the desiring subject on which the cinematic institution depends for its object and accomplice. That institution, Metz tells us, demands an immobile secret viewer who absorbs everything through his eyes. The wheelchair-ridden Jefferies exemplifies this situation of retinal activity and enforced immobility; he is indeed, as Lisa remarks in another context, "travelling but going nowhere." The cinematic apparatus, "prosthesis for our primally dislocated limbs," combines visual hyperperception with minimal physical mobility. Binoculars and a long lens grant Jefferies the illusory godlike power of the "all-perceiving spectator." Hitchcock thus suggests a congruency between the situation of the protagonist, who experiences his reality within the fiction as though he were watching a film, and our own situation as spectators watching the protagonist watch his film.

The identity of Jefferies's situation and our own accounts for a frequent verbal ambiguity in *Rear Window*; the shifter "they" can often refer either to the characters in the fiction or to ourselves in the audience. When Lisa speaks to Jefferies about "rear-window ethics," he remarks: "Of course, they can do the same thing to me – watch me like a bug under glass if they want to." His comment, like virtually everything in this complexly overdetermined film, has more than one meaning. Ostensibly referring to his neighbors, it applies equally to the cinema audience watching Jimmy Stewart "like a bug under glass" as he delivers the line in close-up.

In his state of inhibited motoricity and exacerbated perception, Jefferies embodies the living death of the dreamlike spectatorial experience. The simulation apparatus called the cinema, for Baudry, not only represents the real but also stimulates intense subject effects. The shadowy figures on the screen, the darkness of the theater, the sealing-off of everyday pressures, all foster an artificial state of regression not unlike that engendered by dreams. The cinema, in this sense, constitutes the approximate material realization of the unconscious goal of returning to an earlier state of psychic development, a state of relative narcissism in which desire is "satisfied" through a simulated reality. The first time we see Jefferies, significantly, he is asleep, as if everything we are about to see were in some sense his dream. Indeed, the vacillations in his attentiveness almost seem designed to evoke the diverse points on the continuum of sleep and wakefulness anatomized by Christian Metz in "The Fiction Film and its Spectator" (Part III of *The Imaginary Signifier*). At times, he is sound asleep and presumably dreaming; at others, he dozes intermittently; and at still others, finds himself in a state of animated attention, dreamlike in its intensity, reminiscent of that provoked in the spectator by Hitchcock's own films, of which *Rear Window* is a particularly spellbinding example.

The mechanism of gratification in the cinema, according to Metz, "rests on our knowing that the object being looked at does not know it is being looked at."[5] *Rear Window* constantly underscores the voyeuristic abuse to which the cinema, as the privileged medium of the eye, is so often susceptible. The film proliferates in explicit references to voyeurism, to "Peeping Toms" and "window shoppers," and it is hardly accidental that Stella refers to Jefferies's telephoto lens as a "portable keyhole."[6]

Jefferies, for his part, is a quintessential exemplum of "a race of Peeping Toms." His profession of photojournalism assumes and exploits a kind of voyeurism. (Hitchcock underlines this voyeuristic undercurrent by having his glamor pinups neighbor with his disaster photos.) His leisure mirrors his labor. At work, he observes the world's catastrophes from what is usually a safe distance. At home, he indulges, from his rear-window post, in what Metz calls "unauthorized voyeurism." Overseeing the world from a sheltered position, he indulges his scopic drive, the desire to "take other people as objects, subjecting them to a controlling and curious gaze."[7] His neighbors, with the possible exception of Miss Torso, are nonconsenting exhibitionists, pure objects for his superior gaze. He bears the look that confers power. He is the warden, as it were, in a private panopticon. Seated in his central tower, he observes the wards ("small captive shadows in the cells of the periphery") in an imaginary prison. Michel Foucault's description of the cells of the panopticon – "so many cages, so many small theaters, in which each actor is alone, perfectly individualized and constantly visible" – in some ways aptly describes the scene exposed to Jefferies's glance.[8]

The cinematic spectator is caught in a play between regression and progression. The images received come from without, and in this sense the movement is progressive and directed toward external reality; yet, because of inhibited mobility and the process of identification with both camera and character, the psychic energy normally devoted to activity is channeled into other routes of discharge. It is no surprise, therefore, that the "complement" of Jefferies's voyeurism is a certain passivity. At the beginning of the film, he consistently opts for inactivity and for the inertia of what he himself calls the "status quo." But, although he avoids relationships with friends and lovers and neighbors, he is passionately absorbed in the *spectacle* of his neighbors' lives. Busily spying into the apartments opposite, he can barely pay attention to his interlocutors in the same room. His involvement with people exists in inverse proportion to their distance from him; such is his code of perspective. "Pay attention to me," Lisa demands. "You're not on the other side of the room," Jeff answers, and his response reveals more than he knows. Jefferies prefers his thrills to be vicarious. He would rather watch Miss Torso than touch the flesh-and-blood woman next to him, which is why Lisa contemplates turning herself into a distant and exotic appearance – by "moving into the apartment across the way and doing the dance of the seven veils." The tension between the regressive and progressive paths even takes the form of a physical tussle concerning the direction in which Jeff's wheelchair will face: will it face out of the window toward Miss Torso, and metaphorically the cinema, or will it face toward the apartment, Lisa, and "reality."

Jefferies is our specular reflection, our double. We do not merely watch him performing actions; we perform the identical action – looking. But, at the same time that Hitchcock leads us to participate vicariously in Jefferies's voyeurism, he also frustrates and refuses to satisfy it. An early shot epitomizes this refusal. Two women on a rooftop, presumably Greenwich Village "bohemians," discard their clothes to sunbathe. A helicopter approaches and hovers overhead. The implication: those aboard the helicopter are spying on the women. The helicopter provides a perfect "vehicle" for the spectatorial desire to enjoy a fantasy omniscience, to go everywhere and see everything, and especially for the socially constructed (and largely male) desire to see women in states of undress. The helicopter evokes the technological resources available to the cinema and enlistable in the service of the scopic drive. Yet Hitchcock withholds the "payoff" of these resources by denying us the point-of-view shot from the helicopter. We never see the women; we become aware, rather, only of our desire to see them. The desire is not fulfilled but only designated and exposed.

Jefferies's voyeurism goes hand in hand with an absorbing fear of mature sexuality. Indeed, the film begins by hinting at a serious case of psychosexual pathology. The first image of Jefferies, asleep with hand on thigh, is quietly masturbatory, as if he were an invalid who had just abused himself in the dark. A radio commercial allusion to that "run-down listless feeling" is followed by a series of comments by both Stella and Lisa that might be taken to refer to sexual impotence: "You're not too active...." "How's your leg?" ... "Is anything else bothering you?" Lisa is clearly the sexual initiator – "How far does a girl have to go before you notice her?" she asks – and Jeff the reluctant object of her desire. Stella calls him "reasonably healthy" but wonders about a "hormone deficiency." She berates him for speaking in euphemistic abstractions ("Our relationship is maturing") rather than acting like a sexed human being. Her notion of the normal operations of Eros consists in lust ("You get excited") sanctified by an institution ("You get married"). She defends a kind of *amour fou* – "like two taxicabs crashing" – sublimated and blessed by the state.

As object lesson for Stella's domesticated version of surrealism, Hitchcock has the newlywed couple enter their apartment on their wedding night. The commentative music of "That's Amore!" underscores the paradigmatic nature of their appearance. The couple, eager to consummate their relationship, demonstrate in pantomime the model relationship of which Jefferies has so far shown himself to be incapable. They play out the typical final episode of a classical Hollywood film, generally oriented, as Bellour points out, toward the "constitution of the couple." (That the couple so constituted begins to exhaust the sexual charms of marriage in a matter of days suggests both the limits of Stella's philosophy and Hitchcock's fear of the "desire that speaks in the woman's look.") Jefferies, symptomatically, is bored by this spectacle of consummation, preferring either exhibitionism (Miss Torso) or the morbid concatenation of marriage and violence (the murder of Mrs. Thorwald). Jefferies resists Lisa's sexual demands much as the groom fatigues of the bride's, but in Jefferies's case voyeurism plays a primordial role in sexual apathy. Lisa is more than willing to go to bed, but Jeff prefers to fall asleep with his binoculars. Voyeurism, passivity, and implied impotence are shown to form a melancholy constellation of mutually reinforcing neuroses.

The voyeur, according to Metz, is careful to maintain a gulf between the object and the eye: "His look fastens the object at the right distance, as with those cinema spectators who take care to avoid being too close or too far from the screen."[9] Voyeurism renders desire as a purely visual activity. As long as the voyeur remains hidden, the contradictions of his own perspective can be ignored. His invisibility produces the visibility of the objects of his gaze. But the frame, the rear window, which guarantees the innocuous integrity of the visible for the voyeur and thus his pleasure, remains intact only so long as the viewing remains surreptitious.

The central trajectory of *Rear Window*, in this sense, consists in the progressive shattering of Jefferies's illusion of voyeuristic separation from life and the concomitant rendering possible of mature sexuality with Lisa. This shattering progresses by several stages. At the beginning of the film, Jefferies retains the privileged position of the moviegoer; he observes without being observed. This sheltered position gives Jefferies a factitious sense of superiority; he feels superior, for example, to his double in solitude, Miss Lonelyhearts. But this illusion of distance and superiority soon comes under attack. Lisa tries to keep Jeff from being a mere spectator by turning on the lights and wheeling his chair around away from the window. The danger looms, meanwhile, that Thorwald will discover he is being watched. On Thursday morning, as Jeff tries to persuade Stella that something is amiss in the Thorwald apartment, Thorwald himself comes to the window and looks around the courtyard. Jeff instinctively wheels backward in a kind of panic, and warns Stella to move away from the window.

The next stage in this shattering of illusory distance occurs when Lisa enters Thorwald's apartment. She leaves her seat in the theater, as it were, and enters the screen, the space of the spectacle. When Lisa is threatened by Thorwald's imminent return, Jeff reacts like the naive spectator lurking within even the most sophisticated: he addresses advice to the unhearing screen: "Lisa, what are you doing?" ... "Come on, get out of there!" His reactions mirror our own; he articulates our responses as feeling spectators. But this moment is highly overdetermined and polyvalent. Is this the typical Hitchcockian fusion of danger and desire? Can Jeff love Lisa only when she is threatened with death? Or can he identify only with a Lisa transmogrified into spectacle, framed within the rectangular windows of Thorwald's apartment? What *is* clear is only his own powerlessness. The "blessing" of passive distance has become a curse. The apartment, formerly his sanctuary, and the apartment complex, his panopticon, have now become his trap.

The progressive breakdown of Jeff's voyeuristic passivity is further marked by two particularly chilling moments. In the first he is touched indirectly, by Thorwald's look, and in the second he is violated directly, by Thorwald's hands. The first moment, in which Thorwald looks at Jeff and thus at us, violates the dominant convention stipulating that the film remain radically ignorant of its spectator and that the actor never acknowledge the camera and thus the audience. This moment of the returned glance, of the *voyeur vu*, is often imbued with anxiety in Hitchcock's work. (One thinks, for example, of Melanie caught in Mitch's binoculars as she espies him from Bodega Bay.) It is the moment of a kind of power shift. Thorwald, because of his guilty act, had something to conceal; now Jeff, because of his guilty look, is forced to conceal. Jeff had said of Thorwald at one point that he had a "guilty look," as if he were afraid of being seen. Now that phrase is made to rebound, ironically and retroactively, against Jeff himself. His first reaction, typically, is to turn off the lights – that is, to try to return himself to a privileged cinema-like situation. Like the spectator, he is afraid of the reciprocal glance. Both we and he feel "discovered."

Thorwald's invasion of Jefferies's apartment brings the scopic inversions of the film to their paroxysm. In a narrative chiasmus – the rhetorical figure that operates by the repetition and, simultaneously, the inversion of the relationship between two words in the course of a sentence – Jefferies and Thorwald come to exchange places. Jefferies, delegate for the cinema's all-perceiving observer, has visually "broken into" and "entered" Thorwald's apartment; now Thorwald returns the favor. The spectacle, formerly kept at a safe distance by the no-man's land of the courtyard – figuratively the space between spectator and screen – comes to invade the spectator. Thorwald becomes the ambulatory embodiment of filmic displeasure. King Kong is unchained and attacking the audience. Jeff defends himself by setting off flashbulbs, hiding his eyes with each flash. He treats Thorwald as if he were part of a film to be watched in the dark. If the film becomes too frightening, turning on the lights makes it disappear. Failing that, the childlike spectator can hide his eyes; what is no longer seen is no longer there. From another perspective, Jeff tries to blind Thorwald; his only defense is to deprive the aggressor of the look that confers power. But Thorwald remains menacingly real, demanding reaction as a human being rather than a character in a film. Thorwald breaks down the very condition of Jefferies's voyeurism as the Peeping Tom spectator receives the equivalent of the hot pokers of which Stella had spoken, but with the punishment displaced from the eyes to the second broken leg that Jeff suffers in his (redemptive) fall.

The critique of voyeurism in *Rear Window* is not elaborated only through narrative structure and thematic motifs; it is realized through the manipulation of the precise code most relevant to that critique – the code of point of view. And this manipulation is far more rigorous and subtle than most critics have acknowledged. For many critics, *Rear Window* is largely restricted to Jefferies's point of view. "With the exception of one slow pan across the apartments," writes Donald Spoto, "we see [the neighbors] only as Jeffries [*sic*] sees them."[10] For Robin Wood, only once does Hitchcock grant the viewer information that Jefferies lacks. In all other cases, according to Wood, "we are allowed to see only what he sees, know only what he knows."[11] But, if it is arguably true that we know only what Jefferies knows, it is manifestly not true that we see only what he sees. To begin with the obvious, Jefferies does not see himself as voyeur. "If you could see yourself ..." Lisa tells him, "with binoculars! ... It's a disease!" In the sequences that take place *within* the apartment, moreover, Lisa, Stella, and Doyle are all granted some point-of-view shots. Jefferies's perspective does predominate in the masked, relatively close shots correlated with the binoculars and telephoto lens, but many of the other shots might be more accurately described as from the point of view of the rear window rather than from that of Jefferies himself. Many shots, as we shall see, embody the point of view of *no* character. Some of the most striking subjective shots, finally, are associated not with Jefferies but with Thorwald. Repeated shots render Thorwald's blanched-out vision of Jefferies armed with flashbulbs and trying to blind him. These dazzling shots mark Thorwald's "takeover" of the point of view, and in this sense form an integral part of the film's structure of inversions and reversals.

The credit sequence already "announces" the rift between Jefferies's point of view and that of the authorial instance. This sequence, in which titles are superimposed on a shot of the rear windows of Jefferies's apartment, shows three bamboo matchstick blinds successively rolling up, with no sign of human intervention. The rolling-up of the final blind coincides with the title "Directed by Alfred Hitchcock." The apparently self-generating movement of the blinds, combined with the self-designation of the author, anticipates and "triggers" the subsequent slow pan around the courtyard, a shot pointedly unauthorized by any character within the fiction. Hitchcock further underscores its unauthorized nature by revealing Jefferies only at the conclusion of the shot, sound asleep and turned *away* from the window. The camera then leaves the sleeping Jefferies and makes another self-flaunting tour of the courtyard, this time pausing to inspect specific apartment windows.

The twice-asserted autonomy of this initial pair of counterclockwise pans around the courtyard anticipates a structuring series of similar pans around the courtyard, none of which are from Jefferies's point of view. Each moves counterclockwise around the courtyard and ends with Jefferies in his apartment. In the first two of these pans, he is asleep; in the third, he is being massaged by Stella; and in the fourth, he is being kissed by Lisa. A final pan, during the epilogue, again finds him asleep. Thus Hitchcock repeatedly calls attention to the enunciation, conventionally suppressed in many classical films, by emphasizing the gestural autonomy of the camera and its independence from any particular vision.

These counterclockwise tours of the courtyard also serve to situate Jefferies within the social space of the apartment complex; they tell us that he forms part of this space and cannot therefore be merely its observer or spectator. The film repeatedly contrasts Jefferies's fragmented view of this space with the spatial unity implied by the continuous pans. Jefferies's view of the complex is rendered through the fragmentation of montage: the ping-pong-like play of shots of Jefferies and subjective shots of the apartments. His vision of the courtyard is disconnected; he does not see it as a continuous space. The neighbors do not form part of a community; they are isolated prey for his "controlling and curious gaze." Only gradually does Jefferies realize that he too forms part of the larger social space. His final fall into the courtyard, in this sense, signals his incorporation into that space. His illusion of separation, from Thorwald and the community, has been literally annihilated.

Through Jefferies, Hitchcock indicts not only voyeurism – or, more accurately, he reminds us that he himself, his characters, and the spectators share this penchant – but also the social isolation that makes voyeurism the normal condition. Stated differently, the indictment of voyeurism is intimately linked to the film's valorization of neighborliness. At one point the woman griefstricken over the murder of her dog excoriates all the neighbors for their selfishness: "You don't know the meaning of the word 'neighbors.'" As they stand on their fire escapes or at their windows, she screams: "Neighbors like each other, speak to each other, care if anybody lives or dies. But none of you do!" In short, she accuses all of the neighbors of resembling Jefferies, disengaged onlookers incapable of commitment or solidarity. Her question, "Which of you did it?" is "answered" by an extreme long-shot that includes all the buildings and observers around the courtyard. Thus the film implies a certain collective responsibility and the critique of a social world constituted by isolated monads.

At times *Rear Window* touches on what might be called the political dimension of voyeurism. If the narrative ultimately confirms Jefferies's suspicions of Thorwald, it also sensitizes us to the danger of political abuse of the power conferred by the look. Like Coppola's *The Conversation* two decades later, *Rear Window* is, among other things, an essay on the nature of surveillance.[12] And, if *The Conversation* clairvoy-antly predicted the abuses of Watergate and Abscam, *Rear Window* in some ways echoes the historical ambiance of McCarthyite anticommunism. McCarthyism, after all, is the antithesis of neighborliness; it treats every neighbor as a potential other, alien, spy. It fractures the social community for purposes of control. Jefferies is an anonymous accuser whose suspicions happen to be correct, but the object of his hostile gaze might easily have been as innocent as Father Logan in *I Confess* or Christopher Emmanuel Balestrero in *The Wrong Man*, to cite two other 1950s films with anti-McCarthyite resonances.

Rear Window also explores the sexual politics of looking. Voyeurism in the film is largely defined as a masculine activity, even though the object of that voyeurism, through a kind of displacement, is rendered as male. The cinema, by analogy, is defined as the product of the male auteur/spectator/voyeur who at best enlists some women as accomplices in his voyeuristic activities. (Only Jeff, significantly, is allowed to look through the phallic telephotolens.) But, while Lisa and Stella, at least in the beginning, look directly at Jefferies, he looks away toward women and men transmuted into spectacle. And, when the women turn their eyes toward the spectacle, they see differently, showing enhanced capacities for empathy and com-prehension, especially in relation to other women. Lisa understands instantly that Miss Torso is not in love with the man she kisses on the balcony and knows, with-out ever having met her, what Mrs. Thorwald would or would not have done. The female spectator in the text, in sum, demonstrates a sensibility quite distinct from that of the male.

A simplistic reading of *Rear Window* would monolithically condemn the protag-onist's behavior as totally reprehensible. But in fact the Jefferies of the end of the film is quite different from the Jefferies of the beginning. His ordeal is also a cure, both social and sexual. Although at first impelled by morbid curiosity, Jefferies proceeds, over the course of the film, from scopophilia to epistemophilia, from indifference to concern. The aloof observer is finally compelled to take sides, to intervene, arguably to the benefit of the larger society. While Jefferies's pursuit of Thorwald begins as a voyeuristic game played by a hermeneutic detective, it becomes in the end a response to the dog owner's indictment; Jefferies *does* care "if anyone lives or dies."

Hitchcock, who quite typically superimposes murder and marriage, the herme-neutic and the erotic, has Jefferies's social rehabilitation coincide with a sexual cure whereby the problematic protagonist is divested of his psychosexual impedimenta and rendered ready for marriage. The solution of the murder mystery is made to parallel the evolution of Jefferies's personal relationships. His relationship to Lisa is, at the outset, not unlike his relation to his neighbors. She is acceptable to him only in the form of distant spectacle. The change in Jefferies can be gauged by comparing her first and final appearances. Her initial appearance is as an expressionist shadow crossing Jefferies's sleeping face. She looms above him in outsized close-up, her bright red lips large and somewhat menacing. The *mise-en-scène* renders Jefferies's fear of her closeness as a threat to voyeuristic distance. When she kisses him, he awakens and asks, "Who are you?" She then retreats, re-establishing the necessary gulf, and turns on the lights, leaving him in the shadows, returning him to his spectatorial position. The gap is steadily narrowed throughout the film, however, and by the final shots it is virtually eliminated. Lisa comforts Jefferies after his fall. The shot, with typical Hitchcockian circularity, echoes their initial encounter, yet this time her appearance is not threatening but nurturing, as she holds his head in her lap, bending protectively with the folds of her skirt enveloping him. Jefferies, the paradigmatic spectator, has realized the corollary psychic costs of both voyeurism and solitude. While Lisa may be no expert on "rear window ethics," the film shows Hitchcock to be their brilliant exponent.

Rear Window provides an object lesson in the processes of spectatorship. "Tell me what you see and what you think it means," Lisa tells Jefferies, and her words evoke the constant process of vision and interpretation, inference and intellection, inherent in the "reading" of any fiction film. "I just want to find out what's the matter with the salesman's wife," says Jefferies, thus articulating our wish concerning the film. Jefferies, Lisa, Stella, and Doyle collaborate in producing the meaning of the spectacle before them, much as we collaborate in producing the signification of the film. They pressure the film, as well, with their desire for a story. In fact, some of them would prefer a murder story; they, like us, would be disappointed to discover that Mrs. Thorwald was actually alive and well.

With its insistent inscription of scenarios of voyeurism, *Rear Window* poses the question that so preoccupies contemporary film theory and analysis: the question of the place of the desiring subject within the cinematic apparatus. This theory and analysis shift interest from the question "What does the text mean?" to "What do we want from the text?" "What is it you want from me? ... Tell me what you want!," Thorwald says to Jefferies, and his question, ostensibly addressed to the protagonist, might as well have been addressed to us. What indeed do we want from this film or from film in general? To this question – which filmmakers, critics, and spectators must ask themselves – *Rear Window* offers a complex and multileveled response. The spectators in the film – Jefferies, certainly, but also Lisa, Stella, and even Doyle – want first of all to *see*, to peek into the private corners of the lives of others. The technical instruments at Jefferies's disposal come in answer, as it were, to this primordial desire. Beyond that, these spectators want to identify with the human figures within the spectacle. When Lisa enters into what had been defined as the space of the spectacle – Thorwald's apartment – Jefferies's "investment" becomes clear. Most of all, these spectators want to experience certain "subject effects." They want to find themselves in a heightened state of pleasurable absorption and identification. Jefferies the spectator begins as listless and apathetic, but he gradually comes alive through what he sees. He savors the experience of "coming alive," even though at times it entails pain and anxiety. Furthermore, he shares the experience with others within a kind of ephemeral *communitas* of spectators. His metamorphosis from distant observer into excited vicarious participant "allegorizes" the transformation engendered in us by the narrative procedures and identificatory mechanisms of Hitchcock's cinema, and even that engendered by *Rear Window* itself.

While it is true that *Rear Window* short-circuits voyeuristic involvement by making the audience aware of itself as audience and of the film as artifice, it is also true that our relation to the spectacle remains voyeuristic in the sense that we identify strongly with characters in a fiction and identify even more to the extent that we, like the protagonist, are voyeurs. The distancing of *Rear Window* is not, finally, Brechtian. For Brechtian theater, there is no suspense, no pathos, no catharsis, while *Rear Window* builds to a catharsis that purges the tensions generated by the diegesis. We, like the protagonist, are presumably "cured." *Rear Window* is both indictment and defense of the cinema. Just as scopophilia can incline toward normality (a healthy curiosity) as well as abnormality (a morbid voyeurism), so the cinema can be life-enhancing or destructive. *Rear Window*, at once a cautionary tale for voyeurs and an ode to the cinema, presents both alternatives with extraordinary lucidity.

Notes

We would like to thank Karen Backstein and Louise Spence for their helpful comments.

1. Alfred Hitchcock, "*Rear Window*," quoted in Albert J. La Valley, ed., *Focus on Hitchcock* (Englewood Cliffs, NJ: Prentice-Hall, 1972), 40.
2. Some of the key essays in the discussion of the apparatus are Jean-Louis Baudry, "Cinema: The Ideological Effects of the Basic Apparatus," *Film Quarterly*, vol. 27, no. 2 (1974–5) and "The Apparatus," *Camera Obscura*, no. 1 (1976). Also of interest are Christian Metz, *The Imaginary Signifier* (Bloomington: Indiana Univ. Press, 1982) and Jean-Louis Comolli, "Machines of the Visible," anthologized in Stephen Heath and Teresa de Lauretis, eds., *The Cinematic Apparatus* (New York: St Martin's Press, 1980).
3. Jean Douchet, "Hitch et son public," *Cahiers du cinéma*, vol. 19, no. 3 (1960): 10.
4. We are indebted to Noël Carroll for this insight.
5. Christian Metz, "History/Discourse: A Note on Two Voyeurisms," *Edinburgh Magazine* (1976): 23.
6. Although the cinema is founded on the pleasure of hearing (Lacan's *pulsion invocante*) as well as on the pleasure of looking (scopophilia), Hitchcock throughout emphasizes the visual rather than the aural dimension of voyeurism. Jefferies is granted access to music and noise but not to distant conversations staged as pantomimes. It should also be pointed out, however, that the soundtrack itself makes frequent allusion to voyeurism. The lyrics of Bing Crosby's "To see you is to love you | and I see you everywhere" (ironically superimposed on Jefferies's observation of Miss Lonelyhearts) is in this sense exemplary: "To see you is to want you | and I see you all the time | On the sidewalk | in the doorway | I see you everywhere | To see you is to love you | and you're never out of sight | and I'll love you | and I'll see you | in the same old dreams tonight." A veritable ode to scopophilia, the song fuses sight in desire in its evocation of the distant dreamlike loving common to voyeur and spectator.
7. Christian Metz, "The Imaginary Signifier," *Screen*, vol. 16, no. 2 (1975): 60.
8. Michel Foucault, *Discipline and Punish: The Birth of the Prison* (New York: Vintage, 1979), 200.
9. Metz, "The Imaginary Signifier," 60.
10. Donald Spoto, *The Art of Alfred Hitchcock* (New York: Hopkinson and Blake, 1976), 241.
11. Robin Wood, *Hitchcock's Films* (New York: Castle Books, 1969), 65.

12. Although *The Conversation* is often compared to *Blow-Up*, it actually has more in common with *Rear Window*. Both the Hitchcock film and the Coppola film are structured around the comeuppance of the voyeur, or, in the case of Harry Caul, of the auditeur. Just as Jefferies represents an analogue to the director/spectator/voyeurs, so Harry Caul is sound director, editing different takes into a final text, as well as voyeur/auditeur, eavesdropping on the private lives of others. The "cure," however, is in his case somewhat less effective.

REAR WINDOW (Paramount, 1954). *Producer*: Alfred Hitchcock, *Assistant Director*: Herbert Coleman, *Script*: John Michael Hayes, from the story by William Irish (pseud. of Cornell Woolrich), *Photography*: Robert Burks (Technicolor), *Editor*: George Tomasini, *Sets*: Hal Pereira, Joseph MacMillan Johnson, Sam Comer, Ray Mayer, *Music*: Franz Waxman, *Costumes*: Edith Head, *Players*: James Stewart (L. B. Jefferies), Grace Kelly (Lisa Freemont), Wendell Corey (Tom Doyle), Thelma Ritter (Stella), Raymond Burr (Lars Thorwald), Judith Evelyn (Miss Lonelyhearts). 112 minutes.

Chapter Sixteen

Finding the Right Man in *The Wrong Man*

Marshall Deutelbaum

Because it embodies so many of its director's recurrent themes within its true story, *The Wrong Man* occupies a special place among Hitchcock's films. In it, for once, reality seems to validate the motifs that run through his fictional tales. Now, however, these familiar motifs of the normal world thrown into chaos, the innocent man wrongly accused of a crime, the transference of guilt as an innocent character assumes responsibilities for another's crime, and the uncertainty of appearance are rooted in the true sufferings of Christopher Emmanuel Balestrero, a musician in the Stork Club band. Here, then, it is a real man who is mistakenly arrested for a crime he did not commit and his real wife who irrationally blames herself for his arrest and suffers a nervous breakdown as a result of the unwarranted guilt she heaps upon herself. Here, too, it is only by chance that the real thief is finally apprehended. Thus, in contrast to his other films, no one might object that *The Wrong Man* is woven from artificial coincidence or complain that its sudden turns strain anyone's sense of plausibility. Indeed, Eric Rohmer and Claude Chabrol celebrate the place of *The Wrong Man* in Hitchcock's *oeuvre* for its triumph of fact over fiction, which "brings together the themes scattered throughout his work," while demonstrating their existence in the world.[1]

Hitchcock further underlined the essential truthfulness of *The Wrong Man* by his decision to film the story entirely on location in a semidocumentary style, using many of the actual participants to play themselves in minor roles. The *New York Times* ran two articles describing the location shooting, noting that Hitchcock was "a stickler for fidelity to detail."[2] This same emphasis on the narrative's authenticity marks Hitchcock's long cameo appearance in a precredit sequence as he speaks directly to the audience. Presenting himself in extreme long-shot as a miniscule figure lost in the emptiness of a vacant soundstage – vacant perhaps because this film was shot on location – Hitchcock visually signals the astringent, semidocumentary style of the film to come as he declares its basis in fact:

> This is Alfred Hitchcock speaking. In the past, I have given you many kinds of suspense pictures. But this time I would like you to see a different one. The difference lies

in the fact that this is a true story, every word of it. And yet, it contains elements that are stranger than all the fiction that has gone into many of the thrillers that I've made before.[3]

It should not be surprising in light of such emphasis on the truthfulness of both its story and photographic style that *The Wrong Man* should seem to many to be one of Hitchcock's visually barest and least manipulative films. François Truffaut expresses this attitude best when he describes the feel of the film's story in relation to its stark visual style as "the roast without the gravy, a news event served raw. ...."[4] Yet, despite *The Wrong Man*'s apparent fidelity to truth and its relatively plain visual style, a careful consideration of the film will reveal that Hitchcock manipulates both the facts of the story and the film's images in order to test his viewer's perceptions. A survey of earlier accounts of Balestrero's ordeal will illuminate the ways in which both Hitchcock and the film's images lie when they claim to be transparently true.

Balestrero's misfortune had first been presented to the readers of *Life* magazine in "A Case of Identity," by Herbert Brean.[5] Not only had Balestrero been arrested for twice robbing an insurance office some two blocks from his home but by a bizarre coincidence he had duplicated a curious spelling error in the original holdup note when the police dictated it to him. In the face of this apparently damning piece of evidence and the testimonies of the office clerks who identified him as the thief who had robbed their office on July 9 and December 18, 1952, Balestrero began to assemble the evidence that would prove he could not have been that robber. He hired former New York State Senator Frank D. O'Connor as his attorney and began to reconstruct his activities for those dates. He remembered that on the July date he and his wife, Rose, were guests at the Edelweiss Farm near Cornwall, New York. That particular day had been the birthday of the owner's wife, though a party for her had been cancelled because she was ill. Instead, Balestrero remembered, he had spent the time playing pinochle with other guests. O'Conner took depositions from those players attesting to that fact.

Though it took him a little longer to remember, Balestrero finally recalled that at the time of the December robbery he had been troubled with abscessed teeth. Indeed, a check of his dental records revealed that the right side of his jaw had been so swollen on December 14 that the teeth could not be extracted. Moreover, because the swelling had not lessened by the 22nd (four days after the second robbery), his dentist had sent him to see his family doctor for treatment. Because none of those who identified him as the holdup man had mentioned this swelling, it was unlikely that he was actually the man who had robbed them. The prosecution's case was additionally weakened by the inability of the police to locate either of two items among Balestrero's effects: the lined notebook from which the robber had torn the paper on which he wrote the holdup notes or the blue overcoat worn by the robber during the second robbery. As Rose insisted to the police, her husband owned only a gray topcoat.

At the same time that Balestrero was working to prove his innocence, however, Rose developed the illogical belief that she was responsible for her husband's misfortune because he had gone to the insurance office for her sake. If he had not gone there to borrow money against their insurance policies to pay for her emergency dental work, she reasoned, he never would have been mistaken by the clerks for the robber. Tormented by this thought, Rose suffered a nervous breakdown within a short time and entered a sanitarium in the country. Balestrero was himself such a timid man that O'Conner feared that he, too, might suffer a breakdown during the trial. Indeed, the trial proved to be an unexpected ordeal when, despite the strength of his alibis, it ended in a mistrial when a juror who had already made up his mind interrupted the state's case to ask aloud: "Judge, do we have to listen to all this?" It was only by chance that, before the second trial could start, the actual robber, Charles James Daniell, was caught and confessed to forty robberies, including the two for which he knew Balestrero had been arrested. At the time this story appeared in *Life*, Rose had recovered enough to spend weekends with her family.

These details of the case are worth repeating, for they form the basis for the first dramatization of Balestrero's story, also entitled "A Case of Identity," broadcast on *Robert Montgomery Presents*, on January 11, 1954.[6] Adapted for television by Adrian Spies, the three-act drama managed to fit Balestrero's ordeal within the program's hour length by employing voice-over narration to stitch together its key moments. Despite its hurried pace, it is entirely faithful to Brean's original article and holds up remarkably well in comparison with *The Wrong Man*. Also staged in a semidocumentary style, with filmed footage of Balestrero's neighborhood cut in from time to time, its scenes are often strikingly similar to scenes in Hitchcock's film. The staging of Balestrero's arrest on his doorstep, for example, is quite similar in both the television and the film versions. *Life* celebrated the broadcast with a brief story illustrated by a photograph of Balestrero watching the re-creation of his experiences.[7]

In addition to illustrating the widespread publicity that Balestrero's story received, the original *Life* article and the television dramatization help us realize how much of the true story was eliminated in *The Wrong Man*, despite Hitchcock's declaration to the contrary. While *The Wrong Man* retains the general details of Balestrero's arrest and trial, as well as the details of Rose's breakdown, the weak points of the police investigation, the ease with which Balestrero was able to establish his alibis, and the effectiveness of his attorney have been eliminated from the screenplay. To a certain extent, these excisions make the story more dramatic. Without any mention of the missing topcoat and notebook, the evidence against Balestrero seems more conclusive. The alleged death of all the witnesses who played pinochle with Manny on the July date makes Fate in the film seem all that much more against him. Similarly, O'Connor's claim in the film that he had had little experience with criminal cases makes Balestrero's trial seem all the more chancy. Even the dissolve from Balestrero's face to Daniel's is a dramatic contrivance. Though Balestrero was a religious man and prayed at his trial, Hitchcock embellishes the truth when he dissolves from the accused man's face to the face of the thief, as though to suggest that Manny's prayer is the cause of Daniel's arrest. In fact, as in the television drama, Balestrero was not praying, but playing in the Stork Club band at the time of Daniel's arrest.

Apart from their increased dramatic effect, one might usefully consider these deviations from the truth of the *Life* and televised accounts within the context of the self-conscious conflict between fact and fiction that had become well established in postwar Hollywood films. To be sure, the mixture of fact and fiction in earlier films is hardly remarkable. Much of the output of Warner Bros. since the 1930s had consisted of fictional films based on factual events. Conversely, *The March of Time* series produced by Twentieth Century-Fox between 1934 and 1953 regularly embellished its factually based material with liberal doses of fiction. In the postwar years, however, in a number of the films now associated with film noir, fact and fiction were often presented as antagonists within the same film. In semidocumentary police procedurals, for example, the protocols of fiction came to be associated with duplicitous criminality, while in the fiction film the truth of reality was self-defeating. Two films in particular, *The Naked City* (Universal-International, 1948, directed by Jules Dassin) and *The Glass Web* (Universal-International, 1954, directed by Jack Arnold) epitomize the dynamics of this antagonism and offer a background against which to consider the play of fact and fiction in *The Wrong Man*.

The Naked City grew out of Malvin Wald's experiences making documentaries in the Army Air Corps during the Second World War. When he later proposed to Mark Hellinger that these same techniques might be employed in shooting a feature film entirely on location, Hellinger bankrolled him to a monthlong research trip to New York City to develop a story suited to such a semidocumentary format. Wald spent the time learning the details of police procedures and studying the department's files of unsolved homicides for an adaptable subject. As Wald explains, the police were suspicious about his declared interest in authenticity:

> They started to give me an informal third-degree. No rubber hoses or bright lights. Just the names of a few current murder movies they had seen – and hated. I hadn't written any of the films, but still I started to sweat – a kind of guilt-by-association feeling for the writers who did. Finally I confessed: Many Hollywood writers had gotten trapped in the excitement of their stories and had been careless with the truth. I promised to try to avoid that pitfall – and write an honest film about police detectives, if it ever got produced.[8]

Finally, Wald wrote a story based upon the unsolved murder of a model named Dot King, fashioning a hypothetical solution to the case for the sake of a traditional script.

This mixture of fact and fiction is reflected formally in the finished film as well, for, in place of the traditional written credits, *The Naked City* begins with a combination of voice-over credits and introductory commentary spoken by Hellinger himself and presented against aerial shots of Manhattan:

> Ladies and gentlemen, the motion picture you are about to see is called *The Naked City*. My name is Mark Hellinger. I was in charge of its production. And I may as well tell you frankly that it's a bit different from most films you've ever seen. It was written by Albert Maltz and Malvin Wald, photographed by William Daniels, and directed by Jules Dassin. As you see, we're flying over an island, a city, a particular city. And this is a story of a number of people. And a story, also, of the city itself. It was *not* photographed in a studio, quite the contrary. Barry Fitzgerald, our star, Howard Duff, Dorothy Hart, Don Taylor, Ted De Corsia, and the other actors played out their roles on the

streets, in the apartment houses, in the skyscrapers of New York itself. And along with them, a great many New Yorkers played out their roles also. This is the city as it is – hot summer pavements, the children at play, the buildings in their naked stone, the people without makeup.[9]

Thus *The Naked City* signals its superior truthfulness by replacing the standard printed credits with the conversational voice of Mark Hellinger, the well-known New York newpaperman whose familiarity with the city authenticates his pose as a truthful narrator. Yet in the same way that Wald's story mixes fact and fiction, this opening sequence intercuts authentic shots of New York with staged shots involving the story's fictional characters.

As a police procedural, *The Naked City* follows the homicide squad's investigation of a young model's murder. The search also serves to initiate a young detective, Jimmy Halloran, into the approved, step-by-step procedures under the watchful eye of experienced Lt. Muldoon. While the detectives' work is rational and methodical, the criminals they hunt and the false leads they encounter are based upon fanciful fictions. Indeed, Muldoon identifies their unknown suspect as a fictional character named "J. P. McGillicuddy," his generic term for all as yet unidentified suspects. A sweetly demented woman who tells Muldoon that the killer will confess if a hound dog's tooth is buried at the dead woman's grave, along with a fantasy confession by the dead woman's grocery boy claiming he stabbed her to rid the world of her immorality, point toward the ways that make-believe is associated with the crime throughout the film.

Eventually, the investigation ties the woman's death to a ring of jewel thieves specializing in thefts from wealthy families. Its mastermind, Frank Niles, is an inveterate liar who fabricates all sorts of stories about himself, even when none is necessary to establish an alibi. Niles is a compulsive fabulator, creating a wartime persona for himself and fictionalizing his successes as a businessman before finally admitting that he is a compulsive storyteller. Niles's various stories are so fanciful that Muldoon finally declares, "In a lifetime of interrogating and investigating, you are probably the biggest and most willing liar I have ever met." Niles's admission that he is a liar ties lying to fictional performance as he replies: "All right, I'm a liar. I'm a circus character altogether." The curious phrase, "circus character," points in turn to Willie Garzah, the member of the gang who did kill the model. As it turns out, Garzah was once an acrobat. Significantly, his identity is finally established at a gym. The sequence begins before the investigating detective arrives as a trainer coaches a pair of intertwined professional wrestlers how to grimace and groan as though they were in terrible pain. When the detective introduces himself to the trainer, the wrestlers suddenly pause – clearly in no pain at all – to listen to his questions. Garzah had been a wrestler too, committed like them to performing in the most fictional of sports.

If various sorts of fiction are associated with the criminals in the semidocumentary *The Naked City*, fiction extracts its revenge from fact in *The Glass Web*. Following its credit sequence, the film begins with the apparent murder of a woman at an abandoned desert mine. After the killer dumps her body down the mine shaft, however, the camera pulls back to reveal that the action has taken place in a television studio during the weekly Wednesday night broadcast of "Crime of the Week," a program that prides itself on presenting "the true story as it exactly happened." Within the narrative, the conflict between fiction and fact is embodied in the antagonism between Don Newell, the show's writer, and Harry Hayes, the man who researches the details of the murders and casts each week's show.

Doggedly committed to factual accuracy, Hayes continually faults Newell for valuing dramatic effect more highly than literal truth. One argument between them is worth quoting because it illustrates the conflict inherent in their opposing points of view. Hayes complains that Newell's latest script is flat because he has ignored factual detail:

NEWELL: But who the devil cares about that if the scene plays?

HAYES: Well what we're selling is realism. The people who watch our show every Wednesday night want to eavesdrop on murder. They want to smell the stink of murder. They love it! And they watch our show instead of the others because they know I give them the truth.... I was a police reporter long enough to know that the people buy the little details, the quirks, the idiosyncrasies, the poor slobs in the news.

Over the course of the narrative, the conflict between the two men – concretely, the conflict between fact and fiction – is played out through the murder of an actress with whom they have both been involved, the same actress who is "murdered" in the film's opening sequence. Hayes murders her, then writes a script about her murder for the show, which suggests through circumstantial evidence that Newell was her killer. As one might expect in this fictional work, however, Hayes's passion for accuracy leads him to include details in the script that only the actual killer could know. A fictional work, *The Glass Web* allows the writer of fiction to triumph, as the devotee of fact outwits himself by his slavish regard for it.

Despite their opposite attitudes toward fact and fiction, both *The Naked City* and *The Glass Web* visually signal the antagonism between them through formal devices that strain classical norms – the lack of traditional opening credits in the former and the initial uncertainty of whether the desert murder in the latter is to be read as fact or fiction within its diegesis. In part, some foregrounding of narration in this way is common at the beginning of Hollywood films. As David Bordwell observes:

Classical narration emerges quite overtly in the film's opening moments, during the credits and the early scenes, and then becomes more covert, letting character causality caught in *medias res* carry the narrational burden.... Once the action gets going, the narration slips into the background ... but the narration may become overt again by an anticipatory cut or a stressed sound-image juxtaposition.[10]

These two films differ from the norm, however, because voice-over narration in the one and the constant diegetic conflict between fact and fiction in the other keep narration from ever slipping entirely into the motivated illusion that constitutes classical narration. Narration in these films never quite becomes invisible.

Unlike *The Naked City* and *The Glass Web*, *The Wrong Man* does not present the antagonism of fact and fiction directly within its diegesis. Rather, the film employs a series of markers that question whether its semidocumentary format, as a style, is any more truthful a form of representation, better suited to factual material, than the well-established Hollywood studio style. In their introductory remarks to viewers, both Hellinger and Hitchcock emphasize how different the photographic styles of their films are from studio norms and leave us to infer from the references to "buildings in their naked stone" and "people without makeup," as well as from Hitchcock's stance on a vacant soundstage, that there is some special connection between their comparatively plain visual style and the factualness of the stories photographed in this manner. How different the semidocumentary style was thought to be from studio standards can be gauged from a piece about the location shooting of *The Wrong Man* that appeared in *American Cinematographer*. Frederick Foster quotes Hitchcock's expression of concern that the film's visually bare semidocumentary style might damage the professional reputation of Robert Burks, his longtime cinematographer:

> Perhaps remembering Bob Burks's fine color photography on other pictures and the new prestige he acquired last year as a result of winning an Oscar for the photography of *To Catch a Thief*, Hitchcock said to him: "Perhaps you may not want to do this picture, Bob. I wouldn't want the stark, colorless documentary treatment I expect to reflect on your reputation as a photographer." Burks reassured Hitchcock that if he was willing to risk his reputation on the picture, he'd gladly go along with him.[11]

Burks willingly filmed *The Wrong Man* in this way because he understood that such a plain style authenticated its subject by making it appear unmanipulated, as though it were caught in an actuality. For, as Burks says about filming in a precinct house: "Here, as in all the other interiors, the lighting maintained a stark, natural aspect – free of all the frilly touches that might otherwise be given such a set on a studio sound stage. Hitchcock had emphasized he wanted it to look like a newsreel shot" (Foster, 114). But how true, in fact, are newsreel shots? Some of the changes that Hitchcock made in Balestrero's case, along with some formal features in the film, call the apparent truthfulness of the semidocumentary style into question, encouraging attentive viewers to see it as no more transparent than the classical studio style it seems to refuse. The perceptual problems posed by the film demonstrate that the semidocumentary style offers no more honest or direct a rendering of what transpires before the camera's lens.

The Wrong Man's credit sequence introduces the first of a pair of lap dissolves that embody the problem of perception as a matter of legibility. The initial series of lap dissolves presents an evening at the Stork Club in a temporally condensed manner as dissolves connect separate moments from early evening when the club is filled with patrons to closing time, as the last lingering couple finishes the final dance. The shots are filmed from a fixed setup with the camera aimed across the dance floor toward Balestrero and the band. In condensing the evening in this way, the lap dissolves function in a purely conventional manner, as does the music from the band that helps to hide the eliminated moments by remaining continuous. David Bordwell's comments about the conventional use of diegetic music to mask lap dissolves are worth quoting here because they can help us to understand how unremarkable these are in some ways – particularly because the example he cites is very like the opening of Hitchock's film:

> In the sound film, diegetic music could cover certain gaps at the level of the image while still projecting a sense of continuous time. For example, in *Flying Fortress* (1942) a couple sit down to dinner in a restaurant while a band is playing. The meal is abbreviated by means of dissolves, creating ellipses on the visual track; but the band's music continues uninterrupted. The bleeding of music over large ellipses suggests how easily the temporal vagueness of music can make sound fulfill narrative functions. (p. 46)

However, because the appearance of new credits coincides with the dissolves, the passage of the evening is far less legible than it might be in a series of conventional lap dissolves. Reading the new words makes it doubly difficult to read the new image and vice versa. Thus the sequence formally initiates the question of perception that haunts the text for both characters and viewers until it is resolved in the second lap dissolve, from Balestrero's face to Daniel's.

In contrast to the first, the second lap dissolve could hardly be more legible. Not only is the dissolve so slow that both men's faces merge for a while, but even the soundtrack changes at the point that Daniel's face becomes distinct from Balestrero's. Where there is nondescript music on the soundtrack while Balestrero's face dominates the image, street noises replace the music once Daniel's face is distinct. The fact that the dissolve also conveys simultaneity – Balestrero prays at the same time that Daniel begins the robbery that results in his arrest – further underlines the opposite purposes of this pair of dissolves. The first dissolves confound perception, while the later one insists upon it.

Between these lap dissolves, the same concerns with legibility and perception are manifested in the narrative in a variety of ways. Not only does Balestrero's arrest depend upon the mistaken perception of the office workers who misidentify him, but a curious incident involving his sons just before he leaves for the insurance office points to the same matter in more explicitly dramatic terms. Robert, the elder son, has been practicing Mozart on the piano. He complains that his brother, Greg, has purposely been annoying him by hiding in a closet and playing a different melody on his harmonica at the same time. While Rose struggles to settle their dispute, it finally takes Manny to quiet the boys:

ROBERT: Will you tell Greg to quit playing the mouth organ while I practice!
ROSE: Greg. Greg!
ROBERT: Will you tell him!
ROSE: Gregory!
GREGORY: Yes, mother?
ROSE: Don't play the harmonica while Robert is playing the piano.
GREGORY: But I was playing the same thing!
ROSE: [*to Robert*] Was he?

ROBERT: He thinks he was, but ...
GREGORY: I was!
ROBERT: I don't want you playing, even if it is the same. [*to Rose*] He hides in the
    closet and makes noise.
ROSE: Robert!
MANNY: What's all this?
ROSE: Oh, Robert was playing the piano and Greg was spoiling the music.
GREGORY: I didn't.
ROBERT: You did!
GREGORY: I was playing the same!
ROBERT: You were not!
MANNY: You know, Bob, sounded to me – that last part when Greg was playing along –
    sounded to me like he caught the melody.[12]

Manny finally calms them with the promise of fifteen-minute lessons that night for each boy on his respective instrument. Manny is arrested when he arrives home that evening, however, and never has the chance to give them their lessons.

In a displaced manner, the boys' disagreement concisely encompasses what will become the narrative's main dramatic issues, announcing them as a summary agenda for the remainder of the film to consider in detail. Whether the boys are playing the same or different melodies prefigures the confusion that will develop over whether Balestrero is the same man who twice robbed the insurance company's office or is a different man. More directly related to our purposes, however, Greg's hiding in the closet hints at the phantom presence of Daniel, the real robber, throughout the film.

As a careful examination of *The Wrong Man* reveals, the real thief is often visible in the film as he and Balestrero cross paths. Balestrero actually bumps into Daniel outside the Victor Moore Arcade while on his way to the insurance office inside, where the employees will mistakenly identify him as the man who twice robbed them. After his arrest, the police take Balestrero to a liquor store that had also been robbed in order to give the employees a chance to identify him. As Manny leaves in a squad car afterwards, Daniel walks past the liquor store on the sidewalk. Similarly, after Balestrero is led from a paddy wagon into Felony Court for his arraignment, the camera holds on the scene long enough to show Daniel strolling through the frame after Manny has disappeared from sight. Thus, while Daniel's overt appearance late in the film, in the long lap dissolve that superimposes his face upon Balestrero's, is generally regarded as the film's most striking device, the dissolve simply makes his presence manifest.

As the dissolve and subsequent face-to-face meeting between Balestrero and Daniel in the precinct house reveal, the men share only a slight facial resemblance, much too superficial to register in the long-shots in which they cross paths. Hitchcock takes great pains, therefore, to augment their physical resemblance through the more prominent details of clothing that consistently differentiate them from the appearance of the other men in the film. Both, for example, wear essentially the same hat. In addition, unlike others in the film, they consistently keep the collars of their (different!) coats turned up in a similar fashion. And, while these may seem like negligible details – if there is anything negligible in a drama so closely focused on the misperception of details – the film's dissolves and explicit dramatic concerns about the discrimination of similarities and differences establish a context that urges one to be more attentive to such slight comparisons. Thus Balestrero's promise of music lessons to his sons suggests the film's larger offer of lessons about the apparent legibility of the semidocumentary image. Through these transformations of melodies into men, of a hidden child into a hidden thief, and of promised music lessons into a demonstration of how one must learn to read images too, *The Wrong Man* encourages thoughtful viewers to be more attentive to their own perceptions. Seeing is always problematic, and not even the supposedly objective eye of the semidocumentary camera can relieve the human eye of its responsibility to see clearly by always calling its perception into question. As much as the thematic concerns embodied within Balestrero's case are typical of Hitchcock's narratives, this general truth about perception is one of his abiding concerns, frequently presented, as here, in formal terms.

Notes

1. Eric Rohmer and Claude Chabrol, *Hitchcock: The First Forty-Four Films*, trans. Stanley Hochman (New York: Frederick Ungar, 1979), 145.
2. See "Court Is Turned into a Movie Set," *New York Times*, April 9, 1956, and "All Around the Town with *The Wrong Man*: Hitchcock Troupe Shoots New Thriller at Surface and Underground Sites," *New York Times*, April 29, 1956; reprinted in *The New York Times Encyclopedia of Film* (New York: Times Books, 1984).
3. Here, as elsewhere, all dialogue quoted from *The Wrong Man* has been transcribed from the viewing print.
4. François Truffaut, *The Films in My Life*, trans. Leonard Mayhew (New York: Simon and Schuster, 1978), 84.
5. Herbert Brean, "A Case of Identity," *Life*, June 29, 1953, 97–100, 102, 104, 107.
6. I am indebted to Dan Einstein, Curator of the ATAS-UCLA Television Archives, for arranging for me to view a copy of this dramatization.
7. See "Balestrero's Nightmare: *Life* Story of Musician Falsely Accused of Theft Is Hit on TV," *Life*, February 1, 1954, 45–6. The role of Balestrero was played in this dramatization by Robert Ellenstein. His Balestrero is much more timid than Henry Fonda's portrayal in *The Wrong Man*. Is it merely a coincidence or an example of jokey casting that Ellenstein plays the henchman in *North by Northwest* who mistakenly identifies Roger Thornhill as George Kaplan in the Plaza Hotel's Oak Bar?
8. Malvin Wald, "Afterword," in *The Naked City: A Screenplay* (Carbondale: Southern Illinois Univ. Press, 1979), 138. Wald's claims for the aesthetic reasons for shooting on location ought to be balanced by an awareness of the numerous economic reasons that made location filming attractive in the 1940s. See William Lafferty, "A Reappraisal of the Semi-Documentary in Hollywood, 1945–1948," *The Velvet Light Trap*, no. 20 (1983): 22–6.
9. This speech does not appear in the published screenplay.
10. David Bordwell, Janet Staiger, and Kristin Thompson, *The Classical Hollywood Cinema: Film Style and Mode of Production to 1960* (New York: Columbia Univ. Press, 1985), 69.

11. Frederick Foster, "'Hitch' Didn't Want It Arty," *American Cinematographer*, vol. 38, no. 2 (1957): 85.
12. In Spies's dramatization, Robert becomes angry when his younger brother continues to mimic his every word, including his question about what they are having for dinner. The argument over music, Gregory's hiding in the closet, and the promise of music lessons are newly created for the film.

THE WRONG MAN (Warner Bros., 1956). *Producers*: Alfred Hitchcock, Herbert Coleman, *Assistant Director*: Daniel J. McCauley, *Script*: Maxwell Anderson, Angus McPhail, from Anderson's "The True Story of Christopher Emmanuel Balestrero," *Photography*: Robert Burks, *Editor*: George Tomasini, *Sets*: Paul Sylbert, William L. Kuehl, *Music*: Bernard Herrmann, *Players*: Henry Fonda (Christopher Emmanuel "Manny" Balestrero), Vera Miles (Rose Balestrero), Anthony Quayle (Frank O'Connor), Esther Minciotti (Mrs. Balestrero, Manny's mother), Richard Robbins (Daniel). 105 minutes.

Chapter Seventeen

Male Desire, Male Anxiety: The Essential Hitchcock

Robin Wood

It would be difficult to overestimate the importance – both for Hitchcock scholarship and for anyone who loves the cinema – of the long overdue rerelease of the five "missing" films from Hitchcock's Hollywood period. *Rope* is unique in his career – and indeed in the history of commercial cinema – for its uncompromising use of the ten-minute take; *The Trouble with Harry* – though few will accord it major status – is unique for its tone (not, it is true, the only Hitchcock comedy, but the only truly *Hitchcockian* comedy); *The Man Who Knew Too Much* is self-evidently superior to the British original, though a few diehard British critics still refuse to see this. The real irreplaceable loss all these years, however, has been that of *Rear Window* and *Vertigo*: Hitchcock's reputation does not, of course, stand on them alone, but they are central and indispensable to any valid assessment of his achievement. It is fitting and timely that *Vertigo* is at last inscribed in the final "ten best" list of *Sight and Sound's* 1982 International Critics' Poll.

Twenty years ago, I was writing *Hitchcock's Films*, a book that opens with the question, "Why should we take Hitchcock seriously?" The meaning, at that time, would scarcely have been altered if I had written simply, "*Should* we take Hitchcock seriously?" It would have been unthinkable at the time to refer to "Hitchcock scholarship," whether as something that existed or as something that *ought* to exist (at least in the English-speaking world – a body of such scholarship was already developing in France). Today, the "should" seems to have been answered almost unanimously in the affirmative, but the "why" still remains very much an open question. We have, at any rate, passed far beyond the point where formulas like "skillful entertainer" and "master of suspense" were felt to be adequate. One hopes also for general agreement that the question of the artist's private life – was he lovable, hateful, admirable, despicable, pitiable, and so on? – is one with which serious criticism has no concern, though our society's cult of the individual makes it a recurring danger.

What has happened in the past twenty years is not, of course, a mere shift in the critical consensus on a single director: the entire perspective and objective of film criticism have been transformed. The introduction of semiotics and structuralism, the politicization of film theory during the late 1960s and 1970s, the new emphasis on concepts of ideology, the vital and radical input of feminist theory, the growing importance of psychoanalytic theory (especially as a political weapon) – all these interrelated phenomena have ensured that we can no longer look at the films as we used to, as "works of art" on "universal" human themes. As our culture moves into increasingly fundamental schisms and increasingly polarized confrontations, other, more pressing issues supervene, and *must* do so if the practice of criticism is not to be doomed to triviality: especially, the question of the films' place in culture – their relationship to the "dominant ideology" of patriarchal bourgeois capitalism on the one hand and, on the other, to the progressive and radical movements that seek its overthrow. Instead of "Why should we take Hitchcock seriously?" the opening question of my book, were I writing it today, would be the central question that haunts contemporary Hitchcock criticism in article after article: "Can Hitchcock be saved for feminism?"

At the center of the recent advances in Hitchcock criticism is unquestionably the work of French critic Raymond Bellour, responsible for the development, in North America as well as Europe, of a veritable "Bellour school." (See, among dozens of examples, Deborah Linderman on *Blackmail* and Michael Renov on *Notorious* as well as Bill Nichols on *The Birds*.) It is extremely frustrating that Bellour's work remains, for most of us, so inaccessible, scattered among various periodicals, some of it available in English only in mimeographed seminar papers distributed within obviously limited circles. Now that his essays – in the original French – have been gathered together into a book (*L'Analyse du film*), one hopes that it will be published in translation as soon as possible.

I cannot, in the space available, do even rough justice to Bellour's work for those readers unfamiliar with it (the best introduction is the interview by Janet Bergstrom in *Camera Obscura* (nos. 3–4), which also contains Bellour's essay on *Psycho*). When my own book appeared in 1965, it was praised for its "close reading" of the films. Bellour's work, at the very least, makes such a conception of "close reading" obsolete. His shot-by-shot analyses, his meticulous examination of the functioning of the cinematic codes operative within a given segment, his ability to relate minute specifics to the operation of the film as a whole (and, beyond that, to the operations of the "Hollywood machine") – all this has me lost in admiration.

Which does not prevent doubts from setting in. I am worried by a sense that the overall tendency of Bellour and the "Bellour school" is ultimately reductive. (The same kind of objection applies to Peter Wollen's famous Proppian analysis of *North by Northwest* in *Readings and Writings*: see Seymour Chatman's review of Wollen's book in *American Film*, vol. 8, no. 9 [July–August 1983].) For me, the most important and profitable development in film criticism in the last twenty years has been the concept of "ideological contradiction." The tendency of Bellourian criticism has been to iron out contradiction in favor of demonstrating the workings of "classical narrative," the "classical realist text," the "classical Hollywood film": always the same narrative, always the same film.

At a particularly alarming moment during a film conference in Australia in December 1982, Bellour informed us that there is no essential difference between *Bringing Up Baby* and *North by Northwest*. After all, both end with the hero rescuing the heroine by pulling her up by her arm. The implication seemed to be that there is also no *essential* difference between these and other Hollywood films: they are all "machines for producing the couple" (a formula I find at once marvelously suggestive and profoundly unsatisfying). What semiological criticism crucially, and in some respects disablingly, lacks is a concept of "tone," a factor that may in many cases directly undermine and contradict the conventions of narrative movement. *Rear Window* and *Vertigo* can both, I suppose, be read as "machines for producing the couple" (*Vertigo*, as it were, by default, since the failure of the specific couple confirms the couple's general ideological desirability). That is not at all how I see the films, and the readings I shall offer are completely at odds with it.

The charge of misogyny constantly recurs, and at all levels of critical writing: from personal gossip (Hitchcock treated his female stars – or some of them – callously) to the most meticulously detailed analyses of the filmic texts (for example, Nichols on *The Birds*). I certainly do not intend to claim that there exists in Hitchcock's work an uncontaminated feminist discourse, a view of women that feminism could unproblematically appropriate; nor shall I deny that there erupts periodically in his work an animus against women and, specifically, against the female body. This can be seen at its grossest in *Frenzy* (the rape and murder of Barbara Leigh-Hunt and the notorious potato-sack scene – the latter the more disturbing in that Hitchcock clearly supposed it to be funny). Yet, even there, it is profoundly troubled by contradiction (the two women in question are, after all, by far the most sympathetic characters in the film), and it is precisely this sense of disturbance within the films that opens them up to a feminist analysis. The contradictions have the effect of calling into question, and in some cases disrupting beyond all possible recuperation, the male drives and fantasies that provide the films' initial impulse. At their best, the films dramatize and foreground not merely tensions personal to Hitchcock, but tensions central to our culture and to its construction and organization of sexual difference.

My prime concern here is a rethinking of *Vertigo*. Rereading the original attempt to interpret the film in my book, I find many of the perceptions valid but am greatly dissatisfied with their formulation. That particular chapter, especially, is shot through with a subtle and insidious sexism (at that time I had no awareness whatever of the oppression of women within our culture), and, closely related to this, it strikingly lacks any psychoanalytic account of the nature of "romantic love," accepting it as some eternal and unchangeable given of "the human condition." I want, however, to preface this with a few sketchy remarks about *Rear Window*, "notes toward a reading" that, complete, would require at least an entire issue of *American Film*. I shall consider two interconnected themes of the film that now appear crucial to an understanding of it.

Castration. In *Rear Window* a photographer, wheelchair-bound with a broken leg, whiles away the hours spying on his neighbors with a telephoto lens – until he discovers a murder and becomes determined to catch the murderer. Most critical accounts have centered on its status as "artistic testament." It is a film about the experience of film viewing, with Jefferies (James Stewart) as the spectator, the apartments he watches as the screen. This reading is certainly supported by much of the film's detail and, more generally, by its central tension: the events in the apartments reflect the spectator's fantasies, yet the spectator has no control over them, so that dream can turn to nightmare at any moment. However, such an account requires careful definition. First, it seems quite misguided to see the film as an allegory about "the cinema." Insofar as this works, the film is an allegory about *Hitchcock's* cinema, which is highly idiosyncratic. Second, the spectatorship inscribed in the film is by no means neutral: it is unambiguously male. Far more important, it seems to me, than the "artistic testament" dimension of the film is its dramatization of fundamental male sexual anxieties. Clearly, those anxieties are rooted in the fear of castration, and, equally clearly (from a psychoanalytic viewpoint), castration is represented by Jefferies's broken leg.

The term "castration" has caused certain problems and confusions. Is it meant literally or symbolically? The confusions disappear if one recognizes it as both. Within patriarchal culture, the phallus is the supreme symbol of power; conversely, power is "phallic." Loss of power on any level (money, prestige, social status, authority over women, domination of children, and so forth) is therefore symbolic castration. At the same time, this is seen as reactivating the *literal* castration fears of childhood. Language acknowledges such a connection quite clearly: the word "impotence" (often used to mean "powerlessness") invariably carries sexual overtones.

Castration, then, at the beginning of *Rear Window*, is signified not only by the broken leg but also by the smashed camera. Jefferies's potency as a male expresses itself as much in his role as a freelance photographer as in anything directly sexual, his recklessness and initiative taken as the guarantee of "masculinity." It is the fear of castration and the drive to reaffirm "potency" that the male spectator is invited to identify with. As the film develops, Jefferies attempts to assert his "possession of the phallus" through the power of "the look," a substitute for both the smashed camera and the broken leg (the latter explicitly associated with the deprivation of sexual activity). Hence the significance (and the comedy) of the *growth* of the look as the film progresses: first the eyes, then binoculars, finally a huge erect telescope. But Jefferies's pursuit of power through the look only confirms, repeatedly, his impotence, a point brought home to him (and to us) in the two major climactic scenes: Lisa's search of Thorwald's apartment and the culminating Jefferies–Thorwald confrontation, where the "potency" of Jefferies's flashbulbs proves insufficient to save him.

Marriage. Rear Window is crucially about marriage, and its radicalism lies in the connection it makes between that and the castration theme. Marriage is seen as the castration of the male. Stated like that, the film appears brazenly misogynist, and in many ways it is capable of sustaining such a reading. But only if one ignores other elements. What it is really about is the impossibility of successful human relations within an ideological system that constructs men and women in hopelessly incompatible roles: it relates quite fascinatingly to the "wandering versus settling" antinomy that Peter Wollen sees as central to John Ford and to the Western. At its center are Jefferies, the ideal American male (the "wanderer-adventurer," even if at second hand: he photographs the adventures of others), and Lisa, the ideal American female (settled, eminently civilized, constantly pressuring Jefferies to "settle down" with her, the perfected "object for the gaze"). They are macabrely reflected in the Thorwalds (the wanderer-adventurer reduced to traveling salesman, his wife "settled" to the extreme of being bedridden). All the other apartment-dwellers relate to this theme (with marvelous precision and economy – there is neither redundancy nor irrelevance). They variously embody the twin hells of marriage and singleness, in a civilization that demands the former while rendering its success impossible. What the emphasis on castration and impotence ultimately achieves is the calling into question of our culture's concept of "potency" (masculinity), with the insupportable demands it makes on men and women alike.

With *Vertigo*, I want to examine the first four sequences (culminating in the introduction of Madeleine) in some detail as the basis for a psychoanalytic (and political) reading of the film that I shall subsequently develop. In *Vertigo*, James Stewart plays a detective who falls in love with the object of his surveillance, Madeleine, who eventually commits suicide, or so it appears. Stewart meets Judy, who resembles the dead woman (Kim Novak in both roles), tries to remake her in the suicide's image, and eventually discovers that Judy, in fact, *was* the woman he loved, a part she was playing in a greedy husband's plot to murder his wife.

The opening sequence (the chase, the fall) is among the most succinct and abstract Hitchcock gave us; it is also characteristically fragmented in editing, requiring twenty-five shots. The abstractness is established in the first image: a metal bar against an out-of-focus background that a hand suddenly clutches. Then the camera pulls back, the background becomes a San Francisco cityscape, and three men clamber over the top rung in a rooftop pursuit. We are given only the most minimal narrative information. The second man is a policeman, so the first must be a criminal; the third is Scottie (James Stewart), clearly the male protagonist. He is connected to the cop by being a pursuer, but connected to the criminal by being in plain clothes (nothing tells us at this point that he is a police detective; he might be a reporter or merely a conscientious citizen). The first three shots strongly emphasize the three-character structure: (1) Each man in turn climbs over the bar. (2) An extreme long shot contains all three men within the frame simultaneously. (3) Each man in turn leaps to another roof (Hitchcock cuts before we see Stewart fall and clutch the gutter, an action given us in shots 4 and 5).

At this point begins an alternating pattern – a favorite structural method of the mature Hitchcock, the first of many in the film – that continues almost uninterrupted to the end of the sequence: a series of nine shots, all medium close-up, taken from an identical camera position, of Scottie hanging (nos. 6, 8, 10, 12, 14, 16; then 21, 23, 25); an alternating series, slightly less consistent, of six shots showing Stewart's point of view (nos. 9, 13, 15, 17; then 22, 24; though 15 – the uniformed policeman reaching down – is ambiguous, the position of the camera being inexact). This second series includes, of course, the famous "vertigo" shot (no. 9) with the simultaneous track-out/zoom-in, an effect repeated later in the two tower sequences, at the middle and end of the film. The interruption of the alternating pattern, on which the sequence pivots, gives us the policeman's attempt to save Scottie (with the scene's only dialogue – "Give me your hand") and the start of the policeman's fall (nos. 18, 19, 20), at which point the alternation, thrown temporarily out of rhythm, is resumed.

The sequence represents perhaps the most extreme and abrupt instance of enforced audience identification in all of Hitchcock – an effect to which the technical means (point of view, alternation, vertigo shot, even the jarring rhythmic lurch at the policeman's fall) all contribute. Usually, however, he is far more circumspect, building identification gradually through a complicated process of curiosity, sympathy, emotional involvement (see, for instance, the opening of *Psycho*, where the first clear-cut point-of-view shot – the street crossing seen through Marion's windshield – does not occur until about fifteen minutes into the film). What makes possible this drastic and brutal assault on the spectator? Most obviously, the extreme physical danger, which is the simplest and most basic of the conditions that encourage spectator identification.

It is the most obvious factor but perhaps not the most important. The sequence carries very strong and potent psychoanalytic resonances with as much claim to "universality" as the fear of heights. One such resonance arises from "the fall" itself. One common explanation of dreams of falling (and the sequence's abstraction makes it very dreamlike) is that they reproduce, or at least *refer to*, the birth trauma (from which viewpoint it is interesting that we never see Scottie "let go"). Another, more substantiated by the text, arises from the insistence on *three* characters and their interconnection. They can be taken to represent the fundamental Freudian triumvirate id–ego–superego. The id is associated with unrestrained libido, pursuit of pleasure, which is – in our surplus–repressive culture – commonly associated with criminality. The superego is conscience, the law, the internalized authority of the father – our psychic police officer in fact. The ego is the self, within which the struggle for dominance between the id and the superego is played out. At the opening of *Vertigo*, then, the symbolic father is killed and the "son," if not the actual agent of his death, is responsible for it. The id escapes to wander freely in the darkness, reflected – at the end of the film – in the fact that the murderer, Gavin Elster, is never caught. Scottie is left hanging (we never see, or are told, how he gets down). Metaphorically, he is suspended for the remainder of the film.

The second sequence (in the apartment of Midge, Scottie's ex-fiancée) offers an even more extreme example of the Hitchcockian principles of fragmentation and alternation: more extreme, because the "action" – mainly an extended conversation – could easily have been filmed in a single take, with the exception of a single "subjective insert." Hitchcock breaks it down into sixty-two shots, only five of which contain the two characters in the frame together. The entire scene is constructed in alternating series broken only at certain privileged moments – Midge/Scottie; female space/male space, each defined by the framing and by its own significant object (Scottie's cane, the model brassiere being sketched by Midge, a commercial artist) prominent throughout each series.

Apart from the opening establishing shot (whose function, although both characters are in frame, is to stress the distance that separates them), Midge and Scottie are shown together at three points in the action:

1. Shot 31 (the exact midpoint and pivot shot of the scene, privileged as its only long take): It includes the conversation about the new brassiere with its "revolutionary uplift." Midge remarks to Scottie, "You know about such things – you're a big boy now," as she initiates him into its secrets.

2. Shots 47 and 48: Scottie suggests a method of overcoming his acrophobia, and Midge promptly takes over as organizer, fetching the stepladder. In the ensuing shots (in which the alternation is resumed), she will "push" Scottie – verbally – to the point where he collapses with an attack of vertigo.
3. Shot 62 (the final shot of the sequence): Midge comforts the distraught Scottie in her arms, holding his head to her bosom.

All of these moments have a common theme: the presentation of Midge as mother figure, as made explicit in the dialogue – "Don't be so motherly" (later, in the scene in the nursing home, Midge will say, "Mother's here"). The two come together only in the mother–child relationship; otherwise (and crucially in their discussion of their brief engagement and the possibility that it might be renewed) they are kept rigorously separated.

Of the two, only Midge is permitted close-ups (shots 36 and 38), and they are used to comment on Scottie, to call him into question. They occur during the discussion of the engagement ("Good old college days" – Midge), which lasted "three whole weeks" and was called off by Midge herself (despite the fact that "you know there's only one man in the world for me"). The close-ups emphasize the troubled and enigmatic nature of her glances at Scottie; they suggest an inadequacy in him – an impossibility of a mature relationship – whose nature is left unformulated.

Other components of *Vertigo*'s thematic are introduced during the scene, centered on certain key words or concepts: "free," "available," "wander." Scottie is about to become "free" of the corset he has worn since his fall (if it is valid to relate the fall to birth trauma, the corset logically becomes swaddling clothes). The word "freedom" will recur throughout the film, connected to the word "power" and consistently associated with male prerogative, the freedom and power of domination. Gavin Elster, in the next sequence, refers nostalgically to the "power" and "freedom" of the old San Francisco. The bookstore owner, describing the casting–aside of Carlotta Valdes, the historical figure whose portrait fascinates Madeleine, remarks, "Men could do that in those days – they had the freedom, they had the power." And Scottie, unmasking Judy/Madeleine at the end of the film, asks her contemptuously if, "with all that freedom and all that power," Elster just "ditched" her.

"Freedom," then, is freedom to dominate women or to throw them over – even murder them – when they become inconvenient. It is associated with the past, when "men could do that" – the past to which Madeleine belongs and Midge emphatically does not. Scottie is still "available" for marriage ("That's me – Available Ferguson"); but the film, in a brilliant ellipse, instantly connects this sexual "availability" to Gavin Elster (as the old adage has it, "The devil finds work for idle hands"). Inherent in Scottie's situation is the notion of "wandering" – though the word itself will not occur until the next scene. With the "father" dead and the "id" at large, Scottie's immediate step has been to leave the police force (the "law"); Midge asks what he intends to do now. He will "do nothing for a while." He is free to follow desire wherever it leads, to wander.

The freedom, the availability, the wandering, however, also associate logically with the metaphoric suspension, with the abyss into which Scottie may fall, vividly evoked in what is, remarkably, the sequence's only point-of-view shot, Scottie's hallucinatory vision from the top of Midge's stepladder. Also relevant here is the question of identity: the fluidity, the lack of definition suggested by the range of names Stewart's character accumulates in the course of the film. He will tell Madeleine, "Acquaintances call me Scottie, friends call me John"; he presents himself as "Available Ferguson"; Elster calls him "Scottie"; Midge uses the boylike "Johnny-O" (at one point "John-O"); Madeleine says, "I prefer John," but Judy calls him "Scottie."

The third sequence (divided from the second by Hitchcock's personal appearance and two dissolves, as if to mark it as a decisive new beginning) is also built on alternation patterns, but the series are interrupted much more frequently by two-shots. The main purpose of these is to underline – with the additional emphasis of a low angle – Elster's growing domination of Scottie as he imposes his story on him. Scottie sits, Elster stands; when Scottie rises, Elster moves to the room's higher level, dominating even in long-shot. Though Elster was Scottie's schoolmate, we register Elster as significantly older (partly because we habitually think of James Stewart as young, even in middle age, "boyishness" being one of the basic components of his star persona). Elster becomes, in fact, a new father figure, but a father "outside the law" (the dialogue stresses Scottie's withdrawal from the police force). In terms of the traces of Catholic mythology that linger on in Hitchcock's work, Elster is the devil, his function being essentially that of tempter. He knows Scottie's weaknesses, and in effect offers him his own "wife," Madeleine (the film never invites us to take any interest in his plot to murder his *real* wife).

Madeleine's fascination for Scottie is set up before she appears. Elster presents her as a feminine mirror image. She "wanders" (from this point on the word will weave through the film, repeatedly linking Scottie and Madeleine), and there is also the question of *her* identity (Madeleine Elster, Carlotta Valdes? – though the latter name itself is not introduced until later). Above all, Elster tempts Scottie with "power" and "freedom," marked by a striking cut on dialogue: (1) Back view, Scottie looks at the print of old San Francisco; Elster speaks of "color, excitement, power...." (2) Cut to medium shot of Elster against a window through which we can see the cranes of his shipyard; he completes the sentence: "... freedom." The image associates the term with wealth, industry, and the possibility of escape (abroad or into the past), after which the conversation shifts to Scottie's task, the surveillance of Madeleine.

The fourth sequence, at Ernie's restaurant, offers us (and Scottie) Madeleine. Indeed, it is important that she appears to *offer herself*, at least to the gaze. The fascination is conveyed in the sequence's first shot. Starting from Scottie at the bar, and as if taking its impetus from his look, the camera draws back over the restaurant, turns, cranes, then moves slowly in toward Madeleine's back, her shoulders exposed above an emerald-green stole, the green with which, both as Madeleine and as Judy, she will be associated throughout the film and which links her ironically to the *sequoia sempervirens*, "always green, ever living." It is not – cannot possibly be – a point-of-view shot, yet it has the effect of linking us intimately to the movement of Scottie's consciousness. The camera movement is utterly unlike anything in the film up to that point, introducing a completely new tone, the grace and tenderness underlined by Bernard Herrmann's music. Madeleine is presented in terms of the "work of art," which is precisely what she is. Her movement through the doorway suggests a portrait coming to life, or a gliding statue; when she pauses and turns her head into profile, the suggestion is of a cameo or silhouette, an image that will recur throughout the film. As work of art Madeleine is at once totally accessible (a painting is completely passive, offering itself to the gaze) and totally *in*accessible (you cannot make love to a picture).

At this point it becomes possible to draw all the threads together; but to do so it is necessary to digress again briefly into psychoanalytic theory, to consider the nature of desire and how it is constituted within patriarchal culture. The first love object, prototype of all subsequent love objects, is the mother's breast, to which the infant traditionally is put immediately after birth. The infant is born totally under the sway of the pleasure principle (which Freud associates with the id): she or he has no sense of "otherness," no sense of the mother as an autonomous person; the expectation is of instant, total, always available gratification. This innate "original desire" (I mean the term at once to evoke and oppose the familiar Catholic interpretation of Hitchcock in relation to "original sin") immediately comes into conflict with the reality principle and has to learn to modify itself to accommodate the facts of existence, but it remains the basis on which adult desire is built. It is also, of course, what adult desire must *transcend* if any equality in relationships is to be achieved, though adult desire will still be ultimately dependent on original desire for its energy.

It is essential to the logic of patriarchy that original desire be repressed in women (it would promote bisexuality and sexual activeness, what Freud termed the woman's "masculinity") and encouraged in men. The heterosexual male – our ideological lord of the universe – is taught from infancy to believe in his superiority, his inherited rights, essentially, to "power and freedom." The possibility of regression to the infantile state, the unconditional demand for the "lost breast," is therefore much stronger in men than in women. The most obvious manifestation of this regression is the phenomenon called "romantic love," with its demand for perfect union and its tendency to construct the loved person as an idealized fantasy figure, the necessary condition for "perfect union" being the denial of otherness and autonomy. It is this regression that *Vertigo* so incomparably dramatizes. I know of no other film that so ruthlessly analyzes the basis of male desire and exposes its mechanisms.

Around this, everything falls into place: the reactivation of the birth trauma actually accompanied by the death of the father, the urge for freedom and wandering, the rejection of Midge, the appearance of Gavin Elster as tempter, the gift of Madeleine. One may ask why Midge, who so clearly offers herself as a mother, is impossible for Scottie; there are a number of answers. For one thing, she is too *explicitly* the mother. As such, she is a reminder to Scottie of his dependence. More important, the lost breast is not to be identified with an actual mother. On the contrary, the crucial characteristic of the object of original desire is that it be capable of being totally dominated, with no autonomous existence or desire of its own. As mother, Midge is dominating and active, a defined ego, with her own drives and demands, the chief of which is that Scottie learn to grow up. What she wants is a relationship of equals. Further, she demystifies sexuality (specifically in relation to the breast, explaining the mechanics of the brassiere), and for the romantic lover, sex must always remain mystified. She is finally disqualified by her accessibility.

It is obvious that original desire can never be fulfilled. The lost breast cannot be refound, because it never existed. The fantasy of fulfillment depends, paradoxically, on the inaccessibility of the object. Madeleine dies (both times) at the moments when she threatens to become a real person. It will be clear that, as a construct, a work of art, she perfectly satisfies every condition for the lover's fantasy. When she dies, she has to be re-created; when she is Judy, Scottie cannot bear to touch her. One of the cinema's most perverse (and most "romantic") love scenes – so perverse it could not possibly be filmed – is the scene implied after Scottie brings Madeleine back from her plunge into San Francisco Bay: that he undresses the woman he loves, believing her to be unconscious, while in reality she is *pretending* to be unconscious. It is the nearest the romantic lover can come to physical union without sacrificing something of his fantasy. Judy's unforgivable crime is not accessory to murder or even duplicity; it is that she is not *really* Madeleine.

Madeleine's ultimate fascination lies in her association with death (as Carlotta she is already dead). As original desire can never be fulfilled in life, to surrender to it is to give oneself over to the death drive: hence the Romantic obsession with unions in death, of which Wagner's *Tristan und Isolde* is the supreme expression in Western culture (the "Liebestod" is repeatedly evoked, though never actually quoted, in Bernard Herrmann's score).

Whatever the conscious motivation, the importance of Hitchcock's decision to divulge the solution of the mystery two-thirds of the way through the film cannot be underestimated. Until that point the spectator is locked almost exclusively into Scottie's consciousness (the only exceptions are three brief moments involving Midge, which hint at the possibility of critical distance but are not strong enough to offset the dominant identification pattern): the fascination Scottie feels for Madeleine is also his. (I use the masculine deliberately – the spectator constructed by the film is clearly male.) The shock we experience at the revelation goes far beyond anything that can be accounted for merely in terms of premature disclosure, testifying to the power and "universality" within our culture of the desire drive the film dramatizes. We also, at first, cannot forgive Judy for not being Madeleine, in whose reality we have been seduced into investing so much.

The revelation immediately exposes the entire "romantic-love" project of the first two-thirds of the film as a fantasy and a fraud; thus it turns us back, quite ruthlessly, onto Scottie and ourselves. It also gives us access to Judy, who is not a work of art but a human being, thus exposing the monstrousness of a project built on the infantile demands of the regressed male ego and its denial of woman's human reality. Judy never becomes the film's central consciousness. She is permitted only six point-of-view shots during the entire film (as against the number given to Scottie, which must run into three figures). Four of these (two pairs, precisely symmetrical) are simply shots of trees through the car windshield during the two drives to San Juan Bautista. A fifth is ambiguous: the shot of the broken petals on the water just before Madeleine's false attempted suicide, a shot enclosed within an elaborate structure of Scottie's point of view and equally readable as *his* empathic image of what Madeleine sees. Only one shot from Judy's point of view actually excludes Scottie and comments on him: the shot of lovers on the grass as they walk by the lake and the Portals of the

Past (it stands out the more for being an example of that privileged Hitchcock fingerprint, the subjective forward tracking shot).

Scottie's remains the central consciousness; what changes is our relationship to him. Identification is not so much annihilated as severely disturbed, made problematic. We now know far more than he does, and what we know reflects critically on him, on our own prior identification with him, and on the whole concept of romantic love on which our culture has placed such high ideological value. Throughout the scenes with Judy as Judy, the film's dominant system of alternating series based on Scottie's point of view partly breaks down. Point-of-view shots are not absent (Judy seen in the upper window of the Empire Hotel – as Madeleine was in the McKittrick Hotel – and, notably, the "cameo" shot of Judy in silhouette profile when Scottie brings her home from Ernie's after their first date), but their number greatly decreases, to be built up again strongly as Scottie reconstructs Judy as Madeleine. That the film's efforts to reinvolve us in Scottie's consciousness and the project of reconstructing what we know to be a fantasy are *partly* successful testifies again to the immense power of original desire and its derivative – romantic love – within our culture. (Like the film, I am assuming that the spectator is male; one looks forward eagerly, now that *Vertigo* is once again accessible, to articles on it by women.)

It takes the final agonizing scenes – and Madeleine's second death – to exorcise this decisively, but, of course, the total and unquestioning identification invited by the first part of the film is no longer possible. We are too aware at that point that the fantasy *is* fantasy, and too aware of it as imposition on the woman. The last third of *Vertigo* is among the most disturbing and painful experiences the cinema has to offer.

VERTIGO (Paramount, 1958). *Producers*: Alfred Hitchcock, Herbert Coleman, *Assistant Director*: Daniel McCauley, *Script*: Alec Coppel, Samuel Tayler, from the novel *D'entre les morts* by Pierre Boileau and Thomas Narcejac, *Photography*: Robert Burks (VistaVision, Technicolor), *Editor*: George Tomasini, *Sets*: Hal Pereira, Henry Bumstead, Sam Comer, Frank McKelvey, *Music*: Bernard Herrmann, *Costumes*: Edith Head, *Titles*: Saul Bass, *Nightmare Sequence*: John Ferren, *Players*: James Stewart (John "Scottie" Ferguson), Kim Novak (Madeleine Elster/Judy Barton), Barbara Bel Geddes (Midge Wood), Tom Helmore (Gavin Elster). 128 minutes.

Chapter Eighteen

A Closer Look at Scopophilia: Mulvey, Hitchcock, and *Vertigo*

Marian E. Keane

I

During the past fifteen years, feminist criticism has secured a place of central importance not only within film criticism but within the arena of critical thinking generally. Among the achievements of feminist criticism has been its dedication to employing psychoanalysis and political philosophy in the work of uncovering the meanings of films as they bear directly on and illuminate a cultural consciousness of women. The last decade in particular has seen feminist film critics calling for a revolution, for radical breaks with the established film criticism as well as with the conventional narrative structures of film, which they view as participating in strategies of domination and repression of women.

One of the issues in feminist film criticism has involved the erotic nature of viewing human beings, specifically women, on film. In "Visual Pleasure and Narrative Cinema," Laura Mulvey takes as her "starting point the way film reflects, reveals and even plays on the straight, socially established interpretation of sexual difference that controls images, erotic ways of looking and spectacle."[1] She asserts that "mainstream film encoded the erotic into the language of the dominant patriarchal order" and supports this assertion with a psychoanalytic interpretation of film's presentation of (viewed) human beings to viewers. Formally, Mulvey claims, film relies on a division or "split" between looking, which she calls the active role, and being looked at, which she claims is its passive opposite. On a narrative level, one of the ways in which this division is reproduced is by shots representing the view of one figure by another. In Hollywood films, she maintains, women occupy the passive position of being looked at, whereas men possess the active power of looking.

What draws me to address recent feminist criticism, and Mulvey's essay in particular, is certainly not an argument about the importance and the necessity of feminist criticism. The roles women play in films and the ways films understand and present women are of central importance. I share the aspirations of recent feminist criticism, but I am in disagreement with much of it.

In the case of Mulvey's essay, my disagreement rests with her understanding of the films she calls upon as evidence. It also rests with her reading of texts by Freud that she understands as providing a basis for her psychoanalytic critique of Hollywood films. Finally, and perhaps most importantly, I find inadequate Mulvey's concept of the camera, its powers, and the nature of its gaze. A corollary or consequence of this inadequacy is my dissatisfaction with her understanding of the nature of (human) photogenesis or, as Stanley Cavell has characterized this subject, of what becomes of human beings on film.[2] I understand the problems in Mulvey's critical approach to represent a willingness to repress, or at least an unwillingness to take seriously, the meanings of films that enter or are entered into discussions about the history and the nature of the medium of film. That Mulvey's views have impressed themselves on so many film critics and theoreticians surely means that something is right about them. Film can be used as she says; some films do work in these ways. But it is not the nature of the medium to require this. In particular, it is not true of the films I admire most, for example, *Vertigo*, from which I take and direct my commitments to film.

My dissatisfaction with Mulvey's assertions can begin to be set out in relation to her remarks on Hitchcock's *Vertigo*, her understanding of which is presented in a number of remarks summarizing the film's events and meanings. A problematic consequence of this method is that the film's specific framings, lines of dialogue, and authorship are neglected and lost.

Mulvey finds *Vertigo* "far from simply an aside on the perversion of the police," because the film takes as its subject "the active/looking, passive/looked at split in terms of sexual difference and the power of the male … encapsulated in the hero" (p. 16). Stating that the story is told primarily in terms of "subjective camera," from the point of view of the ex-detective played by James Stewart, she claims that Hitchcock and the camera are unequivocally allied with him throughout the film. She asserts that *Vertigo* goes a step further than most Hollywood films because it turns the "processes" the viewer employs back on himself and thereby demonstrates *how* visual and narrative pleasure are purchased at a woman's expense, but in the final analysis *Vertigo* is still a film in which the man's "curiosity wins through" and the woman "is punished" (p. 16).

In *The World Viewed*, Stanley Cavell observes that "the screen performer is essentially not an actor at all: he *is* the subject of a study, and a study not his own."[3] Since our thoughts in this essay are attuned to qualities of activity and passivity, it would be difficult to overlook Cavell's characterization or definition of all screen performers as more passive than active in relation to the camera and the film's director. Cavell's understanding of the (ontological) passivity of the camera's (human) subjects challenges Mulvey's general assertion that "the image of woman [is the] (passive) raw material for the (active) gaze of man" (p. 17).

Cavell complicates his analytical remark on film acting by inflecting it with a parenthetical remark that qualifies our understanding of the nature of human beings' "passivity" on film. "That is what the content of a photograph is," he declares, "– its subject" (p. 28). Cavell's claim that the content or meaning of a film is absorbed in the camera's attentive recording and the director's thoughtful understanding of the identities, physiognomies, emotions, mannerisms, and thoughtfulnesses of their human subjects is radical. Acknowledging film's photographic basis, Cavell calls upon us to acknowledge that film presents us with projections, hence displaced views, of real human beings who are simultaneously active and passive. Human figures on film reveal or display themselves, participating in the fixing of their presences on film. They are also revealed by the camera's (penetrating) gaze and the director's understanding of the significances inherent to specific human beings' presences on film.

This thesis underlies one of Cavell's central meditations in *Pursuits of Happiness*, where he reflects on the photogeneses of the stars who appear in the remarriage comedies he discusses. These sustained reflections offer concrete evidence for his claim that "the photographic power of the camera [gives] a natural ascendancy to the flesh and blood actor over the character he or she plays on film." The camera's power to displace character and meditate the flesh and blood performer underwrites a profound distinction between the mediums of film and theater, Cavell argues, because it "reverses the relation between actor and character in theater."[4]

For reasons indebted to Cavell's understanding of photogenesis, I will refer to James Stewart and Kim Novak by name in this essay. Insisting upon their flesh and blood identities (or on the flesh and bloodness of a man known as James Stewart and a woman known as Kim Novak) registers the fact of the camera's assertion of the flesh and blood performer over his or her character in a film. It asserts that *Vertigo* is a study of the significances of its leading figures' identities, that who Hitchcock and the camera reveal them to be and what they individually project on film lie at the heart of *Vertigo*'s meaning. Calling them by name is a way of making the claim that their presences on film are subjects for criticism in all of the ways their presences on film are subjects for the film itself.

Chief among the features of Stewart's photogenesis is his capacity for suffering, the most important quality of Stewart's presence on film that Mulvey can be said to ignore in her summary analysis of *Vertigo*. In a series of reflections on Stewart's photogenesis, Stanley Cavell suggests that he "projects a willingness for suffering" and declares further that this quality of Stewart's photogenesis "is [what] would admit him to the company of women [for example, Charlotte Vale/Bette Davis in *Now, Voyager*] whose search for their identities seems to have traced the contours of the subject of film [that I would characterize as] ... the identifying or the inhabitation of a feminine region of the self, whether the person whose self it is be male or female."[5] Cavell's placement of Stewart in "the company of women" directly challenges Mulvey's view of Stewart/Scottie as an exemplar of active male power. Mulvey's view privileges selected features of Stewart/Scottie's identity as a character and reveals that she views him as an actor playing a role (as though *Vertigo* were a play) rather than as the camera's subject. In its denial of the camera's photogenic power and the film performer's precedence over his role, Mulvey's view of Scottie constitutes a profound denial of the medium of film and of the conditions of film acting.

II

Mulvey's denial of Hitchcock and the meaning of the camera throughout *Vertigo* partly gives rise to, and is partly a consequence of, her view that the film (that is, Stewart/Scottie and Hitchcock) subjects the Novak figure to punishment, a punishment partly derived from being looked at, "follow[ed], watch[ed], and fall[en] in love with" (p. 16) by Stewart/Scottie. But Mulvey seems to me to neglect, even to punish, the Novak figure in ways that are similar to, and can be revealed by studying, the Stewart figure's relation to Novak/Judy within the film. Mulvey's blindness to the woman and her central role in the film necessarily entails blindness to Hitchcock as well. In my view, the deepest criticism of Mulvey's reading of *Vertigo* emerges from *Vertigo* itself, from the woman in the film and the film's author.

Mulvey claims that, "apart from one flashback from Judy's point of view, the narrative is woven around what Scottie sees and fails to see" (p. 16). But the "one flashback from Judy's point of view" that Mulvey glosses over, as though it were without importance, constitutes nothing less than the decisive turning point in *Vertigo*. Mulvey's unwillingness or failure to understand this crucial juncture and its significance is a critical error with serious implications.

The flashback sequence is inaugurated by a striking turn of Novak's head toward the camera that culminates in her look into the camera.[6] Her look into the camera registers what she knows, and the flashback that follows represents but a piece of that knowledge. She knows not only all that actually took place on the bell tower but that Stewart/Scottie is right to believe he has found Madeleine Elster again. When she looks into Hitchcock's camera, she is acknowledging her identity as Madeleine, and we cannot assume that we yet know all that this acknowledgment means.

Novak/Judy's look into the camera also declares her awareness of the camera's presence; her look acknowledges Hitchcock and us. During the first part of this scene, when she and Scottie converse in her hotel room, her head is conspicuously turned away from the camera, a precise choreography characteristic of Hitchcock's direction. Novak/Judy turns to face the camera on the heels of Scottie's departure, revealing that she knows she is not alone. The sustained look she gives the camera initiates the camera's possession of her story, represented by the flashback, and establishes a deep bond between her and the camera that is not broken for the remainder of the film. (I am, of course, aware that any specification of what the events – such as a camera movement or placement or a human being's look – in a film "declare" is controversial. Such specifications are acts of criticism, and my own readings of *Vertigo*'s events and declarations are open to further acts of criticism. It is my point that Mulvey's specifications pre-empt such acts of criticism in favor of a theory of film that does not allow criticism to test it. In this sense, it is unempirical.)

When Novak/Judy looks into the camera, her look is fearful. But what is she afraid of? William Rothman argues in *Hitchcock: The Murderous Gaze* that the handful of beings, such as Uncle Charles, Diana Baring, Norman Bates, and, we should add, Judy Barton, allowed the privilege of gazing directly into Hitchcock's camera, all share a singular and profound consciousness of their fates. Their mysteries are the mysteries of Hitchcock's camera. We cannot say all that Novak/Judy is afraid of at this moment. Her fears can only be understood fully when we look at the final moments of the film, when they materialize mysteriously in the shadows of the bell tower. We should expect, however, that what she views there will be, in part, a figure for Hitchcock's camera, an embodiment of its gaze.

After the flashback, we return to Novak/Judy in her room and view her alone, a scene to which Scottie is not privy. She starts to pack but breaks off to write Scottie a letter. Wishing to free him of his guilt and his memory of Madeleine, her letter tells him about Elster's plan to murder Madeleine, that Elster chose him specifically because of his acrophobia, and that the Carlotta Valdes story was part fiction, part truth. "Everything went as planned," she writes, "except I fell in love with you. That wasn't part of the plan." She loves him still, she continues, and if she had the courage she would remain, she would lie about the past and start over again with him. When she tears up the letter, rises, and begins to unpack her bags, her resolve is clear. She has found that courage to start again, to step out of what in *Psycho* is called "a private trap." The remainder of the film is a study of her love for Stewart/Scottie and of his attachment to her.

At no point in *Vertigo* does Stewart/Scottie possess a knowledge of the camera commensurate with Novak/Judy's. In Rothman's terms, we can say that Novak/Judy exhibits hubris when she decides to step out of her private trap and to deny the past. But Stewart/Scottie's hubris is both graver and more complete. His obsessive re-creation of Madeleine is only one level of his hubris. It is equal hubris in the world of a Hitchcock film for him to deny his own participation in his suffering and to deny Hitchcock's camera. It is hubris, too, to deny his passions and sexuality so profoundly, his fears of which are manifest symbolically or symptomatically in his dizziness (such as that sustained during his and Novak's second kiss) and in his fallings (such as happens in his dream).

Mulvey describes the Stewart figure as possessing, brandishing, and relishing a position of active power in relation to the woman, but the truth is that he suffers throughout *Vertigo*. He suffers from the moment he painfully discovers his acrophobia on the rooftop, through his involvement with Madeleine, under the condescending and barbed censure of the court officer at the hearing, and up to his dream, the final nightmare of his life until the end of the film. His dream renders him a catatonic in a sanatarium, immobilized by depression, past the loving reach of Midge (Barbara Bel Geddes), the therapeutic reach of doctors, and even the cobweb-chasing spirit of Mozart.

When Stewart/Scottie emerges from the hospital, his suffering continues. A series of short sequences shows him retracing the steps of his relationship with Madeleine. Each blonde woman in the distance causes his heart to leap as he believes, for an instant, that she has returned. But he is looking for a woman who has died, a ghost.

When he finds Judy, his suffering is not over. He will not be satisfied until the ghost is made flesh, until he has created a living woman out of the dead one. Mulvey claims that Scottie "reconstructs Judy as Madeleine, forces her to conform in every detail to the actual physical appearance of his fetish" (p. 16). "Fetish" and "fetishism" are important terms in Mulvey's understanding of how sexuality functions and is contained in classical films. Mulvey's concept of "fetishism," however, is too extended or metaphorical to bear the weight she puts upon it, as for example when she claims that Scottie is "reconstructing a fetish" when he insists that Judy's clothes and hair style and color match Madeleine's. Stewart/Scottie is not reconstructing a fetish; he is creating a woman in fulfillment of his *vision*. This construction of Judy as Madeleine is, with terrible irony, destructive; it may be even more brutal than Mulvey's idea of "fetish." What is shown to be brutal in *Vertigo* is the nature of human desire and need, not some function of a particular phase of male development whose correction it is fairly simple to imagine.

III

Mulvey's failure to recognize the Novak figure's centrality and Hitchcock's allegiance with her is partly the consequence of her prejudicial understanding of Stewart/Scottie. Mulvey reflects on but half of the man's nature when she isolates his power from his suffering in relation to the woman he loves. Mulvey's understanding of Novak/Judy denies the active aspect of her decision to stay with Stewart/Scottie and it denies his passivity as well – that he is played for a sucker, first by Elster and Judy and then by Judy alone when she withholds from him a fact about her identity: that she is, as Barbara Stanwyck/Jean/Eve is in Sturges's *The Lady Eve*, positively the same woman. Mulvey's partial (or prejudicial) understanding of Scottie is an expression of her theoretical view that sexuality in Hollywood films is founded in a division between looking and being-looked-at, between activity and passivity, between masculinity and femininity.

Mulvey posits that "the image of woman as (passive) raw material for the (active) gaze of man" (p. 17) is at the heart of Hollywood conventions. She claims further that film offers two pleasures to its viewers. She identifies the first as scopophilia, which she takes to be "using another person as an object of sexual stimulation through sight" (p. 10). The second pleasure, "developed through narcissism and the constitution of the ego," derives from the viewer's "identification with the image seen" (p. 10). In male stars and only in males, Mulvey asserts, can the viewer find an ego ideal.

Mulvey claims Freud as the authority on scopophilia:

> Originally, in his *Three Essays on Sexuality* [1905], Freud isolated scopophilia as one of the component instincts of sexuality that exist quite independently of the erotogenic zones. At this point he associated scopophilia with taking other people as objects, subjecting them to a controlling and curious gaze.... In this analysis, scopophilia is primarily active. (Later, in *Instincts and their Vicissitudes*, Freud developed his theory of scopophilia further, attaching it initially to pregenital autoeroticism, after which the pleasure of the look is transferred to others by analogy....) Although the instinct is modified by other factors, in particular the constitution of the ego, it continues to exist as the erotic basis for pleasure in looking at another person as object. At the extreme, it can become fixated into a perversion, producing obsessive voyeurs and peeping toms, whose only sexual satisfaction can come from watching, in an active controlling sense, an objectified other. (pp. 8–9)

Mulvey's account presents itself as simply a transcription of Freud, but it is not. At no point does Freud claim to have a "theory of scopophilia" or that scopophilia subjects others to a "controlling and curious gaze." (This claim makes little sense in any case. If a look is curious – say a child's look at his or her mother's body – it does not know what it will find. How can such a look also be controlling? What can it control?)

Neither does Freud claim that scopophilia is "essentially active." To this last idea he directs a number of remarks in "Instincts and their Vicissitudes," where he declares that "the only correct statement to make about the scoptophilic instinct would be that all the phases of its development, the autoerotic, preliminary phase as well as its final active or passive form, co-exist alongside one another; and the truth of this becomes obvious if we base our opinion, not on the actions to which the instinct leads, but on the mechanism of its satisfaction." Freud provides another sketch of the development of instincts as "a series of separate successive waves, each of which is homogeneous during whatever period of time it may last, and whose relation to one another is comparable to that of successive eruptions of lava." He concludes: "at [a] later period of development of an instinctual impulse, [the fact that] its (passive) opposite may be observed alongside of it deserves to be marked by the very apt term … ambivalence."

In both "Three Essays" and "Instincts and their Vicissitudes," Freud singles out scopophilia-exhibitionism and sadism-masochism precisely because "these are the best-known sexual instincts that appear in an ambivalent manner."[7] His crucial discovery is that these instincts always appear in pairs or, as he puts it specifically, "[a] sadist is always at the same time a masochist" and "exhibitionists … exhibit their own genitals in order to obtain a reciprocal view of the genitals of the other person."[8] Freud's discovery that scopophilia-exhibitionism and sadism-masochism are sexual instincts that occur in ambivalent form constitutes a deep insight into the nature of human sexuality. But of even greater importance is Freud's placement of his study of these instincts at the service of his thoughts about loving, the subject that guides his entire study of human sexuality. Freud's discovery of the ambivalence of these sexual instincts played a crucial role in his deepening understanding of his central subject in both "Three Essays" and "Instincts and their Vicissitudes": the antithetical relation of love and hate.

Mulvey identifies active controlling looks with men and passive looked-at-ness with women, alignments Freud explicitly rejects when he discovers that the active and passive forms of the instincts are always found together in the same human being. She pairs active-male and passive-female in pointed disregard of Freud's statement that "the coupling of masculinity with activity and of passivity with femininity meets us, indeed, as a biological fact; but it is by no means so invariably complete and exclusive as we are inclined to assume" (vol. 14, p. 134).

Acknowledging the confusion surrounding the concepts of "masculine" and "feminine," Freud distinguishes three uses of these concepts in a footnote in "Three Essays." His precisely drawn definitions are valuable to our discussion of Mulvey's views:

"Masculine" and "feminine" are sometimes used in the sense of activity and passivity, sometimes in a biological, and sometimes, again, in a sociological sense. The first of these meanings is the essential one [for psychoanalysis]. When, for example, "libido" was described [in the text] as being "masculine," the word was being used in this sense, for an instinct is always active even when it has a passive aim in view. The second, or biological, meaning of "masculine" and "feminine" ... can be determined most easily [because each is] characterized by the presence of [sexual organs and functions]. . . . The third, or sociological, meaning receives its connotation from the observation of actually existing masculine and feminine individuals. Such observation shows that in human beings pure masculinity or femininity is not to be found either in a psychological or a biological sense. (vol. 7, pp. 219–20)

It is hard to imagine how Freud could be clearer on this subject. He explicitly declares that in psychoanalytic usage the term "masculine" does not indicate a quality that is possessed by men only and that "feminine" does not describe an instinct or quality that can be understood as the special province of women. Freud is also clear on the subject of activity and passivity, in particular in his view that instincts are *always* active, "even if they have a passive aim in view." To arrive at Mulvey's view, one would have to set out an understanding of human sexuality that competes with Freud's on a number of levels, that divides instincts into categories of activity and passivity, and that aligns them according to biological distinctions between the sexes rather than according to the psychoanalytic meanings of the terms "active," "passive," "masculine," and "feminine" that Freud specifies.

IV

Mulvey's view that the camera is an active, controlling male gaze shares the partiality or incompleteness of her understanding of the Stewart figure in *Vertigo* because the camera also possesses both active and passive possibilities or ontological qualities. In his reflections on the camera's nature in *The World Viewed* Stanley Cavell cites drawing the camera back, panning, and close-ups as gestures that exemplify the camera's active possibility. He calls these gestures "images of perfect attention." Cavell continues to reflect on the camera's dual nature and writes: "Early in its history the cinema discovered the possibility of *calling* attention to persons and parts of persons and objects; but it is equally a possibility of the medium not to call attention to them but, rather, to let the world happen, to let its parts draw attention to themselves according to their natural weight" (p. 25).

Every shot in which the camera does not perform a gesture declaring its active attention to persons or parts of persons and objects within the frame realizes and displays the camera's ontological passivity in relation to the world it views. Cavell mentions that certain directors, such as Vigo, Dreyer, and Renoir, explore this possibility in their work. In their films, the conditions of the camera's passivity are meditated and give rise to the conditions, at once moral and aesthetic, that hold in the worlds of their films.

In *Hitchcock: The Murderous Gaze*, William Rothman argues that Hitchcock's films are meditations on the camera's nature, perspicuous critiques of the camera's active and passive aspects. Hitchcock's understanding of the medium of film culminates with *Psycho*, Rothman declares, and with the creation of Norman Bates, a figure at once active (a murderer) and passive (witness to the fact of his "mother's" acts of murder), guilty and innocent, utterly subjugated to his "mother's" will and all powerful. Norman is also the last in a line of Hitchcockian figures, among whom Handell Fane in *Murder!* can be counted, who are sexually ambiguous and ambivalent. These figures, Rothman shows, are surrogates of Hitchcock's camera. Their sexual ambiguity or ambivalence expresses Hitchcock's understanding of the camera as both active and passive.

Their thoughts focused on different features of the medium, Cavell and Rothman both argue that the camera's nature is fundamentally active *and* passive. As Freud argues against separating the active and passive forms of an instinct, so Cavell and Rothman argue against separating the camera's active and passive possibilities. They argue that these two possibilities continuously inform one another and moreover that the ways they inform one another lie at the heart of the medium itself. To separate its active and passive qualities, or to assume that the camera's gaze is only one and not the other, is to deny the camera's nature. To divide the camera's possibilities in relation to Hitchcock's work is to fail to acknowledge his deepest meditations, the deepest meaning of his art.

In *Vertigo*, Hitchcock's camera takes in the world under its gaze; it "lets the world happen." It also performs a number of gestures that constitute declarations about the camera's nature and its powers. These are declarations of Hitchcock's authorship, representative both of what he understands the camera to be and what he understands his act of filmmaking to be. *Vertigo's* central meditations, which must be understood as preoccupations of Hitchcock's authorship and as conditioned by the photogenic qualities of the film's two leading figures, involve a pair of the camera's possible relations to human beings under its gaze. Both of these relations are violent. One is the camera's power to penetrate its subjects to their deepest cores, and both Novak/Judy and Stewart/Scottie are subject to this power. The other is the camera's capacity to display on the screen its (human) subject's inner desires or fears. This complicated power is represented in Stewart/Scottie's view of the world opening up as an abyss beneath him when he grips the rain gutter during his first attack of acrophobia, for instance. Hitchcock also meditates on this power through the Stewart character's obsessive transformation of Novak/Judy into Madeleine. Let me give an example of each of these powers of the camera in relation to Stewart/Scottie.

When Stewart/Scottie sits bolt upright in bed and lunges toward the camera at the end of his dream, his eyes are fixed open and his face is filled with terror. He projects himself directly toward the camera, but his eyes, immersed in his dream, do not take in the camera. (His look at this moment opposes Novak/Judy's look that acknowledges the camera.) His absorption in his inner world blinds him to beings in the world of the film (chiefly to the Novak figure) and to Hitchcock (represented by the camera) who require his acknowledgment. Glassy with horror, his eyes are blinded by the vision of his fate projected in his dream. Therein, with his endless falling into an open grave, he is identified with Madeleine's death. The dream further identifies his desire for her as inseparable from his desire for Carlotta Valdes, the ghost who had possessed Madeleine. Figured in his dream, this man's dread is that he is nothingness, that he can be penetrated completely. We might characterize this as his fear that he too is a ghost.

Just as Stewart/Scottie's dream sketches his deepest fear of being nothingness, the camera, maintaining its fixed position in the face of his lunge toward it, threatens to penetrate him completely, to pierce through him and reveal his insubstantiality. This profound condition of James Stewart on film was discovered first by Frank Capra in *It's a Wonderful Life* (1946). The same look, and the same possibility that the camera might plunge through him, occurs in that film at the moment Stewart, dwelling in the world of his wish turned nightmare, registers his mother's refusal to acknowledge that he is her son. He walks down the porch steps of her house until he fills the frame and stands on the verge of having the camera go through him. Though Hitchcock contemplates the implications of Stewart's photogenesis more completely, both he and Capra reveal that Stewart's curse, at once embedded within him as his deepest private fear and exposed by the camera's power to penetrate its subjects, is that he is insubstantial, incorporeal, nothingness itself.

This is the fear that motivates Stewart's deep attachment to Madeleine, because she too suffers the unrest of a ghost dwelling on earth. It is because he finds a soul with which to identify his own – a lover's aspiration – that he falls in love with Madeleine and re-creates her.[9] And it is because his attachment to Madeleine never acknowledged the real woman, divorced from her relation to Carlotta Valdes, that he can repeat to Novak/Judy on the bell tower that she was always "a counterfeit." Any flesh-and-blood woman is a counterfeit of the ghost he loves.

The second central meditation of Hitchcock's camera is figured in Stewart/Scottie's sustained violations of Novak/Judy. At every escalation of his demands upon her, the film – Hitchcock – indicts his project further. Stewart/Scottie's vision requires violations of Judy on all different levels, but none looms so large and monstrously as his necessary denial of her actual, real being.

When Novak/Judy emerges from the bathroom fully realized as Madeleine, the shot presents Stewart/Scottie's point of view. She is surrounded by glowing, diffused light, and the shot is overlaid with gauze. Suffused with special effects, this shot registers Stewart/Scottie's final violent achievement. This woman is a figment of a dream, an apparition.

A deep issue raised by this shot is that it is not clear whether the vision of Novak/Judy as Madeleine is projected out of the deepest regions of Stewart's being, or if the camera – Hitchcock – subjects him to a view that satisfies his inner desires. This same question applies to all of the vertiginous shots in the film. Are they presented by Stewart/Scottie, or are they the work of a Godlike figure, Hitchcock, who has singled Stewart out and undertaken a special meditation of him? Another way of thinking about this issue would be to ask, is Stewart/Scottie active in his relation to specific views he has, views of the world opening up into an abyss, for example, or the view of Novak/Judy as Madeleine once again? Are these views his projections, hence his work? Or are they Hitchcock's doing, hence views that force Stewart to suffer passively the sight of his deepest fears and wishes?

These shots realize the fears and wishes that dwell in the deepest regions of Stewart/Scottie's being. They are also displays of Hitchcock's authority, declarations of his commanding presence as *Vertigo*'s author. Rothman's readings of Hitchcock's films reveal that Hitchcock consistently uses shots such as those that register Stewart/Scottie's vertigo in order to announce his authorial power and to raise issues about a leading figure's relation to the world of the film. Rothman identifies the cause of a Hitchcock character's vertigo as "the realization that he has been singled out by the agency that presides over the world, that his world has been created in the image of his innermost fears."[10] These shots declare, not Stewart/Scottie's, but Hitchcock's authority over the views that compose the film and the fates of the human beings that dwell in its world.

V

Hitchcock's work, especially in the 1950s, is absorbed in studying specific photogenic features and significances of major stars, and *Vertigo*, in its study of James Stewart's presence on film, is no exception. Like his highly enigmatic surrogate Elster, Hitchcock selects Stewart. Scottie's acrophobia makes him the right man for Elster's job (or should we say, makes it possible for him to be Elster's victim?). Acrophobia is a metaphor for the qualities of Stewart's presence on film that Hitchcock studies and relentlessly exposes throughout *Vertigo*. Within the world of the film, his acrophobia is called a weakness and his selection by Elster cursed as a set up. But what makes Stewart the right man for Hitchcock's job?

In "Visual Pleasure and Narrative Cinema," Laura Mulvey implies that the relationship between *Vertigo* and *films noirs* is central to its meaning when she takes Stewart/Scottie's occupation as a detective to motivate the film's narrative. Earlier I cited Cavell's emphasis on Stewart's projecting "a capacity for suffering" and his consequent placing of him "in the company of women." Mulvey, on the contrary, situates Stewart/Scottie among the heroes of *films noirs* when she claims that *Vertigo*'s narrative is told primarily in "subjective camera." But by allying himself with and privileging the woman's story in *Vertigo* in a way no *film noir* has ever done, Hitchcock breaks with the genre's characteristic absorption in the man's dilemma (falling in love with a villainous woman). While *Vertigo* undeniably invokes *film noir*, it does so, like *Stage Fright*, in order to undermine the genre's central assumption about the camera – that it and the hero's subjectivity are a single "I."

Cavell instructs us to look more deeply at *Vertigo*'s story and figures by revealing their proximity to what are typically called women's films, which Cavell identifies as preoccupied with the search for one's identity and "the identifying and the inhabitation of a feminine region of the self." *Vertigo*'s attentiveness to these subjects in relation to both the man and the woman in the film results in its deep affinity with, not *film noir*, but film melodrama.

The conditions or meaning of Stewart's presence on film, his quest for confirmation of his existence, and his related fear that he is a haunted being are exposed in *Vertigo*. Hitchcock selects and places Stewart in a world where he suffers as both his private dreams of romantic happiness and sexual satisfaction and his deepest fears are presented to him. We might say that *Vertigo* places Stewart in a world designed to gratify him, if we add that we cannot take it for granted that gratification will not expose horrifying truths about one's desires. If Stewart stands to achieve happiness in this film, once Judy's re-creation as Madeleine is complete, he also stands to learn about his desire for happiness, and so to come face to face with his ruthlessness, his violence, and the extent to which his fantasies control him and limit his ability to accept reality and, in particular, Novak/Judy's real existence.

In the world of *Vertigo*, Stewart is not in the happy – if at times difficult – circumstance that Cary Grant enjoys in the world of *North by Northwest*. He is not even offered the reprieve that Henry Fonda is offered in *The Wrong Man*. In each of these films, Hitchcock authors a fate for his leading man that is partly contingent upon the meaning of his individual photogenesis. What this means is that I understand the first occurrence of Stewart's acrophobia, presented in a point-of-view shot that tortures him, to declare Stewart's status as *condemned*. Let me demonstrate what I mean by this by reading the film's closing sequences.

From the start of the closing sequence, during their drive to the mission, Hitchcock presents shots of Stewart/Scottie from Novak/Judy's point of view that were absent in the parallel sequence of their first drive to San Juan Bautista. The most striking and disturbing of these shots is of Stewart/Scottie framed in profile. This shot resembles the stunning profile shot of Uncle Charles (Joseph Cotten) in *Shadow of a Doubt*. Uncle Charles's subsequent gesture of turning his head to meet the camera's gaze distinguishes that moment from this in *Vertigo* and him from Stewart/Scottie.[11] But the shots are deeply related in their announcements of their subjects' villainy. At this moment, we know that Stewart/Scottie is capable of murder.

With each shot in this sequence of their drive, Hitchcock declares his sympathy with Novak/Judy and exposes Stewart's violence and madness. Once they reach the bell tower, things happen very quickly: Stewart/Scottie conquers his acrophobia, learns that Judy was Elster's lover, and pieces together Madeleine's murder. For agonizing moments, we cannot tell whether Stewart will act on the horror of his disillusionment and anger, and so will kill Judy, or whether he will risk the fall that has terrified him figuratively throughout the film, and so will concede to his desire and fall in love. Leaning out of a corner of the tower, Judy tells him all those things are past; all that matters is that she loves him. As she steps forward to kiss him, he murmurs – as she had unforgettably murmured to him during the first scene at the mission – that it is too late. But they kiss nonetheless, and his words are proven false. This time their embrace does not envelop Stewart in a dizzying, exhilarating, and agonizing world of fantasy. For the first time, the woman he loves is not an apparition in his arms.

But turning her head, Novak/Judy again directs a look to the camera. As in the crucial "flashback" sequence, this look declares her knowledge. What she views fills her with terror and she breaks away from Scottie. We cut to a shot of what she sees, a view of an obscured and shrouded figure standing in the recesses of the tower. The figure speaks in a high-pitched voice not unlike Mother Bates's. "I heard voices." We cut back to the shot of Novak, framed by the arch window, with Stewart to the right of the frame. She stares at the figure, turns, and leaps from the bell tower. (It is also possible to think that she falls from the tower, an understanding that implicates Hitchcock further in her death. This is an implication which my understanding of this moment – that she leaps – does not deny but allows.)

What does Novak/Judy see when she looks to the camera? What so fills her with terror? As with Stewart/Scottie, we cannot draw an absolute boundary between what Novak/Judy projects from within herself and what Hitchcock presents for her view. In one reading, then, the shrouded, obscured figure represents to her the being of Stewart/Scottie's vision, and so it is a representation of herself as a spectre. This spectre is what she became in Stewart/Scottie's romantic vision. Judy grasps in an instant the actual figure he desires and grasps at the same moment that this spectre is a consummate denial of her existence. My other reading of this moment (part of whose obscurity is its very fleetingness) is that Novak/Judy, at the moment they kiss, feels herself already a ghost. The figure in the shadows is then a projection of her inner being, the part of her denied and excluded by Stewart/Scottie's vision.

What Novak/Judy reveals that she knows in these charged moments is that their relationship cannot ever fully break Stewart/Scottie's preoccupation with and attachment to nothingness. She knows that his love will never grant her existence the full acknowledgment real love requires. In their kiss, her alternatives have become clear: that she either becomes a ghost, a disquiet and possessed apparition, or she forever agrees to violate her own desires, and her own being, by accepting the conditions of Scottie's love. In either reading, the figure in the shadows emerges as the spectre of a life endured without acknowledgment, her fate if she lives on with this man.

Her leap from the bell tower is both her declaration that she refuses the violations of Stewart/Scottie's vision, and her final and decisive proof to him that she is not a ghost but a living being. Her act forces him to recognize that all along he has been wrong, deeply and profoundly wrong, to deny her his acknowledgment, to desire instead a ghost. Her words in the forest assume the power of prophecy: "Somewhere in here I was born; here I died.... You took no notice." The partiality, the incompleteness of Stewart/Scottie's capacity to acknowledge another's real existence and love stands forever exposed. Harboring the fear that he is himself nothingness, Stewart/Scottie conjured a vision of nothingness and breathed life into it throughout his re-creation of the ghost Madeleine.

A reading of the final sequence is incomplete without understanding that, at another level, what Novak/Judy sees rising up in the shadows of the bell tower is an embodiment of Hitchcock's camera. Once again, Hitchcock acknowledges Novak/Judy's singular capacity to understand the conditions that hold in the world of the film by singling her out as the audience for his theatrical presentation. Reading the shadow-figure as an embodiment of Hitchcock's camera, which itself suffers the conditions of being a spectre, an unacknowledged and sexless existence, does not alter our previous readings. But in this gesture of presenting himself as an exemplar of the horrifying fate that Judy stands to suffer in relation to Scottie, Hitchcock seals his bond with the Novak figure. Hitchcock endorses Novak/Judy's leap because it certifies, as no other act can, her actual existence. The other possibilities – life as a spectre or Stewart/Scottie's life – stand condemned.

VI

If a question lingers, we might formulate it along these lines. Do the similarities between Stewart/Scottie's re-creation of Judy as Madeleine and Hitchcock's work as director naturally align Hitchcock and his leading man more profoundly than each of Hitchcock's announcements of his allegiance with the woman?

I am prepared, in ways Mulvey appears not to be, to claim that Hitchcock reflects upon the act of directing a film through Stewart/Scottie's re-creation of Madeleine. But Hitchcock distinguishes his powers as a filmmaker from Stewart/Scottie's act of "casting" Novak/Judy as Madeleine. In *Vertigo*, as in others of his films, Hitchcock declares that his powers are contingent upon the human beings under his camera's gaze. In his precise meditation of Stewart's and Novak's presences on film he reflects on the fact that he did not, and cannot, create (these) human beings. Hitchcock can place his subjects in worlds tailor-made for the emergence of their inner selves, but he does not have the power to invent these beings. *Vertigo*, like each of Hitchcock's films, acknowledges its medium's ontological condition of tragedy. It calls upon us to acknowledge that its figures possess the causes of their bereavement within themselves.

When Stewart/Scottie "casts" Novak/Judy as Madeleine, he undertakes to re-create a human being who exists in his private fantasies, as though he were casting a part in a play. Novak's photogenic importance to *Vertigo* derives partly from her projection of and the camera's insistence upon her corporeality. This feature of Novak's presence on film measurably contributes to the film's exposure of the ruthlessness of Stewart/Scottie's changes in her appearance, changes that demonstrate, like a proof, Novak/Judy's possession of an inner being that remains constant and in need of acknowledgment. Our and Hitchcock's certainty in and identification with Novak/Judy's inner being are declared in the outrage we feel toward Stewart/Scottie's desires and demands. We and Hitchcock hold against him his failure to acknowledge *her* in each of her theatrical incarnations. The effect of *Vertigo*'s attention to Novak's physicality is as a testament to her metaphysical integrity.

Casting Judy/Novak in the part of Madeleine, Stewart/Scottie denies or opposes the condition of film that Hitchcock meditates. He masks, or violates, her real existence in a way no camera can but, rather, in the precise manner of theater. While it is true (and typical of Hitchcock's work) that Hitchcock presents a version, or an understanding, of directorial powers through a surrogate within the film, it is also true (and equally typical of Hitchcock) that he systematically distinguishes himself from that surrogate and what he represents.

In my reading of *Vertigo*, the Novak figure occupies the center of the film. *Vertigo* offers a lesson to its viewers in which the Novak figure represents the film and Hitchcock, and the Stewart figure stands in for those viewers whose attachments elsewhere make them incapable of acknowledging the film or its maker. *Vertigo* addresses and answers the claim that women can suffer unacknowledgment in a film. The precise ways in which the man's visions deny the woman's own existence are opposed and his inability to acknowledge her is condemned.

Mulvey's account of *Vertigo*, which she grasps as illuminating her ideas, is blind to the woman's role within the film and to Hitchcock's allegiance with her. Mulvey's relation to *Vertigo* is the equivalent of Stewart's relation to Novak within the film. Mulvey is engaged not in changing a woman's hair color or clothing but in fundamentally altering Freud's thoughts and the meanings of films. Where Scottie re-creates Madeleine on the basis of his vision of a ghost, Mulvey re-creates Hollywood films on the basis of her own visions of men, women, and the medium of film. Mulvey's vision denies elements *as fundamental* to the history of Hollywood film and to Freud's thought as Judy's real existence is to the meaning of *Vertigo*. As I hear it, their replies to Mulvey echo Novak's tragic words to Stewart: "Here I was born, here I died; you took no notice." Perhaps because at some level Mulvey's own vision is unacceptable to her, she presents it as though it were an acceptable transcription of Freud and as though she were speaking for all women about things we already know to be true about Hollywood films.

While I demonstrate in my reading of *Vertigo* that the sexual politics and meaning of Hollywood films cannot be presumed in the way Mulvey presumes them, an equally important purpose of the arguments in this essay is to register a claim. If feminist criticism is to understand itself to be deeply informed by Freud's thinking (as Mulvey declares her thinking to be) and by film history (which Mulvey also declares to be the case, though she understands that as a sad rather than wonderful fact), then it must recognize that, as in Freud's work and in films of major importance, its central subject is loving. In my view, feminist thinking cannot contribute as importantly as it should to the fields from which it derives its intellectual power in the absence or the avoidance of reflections on the nature and the meaning of loving that are as serious as those contained in the works feminists refer to and the films they study.

Notes

My thanks are due to William Rothman and Stanley Cavell for their suggestions and editorial remarks on this chapter.

1. Laura Mulvey, "Visual Pleasure and Narrative Cinema," *Screen*, vol. 16, no. 3 (Autumn 1975): 6–18.
2. Cavell's understanding of photogenesis constitutes one of his central arguments about the nature, meaning, and importance of the medium of film. Here I am referring to "What Becomes of Things on Film?," in *Themes out of School* (San Francisco: Northpoint Press, 1984), 173–83, the essay of his that most explicitly reflects on the subject of photogenesis.
3. Stanley Cavell, *The World Viewed: Reflections on the Ontology of Film* (Cambridge, MA: Harvard Univ. Press, 1979), 28.
4. Stanley Cavell, *Pursuits of Happiness: The Hollywood Comedy of Remarriage* (Cambridge, MA: Harvard Univ. Press, 1981), 157.
5. Cavell, "What Becomes of Things on Film?," 179–80. Cavell elaborated his understanding of the woman's film, or film melodrama, in a series of lectures at Harvard University during the spring of 1984 and in his paper "Two Cheers for Romance," delivered at a symposium called "Passionate Attachments: The Essential but Fragile Nature of Love" held in New York on November 10, 1984 and sponsored by the Columbia University Center for Psychoanalytic Training and Research.
6. Disagreements about whether Judy looks directly into the camera, slightly off to the right of the camera, or more than slightly off to the right of the camera can last long into the night. Our inability to determine whether she, or any figure whose gaze is directed at

the camera, looks directly into the camera is not due to a failure of our attentiveness to film. It is the consequence of – hence exposes as an issue – the mysteriousness of the camera's presence within the world of a film. There is no such thing as a direct look into the camera, because there is no equivalent to gazing into the camera's eye; it has no eye, even though, paradoxically, it is only a gaze. Our fascination with determining whether a look is directed at the camera or slightly off masks the deeper issue at hand; that is, what does it mean for that figure to direct his or her gaze to the camera? What does the figure's gesture reveal about the camera?

7. All references to Freud are to *The Standard Edition of the Complete Psychological Works of Sigmund Freud*, trans. and gen. ed. James Strachey (London: Hogarth Press, 1957). All references thus far are to "Instincts and their Vicissitudes," vol. 14, pp. 130–2, hereafter cited in the text by volume and page numbers.

8. Freud, "Three Essays on Sexuality," *The Standard Edition*, vol. 7, pp. 159 and 157, hereafter cited in the text by volume and page numbers.

9. This phrase, "a soul with which …," was written by Bronson Alcott in his diary upon his recognition of his deep love for Abby May, whom he married. For this access to the Alcotts, I am grateful to Madelon Bedell's biography of the family, *The Alcotts* (New York: Clarkson N. Potter, 1980).

10. William Rothman, *Hitchcock: The Murderous Gaze* (Cambridge, MA: Harvard Univ. Press, 1982), 362.

11. Rothman's description of this gesture as one of "meeting the camera's gaze" is perspicuously apt (see p. 216 of *The Murderous Gaze*). The look that Judy gave the camera, discussed earlier in this chapter, is another instance of this gesture. My weighting of her look, whether one agrees that she looks directly at the camera or not, and my claim about its importance within the film are derived from Rothman's recognition that this gesture is repeated and crucial to Hitchcock's cinema, a point of criticism that demonstrates Rothman's philosophical, theoretical, and practical view, which I share, that Hitchcock's allegiances and thoughts are ascertainable only through investigations of the camera's relation to its human subjects throughout a given film.

Chapter Nineteen
North by Northwest
Stanley Cavell

Philosophy's all but unappeasable yearning for itself is bound to seem comic to those who have not felt it. To those who have felt it, it may next seem frightening, and they may well hate and fear it, for the step after that is to yield to the yearning, and then you are lost. From such a view of philosophy I have written about something called modernism in the arts as the condition of their each yearning for themselves; naming a time at which to survive, they took themselves, their own possibilities, as their aspiration – they assumed the condition of philosophy. What I found in turning to think consecutively about film a dozen or so years ago was a medium that seemed simultaneously to be free of the imperative to philosophy and at the same time inevitably to reflect upon itself – as though the condition of philosophy were its natural condition. And then I was lost.

But this is said after the fact. Over and over I have had to find again my conviction in these matters, to take my experience over the same path, finding the idea of film's philosophical seriousness first to be comic, then frightening, then inescapable. To achieve this conviction in the films of Alfred Hitchcock is not something I can imagine apart from a continuing conversation about film and about philosophy with William Rothman, whose conviction in the precision of Hitchcock's self-consciousness and passionate exploration of that self-consciousness in his films has convinced me to find this for myself. My remarks on *North by Northwest* are guided, more specifically, by two ideas from Rothman's forthcoming book on Hitchcock, *Hitchcock: The Murderous Gaze*: first, that Hitchcock's interpretation of the power of the movie camera – for example, its power of interrogation of its human subjects – is something Rothman calls its murderousness; and, second, that the Hitchcock film, hence Hitchcock, is first fully formed in *The 39 Steps*, in its weaving of Hitchcock's interest in his themes of the murder thriller together with the themes of romance.[1]

In *Pursuits of Happiness* I put together seven Hollywood romances of the 1930s and 1940s and claim that they define a particular genre, something I call the comedy of remarriage. It happens that Cary Grant is in four of the seven; Katharine Hepburn is the only other principal to appear in more than one. In my account of Howard Hawks's *Bringing up Baby* (one of the seven films in question) I claim that Grant's saving Hepburn from falling, at the close of the film, by hoisting her hand in hand onto the ledge of a scaffold, a place that also looks like a crib or treehouse, upon which they embrace, is alluded to by the conclusive hoisting in *North by Northwest* from a ledge onto an upper berth. If I will not ask you out of the blue to believe this connection, still less will I ask you to believe an allusion from *North by Northwest* to *The Philadelphia Story*, another of the seven films with Cary Grant, when Grant (or rather Roger Thornhill) early in *North by Northwest* tries to make the police and his mother believe what happened to him at the mansion in Glen Cove, and the place of liquor bottles is shown to be occupied by books. Thornhill's drinking is the subject of much attention in the opening sequences of *North by Northwest*, that is, as long as his mother is present; and C. K. Dexter Haven (Grant's role in *The Philadelphia Story*) cured himself of alcoholism by reading books, a process apparently from which he acquired the authority to affect the destiny of his love. I will wind up saying that *North by Northwest* derives from the genre of remarriage, or rather from whatever it is that that genre is derived, which means to me that its subject is the legitimizing of marriage, as if the pair's adventures are trials of their suitability for that condition. Perhaps this only signifies that *North by Northwest* is a romance. It is in any case the only one of Hitchcock's romantic thrillers in which the adventurous pair are actually shown to have married. It is also the only one in which the man of that pair is shown to have a mother – a mother, needless to say, whom he is shown to leave, and to leave running (out of the Plaza Hotel, away from his abductors, but at the same time away from his mother, who shouts after him to ask whether he will be home for dinner). The fate of the mother in *The Birds* will complicate this story. And naturally certain of Hitchcock's villains, and certain of his heroines, are allowed to have mothers.

But let us begin as uncontroversially as we can. *North by Northwest* contains as one of its stars Cary Grant. It underscores this uncontroversial fact in two principal ways: first, by remark after remark about his nice-looking, vaguely familiar face and about his being irresistible and making women who do not know him fall in love with him, together with several double takes when strangers look at his face (a man going into a phone booth Grant is leaving, a woman who, after as it were seeing who he is, wants him to stop in her hospital room); and, second, by allusions to each of the other films Hitchcock made with Grant. *To Catch a Thief* also has him at the end holding a woman by the hand over a precipice, and in that film he is comically shown to be irresistible; *Suspicion* climaxes with a wild ride down a coast road in a convertible driven by Grant, from which he seems to shove someone out and from which someone who might be poisoned almost falls over a cliff into the sea; and the basic situation of *Notorious* is gone over again (a loose woman's liaison with something like a foreign agent is exploited by an American intelligence agency; the assignment thwarts Grant's desire; it leads to the woman's mortal danger from which Grant rescues her).

There seem to be two immediate reasons in *North by Northwest* for insisting upon the presence of Cary Grant: first to redeem him from certain guilts acquired in those earlier environments, especially in allowing him to overcome the situation of *Notorious*, as if film actors and their characters get stuck to one another, and as if he is being readied for something purer in this context; and, second, to inscribe the subject of film acting, and acting generally, as a main topic of this film, which is to say, a main branch of its investigation of the nature of film. The topic is invoked over and over in *North by Northwest*: Philip Vandamm (James Mason) hardly says a word to Grant that does not comment on his acting; the Professor (Leo G. Carroll) requests him to act a part; and Eve (Eva Marie Saint) compliments him on his performance in the scene they have just acted out for Vandamm's benefit. The theme of theatricality is generalized by the fact that the part Thornhill is asked and forced to play is that of someone named George Kaplan, who does not exist; but to play the part of a fictional character is just what actors normally do. It happens that in the fiction of this film this new fictional identity is imposed by reality, thus generalizing the theme further into the nature of identity and the theatricality of everyday life.

It is, I think, part of Hitchcock's lingo to be referring to these facts, and more, in the exchange on the train between Thornhill and Eve about the monogram on his matchbook. "Rot," he says, "it's my trademark." She asks what the "O" stands for. "Nothing," he replies. In a Hitchcockian context this means both that this man knows that the advertising game (and the modern city generally that it epitomizes) makes up words that are rot but also that it would be rot to think this is all he means. Thornhill and Eve have already questioned his identity and spoken about his familiar face. So in part what or who is "nothing" is the film character (here, Roger Thornhill) in comparison to the film actor playing him. Cary Grant would be more or less who he is if Roger Thornhill had never existed, whereas Roger Thornhill would be nothing apart from Cary Grant (a form of consideration broached as long ago as Erwin Panofsky's "Style and Medium in the Motion Pictures"). "Nothing" equally means that the film *actor* is nothing in comparison to the power of the camera over *him*. This is not so much in need of argument as of interpretation. *North by Northwest* interprets the actor as a victim, as if of foreign views of himself. This thought puts two figures in the film in the role of directors, the Professor and Vandamm, who create scenarios and make up parts for people.[2] On Vandamm's first encounter with Thornhill he draws some theatrical curtains across proscenium-sized windows, shutting the world out, and arranges for Thornhill to be killed, as if punishing him for acting; the Professor lets this go on until forced for the sake of his own script to intervene.

The "nothing," or naught, in the ROT monogram equally appropriately stands for origin, so its simultaneous meaning is that the actor is the origin of the character and also the origin of what becomes of himself or herself on film. The further thought that the human self as such is both an origin and a nothing is a bit of Cartesianism that is conceivably not called for in the context of this film. (To say that Hitchcock is up to it if he wants it is to say that Hitchcock is as intelligent as, say, Samuel Beckett and that he is as good at what he does as Beckett is at what he does.)

But I was trying to begin uncontroversially. The film is called *North by Northwest*. I assume that nobody will swear from that fact alone that we have here an allusion to Hamlet's line that he is but mad north-northwest; even considering that Hamlet's line occurs as the players are about to enter and that *North by Northwest* is notable, even within the *oeuvre* of a director pervaded by images and thoughts of the theater and of theatricality, for its obsession with the idea of acting; and considering that both the play and the film contain plays-within-the-play in both of which someone is killed, both being constructed to catch the conscience of the one for whose benefit they are put on. But there are plenty of further facts. The film opens with an ageless male identifying himself first of all as a son. He speaks of his efforts to keep the smell of liquor on his breath (that is, evidence of his grown-up pleasures) from the watchful nose of his mother, and he comes to the attention of his enemies because of an unresolved anxiety about getting a message to his mother, whereupon he is taken to a mansion in which his abductor has usurped another man's house and name and has, it turns out, cast his own sister as his wife. (The name, posted at the front of the house, is Townsend, and a town is a thing smaller than a city but larger than a village, or a hamlet.) The abductor orders the son killed by forcing liquid into him. It is perhaps part of the picture that the usurper is eager to get to his dinner guests and that there is too much competitive or forced drinking of liquor. Nor, again, will anyone swear that it is significant that the abductor-usurper's henchmen are a pair of men with funny, if any, names and a single man who stands in a special relationship with the usurper and has a kind of sibling rivalry with the young woman that this son, our hero, will become attracted to and repelled by. These are shadowy matters, and it is too soon to speak of "allusions" or of any other very definite relation to a so-called source. But it seems clear to me that, *if* one were convinced of *Hamlet* in the background of *North by Northwest*, say to the extent that one is convinced that Saxo Grammaticus's *Danish History* is in the background of *Hamlet*, then one would without a qualm take the name Leonard as a successor to the name Laertes.

We have further to go. In Saxo Grammaticus's telling of the story the son's enemies send a beautiful woman to seduce him; he is to believe that he and the woman meet by chance. When questioned about what happened between them he says he raped her; she has agreed to back his story since they had known one another in the past. This figure is, as editors have noted, a peculiar prototype for Ophelia, but we can take her as near perfect for Eve Kendall. Thornhill does not, it is true, say that he raped her, but he describes something happening between them, in the name of love, that they both call murdering her. Hitchcock here is following one of his favorite identifications, that of killing with intercourse, the other side of a metaphysical wit's identification of dying with orgasm. It is also to the point, thinking of Thornhill's attention to his clothes, that Hamlet's prototype in Saxo Grammaticus is pictured as covering himself with dirt. That Hitchcock has gone back to the source or origin of the story of Hamlet, as well as to the play, is a reason not to have the title *exactly* from *Hamlet*.[3]

I note two or three further echoes of the play. Thornhill's problem begins when he is confused with, so to speak, someone who does not exist, let us say it is a nothing, or let us say a ghost; and when the woman betrays him he finds her out by following the itinerary dictated by the ghost. And then the son protects himself, saves his life, by what I would like to describe as feigning madness – in the auction scene in which he pretends not to know how you join in bidding for things. The auctioneer at one stage says, "Would the gentleman please get into the spirit of the proceedings?" – that is, be decorous, be socialized; but society has been forcing an identity and a guilt upon him that he does not recognize as his own, so the natural hope for a way out is to abdicate from that society. Thornhill's identifying "rot" as his trademark by now irresistibly suggests to me Hamlet's sense of something rotten.

Allow for the sake of argument that *Hamlet* is present in the film in some fashion. Of what interest is this, I mean of what interest to Hitchcock? I have various speculations about this based on my claim that *North by Northwest* invokes *Hamlet* in conjunction with the source of the story of Hamlet and on my sense that *North by Northwest* plays a special role in Hitchcock's *oeuvre*, a summary role. I take Hitchcock, as it were, to be saying something like the following. Granted that it is not necessary for anyone, let alone a filmmaker, to disclaim the intention of trying to compete with the quality and the importance of *Hamlet*, it is nevertheless my intention, as the filmmaker I am, to compete with Shakespeare in his handling of sources and in this way, or to this extent, to show myself to do whatever it is I do as well as Shakespeare does whatever it is he does. It is with sources as Coleridge famously remarked about Shakespeare's stories: "My belief is that he always regarded his story, before he began to write, much in the same light as a painter regards his canvas, before he begins to paint – as a mere vehicle for his thoughts – as the ground upon which he was to work." But then of course (still speaking for Hitchcock) the question is what one means by "sources." The story is one source, lifted often from indifferent places that would not constitute sources unless I had been inspired to make them such. So is the past body of my work a source, as *North by Northwest* makes explicit. So are what some people call "locations," which for me are places whose genius I wish to announce or to become. So are what other people call "actors," whereas for me what is called "Cary Grant" is considerably more than what that may be taken to mean. So is what you might call the camera a source.... You see the point.

But why is it *Hamlet* about which this is all, according to my speaking for Hitchcock, being said? I think there are two reasons. First, *Hamlet* is perhaps the most popular, or famous, of the greatest works of world literature; the man who on the basis of his kind of thriller became perhaps the most famous director of films in the world, and for a longer period than any other, and whom just about any critic recognizes as in some sense brilliant, may well be fascinated by and wish to comprehend this fact. Surely the play's fame cannot be the result of its actually being *understood*. Second, *Hamlet* is the subject of what is still probably the most famous Freudian interpretation of a work of art, Ernest Jones's *Hamlet and Oedipus*. Given the blatant presence of Freudian preoccupation and analysis in Hitchcock's work, I see in his allusion to *Hamlet* a kind of warning to Freudians, even a dare, as if to say: of course my work, like any art, is subject to your interpretations, but why are these interpretations so often so obvious, unable to grasp the autonomy, the uniqueness, of the object? (Hitchcock would not be the first artist of this century to feel he has to pit his knowledge of human nature against the thought of the man who is said to have invented its science.)[4]

The origin of Eve Kendall in Hitchcock's own past work is explicit enough. She succeeds the prim, good-looking, blonde stranger in *The 39 Steps* whom an earlier Hitchcock hero had met on a train as he was trying to elude the police and get to a person who could clear him of the suspicion of having put a knife in someone's back; and at the end of that train ride there was also a professor. But this time, over twenty years later and in another country, the woman *offers* rather than refuses him help. This proves, initially, to be treachery rather than salvation, but it affords a picture of a relationship to women that this man, now and in the past, had not known. This woman's apparent faith in him succeeds both Madeleine Carroll's early skepticism about his predecessor (Robert Donat), who spends much of *The 39 Steps* trying to overcome it; and her faith succeeds more immediately the skepticism of his mother, to whom he had said goodbye just before encountering Eve on the train. The effect of these substitutions is elaborate and paradoxical, and all in favor of Eve.

Aligning, in retrospect, the Madeleine Carroll figure with the present mother, doubt is cast on the picture of marriage in the final shot of *The 39 Steps*; the man puts his arm around the woman with the handcuffs still dangling from his wrist, a picture suggesting that marriage is a kind of voluntary handcuffing (a portable version of the ball and chain). On the other hand, Eve is made to incorporate both the good woman and the adventuress of *The 39 Steps*, that is, both the marriageable and the unmarriageable woman. The most delicious linking of them is made openly by Eve when she explains her interest in Thornhill to him by saying, "It's going to be a long night and I don't particularly like the book I've started. Know what I mean?" The Madeleine Carroll figure had been reading a book when Donat burst in on her. Thornhill knows what she means, as if seeing a dream coming true. And in that dream, and its responsibilities, the man's task will not be just to save himself and save his country's secrets from leaving it and thus win himself a suitable mate. He has first of all to save the bad woman, to rewrite the earlier plot that in effect began by killing her off, to rescue or redeem or resurrect her, that is to say, to put the good and the bad together. This is rather more like *creating* a suitable mate for himself.

Why is she his to rescue? Both the Professor and Eve tell him he is responsible for her condition, the one because he has cast suspicion on her, the other because men like him do not believe in marriage. But I think the film shows two further causes. First, in addition to her incorporating at least two of the women from *The 39 Steps*, she also incorporates the mother, perhaps the mother he never had, protecting him from the police by hiding him in a bellying container that shows she holds the key to his berth. (This was not necessary: the fact that she subsequently hides him from the porter sufficiently well in the washroom proves that.) It is every bit this birth he is reciprocating in his closing gesture of the film. Second, he has passed some kind of ordeal at her hands in the crop-dusting sequence, and his survival here somehow entitles them to one another – as if his survival, or revival from a Frazerian cornfield, had given them the key piece of knowledge with which to overcome their unlucky erotic pasts, which accordingly would be the knowledge that ecstasy such as she invites is not necessarily death dealing. I am taking it that she is not purely reluctant to send him to meet Kaplan. She is not worried that he is a murderer but that she is. They are both about to undergo an education in these matters. Redemption for them both is under way. But it is not a simple matter to put such knowledge into the world – say, in the form of marriage – and there is danger ahead.

How is it that he is equipped to meet the danger; I mean how does he know that the attempt is the most important thing in the world? I must now put the uncontroversial aside and put forward a bunch of assertions.

I begin by reinterpreting, or interpreting further, Thornhill's survival of the attack by the plane. The attack is the central image of his victimization. I said earlier that this is the form in which his being an actor is to be declared; and just now I said that his sexual redemption depended on what you might call his survival of a kind of victimization by, or a willing subjection to, an assault of feeling. Something cataclysmic happened to Thornhill and Eve the night before, and I understand the attack the next day to be simultaneously a punishment for the night and a gaudy visual equivalent of it. Then I understand the crop-dusting plane, instrument of victimization, as a figure for a movie camera: it shoots at its victims and it coats them with a film of something that both kills and preserves, say that it causes metamorphosis. I claim evidence for the association of the prairie with the, let us say, inner landscape of the train compartment in the way a close-up of Eve's face at the Chicago train station dissolves into the establishing aerial shot of the road and fields of the plane attack. That conjunction of color and mood I claim asks for an allegorical identification of the woman and this stretch of land, but this is just something further each viewer must try out on his or her own. It is on this ground that the man undergoes his Shakespearean encounter of nothings – the nothing of Thornhill meeting the nothing of Kaplan – the attack on his identity, as it were, by itself. The recognition of the plane sent by Vandamm as a figure for the camera accounts satisfactorily for his gathering his stolen secrets on microfilm. This, in turn, would be a way Hitchcock has of saying that film – anyway in his camera – is the recorder of state secrets.

Put this together with the other overt declaration of the movie camera, this time by synechdoche rather than metaphor: I mean the telescope on the terrace of the Mount Rushmore memorial focused on the faces of the presidents. A lot is being woven together here. We have cut to the presidents' faces from a close-up of Grant's face, turned toward us and suddenly illuminated as for examination by a harsh light from what we understand fictively to be a plane turning in his direction, hence what we understand literally and figuratively as a piece of photographic apparatus. We are being told that this face belongs to just one person on earth and that we are going to have to think about what that means. The cut from that image to the image of the presidents evidently poses some matching of Grant's face with the faces of stone, a matching generally prepared of course by the insistent references to the familiarity of his face but prepared more specifically by his having shaved with the minuscule razor and brush. Letting the phallic symbolism alone for a while, the question is certainly being posed about the sizes things are. Thornhill and Eve have had an exchange about whether he is a little boy or a big boy, and now the issue is about what size the human face of flesh and blood is in comparison with faces on the face of a granite mountain and the size of both in comparison with the photographic projection of the human face. A question is thus raised about what Grant is (made of), about what it means that he has become a national monument, and hence about what a monument is. So at the same time a question is raised about what presidents are and about what it means to know and remember them. These comparisons are underscored when it turns out, directly, that our initial view of the presidents' faces is an image of them as seen through a telescope set up for the pleasure and instruction of tourists. The image is possessed for us by, let us say, Thornhill, but there is no reason to think that anyone present would not see the same image, the one we have now. Its being Grant who looks through the telescope at the famous stone faces identifies the conditions of his existence as a screen actor and thus identifies the mode in which we see him and think we know him. And I would be willing to swear from the fact alone of the way Grant is standing behind that telescope that he is also meant as a surrogate for the one who is capturing these images for our pleasure and instruction. But the Professor is there with Thornhill as we cut to him standing before the telescope, so the matter of directorial surrogates must be complicated.

Let us run through the evidence for Grant/Thornhill as surrogate for Hitchcock. There is, first of all, the hint laid down by Hitchcock's having autographed himself in this film as someone who misses a bus: Thornhill is the only (other) character in the film before whom a bus shuts its doors and drives off. Again, however we are to understand Thornhill's participation in the killing of the real Lester Townsend in the United Nations building, we must understand him as what this moment visually declares him to be, someone who betrays by showing a picture, that is, a picture that is, or that causes, a knife in the back – a reasonable, or anyway Hitchcockian, description of Hitchcock's narrative procedure. Now take the telescope and the two men on the terrace. Thornhill's initial reaction to the view through the telescope is to say "I don't like the way Teddy Roosevelt is looking at me." And he will say, "I think he's telling me not to go on with this harebrained scheme." This could be a line Hitchcock is allowing Grant to use about himself, perhaps about his role in this strenuous film, perhaps about his career as an actor. (I would not put it past Hitchcock to be alluding to the fact that Grant shares a name with a president of the United States, one famous for drinking, and one in particular that only Teddy Roosevelt among the four presidents figured at Mount Rushmore would have known was a president.) But the Professor's response suggests something else first: "He's telling you to walk softly and carry a big stick." This makes a certain amount of sense said either to Grant or to Thornhill. It makes much better sense said to Hitchcock, hence said as it were to himself, that is, by one directorial surrogate to another. The exchange about a harebrained scheme and walking softly, as behind a big camera, would express a moment of self-doubt on Hitchcock's part to be overcome by the course of this film; and, since this film is a kind of summary or anthology of his mature career as a whole, the doubt must be about the course of his mature career as a whole. If one were prepared to believe this, one would be encouraged to take the title *North by Northwest* not as naming some odd direction but as titling a search for directedness, a claim to have found it, as of the course of a career. (We will come to a more general reason for taking the title this way.) Hitchcock's identifying himself with the actor figure permits him a certain opposition to the two more explicit director figures, that is, permits him to claim opposition to the way other directors operate; his testimony is to show himself the victim as well as the inquisitor of his trade, the pursued as well as the pursuer, permitting himself to be looked back at.

This prompts me to collect one of the last of Hitchcock's inclusions in his anthology: his reference to *Rear Window*, whose hero (James Stewart) also looks through a telescope, now explicitly a telescopic camera lens and thus more explicitly conferring an identification as a film director, and whom someone or something eventually also looks back at through his telescope in a way he does not like. The Stewart figure has a kind of comic Hamlet derivation in that he sees everything and is debarred from taking action (by a broken leg in a cast). The thing that looks back at him, locking gazes with him, is the man whose murdering of his wife and dismemberment and disposition of the pieces of the body Stewart's camera has divined; and this too feels like an act of identification, between viewer and viewed, between director and subjects. Hitchcock's confession is a terrible one. (It may just be worth remembering that the Hamlet figure in Saxo Grammaticus dismembered the body of the figure that became Polonius and disposed of the parts in a sewer; and just worth putting this together with Thornhill's early dictation to his secretary of a note to accompany a gift of gold-wrapped candy: "This is for your sweet tooth, and all your other sweet parts.") The brighter side of Hitchcock's sensing an identification of himself with Hamlet claims his position as that of an intellectual, as possessed of a metaphysical imagination, and as unknown (partly because of the antic disposition he puts on).

What I just called Hitchcock's terrible confession – it is something I understand by Rothman's detection of Hitchcock's murderous camera – was going to be the guiding subject of these remarks, the thought that filming inevitably proceeds by severing things, both in cutting and, originally, in framing, and that Hitchcock is fully sensible of this fact and responsible to it. While it is buried in *North by Northwest* in the rarified reference to the original Hamlet story, it is, if you allow the subject, blatantly posed by the gigantic heads of the monument and by the matching of Grant's head with them. The suggestion is that these memorializations have required acts of severing. This would be something else Grant does not like when he sees something looking back at him through the telescope. And it is this fate that Thornhill is saved from in earning the rescue from the faces of the monument. So when I say that Grant's looking through the telescope represents our perception of film, of something I mean by viewing, I am proposing that a theory of this mode of perception will be given in a theory of the perception of part-objects, as this is broached in the work of Melanie Klein. Such a theory should be able to help account for a pair of familiar facts in looking at film: that there may apparently be the most fantastic disproportion between what is actually shown on the screen and the emotion this elicits; *and* that this disproportion can be resisted, the emotion fail to appear. After all, many people think, or think they think, that *North by Northwest* is a light comedy. But, while I have left the theme of severed objects as an undercurrent of these remarks, I decided against making it explicit (then I partly changed my mind).

What is it that looks back through the telescope at Thornhill, who presumably has no special relation to those heads (anyway not Grant's relation)? It is puzzling that he should say it is Teddy Roosevelt, since that head is, from the angle taken, quite retracted in comparison to those of Washington, Jefferson, and Lincoln and is not facing in the right direction. We are in any case being asked to let ourselves be puzzled by what it is we see when we are looking at the results of a movie camera and also by what the Mount Rushmore Memorial betokens. I figure what looks back through the lens not to require eyes, not even images of eyes, but to be whatever it is that a movie camera looks at, which is to say, whatever power it is that is solicited from us in perceiving things on film. I once said that the images of photography are of the world as a whole, and now thinking of what looks back at a director – an image's original audience as emblematized by these mountainous heads of the presidents, cliffs turned into faces – I would like to say that what looks back, what reveals itself to the viewer's gaze, is the physiognomy of the world, say the face of the earth. To animate, or reanimate, or humanize the world and so achieve a reciprocity with it is a recognizable aspiration of some poetry and some philosophy, as, for example, when Thoreau writes in the chapter "The Ponds" in *Walden:* "A lake is the landscape's most beautiful and expressive feature. It is earth's eye; looking into which the beholder measures the depth of his own nature." Thornhill's capacity for beholding nature in this way – as unsevered – would be a sign that he is to be saved.

The Mount Rushmore Memorial is a crazy American literalization of this ambition of reciprocity with the world. More specifically it literalizes such an idea as Walt Whitman's that America's mountains and prairies are the greatest of its poems. It is as if the monument proposes a solution to an American ambivalence as old as the pilgrims about the land of America: that it is human, in particular female, a virgin and yet a nourishing mother, but at the same time that we have raped her, blotted nature out by wanting our mark upon her.[5] (I have suggested that the film *North by Northwest*, in the crop-dusting sequence, invokes that ambivalence and calls for a solution to it.) The proposed solution of the monument is that, if the mark is big enough and art enough and male enough, the doom of progress may be redeemed. Hardly a saving message to be drawn from the observation and memory of Washington, Jefferson, and Lincoln.

The *Encyclopedia Americana* notes that the faces of the monument measure some sixty feet from chin to forehead and adds, rather proudly I thought, that this is twice as high as the head of the Giza Sphinx. But what else is there to think about but their monumentality, and what more to conclude on their basis than that America has become twice the land of Egypt, twice as enslaving and twice as mysterious? Hitchcock shows that for a projected screen image to encompass the size of these faces is the work of an instant, and thus he at once declares his work in competition with Mount Rushmore as a monument to America, about America, and asks for a meditation on what can now constitute monumentality, on what can be made so as to show the value in commemorating. This is a reason that this film is at pains to anthologize the whole body of Hitchcock's mature, mostly American, work, to throw it all into the balance as a kind of rededication. Rededication is an appropriate mood before a monument, particularly in a moment of self-doubt. And, even if this monument exemplifies competition and domination as much as it does commemoration, still it is about founding fathers, a wish, however awkwardly expressed, to get back to origins. Hitchcock has been careful to dissociate his attitude toward the monument from Vandamm's contemptuous dismissal of it with his opening question to Kaplan/Thornhill at the cafeteria: something like, "Now what little drama have you invited me to witness in these gay surroundings?" (*This* Englishman does not belong to the place but owns a structure mythically close to it, pitched out from the land, less a dwelling than a space station.) And what better rededication than to compete with this monument's way of remembering by showing your fellow inhabitants a better way – a way that does not attempt to petrify and sever the past but to revise the inheritance of it, to reinherit it?

Before giving the answer I have, I pause to note that we could look back and recount the main topics of *North by Northwest* as topics of seduction – our seduction by one another, by beautiful women and beautiful men and beautiful things, by mothers, strangers, liquor, fame, monuments, politics, America, art, film. The present film asks us to consider our attachments to things less in the light of what things they are than in the light of what mode of attachment we take toward them – for example, fetishistic, scoptophilic, masochistic, narcissistic, or in general, to use a key word of Emerson's, partial. One result of such consideration might be the thought that a healthy suspicion and testing of our attachment to film should extend to our attachment to, say, literature as well and that film and literature are each capable of helping us in this extension.

The mountain-monument seems to have become just another landscape of a cold war, the scene of an escape, as though we had lost the capacity for attachment altogether; but then it is the site of the playing-out of one of drama's oldest subjects, the rights of love against the rights, anyway the requirements, of politics. We might come to think that the escape of this pair is seen by Hitchcock to be of national importance. Who are they, and what are they doing on this monument?

I will, as said, assert that they derive from, or from the same source as, the American comedy of remarriage, which I said means to me that their goal is the thing I call the legitimizing of marriage, the declaration that happiness is still to be won there, there or nowhere, and that America is a place, fictional no doubt, in which that happiness can be found. The structure of these comedies, making the goal achievable, takes responsibility over a longish, extendable list of features, two of the principal ones being the achieving of a new innocence and the establishing or re-establishing of an identity. These are pieces of an ancient Hitchcockian problematic. So are the two further features of remarriage comedies that I call the capacities for adventure and for improvisation. I mean by these capacities the virtues that allow you to become at home in the world, to establish the world as a home. The capacities permit, if necessary, living together on the road, as if loving were the finding of a direction, that is, or a directedness, just, as I mentioned, as Hitchcock's title *North by Northwest* names otherwise than just a given direction. So important is it to get this capacity for adventurousness straight that in the middle of their escape down the monument the pair pause, comically, surrealistically, to discuss it (as silent comics used to pause, in the middle of chasing one another, to catch their breath). After his proposal to her she asks what happened to his two earlier marriages. He says his wives left him because they found he led too dull a life. For Hitchcock so daringly to mock the suspense he has been building up over this escape, virtually declaring that the two are now standing on a platform in a studio, must mean that he wants to illustrate the significance of this exchange, to enforce the assertion that dullness, taken as the opposite of adventurousness, where these are characteristics of human relationship, spiritual matters, is not something that running around the face of the earth proves or disproves, except allegorically. With those wives even this monumental situation of life and death would have been, spiritually speaking, dull; whereas with Eve the "importance" of the time and place is unimportant for the opposite reason, that anything and everything can be an adventure, however untellable as such from outside. (This is roughly the sentiment of *Bringing up Baby*.)

The candidates for remarriage must, further, not be virgins, they must have a past together, and they must talk well and wittily about marriage, especially about whether they believe in marriage. The past the pair share in *North by Northwest* is just one night, but it proves ample enough. And one or both of the pair must maintain an openness to childhood, so it turns out to be to Thornhill's spiritual credit that, although in the course of the film he becomes big, he remains a boy. (The child-like capacity of Grant's temperament on film is stressed, I suppose discovered, in the comedies he made with Howard Hawks.) The man in remarriage comedies is responsible for the education of the woman as part of a process of rescuing or redeeming her from a state in which she keeps herself; this may be characterized as a coldness or an inability to feel, and the education typically takes the form of the man's lecturing or haranguing the woman. In *North by Northwest* Thornhill identifies Eve as a statue and accuses her of having no feelings to hurt, but we are shown by her tears at this moment (at the auction) that what I earlier called the education in his surviving her onslaught has taken effect; to begin her physical rescue, he will later write on his monogrammed matchbook a note that contains information no one else in the world is in a position to impart to her. We may also see in this successful delivery his finally getting a message through to a woman, the difficulty in doing which began this plot.

This is enough to let me outline what I take as the essential difference in structure between the romantic comedies of remarriage and Hitchcock's romantic thriller. The goal of the comedies requires what I call the creation of the woman, a new creation of a new woman. This takes the form in the comedies of something like the woman's death and revival, and it goes with the camera's insistence on the flesh-and-blood reality of the female actor. When this happens in Hitchcock, as it did in *Vertigo*, the Hitchcock film preceding *North by Northwest*, it is shown to produce catastrophe: the woman's falling to her death, precisely the fate *averted* in *North by Northwest*. Here, accordingly, it is the man who undergoes death and revival (at least twice, both times at the hands of the woman) *and* whose physical identity is insisted upon by the camera.[6] Hitchcock is thus investigating the point that the comedies of remarriage are least certain about – namely, what it is about the man that fits him to educate and hence rescue the woman, that is, to be chosen by the woman to educate her and thereby to achieve happiness for them both.

But again, why is the rescue to be achieved from the face of this monument? I have called it the face of the earth, the earth itself become visible, as pure surface. These tiny creatures are crawling between heaven and earth, a metaphysical accomplishment, as if becoming children again. Hamlet, feeling like a child, claims this accomplishment for himself as he decrees that there shall be no more marriages. Thornhill proposes marriage as he and the woman hang from a precipice; a gallant concept, as if marriage were a presence of mind, requiring no assurance of a future. Close-ups of the pair on the surface of the monument faces show them as if on an alien planet. There is no longer nature on the earth; earth is no longer an artifact by analogy, intimating God; it is literally and totally artifact, petrified under the hands of mankind. To place your film in competition with such an achievement is to place it in competition with film's own peculiar power of preserving the world by petrifying it, or anyway fixing it in celluloid. The couple in remarriage comedies are isolated at the end, expected to legitimize marriage without the world, which has no help for pain. The surface of Hitchcock's Mount Rushmore strikes me as a place of absolute spiritual isolation, civilization engulfing even empty space. In one of his first American films, *Saboteur* (to name a final excerpt in this anthology), a man holds a villain from a ledge at the top of the Statue of Liberty, but the villain's sleeve comes loose and he falls to earth. To fall from Mount Rushmore, as I am imagining it, would be to fall off the earth, down the vast edges drear of the world.

Thornhill lifts Eve up directly from the isolation of the monument's ledge to the isolation of the marriage bed, as if identifying both places as the scene of cliff-hangers and declaring that they are at home in both. At the lift Leonard is overcome and drops the statue Eve has been identified with, which breaks against the granite monument, opening to produce some film, I take it the present film. I in effect describe *The Philadelphia Story* as a film produced by a rescue that takes the form of the breaking of a statue in favor of a woman. I also claim that the remarriage is, using a repeated phrase of that film, of national importance. My ground is the thought that, while America, or any discovered world, can no longer ratify marriage, the achievement of true marriage might ratify something called America as a place in which to seek it. This is a state secret.

Notes

1. Rothman's book was published by Harvard University Press in 1982. I am also indebted to Marian Keane's "The Designs of Authorship: An Essay on *North by Northwest*," *Wide Angle*, vol. 4, no. 1 (1980): 44–52. I should like to mention here Robin Wood's *Hitchcock's Films* (South Brunswick and New York: A. S. Barnes, 1969), an intelligent, literate statement about the films of Hitchcock, which, while comparatively early as these things go in English-speaking circles, continues to repay reading. For an account of *North by Northwest* at once more suspicious than mine (about the value of the film) and more gullible (about Hitchcock's remarks about it and about the film's apparently casual evaluation of itself, so to speak), see George M. Wilson's "The Maddest McGuffin: Some Notes on *North by Northwest*," *Modern Language Notes*, vol. 94, no. 5 (1979): 1159–72.
2. A consequent moral equation between these figures is being drawn, another point I took away from a conversation with Rothman and Keane.
3. Subsequent to the original publication of this chapter I looked up another document familiar in *Hamlet* scholarship that Professor Geoffrey Bullough, in volume 7 of his *Narrative and Dramatic Sources of Shakespeare*, describes as "the German prose play *Der Bestrafte Brudermord oder Prinz Hamlet aus Dännemark*, the degenerate version of an

English play probably taken over to the Continent by English actors before 1626" (p. 20). Professor Bullough prints the play (among the Sources, Possible Sources, Probable Sources, Probable Historical Allusions, and Analogues; specifically as an Analogue) in an English translation entitled *Fratricide Punished* revised from one made for H. H. Furness's *The New Variorum Edition* of *Hamlet* of 1877. In this play the Laertes character is named Leonhardus.

I mention this not exactly to clinch my suggestion that the name Laertes may be seen to survive in the name Leonard; and not just to indicate a perfectly obvious place in which Hitchcock might have learned this change of name (Furness's famous editions and compilations), a source he may very well have meant to leave a clue for in his own change; but primarily to make explicit the question of when and how a matter of interpretation gets clinched in one's own mind. It *might*, I think, have happened to me on discovering Leonhardus; but in fact it came with the emphasis on "rot," as read in the paragraph following the one to which this note is appended.

4. Even Raymond Bellour's useful and sophisticated study of *North by Northwest* ("Le Blocage symbolique," *Communications*, no. 23 (1975): 235–350), judging from one hurried reading, has not, it seems to me, cleared itself of this question. My remark is directed only to the first half of this monograph-length paper. The second half, devoted to a geometry of the cropdusting sequence, I have not looked at sufficiently to have a judgment of.

5. Two valuable accounts of the history of American attitudes toward the American land are Edwin Fussell's *Frontier: American Literature and the American West* (Princeton: Princeton Univ. Press, 1965), and Annette Kolodny's *The Lay of the Land: Metaphor as Experience and History in American Life and Letters* (Chapel Hill, NC: Univ. of North Carolina Press, 1975).

6. That a given genre yields an adjacent genre by having one of its features "negated" in this way is something I give a little theoretical attention to in the introduction to *Pursuits of Happiness* (Cambridge, MA: Harvard Univ. Press, 1982).

NORTH BY NORTHWEST (Metro-Goldwyn-Mayer, 1959). *Producers*: Alfred Hitchcock, Herbert Coleman, *Assistant Director*: Robert Saunders, *Script*: Ernest Lehman, *Photography*: Robert Burks (Vista Vision, Technicolor), *Editor*: George Tomasini, *Sets*: Robert Boyle, William A. Horning, Merrill Pyle, Henry Grace, Frank McKelvey, *Music*: Bernard Herrmann, *Titles*: Saul Bass, *Players*: Cary Grant (Roger O. Thornhill), Eva Marie Saint (Eve Kendall), James Mason (Philip Vandamm), Jessie Royce Landis (Clara Thornhill), Leo G. Carroll (the Professor), Martin Landau (Leonard). 136 minutes.

Chapter Twenty

"Oh, I See….": *The Birds* and the Culmination of Hitchcock's Hyper-Romantic Vision

John P. McCombe

A Hitchcock film – and The Birds *is a particularly good example of this – is more analogous to a poem than a novel: Hitchcock focuses the attention and perceptions of the spectator, controls his reactions, through the rhythms of editing and camera movement as a poet controls those of the reader through his verse rhythms; and his films derive their value from the intensity of their images – an intensity created and controlled very largely by context, by the total organization – rather than from the creation of "rounded" characters. (Wood,* Hitchcock's Films Revisited*)[1]*

In the book cited above, Robin Wood initially compares Alfred Hitchcock's *The Birds* (1963) to another ambiguity-ridden twentieth-century text: E. M. Forster's *A Passage to India* (1924). In particular, Wood discusses the similarities between Lydia Brenner's speechless trauma following her discovery of Dan Fawcett's eyeless corpse and the more oblique despair that befalls Forster's Mrs. Moore after her niece's "assault" in the Marabar Caves. Although Wood concedes that the "density and complexity of characterization" are superior in Forster's novel, he also suggests that traumatic horror is better conveyed in Hitchcock's film.[2]

Both Mrs. Moore and Lydia Brenner possess a similar existential dread, but Wood believes that Hitchcock – through the specificity and intensity of his visual images – conveys the source of that horror more powerfully. Further, Wood believes that, because these and other images dominate the filmmaker's language (rather than painstaking character development as in *A Passage to India*), Hitchcock is far more a poet than a novelist. I strongly agree but would hasten to add that any comparison between Hitchcock and the modernists (poets or otherwise), while reasonable, ultimately leads to another productive line of inquiry: the film's clear ties to literary Romanticism.[3]

I need to be very precise about my terms here. I intend to connect *The Birds* to a *particular* version of British Romanticism.[4] As A. O. Lovejoy established as early as 1924, the movement we now identify as literary Romanticism was marked by contradiction and conflict. Lovejoy advocated a thorough and precise "discrimination of Romanticisms," which later critics such as M. H. Abrams, Geoffrey Hartman, Jerome McGann, and others have continued to delineate.[5] In this chapter, my goal is to connect Hitchcock's *The Birds* to a series of philosophical, aesthetic, and religious ideas expressed in Samuel Taylor Coleridge's "Rime of the Ancient Mariner" (1798) and to juxtapose the film more generally with early works by both Coleridge and William Wordsworth. Such an exercise productively illustrates some of the most salient characteristics of Romantic poetry in its "first phase," while also demonstrating how Hitchcock's pessimistic rejection of human rationality in *The Birds* – as well as the educational institutions that serve the cultivation of reason – ultimately extends far beyond the ideology of the British Romantics.

The practice of reading Hitchcock within a literary and historical framework has been rare during the last two decades. Most scholarship on *The Birds* reflects a more general trend: what one might describe as the "Lacanization" of Hitchcock studies. While there are exceptions – for example, Thomas Leitch's refusal to submit the film's characters to the analyst's couch, as well as Christopher Morris's poststructuralist interest in the film as an illustration of the problems of representation – much important work has adopted a psychoanalytic framework.[6] In "*The Birds*: A Mother's Love," Margaret Horwitz offers a heterosexual, Oedipal reading that posits the bird attacks as symbols of a mother's desire to punish her son for his sexual desire for another woman.[7] Also pursuing an interest in the film's complex of desire, Slavoj Žižek argues in *Looking Awry* that, rather than representing an Oedipal desire, the birds actually work to block or mask the unconscious desire in the triangle of Lydia, Mitch, and Melanie, particularly when the latter threatens to undermine the mother's fragile superego.[8]

In *Hitchcock's Bi-Textuality*, Robert Samuels refines the Lacanian paradigm, conceding that the film indeed traces the familiar trauma of the movement from the Lacanian Real to the Symbolic. However, Samuels builds on Žižek's foundation by claiming that what is really being blocked is the fluidity of gender in the film's characters; in other words, Melanie's "punishment" arises from Mitch's denial of his own feminine identifications.[9]

Although I would never argue that the possibilities for further investigations in this complex web of desire are exhausted, another, more historically grounded approach seems timely. As Wood contends in his rejection of such psychoanalytic interpretations of *The Birds*, Hitchcock is a poet in his use of film style. And in his narrative and thematic preoccupations, Hitchcock is hyper-Romantic.

Camille Paglia mentions the idea that *The Birds* is a Romantic text in her recent British Film Institute monograph on the film. In her introduction, Paglia asserts that she places *The Birds* "in the main line of British Romanticism, descending from the raw nature-tableaux and sinister femmes fatales of Coleridge."[10] True to her signature style, Paglia ranges widely from Sophocles to symbolist painting to contemporary film thrillers such as *Basic Instinct* (Paul Verhoeven, 1992), yet she never elaborates on the specific Coleridge/Hitchcock connections. When she does resume the thread of her discussion of the film's Romanticism many pages later, she includes as poetic analogies Percy Bysshe Shelley's "The Witch of Atlas" and William Blake's "The Crystal Cabinet." Although we might anticipate an attempt to historicize Hitchcock and *The Birds* within a specific literary tradition, Paglia quickly reveals a very different agenda: reading Hitchcock's heroine, Melanie Daniels, as the castrating femme fatale carrying a handbag that constitutes "the vagina as a male jail." Such a statement reveals Paglia's real interest: offering yet another psychoanalytic interpretation of *The Birds* in which the film charts, in Paglia's words, "a return of the repressed, a release of primitive forces of sex and appetite that have been subdued but never fully tamed."[11] All of this leads to two points: Paglia says something that rings all too familiar; and there is more to the connection between British Romanticism and Hitchcock than the tyranny of nature or the predatory and devouring Melanie Daniels and her Romantic femme fatale precursors.[12]

"There's an Answer for Everything"

Hitchcock's irony never cuts deeper than when Scottie Ferguson (James Stewart) utters these words in *Vertigo* (1958) in an attempt to interpret the strange dreams Madeleine (Kim Novak) is having of the dead Carlotta Valdes. There *is* an answer, of course, but it is one his fragile psyche will later be unable to accept: the dreams do not exist, because Madeleine does not exist. Scottie's former schoolmate and client, Gavin Elster (Tom Helmore), has duped the former police detective, and the "Madeleine" that Scottie has been trailing (and with whom he has become obsessed) has been as much "the observer" as "the observed." Hitchcock later confirms the predatory nature of Madeleine/Judy with a clever detail in the *mise-en-scène* – a gold brooch of a bird – that links her to the protagonists of two subsequent (and Romantic) Hitchcock films: Marion *Crane* (Janet Leigh) in *Psycho* (1960) and Melanie Daniels (Tippi Hedren) in *The Birds*. During the second half of *Vertigo*, Scottie inhabits a nightmare, one that Penelope Houston describes as a "slow, underwater dream" that possesses "the hallucinatory quality of a nightmare."[13] This nightmarish setting would persist in Hitchcock's films, much like the "waterbound nightmare" of Coleridge's "Rime," in which the ice "crack'd and growl'd, and roar'd and howl'd – | Like noises of a swound [swoon]" (lines 59–60).[14]

One of the key elements of Hitchcock's brand of Romanticism is what John Calabrese describes, in "Romanticism in Alfred Hitchcock's *Vertigo*," as the "dark, sinister aspects of character" that distinguish the Romantic hero: an interest in the mystical, violence, and the grotesque, as well as a "morbid preoccupation with death, and the irrational."[15] Although Calabrese limits his analysis to Scottie Ferguson and *Vertigo*, these qualities also erupt in Norman Bates (Anthony Perkins), the hero (and resident "birdman") in *Psycho*. Perhaps there is ultimately no rational explanation for Norman's strange fits of passion in *Psycho* (although psychoanalytic critics would cast a knowing glance in the direction of dear old Mom), but, regardless of one's explanation for the obsessive behavior in both that film and *Vertigo*, Hitchcock displays an interest also expressed in the first-person speakers of Wordsworth's "Lucy Poems." To paraphrase Wordsworth, Hitchcock traces the fluxes and refluxes of the mind in a state of agitation.[16] In this way, Scottie and Norman become latter-day (and even more extreme) versions of Wordsworth's famous outcasts, "The Idiot Boy" and "The Mad Mother," two marginalized subjects of *Lyrical Ballads* whose ideas and feelings are clearly not, to use the poet's phrase, "in a healthful state of association."[17] Of course, there were also the poems that Coleridge contributed: those verses in which the "incidents and agents were to be, in part at least, supernatural"[18] – the "Poems of High Imagination," which more closely resemble what we see in *The Birds*.

In *The Films of Alfred Hitchcock*, David Sterritt emphasizes what I consider to be the key to the transition from the Wordsworthian to the Coleridgean in Hitchcock's two early-1960s classics:

> *The Birds* is very much a follow-up to *Psycho*, with Hitchcock seeking to go further beyond the bounds of rationality than even Norman Bates's grim adventure allowed. It projects Norman's disequilibrium into the world at large, showing us not an individual but an entire world possessed by madness, confusion, and a rage – erupting not from within but, incredibly, from without – that is as mysterious as it is murderous.... *The Birds* not only depicts the irrational; it *becomes* the irrational by refusing to allow natural (or cinematically naturalized) causal relationships to glue together its hazily separated "real" and "fantastic" elements.[19]

What Sterritt describes in *The Birds* recalls Coleridge's appeal in chapter 14 of the *Biographia Literaria* to the "willing suspension of disbelief." Both *The Birds* and "Rime of the Ancient Mariner" are, among other things, lengthy suspensions of disbelief. Both texts possess an uncompromising ambiguity and blend fantasy with elements of everyday life.

In *The Birds*, a good portion of the chain of cause and effect that typically governs narration in the Hollywood cinema disintegrates after the first thirty minutes, when, in the words of screenwriter Evan Hunter, "a screwball comedy ... gradually turns into stark terror."[20] Initially, the plot concerns a wealthy playgirl, Melanie Daniels, who flirtatiously pursues a San Francisco lawyer named Mitch Brenner (Rod Taylor), by ostensibly delivering two lovebirds as a gift to his younger sister, Cathy (Veronica Cartwright). But, once a seagull dive-bombs Melanie in the middle of Bodega Bay (a sleepy seaside town sixty miles from San Francisco), the romantic comedy becomes subordinated by acts of unspeakable horror. What had been a clear chain of cause and effect is disrupted.

In the early portion of the film, Melanie's trip to visit schoolteacher Annie Hayworth (Suzanne Pleshette) is necessitated by Melanie's attempt to learn the name of Mitch's young sister, and both Annie and Cathy will be crucial to the plot events to come. Similarly, when Mitch's mother, Lydia (Jessica Tandy), makes the fateful trip to Dan Fawcett's farm, she does so to understand why the chickens in Bodega Bay have recently begun to refuse their feed.[21] Such is typical of the way that characters serve as agents of cause and effect and initiate elements of the plot by pursuing their clearly articulated desires.[22]

The complexity of desire in the film extends to the desire of the birds themselves, as their series of bizarre attacks intensifies. When Melanie spends the night at Annie's before attending Cathy's birthday party the following day, a gull flies unexpectedly into the door of the house. Then, during the birthday party, a sustained and more coordinated attack on the children interrupts a game of blind man's bluff. Following this attack, Melanie, in a moment of near-comic understatement, asks, "Mitch, this isn't usual, is it?" Later that day, the highly unusual nature of these acts is confirmed when hundreds of sparrows attack the Brenner home.

Despite the irrationality of the two attacks, the investigating officer insists on a rational explanation: lights must have attracted the sparrows, just as the children must have "bothered" the gulls that disrupted Cathy's party. These explanations are patently ludicrous, but, in a similar way, the viewer attempts to construct a cause for the violent attacks by these normally passive birds. Evan Hunter suggests that the joke is clearly on the audience: "The trouble with our story was that *nothing* in it was real. In real life birds *don't* attack people and girls don't buy lovebirds to schlepp sixty miles upstate for a practical joke."[23] I would disagree with Hunter, since the latter plot development would be very plausible in a screwball comedy. However, from the moment of the first attack on Melanie in Bodega Bay, a truly Coleridgean suspension of disbelief begins in earnest.[24]

In a crucial sequence that plays out in the Tides Restaurant, Hitchcock offers competing explanations for the "cause" of the bird attacks. A local ornithologist, Mrs. Bundy (Ethel Griffies), makes two principal arguments, indicating that she refuses to suspend disbelief. First, the size of a bird's brain pan is too small to permit the planning of a mass attack, and, second, birds do not engage in interspecies flocking. As a result, the attacks that Melanie and the others have described must *not* be happening. As a natural scientist, the ornithologist recognizes only empirical data; the precedent for the attacks by the crows and the gulls must simply not exist.

Moments later, the attacks become impossible to refute, as a filling station erupts in flames. Hitchcock suggests the source of the chaos with a famous point-of-view shot showing Bodega Bay in ruins as the birds circle overhead. Through film style – the careful selection of a high-angle and extreme long shot – Hitchcock offers the possibility that the birds are their own agents, exercising desire and bent on exacting revenge for the unspecified crimes of humanity. This seems plausible when one considers how the characters in *The Birds* do seem to have abused nature throughout the film: the *caged* lovebirds central to Melanie's flirtation, the lush fur coat in which she is attired, and the shouted orders for "three fried chicken!" that provides some of the sly humor and diegetic sound in the Tides Restaurant. But such a "revenge-of-the-birds" scenario is far from the only possibility, as other characters in the restaurant soon suggest.

As one of the diner's traumatized customers proposes, perhaps Melanie really *is* the sinister Romantic femme fatale: "They said that when you got here, the whole thing started. Who are you? What are you? Where did you come from? I think you're the cause of all this. I think you're evil – *evil*!" The speaker is a mother of two children who makes a suggestion that Hitchcock and screenwriter Hunter never directly refute, but this deduction, as any good rhetorician knows, ultimately rests on a post hoc fallacy: nothing directly links Melanie to the attacks by the birds other than her unfortunate and untimely arrival in Bodega Bay.

A more likely explanation for the events – only because it is even more difficult to refute – is offered by an unkempt (and too predictably Irish) drunkard who claims that "it's the end of the world!" According to this religious interpretation, the birds are agents, not for themselves but for a providential deity who is punishing mankind. Although Hitchcock places these words in the mouth of the town drunk (and thereby invites the audience's ridicule), the film's utter lack of closure suggests that, in the end, any of the three possible agents of the destruction – the birds, Melanie, or a divine force – remain a possibility.

The indeterminate chain of cause and effect in *The Birds* operates a bit differently from that in "Rime of the Ancient Mariner." Coleridge's narrative poem possesses a far more explicitly religious quality, given such obvious details as the narrative frame of the wedding feast and the substitution of the albatross for the cross around the mariner's neck. In addition, the mariner returns from his self-imposed world of supernatural horrors in part because he recognizes the beauty of (and also blesses) the "slimy" water snakes. But he also must make a penance in what we can refer to as the "empirical world." By wandering the earth, and recognizing certain souls (like the wedding guest) who *need* to hear his story, the mariner eases his "woful agony" by sharing his didactic imperative: "He prayeth well, who loveth well | Both man and bird and beast" (lines 645–6).

In "Rime of the Ancient Mariner," we have a tale involving a fall and redemption that clearly had profound significance for Coleridge, a writer who would later devote much of his intellectual efforts to exploring the nature of faith. In contrast, the world of *The Birds* is clearly more secular. The Judeo-Christian conception of the wrath of a vengeful God is only one of the many ways in which mankind attempts to explain the unexplainable. In *The Birds*, there is no obvious religious allegory, so the drunkard's religious explanation for the birds' attacks becomes simply another way to impose order and meaning on chaos. But, having said this, there is still an absolute insistence – in *both* "Rime of the Ancient Mariner" and *The Birds* – on a dreamlike world largely without the comforts of an orderly and rational chain of cause and effect.

The narrative frame of "Rime" – in which a wedding guest is detained in order to hear the dreamlike tale of the ancient mariner – is repeatedly interrupted so that the young man may express his fear at the most sensational aspects of what he is hearing. The power of Coleridge's most fantastical images – the storm blast, the polar spirits, the whorelike figure of "Life-in-Death" – derives, in part, from the frequent reminders that return us to the mundane world of the assembled guests, the feast, and the wedding itself. The wedding guest recognizes the disconnect between the image of the world his senses normally permit and the details of dead men piloting a ship and flashes of golden fire in the wake of a school of water snakes; the events in the mariner's tale simply cannot have happened, any more than a seagull attack can derail the children's game of blind man's bluff in *The Birds*. There is no empirical precedent for the ferocity of the birds, and the chain of cause and effect collapses, particularly since the principal objects of the birds' fury become the innocent children of the town, who are surely less culpable (albeit not completely innocent, as we shall see) in the crimes against nature.

This suspension of logic is a crucial governing principle for both Hitchcock and Coleridge. "Rime of the Ancient Mariner" is a poem in which, ultimately, the effect is never even remotely proportional to the cause, although Coleridge initially invites us to understand his poetic narrative in this way. In part I, the mariner's crew feeds the albatross and, as a consequence, "the Ice did split with a Thunderfit" (line 67). Later, when the mariner kills the bird of good omen, he is cursed. But when the fog lifts, in part II, the mariner's actions are praised, since the bird has obviously (to the crew, anyway) been responsible for bringing the fog and mist in the first place. So far, so good. But when the ultimate result of the mariner's cruelty becomes the death of his two hundred crew members in part III, Coleridge overturns cause-and-effect logic. To be sure, the mariner has indeed killed the albatross, an event that breeches the harmony between man and nature, but that killing – thoughtless as it is – hardly seems to justify nature's ferocity and the mariner's life sentence in exile from any human community. The mariner acquires a glittering eye from experiencing these truly fantastical events, while the wedding guest (as well as the reader) has a difficult time accepting "the facts" of the narrative since they are so far removed from the realm of empirical experience.

The eighteenth-century philosophical principle of associationism, one so familiar to Wordsworth and Coleridge, claimed that sensory experience was crucial to cognitive development, but the tale of the mariner exceeds what any rational person was likely to experience with his or her senses.[25] This is precisely Coleridge's point: the wedding guest must accept what he hears regardless of its feasibility. *The Birds* surprises us because of this very same quality of dreamlike absurdity. The crucial difference is that the mariner's story requires a leap of faith on the part of the wedding guest, the faith to accept the improbable, as well as of the larger religious faith that could guide behavior and prevent such disharmony in the future; this is the sort of natural discord in Hitchcock's world from which no escape seems possible. In contrast to "Rime of the Ancient Mariner," *The Birds* depicts a world so violent and illogical that faith and the potential for recognizing beauty in living things are illusions. The ugliness of Hitchcock's world is perhaps best encapsulated by one of Mitch's legal clients – a man who shoots his wife in the head six times simply for changing a television channel. This extreme example of the effect exceeding the cause is but one illustration of the thoughtlessness for which Melanie and the others seem to be paying such a high price. As Leitch suggests in his study of Hitchcock, "the disproportion between the relatively inconsequential behavior in the characters and the magnitude of the threat they face" confronts everyone who interprets *The Birds*.[26] As we have seen, the most popular strategy is to locate answers in the psychoanalytic terrain of the film, while others such as Leitch conclude that the absurdity is part of an extended joke. But to view the film as an elaborate gag is to neglect the film's didacticism, another aspect that connects the work to its distant early nineteenth-century Romantic cousins.

"Let Nature be Your Teacher" (Wordsworth, "The Tables Turned")

Even though Hitchcock eventually goes further in *The Birds* than Coleridge in his resistance to rationality, the audience nonetheless recognizes that a serious breach in the natural order has precipitated the birds' fury. The delicate balance between man and nature that is disturbed (but then restored) in "Rime of the Ancient Mariner" is irrevocably damaged in *The Birds*. As the film concludes, Melanie, like the Ancient Mariner, is too traumatized even to tell her story. Unlike the wedding guest, she may be neither sadder nor wiser; she may not even be conscious. And, even if she were to recover, what meaning could she hope to extract from her experience? As the morning dawns, the appearance of a rainbow could be (and has been) interpreted by viewers as a sign of hope; however, throughout the film, the time of day, the weather patterns, and any "signs" involving the elements are never causally connected to the bird attacks. Further, the cries of the birds, as well as their sheer domination of the landscape as Mitch and Melanie flee from Bodega Bay at the film's conclusion, suggest something more ominous is still to come. Unlike Coleridge's mariner, Melanie is offered no redemption. Whereas the mariner understands that his thoughtless slaying of the albatross initiated his personal nightmare and subsequent penance, Melanie's potential reform – her movement beyond the "thoughtlessness" of her earlier pranks involving smashed windows and naked plunges into Roman fountains – collides with a nightmare that will not relent.

Although Hitchcock's and Hunter's pessimism moves far beyond that of a Coleridgean religious parable involving a fall and redemption, other aspects of *The Birds* link it to early British Romanticism. In particular, both Hitchcock and the Romantics resemble moralists bent on interrogating the relationships between education, knowledge, and something potentially removed from either of these things: what the Romantics regarded as true *vision*.

The motif of the eye is terribly important in "Rime of the Ancient Mariner," as the mariner's eye glitters because he is able to mesmerize the wedding guest and because his experience helps him to see much more profoundly. Following his South Pole voyage, the mariner is able to see beyond the bounds of normal perception; he now has a form of vision that he describes in part VI as absent until the moment when his curse was finally expiated:

> And in its time the spell was snapt,
> And I could move my een [eyes]:
> I look'd far-forth, but little saw
> Of what might else be seen –
> (lines 447–50)

Not only does the mariner no longer see the horrific images of his dead crewmen piloting his ship, but he also no longer sees the natural world in the same way. More than anything, he sees natural beauty that he once took for granted, and "his eye is bright" because true vision implies moving beyond sensory perception to an awareness of the union among "man and bird and beast" (line 646).

The poem that best illustrates the distinction between the two kinds of vision – looking *and* seeing – is Wordsworth's most famous, "Lines Written a Few Miles above Tintern Abbey." The eye that takes *sensory* pleasure in the ruined abbey and its surroundings is the one Wordsworth describes with such brilliant alliteration: "Once again I see I These hedge-rows, hardly hedge-rows" (lines 15–16). But the eye that *really* sees is "the eye made quiet by the power I Of harmony, and the deep power of joy" (lines 48–9). By no accident does Wordsworth invoke "power" twice here; to paraphrase the poet, this sight is more sublime, and it enables him "to see into the life of things" (line 50).

In the words of Jerome McGann, the real landscape of "Tintern Abbey" becomes "the landscape which does not fill the eye of the mind with external and soulless images, but with 'forms of beauty' (line 25) through which we can ... penetrate the surface of a landscape to reach its indestructible heart and meaning."[27] One thing capable of clouding this ability to see beyond the surface – a failure of vision lamented so often in this first phase of Romanticism – is an education that is overreliant on empiricism and on knowledge contained in books.

Despite their many other creative differences, Coleridge and Wordsworth shared a common desire to cultivate this deeper understanding, and such an understanding had to be achieved outside traditional educational institutions. In his analysis of "The Ruined Cottage," McGann describes this essential component of Romantic ideology – the power that nature wields over any institution of human invention:

> Margaret's cottage is gradually overgrown and "ruined" when "Nature" invades its neglected precincts. This – the poem's dominant and most memorable process – finally comes to stand as an emblem of the endurance of nature's care and ceaseless governance, just as it glances obliquely at the pathetic incompetence of individual, cultural, and institutional efforts to give stability to human affairs.[28]

Only those wise enough to recognize the illusory nature of any attempt to contain those natural forces truly possess this Romantic vision. In "The Ruined Cottage," the essentially powerless institutions include Robert's faltering trade (he is a weaver), the army, and the English nation itself. However, of all the Romantic institutions most responsible for projecting a false image of order and stability, the one that Wordsworth and Coleridge most often critiqued was the traditional English school. When Wordsworth speaks in "Expostulation and Reply" of the eye "that cannot chuse but see" (line 17), William, the speaker, reminds his friend Matthew that the light of education transmitted through books is only one of the ways in which we learn. In a companion poem, William concludes his thoughts with some very familiar imagery:

> Enough of science and of art;
> Close up those barren leaves;
> Come forth, and bring with you a heart
> That watches and receives.
>
> (lines 29–32)

In one brief stanza, Wordsworth brings together two alternate forms of "leaves" (with his preference perfectly clear), as well as a heart that "watches," a practice clearly not encouraged in Wordsworth's own classrooms.

Such was clearly the frustration of Coleridge's education as well. In "Frost at Midnight," a poem that appeared slightly later than his and Wordsworth's collaboration, *Lyrical Ballads*, Coleridge provides a more complete statement on the opposition between that "eternal language" of nature and the stuffy schoolroom that suppresses so much imagination, pleasure, and true vision. Coleridge takes comfort in knowing that, in contrast to the London schoolroom of his youth (with its "stern preceptor"), his son will experience a very different form of education, conducted by that "Great universal Teacher!" who "shall mould | Thy spirit, and by giving make it ask" (lines 63–4).[29] Yet, based on what Coleridge describes in chapter 1 of the *Biographia Literaria*, there is much that Coleridge admired about his classical education: while "severe," his schoolmaster was also "sensible." But there were important limits to what Coleridge could learn in Christ's Hospital grammar school. The Rev. James Boyer could introduce him to Shakespeare and to the logic of poetic form, but his school quite literally separated him from the subject of his early poetry; his intellectual and moral development were enhanced in grammar school, but, in the cultivation of his spirit through nature, Coleridge was self-taught.[30]

The hostility to formal education is even more evident in *The Birds*. No viewer of the film can ever really explain why the birds seem to direct much of their rage against children, unless we correctly view them as products of the limits of their education. After all, at the film's conclusion, it is the young Cathy who insists that Mitch allow her to hold on to the caged lovebirds. Although Cathy protests that the birds "haven't harmed anyone," she persists in containing the natural world – most likely as a result of educational conditioning – despite the undeniable evidence that nature is in revolt.

The heretofore indeterminate chain of events achieves a bit of focus when one considers that one of the film's most violent attacks occurs on the grounds of the Bodega Bay school, so that the school, as much as the children, appears to be under siege.[31] This is a much-studied sequence of the film, primarily for documenting how Hitchcock uses editing to enhance suspense.[32] What deserves even more attention is how Hitchcock connects elements of the *mise-en-scène* and sound to the film's ideology.

As is often discussed, Hitchcock indeed creates suspense by showing the silent accumulation of the birds on the jungle gym behind Melanie Daniels, but he also cuts to the interior of Annie Hayward's classroom and layers the sounds emanating from that space over the entire sequence preceding the children's flight from the school. What we see and hear in these moments is crucial to the film's connection to early Romanticism: Annie has arranged the children into perfectly symmetrical rows, and they sing in perfect unison. The banality of all of this provides a counterpoint to the mayhem to come, but it also suggests the limits of imagination in the adult world of *The Birds*. The children's desks further provide a visual parallel to the equally orderly rows of bottles behind the bar in the Tides Restaurant, another conscious choice in the *mise-en-scène* that suggests humanity's futile attempt to impose order on the surrounding world.

The process of imposing order and reason begins in school, a place where knowledge flourishes but true imagination and vision are too rarely cultivated. When Melanie first meets the schoolteacher in the "first act" of the film (the short-lived screwball comedy), Annie speaks of her "compulsive tilling of the soil." Her gardening clothes create a stark contrast between her and Melanie (who is attired in her furs and Christian Dior). But, although Annie may be closer to the land than her society-girl counterpart, Hitchcock's costume choices merely offer us a red herring. Annie's educational practices, as well as the socialization the Bodega Bay School offers, are as much the enemy as any other institution in the town.

The failure of the school to impart any real knowledge seems confirmed as the children are led out of the school in a scene familiar to any of us who, long ago, participated in fire-drill "simulations" in which panic was to be replaced by orderly departure in groups of two. In the case of *The Birds*, however, the well-rehearsed exit merely serves to offer up the children as conspicuous targets for the vengeful crows.

Why *did* Annie escort them to their doom? Regardless of Annie's reasons, the film's argument about the failure of real vision is punctuated in a single shot. During the melee, one of Cathy's young friends falls to the ground as a bird clings to her back. Hitchcock cuts to a close-up of the shattered lens of her eyeglasses.

The Birds is a film (much like *Vertigo*) in which the eye is a crucial motif. In one of the film's recurrent in-jokes, one of the first lines the schoolteacher utters is "Oh, ... I see," in reference to Melanie's plans to deliver the lovebirds to the Brenner house. The phrase "I see" is repeated several times: when Lydia first learns about the lovebirds, again when Melanie informs Annie of her desire to stay for Cathy's birth-day party, and when Lydia speaks to farmer Dan Fawcett on the phone about his chickens. In the first half of the film, such repetition constitutes a joke, but the eye motif becomes less funny when Dan Fawcett's lifeless body recalls the eye-gouged Oedipus or when Mitch screams as the sparrows invade his home, "Cover your faces – *cover your eyes*!" Ultimately, there is no joke, only Hitchcock's grim insistence that those eyes have been covered for far too long.[33]

For the Romantics, the message was much the same. In "London," for example, Blake describes prenatal blindness as a symptom of a greater failure of vision: "the youthful Harlot's curse | Blasts the new-born Infant's tear" (lines 14–15), a scenario much like the one in *The Birds* in that the children pay the greatest price by inherit-ing their parents' and teachers' "mind-forg'd manacles."[34]

As I mentioned in my introduction, much has been made (and naturally so) of the tangled Oedipal complex at the heart of the Lydia/Mitch/Melanie triangle. But I would agree with Annie's assessment in the film that Lydia is less concerned with "losing Mitch" than psychoanalytic critics would permit. "With all due respect to Oedipus," claims Annie, Lydia is neither possessive nor jealous but merely afraid of "being abandoned."

Whereas Paglia sees Lydia as substituting her son for her dead husband[35] – and supports her claim with Hitchcock's own Freudian speculation[36] – Lydia also expresses a profound sense of loss. During her recovery from the trauma of seeing Dan Fawcett's eyeless corpse (yet another instance of the failure of vision), Lydia admits to Melanie that she regrets her husband's passing, in part because of his unique ability *to enter into the world of the children*. Here again Hitchcock is com-menting on the failure of adult imagination and expressing nostalgia for its loss, which appears irrecoverable. This notion is central to Coleridge's "Frost at Midnight," although the poem is much less pessimistic than *The Birds*. Coleridge contrasts his own early education, marked by "mine eye | Fixed with mock study on my swimming book," with a new program of study, in which "thou [his infant son] shalt learn far other lore" because the child will "see and hear | The lovely shapes and sounds intelligible | Of that eternal language" (lines 37–8, 50, 58–60).[37] Such a passage perfectly summarizes Coleridge's fascination with the connectedness of vision and education and nature, a concern Hitchcock shared 150 years later in a world also unable to maintain harmony between humans and nature because it was too often taken for granted.

Conclusion

The link between the "lowbrow" Hollywood filmmaker Hitchcock and his high-brow literary predecessors becomes even stronger when one peruses the recent memoir by Evan Hunter, the screenwriter of *The Birds*. In his book, Hunter discusses Hitchcock's desire for true artistic validation following his disappointment, despite five nominations, to win a single statuette for *Psycho* at the 1960 Academy Awards. " 'True respect' was the engine that propelled the making of *The Birds*."[38]

Although Hitchcock receives no official credit for the script, Hunter confirms Hitchcock's intimate involvement in the creation of the characters and film story, both of which are worlds apart from the Daphne du Maurier short story from which the screenplay was adapted. In place of du Maurier's protagonist, a Cornish farmer, Hitchcock recommended a main character who was, first, more glamorous and, second (and more importantly), a woman who could better serve the film's didacticism. In conversations with Hunter, Hitchcock saw his heroine as representing complacency: "[Hitchcock] said, 'I believe that people are too complacent. People like Melanie Daniels tend to behave without any kind of responsibility, and to ignore the more serious aspects of life. Such people are unaware of the catastrophe that surrounds us all.' "[39]

Hitchcock's dialogues with Hunter resulted in a Melanie Daniels-as-Ancient Mariner, a woman whose initial self-absorption and thoughtlessness come at a terrible price. Throughout Hunter's memoir, one never loses sight of the fact that Hitchcock and Hunter intended to produce a work of serious art; for example, Hunter proposed revisions of an early draft in which the ending was far more horrific than indeterminate. Hunter writes, "It's a little bit hard to be poetic when the roof of the automobile [carrying Mitch, Cathy, and Melanie] is slowly being shredded to bits by attacking birds."[40]

The last quotation returns us to where I began: Wood's notion of Hitchcock as poet. When surveying Hitchcock's complete oeuvre, the first tentative connections between Hitchcock and the early Romantic poets appear as early as *The 39 Steps* (1935). In an early scene in which Richard Hannay (Robert Donat) enters an apartment building, one of the names on the building's directory possesses particular resonance for Coleridge scholars – "Porlock" – a town name crucial to the history of "Kubla Khan." In recounting the vision that first inspired the poem, Coleridge famously also describes how his reverie was interrupted: "At this moment, [I] was unfortunately called out by a person on business from Porlock."[41]

Such intriguing allusions eventually give way to substantive connections in the mature works of the filmmaker. In the works of the Romantics, children – such as the younger version of the poet himself, whom Wordsworth recalls in "Tintern Abbey" – seem closer to that natural world and possess true vision that has not yet been clouded as has the vision of adults. When Wordsworth writes of "the coarser pleasures of my boyish days" and the "glad animal movements all gone by" (lines 74–5), there is an obvious sense of loss but also a sense that the natural world will continue to sustain the poet through memory and imagination. In Hitchcock's case, the expression of true vision – even among children such as Cathy Brenner – seems hopeless. What Hitchcock shares with Wordsworth and Coleridge is the belief that institutions such as schools can often create a gulf that divides us from the natural world. However, for the first-generation Romantics, the solution was expressed rather simply in the Coleridge poem "The Tables Turned":

> Books! 'tis a dull and endless strife,
> Come, hear the woodland linnet,
> How sweet his music; on my life
> There's more of wisdom in it.
>   (lines 9–12)

The poem's speaker advises his friend to "quit your books," the ones assigned in English schools, and simply take a lesson, quite literally, from the song of the linnet, a small finch indigenous to his home in the Lake District. By contrast, although Hitchcock is completely sympathetic to the ideology of the Romantics, the process of man's alienation from the natural world has advanced too far for any such "music" to provide solace. In *The Birds*, that singing linnet has become an avenger, one that preys on the eyes of children, no less – those ostensibly most sympathetic to the beauty of nature.

Notes

1. Robin Wood, *Hitchcock's Films Revisited* (New York: Columbia Univ. Press, 1989), 164.
2. Ibid.
3. Wood invokes the Romantics in his analysis of *Vertigo*. In contrast to the "cards-on-the-table reality of Midge," Madeleine represents a Keatsian "vision" or "waking dream." For Wood, *Vertigo* seems more closely connected to Keats's "Lamia" or "Ode to a Nightingale" than to the genre of the mystery thriller. Ibid., 114.
4. As one of my anonymous readers has suggested, another productive link might be made between Hitchcock and the German Romanticism of Ludwig Tieck and E. T. A. Hoffmann by means of the influence of German expressionist cinema.
5. A. O. Lovejoy, "On the Discrimination of Romanticisms," *PMLA*, vol. 39, no. 2 (1924): 229–53. For more on the further discrimination of the Romantics, see M. H. Abrams, *The Mirror and the Lamp* (Oxford: Oxford Univ. Press, 1953); Geoffrey Hartman, *The Unmediated Vision* (New Haven: Yale Univ. Press, 1954); and Jerome McGann, *The Romantic Ideology* (Chicago: University of Chicago Press, 1983).

6. Thomas Leitch, *Find the Director and Other Hitchcock Games* (Athens, GA: Univ. of Georgia Press, 1991), 225–31. Christopher Morris makes a case for at least one "modernist" preoccupation in *The Birds* (and one shared by postmodernists as well). Morris's argument is that "the problem of representation may always have been the film's proper subject" since "the film's major action consists of looking at birds and speculating as to their meaning." Because that meaning constantly shifts and ultimately eludes the viewer of *The Birds*, the chain of signification constantly breaks down, much as it does in the fiction of E. M. Forster, Virginia Woolf, James Joyce, and their many twentieth-century literary successors. Morris, "Reading the Birds and *The Birds*," *Literature Film Quarterly*, vol. 28, no. 4 (2000): 253–4. David Sterritt arrives at the same conclusion, suggesting, ultimately, that *The Birds* "is *about* the futility of language." Sterritt, *The Films of Alfred Hitchcock* (Cambridge: Cambridge Univ. Press, 1993), 142.

7. Margaret Horwitz, "*The Birds*: A Mother's Love," in Marshall Deutelbaum and Leland Poague, eds., *A Hitchcock Reader* (Ames: Iowa State Univ. Press, 1986), 279–87.

8. Slavoj Žižek, *Looking Awry: An Introduction to Jacques Lacan through Popular Culture* (Cambridge, MA: MIT Press, 1991), 97–106.

9. Robert Samuels, *Hitchcock's Bi-Textuality: Lacan, Feminisms, and Queer Theory* (Albany, NY: SUNY Press, 1998), 127–33.

10. Camille Paglia, *The Birds* (London: British Film Institute, 1998), 7.

11. Ibid., 34, 8.

12. For a more sustained discussion of Hitchcock as a "second-generation" British Romantic, see Richard Allen, "Hitchcock, or the Pleasures of Metaskepticism," in *Alfred Hitchcock: Centenary Essays* (London: British Film Institute, 1999), 229–33. Allen traces the masculine anxiety common in so many of Hitchcock's films to a particular Romantic precursor: John Keats's "The Eve of St. Agnes."

13. Penelope Houston, quoted in Robin Wood, "Why We Should Take Hitchcock Seriously," in Albert LaValley, ed., *Focus on Hitchcock* (Englewood Cliffs, NJ: Prentice-Hall, 1972), 74.

14. This and subsequent verse citations from *Lyrical Ballads* are from William Wordsworth and Samuel Taylor Coleridge, *Lyrical Ballads 1798*, 2d edn., ed. W. J. B. Owen (Oxford: Oxford Univ. Press, 1969).

15. John A. Calabrese, "Romanticism in Alfred Hitchcock's *Vertigo*: Conflicts and Dark Reversals," *Lamar Journal of the Humanities*, vol. 18, no. 2 (1992): 52.

16. See Wordsworth's enlarged "preface" to the 1800 edition of *Lyrical Ballads*, reprinted in *Lyrical Ballads 1798*, 158.

17. Wordsworth's phrase appears in the expanded preface to the 1800 edition of *Lyrical Ballads*. See Wordsworth and Coleridge, *Lyrical Ballads 1798*, 158.

18. Samuel Taylor Coleridge, *The Collected Works of Samuel Taylor Coleridge*, ed. Kathleen Coburn, vol. 7, pt. II (Princeton: Princeton Univ. Press, 1983), 6.

19. Sterritt, 121.

20. Evan Hunter, *Me and Hitch* (London: Faber and Faber, 1997), 17.

21. The problems with "controlling" nature occur almost immediately in *The Birds*, during Melanie's initial flirtatious repartee with Mitch, when she impersonates a clerk in the pet store and a handful of birds escape.

22. One of the most complete discussions of narration in the Hollywood cinema appears in David Bordwell, *Narration in the Fiction Film* (Madison: Univ. of Wisconsin Press, 1985).

23. Hunter, 31.

24. Lesley Brill discusses Hitchcock's recourse to implausible narratives as evidence of his debt to the Romance genre, in which "ordinary constraints of natural law are loosened." See Brill, *The Hitchcock Romance: Love and Irony in Hitchcock's Films* (Princeton: Princeton Univ. Press, 1988), 6.

25. In the "preface" to *Lyrical Ballads*, Wordsworth suggests that one of his goals is to illustrate the principle of associationism: "I have said that each of these poems has a purpose. I have also informed my reader what this purpose will be found principally to be: namely, to illustrate the manner in which our feelings and ideas are associated in a state of excitement." Like John Locke, Wordsworth was fascinated with the notion that differences in ideas seem linked to differences in sensory experience, thus subscribing to Locke's *tabula rasa* theory rather than to that of innate ideas. Wordsworth and Coleridge, *Lyrical Ballads 1798*, 158.

26. Leitch, 230.

27. McGann, *The Romantic Ideology*, 86.

28. Ibid., 83.

29. Coleridge, vol. 16, pt. I, p. 456.

30. Coleridge recounts the details of his early education in chapter 1 of the *Biographia Literaria*. See Coleridge, vol. 7, pt. I, pp. 8–13.

31. Not all critics view the children as "under siege" in this sequence. Richard Allen argues for a parallel between the attacking birds and the children, suggesting that Hitchcock reinforces this analogy by placing both the children and the birds on the same playground equipment and matching the rhythmic sounds of the birds' wings with the children's stamping feet and the birds' screeches with the children's screams. See Allen, "Avian Metaphor in *The Birds*," in Sidney Gottlieb and Christopher Brookhouse, eds., *Framing Hitchcock: Selected Essays from the "Hitchcock Annual,"* (Detroit: Wayne State Univ. Press, 2002), 293–4.

32. For Hitchcock's own comments on his editing style in this sequence (as well as reproductions of his storyboards), see François Truffaut, *Hitchcock*, rev. edn. (New York: Simon and Schuster, 1985), 292–93.

33. Susan Smith discusses the bantering use of "I see" as part and parcel of the film's larger epistemological concerns: the interconnectedness among seeing, knowing, and feeling. Although Smith's argument is often persuasive, the suggestion that the bird attacks provide "the basis for more authentic forms of understanding to emerge" is perhaps a bit optimistic within the world of the film. Perhaps such understanding can be enhanced among Hitchcock's viewers, but little evidence in the film suggests that the characters themselves move from "seeing" to "understanding." See Smith, *Hitchcock: Suspense, Humour, and Tone* (London: British Film Institute, 2000), 125–31.

34. William Blake, *William Blake: The Oxford Authors*, ed. Michael Mason (Oxford: Oxford Univ. Press, 1988), 275.

35. Paglia, 47.

36. In an interview with director Peter Bogdanovich, Hitchcock describes Lydia as "substituting her son for her husband." See Bogdanovich, *The Cinema of Alfred Hitchcock* (Garden City, NY: Doubleday, 1963), 44.

37. *The Collected Works of Samuel Taylor Coleridge*, vol. 16, pt. I, 455–6.

38. Hunter, 16.

39. Ibid., 24.

40. Ibid., 61.

41. *The Norton Anthology of English Literature*, 7th edn., ed. M. H. Abrams (New York: Norton, 2000), vol. 2, p. 439.

THE BIRDS (Universal, 1963). *Producer*: Alfred Hitchcock, *Assistant Director*: James H. Brown, *Script*: Evan Hunter, from the novella by Daphne du Maurier, *Photography*: Robert Burks (Technicolor), *Special Photographic Effects*: Lawrence A. Hampton, Ub Iwerks, *Editor*: George Tomasini, *Sets*: Robert Boyle, George Milo, *Electronic Sound Score*: Bernard Herrmann (consultant), Remi Gassman, Oskar Sala, *Costumes*: Edith Head, Rita Riggs, *Players*: Tippi Hedren (Melanie Daniels), Rod Taylor (Mitch Brenner), Jessica Tandy (Mrs. Brenner), Suzanne Pleshette (Annie Hayworth), Veronica Cartwright (Cathy Brenner), Ethel Griffies (Mrs. Bundy), Charles McGraw (Sebastian). 120 minutes.

Chapter Twenty-One
Mark's *Marnie*
Michele Piso

It's no accident: women take after birds and robbers just as robbers take after women and birds.... What woman hasn't flown/stolen? Who hasn't felt, dreamt, performed the gesture that jams sociality? Who hasn't crumbled, held up to ridicule, the bar of separation? Who hasn't inscribed with her body the differential, punctured the system of couples and opposition? Who, by some act of transgression, hasn't overthrown ...? (Cixous)

The flesh is sad, alas! and I have read all the books. (Mallarmé)

Marnie's reception in 1964 is notable for the popular press's smug disdain of a film now highly regarded by both journalists and academic film theorists. *Time* magazine dismissed *Marnie* as a straightforward case history of a frigid kleptomaniac. Andrew Sarris pronounced it "a failure by any standard except the most esoteric," and, in a strikingly contradictory sentence, described Mark Rutland as both a rapist and a patient husband.[1] Critics found the sets distracting and phoney; the dialogue banal; the plot congealed more than it thickened. The film-critical events leading to *Marnie*'s current revaluation as a masterpiece of modern cinema have come about in three stages.

The first interpretative system to illuminate Hitchcock's work was the French auteur approach pioneered in the 1950s by Eric Rohmer and Claude Chabrol.[2] Behind Hitchcock's Hollywood thrillers they perceived graver themes of sin, guilt, and redemption through confession. Heavily influenced by the auteur method, Robin Wood's later analysis of *Marnie* adopted traditional psychoanalytic concepts in search of the cause of the heroine's disorder and the steps necessary to her cure. In Wood's view the film's world is both bewildering and imperfect, yet in the individual couple a true psychological order and unity may be defined and achieved through the recovery of an unremembered past.[3] A decade later, the more radical social and psychological movement inspired by Louis Althusser and Jacques Lacan challenged the humanism of both auteurist models. This third phase of film interpretation, as practiced, for example, by Raymond Bellour and Laura Mulvey, foregrounds the material production and consumption of film, criticizes the objectification and fetishizing of the female image, and interrogates the filmic text as a bearer of ideology.[4] Their investigations into the complex ways in which film meaning is socially structured replace the metaphysical interpretations of a film's meaning typical of Chabrol, Rohmer, and Wood. More importantly for our purposes here, recent psychoanalytic theory attends to film narrative as an enactment of the Lacanian version of the Oedipal structure, a tangle of desire, sexual differentiation, and identification: the "family romance."

My primary purpose here is to observe the distance between "therapeutic" and feminist rereadings of *Marnie*. But I will question as well the rapport between feminism and Lacanian theories of film meaning that reduce the film to fixed structures of voyeurism, fetishism, and the repetition of a childhood trauma. To perceive Marnie's marriage to Mark as a cure, in my view, is to deny the social misery in the bleak street and cast-off mother imaged at the film's end. It is to accept a melancholic and merely subjective discovery as the salvation of modern life. Further, to endorse as a fuller, more progressive reading of *Marnie* a voyeuristic relation between film and spectator, or to confine its many riches to the mechanics of the Oedipal plot, deprives the viewer of the film's awareness of another fundamental antagonism. Following Marx, therefore, I shall privilege as the film's central tension and particular pathos the class antagonism between Mark and Marnie, with her mother standing not only for a purely private and hideous past but also as the twisted embodiment of social repression and sexual exploitation.[5]

An adequate description of *Marnie* as a nightmare of social exploitation and violation requires a distinction between commodity exchange and gift exchange. Where capital relations generally insist upon division within the labor forces and the further separation of the worker from his or her product, gift relations encourage an imparting of the giving spirit to the thing given and the establishing of communion among segmented parts of society. Drawing upon Marcel Mauss's gift theory, Lewis Hyde describes how commodity exchange stifles any except the most impersonal and objective contact, while gift exchange draws donor and recipient into a feeling bond. Cold to the touch, the purely economic transaction maintains vertical relations of power and privilege. The gift, however, "moves" in circular relations of community, affection, mystery, leaving a "series of interconnected relationships in its wake, a kind of decentralized cohesiveness."[6] In Hyde's view, then, the gift inhibits the threat of domination and inspires social and erotic acts of the imagination: feasts, dances, entertainment, art, and love. French feminist Hélène Cixous would call these "exchanges that multiply," in the sense that they multiply and incorporate human desires and differences as opposed to "hierarchizing exchange" that involves a "struggle for mastery."[7] If the reciprocal social gift holds us to the familiar and conventional, to the beauty of a world held in common, its more heightened form as an artistic or erotic gift bears us away toward the visionary and unexpected. A social gesture calls forth our similarities, while the more intimate gift – a keepsake of some sort – touches in us what is unique; yet both bind us to others. In Hitchcock's films, however, love is suspect and locked within a house set apart from any neighborhood – there are no meals, no parties, no offerings of wine that are not preludes to death.

Personal gifts are contaminated too. "Money answereth all things," mocks Marnie, giving her mother a mink scarf. With a barb, she acknowledges the spread of money and pierces the spiritual generosity of the gift.

Organized around the sexual combat of Mark and Marnie and the familial strife between Marnie and her mother, the film's most general and unresolved social contradiction turns, not surprisingly, around love and money, giving and acquisition. It is precisely this antagonism between the sensual world and the business world that runs through *Marnie*: the world of capital dominates and chills the erotic and creative aspects of life. The real abjection in *Marnie* lies in the blank streets and fast-food restaurants, the alienation from nature, and the replacement of communal spontaneity with the rational corporate hierarchy depicted by Strutt, Ward, and, more suavely, Mark. Think for a moment of the great crowds and collectives of Renoir, whose members gaily redistribute or wreck the wealth and property of the bourgeoisie. Imagine the circles of Fellini, widening to gather whores and intellectuals, producers and pimps. But in Hitchcock, where personal neurosis stands for a more pervasive social ill, multiplicity scatters into an edgy solitude. The group splinters into isolated individuals: Uncle Charlie, Marion Crane, and Norman Bates, saddest of all. The social rituals that create and continue relations between individuals and groups, in whose light a stranger's features flare into a familiarity and collective rapport, burn out in a breach of faith. In *Psycho*, Norman offers bread to Marion and later stabs her to death; in *Shadow of a Doubt*, Uncle Charlie's keepsake to his niece is the emerald ring of his murdered victim; in *Marnie*, marriage is an abduction consummated in rape. Covenants, vows, and promises are reciprocal exchanges that should weave individuals and differences into nets of social and spiritual accord. Yet in the world of *Marnie* community has already broken down into hierarchies fixed in opposition: family/business; men/women; higher class/underclass; north/south; bosses/workers; daughter/mother. Lacking the communal participation that helps dissolve these divisions, *Marnie*'s characters exist unnaturally as separate entities, antagonistic monads. The convergence of differences that could result in a shared public world occurs instead as private collisions, acts of violation, and invasion. In Marnie's case, the invasion is robbery; in Mark's, the violation is rape.

From a Marxist perspective, then, Marnie's frigidity can be read as a metaphor of an oppressed class and as a reflection of the desensualized and rational sphere of business. Anthropologist Mary Douglas describes the body/society relation in similar terms:

> The human body is always treated as an image of society.... [T]here can be no natural way of considering the body that does not involve at the same time a social dimension. Interest in its apertures depends on the preoccupations with social exits and entrances, escape routes and invasions. If there is no concern to preserve social boundaries, I would not expect to find concern with bodily boundaries. The relation of head to feet, of brain and sexual organs, of mouth and anus are commonly treated so that they express the relevant patterns of hierarchy.... [B]odily control is an expression of social control.[8]

Marnie suggests the negative power of private interest penetrating and emptying itself into a woman, invading gestures that – privatized, isolated – are at the same time a struggle against that isolation. Marnie's mother also represents a victimized world – as mother, as prostitute, as underclass. In the struggle between Mark and Marnie, hers is the body to be won or lost, and we must ask ourselves why we think it healthy that Marnie abandon her. Viewed within the context offered by Douglas, *Marnie*'s characters and images not merely depict the psychological problems of individual characters but evoke as well the conditions of the larger organization of society – an ebbing-away of ceremonial culture, the dissolution of vital collective bonds, the isolation of individual action. These are the modern horrors constituting the social vision embedded below the surface of *Marnie*. By grasping the indirect ways its messages are located in the subtext of the film, we can better understand the plight of Marnie and her mother and what it reveals to us of larger patterns of American culture.

Marnie's most consequential act of degraded reciprocity is the mother's first sexual union. Unlike Marnie's trauma, this key episode occurs off-screen and thus makes more complex and elusive the origin of *Marnie*'s pain. At fifteen, Marnie's mother accepts a sweater for her virginity ("He asked me, would I let him?"); deserting her even before the child's birth, the boy violates their union. In a single act, the bartering of virginity for a commodity unites defloration, prostitution, and conception. Yet, in pregnancy, the victimized womb of the virgin/mother/prostitute reflowers and bears Margaret, whose name derives from the Greek and Latin words for flower and pearl. Later in the film we will learn that the mother still has the sweater, as if it were a keepsake, a token of her inner wish to transform degradation and abandonment into a memory of love. With her imagination, the prostitute attempts to turn a different kind of trick – the trade of her body into a gift of love: "Do you want to know how I got you, Marnie? There was this boy, Billy...." With these words, she begins the recitation of her own lonely and impoverished past. The sweater, together with all other gifts in *Marnie* – the mink scarf; the marital ring; the stone animals of the former wife; Forio, the horse that Mark restores to his new wife – all are symbols passed back and forth between one body and another in the hope of an emotional union. Nevertheless, all gifts fall short of their fullest expression in love. They function instead as bribes or swindles and poison the erotic flow. Distortion of life's emotional dimension is implicit in Mark's marriage for money and the mother's sale of her body to get it. The flow of giving and taking implied in Hyde's description of erotic exchange degenerates in *Marnie* to social transgression: Marnie's theft, Mark's marital blackmail, the mother's prostitution.

* * *

Following *Psycho* (1960) and *The Birds* (1963), *Marnie* completes Hitchcock's trilogy of modern despair. Yielding one of America's most rigorously beautiful studies of communal alienation and lost rapport, *Marnie*'s thematic conflicts between reciprocity and exploitation, vulnerability and violation, unfold in a deliberately stiff and rigid *mise-en-scène*. The mortality of the body itself – suggested by Marnie's rape and attempted suicide, the deaths of Forio and the sailor, the mother's injured leg – differs sharply from the stark invulnerability of train stations and offices, their metallic architecture restricted to a design of horizontals and verticals and to colors in primary hues plus white. There are no rounded or soft forms to connote fruitfulness nor tender colors to evoke warmth and calm. The denaturalized purism of style, all fortuitous and distracting elements eliminated, recalls the geometrics of Mondrian, the cropped chasteness of Bresson, the angularity of Antonioni's techno-world. The image is cold, silent, intense; its restricted framing creates an abstract and disorienting relation to the body, as in the early fragmenting shots of Marnie's hands and legs in the hotel and train station. *Marnie* opens with the credits turning as pages of a text, each curling page removing us from reality and preparing us for a narrative. Throughout, *Marnie*'s visual composition is extremely controlled, its formal stylization heightened by the glaringly artificial rear projections of the horse rides and the exaggerated, painterly sets of the Edgar neighborhood and Rutland office. These distortions of outside space are not careless flaws, as lamented by Donald Spoto in *The Dark Side of Genius*.[9] Rather, they are defiantly airless inventions that underscore and condemn the unnatural quality of the film's depicted world. Thus at the end of the Baltimore street, enfolded in silver clouds, lies a false harbor, a painted ship upon a painted ocean. Just as shallow is the façade of the Rutland Company, the harsh jagged lines of its parking lot suggesting the slashes of lightning linked to the storm and the sailor. These outside places associated with the mother's client and Marnie's employer are hollow fabrications propped up under an unreal shell of sky.

Equally claustrophobic are the interior spaces that function less as havens than as torture chambers. Absent are those happy spaces, those dwellings and shelters that can inspire daily chat or nocturnal intimacy. *Marnie*'s domestic spaces are rather marred by violence and transgression: the bedroom where Marnie has nightmares, the deep-freeze kitchen where she is slapped by her mother, the living room where the child-Marnie murders the sailor, the boat bedroom where Mark momentarily covers Marnie's nakedness and then rapes her. Marnie's mother's home has a depressed, banal atmosphere; Mark's mansion is materially bloated, emotionally empty, the site of the father's inertia and Lil's frustrated desire. The aristocratic "home" is a showcase, a display, a façade, a training ground: "This is a drill, dear. Wife follows husband to door, gives and/or gets a kiss, stands pensively as he drives away. A wistful little wave is optional." In Preston Sturges, the absurdity in turning marital intimacy into a martial drill could be funny. In Hitchcock, Marnie's darkly witty reply, "Mark, I, um, I don't have any money," cynically replaces the erotic with the economic and exposes the love union of marriage as a business affair. *Marnie* is built around the similarities and differences between these uncomfortable and unhappy homes; in each, one parent is missing and one child is an outsider, rivalrous for the attention of the surrogate mother or father, as are Jessie and Lil.

Of Hitchcock's work, *Marnie* may be the most unusually severe, its social implications the most bleak. Gone are the quirky minor characters and little bits of goofiness that lighten the earlier films. The shallow surface of the image evokes the impersonality of an advertisement, the cool pragmatism of the business world, and a visual impassivity that suggests daily physical and emotional repression. The peculiarly austere style heightens the image of the body in whose visibility and mortality, its desires so confused and constrained, Hitchcock ultimately places his tenderness. The colder and blanker the world of buildings and nature, the more desolate and unprotected the flesh, its loneliness increased by the dead silence of earth and space. Marnie's cry, "Help me. Oh God, please, somebody help me," wells up from a woman's body, so easily hurt, torn, betrayed. The sense of humiliating exposure is expressed in the "honeymoon" scene. Mark strips Marnie and then shields her nakedness with his robe, as if this covering, like the boy's sweater and the jacket that Mark will finally give to Marnie in the rain, were the male body's promise of protection. Yet Mark's is the gift that takes. Raping her, he breaks all promises.

The modern-day trap of visibility has been commented upon widely, most acutely by Michel Foucault and Jean-Paul Sartre. In *Marnie* the contemporary body is controlled by the totally administered sphere of the Rutland Publishing Company, a symbol of the twentieth-century workplace's estrangement of self and others and the reduction of reciprocal relations to commodity exchange. The Rutland Company is Foucault's "space of exact legibility," an "enclosed, segmented space, observed at every point, in which the individuals are inserted in a fixed place, in which the slightest movements are supervised, in which all events are recorded, in which power is exercised without division ... in which each individual is constantly located, examined and distributed among the living beings."[10] At the racetrack, the office, and the Rutland home, Hitchcock combines planar lighting and the alert gaze of the lens to achieve the visual equivalent of Bentham's panopticon plan of "power through transparency" and "subjugation by illumination." Intended for a more general social application, Bentham's architectural plan for prisons arranged living quarters around a tower from which each prisoner could be watched without knowing when or by whom. As described by Foucault, the primary modern technique of force is an institutional "visibility organized entirely around a dominating overseeing gaze ... which exists to serve a rigorous, meticulous power."[11] Similarly, almost anywhere she is, Marnie's physical and psychological independence is limited by a modern fluorescence that exposes every move. Conspiring with this hostile clarity in a subtle transference of secrecy to visibility, the camera turns from Marnie eyeing the safe to Mark observing Marnie from behind a glass partition. According to Foucault, the anxiety of being observed can be stimulated by anyone; "it doesn't matter who exercises power ... or what motive animates him" (*Discipline and Punish*, p. 202). So Lil spies from a window, a stranger spies at the racetrack, Mark stares from a corner, Hitchcock watches in the corridor. The woman who would prefer to turn her body inward and hide from the air itself (covering her legs, sneers Strutt, "as if they were a national treasure") is the most exposed, "pinned by a look," in Sartre's words, "a butterfly fixed to a cork."[12] In the film's opening shot of Marnie's receding back (Sartre's "blind mass" possessed by everyone before it belongs to the woman), the fixed camera stresses detachment between viewer and Marnie, aligning the viewer's gaze with the "rigorous, meticulous" eye of power, seeing but unseen. In this manner the conventional inscription of a woman's unseen face as enigma is challenged by Hitchcock's knowing eye; the camera follows Marnie, observes her routines, appropriates her smugness. Indeed, *Marnie* is a struggle between absolute surveillance and a woman's camouflage and subterfuge. When Strutt barks "Robbed!," the film's first spoken word, we hear the shout of a blinded eye, a man deceived. Mark's father may think that Marnie will merely bring "a little pizazz" to the farm, but her deeper function is to disorder, to make less perfect the operations of money and power.

The shock of transgression and rupture, of degraded and violent reciprocity, is conveyed through visual and verbal metaphors. By intensifying boundary images that segment space into public and private, familiar and foreign, legal and illegal, social and psychological, the threat of invasion is made more sinister. Theft, staring, interrogation, eavesdropping, rape: all suggest hostile penetration of the hidden and covert. *Marnie* is an intricate design of barriers and enclosures, stressing a theme of secrecy: the threshold of the screen where we watch as Marnie recedes along the cautionary yellow line; the sharp narrowness of the mother's street and stair; the hotel corridor where Hitchcock makes his appearance, catching us watching him watching Marnie; the mother's closed bedroom door; the window mysteriously tapped; the office window and cabinet violently smashed; the safes broken into, hurdles not crossed, silences kept, dreams, a veil of hair; the pecans that spill to the floor, something sweet protected by a hard shell to be broken only by a hard tool, like the fire poker that breaks the sailor's body. Each of these boundaries articulates, traces, invokes the most profound barrier of all, the hymenal membrane enclosed within Marnie and broken by Mark.

* * *

There is an odd moment in *Marnie*, during the first car ride and after the branch has destroyed his dead wife's pre-Columbian art collection, when Mark explains that the storm has not destroyed all that he had left of his wife. Rather, the art collection was all that he had left "that had belonged to my wife." The distinction Mark makes between what had "belonged" to his wife and what he had "left" of her deepens him. Its disclosure stresses a difference between the material and the spiritual, between encased animals of carved stone and the memory of the invisible (abandoned?) woman enclosed within him. If Marnie has nothing, the wife had almost everything, except perhaps love. Why else would she have died of "heart disease," an heiress and collector of precious objects, whose money has kept the Rutland family business afloat? The repressed guilt Mark feels for this bit of familial whoring surfaces as ennui. Mark's material monotony, a dissatisfaction with rank and money, is the source of his attraction to Marnie. Shattering the stone animal and saying "We've all got to go sometime," Mark destroys part of his legacy of hypocrisy and privilege and takes his place with a criminal. He is to do this again, with greater risk, at the "bash," the reception to honor their wedding. To protect Marnie that evening, Mark drops the illicit suggestion before Lil and the Strutts that he and Marnie had known each other during his first marriage. With a destructive social gesture, he cuts his moorings to convention and begins his unruly adventure.

Marnie revolves around the contradictory notion of "belonging" as a matter of possession or domination on the one hand and belonging as a flow of giving and taking, of affinity with a place or a beloved, on the other. The word "belonging" is uttered again when Lil, watching the couple depart after their wedding, tells the money-minded Cousin Bob that Mark spent $42,000 ("plus tax") on a diamond so that Marnie could have "something that had never belonged to anyone else." Finally, Mrs. Edgar, never married, always bought, implies the theme of belonging when she confesses that before she gave birth to Marnie she never had anything of her own. To belong to, or to be loved; to be in possession of, or to give; to gather a thing to oneself and hoard it, or to open and empty oneself in the fullness of love – these are *Marnie*'s opposing values. The film's crucial moments of birth, marriage, and death press possession and love together in confusion. The emotion possible in each instance is either the stasis of property, like the objets d'art impoverished behind glass, thus deprived of their original mystery, inert and mute, or the pouring forth of feeling that both gathers and liberates.

"To possess is to give," wrote Malinowski. Smashing the useless objects or transforming his capital into the marital ring, Mark, like the Haida Indian tribe described by Hyde, is "killing his wealth" (p. 9). The "furtive little wedding," then, is Mark's freest moment, a flight from the hoarding tribe of Cousin Bob, Ward, and Strutt, a release from his role as client in a market that has no imagination for love. "The man is deranged," snorts the sexless cousin, and indeed Mark is, if, after marrying for money and devoting years to acquiring more of it, he suddenly spends it in a fit of love. "What would mother say?" Cousin Bob huffs, implying that Mark is to be as frugal about money as Marnie is to be decent about sex; his cold hard cash and her body are equally frigid, locked up. Neither is to be circulated outside of an elaborate set of governing social and economic conventions. The falseness of money, its utter uselessness in providing happiness, is the secret of the cousin's social reality; it is what makes that world a rigid and unlyrical place. It chills Marnie and stunts Mark's ability to conceive of the ring as more than a right to power and rape, of marriage not as integration but as domination. *Marnie* is as much about a man's inability to free himself from the constraining ideology of his wealth, from the authority and certainty it confers, as it is about a woman's refusal to submit to that ideology.

Mark's first wife was an heiress; the second, a thief. The first gave him the property that the second one steals. Enclosed in the glass cage of the Rutland office, Mark is trapped within what Joan Landes calls "the inherent tension in the bourgeois love match between the demands of the heart and the considerations of property."[13] Mark's marriage of convenience, to save the family business, is an act of prostitution not unlike Marnie's mother's prostitution to save her child from poverty and state intervention. The difference, of course, is that Mark's property identifies him with civil law, while the illegitimate professions of mother and daughter place them at its farthest remove.

That Mark can be tender and arch is evident and attractive. His youth "blighted, dragged down by money, ambition, noblesse oblige," then bored by his corporate interests, a boredom only briefly relieved by his Third World zoology jaunts, Mark's restlessness reflects his desire to escape the bourgeois world. But he is too hemmed in by an arrogant assumption of knowledge, and this assumption, insofar as it is unrecognized and unchanged, is his flaw. Where Marnie has the slyness of an insurgent, Mark merely lacks scruples – as evidenced by his first marriage and his ruthless rebuilding of the Rutland Company. Marnie is the danger zone that Mark enters for a spell, attracted by her parody of the diligent worker ("I want work, Mr. Ward, good, hard, work"), by her mockery of a system that would subject her as it has subjected every other woman in the film, from the secretaries waiting to be called by their boyfriends ("oh, this is the best one you've had"), to the economically dependent Lil, to the waitresses at the roadside restaurant, to the patch-sweatered cleaning woman scrubbing the boss's floor while Marnie, cleverly paralleled in the same frame, cracks the boss's safe. (In the film's trailer, a shot of Marnie breaking into Mark's safe is accompanied by Hitchcock's wry off-screen comment: "Here's Marnie going about her business like any normal girl: happy, happy, happy.") *Marnie* keenly observes a woman's humiliation at job hunting, at having to put out for a job, but to play at being decent. Witness Marnie's rare and wonderful smiles, the calculation and great lies at the interview. With her own private secret, Marnie turns the profession of secretary on its head. Mark wants the outlaw, the criminal, the woman who can jam sociality and ridicule the routine of tea and classy talk, whose glance can foil the snobbery of a spontaneously sprained wrist. He admires the woman who, when asked how she will spend her married days, responds with disdain, "I thought I'd be a society hostess"; the woman who with her wit pierces society's pretensions as well as its safes. He loves her because, tumbling combinations, she dares to challenge the codes, to mimic them in her voice, her dress, her good manners, because perhaps she can smash the glass that surrounds his emotional and sexual desire and free him from the rut that is his life. Unfortunately for Mark, however, he is not Godard's perfect hero, always ready to flee the infinite net of the bourgeoisie. The net is of his own weaving, and with it he captures Marnie. Instead of stealing his property, she becomes it.

Marriage, then, as acquisition. Listen to Sartre on Genet: "The man rarely wishes to seduce by his physical qualities. He has received them, not made them. He makes his woman love him for his power, his courage, his pride, his aggressiveness, in short he makes her desire him as a faceless force, a pure power to do and take" (p. 80). For Mark, marriage is not a reciprocal act transcending the contractual "standpoint from which man and wife are deemed to have property in each other, especially in one another's sexual faculties" (Landes, 129). Elsewhere in *Saint Genet*, Sartre tells us that a man's way of making love reflects his economic situation. What then will Marnie have to look forward to, kidnapped by Mark, coerced, raped, broken at the end of the film, unequal to his stallion powers, as was the wife whose heart failed? ("I'm still a little hoarse today, Mama," whispers Marnie, covering the rape with a cough, and identifying herself with Forio, the beloved animal she will later kill, relieving his misery, reliving her own.) Mark's control is everywhere visible, in his secretaries, in the incompetent subordinate Ward, in the business bearing his name, a name emblazoned on the safe and the black worker's uniform and, presumably, upon the books published by his company. The Rutland family name is a remarkable condensation of trade (a trade name known in the nineteenth century for its roan leather bindings) and periodic sexual excitement, of property and pleasure, money and sex, power and phallus. Mark's unquestioned view of himself as owner and as a man of property leads to the heinous rape. So accustomed is he to owning, so synonymous is his sexuality with social power, that he assumes he can possess Marnie too, violate her, break her down, and then build her back up (in his image, his language, in the image of the "normal" female) in much the same way that he rebuilt the Rutland business. In the most literal and terrible way, Marnie is Mark's.

Because Mark views himself as "criminally and morally responsible" for Marnie, his morality is, finally, inseparable from the ethics of the state. Just as his authority is rooted in the Rutland property, his property is bounded by bourgeois law, a civil preserve from which neither Marnie nor Mark can escape. In the beginning of *Marnie*, Mark makes his first appearance directly on the heels of the police investigating Marnie's robbery of Strutt. His attitude is ironic, detached. At the end of the film he becomes the Law: when the police hear what Mark has to tell them, Marnie will not be arrested. Hitchcock's *Marnie* is about the encounter between Mark, whose name means money and implies the tracing of boundaries, observation and inscription, and Marnie, whose name plays on a virginal Mary and a sexual Mark and also suggests to mar, to damage, to go astray. Mark rapes, Marnie steals; the film's title links and locates both Mar/k and Mar/nie in transgression. Yet, at the film's close, he embodies legal authority, while Marnie loses all autonomy.

Mark's space is full of people and possessions and fixed in place, property, and address; Marnie's is hidden, hymenal, and fluid, like blood, like the water of the port at the edge of her town, the rain of the murder night. Moving from one city to another (mimicking the sailor?), Marnie travels through a no-man's land, without dwelling or love. This lack of place encompasses all of America, its lonely geography characterized by hotels and roadside Howard Johnsons where, recalling Marion Crane, Marnie does not eat. Placelessness is crucial to *Marnie*, identifying woman as wanderer, the one who, crossing borders and thresholds, merely expands a territory of desolation. To be without place is to be without identity; Marnie has had several, none sufficient.

* * *

Genet wrote of the criminal: "I shall so bedeck him with flowers that, as he disappears beneath them, he will himself become a flower, a gigantic and new one."[14] Marnie is the Genet figure in reverse; the unbroken hymen, a symbol of alienation and unhappiness rather than criminal frigidity, is hidden by a thief from a world that renders nearly everything visible. "To escape the eyes of hungry birds," Mark tells Marnie during their honeymoon, "insects disappear in the illusion of a beautiful flower." Escaping within so many aliases, the virgin disappears in the persona of a thief. "Are you called Margaret?" asks Mark, his English accent turning "called" into "cold": "Are you cold, Margaret?" Mark had asked earlier. Margaret, from the Greek *margarites*, means pearl, precious gem; from the Italian *margherita*, it means flower, the pearl-flower that is her sex, unbroken, ungiven, buried within the thief.

At the center of *Marnie* is the virginal hymen, "tainted with vice," says Mallarmé, "yet sacred, between desire and fulfillment."[15] Alluding to Simone de Beauvoir's discussion of adolescent female sexuality, Sartre described the virgin's resistance:

> Girls often force themselves to touch repulsive insects and sometimes put them to their mouths.... We know the reason for these exercises. Out of a mixture of hatred, curiosity

> and defiance, these adolescents are making an effort to perform symbolically and
> through their own initiative the act of deflowering, the obscure presentiment of which
> is sufficient to fill them with horror and which they know will be imposed upon them....
> Since they are unable to escape the future in store for them, all they can do is refuse to
> *undergo* it. Sentenced to death, they demand the right to give the order to fire that will
> kill them. (p. 57)

The shot that kills the beloved Forio appeases the death of the sailor and jars Marnie's
memory of the murder's unleashed violence. "There, there, now," she murmurs,
repeating the words that bind the deaths, her love for Forio purifying the contamina-
tion of the murder. Contrasting with the fox hunt's hypocritical display of killing as
recreation, the death of Forio is both an atonement for murder and a surrender to
marriage. Forio has a direct relationship to Marnie's sexuality, and the violence of
his death on the Rutland property is linked to the violence of her abduction and
rape. The divergent meanings of the scene stem from Marnie's as yet unconscious
desire to clear up the past, made more apparent later when she can no longer steal,
and her dismal realization of her entry into the permanent enclosure of the Rutland
world. That this territory is bounded and closed off, that there are thresholds here
that she cannot cross, is made perfectly clear by the stone wall, the guarded doorway, and the lack of compassion in the tenant from whom Marnie demands the gun.
Shocked by the cruelty of the sport, she has fled the upper-class hunt but cannot
clear the stone wall of the Rutland property upon which Forio is fatally harmed.

We know that Marnie can jump hurdles; she has done it before with ease. But now
she hesitates, and it is her indecision that causes the accident. Her loss of Forio is a
loss of self, and perhaps this loss could be a gain, an emotional clearing in which she
could be free from the past and anticipate the future. But numerous and cheerless
signs – the disgust of the hunt; the rawboned hostility of the Rutland tenant, ingratiating to Lil and repellantly small-minded and mean toward Marnie; Marnie's desperate isolation as she kills Forio – warn against too facile a reading of the scene as
a fruitful breakdown of Marnie's resistances. The way to full consciousness is not
through rape and the enforced subjugation of marriage. Like an animal, Marnie has
been hunted down and broken; her remorse for past crimes is not easily distinguish-
able from the exhaustion and sorrow that result from the crimes presently visited
against her. The blood of the terrified and violated body, the blood of women, of
murder and rape, mingle in the famous red suffusions, the red of suffering. Over the
twisted limbs of Hitchcock's defiled Pietà rise the screams of the mother and her
child, crying for an entire world, not lost but never gained. Love is degraded, a caress
becomes a slap, a marital embrace ends in rape, a drunken attempt to comfort a
child leads to murder. A rape, a hunt, prostitution, and murder – these are Hitchcock's
forlorn instances of violation in marriage, community, and love, where all that
should be held sacred is torn apart.

In a film in which all relationships are characterized by cash, it is misleading, then,
to read *Marnie* merely as a psychological narrative slashed by the blade of the
Oedipal guillotine. To see in the familial trauma only the gash that separates the
daughter from the Imaginary and inserts her precariously on the edge of the Symbolic
is to suppress Marnie's poverty ("We were poor, grindingly poor," she tells Mark at

the racetrack) and the mother's prostitution as the social origins of psychological illness. Marnie's problems are both Oedipal and Capital – her world inhabited by those who can be entertained by suffering, like the hunters swarming around the wounded fox, elite dinner guests by night and, we might infer, corporate executives by day. Threatened by poverty, Marnie's mother sells her body and numbs it in a denial of sexual love. But what is the mother to do, her prostitution not freely chosen, as Marnie's marriage is not? What is Jessie's mother to do, away all day, working to support her daughter but unable to sustain her life with love? What is Lil to do, also motherless, lying around the house all day, taking handouts from Ward? "I thought I'd stick Mark for lunch and you for cash," says Lil, her play on "stick," connoting both "stick up" and knife thrust, linking her to robbery and murder.

After the sailor's murder, the effect of the state's threat to take away the mother's child is an absolute freezing of even the maternal love she bears for her daughter, all she ever loved. The mother's body stiffens in pathetic imitation of social propriety, of an enforced "decency" (a word emphasized throughout) that she must impose on her daughter to save her. Marnie's thievery becomes the mother's economic support, but, while the mother had to forfeit sexual love for sex and money, the daughter drops the sex and just steals the money. Prostitution and frigidity, then, are state products. In Marnie's blank stare, which closes so many of the film's sequences, are the dead eyes of the woman whose sexuality is raped, prostituted, and censored by an authority that is markedly male.

Marnie negotiates the rift between the realm of the mother's prostitution and the Rutland Company's realm of capital. That both places are houses of prostitution is suggested by Mark's first marriage, to save the company. The mother's product is private and nominally denounced; Mark's is public, the literary or scientific books (similar, we might assume, to *Sexual Aberrations of the Criminal Female*) respectably bound and distributed. Marnie represses her memory of the murder, but she also represses knowledge of the "work" hidden behind the mother's closed bedroom door, linked to the closed doors of the Rutland office. Marnie's nightmares contain the truth of her mother's secret profession as prostitute: she dreams that she is sleeping on the sailor's "aloha" pillow, sign of the victim/client; she dreams the mysterious taps of the men in white shirts and feels the "cold" of her dislocation from the mother's bed to the couch, where later, during her honeymoon, she will cringe from Mark as if he too were a sailor. The bed, described by Heidegger as childhood's "hallowed site," serves repeatedly in *Marnie* as the location of bad dreams, rape, prostitution – yet, most movingly, as the place where she free-associates and calls out for help. In the brilliant closing of the film, the mother tells two stories, the one of a psychological trauma of murder, the other of her first act of prostitution as a young girl. Yet the dismal material conditions of her mother's early life and Marnie's own origins remain concealed within a psychological "revelation" of the repressed murder. Seduced by psychology, itself coextensive with social control and normalization, with scientific certainty and the certainty of the Law, Mark hears only one of the narratives, his head turned by his own capital interests.

Mark forces his way into the memories of Marnie and her mother, just as he had earlier penetrated Marnie's body, now forcing confession as before he had caused shame. It is terrible to be a lie and a cheat; not to know the fulfillments of desire, dwelling place, or identity; to be without laughter and unresponsive in erotic love. But what kind of love is this that goes from bad to worse, this submission that claims to represent marriage? "Will I have to go to jail?" asks Marnie in the dazed voice of a child. "I'd rather stay with you." One wonders, a woman wonders, if there is much difference between going off with Rutland or going to jail. For are they not part of the same undifferentiated social space, the Law and psychiatry, the Law and business, widening now to enclose Marnie, to domesticate her, this once cagey woman? "Had you, love?" he responds, framing the film's last spoken words in a fearful ambivalence. The question disturbs, swerves us toward a future more ominous than the past. "The little witch," snaps Strutt at the beginning of the film, "I'll have her put away for twenty years." Instead she marries Mark.

To summarize, *Marnie* entwines two contrasting narrative threads. One weaves the story of a woman who compensates for a traumatic past and need for her mother's love by stealing but is brought to a breakthrough by a man who helps her confront her past and unlock the repressed truth. That is to say, transference occurs in the last scene, when Marnie's head moves from the mother who cannot touch her hair to the man who can and does. On this level, the filmic text projects a therapeutic resolution of social and psychological conflicts, as it allows Marnie to pass from the emotionally troubled domain of the mother to the rational and affluent shelter of the aristocratic male. Unquestioned, however, are Mark's authoritative relation to power and his possession of Marnie-as-child. "I want to know what happened to the child," he asks the detective, "the little girl, the daughter." He has her now.

At this point, a second narrative unravels the Utopian resolution. From the perspective of class (and race, as well, but this requires a future consideration of the Hitchcock production), Marnie's project is to undermine the power of money; yet in the end her class is crushed, her mother is marginalized, and Mark's capital and aggression are victorious. Marnie, who has in effect married the boss, is now a young girl, not a sexually mature woman. She does not know what will happen to her, nor how to protect herself, nor how to face the world. Regressing, she returns to the past so that she may retrieve herself and start out anew from the lost place. But the film gives us no hope that this can be so, for, even though Marnie is no longer frigid, the world is still dead. In the film's final image, the car slowly moves hearse-like toward the fateful ship; it does not clear the frame but intersects with the edge of the false harbor. "Mother, mother, I feel worse," sing the children, frozen on the sidewalk. Like Mark, Marnie leaves with a partial truth, while its entire burden weighs upon the mother, defeated in her last struggle to hold on to her child.

Marnie's climax is thus multiple and leads the viewer in several directions. Mistaken in thinking that the mother was the murderer, Mark is equally mistaken in presuming that Marnie is healed by the knowledge of her trauma. And, if we follow him in thinking that we have found in the murder the secret truth of Marnie's sexuality, we too, like Marnie, are led astray. The presumption of certainty that allowed Mark to misperceive Marnie's mother extends to all who see her as the gloomy figure on the staircase rather than as the woman forsaken once by the child's father, always by her clients, and then, finally, by the daughter Mark takes away. "I'll bring Marnie back," he rules, always the owner. "When a child can't get love," he intones, "it takes what it can get, any way it can get it; it's not so hard to understand." His explanation of Marnie's sickness falls far short of understanding her mother, damaged by the self-hatred of exploitation and prostitution. Mother, daughter, sailor – all are defiled by a history of human misery, its material conditions concealed in psychological mists.

Marnie reveals a woman's pain but cannot heal it, cannot, in the words of Cixous, " 'realize' the decensored relation of woman to her sexuality." Hearing her cry, the film cannot "give her back her goods, her pleasures, her organs, her immense bodily territories which have been kept under seal ... [or] tear her away from the superegoized structure in which she has always occupied the place reserved for the guilty (guilty of everything, guilty at every turn: for having desires, for not having any; for being frigid, for being 'too hot'; for not being both at once ...)" (p. 250). Buried deep within *Marnie* is, not the single trauma of the murdered sailor, but the several wounds of a mother and daughter oppressed by poverty and violated in prostitution and marital rape, of the female body drawn into the categories of illegitimacy and frigidity and supposedly reconstituted in marriage. For Marnie, marriage is not salvation but subjugation, less a recuperation and recovery than the deepening of a wound that will not close.

Finally, *Marnie*'s narrative levels are inconsistent, in tension with one another. While one promotes Marnie's happiness, the other perpetuates pain. In this way, the suspense of the "thriller" is transformed into textual doubt about the unity of a couple linked in violence and the betrayal of social consciousness by a psychological insight that maintains class power and privilege, these wrecking the existence of those who have neither. *Marnie*'s conflicting ideologies delay the resolution of questions about the control of erotic and communal relations by class domination and money. Yet, if *Marnie*'s contradictions hinder a lasting solution to the segmentation and exploitation of class struggle, they do not repress knowledge of its miserable tyranny and destruction.

Notes

1. Sarris's *Village Voice* review is reprinted in *Confessions of a Cultist* (New York: Simon and Schuster, 1970), 141–4.
2. Eric Rohmer and Claude Chabrol, *Hitchcock: The First Forty-Four Films*, trans. Stanley Hochman (New York: Frederick Ungar, 1979).
3. Robin Wood, *Hitchcock's Films*, 3rd ed. (South Brunswick and New York: A. S. Barnes, 1977).
4. Raymond Bellour, "Hitchcock, The Enunciator," *Camera Obscura*, no. 2 (1977): 69–94, and "Psychosis, Neurosis, Perversion" (Chapter 24, below), and Laura Mulvey, "Visual Pleasure and Narrative Cinema," *Screen*, vol. 16, no. 3 (Autumn 1975): 6–18.
5. See Karl Marx and Friedrich Engels, "The Communist Manifesto," in K. Marx, *On Revolution*, ed. and trans. S. K. Padoner (New York: McGraw-Hill, 1971), 81: "Freeman and slave, patrician and plebeian, lord and serf, guild master and journeyman – in a word, oppressor and oppressed – stood in constant opposition to one another, carried on an uninterrupted, now hidden, now open fight, a fight that each time ended either in a revolutionary reconstitution of society at large, or in the common ruin of the contending classes."

6. Lewis Hyde, *The Gift: Imagination and the Erotic Life of Property* (New York: Vintage Books, 1983), p. xiv.
7. Hélène Cixous, "The Laugh of Medusa," in Elaine Marks and Isabelle de Courtivron, eds., *New French Feminisms* (New York: Schocken Books, 1981), 264.
8. Mary Douglas, *Natural Symbols* (New York: Pantheon, 1979), 70.
9. Donald Spoto, *The Dark Side of Genius: The Life of Alfred Hitchcock* (New York: Ballantine Books, 1984), 505.
10. Michel Foucault, *Discipline and Punish: The Birth of the Prison* (New York: Vintage Books, 1979), 197.
11. Michel Foucault, "The Eye of Power," in *Power/Knowledge* (New York: Pantheon Books, 1980), 152.
12. Jean-Paul Sartre, *Saint Genet* (New York: George Braziller, 1963), 49.
13. Joan B. Landes, "Hegel's Conception of the Family," in Jean Bethke Elshtain, ed., *The Family and Political Thought* (Amherst: Univ. of Massachusetts Press, 1982), 136.
14. Jean Genet, *The Thief's Journal* (New York: Grove Press, 1964), 91.
15. Stéphane Mallarmé, "Mimique," in Mary Ann Caws, ed., *Selected Poetry and Prose* (New York: New Directions Books, 1982), 69.

MARNIE (Universal, 1964). *Producer*: Alfred Hitchcock, *Assistant Director*: James H. Brown, *Script*: Jay Presson Allen, from the Winston Graham novel, *Photography*: Robert Burks (Technicolor), *Editor*: George Tomasini, *Sets*: Robert Boyle, George Milo, *Music*: Bernard Herrmann, *Costumes*: Edith Head, Vincent Dee, Rita Riggs, James Linn, *Players*: Tippi Hedren (Marnie Edgar), Sean Connery (Mark Rutland), Diane Baker (Lil Mainwaring), Louise Latham (Bernice Edgar), Martin Gabel (Strutt), Bruce Dern (the sailor), Mariette Hartley (Susan Clabon), Alan Napier (Mr. Rutland). 131 minutes.

Chapter Twenty-Two
The Queer Voice in *Marnie*

Lucretia Knapp

> Mother, Mother, I am ill,
> Send for the doctor over the hill.
> Call for the doctor, call for the nurse,
> Call for the lady with the alligator purse.
>
> Mumps said the doctor,
> The measles said the nurse,
> *Nothing* said the lady with
> The alligator purse.

One of the most intriguing and haunting "voices" in Alfred Hitchcock's film *Marnie* is this jump-rope rhyme familiar to many girls. This song, which refers to Marnie (Marnie is identified with the famous first scene in which we see her from behind, carrying a purse), occurs at the beginning and at the end of the film and in each case is associated with Marnie's visits to her mother. Like other Hitchcock films, such as *Rear Window*, *The Lady Vanishes*, and *Shadow of a Doubt*, subtle songs contain significant clues.[1]

The ambiguity of the rhyme questions gender and creates a riddle concerning "the lady." The song offers four discursive positions for women: the daughter, the mother, the nurse, and the lady, but only one position for men, the doctor. The lady is intriguing because she does not fit within the dualistic economy of male/female, doctor/ nurse, and mumps/measles. The words play on gender identification and therefore the gap in logic creates a mystery, a possible other position for the lady. Like Marnie, the lady from the rhyme does not fit within the oedipal triangle of man, woman, and child. She is the scary spinster with the purse; she is the mysterious other.

Marnie is the story of a woman who has an obsessive need to steal and who makes her living as a thief. Her every move is studied, a performance of survival through manipulation. Marnie steals from patriarchy and returns to a women's space, where her mother lives in a world of fatherless families. Marnie wears the man's desire and distracts him from realizing that he has made a bad deal. Easily and successfully, this trickster hits the man in his most vulnerable spot, the pocket.

After stealing a large amount of money from a company where she was employed as a secretary, Marnie changes identity, goes to ride her beloved horse Forio, and then visits her mother. At her mother's home, it becomes apparent that the color red triggers something in Marnie's past, causing a seizure. Although Mark Rutland is aware of her past thievery, he hires Marnie and then blackmails her into marriage. At Rutland's she meets Lil, Mark's sister-in-law, who takes an immediate interest in Marnie. Mark becomes obsessed with uncovering the causes of her symptoms, reforming her passion for thievery, and curing her lack of heterosexual desire. After her beloved Forio is injured and Marnie kills him, Mark drags Marnie to her mother's home. Finally Marnie discovers she had killed one of the many men that her mother had slept with. In the end, Marnie leaves with Mark.

Like the woman in the rhyme, Marnie is an outsider and is often shown in the film carrying the purse. The striking first image of the film is a close-up, not of Marnie but of her purse. Dialogue that links Marnie to the lady who says "nothing" occurs later in the film, when Mark and Marnie are at the racetrack. He asks her what she believes in and Marnie vehemently asserts, "nothing."[2] Her speech then is that of an outsider, of someone who is hiding something. Just like the lady with the alligator purse, Marnie's not talking, especially not to Mark. This rhyme and the word "nothing" seem to indicate that, whatever it is, she is not telling.

The rhyme, like the film, is compelling because of the questioning presence of the troubling lady. *Marnie* is particularly fascinating because the figure of the outlaw as a motif is resonant for an exploration of how the lesbian is situated both as a viewer and as a figure in film theory. The outlaw in *Marnie* is a figure that exists in two worlds – a white patriarchal world, and a cultural world of women. Masquerading as part of the system, this figure flouts patriarchal authority while using its own laws against it.

My main purpose in this chapter is to redirect attention to those lesbian moments in *Marnie* that have been considered insignificant by other film theorists. Hitchcock's work has provided a cornerstone of feminist theory, yet only recently has the homosexual aspect of his films been examined by theorists such as Robin Wood and D. A. Miller.[3] It only seems appropriate that Hitchcock, the mastermind of celluloid phobia, would find homophobia or homosexuality a costume for some exotic twist. Although Wood and Miller have talked about gay male figures, the issue of lesbianism in Hitchcock's films is relatively unexplored.[4] My interest lies in the possibilities of lesbian positions of spectatorship, or how a lesbian reading may focus on other moments or gazes within films, and specifically in *Marnie*. I will situate the possible positions of the lesbian spectator, first by suggesting that gay presence in feminist film theory has been much like gay presence in traditional Hollywood cinema – there but not there or, quite often, oddly cloaked. Looking at the female space and the female voices in *Marnie* (which have been repressed or overlooked by Raymond Bellour, for instance, who sees in the film nothing but a male oedipal drama) can bring to the viewer another understanding of Marnie and the lesbian spectator. I will assess the limitations of film theory, such as Mary Ann Doane's and Tania Modleski's valorization of the bisexual space and its precursor, the preoedipal, and suggest why these terms are not solely sufficient in theorizing lesbian or gay positions in life or in the theater. I will also consider why the mother has been such a stumbling block in the oedipal scenario in film and in film theory.

I am defining lesbian viewers as those with a consistency of identification (though necessarily in flux like all identifications), one that is part of a lesbian culture, a culture that shares signs, codes, and messages. As part of a subculture, some gays were and still are identified through dress. An obvious example is the lesbian butch, whose male attire no longer signifies gender but desire. In the late 1970s some people wore the color green and/or blue jeans on Thursdays in order to show gay support and, even more importantly, gay visibility. Homophobia was also made visible as many individuals, fearing that they would be suspected of homosexuality, selected another uniform. Women who were athletes or spinsters could trigger the attention of a gay eye. For instance, certain characters on television were suspect, especially lone women. Miss Hathaway on *The Beverly Hillbillies* was quite self-sufficient and not married, and her oddness (being a bird watcher, nerdy, and single) made her a bit queer.[5] I find my own "tomboyish" identification with Peter Pan to be quite significant, especially considering that the character who played Peter was a girl masquerading as a boy.[6]

There are many variables to lesbian identities and many lesbian codes that vary or alter with time – for example, dress, haircuts, sturdy shoes, softball, and cheering for Martina. My desire is to read *Marnie* from such a lesbian perspective. Like Miss Hathaway, Marnie is a spinster, self-sufficient, and banking on her future. And, like some lesbians, she finds it necessary to hide her identity at work. However, I will not argue Marnie is a lesbian character, although her resistance to compulsory heterosexuality could, for someone like Adrienne Rich, define her as such.

During the opening presentation for a lesbian and gay film festival in Urbana, Illinois, Richard Dyer wittily engaged with the question of why gays would be attracted to certain Hollywood films with unflattering portrayals such as *The Killing of Sister George*, *Personal Best*, or even *Desert Hearts*. Dyer argues that, although these films do not accurately portray gays or gay lifestyles, we enjoy watching them because of their campiness and because of something in the film that we identify with. Although *Marnie* does not fit neatly in this category, the film does share some similar stereotypes. *Marnie* is an example of a film rich with campiness and a text that is both corrupt with social and cultural bias while suggesting an existence for Marnie other than a heterosexual one.

Tania Modleski, in *The Women who Knew too Much*, examines the fascination that Hitchcock's films have held for some feminists and suggests that many of his films follow not the traditional oedipal scenario but rather a female oedipal path (although she does not find this to be true of *Marnie*).[7] My interest in Hitchcock's films is likewise driven by his constant obsession with gender play. Not only are feminine bodies quite abundant in Hitchcock's films, but the transversing of both masculine and feminine characteristics makes Hitchcock's characters questionable, alluring, but, almost always, the traps within the narratives.

Modleski suggests that the ambiguous sexuality in Hitchcock's films "destabilize[s] the gender identity of protagonists and viewers alike."[8] Similarly, I find Hitchcock's films to be a bed of paradoxes and ambiguities in which identity is questioned and explored. In her account of the mother in Hitchcock films, Modleski points out that "the misogyny and the sympathy actually entail one another – just as Norman Bates's close relationship with his mother provokes his lethal aggression towards other women."[9] Although I agree with her assessment of the relationship between misogyny and sympathy in regard to the mother in *Psycho*, Modleski stops short of examining the homophobia in which this relationship is inextricably intertwined. This sympathy for Mom is seen for both Norman and Marnie as "unnaturally perverse" and deadly. The closeness to Mom or the corrupt space that she occupies is to blame for the lack of "normal" heterosexual desire (which can be read as gayness). Proximity to the mother or the feminine has always been a problem in heterosexual theory. Male gayness has been blamed on acquisition of the feminine or a frighteningly close relationship with the mother. Today, the preoedipal has become a kind of lesbian landmark for heterosexual theorists – that is, for those who most obsessively seek it, a place of comfort through eventual transcendence. In fact, the preoedipal seems to carry the dubious honor of being the red herring both in the oedipal configuration and in film theory.

In *The Mother/Daughter Plot* Marianne Hirsch redirects attention within the familial structure away from the oedipal of the traditional narrative to preoedipal and maternal structures. Hirsch suggests that, although feminist retellings of *Oedipus* have brought to the forefront a female plot and voice, when it comes to revisioning the oedipal narrative, feminists such as Muriel Rukeyser and Teresa de Lauretis have concerned themselves only with the flamboyant Sphinx character and not with the maternal figure of Jocasta. Hirsch suggests that the maternal is ignored in both male and feminist narratives because "[feminists] are attracted by the enigmatic, powerful, monstrous, and terrifying Sphinx; [but] omit the powerless, maternal, emotional, and virtually silent Jocasta."[10] Although Hirsch claims to be interested in both the Sphinx and Jocasta, her heterosexual, maternal compass seems to be pulling her in one direction only.

Like Nancy Chodorow and Julia Kristeva, numerous theorists of heterosexuality have been obsessed with a mother/daughter relationship often conflated with quasi-lesbian imagery because, I would argue, it serves as an ideal without confronting the cultural complexities of real lesbianism. It is a lesbianism of an unconscious sort, a sexuality that is immature because it is hypothetical, not long lasting. The lesbianism that these theorists invoke exists purely in a phantasmatic space. Hirsch, on the other hand, is concerned not with the idealized preoedipal space and the lesbian bond but with a more adult space of detachment between the mother and daughter. But the fate of the lesbian in Hirsch's adult space is invisibility. Although Hirsch's preoedipal is not the idealized one of most heterosexual theorists, it is, nonetheless, a problematic space for lesbian subjectivity.

Although Hirsch talks a lot about Adrienne Rich and even mentions the term "compulsory heterosexuality," she does so without talking about lesbian subjectivity. Hirsch rethinks the maternal but she does not find a place for lesbian daughters or lesbian mothers. My interest in Marnie and her mother goes beyond the heterosexual (oedipal) bond between the mother and the daughter. I am interested in Marnie as a daughter but also, perhaps primarily, as an outlaw. And, although I am interested in the mother in *Marnie*, my interest is not in maternal subjectivity but in how she too is an outlaw of sorts (a woman who works outside the law) and a very ambiguous figure for Marnie's affection.

Therefore, my concern is not just with the feminine perspective but with a queer perspective that is even more removed from oedipal heterosexuality. In *A Lure of Knowledge*, Judith Roof questions "whether there is a difference between heterosexual and lesbian narratives of [the] mother" and how these "difference[s] might characterize mainstream representations of female heterosexual and lesbian desire."[11] Roof discusses the types of mothers that are mentioned in lesbian novels, mothers who have illegitimate children, who are not a part of the patriarchal world. Thus she describes women who, like Marnie's mother, live outside of patriarchy and thereby "detach[es] maternity from heterosexuality."[12] Roof is engaged by the abundance of heterosexual women theorists who are obsessed by the preoedipal within their work and through this "the lesbian ideal" mother/daughter relationship – and the lack of such an "ideal" relationship in lesbian novels. In some ways, then, Roof and Hirsch are both moving beyond the preoedipal to explore the mother/daughter relationship, though their interests are very distinct. Hirsch is concerned with the heterosexual mother and Roof with the lesbian but not just as daughter.

Although I find *Marnie* rich with queer moments, Raymond Bellour focuses exclusively on a limited heterosexual reading of *Marnie* that covers only the first ten minutes or so of the film and is concerned only with the male inheritance of the gaze.[13] Like Bellour, many theorists have been oblivious to the women's world in *Marnie* and to how it functions to disrupt the heterosexual narrative. The analysis of the gaze and oedipal narrative in Bellour's account marginalizes the two components of the film that threaten to upset the heterosexual space, particularly the female space and the female voice. The female space and female voice have been significant in feminist film theory as a means to explore women's existence or assumed invisibility within a dominant text. Although in *The Acoustic Mirror* Kaja Silverman cites *Marnie* as a film that is obsessed with the woman's voice, she argues that in Hollywood film there is no chance for the female voice to be heard because it is completely repressed. Discussing a number of "talking cure" films, Silverman refers to the last scene of *Marnie* when Marnie visits her mother's home with Mark, and states that Marnie's "voice often seems to circumvent her consciousness altogether. At these times she seeks not so much the language of the unconscious as the language of unconsciousness."[14]

Silverman's account has theoretical similarities with Laura Mulvey's groundbreaking article "Visual Pleasure and Narrative Cinema" in that both agree that women are not represented in cinema, although Mulvey is mainly concerned with the visual while Silverman focuses on the aural content of traditional narrative film.[15] Alternatively, the "other" space and the various voices within the film offer Marnie an escape from the oedipal story. Within this "other" space, there are three principal voices: the rhyme recited outside the mother's home, the occasional contradictory dialogue that moves against the traditional cinematic narrative, and Marnie's own voice, which accompanies her visual "seizures" into the past. These voices make reference to something other than heterosexuality; there is a quirkiness or queerness to the way they operate in the film.

Silverman recounts film theory's historic debates over authorship, citing Bellour's major participation in the quest for the auteur and reviewing his analysis of *Marnie* in his much quoted essay "Hitchcock, The Enunciator." Silverman reiterates Bellour's account of the male possession of the gaze, suggesting why the interconnectedness of authorship and subjectivity should be reconsidered. "The agency of that identification is the image of Marnie, which is passed from the camera to Strutt, Rutland, and Hitchcock-as-fictional-character during the opening three scenes of the film. Ironically, it is only through this radically dispersed and decentered 'hom(m)osexual' economy that Hitchcock-as-director comes to be installed as the point of apparent textual origin, and as the seemingly punctual source of meaning."[16] While Silverman acknowledges the "hom(m)osexual economy," she overlooks queer exchanges between the women. Thus, the identification of the possibility of lesbian desire within the heterosexual world is marginalized or, more emphatically, overlooked.

Although the oedipal narrative is quite obvious in *Marnie*, another subtle narrative wreaks havoc with the heterosexual plot. Curiously, Bellour disregards some of the most striking scenes that involve Marnie's relationships with Lil and her mother in order to discuss the significance of the male as hero, enunciator, or viewer.[17] The explicitly Freudian text is almost too obvious, as if Bellour's discovery is no more than Hitchcock's trap. Bellour's analysis of the purse is just one example of this.

As the film opens we see an extreme close-up of a purse tucked under a woman's arm. This "fetishized" object signifies Marnie's "problem" (her thievery) and her shifting identity (her changing costume). From the outset of the film, then, through the close-up of the purse, the artifice of other accessories such as her hair (Marnie changes her hair from black to blond just at the point when she starts to become a saved good girl), and the sequence of shots that deny the viewer access to her face, Marnie's identity is problematized. We meet her through her "feminine" accessories: the contents of her suitcase, purse, white gloves, compact, nail file, and lingerie. The fetishization itself suggests the difficulty Marnie will have in positioning herself within an oedipal narrative. Her identity, which is not quite heterosexual and law abiding, is also displaced into a series of male fetishes. However, Marnie's identity, when coupled with a homoerotic fetish, coheres in a more convincing manner.

In Bellour's examination of the opening shots of *Marnie* and the fetishized purse, he discusses how the position of "the subject of enunciation" is distributed, like a linear inheritance, among men. He overly simplifies the process of identification and equates the active gaze with a strict division of gender. The possession of the gaze and the possible active positions for the lesbian viewer are more complex. Bellour assumes that women identify only through or with the man's "fear" or fetish. With this narrow definition of identification, the inanimate outcome for women viewers is in the shape of a purse (or as "a man").

Emily Apter, in the conclusion of her book *Feminizing the Fetish*, makes an interesting observation about how male authors, in order to distinguish a difference between the two genders, construct a feminization of the fetish that says more about the man's fear, a male construction of feminization, than about women.[18] Unlike Joan Riviere's argument about the "masquerade of femininity," in which the masculinity of the masculine intellectual "homosexual" woman is being covered over or masqueraded by femininity, Apter is speaking about a "double fetishism whereby male writers are seen to be pretending to be women pretending to be men."[19]

The feminine or homoerotic fetish may be difficult to detect in Hitchcock's films, considering the many layers of male fetishization that are inherent in his work. Hitchcock's scenes are curio boxes neatly arranged with fetishized collectibles – that is, stuffed birds, Norman's taxidermied mother, and phallic ships. In *Marnie*, the maternal is horrifically fetishized as the blood that washes over Marnie's eyes. Mark amasses objects, stuffed animals, and even a token that represents his dead wife, though it is quickly broken. In Marnie's mother's home, fetishized objects are of a domestic kind – knickknacks, vases, and flowers. Just as Marnie seems to be a feminized version of the name Mark, Hitchcock seems to break the fetish up into masculine (dead animals, artifacts) and feminine (domestic) objects. Likewise, fetishism has been regarded as a male terrain that is associated with an active – therefore masculine – gaze of voyeuristic desire. Women have generally been seen as the objects of fetishization, the objects of male desire, and not as the active agents of desire, especially for other women. The male, misogynist fetishization that surrounds Marnie is the veil between a homoerotic fetish and the viewer.

In Riviere's article, masculinity is not questioned, just femininity. The fetish for Riviere is the masculine equivalent of women's masquerade. Apter, in trying to posit a less gender-specific fetish, suggests how femininity may be more than a camouflage for the masculine (or lesbian). As Apter explains, "In this sense we might reread the theory of the masquerade as corrected, so to speak, by sartorial female fetishism, which supplants the notion of femininity as empty content or infinitely layered veil, to replace it with a theory of materialized social construction."[20] Thus, the fetish is seen as a construct, not a cover for the essentialist concept of the masculine.[21]

The fetish or fetishism in *Marnie* can be read in varying ways. Marnie functions by constantly assuming and then denying identities. When trying to define Marnie, we can say what she is not but not, exactly, what she is. A lesbian perspective opens up the possibility of reading the ambiguities in a film like *Marnie*, seeing what is in a film in a different way and therefore constructing a different text than the heterosexual eye might observe. Bellour stirs up masculine myths of authority, in which the male gaze and the fetish remain solid and absolute. More useful is the idea of the fetish as a continuously distorting form through which the complexities of projection are metaphorically sustained. Thus, "the fetish" is not produced out of that which woman lacks but functions as a cover for what she desires.[22]

I am suggesting not that there is not a male fetish in the film but that there is a female fetish, and more specifically a lesbian fetish. For instance, the purse also functions as the fetishized object of a possible homoerotic gaze, specifically, when we hear exaggerated, hypnotic music and see a close-up of Marnie's face as she watches the secretary place the key to the safe in her purse. In certain instances, then, Marnie's gaze is in charge of the fetish. The more typical male-fetishized purse is almost necessary in order to make the women's desire readable or suggested within the heterosexual text. The purse becomes the initial suture of varied exchanges between Mark's secretary and Marnie. (In the scenes with Mark, Strutt, and Hitchcock, Marnie does not return their gaze.) Between the two women the purse is an excuse for looking, a mutual object of interest, and the focal point of Marnie's active gaze. Freud developed the notion of the fetish primarily in terms of the heterosexual male; he does mention a clothes fetish in connection with women, although still in heterosexual terms. Unlike Freud's fetish (which is a replacement for the missing phallus, or desire for the masculine), the fetish suturing the gazes exchanged betwen Marnie and the secretary is desire for the feminine among women. Later, other objects, such as the safe, will become the distracting points of attention between the active gaze of Marnie and the secretary's returning smile.

When considering the idea of the fetish among women, or more specifically among lesbians, I cannot help but reconsider the only exceptional fetish that Freud would attribute to women, clothing, although Freud's clothing was tailored in heterosexuality.[23] It seems that clothing, desire, and gender do not necessarily go hand in hand, and when they do not, it can make people nervous. No wonder some adults become anxious when little girls start eyeing cowboy boots instead of patent-leather shoes. When a lesbian or a gay man hides desire or attire, "being in the closet" seems a significant analogy indeed.

It will come as no surprise that Bellour is interested in reading Forio, the horse, as Marnie's desire for the phallus. I find Marnie and Lil's relationship a more intriguing scenario vis-à-vis the horse. Marnie and Lil's relationship within the often over-looked hunt scene opens up more possible sites of spectatorship. Bellour, again, sees Marnie only in relationship to men, when a crucial part of the film is her relationship to women. Although I would not consider Garrot (the man who hands Marnie her horse) a very active or memorable character, Bellour points out how he is, because of his gender, an extension of Hitchcock and Mark. His gaze, according to Bellour, supposedly acts as some type of trigger. However, it is Lil and Marnie who will fight over the necessity to pull the trigger.

While riding in a hunt Marnie suffers a seizure from her chronic problem, the sight of red. This suggests Marnie's difficulty in both occupying and visually func-tioning within a certain space. The apparent difficulty drives Marnie to flee from the hunt. Unable to scale a wall, she tumbles from her injured horse. In the book *Marnie*, by Winston Graham, Mark comes to the rescue, but in Hitchcock's film Lil steps in as hero. (The other time this happens is when Marnie has a nightmare and calls for her mother. As Mark looks on, Lil touches Marnie and gives her comfort.) Although Lil's curiosity can get the best of her and Marnie, she also comes to Marnie as a protector, comforter, and sympathizer.[24] Just as Marnie must shoot Forio as an active way of protecting that which she loves, Lil is also willing to take on this active role for Marnie.

Lesbianism, Costume, and Spectatorship

As Bellour's analysis is obsessed with dress and accessories (the purse), film theory in general has been obsessed with gender, dress, and desire. The questions of women's desire and women's position as spectators have been a continuing locus of difficulty within feminist film theory. Some theorists still rely on clothing analogies in order to distinguish between male and female spectators and desires in ways that suggest how much lesbians have been a forgotten part of much feminist theoretical viewing. Mulvey's "Visual Pleasure and Narrative Cinema," the classic statement of sexual difference in the cinema, defined the only possible identification for the woman viewer as masculine, or masochistic. Although her work was ground-breaking for feminist theorists, her analysis did not take into account the diffuse complexities of the viewer.

Still struggling to pass through a grid of gender dichotomy, Mary Ann Doane varied the active male and passive female schema by giving the woman viewer another option, that of transvestism.[25] Doane's analysis of the female spectator and, again, the dependence on clothing seems to hint that desire is indeed sex specific, either male or female, and that therefore the "real" woman's identification must be narcissistic, while to identify with the active subject is to be "something other than" woman, to be in drag.

In order to account for the possible position(s) of a lesbian viewer, it is necessary to attend to lesbian codes of desire and to a lesbian culture that is both within and outside of a heterosexual one. Lesbian desire cannot be so simply defined within an "either or" of gender choices. Teresa de Lauretis, in "Oedipus Interruptus," constructs a process of spectatorship that does not rely on simple definitions of masculine and feminine. She suggests that "each person goes to the movies with a semiotic history, personal and social, a series of previous identifications, by which she or he has been somehow engendered." De Lauretis talks of "the project of feminist cinema" as one that "does not destroy vision altogether, but constructs another (object of) vision and the conditions of visibility for a different social subject." Lesbian spectatorship opens up just such conditions of visibility, those possible positions of reading that are more complex than donning a hat, a purse, or both.[26]

Doane's analysis of the woman spectator as transvestite suggests that women can only imagine active agency with men's clothing. Desire is thought in heterosexual terms and thus contained by a dichotomous structure of male and female, masculine and feminine. However, pumps and loafers are not adequate assessments or reasonable representations of desire, for, when we look at the larger picture, opposites do not always attract. Doane suggests that clothes make the man and women are forced into drag. Such an account of spectatorship seems similar to Freud's analysis of the lesbian: if a woman desires a woman, she takes up the position of man. The concept of transvestism is not as threatening to patriarchy as the image of the lesbian is, for transvestism still implies masculine privilege. However difficult she is to imagine, when a woman desires a woman, she is not a man. The lesbian spectator can move into the active position of desire as a woman. In theoretical terms, the lesbian spectator challenges a desire that has always been envisioned as sex specific. Still, in Hitchcockian waters gender seems to be the body that is not so easily kept afloat.

In other films, Hitchcock invests in the tension created between heterosexuality and homosexuality. Of course, a mother is usually mentioned or portrayed as a dominant or domineering figure – e.g., in *North by Northwest*, in *Strangers on a Train*, and of course in *Psycho*. Hitchcock most explicitly plays on homosexuality in the film *Rope*, in which the "initiation ritual" (the murder of a male friend) by two young men is an act with strange sexual overtones that they are proud of and both hide and flaunt before their guests. Robin Wood points out in *Hitchcock's Films Revisited* that, although in 1948 the general audience may not have thought as much, today most read the boy-school characters Brandon and Philip as homosexuals. In "Anal *Rope*," D. A. Miller states: "Until recently, homosexuality offered not just the most prominent, it offered the only subject matter whose representation in American mass culture appertained exclusively to the shadow kingdom of connotation, where insinuations could be at once developed and denied." Miller discusses how the homosexuality in *Rope* is never explicitly shown through kissing, for example, but is hinted at by the "coital nuances of the dialogue" and through stereotypes, such as the boys' prep school. Connotations, such as gazes and phrases, also exist in *Marnie*, although Marnie does and does not conform to lesbian stereotypes. She is the spinster, the outlaw, and a part of the women's community, but she has the invisibility of the femme.[27]

Wood believes that the only lesbian character in a Hitchcock film is Mrs. Danvers from *Rebecca*. I argue that a lesbian would have more to identify with in *Marnie* than in *Rebecca*. Marnie is a less coherent character and therefore offers suggestions of a more complex reading. Marnie is a more appealing spinster, more resourceful, and more easily imagined as having or hiding an erotic life. I would suggest that Marnie opens up possibilities to the lesbian spectator because she does not desire a heterosexual life and a heterosexual male wants to cure her (which is not new to many lesbians). And, like Marnie, lesbians go through the process of "passing" through the heterosexual world while coming out and finding themselves.[28]

Teresa de Lauretis, in "Sexual Indifference and Lesbian Representation," addresses the subtleties of gestures in works in which central characters are not explicitly lesbian. Those who move within the margins are more inclined to notice what may otherwise go undetected to the heterosexual eye because of the shared experience of "passing." In the case of *Marnie*, attention to the set, background, and peripheral characters becomes central to my argument. Marnie is fascinating in her passing because of the tensions that she incorporates, looking feminine but having masculine desires (success in the public world, riding competence, theft). The tension between what she is and what she is not, between stereotype and invisibility, gives Marnie an interesting complexity.

Marnie's voice allots a space that moves against the heterosexual tale of the film. The oedipal narrative of the film does conclude with the male replacing the mother. However, because of visual and audible points of tension, this narrative is resisted. Marnie's voice is not brought to the surface by the male "analyst," Mark, but is activated by the mother's voice and by Marnie's association with her own repressed sounds and images (images that never appear on screen). This contradictory "voice" leaves Mark outside, with access only to the oedipal framework at the end of the narrative.

The discrepancies within the film create tensions on various levels that are never convincingly resolved. An amateur zoologist, Mark wants to "cure" Marnie's "deviant" behavior through scientific means. He reads books such as *Sexual Aberrations of the Female Criminal*, a more than passing hint at lesbianism. The male protagonist wants to recuperate Marnie into a patriarchal narrative progression, which she resists. Once again, a lesbian spectator may be particularly adept at reading these tensions, at attending to Marnie's resistance.

There are many incongruencies between the film's visuals and its soundtrack, and they create a space for Marnie outside the dualistic economies of patriarchy. Marnie speaks to the situation of the young girl enmeshed within an ambivalent mother/ daughter relationship. Although the majority of the film takes place outside of this space, the mother/daughter world is a compelling aspect of the film and is regarded as Marnie's source of trauma. The mother/daughter realm is the film's pandora's box and the key to Marnie's story. Just as Marnie has the ability to "pass" within patriarchy (through clothing and the falsification of her name), there are moments within the film that suggest a women's voice, whereby silence is broken and Marnie's position within a women's space is felt.

The women's space, the mother's world, is presented as a dark cloud that hangs over the heterosexual narrative. When the mother is not physically shown, characters are constantly reminding each other and the viewer of her presence, through general comments about mothers. For example, when Rutland's secretary is talking to a friend, Maude, about weekend plans, she says with regret, "I only thought you said if your mother wasn't coming with us." At another moment in the film, during a discussion with Lil, Mark says, "You should try to be Marnie's friend." She replies, "I always thought a girl's best friend was her mother!" After Mark and Marnie are married, upset with all the money Mark has wasted on a ring and honeymoon, his banker cousin snivels, "He didn't even ask mother [to the wedding]." (This cousin is one of many "single" people in *Marnie* – Mark's secretary, Lil, Marnie, Marnie's mother, Jessie's mother, Mark, Mark's father – and is, to use Miller's term, inflected with connotations of queerness because of his close bond with mother.) And when Marnie becomes worried that she will be found out for her robberies, Mark states, "Didn't your mother ever tell you about sticks and stones?" The mother is someone from whom there is no escape. She is the ruler of the women's sphere, the witch from the fairy tale who is burned in real life. Marnie's journeys always lead back to the mother. To Marnie, her mother represents both anger and pleasure. It is by way of the mother's *voice* that Marnie eventually has access to her past. But the arrival will be greatly hindered by Marnie's ambivalence and the mother's fear.

The space where Marnie's mother lives is a community of women, where little girls inhabit the street, skipping, jumping, and singing rhyme. Marnie's mom tells her that she is thinking of sharing a household with a neighbor girl, Jessie, and her mother. Like a thief within patriarchy, Marnie moves between this women's community and the world of men, stealing from patriarchy and then returning to the mother.

After one of her thefts, Marnie stops to visit her mother. We see, looming in the distance, a giant ship, docked in the harbor, a phallic metaphor par excellence, which also encapsulates the fear and the threat that the mother poses within the oedipal narrative. When Marnie arrives, a small girl, Jessie, whom Marnie obviously considers to be a rival for her mother's affection, greets her at the door. One facet of this mother/daughter relationship, then, is sibling rivalry. Upon seeing the color red, Marnie struggles to stifle a seizure, thus the "repressed memory." Because this reaction initially happens in the mother's home, the first seizure is linked not only to Marnie's mother but to sibling jealousy. The red comes to signify entry into the past, a connection with the mother (birth and menstruation), and the emotion of anger. Marnie quickly removes the indecent color by replacing the gladioli on the TV with a present of white chrysanthemums, thus trying to veil the emotions that surround her early relationship with her mother.

Marnie's disruptive returns to her mother's home, her seizures and thefts, all attest to her internal and external conflicts. At the end of the film, Marnie will learn of her mother's past and realize how she did care for her, although the ambivalence will never be resolved. The voice is, this time, shared by the mother and daughter and moves against the possibility of a successful father-figure replacement. Once Marnie marries Mark, he will try to displace the mother or take Marnie away from the women's space. In Marnie's case, in order legitimately to enter patriarchy or remain true to the traditional oedipal narrative, the mother must be replaced by Mark, the amateur analyst. Mark does not have access to their shared space, though, and therefore he cannot adequately dislodge the mother from Marnie's story. The maternal bond is a threat because it opens up the possibility for a desire that is not informed by, or in harmony with, the masculine.

After Marnie leaves her mother, at the beginning of the film, she takes on a new appearance. She applies for and gets a job as a secretary at Mark's publishing company. While in the reception area, Mark's sister-in-law passes and the women exchange looks. Lil's competent, sensuous, and searching gaze makes Marnie drop her eyes, as if returning the look might disclose some secret. Marnie's glance is curious in that she overreacts to Lil. The gaze is especially significant because the interest between the two women is much like that of the traditional heterosexual gaze of the cinema. When Lil approaches the main office, she looks back at Marnie and says to Mark, "Who's the dish?" This "other" voice of desire suggests a momentary displacement of the heterosexual narrative. At one crucial moment, after Marnie has lied about her mother, Lil catches wind of some trouble. She tells Mark that if he needs any help he can count on her because she does not have any scruples. Fed up with Lil and her advances toward him, Mark, with hostility in his voice, asks her what she's waiting for (in regard to love), and Lil answers, "I'm queer for liars." But Marnie is the liar in the film. Although we are led to believe that this daughter-substitute for Mark is out for daddy, her words indicate that she is possibly after the outlaw, or the other woman without scruples, the liar. Unlike the traditional Hollywood film in which the two women fight over the man, Marnie's interests lie elsewhere. Both Lil and Marnie are lone women, surrounded by the patriarchal Rutland world, and the strong tensions that exist between them are like the intensity or ambiguity that can surround jealousy or desire.

Just as the mother/daughter bond is a threat to partriarchy, much is invested in the desire for jealousy among women. As Irigaray states in *This Sex which Is Not One*, "Commodities can only enter into relationships under the watchful eyes of their 'guardians.' ... And the interests of businessmen require that commodities relate to each other as rivals."[29] In some ways, Lil and Marnie are the familiar rivals of the gothic novel. Within traditional cinema, invested in male desire, women are also often pitted against each other for the affection of the man. There are moments in Hollywood film, though, when the rivalry is disrupted, and through the tension another voice, a voice of contradiction, is heard. These two traditional female figures of the cinema, the blond and the brunette, are both bad girls. Marnie holds Lil's curiosity throughout the film; Lil is an obsessed detective searching out Marnie's identity.

I have discussed the rhyme and the contradictory dialogue as two instances of the other voice in *Marnie*. The third example in the film is Marnie's narration that occurs during her seizures. Before Marnie is blackmailed into marrying Mark, he asks her to work overtime. A high camera angle shows the small figure of Marnie, approaching an industrialized, gothic mansion. In Mark's office, a space of fetishized history, zoology, and cultural artifacts, Marnie has her next seizure. The onslaught of the memory is now produced within both the mother's space and Mark's world. There are some signals that trigger Marnie's memory, or the little girl's experience. Initially, when Marnie is in Mark's office, the lightning frightens her. Soon her terror escalates as a tree smashes through a large wall of glass. Two signals, then, are the lightning and the metaphor of rape, which are indicative of the small girl's narrative or memory. Mark's forced entry, or coercion into the past, reveals a brutality that is determinedly resisted by Marnie. Later the rape during Marnie's honeymoon pushes her toward suicide but also toward further recollection of the childhood trauma that she has repressed.

At the climax of the film, desiring to cure her once and for all, Mark takes Marnie to see her mother. Once she is inside the door, Marnie's fear of lightning activates a seizure. When Mark puts his arms around Marnie gallantly to sooth her, Marnie's mother tells him to "get your hands off of my kid." Mark thinks that he is going to displace the mother but instead he takes up the place of the sailor. The memory of the mother's protective voice and Marnie's desire for something other than the protection of the man uncover Marnie's past.

Although the young Marnie appears to cry because of her fear of lightning, Marnie's words express memories of sexual abuse. Like the gap in time between lightning and thunder, the visual image and the soundtrack of the film do not match. The two ways of reading the scene are like a double exposure, with one perspective always distorting the other. Watching the visuals, you are not sure whether the sailor is harming her, but you see him touching Marnie and kissing the young girl's neck. We are so attuned to direct most of our attention to the visual that the contradiction of Marnie's voice, in contrast to the image, can possibly go unnoticed. "I don't like him to kiss me. Make him go, Mama." The detached voice of Marnie, childlike and screaming, is clearly one of terror that contrasts with the more vague visuals. The "truth" is further dismantled within the image itself. When the sailor first comes out of the bedroom, in the left corner, there is a glimpse of the mother following the sailor. The viewer can assume, then, that the mother is present. This semi-comfort in knowing that Marnie is not alone with this man is undercut as the scene continues and we move into a wider shot. It is disconcerting to see the mother re-enter the living room, once again, as if she had never been there. The disjunction within the image can lead one to think, "Maybe what I saw isn't what I saw."

Marnie's voice explains the mother and daughter's need to protect each other (not necessarily successfully) – the necessity of hiding their story and also the difficulty in telling it. It explains why Mark is never a part of their narrative, because he denies the feminine world and believes in, and is part of, the male fetish and the oedipal scenario. Through tensions within the film that threaten the law of the father, the women's desire constantly challenges and therefore blocks a true recuperation of the heterosexual couple at the end of the film. Marnie's desire is not so much a commitment to Mark or marriage as a desire to avoid going to jail: "Oh Mark, I don't want to go to jail. I'd rather stay with you." As she steps out from her mother's home, a little girl wearing green, who resembles her, makes eye contact with Marnie. In this way, we have the sense that Marnie's spirit has not been curtailed by the man, that the happy ending may not be Marnie's ending after all.

In conclusion, I think that it is critical not only to realize the possibilities of lesbian pleasures in heterosexual texts as well as homosexual or homoerotic texts, but specifically to consider the possible lesbian interest in certain homophobic texts. Why should a text in which a nonheterosexual woman is looking for her past be of interest to a lesbian? *Marnie* affords a lesbian viewer a significant position whereby the status of outlaw becomes a meaningful investment. Lesbians do, after all, function inside as well as outside of a heterosexual world. It is probable that what has drawn theorists to Hitchcock is the very thing that has been swept under the rug. Thus Hitchcock's films are of great interest because, for him, there is nothing sacred about the heterosexual narrative, and he enjoys disrupting social norms with people's fears. What could be a more effective fear to taunt paranoid heterosexuality than homophobia?

A lesbian reading of *Marnie* may open up areas of interest that a heterosexual perspective may overlook or find insignificant, like the voices in *Marnie* or the exchanges between Marnie and Lil. *Marnie* offers the possibility of a lesbian reading, and the lesbian spectator has multiple levels of entry owing to the very ambiguous characters and scenes in the film. On my own informal and unscientific survey, lesbian spectators react with outpourings of anger or comical assertions that, although they know it will not happen in the film, Marnie should pair up with Lil.

That the film centers around the maternal bond, that it is the major problem for Marnie, speaks to the strength of the (maternal) repression and the fear that surrounds it. In *Marnie* patriarchy is so threatened by the women's community and the homoerotic that it fights to pull her back fully into the fatherland. The women's space is seen through a glass darkly, a crippled world where the ambiguous feelings of the mother push you away, after having already swallowed you. At the end of the film, however, it is Mark who has swallowed Marnie.

As Marnie and Mark leave Miss Edgar's home, we see a group of children outside the door. Two boys stand like guards, their backs turned strangely to the viewer. Three girls face Marnie and the viewer, and then we hear the rhyme: "Mumps said the doctor, Measles said the nurse, *Nothing* said the lady with the alligator purse." Or, "Something?"

Notes

I wish to thank Laura George and Judith Mayne for their helpful criticisms. This article is in memory of a very talented artist, Mary Evelyn Knapp.

1. In *Rear Window* a nursery rhyme, "My Hat It Has Three Corners," refers to a murderous "loaded" number 3 and a hat box, where a portion of the dead Mrs. Thorwald is buried. In a less subtle and more literal sense, a tune in *The Lady Vanishes* contains the crucial message of a political spy. In *Shadow of a Doubt* the humming of a song indicates to the young woman Charlie that charming Uncle Charlie is actually a murderer of rich women.

2. Like the psychoanalytic lack, Marnie's "nothing" signifies not simply an absence but a presence that is not easily defined. Teresa de Lauretis suggests the necessity of the concept of castration as a lack not of a phallus but of the feminine body, thus a desire or drive for the feminine. De Lauretis, "Perverse Desire: The Lure of the Mannish Lesbian," *Australian Feminist Studies* (Autumn 1991): 15–26. Judith Roof similarly suggests a lack that engenders a desire to desire the Other (or woman). Roof, *A Lure of Knowledge* (New York: Columbia Univ. Press, 1991). I am hesitant in using the term *lack* because it seems impossible not to associate it with the phallus. However, what we all have in common is the concept of desire for woman.

3. Of course, extensive work has been done in the area of gay theory by film theorists including Judith Mayne, Teresa de Lauretis, Alexander Doty, and Patricia White. See especially Robin Wood, *Hitchcock's Films Revisited* (New York: Columbia Univ. Press, 1989): 232; D. A. Miller, "Anal *Rope*," *Representations*, no. 32 (1990): 114–33.

4. One recent exception was a panel on Hitchcock and Homosexuality at the *Homosexuality and Holiday* conference, Center for Lesbian and Gay Studies, Graduate Center of the City University of New York, March 1992.

5. Lesbian novelist and columnist Marion Garbo Todd makes a humorously similar evaluation of Miss Hathaway in "The Fascination of Television's Perennial Spinster," *Lesbian News*, vol. 16, no. 10 (May 1991): 32–51.

6. Amidst suggesting the destabilizing effect of the transvestite or crossdresser, Marjorie Garber in *Vested Interests* recalls one of the most beloved transvestite figures of all times, Peter Pan, and why it is that this character was played by a woman. Garber, *Vested Interests* (New York: Routledge, Chapman and Hall, 1992), 165–85. I find this character extremely fascinating because he/she was a significant hero that came into my childhood via TV in the late 1950s and therefore is a compelling figure in regard to my developing lesbian viewership.

7. Tania Modleski, *The Women who Knew too Much* (New York: Routledge, 1988).

8. Modleski, 5.

9. Modleski, 5.

10. Marianne Hirsch, *The Mother/Daughter Plot* (Bloomington: Indiana Univ. Press, 1989), 2. It may be that many a lesbian would be drawn to the flamboyant Sphinx because she is not heterosexually defined.

11. Roof, 91.

12. Roof, 106.

13. Raymond Bellour, "Hitchcock, The Enunciator," trans. Bertrand Augst and Hilary Radner, *Camera Obscura*, no. 2 (1981): 66–91.

14. Kaja Silverman, *The Acoustic Mirror* (Bloomington: Indiana Univ. Press, 1988), 65.

15. Laura Mulvey, "Visual Pleasure and Narrative Cinema," in *Visual and Other Pleasures* (Bloomington: Indiana Univ. Press, 1989), 14–26.

16. Silverman, *The Acoustic Mirror*, 204.

17. In Winston Graham's novel *Marnie*, on which the film is based, a male character named Terry is Mark's rival. The character Marnie explains this relationship: "Terry and Mark

really were madly jealous of each other and ever willing to fight over anything; I'd be a new excuse." Graham, *Marnie* (New York: Carroll and Graf, 1961). As is so often the case in soap operas, the replacement of characters is noticeable. But, from the book to the film, it is not only a replacement of looks that is noticeable but a replacement of gender, as Lil takes over the traditionally male position of rival. Considering this gender difference and the desire of Terry in the book, this switch is significant.

18. Emily Apter, *Feminizing the Fetish: Psychoanalysis and Narrative Obsession in Turn-of-the-Century France* (New York: Cornell Univ. Press, 1991).

19. Joan Riviere, "Womanliness as Masquerade," in *Formations of Fantasy*, ed. Victor Burgin, James Donald, and Cora Kaplan (London: Methuen, 1986), 39–40; Apter, 249.

20. Apter, 98.

21. Teresa de Lauretis questions lesbian feminists' refusal of psychoanalytic theory as a means for discussing lesbian sexuality and suggests refiguring lesbian desire through the concept of Freud's negative theory of perversion or the concept of the fetish. De Lauretis finds the reappropriation of the masculinity complex necessary for lesbian theorists in order to move out of the preoedipal realm. For de Lauretis the castration complex is a necessary concept. She uses the character of Stephen in *The Well of Loneliness* to argue that lack is very much concerned with desire for the feminine. In Stephen's case lack signifies a desire for a feminine body and a desire for a feminine lover, a non-narcissistic desire. However, just as de Lauretis believes Freud's masculine complex to forget the feminine lesbian, de Lauretis's fetish positions the butch lesbian as active and the femme lesbian as the passive participant in the fetish. Although I am drawn to the concept of lesbian desire and, through that, the lesbian fetish, I am somewhat perplexed by de Lauretis's rethinking of certain Freudian terms, specifically castration. De Lauretis believes that to "reject the notion of castration is to find ourselves without symbolic means to signify desire." De Lauretis, 17. Although de Lauretis speaks of the desire as not masculine and substitutes the phallus for the fetish, it is difficult to consider the concept of castration without bringing to mind the phallus. My question is, Can you talk about lack without talking about castration? Although I find de Lauretis's fetish compelling, I question the use of the character of Stephen as an appropriate figure at the mirror, for what happens when Marnie looks in the mirror? Typically, unless a woman is considered "masculine" or "butch," her desire is invisible, just as the femme lesbian and Marnie are haunted by their invisibility within film, theory, and psychoanalysis. Elizabeth Grosz in "Lesbian Fetishism?" proposes the possibility of the lesbian fetish by suggesting that it is the masculine lesbian who fetishizes and what she fetishizes is the phallic woman (the mother in Freudian terms) or lesbian, which reduplicates the Freudian model in which only the male fetishizes. This brings to mind Riviere's homophobic text in which the masculine (lesbian) woman becomes feminized or fetishized. I find this analysis problematic because it assumes the relationship of the preoedipal lesbian and phallic mother and the masculine lesbian woman. Elizabeth Grosz, "Lesbian Fetishism?" *Differences*, vol. 3, no. 2 (1991): 39–54.

22. As I mentioned before, I do not suggest a lack of something as de Lauretis and Roof do, but I am equally concerned with lesbian desire and desire for woman (or the feminine).

23. Emily Apter discusses how Freud considered the fetish to be a part of "the male erotic imagination spurred by castration anxiety or repressed homosexuality." Apter, 102. Apter explains that the only fetishistic desire that Freud granted to women was a desire for clothing.

24. In *The Celluloid Closet*, by Vito Russo, the sentence "what the well-dressed lesbian will wear" is the text that accompanies a photo of a costume sketch of Candice Bergen dressed as Lakey, the lesbian in the 1966 film *The Group* (New York: Harper and Row, 1985), 144. Dressed in a black suit, a black derby capping her head, Lakey looks similar to other well-dressed "lesbian" characters such as Theodora in the 1963 film *The Haunting* and Lil in *Marnie*. In fact, in the hunting scene in *Marnie*, while out chasing foxes, both Lil and Marnie are dapperly dressed in black derbies, riding britches, and boots. But Lil and Theo, the lesbian in *The Haunting*, share the mystery of being the dark-haired characters. They are obsessed with the blonde woman's past and present identities and would prefer it if the male characters just left them alone. Each film is obsessed with how the psyche is constructed, and both Marnie and Elizabeth have a past that is tied to the mother, a past that they want to forget. The desire of the viewer to know about each woman's secret is enhanced by the pursuit of the dark-haired, well-dressed, and strong-willed woman. Patricia White has discussed how lesbian characters have been known to haunt film theory as well as horror films and is herself entranced by the characters Elizabeth and Theo. Patricia White, "Female Spectator, Lesbian Specter: *The Haunting*," in *Inside/Out: Lesbian Theories, Gay Theories*, ed. Diana Fuss (New York: Routledge, 1991), 142–72.

25. Mary Ann Doane, "Film and the Masquerade: Theorizing the Female Spectator," 1982, reprinted in *Femmes Fatales: Feminism, Film Theory, Psychoanalysis* (New York: Routledge, 1991), 17–32.

26. Teresa de Lauretis, "Oedipus Interruptus," *Wide Angle* vol. 7, nos. 1–2 (1985) 36, 38. De Lauretis makes this same point in "Sexual Indifference and Lesbian Representation," in *Performing Feminisms: Feminist Critical Theory and Theatre*, ed. Sue Ellen Case (Baltimore: Johns Hopkins Univ. Press, 1990), 17–39.

27. Miller, "Anal *Rope*," 119, 118. In *Marnie* Mark brings Marnie to meet his family, and after Lil shakes Marnie's hand she rubs her wrist. In a gay (generally gay male) stereotyped gesture, Lil's wrist goes limp as she declares, "Oh Dear, I think I rather sprained my wrist this afternoon." After Lil beckons Marnie to her side to pour the tea, Mark makes something of the fact that Lil likes her tea with a slice of lemon, as though she has "weird" tastes.

28. Wood, *Hitchcock's Films Revisited*, 232. D. A. Miller, in "Anal *Rope*," also argues that homosexuality in Hitchcock's films is more complex.

29. Luce Irigaray, *This Sex which Is Not One*, trans. Catherine Porter (Ithaca, NY: Cornell Univ. Press, 1985), 196.

Chapter Twenty-Three
Rituals of Defilement: *Frenzy*

Tania Modleski

Food in Frenzy *is a basic visual metaphor for the devouring abuses of man-against-man. (Donald Spoto,* The Art of Alfred Hitchcock*)*

Seeing a rotten fruit full of worms, Mair, the Urubu demiurge, exclaimed, "That would make a nice woman!" and straightaway the fruit turned into a woman.... In a Tacana myth the jaguar decides not to rape an Indian woman after he has caught the smell of her vulva, which seems to him to reek of worm-ridden meat.... Here again, then, we are dealing with stench and decay which, as has already been established, signify nature, as opposed to culture.... And woman is everywhere synonymous with nature. (Claude Lévi-Strauss, The Raw and the Cooked*)*

Curiosity in an animal is always either sexual or alimentary.... In knowing, consciousness attracts the object to itself and incorporates it in itself.... But this movement of dissolution is fixed by the fact that the known remains in the same place, indefinitely absorbed, devoured, and yet indefinitely intact, wholly digested and yet wholly outside, as indigestible as a stone. (Jean-Paul Sartre, Being and Nothingness*)*

Having begun *The Woman Who Knew Too Much* with a discussion of Hitchcock's *Blackmail*, this study ends appropriately with *Frenzy* (1972), which is concerned with many of the same issues as the early film. In particular, both films include a rape that has proven to be very problematic to Hitchcock's critics, though for opposite reasons: in *Blackmail*, the difficulty is that *nothing is shown* (only shadows of the characters projected onto the walls), whereas in *Frenzy* too much is shown, nothing is left to the imagination. In the later film Hitchcock provides the kind of "incontrovertible evidence" of rape that Durgnat had found lacking in *Blackmail* and that enabled him to disqualify the heroine's view of her own experience.

Some critics have looked at the increasing use of graphic violence in Hitchcock films as evidence of a rather sick mind. For example, in his biography of Hitchcock, Donald Spoto has documented Hitchcock's obsession with filming a rape/murder and has condemned the director as something of a dirty old man. The way the biographer tells it, Hitchcock's career may be seen as one long frustrating bout with cinematic impotence until he managed finally to achieve full orgasmic satisfaction with *Frenzy*: "Unable to realize a rape in *No Bail for the Judge* he had hinted at it in *Psycho*, metaphorized it in *The Birds* and, against all advice, included it in *Marnie*. Now at last – encouraged by the new freedom in the movies – his imagination of this sordid crime could be more fully shown in all its horror."[1]

But precisely *because Frenzy* seems to take crimes against women to new lengths, and because it seems to be the culmination of an entire career, a lifetime of obsession, it provides a good occasion for us to reflect back on and draw together some of the themes that have been important in this study. At the same time I will use this analysis as an occasion to say something about *Psycho* (1960), a film whose impact was such that no subsequent Hitchcock film can be talked about without reference to it. In a way, though, I have never really not been discussing *Psycho* – to my mind, the quintessential horror film.

* * *

After an opening sequence showing the discovery of a woman's body floating in the Thames, a necktie around her neck, *Frenzy* dissolves to a shot of the mirror image of the film's hero/antihero, Richard Blaney (Jon Finch), former Squadron Leader of the RAF, putting on a necktie exactly like the one used by the strangler. He goes into the bar where he works and has a drink, whereupon the proprietor, Felix Forsythe (Bernard Cribbins), enters and reprimands him for stealing. Blaney claims he was going to pay for the drink and is defended by the waitress, Babs Milligan (Anna Massey). From the altercation that ensues, we are made to understand that Forsythe is motivated by jealousy over the relationship between Blaney and Babs. The scene ends with Blaney being fired and having to pay back a loan to Forsythe, so that he is left financially strapped.

Blancy runs into a friend, Bob Rusk (Barry Foster), owner of a wholesale fruit market. Bob is exceedingly friendly, offering money, a bunch of grapes, and a tip on a horse. Instead of betting on the horse, however, Blaney spends all his money on drink, and when he learns from Bob (leaning out over his apartment window to introduce his "old Mum") that the horse has actually won, he walks off in a rage, trampling on the grapes as he goes. He pays a visit to his ex-wife, Brenda Blaney (Barbara Leigh-Hunt), owner of a matrimonial agency, and picks a fight with her in her office. After they make up, she invites him to dinner at her club, where Blaney again becomes enraged at the thought of his bad luck in comparison to his wife's success. He apologizes for his temper when he breaks a brandy glass in his hand, and then the two take a cab to her house. Although Blaney clearly expects to spend the night, the next shot shows him sleeping at the Salvation Army, where an old man tries to steal money Brenda has slipped him on the sly.

In the next scene, Bob Rusk, alias Mr. Robinson, enters Brenda's office. He has clearly been here before, and Brenda, nervous as well as contemptuous, tells him that she cannot accommodate his desire for women who will submit to his "peculiarities." In this prolonged scene, Rusk first intimidates, then rapes, and finally strangles

Brenda, the camera dwelling on every lurid detail of the latter action. The secretary, Monica Barling (Jean Marsh), returning from lunch, sees Blaney go by and after she discovers her employer's body, assumes that Brenda's former husband has committed the murder. Inspector Oxford (Alex McCowen) and his men from Scotland Yard begin investigating the crime, while Blaney, unaware of what has occurred, takes Babs to the fancy Hotel Coburn. After showing them to their room, the porter recognizes the description of Blaney in a newspaper and alerts the police, but the pair have seen the headlines in the newspaper put under their door and have escaped. They find temporary refuge with one of Dick's RAF comrades, Johnny Porter (Clive Swift), whose wife, Hetty (Billie Whitelaw), is convinced of Blaney's guilt and reacts angrily at being forced to shelter him.

Babs returns to the bar the next day and quits after a quarrel with Forsythe. Rusk overhears the argument and offers to put Babs up for the night. They go to his apartment and the camera follows them just to the door and then slowly, silently moves back down the stairs and out into the street. That night Rusk puts Babs's body, stuffed in a potato sack, into a truck and returns home, where he discovers that his tie pin is missing and realizes that it is in the hand of the dead woman. He goes out to the truck, which starts moving after he climbs in, and begins a frantic search amidst the lurching and careening of the truck until he finally reaches the pin clutched in the hand of the corpse. Rigor mortis at first prevents him from retrieving it, however, so he tries unsuccessfully to cut off a finger and then snaps the fingers open one by one to get at the pin.

Blaney's friends refuse to help him after Babs's murder, so he seeks out Rusk, who manages to frame him by hiding him in his apartment and alerting the police to his presence there, having first placed Babs's clothes in Blaney's suitcase. Blaney is found guilty and sent to prison, vowing all the way to avenge himself on Rusk. Meanwhile, the inspector has been discussing the case with his wife (Vivien Merchant) as she serves him grotesque meals she has learned to make at a school for continental cooking (soup with fish heads, pigs' trotters, and so on). Mrs. Oxford insists all along that Blaney is innocent of murdering his wife since a "*crime de passion*" after ten years of marriage seems unlikely. "Look at us, we've only been married eight years and you can hardly keep your eyes open at night." Evidence finally convinces the inspector of his error, but Blaney has in the meantime broken out of prison and returned to Rusk's apartment. He begins to beat the body lying in bed with a tire jack, but it turns out to be another strangled corpse. The inspector surprises Blaney, who for a moment believes himself to be further incriminated. Just then a sound on the stairs causes the inspector to motion for silence, and Rusk enters the room pushing a heavy trunk. The inspector observes mildly, "Why, Mr. Rusk, you're not wearing your tie," the trunk falls, and the film ends.

* * *

Shot in London, *Frenzy* marks a return of the director to his roots, a move that was paralleled by one from the studio to the streets – and hence to a more "realistic" style of filmmaking. This return to London is emphatically signaled in the credit sequence when the camera (suspended from a helicopter) drifts over the Thames and under Tower Bridge. A dissolve reveals an overhead shot of a crowd gathered in front of some large buildings on the banks of the river. As the camera cranes down, the words of the politician haranguing the crowd (among whom stands Alfred Hitchcock in a bowler hat) gradually become audible. The politician is promising to restore the "ravishing sights" of London, to eradicate the "waste products of our society with which for so long we have poisoned our rivers." He continues, "Let us rejoice that pollution will soon be banished from the waters of this river." He is interrupted by one of the spectators who yells out in alarm as the gaping crowd rushes forward to witness the sight of a naked female corpse floating face down in the Thames, a man's tie around her neck. The sequence ends with a male voice saying, "I say, that's not my club's tie, is it?"

This sequence is remarkable for many reasons. While, on the one hand, London is here and throughout the movie strongly evoked, Hitchcock exhibits the utmost contempt for tourism – and most especially for what one might call cinema as tourism (in this respect the film is markedly different from *Vertigo*, which, as Virginia Wright Wexman has argued, indulges us in the tourist's view of San Francisco).[2] Later on two doctors, well-dressed and seemingly eminently civilized men, will reveal just what it is that the tourists crave. As they stand at a bar in a pub, one of them says that in one way he hopes the murderer, who rapes his victims and then strangles them with a necktie, will not be caught because "a good juicy series of sex murders" is "so good for the tourist trade." Foreigners, he observes, "expect the squares of London to be fog-wreathed, full of hansom cabs, and littered with ripped whores." As regards the third expectation, Hitchcock devotes himself with a vengeance to giving the tourists what they want – or at least, if it is not quite accurate to say that the film is "littered with ripped whores," nevertheless, the shots depicting sexual violence or the results of sexual violence are some of the most disturbing ever shown in the cinema. If many critics have found these images to be more palatable than they ought, this is surely at least in part a measure of the extent to which sexual violence is condoned in patriarchal society. As I argued at the outset of this study, whether a viewer endorses or condemns the sexual violence in the film is partly a matter of interpretation, of the viewer's own predilections and experience. To use a metaphor suggested by the film itself, one man's meat may be another man's poison.

At the same time, although by the end of the film we might be inclined to agree with the porter who says, "Sometimes just thinking about the lusts of men makes me want to heave," and although, as Robin Wood has contended, the main female characters are more sympathetic than anyone else in the film, there is little doubt that part of what makes the crime Hitchcock depicts so repellent has to do with an underlying fear and loathing of femininity.[3] This paradoxical state of affairs is simply a more extreme version of the ambivalence toward femininity I have traced throughout this study. In *Frenzy* ambivalence can be related to the polarity woman as food vs. woman as poison (source of "pollution," "waste-product" of society, to use the politician's words). To understand how woman functions throughout the film as both edible commodity and inedible pollutant (the stench of femininity alluded to in the myths studied by Lévi-Strauss) helps us to achieve a deeper insight not only into this particular film, but of some of Hitchcock's major concerns throughout his career.[4]

That eating and copulating have frequently been posited as analogous activities in Hitchcock films has certainly not gone unremarked in the criticism. However, the tendency – most pronounced in the Spoto biography – has been to put this parallelism down to the imagination of an overweight pervert. Such a view has unfortunately obscured the extent to which Hitchcock films put into bold (and rather comic) relief an equation that seems to exist at the heart of patriarchal culture itself. As Lévi-Strauss observes in *The Savage Mind*, there is a "very profound analogy which people throughout the world seem to find between copulation and eating. In a very large number of languages they are even called by the same term. In Yoruba 'to eat' and 'to marry' are expressed by a single verb the general sense of which is 'to win, to acquire,' a usage which has its parallel in French [and also in English], where the verb 'consommer' [to consummate] applies both to marriage and to meals."[5]

In *Frenzy*, when Bob Rusk, owner of a fruit market, forces himself sexually onto Brenda Blaney, he says, "There's a saying in the fruit business, we put it on the fruit: don't squeeze the goods until they're yours. I would never, never do that." (Of course, he proceeds directly to contradict himself and violate "goods" which are not his.) As he sits on her desk, Rusk comments on Brenda's "frugal" lunch, and then he begins to eat the (English) apple she has brought. When he is finished raping and strangling her, he spies the apple, resumes eating it, puts it down, picks his teeth with his tie pin, and again takes up the half-eaten apple (shown in close-up) as he leaves. Now, given the numerous references to gardens in the film (Forsythe sarcastically says to Babs and Blaney when they are talking outside the pub, "This is Covent Garden, not the Garden of Love"; Rusk tells Blaney that his "Old Mum" lives in Kent, "the Garden of England"; and so on), it seems plausible to argue that the Adam and Eve myth is being invoked, but that a deliberate reversal is effected: here the *man* eats the apple, "knows" the woman, and is responsible for her destruction.

In *The Savage Mind* Lévi-Strauss suggests that the common cultural "equation of male with devourer and female with devoured" may be intended to reverse the situation man most fears. Lévi-Strauss refers to the sexual philosophy of the Far East where "for a man the art of love-making consists essentially in avoiding having his vital force absorbed by the women [possessors of the *vagina dentata*] and in turning this risk to his advantage."[6] (We recall the analysis of *Murder!* in which the hero takes the risk of hystericization and feminization in order to achieve masculine control over the narrative.) Thus it is possible to see in the film's brutality toward women still one more indication of the need expressed throughout Hitchcock's works to deny resemblance to – absorption by – the female, a need that for Lévi-Strauss lies at the inaugural moment of culture and of myth (it is no accident that *The Raw and the Cooked* begins with several myths about the disorder introduced by boys who refuse to leave the world of women to enter the separate men's house and ends with a chapter entitled "The Wedding").[7] Yet, as we shall see, the identification of male with devourer and female with devoured may not always have the psychic effect of negating the imagined ability of the female to absorb the male, since food is frequently endowed with the power to transform the eater into its likeness.[8] You are, after all, what you eat.

Lévi-Strauss's linguistic analysis suggests once more the connection we have encountered so often between men's hostility to woman (the need to "win" or conquer her, to "acquire" possession of her) and fear of the female other. Behind all this fear and loathing of woman, this desperation to acquire mastery over her, lies the threat of the devouring mother, a familiar figure in Hitchcock – so familiar indeed that, by the time of *Frenzy*, Hitchcock need do no more than place her picture prominently on display in the villain's apartment, have him quote her on several occasions, and get her to pop her head out the window in a cameo appearance. After *Psycho*, the public understands through these slight allusions and without the necessity of elaborate psychiatric explanations exactly who is responsible for the murderous "lusts of men." We might say (taking our cue again from Lévi-Strauss) that the film *knows so well* who the culprit is and what motivates the crimes that it can dispense with the full articulation of the theme. Traces of it remain, however, displaced into bit parts: for example, when Blaney first visits his wife he observes a brief Thurberesque vignette occurring between a newly paired couple, a large, loud, domineering woman and a meek, mousy, little man. The man suggests they go right for the marriage license, and the woman asks, "What's your hurry? We'll go to my place first." As the two descend the stairs to the street, the camera holds on them in a long take while she tells the man how her late husband used to get up every morning at 5:30 to clean house, a task that he had completed by 9:30 when he brought her her coffee in bed. And he was so quiet the whole time that in thirty years he never woke her once. "A neat man, was he?" her partner asks. "He liked a tidy place," she replies, "So do I come to that."

It has been part of my task in this book to suggest how fear of the devouring, voracious mother is central in much of Hitchcock's work, even where it is not immediately apparent. By "voracious," I refer to the continual threat of annihilation, of swallowing up, the mother poses to the personality and identity of the protagonists. Far from being the mere gimmick criticism has tended to consider it, the mother's psychic obliteration of her child in *Psycho* is paradigmatic of the fear haunting many Hitchcock films, at least since *Rebecca*. Julia Kristeva has theorized that such a threat constitutes the very "powers of horror." In Kristeva's account, phobia and the phobic aspects of religion are all ultimately linked to matrophobia and are concerned with warding off the danger of contact with the mother: "This is precisely where we encounter the rituals of defilement ... which, based on the feeling of abjection and all converging on the maternal, attempt to symbolize the other threat to the subject: that of being swamped by the dual relationship, thereby risking the loss not of a part (castration) but of the totality of his living being. The function of these religious rituals is to ward off the subject's fear of his very own identity sinking irretrievably into the mother."[9] Drawing on the work of Mary Douglas, who considers defilement to be connected with boundaries and margins, Kristeva claims that the feminine/maternal is deemed a "pollutant" because it is experienced as subversive of male symbolic systems and masculine notions of identity and order. Kristeva's language in the above quotation, describing feelings of being "swamped," of "sinking" into the morass of the maternal, uncannily captures the experience of *Psycho*, in which the response of Norman Bates (Anthony Perkins) to his "possessive" mother is to conduct his own ritual of defilement, murdering Marion Crane (Janet Leigh), meticulously cleaning the bathroom of her blood, throwing her body into the trunk of a car, and pushing it into the swamp, which slowly sucks it down. Thus do men's fears become women's fate.

It is commonplace, at least since Rohmer and Chabrol's study, to consider Hitchcock a Catholic director, especially insofar as he is concerned with the themes of guilt and original sin. It seems to me possible to deepen this insight of the religious nature of Hitchcock's work, endeavoring to get beyond the platitudinous in order to understand the strong hold Hitchcock has had on the public imagination right up to the present day. Thus we may speculate that Hitchcock films enact "rituals of defilement," evoking and then containing the fear of women that lies at the heart of these rituals.

The association of women with defilement, with filth, is as strong in Hitchcock as it is in the "savage mind" analyzed by Lévi-Strauss. In *Psycho* Marion Crane is identified with money ("filthy lucre"), bathrooms, toilets, blood, and, of course, the swamp.[10] In an earlier film, *Shadow of a Doubt* (1943), Uncle Charlie (Joseph Cotten), who murders wealthy widows, sees the world as a "foul sty," a "filthy, rotting place," and he delivers a speech (significantly, at the dinner table) in which he speaks of men who work hard until they die, leaving their wives to throw their money away: "Eating the money, drinking the money, ... smelling of money.... Faded, fat, greedy women." In *Frenzy*, the association of women with pollution is made explicitly in the film's opening sequence, and the film is "littered" with shots of grotesque-looking female corpses (Hitchcock had been dissuaded from showing spittle dripping from the tongue of Brenda Blaney in the shocking close-up of her after the murder). Babs's body, dusted with potato flour, spills out of the truck and onto the road, and the potato dust that Rusk brushes off himself after the truck episode is the clue leading to his capture as the murderer. (Earlier Blaney was incriminated for his wife's murder because traces of her powder were found on his money.) Finally, the body of Babs is paralleled with the repellent, virtually inedible food the inspector's wife gives him to eat, food like pig's feet, which the inspector nearly gags on while reconstructing the potato truck episode with his wife. He relates how the corpse's fingers had been snapped open to retrieve an incriminating object, and, as he speaks of this, his wife snaps breadsticks in two and crunches on them.

The corpse of woman is a figure of extreme pollution. "Impure animals become even more impure once they are dead," writes Kristeva; "contact with their carcasses must be avoided" (p. 109). As if reversing the scene in *Psycho*, in which – to the audience's great satisfaction – Norman Bates painstakingly restores the bathroom to its pristine state after stabbing Marion Crane to death there, *Frenzy* shows its villain, who has neatly disposed of the body in the potato truck, returning to the corpse and grubbing around among the potatoes and the body parts, searching for the tie pin that might incriminate him. While critics have frequently noted Hitchcock's detachment in this late film, evidenced in his sparing use of point-of-view shots, it is important to note that this particular sequence employs several point-of-view shots, drawing us into an immediate experience of the man's grotesque encounter with death. The feeling is very much one of violating an ultimate taboo, of being placed in close contact with the most "impure" of "impure animals": the carcass of the decaying female. It is as if Hitchcock is punishing the spectator for years of guilty movie-going pleasures, as if the kick in the face Rusk receives from the corpse's foot is repayment for all the times cinema has fetishized the female body, dismembering it for the sheer erotic pleasure of the male spectator. When Rusk peels back the potato sack to get to the hands (he has, unfortunately, put the body into the sack head first), we are witness to a kind of macabre striptease, a complete deromanticization of the necrophilia that Hitchcock insisted was at the heart of *Vertigo*. Ultimately, the corpse gets its vengeance, since, in spite of his efforts to clean himself. Rusk is unable to eradicate the pollution that has contaminated him. In this way the film works yet another variation on Hitchcock's perennial theme of the powers of a dead woman.

These powers are also exerted on the chief inspector, whose wife forces him to partake of a symbolic feast of the corpse. The later scenes at the dinner table may be paralleled with and contrasted to the earlier one of the rape. In the first scene, Rusk sexually attacks a woman he likens to food; unable to achieve orgasm, he explodes in a murderous rage and strangles her. In the later scenes, the inspector eats food that is likened to a woman; and, though he experiences great difficulty consummating *his* meals, he remains civil to his wife. She, on the other hand, seems to be wreaking revenge on her husband because of his lack of sexual inclination (a deficiency in the "lusts of men"). In contrast to Rusk, then, who exerted brutal control over the woman, Oxford seems very much at the mercy of his wife.

The scenes at the dinner table, flirting as they do with connotations of cannibalism and hence of extreme pollution – that is, the idea of feeding off the "carcass" of the dead woman – are the culmination of the motifs of food and filth pervading the film. According to Kristeva, dietary prohibitions are based upon the prohibition of incest (an analysis confirmed by Lévi-Strauss) and thus are part of the "project of separation" from the female body engaged in not only by the biblical text, which Kristeva analyzes at some length, but by patriarchal symbolic systems in general. Speaking of nutritional prohibitions, Kristeva writes: "the dietary, when it departs from the conformity that can be demanded by the logic of separation, blends with the maternal as unclean and improper coalescence, as undifferentiated power to be cut off" (p. 106). The inspector's cannibalization of the female would obviously be an extreme form of this unclean, improper coalescence, violating in the most immediate way the separation of female body and male law.

Here again Hitchcock makes rather extensive use of point-of-view shots and in so doing it might be said that he forces the spectator into symbolically sharing the unholy feast with the inspector – metaphorically incorporating what he literally incorporates. Interestingly, in film theory incorporation has been considered to be the basis for "secondary identification" – that is, identification with characters: "character representations are taken into the self and provide the basis for a momentary subjectivity."[11] According to Freud, incorporation may be seen as a preliminary stage of identification, one that expresses a fundamental ambivalence toward the object: "The ego wishes to incorporate this object into itself and the method by which it would do so, in this oral or cannibalistic stage, is by devouring it."[12] The ambivalence is such that, on the one hand, the subject wishes by devouring the object to destroy it and, on the other hand, both to preserve it within the self and to appropriate its qualities (this is truly wanting to have one's cake and eat it too).[13] The cannibalism in *Frenzy* seems to me to be the ultimate expression of the ambivalence toward women we have seen to be operating in Hitchcock films, which seek with equal vehemence both to appropriate femininity and to destroy it – hence that curious mixture of "sympathy and misogyny" found in these films.

Kristeva speculates that "defilement reveals, at the same time as an attempt to throttle matrilineality, an attempt at separating the speaking being from his body.... It is only at such a cost that the body is capable of being defended, protected – and also, eventually, sublimated. Fear of the uncontrollable generative mother repels me from the body; I give up cannibalism because abjection (of the mother) leads me toward respect for the body of the other, my fellow man, my brother" (pp. 78–9). At the end of *Frenzy* the film brings together for the first time the three male protagonists – villain, "wrong man," and officer of the law. The chief inspector speaks on behalf of propriety, civilization, and sublimation when he observes wryly, "Why, Mr. Rusk, you're not wearing your tie," thereby restoring us to a world in which men are in control of themselves and their "lusts." It is a world from which women are altogether excluded, having been expelled from it mostly by brutal means, their power throttled. Throughout the film the specter of this power has been continually evoked and subsequently choked off. Babs Milligan is the sexually active woman, unrestrained by marriage (the inspector remarks to Forsythe, who wonders if she will return from her night with Blaney, "Don't worry, these days ladies abandon their honor far more readily than their clothes"). Other women, like Hetty, wife of Dick's RAF buddy, are threatening because they dominate *within* marriage. Still others, like the bespectacled, prudish secretary, keep "a sharp eye on men" and seem to despise them altogether. Finally, Brenda Blaney, as head of a matrimonial agency, is an especially dangerous figure of female power because she has usurped male rights of exchange: no longer are women objects of exchange among men (as, for example they were in *Blackmail*); rather it is the woman who delivers men over to other women who proceed to enslave them. Brenda passes some of the money she makes off this trade to her down-and-out husband, who is embittered because he is not as successful as she, and sends him off to spend the night at the Salvation Army, which he calls the "hotel for bachelors." The film suggests that Brenda's marital and sexual rejection of her husband is avenged by Rusk, since the shot of Dick sitting in the dirty Salvation Army bed holding up the money his wife has given him is immediately followed by the scene of Brenda's rape/murder. As he has done so often in the past, Hitchcock here plays on the notion of the transference or exchange of guilt, only by this point it is clear that such an exchange – the only kind seemingly now possible among men – is a result of women's having usurped male prerogatives and refused to allow themselves to serve as objects of exchange in the usual male rituals like marriage. Thus extreme rituals of defilement become the last, bleak hope for patriarchy.

That *Frenzy is* such an extreme film has generally been attributed to the loosening of censorship that was occurring in the movies at the time it was made and that presumably permitted Hitchcock greater scope for his prurient imaginings. It seems to me more useful, however, to consider *Frenzy* not simply as the reflection of the dirty mind of a frustrated old man nor even of a new "freedom" in sexual mores, but rather as a cultural response to women's demands for sexual and social liberation, demands that were, after all, at their height in 1972 when *Frenzy* was made. In this connection, Mary Douglas's observation about the kind of society in which ideas about sex pollution are likely to flourish is most illuminating. According to Douglas, sex is likely to be pollution-free in a society where sexual roles are secure and enforced directly. "When male dominance is accepted as a central principle of social organisation and applied without inhibition and with full rights of physical coercion, beliefs in sex pollution are not likely to be highly developed."[14] On the other hand, ideas about sex pollution tend to thrive in societies where male dominance is challenged or where other principles tend to contradict it. Douglas's insight is of enormous importance for feminists. It is not because male dominance is so firmly entrenched that ideas about women such as those found in *Frenzy* are held, but rather because it *is not*. These ideas come about as a result of inroads made on the system by women who insist on crossing the borders designed to separate male and female spheres. The resultant "boundary confusion" is threatening to man's sense of social and personal identity, making him feel contaminated, unsafe. In other words, when men are no longer able to use women to consolidate their (oedipal) relations with one another and hence to ensure their separateness from the female, the kinds of psychological fears discussed throughout this chapter – fears of the "totality" of one's "living being" sinking "irretrievably into the maternal" – are aroused.

* * *

This is not to say that the film endorses all the violence it portrays, despite feminist analyses of *Frenzy* that assume Hitchcock's total approbation of his villain's behavior. I have argued in previous chapters that Hitchcock's fear and loathing of women is accompanied by a lucid understanding of – and even sympathy for – women's problems in patriarchy. This apparent contradiction is attributable to his profound ambivalence about femininity, ambivalence that, in *Frenzy*, reaches an extreme form that I have accounted for psychoanalytically by analysis of the cannibalism motif. In Freudian theory, as we have seen, the individual at the cannibalistic stage wants to destroy the object by devouring it, but he also wishes to preserve it and to assimilate it. To say, then, that Hitchcock films seek both to destroy *and* to preserve femininity is not to admit to a failure to arrive at the correct interpretation of the films, an inability to decide once and for all whether or not Hitchcock is really a misogynist. Rather, it is to acknowledge how pervasive and how deep the ambivalence is in these films, and to begin to understand just why it is we *cannot* decide.

By this I do not mean to glorify the undecidability of interpretation the way certain varieties of deconstructionist criticism do. The consequences for women of the negative aspect of ambivalence are too dire. But I do mean to insist on the importance of the fact that woman is never completely destroyed in these films – no matter how dead Hitchcock tries to make her appear, as when he inserts still shots in both *Psycho* and *Frenzy* of the female corpse. There are always elements resistant to her destruction or assimilation. Thus, at the same time that *Frenzy* undoubtedly shares some of the contempt for and fear of women exhibited by the men in the film, it also portrays the main female characters more sympathetically than most of its male characters. Even more importantly, the film links the sexual violence it depicts to a system of male dominance rather than confining it to the inexplicable behavior of one lone psychopath: thus both Blaney and Oxford are shown at different points in the film wearing ties similar to that found on the neck of the corpse floating in the Thames; moreover, this tie appears to be the tie of a certain men's club, as the male onlooker in the opening sequence reveals. Finally, the ironic nature of this sequence, in which the corpse appears as if in response to the politician's remarks about the pollution of the rivers, enables us, if we choose, to take a distance from the equation of woman with pollution and even to see it as a male projection.

In fact, the film provides plenty of evidence of this kind of projection. When a female bartender asks the doctors who have been speaking of the murderer, "He rapes them first, doesn't he?" they reply, "Yes, well, it's nice to know that every cloud has a silver lining." At another point in the film Rusk says, "Mind you, there are some women who ask for everything they get." Yet, in the very way it depicts sexual violence, the film belies the notion, common in patriarchy, that women actually want to be raped and either invite or deserve sexual victimization.

The graphic depiction of sexual violence in *Frenzy* has been the source of some critical controversy, as I mentioned earlier. Donald Spoto, we recall, castigated Hitchcock for showing the "sordid crime" in "all its horror." For Spoto, as for so many critics, much of Hitchcock's distinction had lain in the discretion with which he had treated such subject matter in the past (and notably in *Psycho*): "The act of murder in Alfred Hitchcock's films had always been stylized by the devices of editing and … photographic wizardry. [But in *Frenzy*] Hitchcock insisted on all the ugly explicitness of this picture, and for all its cinematic inventiveness, it retains one of the most repellent examples of a detailed murder in the history of film."[15] Of course, one might ask why, if a sordid crime like rape/murder is to be depicted at all, it should *not* be shown "in all its horror." In fact, it could be argued that the stylization and allusiveness of the shower scene in *Psycho* have provided critics with the rationale for lovingly and endlessly recounting all the details of its signification in the very process of self-righteously deploring its signified, the crime of rape/murder.[16] In *Frenzy*, by contrast, Hitchcock's use of graphic details, his casting of ordinary, non-fetishized women in the various female roles, and his refusal to eroticize the proceedings as he had in *Psycho* – teasing viewers with shots of Janet Leigh in her brassiere and Janet Leigh stripping so that, even while she is being stabbed to death, we irresistibly wonder if we'll get a glimpse of her naked breasts – all this makes the crime he is depicting more difficult for the spectator to assimilate – more "repellent," in Spoto's word. In the assault scene in *Frenzy* the woman's anguish is stressed as the camera shows her in close-up uttering a psalm. These shots and her words clash grotesquely with those of Rusk, to whom the camera keeps cutting and who repeatedly utters the single word, "Lovely" (until, enraged by his own impotence, he yells, "You bitch," and begins to strangle her). In contrast to *Psycho*, which in promotions and in the film itself had titillated spectators with hopes of seeing Janet Leigh's breasts but which had withheld the full sight of the desired objects, *Frenzy* shows an extreme close-up of the woman's breast as she struggles to pull her bra back over it, all the while murmuring the words of the psalm. It is all anything but lovely; it is infinitely sad, pathetic, among the most disturbing scenes cinema has to offer.

The film, then, veers between disgust at the "lusts of men" and loathing of the female body itself, treated in several scenes as an object of ghoulish humor, so that many critics have justly pointed to the film's utter cynicism about sex and the relation between the sexes. This cynicism seems to provide some critics with a convenient excuse for not dealing with the issue of misogyny at all: the logic seems to be that, since Hitchcock shows contempt for women *and* men, there is no reason to single out his treatment of women for special discussion – no reason, then, for considering why women are the exclusive objects of rape and mutilation in the film or why it is their "carcasses" that litter the film's landscape and not men's. The extreme of this blindness can be seen in statements like Spoto's about the "devouring abuses of man-against-man." For feminists there is an obvious need to keep the problem of violence against women at the center of the analysis (as it is at the center of the film); nevertheless, we cannot afford to ignore the full complexity of the film and its attitude toward women.

When Rusk comes to the matrimonial agency, he is, as we learn, in search of a woman – a "masochist," the inspector says – who will submit to his peculiar appetites. The film makes it quite clear that he does not find what he is looking for. At one point Brenda says, "All right, I won't struggle," and he tells her that he wants her to struggle, "some women like to struggle." As Rusk's reply suggests, and as the female spectator very well knows, Brenda's refusal to struggle is not the masochistic submission the man desires – not the acquiescence that in his eyes masquerades as resistance.[17] This is a small detail, perhaps, but it is significant. It provides yet one more indication of the fact that despite the considerable violence visited on women in the movies – and by proxy, women *at* the movies – their capitulation to male desires and expectations is never complete. Or, to put it another way, for a whole variety of reasons which it has been the task of this book to explore, we may suppose that, while women are important consumers of the films, the films themselves do not utterly consume women.

Notes

1. Donald Spoto, *The Dark Side of Genius: The Life of Alfred Hitchcock* (New York: Ballantine, 1983), p. 545. See also the discussion of the reviews of *Frenzy* in Jeanne Thomas Allen, "The Representation of Violence to Women: Hitchcock's *Frenzy*," *Film Quarterly*, vol. 38, no. 3 (Spring 1985): 31. Allen quotes Vincent Canby: "I suspect that films like *Frenzy* may be sicker and more pernicious than your cheapie, hum-drum porno flick, because they are slicker, more artistically compelling versions of sadomasochistic fantasies and because they leave me [*sic*] feeling more angry and more impotent simultaneously."
2. Virginia Wright Wexman, "The Critic as Consumer: Film Study in the University, *Vertigo*, and the Film Canon," *Film Quarterly*, vol. 39, no. 3 (Spring 1986): 32–73.

3. Robin Wood, "Fear of Spying," *American Film*, vol. 9, no. 2 (November 1983): 31.

4. Raymond Durgnat, alone among critics that I am aware of, has noticed that food and pollution function together in an important way in the film. However, he never gets around to saying *how* they function, and is content simply to point out the existence of these elements. See *The Strange Case of Alfred Hitchcock, or the Plain Man's Hitchcock* (Cambridge, MA: MIT Press, 1974), 394–401.

5. Claude Lévi-Strauss, *The Savage Mind* (Chicago: Univ. of Chicago Press, 1966), 105.

6. Lévi-Strauss, *The Savage Mind*, 106.

7. Claude Lévi-Strauss, *The Raw and the Cooked: Introduction to a Science of Mythology*, vol. 1, trans. John and Doreen Weightman (Chicago: Univ. of Chicago Press, 1969).

8. See, for example, Freud's remarks on cannibalism in *Totem and Taboo*. "By incorporating parts of a person's body, through the act of eating, one at the same time acquires the qualities possessed by him." *The Standard Edition of the Complete Psychological Works of Sigmund Freud*, vol. 13, trans. James Strachey (London: Hogarth, 1974), 82.

9. Julia Kristeva, *Powers of Horror: An Essay on Abjection*, trans. Leon S. Roudiez (New York: Columbia Univ. Press, 1982), 64. Kristeva herself has something to say about Hitchcock and horror in her essay entitled "Ellipsis on Dread and the Specular Seduction," trans. Dolores Burdick, *Wide Angle*, vol. 3, no. 3 (1979): 42–7. But her prejudice against anything that has mass appeal is such that she simply cannot see the extent to which Hitchcock's cinema, being an exercise in sustained abjection, is of relevance to her theories. For an extremely interesting discussion of Hitchcock's British film *The Lady Vanishes* in the light of Kristeva's work, see Patrice Petro, "Rematerializing the Vanishing 'Lady': Feminism, Hitchcock, and Interpretation" (Chapter 10, above). Kristeva hereafter cited in the text.

10. For an excellent discussion of these motifs in *Psycho*, see James Naremore, *Filmguide to Psycho* (Bloomington: Indiana Univ. Press, 1973). This analysis is, I believe, the best ever written about the film.

11. Kaja Silverman, "Lost Objects and Mistaken Subjects: Film Theory's Structuring Lack," *Wide Angle*, vol. 7, nos. 1–2 (1985): 24. See also Christian Metz on the relation of the technology of photography to orality. *The Imaginary Signifier*, trans. Celia Britton, Anwyl Williams, Ben Brewster, and Alfred Guzzetti (Bloomington: Indiana Univ. Press, 1982), 50.

12. Sigmund Freud, "Mourning and Melancholia," *Standard Edition*, vol. 14, p. 250. See also *Three Essays on the Theory of Sexuality*, trans. James Strachey (New York: Basic Books, 1962), 64.

13. See the entries on cannibalism and incorporation in Jean Laplanche and J.-B. Pontalis, *The Language of Psychoanalysis*, trans. Donald Nicholson Smith (London: Hogarth, 1973).

14. Mary Douglas, *Purity and Danger: An Analysis of the Concepts of Pollution and Taboo* (New York: Praeger, 1966), 142.

15. Spoto, *The Dark Side of Genius*, 545.

16. As an example, see V. F. Perkins, *Film as Film: Understanding and Judging Movies* (New York: Penguin, 1972), 107–15.

17. I could not disagree more strongly with Jeanne Thomas Allen, who analyzes the rape sequence in detail in order to demonstrate Hitchcock's thoroughgoing misogyny. Allen sees "a suggestion of submissive cooperation" here, in particular in Brenda's request to remove her own clothing rather than have it ripped off by Rusk. "The gesture allows for an element of ambiguity and projection for the male viewer" (p. 34). Later Allen is even

more forceful in her condemnation of the scene, claiming that there is *no* ambiguity whatsoever: "It is the objectification of a particularly pathological but culturally logical male subjectivity in patriarchy, and the film spectator, male or female, is unambiguously forced to share it" (p. 35). See "The Representation of Violence to Women: Hitchcock's *Frenzy.*"

FRENZY (Universal, 1972). *Producers*: Alfred Hitchcock, William Hill, *Assistant Director*: Colin M. Brewer, *Script*: Anthony Shaffer, from the novel *Goodbye Piccadilly, Farewell Leicester Square* by Arthur La Bern, *Photography*: Gil Taylor, *Editing*: John Jympson, *Sets*: Syd Cain, Bob Laing, Simon Wakefield, *Music*: Ron Goodwin, *Players*: Jon Finch (Richard Blaney), Barry Foster (Bob Rusk), Barbara Leigh-Hunt (Brenda Blaney), Anna Massey (Babs Milligan), Alex McCowen (Chief Inspector Oxford), Vivien Merchant (Mrs. Oxford), Billie Whitelaw (Hetty Porter). 116 minutes.

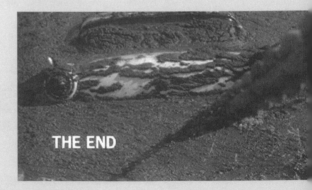

THE END

Part Five

Hitchcock and Film Theory: A *Psycho* Dossier

"*Psycho* is undoubtedly the most obscure of Hitchcock's films," writes Raymond Bellour in "Psychosis, Neurosis, Perversion." This is partly a matter of tone, both visual and narrative. In "none of [Hitchcock's] other films does night seem so black and day so somber," he observes, and this (metaphysical) darkness is unrelieved by clarity of narrative presentation or a resolution of misidentification as it is, on Bellour's account, in *The Wrong Man*. Because *Psycho* appears to contravene the "classical model" wherein "the end must reply to the beginning" – the psychiatric explanation we get at the conclusion of the film leaves Marion's story effectively unacknowledged, and hardly does better for Norman's – the obscurity of *Psycho* "is thus, above all, a rhetorical obscurity."

As the appended bibliography and the three chapters in this "*Psycho* Dossier" attest, another form of rhetorical obscurity confronting the student of *Psycho* is the obsessive and apparently interminable commentary to which writers from numerous disciplines and vantages have subjected it. However eccentric *Psycho* may be to the overall trajectory of Hitchcock's progress and project – by virtue of its low-budget, black-and-white production, its mostly low-rent characters, and its (initial) appeal to the youth market via genre (horror) and stars (Janet Leigh, Tony Perkins) – it is the exception that seems to prove nearly every Hitchcock rule. Thus William Rothman employs nearly 100 densely argued and illustrated pages in *Hitchcock: The Murderous Gaze* to support the claim that *Psycho* "is the masterpiece that culminated the period in which Hitchcock and his public were in closest touch, and announced ... its necessary ending" (p. 248). Similarly, in her chapter on *Frenzy* (reprinted here), Tania Modleski claims that the entirety of *The Women Who Knew Too Much* – its table of contents notwithstanding – has *Psycho* as its subject, as if it were Hitchcock's, and her book's, ever-present unconscious: "In a way, though, I have never really not been discussing *Psycho* – to my mind, the quintessential horror film."

In recent years, doubtless under the influence of Carol Clover's gender-revisionary work on the "slasher film" in *Men, Women, and Chain Saws*, the focus of *Psycho* criticism has shifted somewhat away from the auteurist emphasis on view in Rothman and Modleski and toward debates on film genre and about the film's (or its director's) borderline status as marking (or not) a break between classical and art cinema (Bordwell ("Art Cinema")), between the "image-movement" and the "time-movement" (Deleuze), between the cinema of "sentiment" and the cinema of "sensation" (Monaco), between the modern and the postmodern (Williams), between the cinematic and the televisual (Roth), and so forth. As Raymond Bellour confirms and numerous critics have avowed, the knife that kills Marion Crane in her Bates Motel bathroom effectively cuts the story, if not the screen and the viewer, in two. Thus Norman's story displaces, hence represses and repeats, Marion's story, as if to reverse the film's momentum. As Peter Wollen and others, especially Marty Roth and Laura Mulvey, have described the movie, the forward momentum of Marion's flight from Phoenix to Fairvale circles or doubles back upon itself, so that the last thing we see is the trunk of Marion's second car as it is winched backward from the film's swampy Freudian depths.

In *The Philosophy of Horror* Noël Carroll elaborates his concept of "art-horror" by reference to the figures of monstrousness that give rise to it, the "impurity" of which involves their being "categorically interstitial, categorically contradictory, incomplete, or formless" – both living and dead, both man and beast, and so on (p. 32). Though Carroll doubts the monstrousness of Norman Bates – seeing Norman as psychologically rather than metaphysically damaged – Norman's status as interstitial, "neither man nor woman but both," "son and mother" alike, "both victim and victimizer" (p. 39), is obviously a significant feature of the film. Just as obviously, the cultural categories most in play are those of sex and gender, though *Psycho* is arguably one of Hitchcock's *least* erotic or romantic movies. Indeed, as in the "slasher films" of the 1970s and 1980s discussed by Clover, for which it is in many respects the model, violence in *Psycho* takes the place of sex. More to the point, because slasher films typically appeal to adolescent or young adult males and do so through active female identification figures, the reputed sadism of the male gaze is vicariously confronted and (in many cases) escaped or defeated. Indeed, the heroic success of the "Final Girl" nearly always requires her to "outgaze" her slasher nemesis (pp. 60–1).

The prospect of cross-gender responses to and readings of *Psycho* is fully on view in Jean Douchet's and Robin Wood's respective 1960 analyses of the film (see Douchet's chapter in Part One of the current volume). Both (male) writers assume that Marion Crane is a vehicle for spectatorial projection, the viewer's on-screen agent, enacting our illicit desires. And both subsequently see the viewer entering "completely into [Norman's] thoughts" (Douchet) as he cleans up after "Mother." In contrast to Douchet's invocation of the "occult," Wood's contemporaneous version of this "transfer" scenario explicitly invokes the concept of identification, which became, via its numerous Freudian deployments, central to psychoanalytic interpretations of film in general and of *Psycho* in particular. As Wood put the point in the 1965 version of his essay, eventually the *Psycho* chapter of *Hitchcock's Films Revisited:* "The characters of *Psycho* are *one* character, and that character, thanks to the identifications the film evokes, is us" (p. 147, typo corrected).

Subsequent analyses, Clover's among them, elaborate on the paradox by which a continuity of identity between normal (Marion) and abnormal (Norman) is confirmed by the multiplication or fragmentation of subjectivities, and explicitly across gender lines via the Norman/"Mrs. Bates" conflation, regardless of the gender identity of any particular viewer. Thus Robert Corber argues, regarding the psychiatrist's closure-miming explanation of Norman Bates, that his "reductive use of Freudian categories seems to multiply rather than fix the potential meanings of Norman's behavior" (p. 189). This uncertainty is confirmed by the subsequent scene, in Norman's cell, where "Mrs. Bates" effectively denies that she confessed to the murders, by avowing that she "condemn[ed]" her son to be put "away," and says that Norman "intended to tell them [that she] killed those girls and that man," as if "she" (or Norman) had not already told them. By contrast with *North by Northwest*, where "the discourses of national security virtually guaranteed that gender and nationality functioned as mutually reinforcing categories of identity," asserts Corber, *Psycho* emphasizes "the breakdown of the practices and discourses," such as psychoanalysis, "that anchored and guaranteed the construction of gendered identity" (p. 191). According to Corber, the sexual prohibitions explicitly remarked upon by Sam and Marion (the pleasures of sex in "a cheap hotel," for example) function as fantastic imperatives "that encourage the potentially endless dispersal and displacement of the characters' desire" (p. 210).

The title of Corber's *In the Name of National Security: Hitchcock, Homophobia, and the Political Construction of Gender in Postwar America* makes explicit his interest in "the Cold War Consensus" through which Anti-Stalinist liberals sought to manage the paradoxical task of preserving "the legacies of the New Deal while reclaiming liberalism from the cultural politics of the [1930s] Popular Front." To do so, Corber explains, they "used hysteria over the possibility that the federal government had been infiltrated by Communists, homosexuals, and lesbians to prevent competing constructions of social reality from mobilizing popular support" (p. 3). A critical "node" in this effort was the link between excessive (or regressive) mothering ("Momism," for short) and homosexuality, exactly the cultural logic that Corber sees the psychiatrist in *Psycho* invoking in his explanation of "Mrs. Bates" as a "clinging, demanding woman." (The prospect of the "Monstrous-Feminine," to use Barbara Creed's term, is another link between Hitchcock and the horror genre, and not in *Psycho* alone, as Modleski's discussion of cannibalism in *Frenzy* attests.)

More to Corber's point is the psychiatrist's promptly orthodox refutation of the district attorney's description of Norman as a transvestite. It is not simply that the DA is right; the good doctor wrong. Rather, per Corber, Norman "cannot be adequately explained by the available postwar discourses of identity" (p. 215). A similar logic leads Alexander Doty (in *Flaming Classics*) to suggest that Norman's polymorphous perversity is better seen as "queer," as a way of acknowledging its evident complexities but also as a way of addressing the film's obvious employment of the "dominant cultural trope of mama's-boy-as-homosexual" even while denying it (p. 155). Seeing Norman as queer allows us to go beyond "the established binaries of heterosexual–homosexual and masculine–feminine" (p. 157), says Doty, especially as doing so allows us to complicate our pictures of "Mrs. Bates" (as in wondering why it is "this particular version of his mother" (p. 163) that Norman takes on or becomes) and of Marion (who is Norman-like in being a sexual outlaw, if "Mother"-like in being Norman's victim).

All in all, on Doty's account, *Psycho* is a "dour representation of heterosexuality" as a "rather futile and pathetic activity" (p. 170), most obviously in asking Sheriff and Mrs. Chambers to exemplify the prospect of heterosexual union, most horrifically in the final incestuous union of Norman and "Mrs. Bates." If hope there is, at least for the queerly positioned viewer who finds the film's "crazy-because-he's-gay/queer" (p. 177) portrait of Norman Bates demeaning, it is in seeing Lila Crane as the film's "Final Girl" whose relationship to Norman/"Mrs. Bates" can be taken as a positive model of sexual otherness or outlawry. If taking her own image as that of Mrs. Bates in the *mise-en-abyme* of dressing table and floor mirrors in the latter's bedroom links her to Norman, who also sees himself as "Mrs. Bates," the implied mother/daughter connection, evoking Lila's "Imaginary" or pre-Oedipal relation to her own mother, is not debilitating or infantilizing for her. She is, in Doty's view, "perhaps the most adult character in the film" (p. 177) and succeeds where Arbogast and Sam fail in the investigative task of penetrating Norman's secret. In view of the numerous descriptions of Lila as sexually "restricted" by comparison with Marion, there is room to see Lila's apparent (hetero)sexual disinterest and independence – like Marnie's – as queer, taking the absence of explicit heteronormative markers as allowing the imputation of lesbianism, to the point of seeing Lila, Marion, and Mrs. Bates as a trio of female sexual outlaws, insufficiently "contained" by "the law of the father" that dictates the terms of sexual "respectability."

It is no slight historical irony that the work of Raymond Bellour is so often taken in contemporary film criticism as exemplifying – even as it critiques – the ideological workings and force of "the classical narrative cinema." In his reliance on Jacques Lacan, Roland Barthes, and Christian Metz to model the relationship between culture and language (including "film language"), Bellour effectively wagers everything on the Saussurian or Structuralist axioms that language is a matter of "difference without positive terms" (we recognize "hit" by means of its phonetic difference from "bit" or "kit"); that the linguistic "sign" entails an altogether "arbitrary" linkage of signifier and signified, of figure and reference; and that the "Symbolic" regime of language and culture is effectively coextensive with "reality," though not (perhaps) with the Lacanian "Real," the latter defined (negatively, hence elusively) as what lies beyond language or representation, however much it makes its "impossible" presence felt in its very absence, as symptomatic of castration, loss, or death.

Hence it is possible for Slavoj Žižek to describe Bellour as a "realist" in his taxonomy of realist, modernist, and postmodernist Hitchcock criticisms (see "Alfred Hitchcock, or, the Form and its Historical Mediation"). Indeed, if the reality of our everyday inhabitation – sketched out cinematically in Hitchcock's God's-eye or bird's-eye views of Phoenix in the opening moments of *Psycho* – is in fact the realm of Lacan's "Symbolic" field, in which the Name of the Father ("le nom du père") both engenders and represses desire by means of seemingly arbitrary but forcefully threatening negations, the great Oedipal/patriarchal "No" ("le non du père"), then there is no better guide to Hitchcock's Lacanian/Freudian labyrinth than Bellour. Because the film effectively begins with the primal Freudian scene – displaced just enough to satisfy the Production Code Administration in that we come upon Marion and Sam apparently post coitus – we can hardly be surprised when critics take some form of psychoanalysis as their interpretative model. According to Bellour, *Psycho* reveals this Lacanian "logic of desire" by pressing the "classical narrative cinema" to its limits, hence turning classicism back upon itself, as Norman doubles and turns on Marion. We want to say that Bellour does much the same for psychoanalytic approaches to Hitchcock, both (re)staging the Oedipal mystery and its various investigations, and speculating on his own participation in this heavily "Symbolic" enterprise.

As if enacting this complicity through serial mimicry, Bellour's chapter, like the film itself, shifts terms markedly roughly one-third of the way to the end. In Hitchcock, we shift from Marion to Norman as our main figure of identification in the aftermath of the shower murder. In Bellour, the shift is less figural than terminological. He begins discussing "regulated difference" and "repetition and difference" along auteurist/structuralist lines – employing all the while Freud's dream-work lingo (especially "displacement") and Lacan's developmental terms (especially "Imaginary" and "Symbolic"; see below) – and then goes Freudian, if indirectly or "fictionally," in declaring that *Psycho* is Hitchcock's "reflection on the inevitable relationship, in his art and in his society, between psychosis and neurosis, inscribed respectively in narrative terms as murder and theft." Two complexities here require immediate comment.

First, the "regulation" of difference via "repetition" – which is "structuralist" in the sense that Bellour shows how certain structures of action and desire are repeated across the entire Hitchcock canon and also across the various movements of *Psycho* – is no less dependent on a psychoanalytic model than his subsequent discussion of neurosis and psychosis. Crucial here is Bellour's notion of "Symbolic Blockage," which he elaborates at length in his discussion of *North by Northwest* in *The Analysis of Film*. In the latter case, he associates regularity very explicitly with Oedipus: "The back-and-forth movement that carries the general rhyme from degree zero to the absolute limit of the system is the pulse of the symbolic, commanded from its beginning to its end by the signifier of desire subject to the law that governs it. It makes us hear, as if in a continuous vibration, the destiny of Oedipus and of castration even in the minimal textual operation, the smallest divergence from similarity" (p. 190).

Though he never explicitly mentions Oedipus in "Psychosis, Neurosis, Perversion," Bellour uses the related concept of "family romance" in reference to Norman, Sam, and Marion; and he explicitly links "family romance" to Oedipus and the classical cinema in his interview with Janet Bergstrom, where he remarks upon the historical/ideological conflation of cinema and narrative via "repeated scenarizations of the family romance, which became the object of classical cinema, especially of the American cinema" (p. 103). We could elaborate on the Oedipal "vibrations" of *Psycho* at some length – an abandoned child, mistaken identities, dead or murdered father figures, some version of incest, a dead mother, a tangled search for truth, sightless eyes – but the "Oedipal story," for Bellour as for Lacan, centers on the fact of language or "enunciation" as it pertains, we might say, to the passage from the Imaginary to the Symbolic.

In Lacanian theory, the "Imaginary" is typically elaborated by reference to the "Mirror Stage" of infantile development (of no small interest for students of *Psycho*, wherein mirrors and mirror-like images or appearances are frequently encountered). Here the young child imagines – by reference to a literal mirror image or to the mother's body – "a bodily unity which it still objectively lacks" (Laplanche and Pontalis, 251), and this unity via duality is specular or visual and ontologically or developmentally "mistaken," in that the "roughcast" ego thereby developed involves identification with an external "ideal ego." The "Symbolic" realm, by contrast, is more emphatically "intersubjective," more social, in that it is the realm of language, language understood as "law," "absence," "desire," "castration," and so forth. The "No" of the father splits mother and child. Duality is replaced by Oedipal triangularity, apparent specular similarity by linguistic and sexual difference, presence by absence; indeed, the perceptions of sexual difference and linguistic difference are often conflated, as cause to effect, especially in view of the Lacanian axiom that the unconscious is structured as and by language, by the slide of signifier (meaning) over signified (being). To the extent that the paternal "No" inaugurates language, repression, and desire, one's language is always the "Other's" language, one's desire always the "Other's" desire; the ever-elusive token of desire, Lacan's "objet petit a," is thus the diminutive or derivative of the desire of "The Other" (L'Autre). When Bellour describes Hitchcock as "The Enunciator," then, he implies that Hitchcock is both author and authored, as much the "subject" of the textual system as its ostensible source or speaker.

The "Symbolic Blockage," accordingly, involves a double repetition. Within the depicted (diegetic) world of *North by Northwest*, to use Bellour's example, what *seems* like an Oedipal father/son conflict, when Roger Thornhill escapes the Rapid City hospital against the paternal/national wishes of "The Professor" for the sake of rescuing "Eve" from Van Dam, really entails a successful repetition of the Oedipal cycle, in that Roger "assume[s] his castration" and "substitute[s] Eve for his mother and [can] thus accede to paternal identification through the law the father symbolizes" (p. 98). In taking the law into his own hands, we might say, Roger becomes the father in his turn, and on his (apparently) proper generational schedule. Hence the "rupture" between Thornhill and The Professor functions "in a strictly delimited way, to perfect the Oedipal itinerary of the hero" by confirming "the symbolic alliance between father and son" (p. 100). And this succession or replacement of one authority by another is also played out in the sphere of criticism, where the "family romance" of paternal desire is replayed in the "relay" of looks by means of which Hitchcock's authority is both questioned and thereby assumed by the (often) male critic; in trying to describe and critique the textual system, one risks repeating it.

The other complexity that requires comment – in charting the passage from the "Symbolic" to neurosis and psychosis – is the question and status of "reality" itself. In describing Marion as "the subject of neurosis" and Norman as "the subject of psychosis," Bellour paraphrases Freud's "The Loss of Reality in Neurosis and

Psychosis" to the effect that neurotics lose a piece of reality only in the conflict between id and superego, fleeing or dodging it for the sake of avoiding repression (or repression's failure), while psychotics are those for whom "the Ego is at the service of the Id" and who deny reality (in some of Freud's examples, this involves denying death itself) "in order to reconstruct a better reality." In Freud's own words, "neurosis does not disavow the reality, it only ignores it; psychosis disavows it and tries to replace it" (p. 185). But the reality in question in Freud – despite its obvious connection to the id, hence to desire – is very clearly "the real external world" (Freud, 187). Though Bellour allows Freud's "reality" to go unremarked in the borrowing, he prefaces the use of Freud by discussing, in reference to *Strangers on a Train*, "the fantasy of the murder of the father" that is "necessary to the symbolic resolution of neurosis" as well as "the complementary fantasy" that serves in Hitchcock as "the psychotic's access to the real: the murder of a woman." The Lacanian echoes are clear enough: in suggesting that the real of the Symbolic is already fantastic, and that "The Real" beyond "reality" is only accessible for some via murder, by killing the (M)Other's voice that has already killed The Real.

That "murder" here is a fantasy, and that "fantasy" is less the opposite of "reality" or "The Real" than its necessary supplement, a screen that both censors and reflects, means that fantasy must be "traversed" or gone through, as Žižek often makes the point. ("In the opposition between fantasy and reality," writes Žižek in *The Fragile Absolute*, "the Real is on the side of fantasy" (p. 67).) Indeed, Bellour's association of *Psycho* and film classicism proceeds from the conviction that, in its very perversity and extremity, the film reveals what it would conceal. That we still find the revelation horrifying – even after repeated viewings and all manner of analyses – may mean that we find the reality of our desires too much to bear. Or perhaps it means that we recognize the necessity of confronting "the gaze as *objet a*" in repeatedly facing the traumatic death's-head grin and gaze of Norman/"Mother" when s/he looks straight into the camera in the film's penultimate shot, returning our gaze. As Žižek describes it, what we acknowledge, in gazing back at Norman/ "Mother," is "the subject beyond subjectivization," a "depthless void of pure Gaze" ("'In his Bold Gaze,'" 247, 257–8). This is "the maternal uncanny" (p. 97), in Laura Mulvey's resonant phrase, writ horrifically large.

That language itself may be a "depthless void" endlessly tempting us into futile assertions of truth is an anxiety hardly foreign to Bellour's approach to *Psycho*; it is effectively implicit in the Lacanian twinning of linguistic and sexual difference. But where Bellour emphasizes the force of the repeated assertiveness of language, its Symbolic "reality," Christopher Morris in "*Psycho*'s Allegory of Seeing" tends to emphasize its emptiness, its Imaginary mistakenness. Morris is avowedly "deconstructive" in his approach to the film, though it bears saying that his elucidation of the way in which referentless signifiers are substituted for equally referentless signifiers in an endless "chain of signs" employs much the same (post)structuralist vocabulary as Bellour. Ironically if appropriately, Morris is considerably less tempted to follow that chain to its ostensible anchor point; where Bellour felt compelled to traverse the fantasy of *Psycho*, forcibly to effect the substitution of sign for sign at considerable length, Morris follows his own implicit advice and keeps his explication relatively brief, given his conviction that the "only lesson of the film" is that the "quest for true signification results only in death." Then again, the necessity for mis-reading has the potentially happy effect of postponing, "as if to the end or 'other side' of interpretation, the eventual apprehension of human mortality." And it bears saying that Morris subsequently revised and expanded his original analysis of *Psycho* for inclusion as a chapter in his book *The Hanging Figure: On Suspense and the Films of Alfred Hitchcock*. (Publish or perish, indeed!)

The latter we consider a distinguished contribution to the literature on Hitchcock, and we are happy to include a slightly revised version of his original *Psycho* essay here, as allegorizing the risks interpretation cannot avoid. To the extent that specify-ing those risks serves to remind us that the entirety of *Psycho* is a fictional "play of light and shadow," Morris echoes Bellour in evoking the Platonic critique of art and of representation in general. Moreover, the claim that deconstructing those shadows can be subversive – and that subverting the social and artistic status quo is a primary value of art and of art criticism – has a long and honorable history, as numerous chapters in this collection attest. Morris's chapter on *Psycho* is an exceptionally lucid statement of this perspective.

Two strains of Morris's chapter deserve emphasis. He pays concerted attention, especially in his closing paragraphs, to the film's reflexive dimension. *Psycho* begins, as Morris retells the tale, with a parable of graphic "difference." A gray background is invaded from off-screen by horizontal black stripes, and then by fragmentary white marks, which eventually, after some hesitant horizontal adjustments, become the letters spelling "Alfred Hitchcock's"; then the subsequently all black background is similarly invaded by gray stripes and thence white marks, which finally come together to spell the word "Psycho." Though the letter fragments that eventually coalesce as words "may hint at the popularized understanding of the concept 'split personalities,'" the letters "must first be seen as arbitrary, meaningless marks, which seem to form a referent only in combination." In a kind of mirror-effect, as it were, the shower murder, per Morris, "literalizes the action of *rapid cutting*." Where the credits join to make a temporary meaning, the shower murder severs, slices, frag-ments in such a way as to deanimate, to depersonalize; meaning is as if literally drained away. And the other feature of Morris's chapter worth attending to here is his description of this self-reflective element as "self-parody, which continually mocks the viewer's necessary efforts to glean meaning from the arbitrary flickering of light and darkness in the theater." Hitchcock famously avowed that, for him, "*Psycho* is a film made with quite a sense of amusement on my part. To me it's a *fun* picture" (cited in Wood, *Hitchcock's Films Revisited*, 142). Morris brings that sense of dark humor back into the *Psycho* discourse, from which it had long been ban-ished. That Norman/"Mother's" closing smile hints at an obscene enjoyment or *jou-issance* may mean that s/he is in on the joke, even if it sticks, like the "bone" or "skull" of the Lacanian Real, in our throats.

"On Being Norman: Performance and Inner Life in Hitchcock's *Psycho*" provides yet another way to look at the "void" at the heart of the film. To be sure, in posing her inescapably Freudian questions – "What does Norman know? What does he want? What does it *feel like* to be Norman?" – Deborah Thomas may seem to assume the existence of a potentially coherent Cartesian self at some remove from Žižek's "subject beyond subjectivity." (A major point of Žižek's " 'In his Bold Gaze my Ruin is Writ Large' " is that the "subject beyond subjectivity" just *is* the *cogito*, whereas Morris's anti-Cartesianism seems to follow deconstructive precedent in seeing the "I" of Descartes's "I think, therefore I am" maxim as being a grammatical "subject," a pronoun whose self-identity is no more certain and no less illusory than any other reference point.) Understanding Thomas as an orthodox Freudian, however, is complicated for at least two reasons.

To begin with, Thomas's emphasis on "performance," sparked in part by Hitchcock's famous antipathy to "Method Acting," understands identity retroactively, intersubjectively, almost existentially. Norman's "shrinking postures" – his collar pulled up, his hands clasped together – get their meaning in part by their "contrast with those of Norman-as-mother" and with "those of Sam in the opening scene and [those of] Marion in the shower." Where Sam and Marion are open and vulnerable in their gestures and behavior, Norman is closed-in, angular, almost skeletal; where Norman's body language "continually evokes withdrawal from the surrounding world," Norman/"Mother" is "bold and assertive" both in her voice and in her death-dealing gestures. Whatever "inner life" we attribute to Norman thus derives from perceptions of difference, and these inferences from external behavior depend crucially on things apparently absent or repressed.

Moreover, Thomas views Norman's inner life as comprising mostly a "series of gaps," of "little 'deaths.' " Taking it "as given that Norman is never consciously aware that his mother is dead," Thomas sees something like "emptiness" as the film's primary figure ("Is your time so empty?" Marion asks Norman). Norman describes his "private trap" in avian terms ("We scratch and claw, but only at the air"), and Thomas reads this metaphor as linking inner and outer; Norman thus "presents us with an image of him surrounded by nothing more substantial than empty space, mirroring his experience of much of his life as unfathomably empty time." What Norman knows, "a more general knowledge which Sam and Marion lack," is "that the ways of the flesh are futile, since death inhabits us all." Hence what he wants is "nothingness or annihilation as an alternative to unbearable knowledge and conflicting desires." And this desire is not, in Thomas's view, Norman's alone. Remarking on the numerous gestures and behaviors that suggest a similarity between Norman and Marion, Thomas concludes by wondering if Marion's desire in "stealing the money and running away to Sam" is not really a "desire for her own annihilation," a desire figured as a dream, which starts with the fade to black that (apparently) marks Marion's decision to pull off the road and sleep in her car. As if her death at Norman/"Mother's" hand were *her* dream, her desire; hence her sleep a sleep from which she never awakens, at least not before the film concludes.

If Thomas is a Freudian, then, it is the almost deconstructive Freud of *Beyond the Pleasure Principle* with whom she should be compared, though Thomas does not make this connection herself. We make it now, by way of conclusion, under the influence of Laura Mulvey, for whom *Psycho* literalizes Freud's notion of the "Death

Drive" as exactly that which is "Beyond the Pleasure Principle." Indeed, Mulvey quotes "Psychosis, Neurosis, Perversion" to confirm that *Psycho* exemplifies the original technology of cinematic narrative, which renders the inanimate (the still photo, Mother's corpse) apparently animate via mechanical illumination (the projector, the swinging light bulb in Norman's fruit cellar) only (finally) to return to stillness at "the end." Part of what makes *Psycho* so uncanny on Mulvey's account is the way that, in its penultimate shot, of Norman/"Mother," "the dead merges with the living and movement merges with stillness" (p. 101), and Mulvey subsequently hails Douglas Gordon's *24-Hour Psycho* as marking the "mortality" of cinema itself if also a "point of no return" (p. 102) in the direction of a digitally "expanded cinema" (p. 103). In his discussion of "Freud's Masterplot," from which Mulvey derives at least some of her understanding of Freud's death drive, Peter Brooks offers a picture of narrative that splits the difference between Bellour's attempt to "traverse" the fantasy of *Psycho* and Gordon's slow-motion effort, as it were, to postpone the end: "Repetition, remembering, re-enactment are the ways in which we replay time, so that it may not be lost. We are thus always trying to work back through time to that transcendent home, knowing, of course, that we cannot. All we can do is subvert or, perhaps better, pervert time: which is what narrative does" (p. 111). Psychosis, Neurosis, Perversion. Indeed.

References and Suggested Readings

Bauso, Tom. "Mother Knows Best: The Voices of Mrs. Bates in *Psycho*." *Hitchcock Annual*, 1994, 3–17.

Bellour, Raymond. *The Analysis of Film*. (Cited in Part One.)

Benson, Peter. "Identification and Slaughter." *Cineaction*, no. 12 (Spring 1988): 12–18.

Bergstrom, Janet. "Alienation, Segmentation, Hypnosis: Interview with Raymond Bellour." *Camera Obscura*, nos. 3–4 (1979): 71–104.

Bordwell, David. "The Art Cinema as a Mode of Film Practice." In Leo Braudy and Marshall Cohen, eds., *Film Theory and Criticism*, sixth edition. New York: Oxford Univ. Press, 774–82.

Bordwell, David. "Rhetoric in Action: Seven Models of *Psycho*." In *Making Meaning: Inference and Rhetoric in the Interpretation of Cinema*. Cambridge, MA: Harvard Univ. Press, 1989, 224–48.

Brooks, Peter. "Freud's Masterplot: A Model for Narrative." In *Reading for the Plot: Design and Intention in Narrative*. Cambridge, MA: Harvard Univ. Press, 1992, 90–112.

Brottman, David. "Mrs. Bates in Plato's Cave: Reflections on the Self-Reflexive Signifying Chain Linking the Cellar to Cinema Cells within *Psycho*-tic Experience." In Karl Simms, ed., *Ethics and the Subject*. Amsterdam: Rodopi, 1997, 173–88.

Carroll, Noël. *The Philosophy of Horror: Or, Paradoxes of the Heart*. New York: Routledge, 1990.

Chion, Michel. "Norman; Or, The Impossible Anacousmêtre." In *The Voice in Cinema*, trans. Claudia Gorbman. New York: Columbia Univ. Press, 1999, 125–61.

Clover, Carol J. "Her Body, Himself." In *Men, Women, and Chain Saws: Gender in the Modern Horror Film*. Princeton: Princeton Univ. Press, 1992, 21–64.

Cohen, Keith. "*Psycho:* The Suppression of Female Desire (and its Return)." In James Phelan, ed., *Reading Narrative: Form, Ethics, Ideology*. Columbus: Ohio State Univ. Press, 1989, 147–61.

Cohen, Tom. "Beyond 'The Gaze': Hitchcock, Žižek, and the Ideological Sublime." In *Ideology and Inscription: "Cultural Studies" after Benjamin, De Man, and Bakhtin*. New York: Cambridge Univ. Press, 1998, 143–68.

Corber, Robert. *In the Name of National Security: Hitchcock, Homophobia and the Political Construction of Gender in Postwar America*. (Cited in Part One.)

Creed, Barbara. "The Castrating Mother: *Psycho*." In *The Monstrous-Feminine: Film, Feminism, and Psychoanalysis*. London: Routledge, 1993, 139–50.

Dannatt, Adrian. "*Autours Debates*." In Leigh, *Psycho* (cited in Part One): n.p. Discusses *Psycho* and the Holocaust.

Deleuze, Gilles. *Cinema 1: The Movement Image*. (Cited in Part One).

Doty, Alexander. "'He's a Transvestite!' 'Ah, Not Exactly.' How Queer is My *Psycho*." In *Flaming Classics: Queering the Film Canon*. New York: Routledge, 2000, 155–87.

Durgnat, Raymond. *A Long Hard Look at* Psycho. (Cited in Part One.)

Erb, Cynthia. "'Have you Ever Seen the Inside of One of those Places?': *Psycho*, Foucault, and the Postwar Context of Madness." *Cinema Journal*, vol. 45, no. 4 (Summer 2006): 45–63.

Freud, Sigmund. "The Loss of Reality in Neurosis and Psychosis." In James Strachey, ed., *The Standard Edition of the Complete Works of Sigmund Freud*, vol. 19. London: Hogarth Press and the Institute of Psycho-Analysis, 1961, 183–7.

Griffith, James. "*Psycho:* Not Guilty as Charged." *Film Comment*, vol. 32, no. 4 (July–August 1996): 76–9.

Grimes, Larry E. "Shall These Bones Live? The Problem of Bodies in Alfred Hitchcock's *Psycho* and Joel Coen's *Blood Simple*." In Joel W. Martin and Conrad E. Ostwalt Jr., eds., *Screening the Sacred: Religion, Myth, and Ideology in Popular American Film*. Boulder, CO: Westview Press, 1995, 19–29.

Hemmeter, Thomas. "Horror beyond the Camera: Cultural Sources of Violence in Hitchcock's Mid-Century America." *Post Script*, vol. 22, no. 2 (Winter–Spring 2003): 7–19.

Hendershot, Cyndy. "The Cold War Horror Film: Taboo and Transgression in *The Bad Seed*, *The Fly*, and *Psycho*." *Journal of Popular Film and Television*, vol. 29, no. 1 (Spring 2001): 20–31.

Klinger, Barbara. "*Psycho:* The Institutionalization of Female Sexuality." In Deutelbaum and Poague (cited in Part One): 332–9.

Kolker, Robert, ed. *Alfred Hitchcock's* Psycho: *A Casebook*. New York: Oxford Univ. Press, 2004.

Kolker, Robert, "The Form, Structure, and Influence of *Psycho*." In Kolker (cited above): 206–55.

Laplanche, J., and J.-B. Pontalis. *The Language of Psycho-Analysis*, trans. Donald Nicholson-Smith. New York: W. W. Norton, 1973.

Leitch, Thomas M. "Hitchcock without Hitchcock." *Literature/Film Quarterly*, vol. 31, no. 4 (2003): 248–59.

Lunde, Erik S., and Douglas A. Noverr. "'Saying it with Pictures': Alfred Hitchcock and Painterly Images in *Psycho*." In Paul Loukides and Linda K. Fuller, eds., *Beyond the Stars III: The Material World in American Popular Film*. Bowling Green, OH: Bowling Green State Univ. Popular Press, 1993, 97–105.

Modleski, Tania. *The Women Who Knew Too Much: Hitchcock and Feminist Theory*, second edition. (Cited in Part One.)

Mogg, Ken. "The Dark Side of Genius: Hitchcock's *Psycho*." *The MacGuffin*, no. 4 (August 1991): 9–15.

Mogg, Ken. "Hitchcock Made Only One Horror Film: Matters of Time, Space, Causality, and the Schopenhauerian Will." In Steven Jay Schneider and Daniel Shaw, eds., *Dark Thoughts: Philosophic Reflections on Cinematic Horror*. Lanham, MD: Scarecrow Press, 2003, 84–104.

Monaco, Paul. *The Sixties: 1960–1969*. New York: Charles Scribner's Sons, 2001. Vol. 8 of the *History of the American Cinema*.

Morris, Christopher D. *The Hanging Figure: On Suspense and the Films of Alfred Hitchcock*. (Cited in Part One.)

Morrisson, Ken. "The Technology of Homicide: Construction of Evidence and Truth in American Murder Films." *Cineaction*, no. 38 (September 1995): 16–24.

Mulvey, Laura. "Alfred Hitchcock's *Psycho* (1960)." In *Death 24x a Second*. London: Reaktion Books, 2006, 85–103.

Naremore, James. *Filmguide to* Psycho. Bloomington: Indiana Univ. Press, 1973.

Naremore, James. "Remaking *Psycho*." *Hitchcock Annual*, 1999–2000, 3–12.

Negra, Diane. "Coveting the Feminine: Victor Frankenstein, Norman Bates, and Buffalo Bill." *Literature/Film Quarterly*, vol. 24, no. 2 (1996): 193–200.

Phillips, John. "Psycho-Trans." In *Transgender on Screen*. Basingstoke, UK: Palgrave Macmillan, 2006, 85–114.

Poague, Leland. "Links in a Chain: *Psycho* and Film Classicism." In Deutelbaum and Poague (cited in Part One): 340–9.

Pomerance, Murray. "Marion Crane Dies Twice." In Murray Pomerance, ed., *Ladies and Gentlemen, Boys and Girls: Gender in Film at the End of the Twentieth Century*. Albany: State Univ. of New York Press, 2001, 301–16.

Roth, Marty. "Remembering *Psycho*." *North Dakota Quarterly*, vol. 62, no. 3 (Summer 1994–5): 161–74.

Rothman, William. *Hitchcock: The Murderous Gaze*. (Cited in Part One.)

Schmidt, Johann N. "Literary Adaptation as Pure Cinema: Alfred Hitchcock's *Psycho*." *Anglistik & Englishchunterricht*, vol. 36 (1988): 11–25.

Schneider, Steven Jay. "Manufacturing Horror in Hitchcock's *Psycho*." *Cineaction*, no. 50 (October 1999): 70–5.

Sipière, Dominique. "Telling Eyes in *Psycho*." *Bulletin du CICLAHO*, Nanterre: Université Paris X, 1998, 131–42.

Skerry, Philip J. *The Shower Scene in Hitchcock's* Psycho: *Creating Cinematic Suspense and Terror*. Lewiston, NY: Edwin Mellen Press, 2005.

Staiger, Janet. "Hitchcock in Texas: Intertextuality in the Face of Blood and Gore." In *Perverse Spectators: The Practices of Film Reception*. New York: New York Univ. Press, 2000, 179–87.

Tharp, Julie. "The Transvestite as Monster: Gender Horror in *The Silence of the Lambs* and *Psycho*." *Journal of Popular Film and Television*, vol. 19, no. 3 (Fall 1991): 106–13.

Thompson, David. "Lost Highway." *Sight and Sound*, December 2002, 14–15. Reviews Durgnat's *Long Hard Look at* Psycho.

Warren, Denise. "Hitchcock's *Psycho:* The Spatial Film-Work of Madness." *Interdisciplinary Journal for Germanic Linguistics and Semiotic Analysis*, vol. 5, no. 1 (Spring 2000): 37–70.

Wells, Amanda Sheahan. Psycho: *Director, Alfred Hitchcock*. London: York Press; Harlow, UK: Pearson Education, 2001.

Williams, Linda. "Discipline and Fun: *Psycho* and Postmodern Cinema." In Kolker (cited above): 164–204.

Wollen, Peter. "Hybrid Plots in *Psycho*." In *Readings and Writings: Semiotic Counter-Strategies*. London: Verso, 1982, 34–9.

Wood, Robin. *Hitchcock's Film Revisited*, revised edition. (Cited in Part One.)

Wood, Robin. "Psychanalyse de *Psycho*." *Cahiers du cinéma*, no. 113 (November 1960): 1–6.

Žižek, Slavoj, ed., *Everything You Always Wanted to Know about Lacan (But Were Afraid to Ask Hitchcock)*. London: Verso, 1992. Includes "Alfred Hitchcock, or, the Form and its Historical Mediation" and " 'In his Bold Gaze my Ruin is Writ Large.' "

Žižek, Slavoj. *The Fragile Absolute: Or, Why Is the Christian Legacy Worth Fighting for?* London: Verso, 2000.

Chapter Twenty-Four

Psychosis, Neurosis, Perversion

Raymond Bellour
Translated by Nancy Huston

Barthes said to me the other day: basically, when you give someone something to read, you give it to your mother. (Philippe Sollers)

I

Psycho is undoubtedly the most obscure of Hitchcock's films. Obscure, first of all, in a literal sense, because in none of his other films does night seem so black and day so somber. There is, of course, *The Wrong Man*: exactly like *Psycho* (inscribed between the colorful symphonies of *North by Northwest* and *The Birds*), it left a trail of shadow, three years earlier, between *The Man Who Knew Too Much* and *Vertigo*. The two films do have in common a kind of nocturnal excellence that permeates the gestures, faces, and image tones: Hitchcock sought, in one case, to endow them with documentary value, and entrusted them, in the other case, to a television cameraman. However, this material obscurity – fuller and duller in the realism of *The Wrong Man* – seemed eventually to dissolve away, or at least be balanced out by the exemplary linearity of the screenplay and by the ultimate resolution of the error, restoring to Christopher Balestrero the certainty of his identity, and to his wife the hope of a fragile mental balance. In *Psycho*, on the contrary, to the extent that a surrender to the codifications of romanticism and horror is always possible, the role of shadow grows incessantly, according to the interplay of ordering and disruption that guides the film from its beginning to its end.

The principle of classical film is well known: the end must reply to the beginning; between one and the other something must be set in order; the last scene frequently recalls the first and constitutes its resolution. *Psycho*'s opaqueness is contradictory in this respect: the end, apparently, in no way replies to the beginning: the psychiatrist's commentary on the case of Norman Bates has little to do with the love scene between Marion and Sam in the Phoenix hotel. The specific obscurity of *Psycho* is thus, above all, a rhetorical obscurity. It denotes the fact that the film, in a sense, contravenes the classical model of narrative – as well as that more singular model that is both an eccentric and exemplary version of it: the Hitchcockian system. Obviously, it does so, not in order to elude the system, but rather – through a greater degree of abstraction – to determine its regime(s): the system here performs displacements with respect to itself, designating with extreme clarity the mechanisms that govern its operation.

II

The first sign of this is the radical displacement of the investigation. In the Hitchcockian fable, investigations conform to two major modalities, complementary and interchangeable, in which the relationships of identification are established by the position of knowledge that Hitchcock reserves for himself (and thus for the spectator as well), as opposed to the various subjects (supports) of the fiction. The inquiry represents, first of all, an ideal testing-ground for the hero (or the heroine as mirror-image, or the couple-as-subject), who, constrained by chance and necessity, learns to acknowledge a certain truth about his own desire after a dramaturgy of violence based on the search for the secret. To achieve this the riddle must be solved, and the mistaken identity in which it was cloaked revealed; these two questions may then be traced back to their common origin, resulting in a final equilibrium between desire and the law. This renders possible, through the inclusion–exclusion process of the terms of the destructive drive, the ultimate integration (whether successful or not) of the imaginary into the symbolic by means of a general dovetailing of the textual operations. Such is the exemplary itinerary of *North by Northwest*, but the same model is used in *The 39 Steps*, *Saboteur*, *Foreign Correspondent*, *To Catch a Thief*, and, in a slightly different form, in *Strangers on a Train* and *Rear Window*. In *Notorious*, by displacement, it is the hero, the man of the couple, who is the secret agent invested with the knowledge and initiative usually paradoxically divided up between the police and the false culprit. In *Spellbound*, of the two characters who make up the couple, it is the woman who leads the investigation of which the other is the object. And, in *Shadow of a Doubt*, the investigation is led by both the woman and the policeman, who eventually make up the final couple. Thus, most of Hitchcock's films can be seen as multiple variations or distortions of this same basic model.

Conversely, the second modality consists of denying the hero (or heroine or couple-subject) access to the truth of the investigation: even though they may share its diegetic benefits, they are dispossessed of this knowledge by some external factor. Take, for example, *Dial "M" for Murder*, in which neither the husband nor the wife leads the investigation of which both are the object; or *Under Capricorn*, whose highly improbable plot follows the same model; or even *I Confess*, in which the presumed culprit is, paradoxically, the only one who knows the secret, but can say nothing. However, these narratives in which the hero is deprived of the truth-seeking initiative are, in general, all the more constrained by a uniform dynamic leading from the riddle to its solution (*The Wrong Man*, for example). In addition, they often depend, very naturally, alongside the main couple, on a third important character: in *Under Capricorn*, Charles Adare, the outsider and friend; in *Dial "M" for Murder*, Chief Inspector Hubbard, who unravels all the elaborately tangled threads of the plot.

Psycho, however, apparently conforms to this second model, while breaking the system apart at its very core. Neither of the two main characters is invested as subject during the progression of the investigation; its indices of truth are divided up among Arbogast, the sheriff, Sam, Lila, and the psychiatrist. The former two, a private detective and a policeman, share the partial and misleading truth that is so often allotted them in Hitchcock's films: Arbogast succeeds in tracing Marion but gives credit to the fiction of the mother; the sheriff denies this fiction without being able to account for its effects. Sam and Lila, for their part, seem to fulfill – amidst the scattered functions of the second model – a function proper to the first, that of the couple whose action solves the riddle and opens the way to truth. This is actually due to a displacement, since the solution brings about nothing that concerns them directly (thus Sam and Lila merely mimic the diegetic couple, marking out its absence). In addition – and as a result – their solution is only a half-truth; it immediately requires the mediation of a superior truth. This is provided by the third important character, here embodied in the psychiatrist, with the significant difference that in this case he intervenes, very deliberately, as deus ex machina, a stranger to the action, strictly exterior to what is at stake. This is why the final explanation has sometimes been considered a useless appendix, whereas it is the ultimate result of the work of displacement that has taken place thoughout the film. Thus, from an original dispersion of truth and its diegetic effects, a veritable split occurs between the materiality and the awareness of experience: the division of the investigation merely reproduces the central division organizing the film and determining, at all levels, its regime.

III

Psycho contains two narratives, slipping one under the other, one into the other. This relationship must be conceptualized in order to penetrate to a structural perversion to which Hitchcock opened the way by deciding to "kill the star in the first third of the film."[1] There is, first of all, the story of Marion. The opening scene in the hotel room calls attention to the problematic: marriage; the ensuing theft produces its dramatic effect. This is a weakened version both of *Strangers on a Train* (as regards marriage, Marion and Sam occupying the place of Guy Haines and Ann Morton, with the third person being a first wife, not yet divorced in *Strangers*, already divorced in *Psycho*) and of *Marnie* (as regards the theft). The story could have various outcomes along its own axis: one of these, the meeting between Marion and Norman, has the ambiguous function of ending the story in order to transform it. The second story, that of Norman, might thus be said to begin when Marion arrives at the motel and to continue, slightly altered (because of the persistent pressure of the first story), to the end of the film. Such, indeed, was the case in the novel by Robert Bloch used as a pretext for the film: Hitchcock immediately broke up the overly simple structure of the book, and later justified this in a singularly underdetermined way.[2]

In fact, the first part of the story was a red herring. That was deliberate, you see, to detract the viewer's attention in order to heighten the murder. We purposely made that beginning on the long side, with the bit about the theft and her escape, in order to get the audience absorbed with the question of whether she would or would not be caught. Even that business about the forty thousand dollars was milked to the very end so that the public might wonder what's going to happen to the money....

The more we go into the details of the girl's journey, the more the audience becomes absorbed in her flight. That's why so much is made of the motorcycle cop and the change of cars. When Anthony Perkins tells the girl of his life in the motel, and they exchange views, you still play upon the girl's problem. It seems as if she's decided to go back to Phoenix and give the money back, and it's possible that the public anticipates by thinking, "Ah, this young man is influencing her to change her mind." You turn the viewer in one direction and then in another; you keep him as far as possible from what's actually going to happen.[3]

This statement focuses on what constitutes, properly speaking, the center of the narrative, its moment of extreme fascination. However, it denies the fact that, from this very moment onwards, the constitution of the "first story" is supported by its inscription within the "second," both at the level of narrative identifications and at that of the logic of its occurrences. Denied, too, is the subtle movement by which the narrative both masks and accentuates the division constituting its paradoxical unity. The singular genius of the film consists of indissolubly mixing together the two narratives that it is composed of by using the meeting of the two characters as the means of their substitution.

Everything contributes to this.

1. The time allotted to the meeting, which by itself takes up, strictly speaking, one-fifth of the film (more, in fact: a third, counting the rather short sequence that leads Marion, caught in the storm, to the Bates Motel, and the much longer sequence between the murder and the disappearance of Marion's car in the marsh).

2. The violence that concludes the meeting, which is so incredible that it obfuscates its own secondary effect: namely, the determining fact of the passage, in a sense, from one character to the other.

3. A major rhetorical shift contributes to this displacement and facilitates the reversal. Whereas the segmentation of the rest of the film systematically employs, in a highly classical manner, the three criteria of segmental demarcation, the scene of the meeting (in the extended sense) is devoid of all punctuation: there is not a single fade-out between the moment Marion abruptly leaves the garage where she has traded in her car and the moment her new car sinks into the marsh.[4] This does not mean that thirty-five minutes of the film make up a single segment; the two other criteria of demarcation do intervene, although much less distinctly than in most classical films. It is as though the sudden absence of punctuation were responsible for creating the illusion of segmental continuity, isolating the time of the meeting within the construction of a whole in order to give it a greater fluidity and the logical evidence necessary to carry out the substitutive shift.

4. Finally, "naturalness" acts like the musicality of a fiction, integrating with misleading obviousness the elements of the first narrative that contribute to the construction of the second.

IV

The perfection of the ternary composition both conceals and reveals the binary division between the narratives and the characters. Three movements, reiterated to harmonize term-to-term in coupled oppositions, reinforce the unfolding of the fiction and its organic cohesion by establishing a very stable hierarchy of repetition and difference. All three involve an itinerary leading to the motel, and all three end in a murderous aggression punctuated by strident music. The first takes Marion Crane from her room in Phoenix to the motel room, where she is assassinated by "the mother"; the second takes Arbogast from Sam's store in Fairvale to the motel and then to Norman's house, where he in turn is assassinated by "the mother"; the third takes Sam and Lila from Sam's store to the motel and then to Norman's house, where Lila escapes aggression by "the mother" only thanks to the intervention of Sam, who recognizes Norman through the disguise.

It is immediately clear, limiting the discussion at first to murder, what movements 2 and 3, 1 and 2, have in common, respectively and by pairs: the aggression is a response, in the two latter cases, to an intrusion into the house, first by Arbogast, then by Sam and Lila (whereas Marion's assassination takes place at the motel); but – conversely – in the first two cases the murder is accomplished, whereas its failure in the third case lifts the veil of mystery and carries the film to its resolution. Thus, with the benefit of an equivalence by pairs (1 = 2, 2 = 3), the third movement recalls the first, thus accentuating the repetitive circulation.

Nevertheless, on closer examination it can be seen that an intrusion into the house is suggested during the first movement, though in unlike manner, when Norman invites Marion to share his meal, provoking the indignation of "the mother" and, eventually, the murder and everything that ensues. Thus, by a regulated difference, the circularity of the fiction is ensured – what might be called its narrative (dis)similarity. In the same way, just as movements 1 and 3 are organized around the repeated motif of the rooms rented first by Marion, then by Sam and Lila, the second movement includes Norman's very natural proposal of his room to Arbogast (and later, failing that, his less natural proposal that Arbogast come and help him change the beds).

Again, one could evoke the three scenes of shot–reverse shot, identically distributed throughout the three movements, in the small motel office (with Norman on one side of the counter, Marion, Arbogast, Sam, and Lila on the other, reflected in the mirror). However, in the third case, there is a repetition: Sam is later seen alone with Norman in the office (while Lila is on her way up to the house). Thus, the third movement constantly doubles back on itself to emphasize, within the regulated difference, the progression and accomplishment of the narrative. It has been seen that movements 2 and 3 are defined by an identical trajectory: from Sam's store to the motel and then to the house. However, in the third movement this trajectory is split in two by the emergence of the mystery, which constitutes a turning point.[5] When Sam goes to the motel the first time to look for Arbogast, he sees "the mother." He undertakes the same visit with Lila in order to initiate her fully into the secret; thus they follow, together, the whole itinerary leading from their rented room to Marion's, and then, separately, from Norman's office to the mother's room, and from Norman's boyhood room to the cellar where his mother is concealed. The (dis)similarity ensures the circular identity of the narrative by guaranteeing its unpredictable advance toward a final result.

Within this regulated succession, this elaborate interplay of identities, separations, intimations, and revelations that correlatively ensure the superimposition and interchangeability of the two narratives, the second movement, much shorter than the first, has a specific transitive value: following Marion's disappearance, it emphasizes the role of Norman, progressively establishing him as the new hero of the narrative before making him the center of the mystery. The latter is accomplished by the third movement, for which Hitchcock cleverly reserves the sheriff's revelation concerning the mother's death – since, logically, if Sam and Lila were preoccupied only with Marion's fate and the stolen money, the spectator could only expect, and dread, the solution of the undoubtedly horrendous mystery hidden within Norman.

V

This circular orchestration, by the very progression of its three movements, has a secondary effect: it sets off all the more plainly the segments bordering it on either side (the opening and closing scenes), and, within these segments, rigorously heterogeneous and yet connected, the speech of the psychiatrist and the love scene in the Phoenix hotel.

The speech of the psychiatrist, in the course of which those parts of the mystery still remaining obscure are finally illuminated, is the logical consequence of the radical exclusion of the first narrative. The speech concerns Norman; it is a commentary and explanation of his case: it says nothing about Marion, who has become the pure object of a murderous desire, and even less about Sam, who can only listen, at Lila's side, to an analysis that excludes him from the diegesis of which he too, through Marion, had been the subject.

This raises a series of questions. Why is this film about psychotic dissociation organized with respect to an original plot that, while supporting it to the point of appearing indispensable, nevertheless remains, in a sense, totally foreign to it? In this highly classically orchestrated film, whose three movements recall the hermeneutic tripartition of *North by Northwest*, how is the internal principle of classical film satisfied – namely, that the end must always reply to the beginning? In what way does the last scene provide a solution, or even an echo, to the first? I think it is necessary, here, to conceive of Hitchcock as pursuing, through fiction, an indirect reflection on the inevitable relationship, in his art and in his society, between psychosis and neurosis, inscribed respectively in narrative terms as murder and theft. These are general instances, fictional rather than clinical, those of a civilization in which a certain subject, who is both a singular subject and the collective agent of enunciation, finds a way to structure his fantasy and determine his symbolic regime. What appears from the fact that the subject of neurosis is offered up in the logic of the narrative to the violence of the subject of psychosis, man or woman, mutually interchangeable throughout the course of the narrative, is the obscure numinous point of a fiction that carries to a vertiginous degree of duplication the fascinated reflection on the logic of desire.

This position is a familiar one within the twists and turns of Hitchcock's labyrinthian scenarios. It is already enunciated with incredible precision in *Shadow of a Doubt* by the doubling of uncle and niece, manifested in the Christian name they share as well as in the repeated motif of the bedrooms (the uncle's hotel room and the niece's family room: both characters are revealed, lying in bed, by a single movement of the camera; and, in a pure mirror-effect, there appears in the first shot, from the left, the woman who runs the hotel, and in the second, from the right, the young girl's father; thus is prepared the substitution that will later place the uncle in the niece's room). On the one hand, there is Charlie's – the niece's – profound, inexpressible dissatisfaction, the neurotic lack that she hopes will magically disappear thanks to Uncle Charlie; on the other, there is the uncle's psychotic split, the return of his childhood trauma that is compulsively acted out in the murder of widows, and that ultimately, because of the progression of the inquiry, turns upon the young girl as the logical object of its deadly desire. Thus, as in *Psycho*, woman, the subject of neurosis, becomes the object of the psychosis of which man is the subject. This is a fundamental aspect of the Hitchcockian constant according to which, given a certain order of desire, it is above all women that get killed.

That is not to say:

1. That women do not kill. But the murder they commit is always the reverse side of the "psychotic" aggression of which they are the object. It is thus that, in *Shadow of a Doubt*, the uncle, in his struggle, falls off the train from which he had tried to throw his niece; in *Blackmail* the young woman kills the painter who had tried to rape her; and, in *Dial "M" for Murder*, the husband's murderous desire having replaced, as in so many of Hitchcock's and other films, the psychosis he conceals, the woman kills to defend herself from the assassin he has hired. This is why, in a rigorously complementary manner, women may – or must – seem in the position of symbolic murderers: thus, in *North by Northwest*, Eve's fictitious murder of Thornhill is woman's response to the murderous desire she awakens in man – if only metaphorically, as a sexual object.

2. That women cannot "manifest psychotic tendencies" (as can be seen in *The Wrong Man* or in *Under Capricorn*). But that they do so only to the extent that the hero has suffered a loss of identity, and never from the same demented object-desire as he. This is why women can tolerate madness in men only if they can save them from it (*Spellbound*: even at the cost of awakening their murderous desire; or, in a totally different way, *Rebecca*). This modality may also be that of men (*Marnie*), but it then involves only, so to speak, a semimadness, and this at the price of a fetishistic position that reinforces love and is related, through scoptophilia, to murderous desire, of which it is the mitigated, possessive form.

Vertigo constitutes, in all respects, a marvelously complex counterexample. The woman is the object of an illusory psychosis; she is an image of psychosis, turned toward death in a twofold manner, through the image-painting of Carlotta Valdes. She awakens a passion in the man: the desire to see, mesmerized by death; this is the moment when Scottie tears Madeleine away from what fascinates him. Later, after the false–real death of Madeleine, the man wanders on the borderline of madness (between neurosis and psychosis: narcissistic neurosis, mourning, and melancholia). Still later, when the false living woman reappears, the desire to kill re-emerges: an image must be modeled so that the "real" can at last be transferred onto it, thus accomplishing – with the help of God if necessary (the appearance of the nun dieget-ically motivating the second fall) – the subject's desire, sublimated in the scopic drive that transfixes the male subject.

3.   Finally, this is not to say that men cannot be the subject of neurosis. Such, indeed, is their most common lot. Neurosis is what occurs when an encounter with the extraordinary, by way of the inevitable ritual testing of murder-psychosis, deter-mines for the hero the resolution of the symbolic. There is always a "madman" who kills for the hero, turning the subject of neurosis into a false culprit, and thus inciting him – through a displacement in which neurotic guilt is resolved in the reality of action – to rediscover a certain truth of his desire. Here again, the itinerary of *North by Northwest* is exemplary.

So, in another manner, is that of *Strangers on a Train*, through the meeting of the characters and the fiction of the exchanged murders. The issue of marriage, or in this case remarriage (elsewhere it is the question of stabilizing or restabilizing the couple: *Suspicion*, *The Man Who Knew Too Much*), serves to sustain what can be called Guy's "neurosis": the basic neurosis of American cinema. By a diabolical twist, this issue – in the interests of its own resolution (final marriage) – provides psychosis with its object. Because of the exchange of murders, Miriam, Guy's wife, comes to occupy the place of Bruno's father, whom Bruno has vainly appealed to Guy to murder. As a part of the fantasy of the murder of the father, necessary to the sym-bolic resolution of neurosis, Miriam thus embodies the complementary fantasy that indicates, for Hitchcock, the psychotic's access to the real: the murder of a woman (and, through her, of the too-well-loved mother; such films as *Shadow of a Doubt*, *Strangers on a Train*, and *Frenzy* are directly connected around this motif).

* * *

These, then, are the terms that *Psycho* sets into play, frontally, through a reversible effect of the articulation between the two psychic structures, grasped in a doubling relationship carried by sexual difference. The criterion used here to associate and dissociate neurosis and psychosis remains, overwhelmingly, the one used by Freud: both are avatars of desire that bring about an unsettling of the subject's relationship to reality.[6] But whereas in psychosis the Ego is at the service of the Id and eludes what it finds intolerable in reality, in neurosis the Ego is the stage of a conflict between the Id and the Superego, such that the loss of reality "affects precisely that piece of reality as a result of whose demands the instinctual repression ensued."[7]

This is Marion's situation in *Psycho*: the theft that draws her into this loss is her response to the sociosexual aggression on the part of the "millionaire" in Lowery's office, of which she was, metaphorically, the object. But, on a much deeper level, it is her response to Sam's aggression, of which she feels herself to be the object, in the sordid clandestineness of the hotel room, when the conflict between the intensity of her sexual demand and her wish to have it legally sanctioned by marriage (continually postponed because of Sam's financial position) comes to a head.[8] This explains the focus, just as later on in *Marnie*, on money, that polyvalent signifier of desire (sexual or social) that also serves, even better than hysterical conversion and perhaps with greater conformity to unconscious logic, the logic of the fiction.[9] This is what Marion's theft attempts to resolve, magically, "by a sort of flight," as Freud says of neurosis, dodging the fragment of reality that psychosis, for its part, simply denies in order to reconstruct a better reality.

VI

The long segment during which Marion and Norman are face to face in the small reception room of the motel thus places face to face, fictitiously, two psychic structures: man and woman, the latter destined to become the prey of the former. The mirror arrangement that organizes their dialogue in a regulated alternation of shot-reverse shots ensures, between the two characters, the interchangeability necessary to their future substitution. It is here that Norman's family romance is presented, in the deceptive form in which it has been restructured by his desire, by the truth of his delirium, thus echoing the more disparate elements of Sam's and Marion's family romances, scattered throughout their dialogue in the hotel room.[10] Thus, the two mental forms are brought together by similarity and exclusion: Marion grows aware of her own derangement because of the much more absolute derangement she senses in Norman. Their differential assimilation is concentrated in a metaphor with endless ramifications. "*Norman:* You – you eat like a bird." The metaphor is no sooner spoken than it is denied. "Anyway, I hear the expression 'eats like a bird' – ... it – it's really a fals-fals-fals-falsity. Because birds really eat a tremendous lot."[11] Marion has to be a bird, in order to be constituted as a body potentially similar to that of Norman's mother, object of his desire, stuffed just like the birds who survey their exchange. But Marion cannot really be a bird, because the bird's "psychotic" appetite has been reserved for Norman, as the body transformed into the mother's body (even if, by a remarkable reversal, Norman eats nothing during the entire scene: "It's all for you. I'm not hungry").

* * *

The reception-room scene is meticulously organized to lead up to the murder scene. After an opening shot during which Norman appears amidst the stuffed birds disposed about the room, there are four shots showing Marion, standing, in alternation with the birds: the order of these shots (bird *a* – Marion – bird *b* – Marion) denotes her feeling that she is seen by the birds as much as she sees them, and that this disturbs her. After a repetition of shot 1 (Norman standing), there is a shot showing Norman and Marion together, seated on either side of a tray of food pre[...] by Norman. Then a classical alternation is established, dividing the shot betwee[n] two characters to distribute their dialogue. At the same time, a formal opposition emphasizes the fact that Norman, in this second alternation, has come to occupy, with respect to Marion, the place of the birds. In the various ways in which Norman is framed, he is associated with the outstretched beaks and widespread wings of one or several of the stuffed birds. Conversely, Marion is defined successively in two framings: she is beneath an oval painting whose theme was clearly visible during the second bird shot of the preceding alternation. The painting distinctly shows a band of angels, or, more precisely, a group of three women in which the central figure seems to be rising up to heaven, wings outspread. Next to the painting, in the same shot, the menacing shadow of a crow is projected onto the wall, penetrating the picture like a knifeblade or a penis. It is this complex whole that rivets Marion's attention, then splits apart when she takes her seat beneath the painting and becomes – through a double, metaphorical-metonymical inflection – defined by it, just as Norman is later emblematically defined by the birds. Thus the differential assimilation is continued: Marion, angel–woman–bird; Norman, bird–fetish–murderer. And thus is prefigured, in the intertwined motifs of alternation, the aggression of which she is soon to be the object (announced, when she rises, half concealing the painting, by the black beak of the crow that reappears inside the frame).

A few shots later, the alternation between Norman and Marion recommences, this time through an apparatus that mimics the cinematographic apparatus itself. Norman is concealed, significantly, by a painting that prefigures the effect he is to produce: *Susannah and the Elders*, virtually at the moment of the rape. Beneath the painting is a large hole that reveals, in the wall itself, the tiny luminous hole to which Norman puts his eye, creating – just like the projector's beam – an image that is for us virtual and for him almost real: Marion undressing, once again in the proximity of two birds, the portraits hanging on the wall of her bedroom near the bathroom door. The alternation then continues, obsessively marking the insert of the bulging eyeball, and shifting from the relationship between shots to the relationship between segments (or subsegments).

The next double series of shots, postponing voyeurism, intensifies it to the extreme:

(a) Norman, under the influence of what he has seen, goes back to shut himself up in the house in order to imagine what will happen next – or better yet, what will happen metaphorically for him, given the premises that catalyze his desire.

(b) Marion, in her room, soon gets into the shower: the spectator, by this advance intrusion, is witness to the scene for which Norman's obsession has prepared the way.

The moment of the murder marks the invasion by the subject (hero and spectator together) of the constituted image of his fantasy. Here, alternation must be abandoned; it is ruptured by the brutal inscription on the image of the living body–knife–bird of

Norman–the mother, the reiterated fragmentation of Marion's body, the insert of her mouth agape in a horrendous scream and that of the dead eye that answers – at the opposite extreme of this very long fragment – the bulging eye of Norman given over to the inordinate desire of the scopic drive.

VII

That only men are subjects of psychosis (or that women are psychotic only by default, or by reflection) here implies, above all, something else: that only men are subjects of perversion (here and elsewhere, given a certain regime of fiction, and a certain order of civilization).

It should be recalled that the manner in which psychosis and perversion can both be defined – although not in the same way – is by their difference from neurosis, through their common allegiance to the wishes of the Id: the former, as has been seen, by its indulgence in a form of delirious reconstruction, through an infinitely more radical loss of reality than in neurosis, implying a lesser subservience to repressive mechanisms; the latter, in the sense of the famous formula: neurosis is "the negative of perversion." Though it must not be taken literally – as its reversal (perversion is the negative of neurosis) would tend to define perversion as nothing but the raw manifestation of infantile desire – Freud's formula does imply, however, that perversion provides a more direct access to the object of the drive, according to its own defense mechanisms (denial of reality, splitting of the Ego), which in some ways link it to those of psychosis.[12]

More specifically, it can be seen how this twofold difference is articulated here with respect to the inscription of the scopic drive and its destiny. To go back to the beginning of the film: there is the first, continuous shot during which the camera wanders down from a high angle over the rooftops of a city, progressively closing in on a window with half-raised blinds, then going beneath these blinds to reveal, in a bedroom, a couple that has just been making love. Thus, from the start, emphasis is placed on the voyeuristic position, which deliberately constitutes the position of enunciation.[13] It is highly remarkable that this opening shot, quite common in Hitchcock's films (cf. *Shadow of a Doubt*), is especially reminiscent of *Rope*, in which the first interminable shot focuses – having passed through a similar window/screen – on the cold fury of a murder.[14] In this interplay of forms based on an endless interchangeability between murder and the sexual act (cf., for example, the scene of the kiss in the train in *North by Northwest*), it is clearly the "unseen" of the primal scene in the hotel room that, at the level of the enunciating instance itself (Hitchcock–the camera), is displaced from neurosis to psychosis, from the hotel room to the motel room.[15]

Thus, Norman obviously comes to occupy, with respect to Marion, the place of Sam (whence the resemblance, for some striking, between Sam and Norman, particularly during the scene of their confrontation across the counter in the motel office).[16] However, the substitution occurs at the price of a displacement, imputable to the respective identifications between Hitchcock and the two male characters. In the first scene, the camera almost always remains at a distance from Sam: he is held, like Marion, and usually with her, within the frame – that is, within the neurotic field that the two of them circumscribe. An essentially diegetic identification is thus set up (for the male spectator, who is *primarily* addressed), at the level of the sexual possession of which Marion has been the object, when Sam renews his demand and hears it refused.[17]

Conversely, in the shots preceding the shower scene, the camera reduces to an extreme degree the unforseeable effect of the distance separating it from what is being filmed: it virtually coincides with the insert of Norman's bulging eye, owing to the metaphor of the apparatus thus constituted. This is the point of maximal identification between the character and the instance of the *mise-en-scène*; it can only be surpassed by its own excess, when the eye–camera becomes a body–knife, entering the field of its object and attempting in vain to coincide with it.

However, in order to go from one man to another, and from one position to another, the camera must also embody the woman and adopt her look, conserving a strong identification – diegetic, of course, but more specifically specular, determined by the organization of the point of view – with the subject it has taken as its object. (The latter can be maintained in a position of fundamental subjection through a series of carefully planned relays – the policemen, the service station attendant – that reiterate the question of which she has been the object from the start.) In conformity with its basic path, that of perverse structuration, the transformation from neurosis to psychosis is brought about by woman, who is both its foundation and its indispensable form.

This explains the lengthiness of the first half of the first movement, organized around theft and escape. It also explains the systematic series of shot-reverse shots that mark Marion's itinerary up until the moment of blindness (a mixture of fatigue and hypnosis) that causes her to turn off the wet highway and head for the motel. It explains, finally, the resumption and redoubling of these shots as a preparation for the moment of reversal, during the confrontation between Marion and Norman. In this manner, the diegesis participates directly in the aggressive potential, carried to an extreme by the reciprocity of the looks in the alternation of shot–reverse shots. The effects of this cinematographic code par excellence evoke the structure of the cinematographic apparatus, and thereby of the primitive apparatus it imitates – namely, the mirror wherein the subject structures himself, through a mode of narcissistic identification of which aggressivity is an indelible component.[18] However, this reference only makes sense – here very specifically (as in all of Hitchcock's films, and classical cinema in general, particularly American) – within the global system in which the aggressive element can never be separated from the inflection it receives from sexual difference, and the attribution of this difference to the signifier that governs it. In other words, it is directed from the man toward the woman, and that difference that appears due to woman is nothing but the mirror-effect of the narcissistic doubling that makes possible the constitution of the male subject through the woman's body, ordered by a double play of differentiated identity, based on an effect of imaginary projection subjected to the constitutive pressure of a symbolic determination.[19]

* * *

Between man and woman, through woman's look as appropriated by the camera, this mirror or doubling-effect (hence also one of denial and splitting) serves to structure the male subject as the subject of a scopic drive – that is to say, a subject who imaginarily attributes to woman the lack he himself has been assigned, in response to the anxiety created by the fantasized threat of this lack within his own body. This is the classical dialectic – as described by Freud and Lacan – of the phallus and castration; its implications with respect to perversion (the conjugated motifs of voyeurism and fetishism) have been astutely analyzed by Guy Rosolato.[20] Lacan refers this dialectic, particularly as regards the scopic drive, to the lack – unevenly divided between the two sexes – of the signifier that structures it; it is this signifier, castration, that determines "the gaze as *objet a.*"[21] In a different perspective, the same dialectic has been relativized by Luce Irigaray, who denounces the fact that in men (that is, in Sam, Norman, Hitchcock, Freud, Lacan, the subject writing these lines in an attempt to fissure the system that holds him) "the scopic drive is predominant."[22]

This is why, theoretically, there are no women fetishists; nor even, more broadly speaking, women perverts: either because, in psychological terms, "perverse" as applied to women connotes perversity rather than perversion, or because theory – elaborated or directed by men – has avoided acknowledging perversions in women, not having discovered *perversion* itself.[23]

This explains the fact that Norman's psychosis, his inordinate object-desire that rushes headlong into murder, is entirely structured by a fetishistic aim carried to the point of madness. Psychoanalytically, it might be said, Norman is a collage (which neither confirms nor denies his clinical possibilities, which are not in question – simply because, for me, that is not the question). He seeks to construct a chain in which the excessiveness of the psychotic-perverse desire of the male subject can be structured – from the man to the camera, his true measure – during the scene where he establishes his presence at a distance, fascinated, in vertiginous mastery. This chain may be written: phallus–bird–fetish–mother–eye–knife–camera. A terrifying play on words (suggested, rather than made explicit, in the film) connects this chain to the omnipotence of infantile desire turned toward death: *Mommy, mummy*: the mother's body, fetishized to death, so to speak, becomes the body that murders, in keeping with the desire awakened in the eye of the subject possessed by it.[24] Through the incredible incorporation of a metaphor-become-reality, Norman's fascinated look carries within it the phallus immemorially attributed to the mother. But he can acknowledge it in himself only on condition that he ceaselessly encounter it in his mirror-image – namely, in the body/look of woman (which engenders the mirage), and as an absolute threat to which he must respond; otherwise, it is his own body that will desert him. Such (to complete the psychiatrist's speech) might be the motivations behind the genealogy of the case: the reiterative passage from the former murder (that of the mother) to the murder of Marion of which Norman–the mother is the agent, emphasizing in both cases, given an original identificatory fantasy, the literally impossible desire for possession and fusion that is at stake.

* * *

This allows us to describe the distribution of the three terms (psychosis, neurosis, perversion) within the logic of the process of enunciation. These terms define the primordial relationship between the two scenes that most closely circumscribe this process (the hotel and the motel), through a "breathing space" during which the subject is presented as such. The possessive form used in the credits – "Alfred Hitchcock's *Psycho*" – is a mark of enunciation that may be said to have a double meaning: this film belongs to me; this psychosis is mine, or would be mine if ... if it were not, precisely, for this film, which both involves me in and frees me from psychosis, positioning me elsewhere. A special lettering effect (something like the bulging eye during the credits of *Vertigo*) contributes to the singularization of this relatively common signifying arrangement: a vibrato twice causes the center of the letters to shift back and forth, first for the title *Psycho*, and then for the name in the final enunciation: "Directed by Alfred Hitchcock." In addition, the opening scene immediately reiterates the interplay of black and white lines that had striated the credits from top to bottom: the camera must pass under venetian blinds to enter the room at the end of its movement, and it is on the background of these horizontal lines, in the second half of the scene, that Sam and Marion are seen in reverse shot, separately or together. Thus, by displacement and metaphor, what is inscribed in this space communicates an implied relationship between the title and the name.

In the first scene, the camera's power is intrinsically expressed by the bird's-eye view of the city and its rooftops, then emphasized by its concentration on the voyeuristic point of reference: the couple in the bedroom after lovemaking. The "after" is important, since, in a sense, the camera intervenes in place of what happens between man and woman at the literally mythical level of the primal scene: it is a continually withdrawing instance, collecting – at the purified level of vicariousness – what is fundamentally perverse and psychotic, given the logic of this perspective, in man's desire for woman, even within the neurotic configuration that is its most common destiny. The camera becomes, it might be said, the eye–phallus, projected and reprojected from one sex to the other, but [one which,] on the basis of a signifying privilege assigned to only one sex, transforms the camera into pure eye, look, dissociated from the scene, in proportion to the lack of the phallus of which it circumscribes the representation so that – and because – it is represented in it.[25] It is this dialectic, in slightly different terms, that emerges during the second scene, through a temporal actualization: "that which may not be seen" seeks to show itself, to break into awareness (into reality), but displaced from the act. The camera must still, obviously, remain outside its object. Yet it is also doubly inscribed within it, as has been seen: first by the mediation of the apparatus set up around Norman, and, secondly, through the invasion, by the subject of the apparatus, of the tableau of his own vision. From its perverse situation, already enhanced by an identification with the subject of the diegesis, the camera thus fully assumes the psychotic function that was potentially circumscribed during the first scene. However, it can of course attain only a more extreme perversion, since it is filming its metaphorical invasion of its own field. It thus reaffirms all the more strongly, by its very division, the unforeseeable effects of distance, lack and denial that make it up – everything that psychosis (Norman–the camera) is at that very moment attempting to exorcize by presenting as real, through a rape ending in murder, the imaginary and ungraspable relation of the primal scene.

Within this configuration, one thing seems to me to be essential – namely, that it is through woman's pleasure (*jouissance*) that the perverse projection and psychotic inscription are carried out (just as it is through her actions, her body, her look, that the film moves from one scene to the next). The emphasis on Marion's pleasure in the shower goes well beyond all diegetic motivation: close-up shots of her naked body alternate with shots of gushing water; she leans into the stream, opens her mouth, smiles, and closes her eyes in a rapture that is made all the more intense because it contrasts with the horror that is to come, but also because the two are linked together. By a subtle reversal, the pleasure that Marion did not show in the opening love scene at last appears. However, the pleasure is for herself (even if it can only be so for the camera, because of the image-nature assigned to her by the camera); it takes the form of narcissistic intimacy that poses, for men, the question of sexual pleasure itself, with woman's body instituted as its mythical site. The masculine subject can accept the image of woman's pleasure only on condition that, having constructed it, he may inscribe himself and recognize himself within it, and thus reappropriate it even at the cost of its (or her) destruction.[26]

VIII

Briefly, to resume and strengthen what has been said by considering several points in a spiral-like movement, that is, together, as a text does whenever one tries to make it appear as what it is, that is to say, as what it becomes, virtually, always in analysis: a *volume*.

1.   The first scene(s) is (are) programmed as a matrix whose elements are distributed throughout the whole text by effects of dispersal, rebound, and repetition. This is one of the laws of classical film (see, in particular, the analyses of Thierry Kuntzel).[27] In *Psycho*, this process is at first carried out at a very general level. The first scene, through the shift in the screenplay, primarily serves as a preparation for the succession of scenes between Marion and Norman: their tête-à-tête in the reception room, the series of shots setting up Norman as apparatus, the murder in the shower. From this is derived, at the end, the scene with the psychiatrist, which resolves not only the enigma, but the (psychic) mystery of the murder: this final scene only replies to the first one at the price of the initial displacement caused by the shift in the screenplay.

There is also, however, the way in which the first scene inaugurates the sequence of bedrooms: the motel rooms, Marion's room, Arbogast's room (suggested), Sam and Lila's room, and thence, at the end of the third movement, the intrusion into the bedrooms of the house, especially Norman's and the mother's, under Lila's discovering look.

More subtly, there is a thread that leads from the first shot, to Norman as apparatus, to the next to last shot. Norman–the mother is seen in a medium shot against the naked wall of his cell, smiling, while on his face is gradually superimposed the skull that will make of him, irremediably, the mother. Her voice is heard: "I hope that they are watching, they will see, they will see and they will say, 'Why she wouldn't even harm a fly'."[28] This circular play on words goes from the fly to the bird, to the body-fetish of Norman–the mother. But it goes further still: to the omnipotence of the scopic drive. Norman's words are addressed to all the guardians of the law (police-men, judges, psychiatrist), presumably gathered on the other side of the door and peering at him through the keyhole. How ⬛⬛⬛ough them, his words are addressed to the spectator, who is trapped in the mi⬛⬛⬛ Norman's eyes, staring right into the camera as though to conjure away the ⬛⬛er it exerts. The spectator is thus confronted, from within the shot itself, with the "non-authorized scoptophilia" that places cinematic voyeurism "in the direct lineage of the primal scene."[29] Thus, all of the opening shots have been condensed into the body-look of Norman–the mother, revealing the reflective structure of the apparatus, before the final shot, with an ultimate effect of resolution, brings the film to its close (in a single sweep, using a very long dissolve to link the last and next-to-last shots through the superimposition of the skull). In this way, two screenplays intermingle: male (Sam, Norman, and – in both – Hitchcock) and female (Marion, the mother); and the end, after a monstrous detour, replies to the beginning. Marion's dead body reappears in the white car dragged from the marsh only because it has been, from the beginning, the object of the conjugated desire of a man and the camera.

2.   The apparatus is therefore present in the film, though not – as in *Rear Window* – by a mirror effect. Here, a certain rhyming effect of two images strikes me; first, on the roadside at dawn, the close-up of the policeman coming upon Marion asleep in her car; and, secondly, in the cellar, the close-up of the mother's skeleton. The latter is seen twice, once when Lila puts her hand on Mrs. Bates's shoulder and the draped skeleton slowly swings around toward her, and again at the end of the segment, after Norman's intrusion. There is a similarity between these two faces, sustained by a striking reversal: the eyes have disappeared; in the second case they are nothing but hollow sockets, and in the first they are totally hidden by dark glasses. This is a way of signifying, by its very absence, the unbearably excessive nature of the look. The dark glasses especially (like Mitch's binoculars in *The Birds*) suggest a metaphor of the photographic lens: super-vision of the law, symbolized by its representative; excess of the symbolic itself, which triumphs at the end "in the prolixity of the psychiatrist."[30] Film, both as discourse and as an institution, is subject to an order that is marked by the monolithic power of its ruling signifier. However, this super-vision is also that of disorder, the breaking of the law, of which fetishistic psychosis is the most inordinate form. Moreover, the signifier is perpetu-ally imaginary, subject to denial and splitting. The hollow eye sockets of the mother are the verso of an apparatus whose recto is the policeman's dark glasses. There is an endless circularity between desire and the law, both of which, taken to an extreme, inspire terror (in Marion, in Lila).

Here, I cannot resist associating more or less freely. When Lila enters the cellar she sees, from behind, a woman seated. In the foreground to the right, in the upper part of the frame, there is an electric light bulb so alive, so enormous, and disposed in such a manner that it seemed to me – at first sight and at each successive viewing, despite critical distance – to simulate a spherical screen, casting a blinding light onto the brick wall across from Mrs. Bates. The mother occupies, in this virtual image, the place of the spectator, thus evoking the real spectator, and even more so his mirror image (the fetish inhabited by the death wish) when she looks at him directly during the next two close-up shots. This is particularly true the second time, when Lila's terror causes her to knock against the light bulb, making it swing back and forth. The vacillation in the lighting thus produced is repeated and amplified later (when Norman bursts in, unmasked and overcome by Sam): the skull seems to be animated by this vibration – this play of lights and shadows that also designates the cinema itself.

Following this, representation dissolves into the very image of the law (a metaphorical reappearance of the policeman): a general shot of the courthouse introduces the psychiatrist's speech.

3. That everything in *Psycho* seems immediately doubled must be seen as the effect – with repercussions in concentric waves down to the microsystematic level of the smallest signifying units – of the two main rhetorical axes that organize the film, namely, its ternary composition and its two screenplays. Other of Hitchcock's films also manifest, by their very structure, the specific pressure of the doubling process that underlies all his films: *Shadow of a Doubt*, with the determining superimposition of the uncle's and niece's names (Charlie); *Strangers on a Train*, with the exchange of murders; *Vertigo*, with the mirror-effect of the double heroine (Madeleine–Judy). However, this doubling process is, so to speak, exacerbated in *Psycho* by the crisscross effects of substitution, division, and echo among characters. The first couple, Sam and Marion, engenders the second, Norman and Marion: Norman has thus taken the place of Sam. Yet he has actually, diegetically speaking, taken the place of Marion, given the mirror dialectic between the sexes and their psychic structurations. Lila's appearance at the beginning of the second movement causes this network of transformations to double back on itself: she represents the return of the indispensable heroine, Marion's reappearance (like Judy's in *Vertigo*) in the form of her sister. Thus, the film could be said to be organized in yet another way with respect to woman's body-look, because of the long sequence taking Lila from the motel to the cellar where she discovers – with an absolute horror that obviously recalls that of Marion in the shower – the stuffed body of the mother. Thus the diegetic couple disjoined at the end of the first segment is reconstituted as a shadow: Sam and Lila, pretending to be married – as Sam and Marion were intended to be – approach the motel where Marion first met Norman on the path that was supposed to lead her to Sam. The function of this shadow-couple reveals in an exemplary way, through repetition and mimed (undermined) resolution, the deep structural subversion of sameness that is here carried out.

4. To conclude, we might point out the constellation of signifiers that disseminate and recenter the differential doubling between men and women to which the fiction is continually and completely subjected.

- *Norman–Marion*: Christian names in mirror-relation to one another, interchangeable but for a single phoneme (Marion was chosen instead of the Mary of Bloch's novel).
- *Norman*: he who is neither woman ... nor man, since he can be one in the place of the other, or rather one and the other, one within the other.

- *Marie Samuels*: the name used by Marion to sign the motel register, derived from Sam's first name.
- *Phoenix* (superimposed on the first shot to situate the action): again, a bird; the bird that dies only in order to be transformed (as is here the case, through murder, of one character, one sex, one story) into another. In fact, there is a double metamorphosis: a diegetic one (Marion becoming Norman) and a formative one (Norman becoming a living bird–mother) that renders possible the former.
- *Crane*: Marion's last name; once again a bird's name. It marks her body with the signifier that appears, to Norman, as a lack or an excess. But the word "crane" also means something else: the machine that embodies above all others, in the image-taking apparatus, the omniscient power of the look, what might be called the bird's-eye view. This is to say, once again, but here with an element of humor, that the camera becomes one with woman's body, and that in this sense it is itself the fetish, adopting the forms of the bird and of Norman–the mother, going through the whole circuit of the fiction, only to be immediately acknowledged as the enunciating index, at the level of the apparatus that makes fiction possible.

Whence, indissolubly, here, it can be said of film and cinema, that they are the very institution of perversion.

Notes

1. François Truffaut, *Hitchcock* (New York: Simon and Schuster, 1967), 206.
2. Cf., on the relationship between the film and the original narrative, James Naremore, *Filmguide to* Psycho (Bloomington: Indiana Univ. Press, 1973), 23–4, 33–4. I found in this short essay, after having written a first, summary version of the present article ("Psycho," *Dossiers du cinéma, Films II* (Paris: Casterman, 1972)), several observations along the same lines as my analysis. Some of the elements organized around Marion during the first section of the narrative appear, in Bloch's novel, as mental flashbacks to scenes that comprise, in Hitchcock's film, the second section.
3. Truffaut, 206.
4. Syntagmatic change, punctuation, diegetic unity. Cf. Christian Metz, "Ponctuations et démarcations dans le film de diégèse," in *Essais sur la signification au cinéma*, II (Paris: Klincksieck, 1972), 126–8. Cf. also on this point my study of Minnelli's *Gigi*, "To Analyze, to Segment," *Quarterly Review of Film Studies*, vol. 1, no. 3 (1976): 331–53.
5. Sheriff Chambers expresses this in two sentences, the second of which closes the scene on a note of horror: "Norman Bates's mother has been dead and buried in Greenlawn Cemetery for the past ten years." "Well, if that woman up there is Mrs. Bates, who's that woman buried out in Greenlawn Cemetery?" Richard Anobile, ed., *Psycho* (New York: Avon, 1975), 193, 195.
6. Sigmund Freud, "Loss of Reality in Neurosis and Psychosis" (1904), *Complete Works*, Standard Edition, vol. 19, pp. 183–7.
7. Freud, "Loss of Reality," 183.

8. MARION: Oh, Sam, I hate having to be with you in a place like this.

   SAM: I've heard of married couples who deliberately spend an occasional night in a cheap hotel. They say it's very exciting.

   MARION: Oh, when you're married you can do a lot of things deliberately.

   SAM: You sure talk like a girl who's been married.

   MARION: Sam, this is the last time.

   SAM: Yeah? For what?

   MARION: For this. For meeting you in secret – so we can be secretive. You come down here on those business trips and we steal lunch hours and – Oh, Sam, I wish you wouldn't even come....

   SAM: I sweat to pay off my father's debts and he's in his grave. I sweat to pay my ex-wife's alimony, and she's – living on the other side of the world somewhere!

   MARION: I pay, too. They also pay who meet in hotel rooms.

   SAM: A couple of years and – the debts will be paid off and – if she ever remarries, the alimony stops and –

   MARION: I haven't even been married once yet!

   SAM: Yeah, but when you do you'll swing!

   MARION: Sam, let's get married! (Anobile, 15–16, 19–20)

9. It might be added, for the pleasure of the "intertext," that the amount of money stolen by Marion ($40,000) is the same as the amount spent by Mark, in *Marnie*, on the wedding ring he offers Marnie. Moreover, this money was intended by the millionaire, who shows it off to Marion, for the purchase of a house as a wedding gift to his daughter.

10. *Norman's version*: Father's death when he was five. Some years later, his mother falls madly in love with a man who encourages her to build the motel. When he dies, the mother goes crazy.

    Sheriff's version (emergence of the mystery in the middle of the third movement): Norman poisons the lover. The mother, in turn, poisons herself.

    Psychiatrist's version (solution of the mystery): Norman poisons the lover and his mother.

11. Anobile, 77.

12. J. Laplanche and J.-B. Pontalis, *The Language of Psycho-Analysis* (New York: Norton, 1973), 309.

13. HITCHCOCK: "It also allows the viewer to become a Peeping Tom" (Truffaut, 204).

14. No contradiction is implied by the fact that in *Rope* it is a man who is being killed. Men, too, are killed in Hitchcock's films – and often – in more or less direct or displaced reference to the murder of the father. In *Rope*, the object of the murder may also be referred, in a complementary manner, to the virtually manifest homosexuality of the two murderers.

15. Cf. my analysis, "Le Blocage symbolique," *Communications*, no. 23 (1975): 251–6.

16. Cf. Naremore, 66.

17. SAM: We could laze around here a while longer.

    MARION: Checking out time is three p.m. Motels of this sort – are not interested in you when you come in, but when your time is up –. (Anobile, 15)

18. Jacqueline Rose, "Paranoia and the Film System," *Screen*, vol. 17, no. 4 (1976–7): 85–104.

19. Cf., for a historical perspective on the symbolic constitution of the male subject, my study "Un jour, la castration," *L'Arc*, no. 71 (1978).

20. Cf. in particular "Perversions sexuelles," in *Encyclopédie médico-chirurgicale* (Paris, 1968), 37392 CIO: 8–9.
21. Jacques Lacan, *Les Quatre Concepts fondamentaux de la psychanalyse* (Paris: Seuil, 1973). English translation by Alan Sheridan, *The Four Fundamental Concepts of Psycho-Analysis* (London: Hogarth Press, 1977).
22. "Misère de la psychanalyse," *Critique*, no. 365 (October 1977): 900. Cf. also *Ce sexe qui n'en est pas un* (Paris: Minuit, 1977), 25.
23. ROSOLATO: "This perversion [fetishism] is practiced exclusively by men," *Encyclopédie médico-chirurgicale*, 9.
24. I owe this to the friendship of Thierry Kuntzel.
25. On the eye–phallus relationship, cf. Lacan, *The Four Fundamental Concepts of Psycho-Analysis*, 101–4.
26. *Marnie*, in this regard, deals with the reappropriation of the image, whereas *Psycho* deals with its destruction. Cf. my article "Hitchcock, The Enunciator," *Camera Obscura*, no. 2 (1977): 69–94.
27. "Le Travail du film, 1," *Communications*, no. 19 (1972); English translation, *Enclitic*, vol. 2, no. 1 (1978): 39–64. "Le Travail du film, 2," *Communications*, no. 25 (1975); English translation, *Camera Obscura*, no. 5 (1980): 6–69. Cf. also my article "Hitchcock, The Enunciator," and similar themes in my articles "Les Oiseaux: analyse d'une séquence," *Cahiers du cinéma*, no. 216 (October 1969): 38; "Le Blocage symbolique," 349; "To Analyse, To Segment."
28. Anobile, 255.
29. Christian Metz, "Le Signifiant imaginaire," *Communications*, no. 23 (1975): 45. English translation, *Screen*, vol. 16, no. 2 (Summer 1975): 14–76.
30. Roger Dadoun, in the few suggestive lines devoted to *Psycho* in "Le Fétichisme dans le film d'horreur," *Objets du fétichisme, Nouvelle Revue de Psychanalyse*, no. 2 (Autumn 1970): 238.

PSYCHO (Paramount, 1960). *Producer*: Alfred Hitchcock, *Assistant Director*: Hilton A. Green, *Script*: Joseph Stefano, from the Robert Bloch novel, *Photography*: John L. Russell, *Editor*: George Tomasini, *Sets*: Joseph Hurley, Robert Claworthy, George Milo, *Music*: Bernard Herrmann, *Costumes*: Helen Colvig, *Titles*: Saul Bass, *Players*: Anthony Perkins (Norman Bates), Janet Leigh (Marion Crane), Vera Miles (Lila Crane), John Gavin (Sam Loomis), Martin Balsam (Arbogast), John McIntire (Sheriff Chambers), Lurene Tuttle (Mrs. Chambers), Frank Albertson (Tom Cassidy), Simon Oakland (psychiatrist), Patricia Hitchcock (Caroline). 109 minutes.

Chapter Twenty-Five

Psycho's Allegory of Seeing

Christopher D. Morris

Recent studies by Rosalind Krauss and Martin Jay consider surrealist photography and film as part of a more generalized revolt against the philosophical tradition of the Cartesian self; for both writers, surrealism's protest often took the form of an assault against ocularcentrism – against the privileged status accorded the sense of vision as the correlative of the grail of hermeneutics, the achievement of some true theoretical perspective. For Krauss and Jay, Bataille's enucleated eye, Magritte's *trompe d'oeil*, and Dali's sliced-eyeball are artistic anticipations of the philosophic interrogation of hermeneutics intensified later in the century by deconstruction.[1] Of course, Hitchcock's admiration for Dali is well known; their collaboration on *Spellbound* (1945) reflects a fascination with the eye as a metaphor that recurs in *Vertigo* (1958) and *Psycho* (1960).[2] At the center of *Psycho* is Marion Crane's dead eye, which, in a famous dissolve, gradually replaces the image of a bathtub drain. Critics have interpreted the dissolve in many ways, without consensus.[3] Following Krauss and Jay, I will examine it and the film as a whole as an extension of the same subversion of hermeneutics they find manifested in surrealism. At the same time, adapting the thesis of Paul de Man, I explore *Psycho* – in both its plot and its reflections on itself – as an allegory of seeing in the figurative sense of understanding – a dramatization of the necessity for the seer/interpreter to mistake a sign for a signified presence.[4]

If Marion's eye only apparently sees, it may signify the illusion of true vision or reading; its emergence from the dissolving bathtub drain suggests how both may be considered apertures to nothingness. By this reasoning, what the eye takes in, in viewing or reading, is like diluted blood down the drain – a sign only of emptiness and death. What the world calls perception may be no more than illusions that temporarily keep mortality at bay. On this level, what we see or read in *Psycho* is reducible to the drain–eye image that subverts psychologies and perceptions as mistakings of absences. No one – not Marion, Norman, Arbogast, Sam, Lila, the psychiatrist, or the critic – ever sees truly; each is condemned to the search for a signifying presence ultimately exposed as illusory – love or money, reason or cause, theme or meaning – as a substitute for nothingness.

Psycho allegorizes this universal delusion by showing that its characters' hunts for signified presences are mistaken. Marion Crane's search for love necessitates, first, a search for money. It is as if an advance toward a goal requires first a retreat, a substitution, a mistaking; the embezzlement is a literal example of "taking" new signs. (Of course, the necessity to "take" signs as real is as fundamental to reading or viewing films as it is to love, so Marion Crane's misappropriation only repeats as it exposes, belatedly, the viewer's act in taking as real a cinematic play of light and dark signs.) The idea that Marion's substitute goal, cash, consists of new signs momentarily taken as referents is reinforced when Marion hides it, like a signified message, inside an envelope. The idea that cash functions as the object of the viewer's curiosity is reinforced by the way the camera lingers over it.

If we take Marion's cash as a metaphor for the sought-after locus of signified meaning – the goal of hermeneutics – we can observe how the film dramatizes the futility of its pursuit. The cash or putative meaning is wrapped in an envelope and also a newspaper, like the destination of a reading, and it is this signifier that provides the rationale for Arbogast's interpretative quest (which in turn triggers Lila's, which triggers the psychiatrist's and then the reader's). Marion converts some of her signs into a new putative signified, a car, and hides the rest, which Norman unknowingly returns to her car. In the end, signifier and an interchangeable putative signified – cash, car, Cartesian self – sink into the quicksand, down the drain, into oblivion. So by the end of the film, there is some suggestion that the object of the circular pursuit of meaning is all the time not some stable referent but only other signs, and that it leads to a nothingness comparable to that of a drain or dark swamp.

(Of course, the film's final scene depicts a wrecker's winch beginning to pull the car out of the swamp. Is there some prospect that the cash and car will finally be brought to light? This eventuality exists only in prospect, outside the film, deferred. It is as if art has the capacity to hold forth the prospect of some bringing-to-light but can never fulfill it. In any case, since cash and car are both parts of a chain of signs, their eventual discovery will only provoke new mistakings. In this respect, the ending implies that art consists of signs that momentarily give its interpreters the illusion of waiting for meaning to be brought to light elsewhere.)

The principal hermeneutic "meaning" within the film – Norman's motivation – is personified in "Norman's mother," but events show us that "Norman's mother" is chimerical, ungraspable. Even to name her or "represent her" in a pronoun is already to be in error. Like the cash, Norman's mother is frequently the object of mistaken sight. Arbogast and Lila think they see her at the window; Marion and a first-time viewer may even "see her" attacking. Of course, we cannot simply say, either, that Norman's mother "doesn't exist." This is the effect of the scene with Sheriff Chambers, who exclaims, "If Norman's mother is up there, who is in the grave?" (Since the dead "exist" as corpses and also as memories, their names may be humankind's first experience of signifiers that promise but withhold a signified. *Psycho*, like many literary and cinematic predecessors, equates the dead with the larger entity "psychological motivation." Invoking either in seeing or reading raises prospects of signification that are not fulfilled.)

This impression of necessary misinterpretation is strengthened by the psychiatrist's explanation. The very conspicuousness of his speech at the end of the film makes it seem a parody of the "explanation at the end of the mystery," as common to the genre of detection and crime fiction as it is to Greek tragedy. The unnamed psychiatrist is the modern world's equivalent of the "Deus ex machina," and his explanation has just the right blend of plausibility and outrageous arrogance to bestir in audiences the grudging acquiescence and objections that have characterized critical responses to the scene.[5] But to cast the critical problem as whether or not to agree with the psychiatrist is already to miss the film's dramatization of interpretation as *necessary* mistaking. The psychiatrist – like Arbogast, Lila, and Marion – must confront "Norman's mother," must frame a hypothesis about intention-as-presence as a condition of perception and discourse. He can no sooner see Norman as motiveless than viewers can see him as an alternation of light and shadow.

It is notable that the psychiatrist delivers his explanation as a kind of lecture before a seated audience, in one room, while the presumed "object" of his discourse is seated alone in an otherwise empty room; of course, the true "object" of the psychiatrist's discourse – "Norman's mother" – is absent, invisible. The emphasis on the separation of signifier and signified is then repeated by the disembodied woman's voice, which purports to be that of Norman's mother. Hitchcock's penultimate scene does not support or dramatize the psychiatrist's conventional split-personality theory; on the contrary, it contradicts that theory (and perhaps all Cartesian theory) by dramatizing the independence of language from the speaking subject. The voice-over shows us language separated from human subjectivity.[6]

The idea that all searches for signification, like the psychiatrist's, can never escape a world of referentless signs – of optical illusions – is dramatized in the quests of Arbogast, Sam, and Lila. Motivated by Marion's mis-taking of cash, Arbogast nonetheless cannot doubt the existence of referents for signs, like his photograph of Marion, now dead. His deduction, that Norman's mother actually exists, proceeds from a visual delusion. His quest for true signification results only in death; this is the only lesson of the film. Answering the plot question of whether Arbogast or Marion is "demystified" at the moment of death – by seeing Norman's mother as unreal – only establishes more clearly the interminableness and futility of hermeneutics. If they see "Norman's mother," they die in palpable illusion. But if they see "Norman disguised as his mother," as Sam and Lila do, they are still deluded, just as much as the viewer is, since the hermeneutic question of the meaning of or motive for Norman's attack is still deferred, until we come to the psychiatrist's "explanation," which itself becomes the object of critical interpretation in an endless series.

That Sam's quest begins in referentless signs and optical illusion is made clear by the letter he is writing to Marion:

> Dearest right as always Marion, I'm sitting in this tiny back room which isn't big enough for both of us, and suddenly it *looks* big enough for both of us. So what if we're poor and cramped and miserable, at least we'll be happy. If you haven't come back to your senses and still....

Here the idea of the visual delusion is explicitly connected with the futility of signs – the letter Sam is writing (like all letters?) is already precluded from reaching its

364 *Christopher D. Morris*

destination. The fragment makes a clear connection, too, between the delusion of signification and moral undecidability. We are invited to consider the sense in which Marion is "right as always." Sam's implied praise – that Marion is right to prefer love to money – is neutralized first by his observation that she is out of her senses and also by her embezzlement.

Moreover, the question of Marion's "true" intention cannot be finally answered. Just before her death she sits at a writing desk and subtracts 700 from 40,000; then she rips up this calculation and begins to throw it in the wastepaper basket; again she changes her mind and throws the paper in the toilet. From these actions critics usually conclude that she has decided to return to Phoenix and make restitution; this may also be Lila's conclusion when she comes upon the remaining scrap of paper. But it is clear that no interpretation of Marion's motivation can be based on a torn piece of paper. We cannot know if she decided to return the money or to continue in pursuit of her goal, because no interpretation of what is only silence and visual ambiguity can be successful. On the contrary, what the scene does dramatize is precisely the effect that its true interpretation is impossible. The sign Lila reads, a fragment not yet flushed down the drain, is meaningless in itself. It is analogous to the psychiatrist's interview with Norman, to the film *Psycho*, to interpretations of it (like this one) or in fact to any text – a meaningless sign temporarily preserved from extinction is read in terms of an absent, invisible intention. In fact, this scene dramatizes the wholly constructed and fictional nature of human motivation and interpretation.

As does Lila's quest. In her exploration of Mrs. Bates's and Norman's rooms, the camera dwells on portentous, seemingly talismanic images that reveal, after all, only the waywardness of the search. If we understand her journey as the hermeneutic quest for true interpretation, we are everywhere reminded of its futility. We see absences (an empty sink and fireplace, the outline of a body in a bed); simulacra of life (the folded hands on the jewelry box, single and double mirror-reflections, a stuffed bunny); and signifiers of signifiers (a phonograph of the Eroica symphony, a book whose contents remain undisclosed). Lila's search through these rooms has important consequences. First, it vitiates in advance the psychiatrist's analysis by showing us that – just as in the case of the scrap of paper rescued from the toilet – no accumulation of biographical signifiers or "details" can amount to or validate a Cartesian subject with determinable motivation. Is the stuffed bear a signifier of psychotic regression or of normal sentimentality? Is there any way such mute details could interpret themselves, without irony? Second, the succession of details "ends" with Lila's confrontation with the corpse of Mrs. Bates, thereby strengthening the sense, noted earlier, in which the film's signs seem only to occlude, defer, and evade the fact of mortality. Most crucially, as dead representations of life, the details Lila and the viewer scrutinize recall Norman's stuffed birds and Marion's dead eye. We are now in a position to see how such signs suggest the death of theoria, or interpretation, itself. It is instructive that the etymology of "theory" is rooted in the visual sense – the words "idea" and "video" proceed from a common ocularcentric root. *Psycho* first shows us the failure of Marion's and Norman's visual quests – their literal and figurative searches for insight; these failures are then repeated by the film's theory-makers (Arbogast, Lila, the psychiatrist). It is as if the quest for interpretation is unstoppable, even in the face of the dead eye. And, like the film's theory-makers, viewers come up lamely behind, adding their own redundant interpretations to a sequence of "ideas" already shown to be dead.

II

In the foregoing we looked at the film's plot as an allegory of seeing as interpretation and proposed that Marion's quest and the repeated interpretative quests of Arbogast, Lila, and the psychiatrist may be read as redundant mistakings of signifiers for signifieds. In this extension of Paul de Man's argument, the story of *Psycho* illustrates a necessity for misreading by continuing while mortal cycles postpone, as if to the end or "other side" of interpretation, the eventual apprehension of human mortality – human seeing (or understanding) is a delusion comparable to a dead eye. In this regard, *Psycho*'s effect resembles that of surrealist painting, in impugning human understanding through an assault on ocularcentrism and all theoria, especially psychoanalytic discourses. Of course, at the same time, the film also indicts itself as a visual spectacle helpless to offer a valid alternative to the delusions it dramatizes. The primary means for achieving this simultaneous self-indictment is through its running self-parody, which continually mocks the viewer's necessary efforts to glean meaning from the arbitrary flickering of light and darkness in the theater.

Many critics have noticed self-reflective features in the film, from the opening tracking shot and subjective camera to the swinging light bulb in the root cellar.[7] These studies have established the extent to which the film makes the viewer complicit in Norman's voyeurism and aggression; they have identified numerous ways in which the viewer is forced to acknowledge film artifice while interpreting the story. But, in a deconstructive analysis, these details function even more subversively by forcing the viewer to acknowledge, belatedly, the arbitrary character of all interpretation – even of the status of director and viewer as sender and recipient of a supposed message of complicity.

The titles may illustrate this difference in subversion. The separated letters of the word "Psycho," which momentarily join together, may hint at the popularized understanding of the concept "split personalities" – the concept endorsed by the psychiatrist at the end of the film. But even before the semantic value of these broken letters can be established, they must first be seen as arbitrary, meaningless marks, which seem to form a referent only in combination. Reading the film's title presupposes the imposition of meaning on arbitrary signs – just as the quests of Marion, Norman, and Arbogast require mistakings of absences for presences. Of course, such a mistaking is necessary – as necessary as attributing a name or a voice to a face. So *Psycho* begins with the idea that psychoanalytic discourses are first *constructed*, from arbitrary signs.

The opening tracking shot makes the viewer an eavesdropper and voyeur. But, as Sam and Marion talk, we become conscious of a second aperture – the window, whose shades Sam adjusts. Thus, from the outset there are two focused "points of view" on the affair – ultimately, of course, there is an infinite number – and each is constructed of light and shadow. The viewer as voyeur is no more privileged than any other percipient of the scene. The shafts of light here suggest the subject/viewer's self-construction in the filmic analogue of the mirror-stage, as Christian Metz argues; however, this erotic identity is derived from a play of light and shadow.

The fact that the murder is committed by someone impersonating someone else is enough to make viewers aware of the fiction on which interpretations rest. An even more telling instance of the same subversion is the famous editing of the shower sequence, which literalizes the action of *rapid cutting*. That these actions take place with shadows cast upon a screen only further reminds us of the mistakes we cannot help making while viewing. As viewers, our quest for some stable referent of the hermeneutic quest is frustrated in just the same manner as those of the characters. Although Norman sees Marion naked through the peephole and in the shower, we are never vouchsafed those visions. After we understand the shortcomings of the hermeneuts, through the psychiatrist's speech, we are returned to the scene of a face dissolved in a skull and to the image of eyes dissociated from words. These images reiterate the idea that seeing may be dead seeing. But interpretation can never rest, even at this point of subversion. As noted earlier, the final image of the emergent car promises only that something – something that will finally link signifiers like the cash and the newspaper with the fact of mortality, Marion's dead body – may someday be brought to light. Art can bring us to this threshold of understanding the contradictions of its expressions, but afterward it leaves the viewer in silence and darkness.

Notes

1. Jay, 32, 37, notes the relation between surrealism's anti-ocularcentrism and the work of Derrida. For the general distinction between hermeneutics and deconstruction, see the collections edited by Caputo and by Shapiro and Sica.
2. For an account of Dali's work on *Spellbound*, see Phillips, 117–18.
3. For Rothman, the dissolve is an image of birth (p. 308); for Brill, the failure of hopes for renewal and regeneration (pp. 221, 227); for Leitch, 217, the moment when the film's mode "switches decisively from psychological drama to black comedy" (p. 217).
4. De Man's most sustained exposition of this thesis is *Allegories of Reading*. Deconstructive film criticism is relatively recent; examples derived from the work of Derrida include *Screen/Play*, and the essay by Brunette.
5. Schneider uses this metaphor in arguing that the psychiatrist's presence reassures viewers of both the legitimacy of their presence in the theatre and the superiority of their insight. Naremore points out that the "best critics of *Psycho* have argued that the scene is ironic"; he himself finds it "flat, dull, and pompously acted" (pp. 68, 69). Brill concludes that, despite the psychiatrist's fatuous manner, "much of what he says is plausible enough" (236). Numerous challenges to the psychiatrist's reliability are raised by Rothman, 332–40.
6. These considerations suggest ways in which the psychiatrist's pop Freudianism may be critiqued from the vantage-point of Lacanian psychoanalysis. For one connection between Lacan and the surrealists, see Jay, 27.
7. Recchia interprets the film's reflexive devices as establishing the viewer's complicity with its dark themes. For other hermeneutic analyses of these devices, see the appropriate chapters in the work of Leitch and Rothman.

Works Cited

Brill, Lesley. *The Hitchcock Romance: Love and Irony in Hitchcock's Films*. Princeton: Princeton Univ. Press, 1988.

Brunette, Peter. "The Three Stooges and the (Anti-)Narrative of Violence: Deconstructive Comedy." In Andrew Horton, ed., *Comedy/Cinema/Theory*. Berkeley: Univ. of California Press, 1991.

Brunette, Peter, and David Wills. *Screen/Play: Derrida and Film Theory*. Princeton: Princeton Univ. Press, 1989.

Caputo, John D., ed. *Radical Hermeneutics: Repetition, Deconstruction, and the Hermeneutic Project*. Bloomington: Indiana Univ. Press, 1987.

De Man, Paul. *Allegories of Reading: Figural Language in Rousseau, Nietzsche, Rilke, and Proust*. New Haven: Yale Univ. Press, 1979.

Jay, Martin. "The Disenchantment of the Eye: Surrealism and the Crisis of Ocularcentrism," *Visual Anthropology Review*, vol. 7, no. 1 (Spring 1991): 15–38.

Kraus, Rosalind. "The Photographic Conditions of Surrealism." In *The Originality of the Avant-Garde and Other Modernist Myths*. Cambridge, MA: Harvard Univ. Press, 1985.

Leitch, Thomas. *Find the Director and Other Hitchcock Games*. Athens, GA: Univ. of Georgia Press, 1991.

Naremore, James. *Filmguide to* Psycho. Bloomington: Indiana Univ. Press, 1973.

Phillips, Gene D. *Alfred Hitchcock*. Boston: Twayne, 1984.

Recchia, Edward. "Through a Shower Curtain Darkly: Reflexivity as a Dramatic Component of *Psycho*," *Literature/Film Quarterly*, vol. 19, no. 4 (1991): 258–66.

Rothman, William. *Hitchcock: The Murderous Gaze*. Cambridge, MA: Harvard Univ. Press, 1982.

Schneider, Irving. "Deus Ex Animo, or Why a Doc?," *Journal of Popular Film and Television*, vol. 18, no. 1 (1990): 36–9.

Shapiro, Gary, and Alan Sica, eds. *Hermeneutics: Questions and Prospects*. Amherst, MA: Univ. of Massachusetts Press, 1984.

Chapter Twenty-Six

On Being Norman: Performance and Inner Life in Hitchcock's *Psycho*

Deborah Thomas

I would like to offer a tentative exploration of performance in Alfred Hitchcock's *Psycho* (1960), concentrating on Anthony Perkins in the role of Norman Bates. This is far from straightforward. For one thing, Hitchcock is famous for his dismissive attitude to the importance of acting in creating our sense of characters in his films, adhering to the conclusions reached by Kuleshov to the effect that audiences use clues around an actor's appearance (such as the imagery of adjoining shots) to project onto the character their own expectations and responses, the actor's expressions having little to do with their readings. Although Hitchcock would be reluctant to admit it, such clues may not even be primarily *his*, as a television programme on the music of Bernard Herrmann attempted to demonstrate by showing part of the sequence where Marion Crane (Janet Leigh) drives toward the Bates Motel both with and without the accompanying music, our sense of Marion's state of mind very different in each case. Nevertheless, it has also been generally acknowledged, despite Hitchcock's apparent belittlement of actors, that there are fine and complex performances in his work, and that Anthony Perkins as Norman Bates is one of them.

If disentangling Hitchcock's and Perkins's contributions from each other presents one sort of challenge, there are further difficulties in distinguishing amongst the various performances at stake, given that Norman himself "performs" a number of roles, both as himself and as his mother, and to a number of different audiences (us, Marion, Arbogast/Martin Balsam, Sam/John Gavin, and Lila/Vera Miles, the Sheriff/ John McIntire, and – in their conversations together, where he plays both roles – his "mother" and himself). There are complications too, perhaps, in the fact that the roles played by Norman exceed those played by Perkins: as Stephen Rebello points out (in *Alfred Hitchcock and the Making of Psycho*, Mandarin paperback edition, London, 1992), the voice we hear as "Mother" does not belong to Perkins, but is "spliced and blended" from "a mixture of different voices" (p. 133), nor is Perkins the figure who murders Marion in the shower: "Stuntwoman Margo Epper portrayed Mother in the sequence. An amused Tony Perkins recalled: 'The crew always referred to Mother and Norman as *totally* separate people'" (p. 113). However, such details need not detain us, since it is a commonplace that stand-ins are used from time to time, and this seems a similar sort of case (if more heavily foregrounded in the case of the voice). Still, we shall need to be careful not to attribute the construction of "Mrs. Bates" to Perkins himself, even though we may reasonably attribute it to Norman.

My interest is in the link between an actor's performance and the "inner life" of the enacted character. In other words, in the present case, what conclusions can we draw about Norman's awareness, motivations, and feelings from the performance details available to us? What does Norman know? What does he want? What does it *feel like* to be Norman? Yet another complication in this very complicated film is that what *we* know, as opposed to what Norman knows, is radically different on a first and second viewing, given the suppression of our knowledge that Norman's mother is dead until very late in the film. Does this change the way we think about Norman on subsequent viewings? Clearly, in some sense, it does, yet oddly enough not in terms of the questions just posed (his knowledge, motives, and feelings). If Norman is deceiving us, it is only because he is deceiving himself, or, rather, his deceptions are to prevent his "mother" from being found out for Marion's murder, so what he tries to hide from Arbogast, Sam, and Lila, but not from us (that Marion was at the motel, that she – and, later, Arbogast – are dead), is a product of the larger illusion, which we share with him, that his mother is still alive. In contrast to his deceptiveness toward those investigating Marion's disappearance later, with Marion herself he is largely truthful, at least in terms of what he himself believes to be true. This sincerity is conveyed by his ready and disarming smiles and the raised eyebrows above wide-open eyes – in Norman's own words to Arbogast, "I must have one of those faces you just can't help believing" – as well as by the intensity of his more serious moments when he is critical of the facile nostrums Marion offers for his ills.

Our first view of Norman is not as himself, but as "Mother," visible through the window of the house behind the Bates Motel. His mother appears in two forms in the film: as Norman's enacted version of her and as a corpse. The fact that what we have here is Norman-as-mother, rather than his mother's corpse, is made clear by the fact that the figure is walking past the window, rather than sitting still. However, once Marion attracts Norman's attention by honking the horn of her car, he appears as himself, hurrying down the stairs from the house, having cast off his wig and dress very quickly indeed. In a gesture that will be repeated later in the film, Norman holds the upturned collar of his jacket tightly closed against the rain, as he lopes down the stairs toward Marion. Hitchcock's withholding of the fact that Mrs. Bates is dead depends on our never seeing Norman in a transitional state between being himself and being his mother (that is, we never see him *becoming* "Mother"). In fact, even with the final revelation near the end of the film, when Norman's "costume" falls off, revealing him beneath the wig and dress, we do not see his psychological change from one identity to the other, but rather see him in a state of crisis that, as we later learn, leads to his remaining immobilized in his identity as "Mother," finally unable to return to being Norman, as he does so quickly and seamlessly off-screen when Marion first arrives at the motel and makes her presence known.

I think we must take it as given that Norman is never consciously aware that his mother is dead. This carries with it as a consequence, however, that he must also have no conscious awareness of his transformations into his mother and back again to himself, but must be in some sort of trance, his behavior that of an unthinking automaton throughout these off-screen moments, with no memory of them but just a vaguely troubling sense of a series of gaps. That these gaps add up to a substantial part of his life is already suggested in our first view of him. Clearly, when no customers are around, he spends much of his time in this state. His "hobby" is not so much taxidermy (as he tells Marion) as "being Mother." In this context, both his wistful comment that "a hobby's supposed to *pass* the time, not *fill* it" and Marion's question in response – "Is your time so empty?" – pinpoint his situation with some accuracy. His time is empty not in the sense of its lacking purpose, but in its being short of memorable events, or at least of those that he can consciously acknowledge. Norman's backtracking in answer to Marion's question – "No ... uh ... Well, I ... I run the office and ... uh ... tend the cabins and grounds and ... and do little ... uh ... errands for my mother, the ones she allows that I might be capable of doing" – is also significant. Of all his on-screen moments, it is precisely as he is cleaning up after Marion's murder shortly afterward – when he is "tending" the cabin and doing an "errand" for his mother by hiding the evidence of "her" guilt – that he comes closest to seeming "entranced" in the sense I suggested earlier, at least after the initial shock of Marion's murder has worn off. His face has none of the mobility and apparent readability he seemed to offer Marion earlier, but appears emotionless and completely caught up in the performance of the task in hand.

The film makes clear that "Mrs. Bates" has killed before. Therefore, Norman's claim, in his conversation with Marion, that his mother is "harmless" and *not* "a raving thing," seems to be an outright lie, unless this too can be taken as an example of the extent to which his knowledge of the truth is suppressed and denied. Surely it is no more outlandish to suppose that he can clean up after a murder, while suppressing any knowledge of his mother's guilt (not to mention his own), than it is to suppose that he can look upon and address her corpse while denying her death. Norman's mental obliteration of painful realities, while he nonetheless behaves as required to uphold his illusions, fits in with his expressionless demeanor as he tidies up. And yet, a number of aspects of Perkins's performance reveal that, at some level that is not quite fully conscious, Norman *does* know more than we may think. (Indeed, the claim that his mother is "harmless" is, in one sense, absolutely true, if we allow Norman to be referring to his mother's corpse, and not to himself-as-mother.) The self-satisfied smiles that cross his face when what he knows gives him pleasure (smiles that are very different from the friendly and ingratiating ones he gives Marion at other points), and the way he trips over his words when the knowledge is painful, are partial evidence of his struggles with the truth, as are his hesitations at several key moments.

In many ways, Norman is quite astute, with an ironic appreciation of Marion's pretenses. For example, he picks up very quickly on her reluctance to write her address in the motel register and tells her that the town will do, and, when she tells him her real name later, he remembers that she had signed in under another one. Equally, he is able to be ironic about himself, as when he points out the motel stationery and tells Marion she can use it if she wants to fill her friends back home with envy.

So Norman's naivety as a wide-eyed and friendly young man is undercut by the sharpness and accuracy of his critical assessment of Marion, particularly when he takes offense at her suggestion that he put his mother away in an institution and condemns her hypocritical complacency. His shrewd tight-lipped hint of a smile when he checks her false name in the register matches his smile when the car with her body in it sinks into the swamp, implying a moment of much fuller awareness and satisfaction than his behavior as a dutiful son cleaning up after his mother would suggest. That many of his stammerings are on words with heavily weighted significance is also relevant here. Thus, he tells Marion he will be back "with m ... with my trusty umbrella," and that "the expression 'eats like a bird' is really a fal ... fal ... fals ... falsity," and his later stammering description to Arbogast of his mother as an "invalid" opens up questions (both for Arbogast *and* for Norman) as to her actual state while simultaneously raising issues of validity and invalidity in their epistemological sense, akin to the respective issues of trustiness and falsehood in the other examples.

Norman's lack of conscious knowledge of his mother's death, and thus of his own guilt, is very precariously suppressed, and this is made possible, as we have seen, only by transforming much of his life into a series of inexplicable gaps. His description of being in a private trap – "We scratch ... and claw, but only at the air ..." – presents us with an image of him surrounded by nothing more substantial than empty space, mirroring his experience of much of his life as unfathomably empty time. His posture continually evokes withdrawal from the surrounding world, whether through the way his coat collar is held tightly closed against the rain when Marion first arrives, or the way he keeps his hands in his pockets as he enters the kitchen after spying on Marion and, later, as he greets Lila and Sam on their arrival at the motel, or the manner in which he sits in the parlor with his hands clasped as Marion eats. This is a body making as little space for itself in the world as possible, pulling back from contact with its troubling realities, which present themselves to him as thin air. Such postures get part of their meaning in contrast with those of Norman-as-mother, when both her strong voice and the stabbing motions of her powerful arm carve out a place for herself in the world with bold and assertive strokes. However, Norman's shrinking postures also get much of their meaning in contrast with those of Sam in the opening scene and Marion in the shower.

Sam and Marion are presented from the start of the film as creatures of the flesh, their half-naked states emphasizing the softness and vulnerability of their bodies. (Indeed, as Marion drives away from Phoenix with the money she has stolen from Cassidy/Frank Albertson, an unpleasant wealthy client of her boss, the point is made explicit as she imagines Cassidy threatening to replace the money with "her fine soft flesh.") As Sam sprawls in a chair, his legs apart, and talks to Marion about seeing her again, agreeing to her conditions that they meet in more respectable circumstances than in a cheap hotel, he spreads his arms, the palms facing outward, both displaying his half-naked body and seeming to offer it to Marion, just as she will appear to surrender her body to the stream of water from the showerhead just before her murder. The cheap hotel where Sam and Marion have stolen a lunch hour together, and Marion's unfinished sandwich lunch, will find their equivalents in the

Bates Motel and the sandwich supper that Norman provides. But if Norman is thus, in some sense, another version of Sam, his hunched-up posture and the gesture of holding up his hand as though to ward off the world, rather than to offer himself to Marion, are very different. In place of Sam's "fleshiness" is Norman's angularity, his thin, bony shoulders and the workings of his jaw as he munches candy throughout the film reminding us of the skeleton beneath the skin. If Norman has no conscious knowledge of his mother's corpse, his own body reminds us of the corpse within us all, his repressed memories surfacing in his own body, which bears the marks of his mother's fate.

Similarly, the physical coldness of Norman's world contrasts with the heat of Sam's and Marion's. Clearly, their hotel room is warm enough for them to sit and talk in comfort without being fully dressed, whereas Norman seems always to be cold, both on his first appearance in the rain when he holds his jacket closed at the neck and when, as "Mother" at the end of the film, he asks a policeman for a blanket, which he clutches around him in a similar way. If the atmosphere in Marion's office is described by Cassidy as being "hot as fresh milk" (an image of suffocating maternal warmth), Norman talks, in contrast, about how his mother's room would become "cold and damp, like a grave" if he were not there to light the fire, later telling Arbogast that he always changes the motel sheets each week, whether they have been used or not, since he hates the smell of dampness ("such a creepy smell"). Despite all Norman's efforts at wiping out his knowledge of the past, he carries it with him as the cold, "creepy" touch of the grave. On the one hand, the film offers us a vision of warm flesh and a heavy oppressive atmosphere as hot as fresh milk. On the other hand, Norman's world is cold and damp, like the grave, its atmosphere thin and anemic, his angular body a reminder of the skeletons within us all.

What we have seen so far is that the question "What does Norman know?" has no easy answer. Although, in one sense, he knows very little, this is continually belied by the deeper knowledge carried by his body and by Perkins's performance. The contrast between his ready and disarmingly friendly smiles to Marion and his more private knowing smirks, as well as his stammerings when issues of truth and falsehood arise, suggest a constant battle between acknowledging and suppressing darker areas of awareness and a darker aspect to his psyche. But beyond the specific question of whether Norman knows that his mother is dead and that he is complicit in the murders she commits, Norman's body carries within it a more general knowledge that Sam and Marion lack: the apprehension that the ways of the flesh are futile, since death inhabits us all. This pessimism inheres in Norman's experiencing the world as cold and sparse, rather than as warm and full-bodied, and in the consequent way his body seems to contract and pull back from the world around it. Closely connected to the discussion so far is the second question about Norman's inner life: What does Norman *want*?

The question of Norman's motivation is even more difficult to work out than that of the extent of his knowledge, given both the extreme attenuation of his inner life and his lack of insight into the conflicts in his desires, which are represented by his identity as Norman and his acquired identity as his mother. Even as Norman, he both owns up to and disavows his desires: for example, he tells Marion he no longer minds having been born into his private trap, but when she challenges him by saying he *should* mind, he quickly adds, "Oh, I *do*, but I say I don't." So we will need to pay attention to something other than his words. I would like to concentrate on the moments that lead up to Marion's murder and to raise the question of what Norman wants as he returns to the house after watching Marion undress.

Norman's voyeurism confirms that, as we have already seen, his identity as Norman is divided between the friendly open-faced sincerity he offers Marion and the slyer, more secretive pleasures he takes in various private moments when he is somehow getting the better of others (seeing that Marion has used an alias, watching her undress, hiding her body in the swamp). In addition, his identity as Norman in both its aspects appears to contrast with his identification with his mother in both of *her* manifestations: as the argumentative knife-wielding figure he enacts through his own voice and body who inhabits the world with such bold and sweeping strokes, and as the passive corpse that can do no harm. So his desires are much more complex than the psychiatrist at the end of the film would have us believe when he contrasts Norman's sexual desires for women with the jealous rages of the "mother" side of himself who kills such women in retaliation, since both Norman-as-himself *and* Norman-as-mother have two sides. Further, the psychiatric explanation makes no sense of the killing of Arbogast and the attempted killing of Lila (neither of whom arouses Norman's desires), since the covering-up of the crimes and the deflection of curious intruders have so far seemed to be Norman's responsibility in his own guise and not in that of his mother, who has little apparent concern with being found out.

Rather than reducing Norman's desires to the sexual and the aggressively punitive, we need to look more carefully at the meaning of the hesitations that punctuate Perkins's performance at several points. For example, what are we to make of the way Norman hesitates as he chooses a cabin for Marion, his hand hovering and finally selecting the key to the cabin adjacent to the office? Is he wavering between his desire for a chance to spy on Marion and the jealous disapproval he knows his "mother" would feel, as the psychiatrist would have us believe? Or between his desire to spy on Marion and his own sense – as the friendly, smiling version of Norman, rather than the furtive, smirking one – that this would be wrong? Or is he struggling between the belief that he means what he says about the convenience of Marion's being so near the office if she should need anything, and the realization that his motives are less pure? Or, finally, is his desire to see Marion undress in conflict with a memory of a previous murder by his mother of another woman in the same cabin and a wish to protect Marion from a similar fate? (His inability to pronounce the word "bathroom" when showing Marion her room may also be the result of a half-remembered murder there, rather than excessive prudery, especially as he talks about his mother's lover readily enough.) Of course, there is no way of answering such questions with any certainty. That his mother is, somehow, a factor in his hesitation may be implied by the slight movement of his head as he gazes over his left shoulder (a look to the left of the screen that he repeats more firmly after the spying scene itself, when it is more clearly directed toward the house and his mother inside it). However, unless Norman "knows" that he and his mother are one and the same, it is difficult to see why he would imagine that Marion's being in one cabin rather than another should make much difference to her. Again, we are back to the fact that Norman's knowledge is very precariously suppressed, and his identification with his mother and her desires invades even those moments when he is being Norman.

The murder of Marion has been spoken of as a sort of displaced rape (see, for instance, Robin Wood's account in *Hitchcock's Films Revisited*, Faber and Faber, London, 1989, p. 149). This too makes it hard to see the murder merely as an act of jealous retribution on the part of "Mother" or to see the conflict between seeing and desiring Marion, on the one hand, and punishing her, on the other, as a satisfactory description of Norman's contradictory desires. Given Norman's clear desire to spy on Marion and thus to assert himself by intruding upon her privacy and space, though still from a distance, the stabbing is more akin to an intensified version of the same thing than to a simple act of jealous rage. The invasive act of spying is a tentative reversal of the contraction of his body that characterizes Norman at other moments, and the stabbing extends this invasion of Marion's world to its full extent. Thus, Norman-as-mother is a Norman able to make his mark upon the world, rather than remaining a nervous young man unable to do more than keep his distance. The voyeurism is an intermediate stage in this journey from Norman to "Mother."

In this light, Norman's return to the house behind the motel after he spies on Marion becomes all the more moving when he hesitates about going upstairs (to check on his mother? to *become* his mother?), before going into the downstairs kitchen instead. The vision of him seated at the kitchen table, hunched over, as usual, and lost in his thoughts, is an affecting sign of his resistance to what is to follow. However, it is impossible to imagine what he can be thinking at this point, assailed as he must be by so many conscious and semi-conscious feelings at odds with each other and no sooner acknowledged, perhaps, than suppressed (the desire for Marion, the sense that it is wrong, the fear that "Mother" will strike again, the submerged sense that she is already beginning to take him over, and so on). Here, as elsewhere, he is presented as a figure besieged by and withdrawing from the world around him, a world that manifests itself to him in the form of unspoken terrors lurking in the empty air. Thus, when he is tidying up the murder scene soon afterwards and comes out to Marion's car holding the bucket and mop in one hand and Marion's suitcase in the other, a passing car causes him to freeze in his tracks, like a scared animal in the headlights of a car, the case and bucket hastily placed on the ground as he looks anxiously about him. Similarly, a bit later, when the car momentarily stops sinking into the swamp, he again looks around him, giving the same impression of being completely at a loss. He is not so much helpless at such moments as *bewildered*, as if the world's workings are arbitrary and beyond his comprehension.

So Norman's desires can be said to assail him in a random and chaotic way, belonging to various separate and conflicting sides of himself rather than to a coherent personality with an organized sense of purpose, or even to two such personalities with clear battlelines between them. At those moments when we would most expect such confusions to prevail, he seems to hesitate, freeze in his tracks, or go blank (or, as I described it earlier, become "entranced"), as the only way of avoiding his identity shattering into pieces in the face of his contradictory desires. These little "deaths," as he appears to go blank, suggest that his ultimate desire may be a wish for nothingness or annihilation as an alternative to unbearable knowledge and conflicting desires, a wish to be "Mother" not in her aggressively punitive version but as a corpse, which is finally fulfilled at the end of the film in Norman's stillness and passivity as the skeletal grin of his mother as corpse is superimposed on his smile.

By looking closely at the details of Anthony Perkins's performance as Norman – as well as at Norman's performances of various roles within the narrative, both as himself and as his mother – we have pinpointed some of the difficulties and some of the possible conclusions we may reach in trying to determine what Norman knows and desires. What it *feels like* to be Norman follows on from the results of this exploration. The chaos of Norman's conflicting desires and of the conflicting aspects of his personality is countered by his partial refusal of such knowledge, leaving him with an attenuated version of himself on the road to nothingness: in this state, he feels cold, he feels empty, he feels something like death. In one way, the psychiatrist is correct in saying that, after Marion's murder, "Norman returned as if from a deep sleep," though I would want to emphasize the continuing sense of absence and bemusement – the lack of fullness in his life, the sense that he lives a waking dream – which remains through much of his time as Norman, and not merely during those moments when the vengeful mother takes him over. For all these reasons, Norman remains a sympathetic figure even on repeated viewings of the film.

I have not offered a reading of *Psycho* as a whole. There are many excellent accounts to which I have added very little. Instead, I have attempted to look at a single character and the way our sense of him is not only a matter of such things as dialogue, visual treatment, narrative strategies, and so on, but of such details as bodily posture and movement, facial expressions, gestures, hesitations, and vocal delivery as well. However, if the performance details of a given character can never be understood fully in isolation from those meanings that are provided by the techniques and strategies of the film as a whole, neither should they be seen apart from the performances of other characters in the film, since part of their significance may be a structural matter, dependent on how one character's performance mirrors or contrasts with those of other characters in various ways. Therefore, I would like to conclude with a brief look at Marion asleep in her car in the course of her flight from Phoenix, as Marion too, like Norman, appears to waken "from a deep sleep."

The landscape around Marion's car is barren and deserted and is reminiscent of the desert landscape that hangs on the wall above her desk at work, while simultaneously providing a link with our later sense of Norman as surrounded by empty space. Many of her facial expressions throughout her drive toward Norman are similar to his: the wide-open eyes and furrowed brow, the sly smile as she too takes pleasure in her having got the better of someone else (Cassidy, in this case, whose money she has stolen). Like Norman later in the film, Marion hears voices in her head in the course of her drive. She imagines the reactions of her boss, of Cassidy, and of various others to the discovery of her disappearance and theft, as well as Sam's reaction to her turning up with the stolen money. William Rothman suggests that Marion's imaginings comprise a sort of "private film" that is "projected onto the inner screen of her imagination" (*Hitchcock: The Murderous Gaze*, Cambridge, MA: Harvard University Press, 1982, p. 261).

I would like to explore a slightly different way of construing her subjective experiences in the course of her journey, centered upon the abrupt fade to black that accompanies and, presumably, represents the sudden break in Marion's consciousness as she falls asleep. It may seem odd that Hitchcock has chosen to present *this* moment as such a rupture, through his use of the fade, rather than the much more severe break in her consciousness when she is murdered in the shower. Perhaps one explanation, which links her to Norman, is that the fade marks a break in the narrative where all that follows can be seen as Marion's dream. We have seen how Norman's desire to carve out a space in the world by becoming the vengeful version of "Mother" may be seen to screen a deeper desire for death and nothingness, a desire to become his mother-as-corpse. Perhaps we can understand Marion's desires in a similar way. In other words, her vengeful pleasure in stealing the money and running away to Sam (a kind of revenge on Sam, as well as on Cassidy, both in implicating him in her crime and in giving him no further grounds to put off their marriage) may be seen to screen a desire for her own annihilation.

Index

Note: "n" after a page number refers to a note on that page.